PATHWAYS THROUGH
MINNESOTA

An insider's guide to the best, most unusual, and unique travel selections in the Land of 15,293 Lakes. Includes lodging, bed & breakfasts, specialty shops, restaurants, attractions, festivals, and much, much more.

Alex B. Marshall

CLARK & MILES PUBLISHING, SAINT PAUL, MINNESOTA

Published by:
Clark & Miles Publishing
1670 S. Robert St. Suite 315
Saint Paul, Minnesota 55118
(612) 454-8212
(800) 728-9972 outside the Twin City metro area

Although the author and publisher have exhaustively researched all sources to ensure the accuracy and completeness of the information contained in this book, readers are advised that conditions of the businesses and attractions profiled can change over a period of time. We therefore assume no responsibility for errors, inaccuracies, omissions or any other inconsistency herein.

Printed and bound in Minnesota, U.S.A.

Publisher's Cataloging in Publication
(Prepared by Quality Books Inc.)

Marshall, Alexander B.
    Pathways through Minnesota / Alex B. Marshall.
    p. cm.
    Includes index.
    ISBN 0-9626647-0-7

    1. Minnesota--Description and travel.   I. Title.

F604.3   977.6

                                          QBI91-1419

ACKNOWLEDGMENTS

Many people have been instrumental in the research and production of this book. Hats off to everyone who participated, believed in, and supported this worthwhile project. Without their determination, this book would not have been possible. I would especially like to thank Becky, Bjorn, Jackie, Stuart, and Ellen for their drive and extensive research that was essential in making this book complete. I would also like to thank Claudia and Rebecca for their many hours of editing and layout. And finally a special thanks to Ross for the faith and insight that have been expressed in seeing this project to completion.

PATHWAYS THROUGH MINNESOTA

Research and Production
Pathway Publications

Travel Researchers
Rebecca Ketola
Myra Swanson
Stuart Mensinger
Ellen Magratten
Connie Clark
Andria Zimmerman
Irving F. Maxwell

Research Coordinator
Randall C. Bird

Contributing Writers
Alex B. Marshall
John Shepard
Bjorn Sletto
Jackie Sletto
Carla Waldemar
Sheila Gregory
Nina Wegryn
Marcia Sanoden
Kathy Kilmartin
Martha Ricketts

Editing and Layout
Debner Publications Group

Text Design and Maps
Charlie Olson

Special Projects
Teresa Fudenberg

Account Manager
LuAnn Munger

Artwork
Harvey Bernard
Martiena Richter
Bob Negaard

Cover Photo
Bob Firth

Cover Design
Randall C. Bird

Cover Layout
DPS Creative

Publisher
Randall C. Bird

*Special thanks to Tom Crain and
the Minnesota Office of Tourism for
their help and information supplied.*

CONTENTS

ARROWHEAD

B LUFF COUNTRY

HEARTLAND

METROLAND

PRAIRIELAND

PREFACE

The very idea for this travel guide emerged because we felt there was a need to probe deeper into the travel and sightseeing opportunities in Minnesota. The "Land of 10,000 Lakes" could have easily been a book of 10,000 destinations due to the tremendous number of attractions in this state.

Even after devoting 18 months to travel and research throughout Minnesota, we were unable to visit every one of close to 1,000 communities that constitute this vast state. Nonetheless, we have journeyed thousands of miles to discover the unique and interesting destinations that make Minnesota special.

While we have made every effort to ensure that this book is complete, there are bound to be some unavoidable exclusions. We would love to hear about those places that merit inclusion in our next edition.

What separates us from other travel guides? We simply do not just compile information. We have based the selections in this book from research and interviews conducted with residents of each area. We have asked them to recommend businesses and attractions that are unique to their community and worthy of a visit. The profiles and listings are not designed as critiques in any way, but rather to help travelers select what is of special interest to them.

It is a thrill to bring you the best along *Pathways through Minnesota*. Every member of our staff has found this to be a most enlightening experience, and we are sure not to forget all the wonderful people we have met along the way. We sincerely hope your experience with this publication is as fantastic as ours.

Many of the businesses have shown us their support by granting extensive interviews and helping to distribute books to their customers. Once again, thank you to all participants who, together, helped make this Minnesota's newest, most complete travel guide.

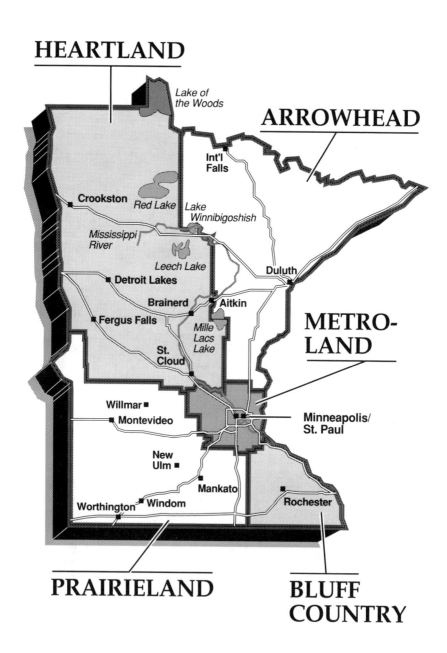

HEARTLAND

ARROWHEAD

Lake of the Woods

Int'l Falls

■ Crookston

Red Lake

Lake Winnibigoshish

Mississippi River

Leech Lake

■ Detroit Lakes

Brainerd ■ ▪ Aitkin

Duluth

METRO-LAND

■ Fergus Falls

Mille Lacs Lake

St. Cloud

Willmar ■

■ Montevideo

Minneapolis/ St. Paul

New Ulm ■

■ Mankato

Worthington ■ Windom

■ Rochester

PRAIRIELAND

BLUFF COUNTRY

Minnesota: A State of Enchantment

by John G. Shepard

To experience Minnesota-style enchantment, gaze at a northern lakeshore as a crystal spring or summer day turns to night. A hush sets in just as the sun drops below the trees, and the radiant orange and red near the western horizon climbs to a fantastically rich indigo at the zenith. An imperceptible breeze over the lake kicks up an intricate pattern of ripples to dance in the spectacular light.

The planets and brighter stars begin glimmering. Slowly, the exquisite indigo overhead grows deeper and denser, as if the air itself were thickening with sleep. The purplish darkness creeps downward to all corners of the sky, snugly wrapping the world in a velvet quilt stitched with starlight.

As the last traces of sunlight leave the sky, a loon calls into the impending night. Her message is filled at once with welcome, longing, and something unrecognizable — something beyond what we know.

From Iowa to Canada and from Wisconsin to the Dakotas, spectacles like this are repeated many times each year on more Minnesota lakes than you'd care to count. The North Star state's motto, "the land of 10,000 lakes," is in fact a typically Minnesotan understatement. In a wet year, the actual number of glacially carved lake basins brimming with water can be thousands higher.

These lakes and a labyrinth of rivers and streams support an abundance of water recreation. Anglers fish year-round for walleyes, bass, trout, muskies, and other freshwater fish. The Boundary Waters Canoe Area wilderness attracts solitude-seeking canoeists and hikers. Sailors, power boaters, jet skiers, and house-boaters have many thousands of watery acres from which to choose.

In autumn, the dazzling hues of Minnesota's hardwood forests are a visual symphony of color. With the maples' showy reds and the rich golds and rusts of the oaks, September and October are magnificent months for hiking, biking, or boating. Hunters find forests, fields, and wetlands abundant with wild turkey, deer, bear, moose, and game birds.

Then comes winter, and the landscape is transformed once again — this time into a pristine adventureland for skiers, snowmobilers, dog sledders, and ice fishermen. Hundreds of miles of cross-country skiing and snowmobile trails dissect the state. Minnesota's downhill ski areas—especially those in the rugged Arrowhead region — are among the best in the Midwest.

Minnesota's diverse ethnic traditions and variations in geography make for a landscape of sweeping contrasts and delightful surprises. Nature's endowments include three continental divides, three distinct ecological regions — boreal forest, hardwood forest, prairie — and enough untrammeled woodlands to support the largest surviving wolf population in the lower 48 states. We have a lake (Superior) that could almost pass as an ocean and a string of hills that we encouragingly call mountains (the Sawtooths). Certainly, those who have survived a Minnesota winter won't argue that the seasons lack variation.

To the south and west is rolling prairie country. At one time or another, it has been rangeland for bands of plains Indians, massive herds of bison, legendary (if not mythical) Viking explorers, and generations of stoic, sodbusting Norwegian and German farmers.

A day's drive to the northeast leads into the heart of Minnesota's densely forested and lake-strewn wilderness. Over the centuries, these woodlands have hosted native Dakota and Ojibwa tribal groups, French fur traders, thousands of miners from Europe, and an equal number of larger-than-life lumberjacks.

Between the prairie and the wilderness, the Mississippi River is straddled by Minneapolis and St. Paul. These eminently cosmopolitan cities trace their present glory to an unlikely, and at times most unloving, marriage of Protestant millers, Irish Catholic railroad magnates, and German beer barons.

Even the name of many a Minnesota town playfully suggests something of these colorful historical and ethnic traditions. Upon visiting Beaver Bay, for example, one might expect to encounter plucky French-Canadian fur traders packing their heavy fur bundles for the voyageurs' rendezvous. Travelers of refinement might shun the riffraff of Thief River Falls and the uncouth citizens of Savage, preferring instead the classical elan of Homer, the scholastic milieu of Cambridge, or the utopia of Harmony. Those with even more exotic tastes could book passage to Santiago or Ceylon. They might also go to Alexandria, where the breezes would carry the salt scent of the Mediterranean.

Though every Minnesota town may not live up to the promise of its name, you can expect a well-honed sense of hospitality from the people you meet and an equally generous reception from Minnesota's ever-giving land and waters. And at the end of each day's adventures — whether it's bird watching at Pelican Rapids, or an "international" road trip from Oslo to Cologne to Milan to Delhi — you can count on finding some quiet little hamlet with a name like Sleepy Eye to welcome you for a good night's rest.

For more information about Minnesota, call (800) 657-3700 or (in the Twin Cities area) 296-5029. You can also write to the Minnesota Office of Tourism, 275 Jackson Street, 250 Skyway Level, St. Paul, Minnesota 55101-1848.

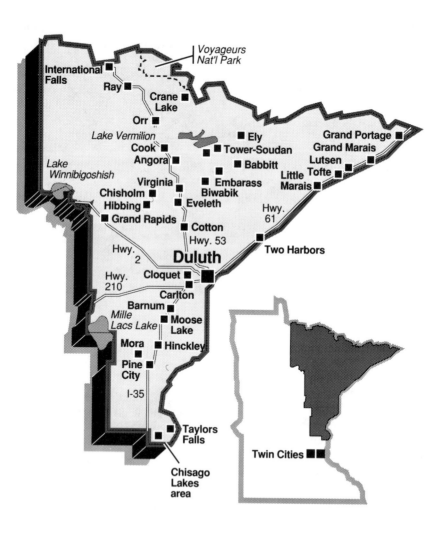

Voyageurs
Nat'l Park

International
Falls

Ray

Crane
Lake

Orr

Lake Vermilion

Cook

Angora

Ely

Tower-Soudan

Babbitt

Grand Portage

Grand Marais

Lutsen

Tofte

Lake
Winnibigoshish

Virginia

Embarass

Biwabik

Little
Marais

Chisholm

Eveleth

Hibbing

Grand Rapids

Cotton

Hwy.
61

Hwy. 53

Duluth

Two Harbors

Hwy.
2

Cloquet

Hwy.
210

Carlton

Barnum

Mille
Lacs Lake

Moose
Lake

Mora

Hinckley

Pine
City

I-35

Taylors
Falls

Chisago
Lakes
area

Twin Cities

ARROWHEAD

by John G. Shepard

The pristine wilderness forests and crystal lakes of Minnesota's Arrowhead region, while forming a land distinct unto itself, have an intriguing way of calling up associations with places elsewhere on the globe. Woods thick with pine and underlaid by rugged bedrock suggest the vast Canadian and Alaskan frontiers. Towns that sprang up early in this century near the region's mammoth iron-ore mines attracted workers from dozens of Old World countries, and the richness of their ethnic traditions still flourishes. Lake Superior itself, with its infinite horizons, powerful moods, and spectacular shoreline, has more the character of an ocean than a mere "lake."

In the harbor at Duluth — the Arrowhead's cultural and economic center — huge freighters that have labored up the St. Lawrence Seaway and climbed to the head of the Great Lakes bear flags from around the world. A good place to see them is from the breakwater that juts out into the lake from Canal Park, found next to Duluth's most famous landmark, the aerial lift bridge. Ocean-sized waves break against the shore, seagulls call stridently overhead, and the exotic flags and foreign ship names can transport your imagination far from the American heartland.

The Arrowhead is a great year-round adventure/travel destination too. Thousands of canoeists and anglers from all over the country annually find solace in the million-plus acres of the Boundary Waters Canoe Area (America's largest wilderness east of the Mississippi River) where one can paddle through a glacier-carved landscape that is home to delicious walleye and lake trout as well as timber wolves, moose, and eagles.

In winter, the 70-100 inches of snow that covers this pristine terrain supports hundreds of miles of well-maintained cross-country ski trails served by hospitable lodges. There are also excellent resorts for alpine skiers and vast networks of snowmobile trails.

The history of the Arrowhead is closely bound up with the wealth of natural resources that have been systematically exploited in wholesale fashion since the first Europeans entered the scene some 300 years ago. Native Ojibwa bands began trading furs with French and French-Canadian voyageurs in an enterprise that eventually grew to continental proportions and nearly wiped out the beaver, whose pelt was the fur of choice. Grand Portage National Monument, found at the Arrowhead's northeastern tip, was a major hub of this activity. Today, it is an excellent place to gain an appreciation of how the fur trade worked and of its impact on the state's original inhabitants, whose culture and lands were altered forever. The reconstructed North West Company fur trade post near Pine City gives yet another glimpse of life during this fascinating era.

Logging and mining were the next industries to leave their indelible impressions on the land. There are excellent historic sites pertaining to each of these economic enterprises found throughout the Arrowhead. Logging history comes alive at the Forest History Center near Grand Rapids, where not far away huge paper mills are still in full operation. Mining history can be explored at the excellent exhibits of Chisholm's Ironworld USA, in the deep passages of the Soudan Underground mine at Tower, and on the slopes of the Hill Annex open-pit mine near Calumet.

Babbitt

The home of Minnesota's taconite industry, Babbitt had an inauspicious beginning in 1916 as a campsite for mining engineers experimenting with processing taconite — a hard rock with a low iron content. For the next 30 years, Babbitt remained an obscure Iron Range community, awaiting the day when taconite mining would become economically feasible. Finally, in the 1950s, when the more valuable iron reserves were depleted, Reserve Mining Company began constructing a pit mine and processing plant nearby, along with an entire town of 80 new homes, shops, and community buildings to house its workers.

Today, Babbitt is a prosperous, modern city of 2,000, complete with schools, medical facilities, and a community business center. Reserve Mining is still the largest employer, producing 30 million tons of crushed taconite iron ore annually. But the city has also attracted other industries to its serene northwoods location, earning it the first Iron Range designation as a Minnesota Star City for Economic Development.

ATTRACTIONS

The mining industry is, naturally, a focus for Babbitt's attractions. Every summer from Memorial Day to Labor Day, *Reserve Mining* arranges fascinating tours of the company's gigantic open pit mine and processing facilities. Mining equipment ranging from a mammoth mining truck to a modern jet drill is also on display — a must for those curious about the intricacies of large-scale mining and a sure hit with the kids. In addition, since Babbitt is located in the heart of the lake district near *Boundary Waters Canoe Area,* it offers excellent opportunities for sportfishing, hiking, and camping. The city maintains two-and-a-half miles of paved trails from the city through the forest to *Birch Lake,* which has a public beach and boat landing. City and school facilities open for public use include an all-weather tennis court, baseball and softball fields, an exceptional indoor ice arena, and a nine-hole golf course.

For more information of Babbitt, contact:

BABBITT-EMBARRASS AREA DEVELOPMENT ASSOCIATION
City Hall
12 Babbitt Road
Babbitt, MN 55706
(218) 827-3423

L ODGE & HOUSEBOATS

■ TIMBER BAY LODGE & HOUSEBOATS
P.O. Box 248
Babbitt, MN 55706
Tel: (218) 827-3682
Winter address from Oct. 15-May 1:
10040 Colorado Road
Bloomington, MN 55438
Tel: (612) 831-0043

For those who enjoy the outdoors, but who don't want to give up on modern conveniences, there's Timber Bay Lodge and Houseboats. Located in the heart of Superior National Forest in northeastern Minnesota, Timber Bay is modern, yet friendly and rustic. Open from May through September, the lodge offers comfortable log cabins equipped with televisions, gas heat, showers, gas ranges, dishes and cooking utensils, refrigerators, and Franklin Stove fireplaces.

For guests who prefer their dinner grilled rather than oven-baked, each cabin comes with a deck complete with patio furniture and a charcoal grill. But most importantly, the log cabins are located just a stone's throw from Birch Lake — 20 miles long, island-studded and undisturbed. Most activities at the lodge are connected with the lake. Visitors can swim in supervised swimming areas, or use the lodge's free canoes, water skis, and sailboats. Fishing is another popular choice, either from shore or from one of the lodge's pontoon boats. For those who enjoy the links, Babbitt Golf Club is nearby. Guests can also rent a houseboat and stay overnight on the lake, anchored in a secluded bay where the only sounds are the call of the loon and the wind whispering in the pines overhead.

S PORTS CAMP

■ KIWADINIPI SPORTS CAMP
c/o Bryant Center Mall
10 Babbitt Road
Babbitt, MN 55706
Tel: (218) 827-3743
Hrs: (May 1 - Oct. 1)

Hockey Camp during last two weeks of July and first week of August, led by Doug Woog, head coach of the University of Minnesota.

Basketball Camp during last week of June and first two weeks of July, led by Paul McDonald, head coach of Vermilion Community College, Ely, MN.

When the kids get restless and want something active to do, send them to Kiwadinipi Sports Camp located just 20 miles south of Ely, MN — famous for the Boundary Waters Canoe Area — and 20 miles east of Babbitt, MN. For 17 years, youngsters have been coming to Kiwadinipi to improve their sports ability and to just have some good old-fashioned fun.

At the camp, both boys and girls can practice and improve their basketball techniques and boys can work on their hockey skills — if they choose to attend the special camps for those sports. Those who just wish to enjoy an eclectic mix of sports such as swimming, volleyball, ping pong, billiards, and softball are also welcome. A new soccer field has just been built, and the camp will be setting up a volleyball program in the near future. Other allied group inquiries are welcome. In addition to the sports camp programs, Kiwadinipi provides rustic bunking facilities and all meals for camp residents. A full-time nurse is always on the premises to see to any health problems, and counselors stay with campers in their cabins. Every Friday, the parents of camp participants are invited to a special barbecue where they can mix and mingle with campers, picking up the latest scoop on the week's power plays and free throws.

Under the watchful eye of professional athletes and coaches, boys and girls ages nine to 16 have the invaluable chance to develop their skills and challenge their sports abilities. No matter what sport they're interested in, Kiwadinipi promises an unforgettable summer experience.

Barnum

T he "Gateway to the Northwoods," Barnum is a low-key alternative to the more crowded resort areas of the region. Although many visitors have fallen for its tranquility and have built vacation or permanent homes along one of the many lakes in the area, the small village still maintains its friendly small town atmosphere. In the way of attractions, Barnum offers a multitude of lakes, unspoiled wilderness, and a rare chance to picnic, canoe, hunt, fish — or simply to get in touch with nature again. Barnum is the starting point for the *Kettle River Canoe Route,* and the city boasts many excellent camping areas, including *Bear Lake County Park, Park Lake Resort, Good-dale Acres* on popular *Bent Trout Lake,* and *Jay Cooke State Park,* all conveniently located near the town. In addition to camping, visitors often join the locals in a more curious and exceedingly popular activity: hunting for *agate,* a fine-grained, multi-colored stone. Although small, the town organizes a series of events, including the fishing contest *Trout-O-Rama* on the first Sunday in January; *Canoe Races, Dairy Day,* and a *Horse Show* in June; and the popular *Carlton County Fair* in August. Featuring tractor pulling, horse racing, a demolition derby and a historical museum, the fair has provided many a visitor with a boisterous, fun-filled counterpoint to an otherwise restful summer.

For more information on Barnum, contact:

BARNUM TOURIST INFORMATION CENTER
Northwoods Motel
904 E. Main Street
Barnum, MN 55707
(218) 389-6951

ACCOMMODATIONS

■ NORTHWOODS MOTEL
904 E. Main Street
Barnum, MN 55707
Tel: (218) 389-6951
Hrs: Open year-round
Visa, MasterCard, and Discover are accepted.

Overlooking beautiful Bear Lake in Minnesota's River Country, the Northwoods Motel has the ultimate access for snowmobile enthusiasts and travelers. It is located just off I-35 about 110 miles north of Minneapolis-St. Paul, exiting on County Road 6.

With over 500 miles of well-groomed trails through the motel's backyard, snowmobilers come from miles around to stay the evening or just a "pit stop" as they are passing through. The public beach on Bear Lake, and picnic and play area provide for a very relaxing summer outing. Each of the 15 units has all the modern amenities needed for a comfortable stay, including coffeemakers, tub and shower combinations, color television, guest-controlled heat and air conditioning, and direct dial telephone. Just a few steps away are a 24-hour restaurant and gas service.

The motel's setting is spectacular, the service courteous and friendly, and the rooms clean, comfortable, and reasonably priced. Minnesota's river country is a land of rugged beauty and charm. Quaint motels like the Northwoods Motel make a stay in the area memorable.

F AIR

■ CARLTON COUNTY FAIR
Highway 61 South (Front Street)
P.O. Box 216
Barnum, MN 55707
Tel: (218) 389-6737
Held in mid-August for four days

For some old-fashioned family entertainment, stop by the annual Carlton County Fair held the weekend of the third Saturday in August. It includes all the traditional events and exhibits from horse racing and livestock judging to figure 8 auto racing.

In 1990, the fair celebrated its 100-year anniversary, and it is the only county fair in Minnesota to offer 99 continuous years of horse racing. In addition to such time-honored traditions as needlework exhibits, flower arranging, and fruit and vegetable competitions, the fair also features a Gospel Fest, a teen dance, and an Outstanding Senior Citizens Awards Program. Other popular events include a demolition derby and a draft horse show. Visitors will find an authentic farmstead from the 1890s, a DNR forestry ranger cabin from the 1940s, and an old train engine and caboose.

With so much to do and see, Carlton County Fair is truly an event the whole family can enjoy.

Biwabik

L ocated in the heart of the northwoods, Biwabik is not only an excellent vantage point for summer fishing and camping expeditions, it is a dream-come-true for the winter outdoor sports enthusiast. Foremost among Biwabik's ski facilities is *Giants Ridge Ski Area,* headquarters of the *United States Ski Association Training Center.* Located one-and-a-half miles east of Biwabik on Highway 135, Giants Ridge features four high-speed chairlifts and 15 challenging slopes with full snow-making, lighting, and power tilling capabilities. For those interested in cross-country skiing, there are more than 30 miles of groomed trails available, many of them located within the untouched beauty of the *Superior National Forest.* In addition, the center provides a rental and pro shop, restaurant, lounge, cafeteria, locker room with showers, waxing room and sundeck, making it one of the premier recreational ski areas in the United States. The Biwabik area also offers excellent snowmobiling opportunities. Through the *Laurentian Trail,* snowmobilers can reach hundreds of trails for extensive excursions throughout the region. In addition to outdoor activities, Biwabik regularly celebrates its varied ethnic heritage. During the Christmas season, *Weihnachtfest* illuminates the city and its parks with thousands of lights, while the pre-Lenten sliding festival *Laskiainen* pays tribute to Biwabik's Finnish heritage.

For more information on Biwabik, contact:
BIWABIK TOURIST INFORMATION
P.O. Box 529
Biwabik, MN 55708
(218) 865-4403

C IVIC ASSOCIATION

■ BIWABIK AREA CIVIC ASSOCIATION
P.O. Box 304
Biwabik, MN 55708
Tel: (218) 865-4335
Special events all year-round

Biwabik, MN, celebrates throughout the year. From dog sled races, to triathlon, to Fourth of July parades, the fun never ends in this Iron Range town.

The excitement starts in January when Biwabik hosts sled dog sprint races. The races attract top dog-sled racing teams from across the United States and Canada who compete for cash and prizes worth more than $5,000. Later in the month, the city is the site for the Pepsi Challenge Ski Cup. The Pepsi Challenge tests amateur skiers on a 50 kilometer cross-country course. Skiers who prefer less arduous competition can compete in the 25K Laurentian Loppet or the 10K Mini-Challenge run concurrently with the Pepsi Challenge Cup. After the ski excitement, Biwabik cools down for a few months until the Fourth of July when the town goes all out for the annual Calithumpian Parade, followed in September by the Giants Ridge Triathlon. During the triathlon, participants compete in running, canoeing, and bicycling; and the athlete with the fastest time in all three races is the combined winner of the event. In December, Biwabik gears up one more time for the annual Weihnachtfest Christmas festival, which features giant Christmas postcards, lavishly decorated houses, horse and sled-dog rides, and other entertainment.

S NOW SKIING

■GIANTS RIDGE
P.O. Box 190
Biwabik, MN 55708
Tel: (218) 865-4143 or (800) 475-7669
Hrs: Mon. - Fri. 10 a.m. - 9 p.m.
    Weekends and holidays 9 a.m. - 9 p.m.

Located in the great northwoods, Giants Ridge is surrounded by more than 2,000 acres of the Superior National Forest. Created to satisfy every type, style, and ability of skier, there are 19 ski runs.

At Giants Ridge, the skiing is at its best, and night skiing in both cross-country and alpine are offered. More than 55 kilometers of cross-country ski trails wind through the terrain, with three kilometers lighted for night skiing. Also known as the USSA Nordic Training Center, Giants Ridge has been a leader in hosting state, national, and world-class events. The resort has made a name for itself with excellent snow and snow conditions, along with perfected groomed trails and runs for the recreational as well as the competitive skier.

Giants Ridge is the best family recreational ski area in the Midwest as well as a training center for future ski champions. There are many motels in the area offering special package rates. Giants Ridge offers skiing, snowmobiling, and many other kinds of pure winter fun, all in a world of Scandinavian-style charm.

Carlton

A quaint, sleepy railroad town only a short drive from Lake Superior, Carlton is known for the array of river-related excursions available to the out-of-town visitor. The wild and scenic *St. Louis River* makes the town a paradise for canoeists, kayakers, and fishermen. During the summer, Carlton comes alive with national and international *whitewater slalom competitions* — fast and fascinating kayaking events where participants dodge obstacles during a race down furious rapids. Carlton is also the gateway to scenic *Jay Cooke State Park,* featuring 80 campsites, picnic grounds, and an interpretive center. For those looking for physical exertions, there are no less than 50 miles of hiking, 36 miles of ski touring, and ten miles of horse trails available in Jay Cooke. On an entirely different note, Carlton is also home to *Charlotte's Motel & Coffee Shop.* Owned and operated by Charlotte Zacher, Charlotte's has been featured on the national television shows "Real People" and "PM Magazine" and has been responsible for putting tiny Carlton on the map. A visit to the coffee shop may find Charlotte cooking her delectable country-style meals in a long chiffon gown or dancing for her appreciative customers in shorts and "go-go" boots. Visitors to Carlton can also choose to make Charlotte's or some other motel their restful base from which to explore all the activities and sights of cosmopolitan *Duluth,* located only a few miles away.

For more information on Carlton, contact:
MINNESOTA EXTENSION SERVICE — CARLTON COUNTY
P.O. Box 307
Carlton, MN 55718
(800) 862-3760

RESTAURANT & LOUNGE

■COZY RESTAURANT
210 Chestnut Street
Carlton, MN 55718
Tel: (218)384-4801
Hrs: Mon. - Thur. 7 a.m. - 9 p.m., Fri. 7 a.m. - 10 p.m.
    Sat. 8 a.m. -10 p.m.
    Sun. 9 a.m. - 3 p.m.

The Cozy Restaurant and Lounge opened in 1986, expanding on the original cafe setting that had opened in 1983. Currently the Cozy Restaurant and Lounge is a full service establishment. Fine food and friendly service are offered with a small town atmosphere.

Some of the more popular items are the Mexican dishes served on Fridays. These dishes offer an exceptional way to kick off the weekend. Prime rib is the speciality on Thursdays and Fridays. All dinners include a choice of soup or fresh garden salad, choice of potato, and hot fresh bread loaf.

All of the food is made from scratch, including the soups, which include an especially delicious chicken dumpling and vegetable beef. Chef's specials are offered daily for noon lunches with everything from hot dishes, to meat loaf and prime rib sandwiches. A full breakfast menu is also available to give the morning a cozy start.

R ESTAURANT & TRAVEL CENTER

■ JUNCTION OASIS RESTAURANT & TRAVEL CENTER
I-35 and Highway 210
Carlton, MN 55718
Tel:(218)384-3531
Open daily 24 hours-a-day
Visa, MasterCard, Amex, Discover, and Unocal are accepted.

Convenience for truck drivers, travelers, and local customers is the primary goal at Junction Oasis. It is a service station, a restaurant, a truck stop, and a store. Over the last 30 years this oasis at the junction of I-35 and Highway 210 has evolved into a comprehensive facility, providing supplies for drivers and fuel and basic services for cars, motor homes, and tractor-trailer rigs.

The experienced cooks at Junction Oasis Restaurant prepare affordable daily specials with care, and friendliness prevails at this family restaurant. An all-you-can-eat fish fry every Friday night draws dedicated customers from miles around. The menu also features various meat entrees, sandwiches, salads, and burgers as well as the restaurant's homemade specials, soups, and freshly baked breads and desserts.

Junction Oasis Union 76 Truck Stop provides multiple services, including full- and self-service diesel, propane, unleaded, super unleaded, and regular gasoline at competitive prices. Well-trained and friendly attendants mount new tires, repair flats , install batteries, and provide numerous other automotive services. In addition to regular truck stop services, hot showers are available for truck drivers. While their cars are being serviced, customers find groceries, travel necessities, books and magazines, car accessories, cassette tapes, baked goods, and fast food in the Junction Oasis convenience store.

Chisago Lakes Area

E ncompassing the communities of Chisago City, Center City, Lindstrom, Shafer, and North Branch, the Chisago Lakes area is a land of tranquil waters and rolling farmland. The region was almost exclusively settled by Swedish immigrants, and this heritage is reflected in traditional craft and antique shops, ethnic eateries, and historic monuments and buildings. In fact, Center City is the first permanent Swedish settlement in Minnesota, and the historic *Chisago Lake Swedish Evangelical Lutheran Church* is the second oldest Lutheran church site in Minnesota. The renowned Swedish author Wilhelm Moberg conducted his research for the heartbreaking immigrant saga *The Emigrants* in this area, and the movie by the same name was filmed here. In Lindstrom, a statue of Moberg's characters *Karl and Kristina Oscar* has been erected as a tribute to the Swedish settler spirit. Among other celebrated historical sites are the *Gustaf Anderson House* and *Fridhem House* in Lindstrom, and the *Historic District* and *Chisago County Courthouse* in Center City.

Center City, along with Chisago City, is also known for its proliferation of antique and craft shops, and charter companies in the Twin Cities regularly offer antique-shopping tours to the Chisago Lakes area. Shafer, meanwhile, is home of the intriguing farm museum *Yesterfarm of Memories.* The historical roots of these cities are celebrated in area festivals, including Lindstrom's

Karl Oscar Days, the *Center City Days,* and the *Ki-Chi-Sago Days* in Chisago City during the third weekend in September.

For more information on Chicago Lakes, Center City, Lindstrom, Schafer, and North Branch, contact:

LINDSTROM CHAMBER OF COMMERCE
P. O. Box 283
Lindstrom, MN 55045
(612) 257-2282

A NTIQUES

■ MURIEL'S ART AND ANTIQUES
10635 Railroad Ave.
Chisago City, MN 55013
Tel: (612) 257-8325
Hrs: Mon. - Sat. 10 a.m. - 5 p.m.
　　　Sun. noon - 5 p.m. Closed Tuesdays
Visa and MasterCard are accepted.

Muriel Bacon has a talent to recreate drab merchandise into beautiful reconditioned antiques. Using the technique of faux marbling, she can paint wood items to have the effect of marble. Whether painting, decorating, or creating something new, her talent is clearly demonstrated in the display of work seen throughout her store.

As customers walk through the front French-glass doors, the soft music and aroma of spice potpourri sets the mood. An assortment of linens, hand-painted carousel horses, handmade wreaths, dried flower arrangements, glassware, furniture, jewelry, dolls, and a variety of other antiques and collectibles can be found.

Muriel's Art and Antiques is a special place for the avid "antiquing" person or just the casual browser.

B ED & BREAKFAST

■ COUNTRY BED & BREAKFAST
32030 Ranch Trail
Shafer, MN 55074
Tel: (612) 257-4773 Call for reservations in advance.
No pets. Children must be 12 and over. No smoking.

The 1880s red brick farmhouse surrounded by quiet country-side invites guests to relax in rooms of white wicker and soft floral wallpaper, with handmade comforters on comfy beds. The lavender, rose, and green colors permeate each of the three bedrooms — one with private bath, and two with a shared bathroom. Guests enjoy an unforgettable breakfast of Bud's special omelettes and Lois's buttermilk pancakes; complemented with a fresh fruit bowl; juice;

sizzling ham, bacon or sausage; maple syrup; and aromatic "Swedish egg coffee."

The pillared front porch and patio beckon guests morning or evening to listen to the birds and the sounds of the meadow, also the country lane for moonlit walks. Located only a few miles from many recreational site-seeing attractions, guests can visit nearby museums, pottery shops, antique stores, and fine restaurants. Ki-Chi-Saga Lakes and the Sunrise and St. Croix rivers offer riverboat cruises, tubing, canoeing, swimming, and fishing. Wild Mountain and Trollhagen offer excellent downhill skiing, and Wild River State Park has 40 miles of groomed cross-country skiing and nature hiking trails.

Country Bed and Breakfast is located two miles north of Shafer and five miles west of Taylors Falls. The home was originally built by Swedish immigrant Lars Thorsander, and it remains in the family with Lois and Bud Barott.

C HEESE & GIFT SHOP

■ EICHTEN'S HIDDEN ACRES CHEESE & BUFFALO FARM

Highway 8
Center City, MN 55012
Tel: Store: (612) 257-1566, Mail order: (612) 257-4752
Hrs: Daily 10 a.m. - 6 p.m.
    Hours are extended during the summer.
Visa and MasterCard are accepted.

Eichten's Hidden Acres is not only unique as a Cheese House shop and factory, but the newest addition is a herd of American Bison (buffalo). It is one of just a few herds of its size privately owned. Joe and Mary Eichten and their family have been in the cheese business since 1976, specializing in European style cheese including Dutch gouda, Danish tilsit, baby Swiss, and several more.

Along with the buffalo meat and nationally acclaimed award winning cheeses sold, imported candies and jams, maple syrup, honey, and craft items have been added to the gift shop. The American public likes the buffalo meat because it is lower in cholesterol, fat and calories than chicken; higher in protein than beef; and tastes the way beef used to. For convenience and gifts, selections can also be purchased through the Cheese House mail order department.

Bring the family and watch for the Dutch windmill and the buffalo herd! Children will enjoy "Grandpa Joe's Barnyard," where they can get a close look at a variety of animals, including buffalo and llama.

F OOTWARE

■ SVEN'S SWEDISH CLOGS AND QUALITY FOOTWARE
10,000 Lake Boulevard
Chisago City, MN 55013
Tel: (612) 257-4598
Hrs: Mon. - Fri. 10 a.m. - 6 p.m., Sat. 9 a.m. - 5 p.m.
   Sun. 11 a.m. - 5 p.m.
Visa, MasterCard, and AmEx are accepted.

Service and top quality are Sven Carlsson's priorities. He has been making clogs for close to 50 years, and customers are assured of obtaining the absolute finest when they stop at Sven's Swedish Clogs and Quality Footwear. With a factory outlet right on the premises, customers are also assured of finding the best possible prices.

An authentic Swedish windmill greets all who enter the comfortable shop. The main attraction is Sven's handcrafted Swedish clogs, but other items are also on hand. Sven offers a line of very soft Romika shoes, sheepskin boots and Bout Clarks of England liners, Weinbrenner workboots, SAS shoes, and Minnetonka moccasins.

Sven's handmade clogs are created with wooden bases imported from Sweden. He prepares the bases and attaches all leather uppers, cut and sewn in Chisago City, available in a variety of colors. Sven makes clogs for men, women, and children and welcomes custom orders at no extra charge.

Wood-O-Flex clogs are among the newest items available; the flexible sole is so comfortable that wearers hardly feel they have anything on their feet. Wood-O-Flex has a shock-absorbing sole, and the anatomically correct wooden base follows the movements of the foot and adjusts for temperature and moisture.

G IFT SHOP

■ GUSTAF'S FINE GIFTS & COLLECTIBLES AND GUSTAF'S WORLD OF CHRISTMAS
13045 Lake Boulevard
Lindstrom, MN 55045
Tel: (612) 257-6688 - Gustaf's Fine Gifts
   (612) 257-4945 - Gustaf's World of Christmas
Hrs: (Spring, summer, fall)
   Mon. - Sat. 9:30 a.m. - 5:30 p.m., Sun. noon - 5 p.m.
   (Winter: Thanksgiving through Christmas)
   Mon. - Fri. 9 a.m. - 8:30 p.m., Sat. 9 a.m. - 6 p.m., Sun. noon - 6 p.m.
Visa, MasterCard, AmEx, and Discover are accepted.

Built in 1879 by Gustaf Anderson, known as "Guldgubben" (old gold man, or old man of gold), this historic house is now the home of Gustaf's Fine Gifts and Collectibles. Next door is Gustaf's World of Christmas.

Gustaf's has a magnificent display of gifts that will be of interest even to the youngest member in your family. There are many Scandinavian and German items. Gustaf's has one of the largest collections of Hummel figures, along with many collectibles of porcelain and crystal. It carries the finest lines in Orrefors (from Sweden) along with Kosta Boda, Iris Arc, and Swarovski Crystal. There are Department 56 houses, Nativities, Santas, collector cars, Russian boxes made of paper-mache, music boxes, wood carvings, steins, stuffed animals, collector dolls, toys, and many more gifts and decorations from around the world.

Gustaf's World of Christmas houses an imported life-like Santa from Sweden. Children love to listen to Christmas stories as Santa reads to them in Swedish. Room after room are filled with Christmas items, and there are also other holiday items, including Easter and Halloween collectibles and gifts.

Chisholm

A lthough Chisholm was home to Dr. A. W. Graham, who was a character in the movie "Field of Dreams," the city is best known as an historic Iron Range mining community. Like its neighbors — Hibbing, Eveleth and Virginia — Chisholm's fortunes have waxed and waned in tune with the mining industry. In later years, however, tourism has become a major and stable source of revenue.

Most of these out-of-town visitors head for *IronWorld USA,* a major historical center dedicated to the unique heritage of northern Minnesota. It features a *Festival Park* with brooks, waterfalls, and rustic bridges; ethnic dances, crafts, and foods; and an *Interpretive and Research Center* with exhibits relating the fascinating history of iron ore mining.

In addition, railway and trolley rides take visitors along the open-pit *Glen Mine,* and during the summer, top entertainers perform in the 3,000-seat, open-air amphitheater. Chisholm is also home to the *Minnesota Museum of Mining,* featuring old mining equipment ranging from a 1907 steam locomotive to a modern jet drill, as well as a replica of an underground mine and a restored early mining village. The 36-foot brass and copper *Iron Man Memorial* dominates the grounds in front of the museum entrance.

Chisholm's early settlers hailed from a number of different European countries, and to celebrate their checkered heritage, the residents of Chisholm have erected a *Bridge of Peace* — a huge outdoor display of all the world's flags. They also stage the annual *Minnesota Ethnic Days,* a 12-day extravaganza held at *Ironworld USA* which includes ethnic foods, crafts and music. Two other popular events in Chisholm are the *Polka Fest* and the *Iron Country Hoedown* (a big-name country music festival), also staged at Ironworld USA.

For more information on Chisholm, contact:
CHISHOLM CHAMBER OF COMMERCE
327 W. Lake Street
Chisholm, MN 55719
(218) 254-3600
(800) 422-0806 (In Minnesota)

A NTIQUES

■ DREAM COTTAGE ANTIQUES
300 N.W. First Street
Chisholm, MN 55719
Tel: (218) 254-2153
Hrs: (Summer) Tue. - Thur. 4 p.m. - 7 p.m., Sat. - Sun. 11 a.m. - 4 p.m.
(Winter) Thur. 4 - 7 p.m., Sat. 11 a.m. - 4 p.m.

Dream Cottage Antiques truly is a collector's dream: an entire house filled with old treasures and collectibles. The Dream Cottage itself also is an antique: look for a cozy turn-of-the-century stucco house on the corner of First Street N.W. and Highway 73 in Chisholm.

As Millie Muhar, life-long collector and owner, says, there is "something for the collector in all of us." Two floors and a basement of Dream Cottage Antiques are carefully arranged to show items as they might actually be used. Glass and kitchenware are displayed in the kitchen; pictures are displayed on the walls. Browse through the rooms of furniture, jewelry, books, magazines, old records, sporting collectibles, and dolls, including an extensive Barbie doll collection.

Early mining memorabilia and handcrafted items from the Iron Range also are available. Services include shipping.

T HEME PARK

■ IRONWORLD USA
P.O. Box 392
Chisholm, MN 55719
Tel: (218) 254-3321 or (800) 372-6437 (In Minnesota)
Hrs: Seasonally from 10 a.m. - 7 p.m. daily

In the heart of the Iron Range is a theme park, IronWorld USA, dedicated to the preservation and celebration of the region's cultural heritage. There are numerous things to do and places to see at IronWorld USA, ranging from the educational to just plain fun. From the Interpretive and Research Centers to the flag-lined walkways of Festival Park, one can see exhibits, visit the library and archives, or enjoy the ethnic crafts, strolling musicians, and delicious food of Festival Park. Ride the electric trolley along the edge of an open pit mine, or have the children enjoy the Carousel, Merry-go-round, and remote control boats. Enjoy a meal in the ethnic restaurant, and see one of the many daily live shows in the outdoor amphitheatre.

IronWorld USA, which opened in 1986, is owned by the Iron Range Resources and Rehabilitation Board of the State of Minnesota. Located on three hundred acres at the site of a former ore mine, Ironworld USA employs nearly 100 full-time and seasonal employees.

Ironworld USA hosts several annual summer festivals: International Polkafest, Minnesota Ethnic Days, Fabulous Fifties, and Iron Country Hoedown. The entire park is wheelchair accessible, and a shuttle service is available at the entrance.

Cloquet

S et in the heart of vast forests on the banks of the scenic St. Louis River, Cloquet has long been a center for northern Minnesota's wood products industry. Among the giant companies that provide jobs and economic stability for this friendly town are *Diamond International Corporation* — one of the largest wooden stick match mills in the world — and the *Potlatch Corporation,* a leading manufacturer of high-grade printing, writing and converting papers. The University of Minnesota's *Cloquet Forest Research Center,* with its experimental forest research, fire towers and picnic and cross-country skiing areas, underscores Cloquet's significance as a logging center. Before the advent of the logging industry, however, the Chippewa Indians reigned supreme in the area. Today, small stores on the *Fond du Lac Indian Reservation* are excellent sources for handmade souvenirs and delectable, hand-harvested wild rice. Located in the northwoods, the entire Cloquet area offers excellent fishing, hiking, canoeing, and camping opportunities, in addition to the more curious activity of hunting for agates, visitors to Cloquet shouldn't miss *Best Service,* the only gas and service station designed by Frank Lloyd Wright, located at the corner of highways 45 and 33. For those with a zest for the traditional, the *Lumberjack Days* in June feature a variety show, arts and crafts, displays, a parade, and other fun festival fare for the entire family.

Meanwhile, the focus is on country music at *North Country Shindig*, a "Grand Ole Opry" style show held every Saturday night at the Cloquet National Guard Armory.

For more information on Cloquet, contact:
CLOQUET CHAMBER OF COMMERCE
P. O. Box 426
Cloquet, MN 55720
(218) 879-1551

CAMPGROUND & RESTAURANT

■CLOQUET KOA CAMPGROUND/JIM & JOE'S STEAKS N SEAFOOD
1479 Old Carlton Road
Cloquet, MN 55720
Tel: (218) 879-5726
Hrs: Open daily (summer) 7 a.m. - 10 p.m., (winter) 11:30 a.m. - 9:30 p.m.
Visa, MasterCard, and AmEx are accepted.

Imagine a 70-site KOA campground with heated pool and sauna, combined with a cozy full-service restaurant. If the scenario sounds like camping heaven, wait no longer. Take the short jaunt to the Cloquet KOA campground, just outside Duluth.

Full RV hook-up, a tent area, laundry facilities, and showers are just some of the amenities at the campgrounds. After they settle in, guests can also dine at Jim & Joe's Steak N Seafood restaurant where they'll find a cocktail lounge as well as banquet facilities. The menu offers such specialties as fresh fish, certified Angus beef steaks, and barbecued ribs. Lunch and dinner are available year-round, while a breakfast buffet is offered only in the summer.

At the Cloquet KOA, there is everything needed for an unforgettable camping experience.

Cook/Lake Vermilion Area

A resort community two hours north of Duluth, Cook is an excellent vantage point for fishing and camping expeditions into the famed *Boundary Waters Canoe Area*, the remote, untouched home to timber wolves, black bears, and bald eagles. The town offers a wide variety of resort accommodations, ranging from rustic cabins to luxurious rooms. Many offer top-notch outfitting services and boat rentals designed to make the visitor's wilderness experience an exciting yet comfortable adventure. However, Cook is not simply a collection of resorts, but a complete, rustic community with gift shops, supper clubs, grocery stores, and auto services, all carefully geared to the traveler's needs. Located just off *Lake Vermilion* — with its 40,000 acres of sky-blue waters, 365 islands, and 1,200 miles of scenic shoreline — Cook is a fisherman's dream-come-true. The Minnesota Department of Natural Resources has maintained a hatchery and stocking service at Lake Vermilion since 1969, making the lake one of the premier walleye lakes in Minnesota. For those who want a break from fishing, the Cook/Lake Vermilion area also offers fine golf courses, tennis courts, horseback riding, and miles of hiking trails in the quiet woods.

For more information on Cook and the Lake Vermilion area, contact:

CₒₒK VɪsɪTORS Iɴғᴏʀᴍᴀᴛɪᴏɴ Cᴇɴᴛᴇʀ
P.O. Box 155
Cook, MN 55723
(218) 666-5850

G IFT & COFFEE SHOP

■ CₒᴜɴᴛRY Rᴏᴀᴅs
8547 Highway 53
Angora, MN 55703
Tel: (218) 749-6346
Hrs: Mon. - Sat. 9:30 a.m. - 6 p.m., Sun. 11 a.m. - 6 p.m.
Visa and MasterCard are accepted.

Country Roads is in a historic Finnish Lutheran Church built in 1908, just north of Virginia on Highway 53.

This charming country church has a closed-in veranda around the building. The church altar was remodeled into a kitchen and seating area for lunches, and the choir loft now holds a beautiful Christmas display of gifts. The shop also offers other handcrafted items with a country flair, such as artwork, wall decorations, baskets, cosmetics, pottery, quilts, rugs, table linens, collector dolls, plush toys, and wood carvings. The coffee shop is truly country, serving menu items baked the old-fashioned way that include homemade ice cream, breads, muffins, pies, salads, and soups. Among the selections are luncheon specials prepared with Minnesota-grown wild rice and blueberries.

Country Roads is a delightful treat. Experience the taste of an earlier time.

R ESORTS

■LITTLE SWEDEN RESORT
9084 Little Sweden Road
Cook, MN 55723
Tel: (218) 666-5568 or (800) 777-8480
Hrs: (Summer) mid-May through September, Closed winter
Visa and MasterCard are accepted.

Looking for a memorable vacation experience? Built in the late 1930s, Little Sweden is a charming family resort in northeastern Minnesota nestled amid the pine and birch of Lake Vermilion, just 10 miles north of Cook on Highway 24.

The resort has seven cozy and comfortable housekeeping cabins, each designed to be different from the others. Each cabin is named for a province in Sweden and features traditional Swedish decor. The lodge is the center of hospitality where guests can relax by the fireplace or watch television. Games, ping-pong, and pool table are also available. There are groceries, souvenirs, fishing tackle, licenses, maps, bait, gas, and snacks for sale, along with boat and motor rental. Canoes are available at no extra charge. The gift shop, which is built around a large granite glacier boulder, is filled with beautiful Scandinavian imports and many other gift and souvenir items. Waterfront activities revolve around a large lighted dock area. Children enjoy fishing from the dock and playing in the safe, sandy swimming area as well as a large play structure built for kids of all ages. Lake Vermilion has long been famous for its fine catches of walleye, northern pike, large and smallmouth bass, panfish, and muskie. A fish cleaning facility and large freezer are available to guests. Guests are enticed to unwind with a Swedish full body massage.

Wildlife complements the beauty of the northwoods, and there are plenty of nature trails to explore beyond the resort's own self-guided trail. Guests relax in this quiet and peaceful Scandinavian atmosphere.

■LUDLOW'S ISLAND LODGE
Lake Vermilion
Cook, MN 55723
Tel: (218) 666-5407 or (800) 537-5308
Hrs: Daily, May through Oct.
Visa, MasterCard, and AmEx are accepted.

Ludlow's Island Lodge is a 19-cottage resort situated on the main island and two adjacent shorelines of Lake Vermilion in northern Minnesota. It is the highest rated AAA and Mobil Guide resort of its type in the state. Ludlow's Island is also the only resort in the state to receive *Family Circle* magazine's "Family Resort of the Year" award for 1990.

The cottages, ranging from one to five bedrooms, have fireplaces, decks, knotty pine or cedar interiors, and are equipped with Weber grills, dishwashers, microwaves, blenders, drip coffeemakers, and popcorn poppers. The cottages are nestled privately among pine and birch, each with an excellent view of the lake and not another cabin. The guests may choose from a variety of activities or simply enjoy the solitude.

The resort facilities include a camping island for kids, tennis and racquetball courts, canoes, paddleboats, power boats, kayaks, sailboats, a waterslide, a play-ground with a treehouse, sauna, a protected sandy beach swimming area, lodge, and game room. The guests can also shop for groceries in the "Gourmet Pantry," a self-service mini-grocery open 24 hours a day. Golf is nearby.

Mark and Sally Ludlow and their four children operate the resort from mid-May until October. The Ludlows and their staff emphasize personal service for their guests.

■ PEHRSON LODGE RESORT
2746 Vermilion Drive
Cook, MN 55723
Tel: (218) 666-5478 or (800) 543-9937
Hrs: May 15 - Sept. 30

Pehrson Lodge Resort on scenic Lake Vermilion features 21 carpeted, well-furnished cabins complete with linens and microwaves. All cabins, which are either located directly on the lake or include a good view of the lake, come with sundecks — some even have fireplaces.

The resort is situated on 68 wooded acres with 1,800 feet of shoreline and a 600-foot gradual-sloped natural sand beach. The cabin rate includes a naturalist program for children ages 4-12 from June 15 to August 15, and the use of a sailboat, canoes, paddleboats, and windsurfers to explore some of the 300 islands dotting the lake. From May 15 to August 30, visitors can attend a weekly fishing seminar given by a professional guide. In the seminar, they gain invaluable insights into the intricacies of fishing walleye, northern pike, bass, and crappie. Lake Vermilion, a stunning northwoods lake with 1,200 miles of shoreline and 40,000 acres of water, is restocked yearly with walleye to maintain a healthy supply of trophy fish.

For a truly relaxing vacation, one will enjoy the comfort of Pehrson Lodge, and the tranquility and beauty of Lake Vermilion.

■ VERMILION DAM LODGE
Lake Vermilion
P.O. Box 1105-B
Cook, MN 55723
Tel: (218) 666-5418 or (800) 325-5780
Hrs: (Summer) daily May 11 - October 1
Visa, Mastercard, and AmEx are accepted.

Lake Vermilion has been classified as one of the three most beautiful lakes in the world by a journalist for *Redbook* magazine. Vermilion spans 40 miles from east to west, and encompasses some 1,200 miles of shoreline, including 365 islands. Visitors can fish, hunt, hike, canoe, sail, swim, water ski, or just enjoy nature, all on Lake Vermilion while staying at Vermilion Dam Lodge.

Twenty-one miles north of Cook, MN, Vermilion Dam Lodge has much to offer guests who come to unwind in the northwoods. Clean, comfortable cabins close to the lake accommodate 2-12 persons. The knotty-pine elegance and efficiency of the vacation homes make visitors' stay a pleasure. At the end of a busy, fun-filled day, relax and soothe muscles in the sauna and heated swimming pool. Then head for the main lodge to socialize, or retire to the luxury of the cabin to rest up for the next day's adventure.

R ESTAURANT

■ THE LANDING RESTAURANT
3096 Vermilion Drive
Cook, MN 55723
Tel: (218) 666-2201
Hrs: Varies with season
Visa and MasterCard are accepted.

The Landing, on the shores of the Head of the Lakes Bay of Lake Vermilion, is a full-service marina able to dock up to 40 boats and readily available to snowmobilers in the winter looking for terrific food and a warm atmosphere. The Landing was a marina for years but now has devoted its existence to sumptuous food for tastes of all kinds.

All the dishes are made from scratch using fresh herbs grown on the premises, fresh produce from local farmers, and wild rice handpicked locally. Original recipes appear nightly. Unique dishes to The Landing are Deep Fried Chevre, Coconut Tempura Shrimp, Italian Tropical Sandwich, Wild Rice Shrimp, Pork Chop Extraordinaire, Minnesota Walleye, and Pacific Pan-Fried Oysters.

There are plans to expand the restaurant to offer an even better view of Lake Vermilion and the surrounding scenery. Visitors may sit on the outside deck and take in the sights and sun as well as libations served from the bar. Fantastic food and the charm and tranquility of Minnesota's outdoors — a truly perfect match.

Cotton

A lthough the early settlers of northeastern Minnesota were used to living in remote areas, Cotton was going too far for most of them. Originally settled in 1897 by a dogged individualist known as "Charlie in the brush," Cotton did not have a paved road connection with the rest of Minnesota until 1922. Fortunately for the scattering of families in the young town, however, the long-awaited road didn't turn Cotton into a big-city competitor to Duluth, located 40 miles to the south.

Although Cotton today boasts three restaurants, a bakery, motel, and a handful of other service businesses, its 600 inhabitants zealously guard its peaceful small-town atmosphere. On the fourth weekend in August, however, the calm is shattered. It's time for the annual *Minnesota State Old Time Fiddle Championship*, a highly popular event attracting top fiddlers from across the United States and Canada, and a respectable crowd of spectators. In addition to top-caliber fiddle music, the event also includes a Festival with mouthwatering pancake breakfasts, arts and crafts displays, games for children, and an eccentric sheep-to-shawl contest.

As a natural companion to the fiddle championship and festival, Cotton arranges an *Old Time Scandinavian Dance* in the community center the first weekend of each month from October through June. Featuring live music in the genuine Scandinavian immigrant tradition, the dance is a fitting tribute to the first settlers who braved the isolation on Lake Kauppi.

For more information on Cotton, contact:
MINNESOTA STATE OLD TIME FIDDLE CHAMPIONSHIP
P.O. Box 205
Cotton, MN 55724
(218) 482-3430 or (218) 482-5549

C AFE & BAKERY

■ SUE'S SWEET SHOP
Highway 53
Cotton, MN 55724
Tel: (218) 482-3281
Hrs: (Summer) Mon. - Sun. 6 a.m. - 8 p.m.
    (Winter) Mon. - Sun. 6 a.m. - 7 p.m.

What began as an idea for a coffee shop opened in May of 1985 as a restaurant where everything on the menu is home cooked and baked. Built by the owner and her family, Sue's Sweet Shop is actually three times the size originally planned.

Sue Erjavec and her crew serve up a menu featuring roast turkey, baked ham, and roast beef with "real" mashed potatoes and gravy, and a warm country atmosphere. Several kinds of pies, made from scratch daily, also are offered on the menu, as well as bread pudding, cookies, sandwiches, and breakfast items. Coffee here is a favorite in the area, especially when accompanied by a homemade cinnamon or pecan roll. Ice cream treats from the soda fountain include sundaes, malts, floats, and cones.

Sue is planning to share her home cooking secrets in a cookbook, to be available soon. Visitors may not find the standard hamburger and fries fare at Sue's Sweet Shop, but they will find good home cooking and tasty desserts. Remember to ask about the daily specials for meals and soup. The restaurant is open for breakfast, lunch, and dinner.

Crane Lake

O nce part of the great fur trade route, Crane Lake is today a modern northwoods resort community. A host of wilderness lodges, marinas, outfitters, and campgrounds make the town an ideal starting point for a journey into the serene lakes and rivers abutting the U.S.-Canada border. But despite all the conveniences offered to visitors, Crane Lake offers a genuine wilderness experience for those looking for a few days of solitude accompanied by a few friends and, most likely, a fine selection of walleye for dinner. Although the whispering woods and sky-blue waters are outstanding attractions in their own right, the Crane Lake area also offers intriguing glimpses into three distinct historical epochs. First came the Indians, who left behind the *Painted Rocks* at *Lac La Croix* and *Namakan*. Painted hundreds of years ago, these pictographs are the last traces of the first people who enjoyed the bounty of this vast lake area. By *Crane Lake Gorge,* visitors can see the remnants of a late 18th-century voyageurs wintering camp, while the *Kettle Falls Motel* is a memory of the logging boom of the early 20th century. Built in 1913, the hotel is now listed on the National Register of Historic Places.

For more information on Crane Lake, contact:

CRANE LAKE COMMERCIAL CLUB
Crane Lake, MN 55725
(218) 993-2346

R ESORT

■ NELSON'S RESORT
Crane Lake, MN 55725
Tel: (218) 993-2295
Hrs: Open May 15 through Sept. 30
MasterCard and Visa are accepted.

Nelson's Resort is easy to find on the Minnesota-Ontario border waters at Crane Lake, MN. A haven in the wilderness, it is on the fringes of the Superior National Forest, the Boundary Waters Canoe Area, Voyageurs National Park, and Canada's Quetico Park. Guests come to the resort by automobile, or private and commercial planes, via the shuttle service available from airports in Orr and Hibbing, MN.

Boating enthusiasts will delight in over 40 miles of continuous waters from Crane Lake into Sand Point and Namakan and up to Rainy Lake, all without a portage. Nelson's can arrange all types of boat trips, from fishing and camping to fly-in or wildlife camera excursions. Boat rides with shore lunch prepared for visitors by the guide are especially popular. Nelson's offers the convenience of furnishing whatever is needed for each trip, from boat and motor, to gear, tackle, and even weather reports. Fishermen of any caliber will find championship fishing at the resort because the border waters are teeming with walleye, northerns, lake trout, and bass. Many other activities such as snorkling, water skiing, swimming, and canoeing are available. Three miles of nature trails can keep photographers, bird watchers, and hikers busy for hours. Ping-pong and pool tables, the sauna, and a crackling fireplace provide a pleasant, less strenuous diversion.

The resort has its own store, gift shop, and laundromat; and it can arrange for babysitters. Accommodations are available for individuals, families, conventions, and corporate functions, with rates ranging from European to full American plans.

Duluth

Duluth is Minnesota's best-kept secret, a fascinating cosmopolitan city steeped in tradition, but with an eye on the future. Set on the shores of vast Lake Superior, Duluth has always been a gateway to the world. Claimed for the French in 1679 by the explorer Daniel duLuth, the city passed a couple of centuries as a fur trading post. But already in its early days Duluth's significance as a port became evident, and in 1871 the Duluth ship canal was cut, firmly establishing the city as a major shipping center. When the St. Lawrence Seaway opened almost a century later, Duluth became the country's westernmost Atlantic seaport.

Today, Duluth is a world seaport with 49 miles of docks, shipping 40 million metric tons of cargo every year. Every day in the shipping season, ships from all nations glide through the canal beneath the Aerial Lift Bridge, one of only two of its kind in the world. Ship watching is a favorite Duluth pastime — there's even a Boatwatcher's Hotline (218-722-6489) to call for up-to-the-minute information on arrivals and departures.

Not surprisingly, since the waterfront is the center of the city's bustling commercial life, it has been the focus for an impressive rehabilitation project earning Duluth a national City Livability Award for Outstanding Achievement and an All-America Cities Award. The hotels, restaurants, unique shops, boardwalks, horse-drawn carriage paths, and occasional festivals make this restored port area a hub of activity during the summer months and a natural starting point to explore the city's many other attractions.

ATTRACTIONS

The harbor area offers a series of sights and activities, including the newly built *Corps of Engineers Canal Park Marine Museum*, with exhibits related to the marine history of Lake Superior, including shipwreck relics and model ships; the *William A. Irvin*, former flagship of the U.S. Steel Great Lakes Fleet, now a 610-foot floating museum; and *Vista Fleet Harbor Cruises* offering boat tours that take visitors close to loading docks, visiting ships, and to the lift bridge, which rises to its full height of 138 feet in 55 seconds. The *Downtown Lake Walk*, a two-mile, landscaped pathway running from *Leif Erikson Park* to *Canal Park*, provides an excellent view of Lake Superior and the harbor area. Also located on the waterfront, but connected to downtown through the skyway system, is the *Duluth Entertainment Convention*

Center (DECC), a center for conventions as well as sporting events, cultural activities, and other entertainment. Further into town, the restored train station (a Chateauesque-style landmark officially named the St. Louis County Heritage and Arts Center but commonly known as *The Depot*) houses three museums, a visual arts institute, and three performing arts organizations. Other sights of historic interest include *Glensheen* mansion, a 39-room Jacobean mansion with original furnishings and carriage house owned by the University of Duluth, and the more down-to-earth *Fitger's Brewery* — a renovated brewing complex with a 48-room inn, a restaurant, and 35 specialty shops. For a different perspective on the city, visitors find their way to the popular *Spirit Mountain Ski Area* with its excellent hills and views of Lake Superior and the surrounding area, drive the marked *North Shore Drive* with its spectacular views, or travel on the *North Shore Scenic Railroad* in a restored Budd Car. The North Shore Drive is also an excellent vantage point from which to enjoy the spectacular explosion of color when the leaves turn in the fall, or to watch the fascinating salmon run. Ask any bait shop operator for viewing sites and times. Finally, there's the new *Lake Superior Zoo,* home to animals more exotic than the famed salmon.

Some of the best-known events in Duluth take place in the winter. The *John Beargrease Sled Dog Marathon,* held every January, is the premier sled dog race in the lower 48 states and attracts top mushers. It is arranged in conjunction with the *Duluth Winter Sports Festival,* a frisky tradition featuring auto ice races, skating competitions, and 60 other events. In the summer, meanwhile, *Grandma's Marathon* has become one of the country's top races, attracting athletes from 15 countries. At the *Bayport Blues Festival* in August, residents and visitors are treated to free performances by a dozen world-renowned bands. Later that same month the fascinating *International Folk Festival* springs into action, providing a taste of food and entertainment from around the world.

For more information on Duluth, contact:
Duluth Convention and Visitors Bureau
100 Lake Place Drive
Duluth, MN 55802
(218) 722-4011 or (800) 4-DULUTH

ACCOMMODATIONS

■ PARK INN INTERNATIONAL
Duluth Lakeshore
250 Canal Park Drive
Duluth, MN 55802
Tel: (218) 727-8821 or (800) 777-8560
Visa, MasterCard, AmEx, Discovery, and Diners are accepted.

Park Inn International is located on the lakeshore in downtown Duluth. Situated in the heart of beautiful Canal Park, it is only steps away from the aerial lift bridge, ship canal, and the Marine Museum. There is easy access to I-35 and the scenic North Shore Drive.

The two-story hotel has 145 recently remodeled guest rooms. Guests have the choice of luxury whirlpool suites, executive "king" quarters, or rooms with a view of the city or lake. The lakeshore deck is available for lounging. Indoors, the hot tub or sauna may prove relaxing, or a dip in the pool may be refreshing. The restaurant, at street level, offers a casual yet elegant dining experience. Fresh seafood, ribs, homestyle dinners, and gourmet soups are served by friendly staff. The days end with music at the Schooners Beach Club Lounge. Seven nights a week live jazz, rhythm and blues, variety, and Top 40 bands can be heard there. Special services offered by Park Inn include discount ski weekends, group rates, and Schooner's Charter packages for fishing on Lake Superior.

The Inn is convenient to Duluth's downtown business district, shopping, the Depot Train Museum, Fond-du-Luth Gaming Casino, and the Duluth Civic Center.

ACCOMMODATIONS & RESTAURANT

■ FITGER'S INN/AUGUSTINO'S
600 E. Superior Street
Duluth, MN 55802
Hrs: Open daily
Tel: (218) 722-8826
All major credit cards are accepted.

Fitger's Inn lies at the end of Fitger's Brewery Complex, which houses assorted specialty shops. It is on the bank of Lake Superior and occupies what used to be the bottling area of Fitger's Brewery in Duluth. Preservation of the landmark building can be seen in the surroundings of the Inn. Reminiscent of the 1850s, victorian styled settings captivate the guests. Fitger's Inn contains 48 rooms and suites, most facing Lake Superior, but providing cozy alcoves in which to enjoy the beauty of the scenery without enduring the chill.

Augustino's Pasta, Seafood and Steaks is located near the inn. Originally from the New York Culinary Institute, the chef displays his culinary expertise, specializing in authentic Italian dishes. Recommended dishes are the Carpaccio Classico for an appetizer and the Flaming Spinach Salad to start the meal. Chargrilled pesce of the day, which is mesquite-grilled, or Fettucine Carbonara are endorsed entrees as well as the Lake Trout Augustino and the Chicken Florentine. All of the pasta is made from scratch.

A full view of Lake Superior surrounds the restaurant, and a fully stocked bar is on site. A pastry chef is also on staff for a sweet end to the meal. New delights are always appearing on the menu to tantalize returning guests. Fitger's Inn and Augustino's complement one another in the panoramic setting of Lake Superior.

■ HOLIDAY INN-DULUTH
207 W. Superior Street
Duluth, MN 55802
Tel: (218) 722-1202

The Holiday Inn-Duluth marked the completion of a $9.5 million addition in the fall of 1990, which now ranks as one of Minnesota's ten largest hotels with 353 rooms and suites. They have been the recipient of two "Superior Hotel" awards in recognition of the excellent service to their guests and the coveted "Torchbearers Top 20" award ranking them as one of the Top 20 Holiday Inns in the international Holiday Inn chain of 1600 affiliated hotels. The Holiday Inn is Duluth's Convention Center Hotel and is connected by skyway to the Duluth Entertainment Convention Center (DECC).

There are several eateries to choose from, ranging from casual to elegant dining. Porter's Restaurant provides a more formal setting in which to enjoy fresh seafood specials, prime rib, steak, and an excellent Caesar's salad. For a more casual setting, Sneakers Sports Bar and Grill has a tasty burger, sandwich, and salad menu and a satellite television system. Porter's Pub offers a second alternative to casual dining and friendly conversation. The Greenery-Vie de France bakery stirs up visions of a European sidewalk cafe with a fresh selection of croissants, sandwiches or baguets, and cappucino.

To work off those meals, the Holiday Inn has two heated indoor pools, a workout room, sauna, and two whirlpools. Outside, downtown Duluth presents an array of sights, attractions, shops, and more restaurants all within walking distance. Duluth's exquisite beauty is displayed in and around this lavish hotel where comfort and cuisine abound.

B AKERY

■ PATTY CAKE SHOP
15th Ave. E. & Superior Street
Duluth, MN 55805
Tel: (218)728-4219
Hrs: Mon. - Sat. 7 a.m. - 5 p.m.

The Patty Cake Shop has been in the bakery business for 40 years and the experience can be tasted in every bite. A Bavarian atmosphere surrounds the shop run by Jack and Virginia Soetebier. Specialities offered by the shop include cake decoration as well as danish rolls and doughnuts.

A delicious assortment of French, Viennese, and German pastries tantalize visitors as they decide which to choose. All of the tempting treats are baked fresh each day and have kept customers coming back for more year after year. The expansive product line provides an overwhelming number of temptations such as Black Forest torte, Hungarian apple cake, and Prince of Wales pie, to mention just a few.

The Patty Cake Shop has provided birthday cakes for celebrities such as Sam Sheppard and Patty Duke while filming on location in Duluth. For a mouth-watering treat, take a side trip to Bavaria — visit The Patty Cake Shop just two blocks off of Highway 61.

B ED & BREAKFASTS

■ BARNUM HOUSE BED & BREAKFAST
2211 E. 3rd Street
Duluth, MN 55812
Tel: (218) 724-5434 or (800) 879-5437
Hrs: Open daily
Visa and MasterCard are accepted.

Barnum House Bed and Breakfast is an elegant haven in Duluth's historic east end. Built in 1910, it is surrounded by stately homes of historic and architectural significance. The house was built in reflection of the wealth and taste of its owner George G. Barnum, who was a successful businessman and world traveler. He is credited with bringing the first passenger train to Duluth.

Generous as well as wealthy, George Barnum received the Duluth Hall of Fame Award for his contributions to charity.

A reflection of Barnum's good taste and love of life is apparent in the Barnum House. Ideally located on a quiet cul-de-sac adjoining a brook running through a heavily wooded ravine, the inn is a refreshing retreat for those who long for a sense of history, quality, antiques, and luxury. Four rooms are featured: the Barnum suite furnished with a massive 1880s queen bed set, private bath, fireplace, and veranda; the Humes suite offers a king-size bed, fireplace, private bath, and veranda; the Isle Royale room is rich in architectural detail and has a king-size bed complemented by wicker furniture and antiques as well as a private bath; the Brookside room has a queen-size Golden Oak bed, private bath, and private veranda overlooking the creek.

The Barnum House provides breakfasts that are as distinctive as the guests. Summer breakfasts are served on the spacious veranda where the warm breezes and sunshine enhance the meals. In the fall the warmth of the crackling fire in the enclosed veranda warms the crisp air. Winter brings a cozy setting by the fireside in the Stair Case Hall or the formality of the 1880s dining table. Whatever the season, indulge in a delicious full breakfast with fresh fruit, juice, baked muffins or breads, a main entree, and freshly ground gourmet coffee or tea.

■ THE MANSION
3600 London Road
Duluth, MN 55804
Tel: (218) 724-0739
Hrs: Open six days a week (closed Wed.) from mid-May to Oct.

The Mansion is a magnificent home built between 1928 and 1930 by Marjorie Congdon Dudley and her husband Harry C. Dudley. The seven-acre estate is situated along 525 feet of the Lake Superior shore, with beautifully tended lawns and lush woods and gardens. In 1983, Warren and Sue Monson opened The Mansion as Duluth's first bed and breakfast inn. The historic mansion is being preserved as it was when it was built, and features ten bedrooms in the main house and a three-bedroom apartment in the carriage house. Overnight guests are welcome to make themselves at home on the grounds as well as the common areas of the house. Elegant woodwork, leaded windows, and comfortable furnishings are seen throughout the library, living room, summer room, gallery, and trophy room. A hearty country breakfast is served in the dining room.

Rooms overlook different views of the estate, some facing the lake, and have varying degrees of privacy. Room size and difference in bathroom facilities are reflected in the room rates. The Mansion is open to groups all year by special arrangement.

■ MATHEW S. BURROWS 1890 INN
1632 E. First Street
Duluth, MN 55812
Tel: (218) 724-4991
Hrs: Check-in 4 p.m., Check-out 11:30 a.m.
Visa and MasterCard are accepted.

Built in 1890 as a refined residence for notable clothier Mathew S. Burrows, this Victorian house features original stained glass and beautifully carved woodwork. Porches filled with wicker furniture and a porch swing create an especially casual elegance. Guests at the Mathew S. Burrows 1890 Inn appreciate the luxurious ambiance which allows them to escape the pressures of work and urban life.

In 1988, Pam and Dave Wolff transformed their home into the bed and breakfast inn to continue the distinguished history and hospitality of the home. Guests at the inn will encounter a smoke-free atmosphere throughout the house. The four guest rooms are decorated with luxury in mind, and each offers its own exquisite features. All have private baths, and the master suite has a wood burning fireplace. Large, comfortable beds and antique furnishings along with other appointments reflect the Victorian charm of this romantic getaway for adults. Guests are invited to relax on one of the two porches, bask in the sunshine of the inn's cozy solarium, or enjoy the comfort of the library and music room with its 1910 player piano.

In addition to the inn's charming amenities, a sumptuous candle-lit breakfast including freshly baked breads and muffins, in-season fruits, juice, coffee, teas, and a special entree are served in the dining room every morning. Pam and Dave invite guests to "leave your cares behind" as you enter the portals of a bygone era and enjoy the ambiance and comfort of the Mathew S. Burrows 1890 Inn.

CANDY STORE

■ CANELAKE'S CANDY
Fitgers On The Lake
Duluth, MN 55802
Tel: (218) 722-4609
Hrs: Mon. - Sat. 10 a.m. - 9 p.m., Sun. noon - 5 p.m.

Canelake's Candy truly is a real tradition of old-fashioned homemade candies. Originally started in 1905, the founder of Canelake's Candy Kitchen believed in making his candies with the freshest ingredients. The tradition of hand-roasted nutmeats, hand-dipped chocolates, and hand-decorated candies is still carried on. Along with quality chocolates, other selected candies include caramels, dipped nuts, toffee, creams, brittles, bars, and much more. Mail orders are accepted.

CHARTER FISHING

■ DEEP SECRET CHARTERS
5254 Albert Olson Road
Duluth, MN 55804
Tel: (218) 525-6733
Hrs: May - Oct. Daily trips

Serious fishermen now and then are afflicted with an irresistible itch to troll the depths of Lake Superior. They "scratch" that itch by arranging a charter with Deep Secret Charters and going after the truly big ones on the largest freshwater lake in the world — a fisherman's dream, brimming with lake trout, steelhead, and coho, chinook, and Atlantic salmon.

Deep Secret Charters operates out of the beautiful port of Knife River, just 15 minutes northeast of Duluth on Old Highway 61. Deep Secret is run by Captain Gordon Olson, a North Shore resident and experienced guide. Captain Olson is licensed by the U.S. Coast Guard; he is a Minnesota state licensed guide (#16); and he is a member of the North Shore Charter Captains Association. His 31-foot Sportcraft Sport Fisherman, Deep Secret, features everything needed or wanted in a charter boat. Deep Secret sports a flying bridge, heated cabin, and large fishing deck; and it is furnished with all the necessary deep-sea trolling gear. Also provided is the latest in electronics, including radar, Loran C navigational device, and a color videograph-depth finder. The Deep Secret is fitted with U.S. Coast Guard-approved safety equipment, and she can accommodate up to six people. Children are welcome.

This is a vacation the whole family will enjoy, whether determined to hook a feisty fish or just to spend a day out on the big lake.

FISH MARKET

■ KEMP'S FISH MARKET & GRILL
11-15 Buchanan Street
Canal Park
Duluth, MN 55802
Tel: (218) 727-4800
Hrs: Hours vary

Kemp's is a family-run business with over 60 years of expertise in local and national fish markets. Located on one of the busiest corners in the popular Canal Park district, Kemp's Fish Market occupies a section of what was once a warehouse. The market has a large selection of fish, available fresh and frozen. Alaskan king salmon, flown in several times a week, and Canadian walleye are favorite domestic species. Popular, more exotic fish include shark, swordfish, mahi-mahi, and halibut as well as seafood such as crab legs, shrimp, and scallops. Kemp's also specializes in smoked fish, and offers choices from king salmon to ciscos. Guests can have their orders grilled right at Kemp's and dine in the waterfront atmosphere. High timber-beamed ceilings, wood floors, and fish nets on the walls and ceilings set the mood. Mounted fish and an aquarium with footlong rainbow trout complete the picture.

In the summer, the outdoor deck on the lakeside corner offers a place for a warm sunny or cool evening meal. A wide variety of fresh and saltwater entrees may be chosen from the menu, and each includes a baked potato or wild rice dish with an order of fresh coleslaw, all for a most reasonable price.

GAMING CASINO

■ FOND-DU-LUTH
129 E. Superior Street
Duluth, MN 55802
Tel: (218) 722-0280 or (800) 777-8538
Hrs: Open 11 a.m. daily

Las Vegas gambling excitement can be found along the North Shore of Minnesota. One-thousand miles closer to home is the Fond-du-luth Gaming Casino. The Fond-du-luth Casino lights up Superior Street in Duluth; inside, the gaming tables heat up the interior. Admission to the casino is free, providing an opportunity to observe the games and choose favorites on which to wager. For the novice gambler, $9 may cover an entire evening of gambling, for the high roller, the deluxe packages of up to $81 are available.

There are several games of chance to choose from: video poker, video blackjack, video horse racing, high or low stake bingo, pulltabs, videogames, and casino bingo table that are similar to Vegas-style B blackjack except bingo balls numbering from one to ten are used instead of cards. Chips may be purchased at the gaming tables in dollar denominations, $2 minimum wager and $25 maximum wager. Payouts are naturally dependent on what and how much is chosen to play. Pulltabs are worth up to $25,000, and regular bingo generally pays out about $8,000 per session.

The casino opens daily at 11 a.m. with late night sessions on Friday and Saturday evenings beginning at 10:45 p.m. There is a refreshment area on both of the two floors, with beer and wine available on the first floor only. A concession area and a Casino Gift Shop are also readily available for patrons. Fond-du-luth is adjacent to a 300-car parking ramp; one-hour complimentary parking is available for casino customers.

G IFT SHOPS

■ MADE IN THE SHADE
Fitger's Brewery Complex
600 East Superior Street
Duluth, MN 55802
Tel: (800) 777-8538
Hrs: Mon. - Sat. 10 a.m. to 9 p.m.
    Sun. 11 a.m. to 9 p.m.
Visa, MasterCard, AmEx, and Discover are accepted.

This fascinating gift shop features a variety of functional and decorative gifts, all individually created by American artisans. Made In The Shade's selection has come to exemplify the growing diversity and creative excellence of fine American designers since it first opened its doors in 1976, offering one-of-a-kind treasures for everyone.

The popular jewelry selection includes sophisticated glass beads and whimsical creations as well as intricate hand-crafted designs that feature semi-precious stones. Gourmet and weekend cooks alike will enjoy Made In The Shade's sculpted stoneware and also its porcelain and cookware. Many kinds of preserves, teas, and candies by Crabtree & Evelyn make excellent gifts for food lovers of all persuasions.

Made In The Shade also features Native American artifacts. Items such as birch bark baskets, miniature Papago ornaments woven from horsehair, and decorative peace pipes celebrate the rich diversity of the Native American culture. This unusual shop is full of unique gift ideas and is worth a visit when spending time in the Duluth area.

■ ONCE UPON A TIME
5103 North Shore Drive
Duluth, MN 55804
Tel: (218) 525-3029
Hrs: Open daily, closed Jan. - March
Visa and MasterCard are accepted.

Located on the beautiful north shore of Lake Superior, this Victorian style gift shop has been fashioned to look like the fabled gingerbread house with the interior holding surprises for all. Six rooms display charming gift selections and are decorated differently from one to the other. The Minnesota room features items made and representative of the Land of 10,000 Lakes. The Christmas room displays treasures of the holiday season. These items complement the authentic Swedish fireplace, which is an attraction in itself. Reproductions of old prints are special items available at Once Upon a Time. Cards, prints, gift bags, and books by Swedish artist Lissi Martin are featured as well as Sara's Attic collectibles and David Winter Cottages.

For the decorator, lace curtains and doilies will help round out that special room. Wonderful treasures line the shelves of Once Upon a Time, helping to bring the fairy tale in all of us to life.

HERITAGE & ARTS CENTER

■ THE DEPOT
506 W. Michigan Street
Duluth, MN 55802
Tel: (218) 727-8025
Hrs: (May - mid-Oct.) daily 10 a.m. - 5 p.m.
      (Mid-Oct. - April) Mon. - Sat. 10 a.m. - 5 p.m., Sun. 1 p.m. - 5 p.m.

Built in 1892 as a train station, the Depot is now one of Duluth's favorite attractions. The Chateauesque-style building, listed in the National Register of Historic Places, has become the cultural center of the northland. Eight organizations (including three museums, a visual arts agency, and four performing arts organizations) are housed in the historic landmark. The Depot's museum complex offers a variety of experiences for visitors — train, historical, and children's museums as well as art galleries.

The A.M. Chisholm Museum, featuring educational displays and one of the largest train museums in North America, is housed in the Lake Superior Museum of Transportation. See the past come alive in the St. Louis County Historical Society's exhibits and catch a glimpse of 1910 Duluth by strolling or taking a vintage trolley through Depot Square. (The trolley runs Memorial Day through Labor Day.)

Also in the museum complex are the Duluth Art Institute's galleries, featuring exhibits by local and regional artists.

In the performing arts wing, performances are scheduled by the Duluth Ballet, the Duluth Playhouse, the Duluth-Superior Symphony, or Matinee Musicale.

R ESTAURANTS

■GRANDMA'S SALOON & DELI
522 Lake Ave. S.
Duluth, MN 55802
Tel: (218) 727-4192
Hrs: Hours vary
All major credit cards are accepted.

Vintage decor, Italian pasta, and overstuffed sandwiches headline the bill of fare at Grandma's Saloon & Deli. Specialty drinks and desserts, including award-winning cheesecake, can be enjoyed in a fun, casual atmosphere. A popular restaurant and night spot in Duluth, look for Grandma's in Canal Park on the historic waterfront. Grandma's Original Saloon & Deli is joined by Mickey's Grill and Grandma's Comedy Club in a lively complex on Lake Avenue. Mickey's Grill is known for its choice steaks, plump poultry, and fresh seafood hot off the grill. The Comedy Club features local and national talent provided by Scott Hanson's Comedy Gallery in Minneapolis. Grandma's Sports Garden, right across the street, dishes up pizza, sandwiches, and burgers, as well as providing a large arcade, billiards, and live television sports.

Upstairs, Grandma's Canal Park is kept jumping with dancing every night. One of the largest decks overlooking Lake Superior gives a great view of the beach for outdoor drinks and dining in the daytime or evening. For people on the go, take-out is available from both Grandma's and Mickey's Grill.

The name "Grandma's" may sound familiar to many because they have heard of Grandma's Marathon, an event held each year in June. In Minneapolis, Grandma's Saloon & Deli is located on the West Bank.

■ LOMBARDI'S ITALIAN CAFE

201 E. Superior Street
Duluth, MN 55802
Tel: (218) 722-0190
Hrs: Open daily
Visa and MasterCard are accepted.
Delivery available.

Lombardi's Italian Cafe is the newest addition to fine dining in Duluth. This cafe provides an intimate and relaxing setting in which to enjoy exceptional Italian cuisine. The number one priority is the outstanding quality and freshness of the pastas, sauces, and unforgettable gourmet pizzas. Specials are offered daily, providing an opportunity to experience other fine dishes not offered on the menu. Cappuccino, espresso, beer, and wine are available as well.

During the summer, cool jazz is presented with hot Italian food providing an entertaining yet tasteful way to spend Sunday evenings. Lombardi's Italian Cafe offers an enjoyable dining experience at reasonable prices.

R ESTAURANT & MOTEL

■ LAKEVIEW CASTLE

5135 North Shore Scenic Drive
Duluth, MN 55804
Tel: (218) 525-1014
Hrs: (Restaurant) 8 a.m. - 10 p.m.
    (Lounge) open until 1 a.m.
All major credit cards are accepted.

Lakeview Castle offers royal dining and lodging along the scenic North Shore Drive in Duluth. The restaurant and lounge area were built 11 years ago, staying true to the stone and woodwork material maintaining the look of a castle. In 1914 Lakeview Castle began as a fish stand and coffee shop. Over the years it has evolved into a nightclub with cottages available in the summer. Steaks, seafood, and Greek specialities such as Dolmades and Pastisio highlight the menu. The Castles' own seafood platter combines scallops, shrimp, trout, and crab to bring together a nautical feast. Breakfast and lunch are served as well and reasonable prices. Off sale liquor is also available.

For those who desire a more intimate setting, the lounge has weekly entertainment in a friendly and spacious atmosphere.

Lakeview Castle offers the mystery and romance of the medieval ages enhanced by the beauty of the North Shore.

$\boxed{S}$ HOPPING

■ DeWitt-Seitz Marketplace
394 Lake Ave. S.
Duluth, MN 55802
Tel: (218) 722-0047

The DeWitt-Seitz Marketplace is a collection of 15 unique variety shops and restaurants located in the renovated DeWitt-Seitz Building on the Duluth waterfront. This building is on the National Register of Historic Places and was the home of the DeWitt-Seitz Company, a furniture jobber and a mattress manufacturer.

The 1909 warehouse's renovation began in 1985. The first and second floors were turned into the DeWitt-Seitz Marketplace, while offices were constructed on the lower level and on the third and fourth floors. The renovation complemented the buildings' post and beam construction; the original hardwood floors were kept while a wooden staircase was added. An adjacent building was purchased in 1987 and became part of the complex in 1988.

The marketplace is located in Canal Park, conveniently near the Aerial Lift Bridge, the canal, and the new Lake Walk.

■ Fitger's Brewery Complex
600 E. Superior Street
Duluth, MN 55802
Tel: (218) 722-8826
Hrs: Mon. - Sat. 10 a.m. to 9 p.m., Sun. 11 a.m. to 5 p.m.
All major credit cards are accepted.

Fitger's Brewery operated successfully from 1881 to 1972, and currently houses various shops, restaurants and an inn. The weathered brick building, which is listed on the National Register of Historic Places, overlooks Lake Superior and still maintains the turn-of-the-century motif throughout the interior.

Fitger's Inn has 48 rooms and suites, each decorated differently and most providing a view of Lake Superior and the ships anchored along the harbor coast. This luxury inn has maintained many of the 19th century classic fixtures of the original structure. The Spirit of the North Theatre, occupying the third level of the complex, seats up to 160 and accommodates the presentation of seminars, plays, and closed circuit and satellite teleconferencing. Adjacent to the theatre is the August Fitger Room, often used for banquets and entertainment.

Thirty speciality shops adorn the interior of the complex, ranging in merchandise from South America to Germany. Fitger's restaurants offer late night dining in order to provide a spectacular view of the harbor lights.

The Lake Walk begins at Fitger's and winds along the waterfront with a captivating view of Lake Superior, the canal, and the aerial lift bridge. A parking ramp is adjacent to the complex, providing free parking to patrons and handicapped accessibility.

S PECIALTY SHOP

■ USA FOXX & FURS
9 N. Fourth Ave. W.
Duluth, MN 55802
Tel: (218) 722-7742 or (800) USA-FOXX
Hrs: Mon. - Sat. 9 a.m. - 5 p.m.
AmEx, Visa, MasterCard, and Discover are accepted.

USA Foxx & Furs is owned and operated by Wayne Nurmi, a man known throughout the fur industry for his knowledge of furs. For several years, Nurmi raised mink, fox, and sable in the Two Harbors area. He then started in retail and has been in business for more than ten years. In addition, he operates a national mail order fur garment business.

The boutique in downtown Duluth has a show floor and fur room with a large selection of fur coats, jackets, car coats, the popular strollers and hats, muffs, and boas. Fur hats and mittens are designed and made on the premises by Anja Sikio.

Nurmi assists in finding a specific style and color of fur as well as in designing and making the garment for individuals. USA Foxx & Furs offers repair and alteration service, as well as cleaning and storage of furs.

T EA ROOM

■LAKE SUPERIOR TEA ROOM
5363 North Shore Drive
Duluth, MN 55804
Tel: (218) 525-3503
Hrs: Open June - Sept. 7 a.m. - 4 p.m. Closed Tuesday

The Lake Superior Tea Room was established in 1986 to continue the tradition of relaxation and socialization associated with drinking tea. Located on the scenic North Shore at the French River, travelers can enjoy a "spot" of tea along with the breathtaking view of Lake Superior's shoreline.

This cozy tea room serves morning, noon, and high tea, along with menu items featuring muffins, nutbreads, fresh fruits, cheeses, smoked fish, and delicious desserts. The atmosphere is casual and relaxed, complemented by folk and classical background music. Customers can also take a packaged box lunch to enjoy on their North Shore adventures.

T OURS

■GLENSHEEN
3300 London Road
Duluth, Mn 55804
Tel: (218) 724-8864 (reservations) or (218) 724-8863 (recorded information)
Call ahead for tour times and admission fees. Reservations are recommended.

Near the turn of the century, the iron mining industry played an important part in transforming Duluth into a prosperous city with a sophisticated lifestyle. Beautiful, stately homes were crafted for the financially successful. Glensheen was built in the style of an early 17th century English country estate with a 39-room Jacobean-style manor house. It was completed in 1908 for Chester Adgate Congdon, an attorney, legislative member, philanthropist, and self-made millionaire.

Set on 22.7 acres, Glensheen took three years to complete, at a cost of nearly $1 million. In 1968, members of the Congdon family gave the priceless estate to the University of Minnesota so that it would be preserved for public use and educational purposes. Glensheen was opened to the public in July, 1979. Children and adults enjoy visiting the manor house, where the Congdon family and their six children once resided. A tour of the estate, including the bowling green, coach house, boat house, formal gardens, and gardener's cottage shows the intricate attention to detail that brings students of architecture, interior design, art history, and horticulture to Glensheen. Reservations and special tours can be arranged for schools and groups of 20 or more.

Ely

S ettled in 1883, Ely offers an excellent vantage point for northwoods canoeing and fishing tours. Once a mining town, it prospers today as a tourist and outfitter center and is home to renowned wilderness explorers Will Steger and Paul Schurke. Few other cities house as many sled dogs as Ely, a curious fact that has earned the town the nickname "Sled Dog Capital of America." Ely arranges the *All-American Sled Dog Championships* in January, an international-level competition attended by the top mushers from across the country. In the warm season in late July, the *Blueberry/Art Festival* and *Heritage Days* give visitors a taste of genuine North Country hospitality. The *International Wolf Center,* is a premier nature center featuring wolf exhibits, interactive displays, and live wolves. The *Vermilion Interpretive Center* presents the intriguing history of the industrial development of the Vermilion Iron Range.

For more information on Ely, contact:
ELY CHAMBER OF COMMERCE
1600 E. Sheridan
Ely, MN 55731
(218) 365-6123

A IR SERVICE

■PORTAGE AIR
1583-A Highway 1
Ely, MN 55731
Tel: (218) 365-5600
Hrs: Daily, 24-hours-a-day
Visa, MasterCard, Multi-Service, and Phillip 66 are accepted.

"Portage Air" says it all, a full-service airport and seaplane base that brings flying adventure to everyone. Because there is so much to see in this north country, portaging by air is a great way to do it. This year-round wilderness flying service includes fly-in canoeing, fly-in fishing trips in the U.S. and Canada, moose hunts, polar bear sightseeing tour and other wildlife scenic flights, waterfowl hunts, winter dog sled, and ski trips. Portage Air also has a two-year professional flight training program that is affiliated with the Vermillion Community College in Ely.

All of these adventures are enhanced when you realize that Portage Air has an excellent safety record and high quality aircraft. The wilderness aircraft include a DeHaviland Beaver, Cessana 180, and Super Cub on skis and floats. Other charter aircraft include a Seneca III and a Cessana 172XP. Training aircraft includes Cessana 152's, Piper Arrow, and Seneca III. All commercial and private single- and multi-engine ratings plus wilderness ratings are available. The pilots know the territory and are experienced flying across the lakes and forests of the north country.

The 5,600-foot asphalt runway at the airport is six miles south of Ely and a 15,000-foot seaplane runway at Shagawa Seaplane base is one mile northwest of Ely. Portage Air has airline connections from Minneapolis-St. Paul and Duluth to the Arrowhead region. The hanger facility can accommodate a King Air. Aircraft maintenance and 100LL and jet fuel are also available.

B ED & BREAKFAST

■THREE DEER HAVEN BED & BREAKFAST
1850 Deer Haven Drive
Ely, MN 55731
Tel: (218) 365-6464
Hrs: Closed April and November
Visa and MasterCard are accepted. Personal checks are preferred.

"A tempered wilderness experience" accurately describes this contemporary northwoods home — in summer or winter.

Located on Clear Lake, 11 miles west of Ely near the Boundary Waters Canoe Area, guests can canoe, swim, hike, fish, or cross-country ski right from the front door. Beautiful grounds utilizing rock gardens, wild flowers, and nature's woodlands make for a picture perfect setting. During cool weather, a fire burns brightly in the living room fireplace, inviting guests to relax and visit. The wood-burning sauna is fired up for a truly "Finnish" sauna for bathing. Private or shared baths are available.

Anna Randall, hostess, loves pretty surroundings. Her first-class table settings, oriental rug in the dining room and many lovely, interesting art pieces and furnishings throughout the home attest to her talents for tastefully decorated rooms. Three bedrooms can accommodate up to seven people. A full breakfast is served, often featuring blueberry and raspberry items.

CLOTHING STORE

■ BOBBY JOHNS
145 E. Chapman Street
Ely, MN 55731
Tel: (218) 365-6081
Hrs: (Summer) Mon. - Fri. 9 a.m. - 6 p.m., Sat. 9 a.m. - 5 p.m.
　　　Sun. 11 a.m. - 3 p.m.
　　　(Winter) Mon. - Sat. 9 a.m. - 5 p.m.
　　　Closed Sunday
Visa, MasterCard, and AmEx are accepted.

A fashion experience awaits customers at this specialty clothing store for little boys and girls of all ages. The outside mirrored panels on the gray and mauve building seem to say, "We can reflect your image, old or new, just step on in." A personalized fashion look is fulfilled by their experienced, courteous sales personnel.

The main floor houses a charming junior-missy department that carries brand names such as Pykettes, Graff, Koret, Don Kenny, and Platex. A junior department carries major name brands of Ocean Pacific, Bugle Boy, Ultra Pink, and Bee Wear. On the second level is a compact, complete children's clothing section that carries brand names such as Carter, Health Tex, Quiltex, London Fog outerwear, Bugle Boy, and many more. A playhouse is set up within the department for the little one's amusement while Mom and Dad shop.

A full line of accessories of purses, scarves, hosiery, and jewelry give a full-fashion flair. Look closely at the detailed displays. Their colors and coordinates make beautiful statements.

GALLERY

■ BOIS FORT GALLERY
130 E. Sheridan Street
Ely, MN 55731
Tel: (218) 365-5066
Hrs: (Summer) Mon. - Sat. 9 a.m. - 6 p.m.
    Sun. 11 a.m. - 3 p.m.
    (Winter) Mon. - Sat. 9:30 a.m. - 5 p.m.

A faction of the Ojibwa Indian tribe native to northern Minnesota was dubbed by their fellow tribesmen the "Sagwadagawiniwag," or "Men of the Thick Fir Woods." Early French explorers shortened the title and put it into their own language, calling the band "Bois Forts" or "Strong Woods." So is named the rustic fine arts gallery started by Carl Gawboy, himself a member of the Bois Fort band. Gawboy, an Ely native, opened the gallery in 1973, 14 miles east of Ely on the Fernberg Road. Relocated in 1975, the gallery now sits in downtown Ely and welcomes the visitors and natives who are drawn to its selection of quality artwork.

Gawboy began the gallery to provide an outlet for his art and that of other fine artists of the area. Currently owned by Judy Danzl, the gallery continues to house the quality work of northwoods residents, while also drawing pieces from other areas of Minnesota and the rest of the country. A variety of media and artists are displayed here.

Among some of the current artists displayed are Gawboy, a regional painter; Gerald Brimacombe, a photographer and painter; and Terry Palm, a watercolor painter. Many limited-edition prints are available by such noted artists as Les Kouba, Terry Redlin, Carl Brenders, and Robert Bateman. Stoneware by Pat and Ken Larson and jewelry by Wildbryde, M'Lou Brubaker, and others grace the shelves and walls. The gallery's structure and decor, like the art it displays, remain in the tradition of the rustic northwoods. Its wood-frame structure was built in the 1890s, and restored hard-wood floors in the loft display area and warm-wood shelving throughout create a befitting backdrop for the work displayed.

A recent addition to the gallery is a room called "Creations for Kids." This section features quality activity toys and books for children, uniquely designed to nurture their creative spirit. A full-service custom frame shop stocks more than 300 moulding samples and offers museum mounting. All this aims at holding up the Bois Fort Gallery's motto: "Because you like your ordinary things to be special!"

GIFT SHOP

■ MEALEY'S
124 N. Central Ave.
Ely, MN 55731
Tel: (218) 365-3639

Ely is one of the best-known small towns in northern Minnesota and Mealy's is fast becoming one of the best-known small gift shops in this town.

Originally built in 1889, the building of Mealey's gift shop has been totally renovated. The owners have retained the original store front, wood siding, embossed tin ceiling and walls, and hardwood floors reflecting the fine craftsmanship of a past era.

Appropriately, the fine craftsmanship of this era is evident in the many handmade wood products available at the gift shop. Assorted planters, log bird houses and feeders, toys, and furniture are just a few items available. Scandinavian rugs, scented candles, wooden candles and carvings, along with handblown glass items are other novelties offered. All at affordable prices.

An open porch leads into a custom "sauna" shop addition built in 1985. Many hard-to-find "sauna" buckets, ladles, mats, pillows, back rests, switches, and soaps give the shop a uniqueness. They have a barrel sauna that will hold up to six people. Very unusual. For those who are unfamiliar with the term "sauna," it is a Finnish word meaning steam bath. For those who purchase one, Mealey's will deliver.

OUTFITTERS

■ BOUNDARY WATERS CANOE OUTFITTERS, INC.
1323 E. Sheridan Street
Ely, MN 55731
Tel: (218) 365-3201 or (800) 544-7736
Hrs: (Summer) May 1 - Oct. 1, daily 7 a.m. - 8 p.m.
Office phone answered all year 7 a.m. - 8 p.m.
Visa, Mastercard, and Discover are accepted.

It's best to be prepared if you plan to spend some time paddling through the wilderness, and Boundary Waters Canoe Outfitters provides personal service for the novice as well as for the experienced. Family-owned and operated, the headquarters and motel are conveniently located on the main street of Ely. It is one of the largest canoe outfitters serving the Boundary Waters Canoe Area.

Five types of trips are offered, including the deluxe complete outfitting canoe trip, deluxe lightweight, econo-canoe trip, partial outfitting, and fly-in canoe trips. The company has private landings at three major entry points: Moose, Mudro, and Lake One. Staff members with years of experience on the trails plan trips well-suited to your capabilities and desires. Points of interest, fishing spots, and campsites can be incorporated into your route. Once your maps and route have been determined, you can have an orientation session explaining each piece of equipment and how to use it. Only high quality, trail-tested equipment, canoes, and camping gear can be found at Boundary Waters Canoe Outfitters. They also have one of the largest stocks of fishing tackle to be found in northern Minnesota.

Boundary Waters Canoe Outfitters has been in business since 1959. Owners Marty and Nancy Lakner make it a point to see that their customers receive personal service, and in addition to motel accommodations, provide transportation to the major landings, canoe tow service, and have camping permits and fishing licenses available.

■CANADIAN WATERS, INC.
111 E. Sheridan Street
Ely, MN 55731
Tel: (218) 365-3202 or (800) 255-2922
Hrs: (Summer) May 1 - Oct. 15 daily 6 a.m. - 9 p.m.
 Office: Mon. - Fri. 9 a.m. - 5 p.m.
Visa, MasterCard, AmEx, and Discover are accepted.

Twenty-five years of providing some of the finest outfitting facilities in the country has earned Canadian Waters, Inc. a world-class reputation. Jon and Dan Waters, owners and operators, are eager to share with you the skills and knowledge they used to build their business.

Canadian Waters, Inc. has a large base on Moose Lake, but the main base is located in downtown Ely, the center of the southern boundary of the Boundary Waters Canoe Area Wilderness. Knowledgeable guides, routers, equipment packers, and sales personnel with hands-on experience are part of the team involved in planning your trip, whether you need complete or partial outfitting. Fly-in canoe trips are available for extended trips when time is limited. Wilderness canoe trips can be designed especially for families with children under 12. You will be provided with canoe country maps and charts, all reviewed in the briefing areas provided at headquarters. To take advantage of the fine fishing offered by the clear freshwater lakes, boat and motor fishing trips can be arranged. Specially designed camping equipment, fishing tackle, and outdoor clothing are indicative of the quality found at Canadian Waters. And since no trip would be complete without top grade canoes, the outfitting fleet includes Grumman, Aluma Craft, and Old Town canoes. Other services available include airport pickups, ground transportation to departure point, tow service, motel accommodations, and emergency services.

Warm, friendly, and competent outfitting service at Canadian Waters, Inc. allows guests to enjoy the peace and solitude of a canoe trip, whether they prefer the booming rapids and falls of the Basswood River or the serenity of a quiet lake.

■TOM AND WOODS' MOOSE LAKE WILDERNESS CANOE TRIPS
P.O. Box 358
Ely, MN 55731
Tel: (218) 365-5837 or (800) 322-5837
Hrs: May 1 - Sept. 25, daily 24-hours-a-day
Visa and MasterCard are accepted.

Whether canoeists are novice or experienced, Tom, Woods, and their staff will cater to their every need. Canoe country lies within the Rainy River and Hunters Island districts of Ontario, bordered on the south by Superior National Forest. And, nowhere in North America can such a variety of freshwater gamefish be found.

As North America's only outfitter specializing in ultra-lightweight outfitting, the canoes, tents, sleeping bags, packs, and food are custom-made to their own specifications. Every detail of the trip is discussed prior to embarking. All camping equipment is reviewed. Techniques of outdoor cooking and food preparation are given. Map work and routes are selected, and an orientation is held on how to correctly handle a canoe, choose a good tent site, and erect the tent. Before the trip and after they return, guests may enjoy overnight accommodations of private double bedrooms as well as private bunk rooms, showers, and a family-style guest dining room overlooking Moose Lake.

Reservations are necessary because a permit is required to get into the Boundary Waters Canoe Area. All canoe trips are arranged for a specific number of days so reservations should be made as early as possible.

R ESORTS

■ BREAKER'S ON SNOWBANK
P.O. Box 128
Ely, MN 55731
Tel: (218) 365-6032 or (800) 777-7162 Ext. B.C.
Hrs: Daily 24-hours-a-day
Visa and MasterCard are accepted.

For a quiet getaway with a wide variety of activities any time of the year, Breaker's on Snowbank provides a refreshing change of pace. Located in the unspoiled wilderness, it supports wildlife, including moose, deer, otter, ducks, loons, bald eagles, and more.

Snowbank has 98 percent undeveloped lakeshore and numerous tree-packed islands.

The resort offers services to canoeists headed to Lake One and Moose Lake entry points into the Boundary Waters Canoe Area. These include canoe tow and transportation for canoeists and equipment. Hiking enthusiasts can take advantage of 41 miles of trails around Snowbank Lake and nearby lakes, including a loop winding through giant white pines hundreds of years old. There is a hiking trail pickup service, so hikers do not have to pack everything in. Cross-country skiers can indulge in the 8-kilometer trail that begins from the lodge, or any of the other 20 kilometers of nearby trails. Some of these are groomed and offer uncrowded paths of varying degrees of difficulty. Advance reservations may be made for dog-sled trips. Hunters can be guided to choice areas for duck, grouse, deer, moose, and bear. Excellent summer and winter fishing can be found on Snowbank and surrounding portage lakes. Heated ice fishing houses are available in the winter.

Breaker's overnight accommodations include motel rooms and housekeeping suites in a fully modern lakeside building. There are suites with dining/living areas and all utensils for cooking and eating. Visitors may also enjoy their meals in the dining room in true family style. The lodge and general store at Breaker's stock seasonal equipment as well as groceries, snacks, and souvenirs, rounding out a comfortable place to view the wilderness in a relaxed friendly atmosphere.

■ RIVER POINT RESORT
P.O. Box 397
Ely, MN 55731
Winter Address: 12410 44th Place N., Plymouth, MN 55442
Tel: (800) 777-7082 or (218) 365-6604 or (612) 559-8231 (in winter)
Hrs: Open mid-May to mid-October and selected winter weekends.
Visa and MasterCard are accepted.

River Point Resort lies on a 2,000-foot secluded peninsula where the Kawishiwi River joins beautiful Birch Lake. This ideal vacation spot is located among the tall pines and serene wooded areas of the Superior National Forest. In 1982, River Point Resort was the site of the nationally significant archaeological find of the Laurel Indian culture dated 500 B.C. Back then, as is the case today, the beauty and desirability of this most private site was recognized.

Vacation homes and villas face south and are right at the water's edge, 75 to 100 feet apart. They have paneled or knotty pine interiors, baseboard heat, electric refrigerators, ranges, microwaves, dishwashers, and all the small electric appliances. Spacious screened-in porches, huge sundecks, picnic tables, barbecue grills, private docks, and laundromat are some of the amenities of the resort facility. Select one- to four-bedroom homes for family, fishing groups, or a conference retreat. In 1990, one- and two-bedroom luxury and queen-size beds were completed. The knotty pine guest lodge, with stone fireplace, trading post, gameroom, and meeting room, was also completed. The naturalist program and free fishing seminar are held in the lodge.

The swimming beaches are spacious and safe. Relax in the authentic Finnish sauna. Enjoy the sailing, windsurfing, waterbiking, funbugging, and kayaking, or go on an outing on the pontoon boat. Paddle a canoe up the South Kawishiwi River or take a day canoe trip into the Boundary Waters Canoe Area. Hiking trails are well marked and are abundant with wildlife.

Beautiful views, spacious grounds, comfortable accommodations and an abundance of recreational activities all blend into the calmness present in this natural setting of the lake, river, and peninsula. Such privacy. No wonder they have been attracting generations of guests.

R ESORTS & RESTAURANTS

■ BURNTSIDE LODGE
2755 Burntside Lodge Road
Ely, MN 55731
Tel: (218) 365-3894
Hrs: Late May to mid-September
Visa, MasterCard, AmEx, and Discover are accepted.

Burntside Lodge, originally known as Brownwell Outing Company, was established as a hunting camp in the early 1900s. The Chippewa Indian tribe lived on the lake and gave it the name "Burntside" after the north shore of this glacier-made lake was devastated by a forest fire. Burntside has been a resort since 1913 and is listed on the National Register of Historical Places. Its designation is due to the high integrity and large collection of log buildings that remain in a remarkable state of preservation.

Most of the handcrafted pine and hardwood furnishings presently being used in the lobby and dining room are part of the original rustic furniture built in the early 1920s. There is a unique variety of one-, two-, and three-bedroom log cabins to choose from; many are located lakeside. Accommodations are comfortable; some with light housekeeping facilities. Burntside

Lodge also offers a dining experience unmatched in the area. A full menu includes over 20 entrees with salad bar and an excellent choice of homemade desserts. Chef-prepared walleye pike, lake trout, seafood, steaks, and barbecued ribs are popular selections. Chef specials include Saturday night prime rib, Steak au Poivre, Steak Neptune, as well as other specials. Launching and dock space are generally available to all guests, along with boat and motor, canoe, pontoon, and paddleboat rentals. Burntside Lake is an exceptional lake trout and small-mouth bass lake. Guided day trips into the Boundary Waters on Basswood Lake, Burntside, or other lakes are also available. Other resort activities include a sandy swimming beach; children's playground; shuffleboard; and a recreation building with a pool table, ping pong, and video games.

Burntside Lodge is a place where families have come for over 75 years to share a good time in the beauty and quiet of the Minnesota northwoods. For many, the annual return to Burntside is a tradition.

■ VILLAGE OF OLSON BAY
2279 Grant McMahon Boulevard
Ely, MN 55731
Tel: (218) 365-4876 or (800) 777-4419
Hrs: Pier 88 - mid-May through September: 11 a.m. - 8 p.m.
    Oct. through mid-May, Thur. - Sun. 5 p.m. - 9 p.m.
    Cottages available May through October
Visa, MasterCard, American Express, and Discover are accepted.

The main lodge of the Village of Olson Bay Resort was built in the late 1800s. One of the first buildings in the area, it served as the community hall for the Finnish immigrants. The building was moved in 1946 from its site in nearby Winton to where it rests today on the shore of scenic Shagawa Lake.

The lodge now houses the popular Wilderness Inn Supper Club. Guests become acquainted with Paul Bunyan's "Mountain of a Dinner" menu. Outdoor dining by the lake is offered at "Pier 88."

The newly renovated cottages accommodate vacationers who want to "rough it in comfort." Each is equipped with modern bathroom and kitchen facilities, including a microwave oven; plus color television, new mattresses, and a 14-foot aluminum boat. Large patio decks have furniture and Weber grills. Beginning with a campfire and get-acquainted evening, guests can take advantage of wide-ranging resort activities. On the water there is great fishing, canoeing, sailing, and paddle boating, as well as swimming at the sandy beach. There is free use of bicycles, badminton, volleyball, and horseshoe equipment, in addition to nearby golf, tennis, and hiking trails. Children enjoy the playground and special, organized activities.

The "Village" features Bunyan's Ice Cream Palace, Shagawa Lake Marina, and a log cabin arts and crafts gift shop, "Country Simple Pleasures." Here local artists and craftsmen demonstrate their talents. The Fleischman family has run the resort since 1976, creating a special atmosphere for the "Village" and offering a fun, carefree vacation for the entire family.

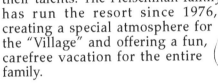

▊R̲ ESTAURANT

■ SIR G'S ITALIAN RESTAURANT
520 E. Sheridan Street
Ely, MN 55731
Tel: (218) 365-3688
Hrs: (Summer) daily 11:30 a.m. 11 p.m.
      (Winter) daily 4 p.m. - 9 p.m.
Visa and MasterCard are accepted.

Although the sign "Sir G's Pizza" is small, the exquisite Italian foods served in this restaurant are big — big in flavor and big in portions.

The present owner purchased the restaurant in 1982 from a native of Italy. Authentic Italian recipes were part of the acquisitions from Sir G. Over the years, chef-owner Neil has expanded the menu and added several of his own specialty creations. The homemade pastas of ravioli, cannelloni, lasagne, and spaghetti are just the beginning of some delicious dishes. His flair for delicate seasonings are also carried forth in the Italian gravies, sauces, and salad dressings. A special antipasto salad is a must when ordering, but here is a tip: "it's large enough to serve two people." The pizza rollers and ovens are in plain view to patrons of the restaurant, so they can watch the chef prepare their order. Generous garnishments and toppings abound. Beer and wines are available with meals. Carry-out service also is available.

Sir G's Italian Restaurant continually receives high ratings from tourists and locals alike. Comfortable tables and booths, with an Italian color scheme of red, white, and green — complete the decor of the dining area. Service is always reasonably quick and courteous.

WILDERNESS TREKS

■ WINTERGREEN
1708 Savoy Road
Ely, MN 55731
Tel: (218) 365-6022
Minnesota treks offered through the winter, and Soviet Arctic trips offered late spring to early fall.

Winter can be the most wonderful time of the year and Paul Schurke, owner of Wintergreen, will take trekkers on a wintertime wilderness adventure that will forever change their perceptions of this misunderstood season.

In 1986, Paul was the co-leader with Will Steger of the North Pole expedition, and in 1989, he led a U.S.-Soviet dogsled expedition from Siberia to Alaska. Now he has started his own wilderness trekking and camping program and helps his wife, Susan, sell her handcrafted line of winter apparel. Both ventures are under the umbrella name of Wintergreen.

During a typical Wintergreen camping trip, participants venture out into the wilderness in groups of eight to 12 with sled-dogs and top-quality winter survival gear provided by the program. Under the guidance of experienced Wintergreen staff members, they learn to both drive the dogs and to care for them in their off hours. They also master such basic skills as cross-country skiing, snow-shoeing, map and compass reading, and snow shelter building. Trips may last from a few days to a few weeks. In addition to

Minnesota adventures, Wintergreen also offers an extensive array of Soviet Arctic programs designed to bring Soviets and Americans closer together as they meet and learn from each other.

Embarrass

The tiny Iron Range community of Embarrass has gained more national acclaim than cities ten times its size. Primarily a Finnish farming settlement until the early '50s, when taconite mining transformed the area, the town is now celebrated in architecture circles for its numerous original log buildings. Thankfully, the cold climate has preserved the century-old buildings remarkably well, and when the mining industry took a downturn in the early '80s, the townspeople set out to rejuvenate their heritage.

At the heart of the restoration efforts that have earned Embarrass time on the "McNeil-Lehrer" show, as well as its own PBS documentary, is the local organization *SISU Heritage.* Through the work of SISU, seven of these log buildings have been saved from demolition and have been listed on the National Register of Historic Places. For the enjoyment of visitors, the organization offers reasonably priced *Heritage Homestead Tours* of restored homesteads, saunas, and a rare housebarn. In the quaint *SISU Tori* ethnic craft shop, people can purchase finely crafted items. Another eccentric attraction is the newly built *Evangelical Free Church,* patterned after the vaguely oriental-looking Norwegian stave churches and fondly referred to by the local children as "the chocolate chip church" because of its appearance. SISU also sponsors the *Summer Festival* — fun, family entertainment packed with music, Finnish foods, dancing, and arts and crafts. Then, in December, the organization arranges a *Finnish Christmas* celebration that includes Finnish cooking, Finnish Christmas carols, and horse-drawn sleigh rides to the cemetery so participants can see the lighted candles that have been placed along the way in memory of departed loved ones. In addition, the city stages the *Embarrass Region Fair* — including a Mud Run, tractor pull, and antique car and horse shows — on the weekend nearest the 25th of August.

For more information on Embarrass, contact:
TOWN OF EMBARRASS
7503 Levander Road
Embarrass, MN 55732
(218) 984-2672

H ERITAGE ORGANIZATION

■ SISU HERITAGE
P.O. Box 127
Embarrass, MN 55732
Tel: (218) 984-2672

SISU is an organization started by townspeople to promote and preserve their Finnish heritage. Embarrass is of national significance because of its highly preserved turn-of-the-century buildings built by Finnish settlers. Seven of these buildings are currently on the National Register of Historic Places with more being added every year. Through the work of SISU, many of these derelict farmsteads have been stabilized and saved from demolition. The organization offers historic tours of the area for a reasonable fee. Guests can also visit the quaint, SISU Tori ethnic craft shop where they can purchase finely crafted items. In addition, SISU sponsors the Summer Festival — fun, family entertainment packed with music, ethnic foods, dancing, and arts and crafts. Then, in December, the organization arranges a Finnish Christmas celebration that includes Finnish cooking, Finnish Christmas carols, and horse-drawn sleigh rides to the cemetery where lighted candles are placed along the way to remember those who were once alive.

Embarrass also hosts the Embarrass Region Fair in August, which gives visitors even more to see and do. Every year the fair gets bigger as more entertainment and events are added. This event also is a good opportunity to visit the many fine local businesses serving the community.

Eveleth

K nown as the "Hockey Capital of the Nation," Eveleth owes its founding to the rich deposits of iron ore in the region. Before the city spawned the hockey greats — Frank Brimsek, Sam LoPresti, and Mike Karakas among others — that gave it its nickname, Eveleth prospered as the center for the Adams-Spruce and Leonidas iron mines.

Today, the city still benefits from the mining of taconite, but is also swiftly becoming the hospitality center of the Iron Range. Although in the beginning the city consisted of a tiny settlement of five buildings and a handful of people subsisting on moose meat, it is now a bustling town of 5,000 with four hotels, an airport, a technical college, and a series of restaurants.

ATTRACTIONS

In the spirit of its original die-hard founders, the city offers an array of sports-related facilities, including a series of hiking and biking trails in the *Fayal Pond Trail* system, ten tennis courts, the *Eveleth Hippodrome,* and the *Giants Ridge Ski Area.* On the less strenuous side, there's the *Eveleth Curling Club* and the nine-hole golf course along *Ely Lake.* In a similar vein, a climb to the *Leonidas Overlook* — the highest man-made point on the Mesabi Iron Range — will provide a spectacular panorama of the Eveleth Taconite Operations and the Minntac Mine.

The most intriguing sight in town is the *U.S. Hockey Hall of Fame,* a mecca for sports fans, featuring historical displays, a Zamboni, old artifacts, a film library, an Olympic Champions display, and even a shooting rink.

Hockey is also the focus for some of Eveleth's major events, including the *Sam LoPresti* and *John Mariucci hockey tournaments* in January and February, respectively. In October, it's time once again for the *U.S. Hockey Hall of Fame Enshrinement,* an event recognizing outstanding contributors to the sport.

For more information on Eveleth, contact:
IRON TRAIL CONVENTION AND VISITORS BUREAU
P.O. Box 559
Eveleth, MN 55734
(218) 744-2441 or (800) 777-8497

ANTIQUES

■ THE UNUSUAL PLACE
113 Grant Ave.
Eveleth, MN 55734
Tel: (218) 744-4714
Hrs: Mon. - Fri. 9 a.m. - 5:30 p.m., Sat. 9 a.m. - 5 p.m.

Visitors to the Unusual Place can see that it does indeed live up to its name. Located in a big blue building on the main street of Eveleth, it is certainly easy to find. The shop is clean and neatly arranged to allow easy access to the many collectibles from around the world.

Numerous antiques, primitives, collectibles, and nostalgia have people coming back with friends to explore the shop. Visitors are welcome to a complimentary cup of coffee as they browse. A nearby warehouse has many other items.

An interesting find at the Unusual Place is Native American, hand-processed wild rice. The friendly owners are always happy to share their favorite wild rice recipes.

A NTIQUES & GIFTS

■ THE GARDEN COTTAGE
Junction of Highways 53 and 16E
Eveleth, MN 55734
Tel: (218) 744-5199
Hrs: (Summer) Mon. - Sat. 10 a.m. - 6 p.m., Sun. noon - 5 p.m.
    (Winter) Dec. 25 - April 1, Call for hours
Visa, MasterCard, and Discover are accepted.

A retired banker, Eileen Mickelson, fulfilled a lifetime dream when she transformed a vine-covered guesthouse into an antique and gift shop. The Garden Cottage sits among 30 acres of pine trees overlooking a pond, just steps away from the family-owned Swanson Greenhouses. It is 40 miles north of Duluth on Highway 53. This quaint cottage has an everchanging variety of antiques, art, handcrafts, and books in all price ranges. It is ideal for those who are looking for unique, one-of-a-kind decorating ideas for their homes.

On any day you might find a Maxfield Parrish print hung next to the bright collection of depression glass, a Raggedy Ann nestled among the chintz pillows on the antique oak rocker, contemporary metal and stone sculptures intermingled with the handcarved Minnesota woodland creatures. In the farm kitchen, the old iron cookstove is covered with antique kitchen gadgets between the yellowware bowls and the Griswold pots. Contrasts abound, with exquisite porcelain and antique dolls surrounded by handmade quilts and rugs on the rustic twig loveseat. You will also find books for gardeners, cooks, nature lovers, and collectors everywhere. Books, too, are in the children's corner along with antique and handcrafted toys.

The Garden Cottage is the ideal browsing stop on the way to or from the beautiful northern Minnesota lakes, or when visiting Ironworld U.S.A. in Chisholm to explore the history of the Iron Range mining industry.

ART GALLERY

■ WINDFALL STUDIO
Grant and Jones
Eveleth, MN 55734
Tel: (218) 744-3004
Hrs: Mon. - Fri. 10 a.m. - 5 p.m., Sat. 10 a.m. - 3 p.m., Closed Sun.
Visa and MasterCard are accepted.

The open door at Windfall Studio beckons invitingly to browsers and serious collectors alike. See limited edition prints by nationally known artists such as Robert Bateman, Carl Brenders, P. Buckley Moss, Terry Redlin, Les Kouba, and northern Minnesota's own Brian Jarvi.

Enjoy original watercolors by another northern artist, Terry Palm, who draws inspiration from this beautiful vacation area. Choose from Mill Pond Press, Greenwich Workshop, Hadley House, Moss Portfolio, and other publishers.

At Windfall's custom framing service "almost anything is frameable," whether it is a golf ball on a tee, a photo layout, or a fine old painting.

RESTAURANTS

■ K & B DRIVE INN
Highway 53
Eveleth, MN 55734
Tel: (218) 744-2772
Hrs: (Summer) 10:30 a.m. - 10 p.m.
       (Winter) 10:30 a.m. - 7:30 p.m.

Well-known for making the best burger around, K & B offers quick service in the style of an old-fashioned drive-in. Driving down Highway 53 south of Eveleth, customers know they are there when they see the big arrow pointing at the edge of a grove of birch and aspen trees.

At the bright red and white painted building, driveup customers will have their orders taken by a "car hop" the way it was in the 1950s when K & B Drive Inn first opened. Those who prefer to eat in the dining room will find it a quiet, relaxing place to enjoy the house specialty, the "Sizzler." Fresh hamburger from a local store and fresh-baked buns make this sandwich delicious. The menu includes more tasty burgers: the double cheeseburger is a favorite, as is the pizzaburger with pizza sauce made from scratch and topped with mozzarella cheese. Other grilled sandwiches, dinners, munchies, and assorted ice cream desserts round out the selection.

Kathy Klune became owner of the K & B Drive Inn in the 1980s. She and her friendly staff invite customers to satisfy their craving for a burger at this one-of-a-kind roadside haven for hungry travelers.

■ THE LANTERN FAMILY RESTAURANT
3147 Miller Trunk Road
Eveleth, MN 55734
Tel: (218) 744-9931
Hrs: (Summer) daily 7 a.m. - 10 p.m.
    (Winter) daily 10:30 a.m. - 10 p.m.
Visa, MasterCard, AmEx, and Discover are accepted.

When this establishment first opened in 1931, it served a barbecue sandwich brought to the car by carhops. This service caused quite a stir in the community. Over the years, additional eating services have expanded the once small drive-in to a restaurant with a seating capacity for 175 people. Breakfasts, lunches, and full dinners are served as well as cocktails. The three

dining areas, lend themselves to business meeting rooms, reception areas and private party rooms when necessary. Other interior improvements of wall paneling and wallpapers, picture windows, and fully carpeted floors add to the enjoyment of pleasant, comfortable surroundings.

New ownership in December 1989 has brought about more interior decorating improvements and plans for outdoor eating accommodations and recreational fields for summertime activities. Stressing a "family" restaurant atmosphere, cleanliness, reasonable prices, and generous portions, the friendly host and hostess aim to please. Chef Greg Moe has 13 years of experience creating his own special recipes. He enjoys whipping up fresh omelettes, cutting his own steaks, and having customers try it all. The prime rib dinner, barbecue pork ribs, fresh walleye pike, and tenderloin are supreme. He may just insist you try the cheesecakes.

Located five miles south of Eveleth, 20 miles east of Hibbing, and 50 miles north of Duluth, at the junction of Highway 53 and 57, this family-owned and operated business is still a dining landmark.

S PECIALITY GROCERY STORE

■ PAUL'S ITALIAN MARKET
623 Garfield Street
Eveleth, MN 55734
Tel: (218) 744-1244
Hrs: Mon. - Fri. 8 a.m. - 6 p.m., Sat. 8 a.m. - 4 p.m., Sun. 9 a.m. - 2 p.m.

In the early 1900s, Paul's Italian Market moved to its present location in a three-story stucco building over 100 years old that was once the Rex Hotel. As they walk over the wooden floors, visitors can see that the market carries imported bulk pasta in the same way it has for many years. The little market has a steady clientele, which enjoys the many Italian foods sold here. Among these are a large selection of domestic and imported cheeses, homemade antipastos, and Italian breads and muffins that are baked fresh in the store.

In the meat section, customers are assisted by a butcher in choosing from the selection of fresh and imported meats, homemade sausages, and especially Italian sausage, porketta, and beeffetta products. Holiday roasts are also available. The market has recently introduced its line of Famous Fonti Family homemade pasta. Paul's Italian Market also offers shipping in addition to full service groceries.

Grand Marais

Today a center for "deep-sea fishing" in Lake Superior, Grand Marais was only officially incorporated as a village in 1903. Originally, the Ojibwa Indians (also known as Chippewa) lived in the area and called the natural harbor along Lake Superior Gitch-be-to-beek (Big Pond). In the 1700s, French fur trappers passing through the region took on the Ojibwa's name for the bay, calling it Grand Marais (Big Marsh) in French. Many years passed, however, before anyone attempted to settle permanently near the bay. Then, in 1854, fur trader Richard B. Godfrey erected a rough shelter and became the first postmaster for the area. But times were hard, so he soon returned to the East. About 20 years later, more settlers came and put down roots, finally founding a real community.

At the turn of this century, Grand Marais was a small, bustling town dependent on logging, commercial fishing, and farming. Settlers with dreams of wealth continued to move into the area, and the town flourished despite the relative isolation of the North Shore. Although logging and lumbering are still economically important to Grand Marais — which has a population of 1,500 — tourism has actually become the backbone of the town's economy. Many comfortable accommodations are now available, scattered throughout the quaint streets and in the lovely wilderness on the outskirts. In addition, visitors can take their pick from a variety of eating establishments, serving everything from homemade pizza to blueberry buttermilk pancakes. And Grand Marais also has some intriguing shops that sell such hard-to-find items as paintings by local artists, fresh smoked fish, and Swedish antiques.

ATTRACTIONS

No matter the season, the surrounding northwoods always beckon those who love the outdoors. Hiking trails abound in summer, and in winter, cross-country ski trails and snowmobile trails offer an alternative to those cold weather blahs. Of course, there's always plenty of fishing in rivers, smaller lakes and *Lake Superior* itself, as well as berry picking throughout the summer, camping, rock hunting on the shore of Lake Superior, and canoeing. The nearby *Boundary Waters Canoe Area Wilderness* holds 1,100 lakes within its one million acres — truly a canoeist's paradise. Within Grand Marais's city limits, visitors can camp at one of the 300 camping spaces available, or hike the two-mile-long nature trail in the *Grand Marais Tourist Park.* Then there's always golfing at the rugged nine-hole golf course on the outskirts of town or swimming in the olympic-size municipal pool with its adjacent sauna and whirlpool.

In addition, Grand Marais boasts a Playhouse now located in the 80-year-old structure that was once the Norwegian Lutheran Church. Plays are performed there throughout the summer season. The town also hosts some special events during the year. In mid-January, it's the *John Beargrease Sled Dog Marathon* — the premier sled dog marathon in the lower 48 states — and in February, the winter heats up with the *International-500 Snowmobile Race.* Mid-June finds the town celebrating *Scandinavian Days,* while the first week in August is the date for the annual *Fisherman's Picnic,* five days of non-stop entertainment and delicious food.

With its ideal location on the shores of Lake Superior and its four-season outdoor activities, Grand Marais offers visitors all the fun and fresh air they can handle — and some breathtaking scenery, too.

For more information on Grand Marais, contact:
TIP OF THE ARROWHEAD ASSOCIATION
P.O. Box 1048
Grand Marais, MN 55604
(218) 387-2524 or (800) 622-4014

◼C LOTHING & GIFTS

◼ LAKE SUPERIOR TRADING POST
On the Harbor
Grand Marais, MN 55604
Tel: (218) 387-2020
Hrs: (Summer) Mon. - Sat. 9 a.m. - 8 p.m., Sun. 9 a.m. - 5 p.m.
      Winter) Mon. - Sat. 9 a.m. - 5 p.m.
Visa, MasterCard, AmEx, and Discover are accepted.

This authentic constructed "trading post" specializes in outdoor clothing, footwear, and sporting goods. Here are brand names such as Woolrich, Patagonia, Columbia, North Face, Timberland, and Vuarnet.

Visitors can find everything from greeting cards to bird feeders. With the wide selection in clothing, they can also choose from many other gift items such as dolls, baskets, wildlife prints, Scandinavian jewelry, crystal, wood boxes, rugs, and candles.

While in the Grand Marais area, be sure and take in the Cook County Museum, which houses a display depicting the history of the area. There are also many hiking trails, parks, waterfalls, and the wilderness of the Gunflint Trail to enjoy. For some of the best gift choices in the Grand Marais area, the Lake Superior Trading Post is a must.

◼M ARINA & RESTAURANT

◼ NORTHWIND SAILING AND THE ANGRY TROUT CAFE
Grand Marais Harbor
Grand Marais, MN 55604
Tel: (218) 387-1265
Hrs: (May 20 - Oct. 1) 10 a.m. - 8 p.m.
Visa and MasterCard are accepted.

Northwind Sailing and The Angry Trout Cafe are located on Grand Marais Harbor just off Highway 61. Here is a small marina of sailboats and fishing boats moored only a few feet from the deck of Grand Marais's famous open-air eatery.

At the Northwind docks, guests will find a variety of way to get out on the waters of Lake Superior. A classic 26-foot motorlaunch gives a leisurely one-half hour tour of the Grand Marais area. For the more adventurous, tours of up to two hours are given aboard 23-foot sailboats. Northwind's sharply maintained tour boats provide a remarkably stable ride, and will hold up to six passengers in a roomy, comfortable cockpit. Skippers are U.S. Coast Guard licensed. This really is a great way to get out on the water and experience the vast beauty of Lake Superior. Also available are sailboat rentals and lessons, paddleboat rentals, and fishing charters for trout and salmon.

Northwind offers two- to 14-day captained and bareboat sailing charters to Isle Royale National Park aboard performance 36-foot and 43-foot sailing yachts. Sailing around Isle Royale provides an incredible insight into this wilderness preserve of rocky shorelines, fjord-like harbors, and deep forests. The Park Service maintains a network of foot trails, docks, and two small ranger stations with showers and other facilities. Write or call for more information and a free brochure on Northwind's sailing charters.

And...if looking for a delicious meal, try taking in the harbor scene from The Angry Trout Cafe where diners can relax and enjoy their favorite import beer or a cup of freshly ground espresso. The Trout's specialties include smoked Lake Superior lake trout, fish and chips, shrimp, butcher-shop hot dogs and polish sausage, and an assortment of sandwiches, soups, and salads. Seating is both indoor and outdoor.

OUTFITTERS

■GUNFLINT NORTHWOODS OUTFITTERS
750 Gunflint Trail
Grand Marais, MN 55604
Tel: (218) 388-2296 or (800) 328-3325
Hrs: (May 1 - Oct. 20) Mon. - Sun. 7 a.m. - 7 p.m.

It was 1927 when the Kerfoot family first arrived in Gunflint. Since building their homestead on remote Gunflint Lake, which bumps up against the Canadian border, the family has weathered the Depression, two wars, and decades without electricity, telephones, or roads. By the 1950s, the modern world began to encroach, attracted to the beauty of the largest canoe area in the world.

Thus, the Kerfoots built an outfitting post to accommodate their adventures. The family is still at it, and over the years they've built bigger and better facilities, expanded the services offered to their visitors, and accumulated top quality equipment and first-hand knowledge about the wilderness.

Gunflint Northwoods Outfitters makes the logistics of canoe adventuring easy for Boundary Waters Canoe Area visitors. A large outfitting headquarters includes a room for trip planning and equipment packing. Bunkhouses with showers and a sauna accommodate overnight guests before and after trips, and vans and buses are available for transportation to various canoe landings. There is also a lodge with stone fireplaces and open-beam ceilings for more modern accommodations and delicious home-cooked meals. A full-time naturalist is on staff to review paddling and portaging skills with guests. A trading post supplies fishing tackle, clothing, gifts, etc.

The Kerfoots pride themselves on a tradition of personalized service. Lifetime experts in the canoe area, they help visitors plan their trips from beginning to end, gauging experience and skills and tailoring the routes accordingly. Sitting around the planning table, staff and visitors choose from one of more than 50 routes and work through all the details.

Committed to low-impact wilderness use, the outfitters educate their visitors about the U.S. Forest Service rules, brief them on wildlife they're likely to see, and on campsite clean-up. They provide only functionally and environmentally safe equipment and packaging.

Several specialized packaged trips are available through the outfitters, including air transportation packages, wilderness-skills workshops, and deluxe trips including lodge stays and guides. Whatever level of comfort and attention is preferred, an experience in the Boundary Waters is an experience of a lifetime, and Gunflint Northwoods Outfitters provides the service and the knowledge to make it the best it can possibly be.

■HUNGRY JACK CANOE OUTFITTERS & CABINS
434 Gunflint Trail
Grand Marais, MN 55604
Tel: (218) 388-2275 or (800) 648-2922 (for reservations)
Hrs: May - Oct., daily 7 a.m. - 9 p.m.
Visa and Mastercard are accepted.

The Boundary Waters Canoe Area, an unparalleled, remote, and beautiful wilderness; draws refugees from the fast lane to its silent and serene labyrinth of lakes. Ready with the welcome mat and carefully prepared staples, canoes, packs, tents, and experienced, sound advice, Sue and Jack McDonnell outfit and shelter many grateful adventurers.

Located on the Gunflint Trail, on the shores of gorgeous Hungry Jack Lake, the McDonnell's outfitter operation offers individualized service to its customers. Complete meal packages with various menus, top-quality equipment, orientation courses, and extensive trip routing combine with personal attention to ensure unforgettable experiences for the novice and the expert alike. Several varieties of canoes and tents, lightweight and ultra-lightweight gear, and food packages are available. In addition, the outfitters handle the necessary permits needed to enter the wilderness area. A head-start tow service is available across Saganaga Lake for those entering Quetico Provincial Park or traveling the border. Hungry Jack Outfitters also boasts two lake-side cabins, full of all comfortable amenities, for those who prefer to take day canoe trips. A bunkhouse is available as well and is much appreciated by canoeists both before and after their expeditions.

The McDonnells promote and aid low-impact canoe adventures in a fragile and precious natural wonderland. The canoe area offers wildlife, silence, and communion with the earth that all who experience appreciate.

R ESORT

■BEARSKIN LODGE
HC64, P.O. Box 275
Gunflint Trail
Grand Marais, MN 55604
Tel: (218) 388-2292 or (800) 338-4170
Visa, MasterCard, and AmEx are accepted.

Along a secluded bay of East Bearskin Lake on the border of the Boundary Waters Canoe Area Wilderness is a modern, quiet, family resort — Bearskin Lodge. Originally built in 1925, this rustic fishing camp has grown to a well-crafted year-round resort and has built its reputation on quality accommodations and equipment with hospitable service.

While at Bearskin Lodge, guests may choose to stay in one of the lakeside, housekeeping cabins or lodge townhomes. The cabins are secluded along the bay and each is set back in the trees for a true northwoods atmosphere. Accommodations have fully equipped kitchens, private baths, dining and living room area, and free-standing fireplaces. The main lodge has a comfortable lounge area with a massive granite fireplace. Meals are served in the dining room. A gift shop and private sauna are also available for Bearskin Lodge guests. East Bearskin is a 440-acre lake with 14 miles of shoreline and is excellent for swimming and fishing. Smallmouth bass, walleye, and northern pike inhabit its waters. Guide service, tackle, and live bait are also available. A full-time naturalist coordinates summer activities for people of all ages, which include special nature hikes, environmental games, and slide presentations. "Kids Korner," the children's activities program for ages 3-13, will keep kids busy with supervised activities. Winter activities include 48 kilometers of well-groomed and marked wilderness ski trails, excellent for cross-country skiing, snowshoeing, and dogsledding trips. After an invigorating day of skiing, enjoy the relaxing sensation of a "Swedish massage." Massages are available year-round.

RESORT & OUTFITTERS

■ GUNFLINT LODGE
750 Gunflint Trail
Grand Marais, MN 55604
Tel: (218) 388-2294 or (800) 328-3325
Hrs: Open year-round
    Mon. - Sun. 7 a.m. - 10 p.m.
Visa, MasterCard, AmEx, and Discover are accepted.

In northeastern Minnesota along the Canadian border and right next to the Boundary Waters Wilderness, Gunflint Lodge is a world of serene beauty for hiking, fishing, canoeing, cross-country skiing, or just relaxing.

The main lodge, built in 1953, is decorated with voyageur artifacts, carved birds, and Indian crafts. Accommodations vary from one to four bedrooms in size and are comfortably furnished with a fireplace in each living room. Many of the cabins have complete kitchens, private saunas and whirlpool tubs, and the deluxe two-bedroom units also include a microwave, CD music system, and VCR.

Fishing and the northwoods seem to go together. Fishermen travel to Gunflint Lake for its walleye, smallmouth bass, and probably the finest inland trout fishing in Minnesota. Top quality boats and motors, canoes, kayaks, and rafts are available. The lodge's Gunflint guides are the best in the area to help guests become acquainted with the lakes and fishing styles. A day with a guide also includes a complete fish fry for a shore lunch. Children will enjoy swimming, the recreation area, half-day fishing trips, nature hikes, and other family fun. The dining room is open for three meals a day, offering a different menu each night. Enjoy a picnic lunch to take fishing or while exploring the wilderness and wildlife, or visit any of the secluded beaches. Visit the Trading Post for fishing, groceries, gifts, and other necessities. There are several accommodation packages to choose from, with the most popular being the American Plan.

Outdoor enthusiasts will enjoy a variety of season trails for mountain bikes and cross-country skiing. Mountain bike, ski, and snowshoe rentals are available. Gunflint Lodge is also the only resort in Minnesota offering scenic, moonlight, and Northern Lights dogsled rides.

■THE NOR'WESTER
Gunflint Trail
P.O. Box 550
Grand Marais, MN 55604
Tel: (218) 388-2252 or (800) 992-4FUN (for reservations)
Hrs: Open year-round
Visa and MasterCard are accepted.

Dreaming of a cozy cabin on the shore of a sun-dappled, spring fed lake? A wilderness hideaway, where cool breezes carry the scent of the tall pines? Nestling beside a cracking fire at night to watch the stars come out?

On the shore of Poplar Lake, Nor'wester has been family owned and operated for more than 50 years. It is AAA and Mobil rated with a wide variety of accommodations to offer. Carl and Luana Brandt give every guest a personal welcome. Carl brings the expertise of his years of canoeing to their outfitting service and ensures that everyone has the gear and knowledge needed to make the canoe adventure a memorable experience. Poplar has four entry points into the Boundary Waters Canoe Area, but every trip is tailored to meet the needs of their guests. Especially popular is the rustic log dining room which Luana has filled with beautiful antiques. The Brandt's famous homemade bread and pies are baked fresh daily. Enjoy dining at its finest, while relaxing in comfort and savoring the view through large windows overlooking the lake. From sun glinting on the water as children swim, to the many shades of a beautiful sunset, nature is always entertaining.

The area abounds with wildlife to photograph, trails to explore, and fish to catch. Guests quickly become friends in this historic "Land of the Voyageurs!"

■R ESORTS & RESTAURANTS

■CASCADE LODGE AND RESTAURANT
P.O. Box 693-HCR3
Grand Marais, MN 55604
Tel: (218) 387-1112
Visa, MasterCard, and AmEx are accepted.

Cascade Lodge offers the seclusion for honeymooners, natural forest beauty for nature lovers, and superior accommodations in a wilderness setting for everyone.

There are several mini-vacation packages from which to choose: guest rooms at the main lodge, kitchenette facilities, or rustic log cabins for a more romantic or private atmosphere. Summer provides endless activities of hiking and fishing at the lodge, and tennis, golf, sailing, swimming, and horseback riding nearby. Wildlife is not uncommon to see during a nature walk through Cascade River State Park which surrounds the lodge. Enjoy the breathtaking sunsets and sunrises over the lake. During the winter months there are over 32 miles of groomed cross-country ski trails from the front doors of Cascade Lodge, along the Cascade River, and to Deer Yard Lake. Ski and snowshoe rentals are available and an extensive snowmobile trail system is accessed from the lodge. Just minutes away are downhill skiing at Lutsen Mountain Ski area and ice fishing on nearby inland lakes. There are planned activities every day in the summer. In the winter, guests relax in the warmth of the Fireplace Room.

Overlooking the lake, the restaurant provides a superior selection for breakfast, lunch, and dinner. The ambience is warm and wholesome, and the menu selections and service are superior.

■NANIBOUJOU LODGE & RESTAURANT

HC1, P.O. Box 505
Grand Marais, MN 55604
Tel: (218) 387-2688
Hrs: (Restaurant) Mon. - Sat. 8 a.m. - 10:30 a.m. and 11:30 a.m. - 2:30 p.m.
    Tea 3 - 5 p.m. and 5:30 p.m. - 8:30 p.m.
    Sunday brunch 8 a.m. - 2:30 p.m.
Visa, MasterCard, and Discover are accepted.

Built in 1928 as an exclusive private resort, the unique Naniboujou Lodge has served such members as Babe Ruth, Jack Dempsey, and Ring Lardner. Still reflecting the noble style of the 1920s, Naniboujou is now on the National Register of Historic Places.

Although the original plans for the club were abandoned during the Depression, the rustic lodge with its beautiful and original brightly painted interior still remain. Minnesota's largest native stone fireplace made with 200 tons of lake rocks and decorated in Cree Indian design stands in the dining room. Maintaining its historical ambience, restoration still allows for a choice of modern amenities. A variety of queen, double, and twin beds in guest rooms and connecting suites are available. Fireplace rooms are also available for an additional charge. There are no televisions or telephones in the rooms, providing a true sense of "getting away from it all."

Breakfast and luncheons provide wholesome, northwoods selections. Dinner entrees include an exquisite selection of fresh Lake Superior fish, chicken breasts sauteed with fresh tomatoes, and boneless barbecued pork ribs.

With the area's reputation of unspoiled forest, guests can enjoy scenic drives and nature walks through the Boundary Waters Canoe Area, the Gunflint Trail, or Superior National Forest. There are several trout fishing "hot spots" to discover and an abundance of gift and souvenir shops.

R ESTAURANTS

■ BIRCH TERRACE AND TERRACE LOUNGE

6th Ave. W. on Highway 61
Grand Marais, MN 55604
Tel: (218) 387-2215
Hrs: (Summer) daily 11:30 a.m. - 3 p.m. and 5 - 11 p.m.
  (Winter) daily 11:30 a.m. - 2 p.m. and 5 - 10 p.m.
Visa and MasterCard are accepted.

Birch Terrace was built in 1889 out of pine logs by the Charles Johnson family. Johnson was a logger and would occasionally trade furs in his home with trappers and local Indians. When building this northwoods mansion, he discovered that the front yard was an Indian burial ground. To this day it remains untouched. The early governors of Minnesota were often entertained here, and it was here that the bill was signed by Governor Preus to start the construction of the Gunflint Trail.

The Birch Terrace restaurant's glass enclosed sun porches overlook the Grand Marais harbor. The four original rooms of the

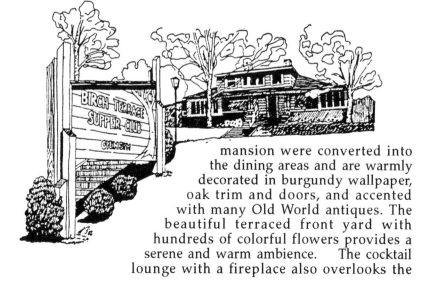

mansion were converted into the dining areas and are warmly decorated in burgundy wallpaper, oak trim and doors, and accented with many Old World antiques. The beautiful terraced front yard with hundreds of colorful flowers provides a serene and warm ambience. The cocktail lounge with a fireplace also overlooks the harbor, lighthouses, and Lake Superior, providing entertainment on Saturday nights. The restaurant provides a full menu with steak, seafood, and other specialties, serving only the freshest Lake Superior fish. A full lunch menu includes a different house feature daily. Complete catering service is available for weddings and banquets.

The Birch Terrace is one of the North Shore's most beautiful and historic restaurants. The commitment to excellent food and service is recognized statewide and across the border.

■BLUE WATER CAFE/UPPER DECK

Wisconsin and First
P.O. Box 302
Grand Marais, MN 55604
Tel: (218) 387-1597
Hrs: (Summer) daily 5 a.m. - 9 p.m.   (Winter) daily 6 a.m. - 8 p.m.
     Closed holidays
Visa and MasterCard are accepted.

The Blue Water Cafe is truly "the meeting place in Grand Marais." It is a popular place for local residents as well as tourists. It comprises the first floor of a corner building located on the harbor of downtown Grand Marais. The walls of the cafe are decorated with interesting pictures of early settlers in the area.

Dinner entrees feature house specialties such as Lake Superior trout, herring, chicken, and steak. The second floor is called the Upper Deck. It has a nautical decor and allows diners to enjoy a fantastic view of the harbor and town of Grand Marais.

While in the area, don't forget to enjoy the great scenery and hiking that Cascade River State Park — located nine miles south of Grand Marais — has to offer.

■SVEN & OLE'S

9 W. Wisconsin Street
Grand Marais, MN 55604
Tel: (218) 387-1713
Hrs: Sun. - Thur. 11 a.m. - 10 p.m., Fri. - Sat. 11 a.m. - 11 p.m.
AmEx is accepted.

Delight is the only word for this comfortable, family restaurant. The complete menu includes appetizers, pizza, deli and hot submarine sandwiches, "Lena's" croissants, and salads. Specialty pizzas include the Uffda Zah, Vild Vun, Meat Zah, Vegie Zah and Haviian Zah. Eat-in, take-out, and delivery are available. All recipes are made from scratch and during the summer months, on Friday, a Scandinavian fish cake is made from fresh herring of Lake Superior.

"The Pickle Herring Club," located on the upper deck, offers 65 imported and domestic beers and a fine selection of wines and wine coolers along with live entertainment on weekends.

The key word is "fun" and "yew" are invited to stop with family and friends and enjoy some Scandinavian hospitality. "Yew hevn't bin tew Grand Marais until yew've bin tew Sven and Ole's!"

Grand Portage

One of the most scenic spots along the North Shore, Grand Portage was founded on the fur trade, the industry that opened up the Northwest to exploration in the 18th century. The original Grand Portage — "Great Carrying Place" in French — was a bypass past the rapids of the Pigeon River in the hilly woodlands just off Lake Superior. Soon, it became the prime thoroughfare between the East and Canada's great fur country. In 1784 the British fur trade empire known as the North West Company established a trading post here. Every July the company organized a "rendezvous," an early form of trade convention and festival wrapped into one when winter-based traders — or voyageurs — from Canada and the resident Ojibwa and Cree Indians would trade beaver furs for supplies brought by other voyageurs from Montreal.

ATTRACTIONS

The North West Company fur post with its 16 buildings fell into disuse when the company moved across the border to Canada in 1803, but in the 1950s the site was declared a national monument and restoration began. Today, the *Grand Portage National Monument* includes accurate replicas of the Great Hall— the meeting place for fur traders: a kitchen, a fur press that once converted 60 bulky beaver furs to compressed 90-pound bales, a stockade, and a warehouse. Every August, a modern reenactment of the early rendezvous takes place at the national monument. The *Rendezvous Days* include canoe races, ax throwing contests, and leg wrestling — all events popular with the famed voyageurs of the 1700s. A highlight of the reenactment is the *Ojibwa Indian Pow Wow* arranged by the Grand Portage Ojibwa Reservation, which in 1958 donated the land that became the Grand Portage National Monument. The tribe also operates the *Grand Portage Lodge,* a full-service hotel with indoor pool and sauna that also features a dinner theater.

The area is known for its scenic trails and camping sites, as well as the *Witch Tree,* the 300-year old twisted cedar at Hat Point that alone has witnessed the ebullient history of Grand Portage.

For more information on Grand Portage, contact:
TIP OF THE ARROWHEAD ASSOCIATION
P. O. Box 1048
Grand Marais, MN 55604
(218) 387-2524 or (800) 622-4014

R ESORT

■ GRAND PORTAGE LODGE
P.O. Box 307
Grand Portage, MN 55605
Tel: (218) 475-2401 or (800) 232-1384
All major credit cards are accepted.

Grand Portage Lodge, a year-round resort just 150 miles northeast of Duluth on Highway 61 and located on Lake Superior's shoreline, is one of the most scenic, historic, and unspoiled areas in the country. The Grand Portage area has lured travelers since time began. First used as a gathering place for Indian people of many nations, it became Minnesota's first white settlement in 1731. Today, guests can relive this exciting history at the National Park Service's reconstructed Fur Trading Post. Tours, exhibits, movies, and demonstrations show how people lived, traveled, and did business 200 years ago.

The Lodge is an ideal spot for vacations and well suited to groups of all types and sizes. It offers 100 spacious guest rooms, lakeview restaurant, sauna and swimming pool, direct pay "slots," cocktail lounge, lobby fireplace, and banquet facilities accommodating up to 300 people. The restaurant features dining in casual elegance with a wide menu selection, including fresh locally caught Lake Superior fish, wild rice, homemade pastries and desserts.

Summer visitors will enjoy the tennis courts, hiking, nature programs, and birdwatching, along with daily boat service to Isle Royal and guided interpretative tours of the historic Grand Portage National Monument. The highest waterfall in Minnesota is only five miles away. On weekends enjoy an evening cruise of the pristine Susie Islands. Guests will enjoy Minnesota winter to its fullest on one of the largest, most scenic cross-country ski trail systems in the Midwest. A 170-kilometer network of trails provides an unforgettable wilderness experience.

All the lodge accommodations meet or exceed expectations. Let the Grand Portage Lodge pamper and please with one of the several package plans designed to fit the needs of today's travelers, without giving up the amenities of a luxury resort.

Grand Rapids

M ississippi River navigation begins below a series of turbulent rapids by Grand Rapids — once the rugged home of lumberjacks, today the heart of one of the most popular fishing and camping resort areas in Minnesota. Soon after its founding in 1877, Grand Rapids became a center for the logging industry, serving as the starting point for the historic log drives to Minneapolis. Logging was eventually superceded by the great industry of the area — iron mining and processing — and dams soon tamed the rapids that had given the city its name a few decades earlier. Today, iron processing is still a major industry, but the city is also a retail center with a wide selection of shops, hotels, restaurants, parks, and wide, tree-lined streets.

ATTRACTIONS

Grand Rapids was founded on the resources of the surrounding forests, and several attractions celebrate this natural heritage. The *Chippewa National Forest* includes 1,312 lakes with excellent swimming, boating, canoeing, and even bald eagle viewing sites. The *Forest History Interpretive Center* features an authentically reconstructed logging camp from 1900 complete with costumed guides, and a "wanagan," a combination cook shack and store that floated along with the loggers on the log drives to Minneapolis. During the *Tall Timber Days* in August, modern-day lumberjacks compete in wood chopping, buck sawing, and pole climbing, along with other lumberjack events. Still, the festival is not only for lumberjack aficionados since it also includes chainsaw sculpturing, musical entertainment, dances, children's games, and more. Grand Rapids is also the hometown of Judy Garland, and the town celebrates its famous daughter with the *Judy Garland Museum* and the *Judy Garland Festival* in June. Continuing in a musical vein, visitors can also enjoy the *Mississippi Melodie Showboat*, a riverboat presenting 19th-century song, dance, and comedy during weekends from mid-July to early August. In January, the *Grand Vinterslass* with its snowmobile races, curling tournaments, and other family fun heats up the town.

For more information on Grand Rapids, contact:
1000 GRAND LAKES VISITOR AND CONVENTION BUREAU
1 Third Street N.W.
Grand Rapids, MN 55744
(218) 326-1281 or (800) 472-6366

▮A CCOMMODATIONS

■ SAWMILL INN
2301 Pokegama Ave. S.
Grand Rapids, MN 55744
Tel: (218) 326-8501 or (800) 235-6455
Hrs: Open year-round
All major credit cards are accepted.

On Highway 169 South, the Sawmill Inn of Grand Rapids has ideal accommodations for the champion vacationer as well as the travel-weary business person. The Sawmill Inn lobby greets visitors with history of the wild north country, seen in the wood beams, old logger tools, and photos that are part of the decor. There are 125 suites and guest rooms to choose from, half of which are conveniently located adjacent to the pool. The indoor domed pool and recreation area is climate-controlled for year-round comfort. With two saunas, and whirlpool, heated swimming pool, and a putting green, it is the perfect place for lounging and relaxing with friends and family. At mealtime, savor the Cedars Dining Room featuring renowned walleye pike, homemade soups, and seasonal menus. A central fireplace adds warmth and ambience, especially on those chilly evenings.

The Cedars Lounge is a quiet place to unwind, and the Sawmill Lounge and Nightclub provides live entertainment and dancing. For business meetings and banquets, the Sawmill Inn can provide the appropriate setting. Staff members offer professional planning and handling of each event, providing room set-up and a wide variety of audio-visual equipment. Facilities for up to 500 people may be arranged, as well as outdoor catering services for anywhere in Itasca County. When it's time for a break, Sawmill Inn assists in setting up hunting, skiing, golfing, or fishing trips.

▮H ISTORIC SITE

■ FOREST HISTORY CENTER
A Minnesota Historical Society Site
Near Highways 169 and 2, Grand Rapids
Mailing Address: 2609 County Road 76, Grand Rapids, MN 55744
Tel: (218) 327-4482
Hrs: May 15 - Oct. 15 (logging camp and visitors center) daily 10 a.m. - 5 p.m.
Oct. 16 - May 14 (visitors center only) daily noon - 4 p.m.

At the end of the nineteenth century, the mighty white pine ruled the forests of northern Minnesota, and lumberjacks came to harvest them. All through the long, cold winter, the lumberjacks felled the trees and prepared them for the spring log drive down the rivers to the sawmills. The Forest History Center offers visitors the chance to experience the life of these turn-of-the-century lumberjacks at its authentic reproduction of a logging camp. At the camp, costumed staff recreate the lifestyles of the camp blacksmith, saw filer, clerk, cook, and the lumberjacks themselves. Down a short path near the logging camp, visitors also will find a river wanigan floating in the Mississippi River. This boat, used in log drives, is the ticket to the river's past. Board the wanigan, and listen to the exciting tales of log jams, fast water, and the history of the mighty Mississippi.

In addition to the logging camp, the Forest History Center offers dramatic displays of forest history in its interpretive building. Here visitors can learn about the four themes of forest history: the forest and the Indians, the forest and the lumbermen, the forest in transition, and the forest of today. Nearby, find a Minnesota Forest Service cabin from the 1930s with a costumed guide who will tell of the lonely life of a forest service patrolman, as well as describe the role of the Minnesota Forest Service in protecting forest resources. A woodland trail winds along the Mississippi River where nature lovers can study a secondary growth forest and learn to identify trees common to northern Minnesota.

A visit to the Forest History Center is a great introduction to the fascinating life cycle of forests and ways people have used this resource throughout the centuries.

Museum, Shopping & Food

■ Central School
10 N.W. Fifth Street
Grand Rapids, MN 55744
Tel: (218) 327-1843

To the founders and early residents of Grand Rapids, Central School was a most important institution, offering their children a ladder leading to professional careers, public service, and social and cultural richness. Central School was built in 1895 and served as a public school until 1972. At one time it was the only high school in northern Minnesota. Today, this landmark is listed in the National Register of Historical Places and the Minnesota Inventory of Historic Places. Located in the heart of Grand Rapids, people have come from all over the United States and other countries to appreciate its Romanesque Revivalist style of architecture and the many attractions within the school.

Shops now occupy the circular floor plan where there once were classrooms. On the first floor, framed by the original hardwood floors and pressed metal ceilings are a small restaurant, antique shop, and craft store. An elevator or double staircase with carved handrails and an extraordinary oak balustrade lead to the second floor, where the Itasca County History Museum and Store is devoted to preserving artifacts of past generations who shaped Itasca County. The third floor, with exposed rough-hewn local timbers, honors a most beloved Grand Rapids resident with the Judy Garland Museum.

The "Yellow Brick Road" through the Central School gardens was established during the 50th anniversary of the filming of "The Wizard of Oz." Nearly 1,300 messages are etched in the yellow bricks. Central School also serves as headquarters for several non-profit public service organizations, maintaining its central role in the community life of Grand Rapids.

Hibbing

S ite of the world's largest open pit mine, Hibbing's fate has always been intertwined with iron ore. The city was founded in 1893 by Frank Hibbing, a German immigrant who had turned to iron prospecting in his new homeland. Only one year earlier, Hibbing had led an expedition to the area, and during a particularly freezing January morning he had emerged from his tent and declared: "I believe there's iron under me. My bones feel rusty and chilly." He was right, of course, and by World War II the *Hull Rust Mahoning Mine* produced one quarter of all iron ore mined in the United States. Today, the enormous three-mile-long, 600-foot-deep mine can be observed from an observation building, where a video exploring its colorful history is also available for viewing. A bus tour offered Monday, Wednesday, and Friday afternoons takes visitors on tours of the *Hibbing Taconite Company,* one of the city's largest employers. For further insight into the fascinating history of the "Iron Ore Capital of the World," the *First Settlers Museum* relates the story of how the entire community had to be moved when the giant pit mine encroached on the town. In July, the *Hull Rust Days* features parades and the *Mines and Pines Art Festival.*

But all is not iron ore and mines in Hibbing; this intriguing town is also the hometown of famed folk singer Bob Dylan and pro basketball star Kevin McHale. The local bus line that started here in 1914 with an open touring car is now the nationwide

Greyhound Bus Company. The *Greyhound Bus Origin Center* features exhibits celebrating the founding of the company.

For more information on Hibbing, contact:
HIBBING CHAMBER OF COMMERCE
P.O. Box 727
Hibbing, MN 55746
(218) 262-3895

B AKERY

■ SUNRISE BAKERY
1813 Third Ave. E.
Hibbing, MN 55746
Tel: (218) 263-4985, (218) 263-3544, or (218) 533-9066
Hrs: Mon. - Fri. 6:30 a.m. - 5 p.m.
Visa and MasterCard are accepted.

You have to be good to stay in business for over 70 years. The Sunrise Bakery has done just that. They have been a family-owned and operated business for over three generations.

Bakeries always have a wonderful aroma, but when the products are made from scratch, contain no preservatives, have consistency in their texture and wonderful flavor, not to mention racks and racks of freshly baked cookies, breads, muffins, buns, and rolls to make a selection from, what else could a customer ask for? Other specialty products can be found in the store, including pastas, vinegars, meats, homemade soups, specialty sandwiches, and cheeses.

Deliveries begin early in the morning to provide area restaurants with pastries and bread items. Area grocery stores carry a fine selection of Sunrise Bakery products on their shelves. A mail order business is available for selected items. The favorite item is the Yugoslavian Walnut Potica (Po-tee-zah), a rich nut roll.

Located just off Main Street in Hibbing, in an unpretentious white building, visitors have to look carefully to find the entrance. The comings and goings of happy customers will help them find the doorway to an excellent bakery.

DELI

■ SUNRISE DELI
2135 First Avenue
Hibbing, MN 55746
Tel: (218) 263-5713
Hrs: Mon. - Fri. 8 a.m. - 6 p.m., Sat. 8 a.m. - 4 p.m.
   Closed Sunday

Located in a theatre once known as the Lybba is Sunrise Deli, renovated in 1987 into a bakery, deli, and cafe.

The grocery items include olive oil, Italian pasta, and Minnesota's famous wild rice. The chef makes all bakery from scratch, offering a variety of breads, muffins, apple strudel, eclairs, bread sticks, and homemade cookies, homemade candy, pies, and bars. One look in the glass display case makes customers want to order one of everything. A full line deli counter includes a variety of meats and cheeses such as roast beef, ham, turkey, capocollo salami, pepperoni smokey and mild cheddar, provolone and parmesan cheeses, and much more. Daily dinner specials include meat, potatoes, gravy, vegetable, and roll, priced very reasonably. Other menu items include a wide variety of sandwiches and box lunches from broasted chicken, croissants and submarines, to fresh cold cuts, cheeses, and hot meat sandwiches. Barbecued ribs, sarmas, egg rolls, and chimichangas are among the daily favorites. An appetizing selection of homemade soups and salads is offered to complement meals. Freezer items to take home also include ravioli and lasagna. Deli party trays feature any selection desired and are perfect for luncheon snacking, for a buffet, cocktail party, or any other special get-together.

Indulge in the freshness of Sunrise Deli. Whether it's for lunch, dinner, or catering a party, the choices are endless and superb.

ENTERTAINMENT

■ PAULUCCI SPACE THEATRE
Highway 169 and E. Twenty-Third Street
Hibbing, MN 55746
(Located on the Arrowhead Hibbing Community College campus)
Tel: (218) 262-6720
Hrs: (Jun. - Aug.) 2 p.m., 4 p.m., 7 p.m.
   (Sept. - May) Fri. 7 p.m., Sat. - Sun. 2 p.m., 3 p.m.

"Come Voyage with us!" beckon the brochures. Voyage to the landscapes of pre-history when only dinosaurs stalked the earth. Voyage through the dark, mysterious reaches of the solar system and outer space. Voyage dangerously near jagged, sea-side cliffs on the soundless wings of a hang-glider. Voyage to the Paulucci Space Center. Proposed in 1974, constructed from 1977-1979, and dedicated in 1980, the Paulucci Space Center was co-funded by Jeno F. Paulucci and the Paulucci Family Foundation, the Upper Great Lakes Regional Commission, the U.S. Dept. of Commerce and Energy, and the Iron Range Resources and Rehabilitation Board. Underneath its vaulted dome await the marvels of the earth and sky brought breathtakingly close by thrilling visual illusions.

Catering to the curious of all ages, the theatre offers both educational and entertaining multi-media shows. An astronomy curriculum sequence teaches the wonders of the heavens to students in kindergarten through ninth grade. First-grade classes are introduced to easily identifiable constellations, while ninth graders come away talking about neutron stars, white dwarfs, pulsars, and black holes. The theatre, crowned with a 40-foot diameter dome, features a C 360 movie projection system. Using a fish-eye lens, films are projected over most of the dome's interior surface, an effect which totally immerses audiences in spectacular cinematography. A central computer console controls all the shows and utilizes 25 slide projectors and a dynamic multi-track sound to whisk audiences away on unforgettable journeys.

In addition to its regular programs, the theater schedules a wide variety of special workshops and symposiums, offers money-saving memberships, and houses a gift shop filled with unusual educational items and novelty toys. A visit to the Paulucci Space Theater is like a visit to another world.

HISTORICAL SOCIETY

■ HIBBING HISTORICAL SOCIETY
Twenty-first Street and E. Fourth Avenue
Hibbing, MN 55746
Tel: (218) 262-3486, Ext. 28
　　　(218) 262-4900 (Hull-Rust-Mahoning Mine)
　　　(218) 262-3895 (Chamber of Commerce)
Hrs: (Summer - May 15 through Sept. 30)
　　　Mon. - Fri. 8 a.m. - 4 p.m.
　　　(Winter - Oct. to May 15)
　　　Tue. - Thur. 8:30 a.m. - 4:30 p.m.
　　　Hull Rust Mineview (Summer only - May 15 to Sept. 30)
　　　Daily 9 a.m. - 7 p.m.
　　　Tours - Call Chamber of Commerce for reservations.

The Hibbing Historical Society operates the First Settler's Museum that was established by the First Settler's Association, the people who settled in North Hibbing. North Hibbing was built in 1893 atop one of the richest iron ore bodies in the world, The Hull-Rust-Mahoning Mine, which is now a National Historic Landmark site. Immigrants from 43 different nationalities came from all over Europe to earn their livelihood mining. The town had to be moved two miles south to make way for mining.

The First Settler's Museum was established in 1958 on the first floor of City Hall and displays artifacts and memorabilia from North Hibbing. Each case depicts a specific theme or subject. There are many areas of interest for the young and old. In 1976, a model of North Hibbing was built in the old municipal courtroom on the third floor of City Hall which is a museum room in itself because of the decor of the 1920 era. Tourists can view exhibits and pictures on Indian culture, mining, railroading, geological rocks, logging, and many other artifacts from days gone by.

Visit the Hull-Rust-Mahoning Mineview site by going north on Third Avenue in the present day Hibbing. Since 1895 over 1.4 billion tons of earth have been removed, creating this "Man-Made Grand Canyon of the North." There is a spectacular view from the lookout just behind the mineview building where visitors can see a vast pit yawning more than three miles long, up to two miles wide, and 535 feet deep. The Hibbing Taconite Company continues mining taconite in full view. A slide presentation in the Observation Building travels through the colorful history of the Hull-Rust-Mahoning Mine and early mining activities. A bus tour, offered weekdays in the summer, takes visitors on a tour of all points of interest to coordinate the history of the "Town That Moved."

Hinckley

On Saturday, September 1, 1894, one of the worst fires in history ravaged the young railroad town of Hinckley and five other surrounding communities in eastern Minnesota. When the catastrophe was over, 400 people had perished in the flames. But Hinckley rose from the ashes and grew into a successful, prosperous industrial and agricultural city of 1,000 inhabitants. The city also benefits from its convenient location just off I-35 halfway between Duluth and the Twin Cities, and numerous restaurants and motels have been built to serve motorists.

ATTRACTIONS

The most notable attraction in town is the *Fire Museum,* housed in the rebuilt *St. Paul and Duluth Railroad Depot.* Listed on the National Register of Historic Places, the depot burned in the 1894 fire. Exhibits, including a slide show, relate the events connected with that great tragedy, but the museum also features agricultural and logging artifacts from the period before the fire. After perusing the Fire Museum, visitors may choose to take a steam-powered train one-half mile south to the highly popular *Mission Creek,* an 1894 theme park featuring village shops offering gift items and foods; Froggy's Saloon with its honky-tonk piano; the Frontier Fort where the village blacksmith plies his trade; or the authentically recreated Chippewa Indian village and Voyageur Camp and Trading Post. At the *Mission Creek Amphitheater,* big-name artists perform throughout the summer. In addition to cultural entertainment, Hinckley is located near the magnificent *St. Croix State Park* with its campgrounds, 100 miles of foot trails, and 75 miles of paths for horseback riding by scenic *St. Croix River.* The *Moose Lake-Hinckley Fire Trail* is a must for bikers — an asphalt trail winding its way through aspen, pine, and hardwood forests for 32 miles from Hinckley to Moose Lake. Back in town, the *Korn & Klover Karnival* during the first weekend in July boasts one of Minnesota's best parades, including extravagant floats and top-quality marching bands, and drum and bugle corps.

For more information on Hinckley, contact:
HINCKLEY AREA CHAMBER OF COMMERCE
P. O. Box 189
Hinckley, MN 55037
(612) 384-7837

B ED & BREAKFAST

■ DAKOTA LODGE
R.R. 3, P.O. Box 178
Hinckley, MN 55037
Tel: (612) 384-6052
Hrs: Open year-round
Visa and MasterCard are accepted.

The Dakota Lodge is a new bed and breakfast that offers privacy in a relaxing atmosphere. Seven different rooms are available, each decorated in its own individual style. Carefully chosen antiques adorn each room to provide a rustic atmosphere. Two of the rooms have private, two-person whirlpools as well as fireplaces. Five of the rooms have private baths, with the remaining two sharing a bathroom. A living room area has been designed for guests to sit by the fire and socialize or take in a good book selected from the 1,000 plus titles available in the lounge area. The Dakota Lodge is built on seven beautiful acres and is only four miles from St. Croix State Park. For a quiet retreat from the world, the Dakota Lodge provides the perfect haven.

O UTDOOR & SPORTING GOODS & GIFTS

■ OUTDOORSMAN OF TOBIE'S MILL
Tobie's Mill
I-35 and Highway 48
Hinckley, MN 55037
Tel: (612) 384-7469
Hrs: Open daily
Visa, MasterCard, and AmEx are accepted.

Outdoorsman of Tobie's Mill offers the right equipment for the expert or the novice sportsman. Owners Mike and Linda Welch strive toward their goal for the store to offer something for the entire family, not just the hunter. Unusual items are on display as well as a full selection of hunting and sporting accessories that would please even Daniel Boone. A complete selection of rifles, shotguns, and handguns are available as well as compound bows and arrows. Tents, backpacks, and camping supplies can all be purchased in one stop. Mountain and touring bikes are featured for the cycling enthusiast to take in the beauty of the north woods. In the loft area customers will find a complete selection of both downhill and cross-country skis, boots, bindings, and apparel. Shoppers have the opportunity to view bear, deer, elk, and even lion mounts that tastefully decorate this store. The Outdoorsman offers the equipment for every sport.

Gifts and collectible items also line the shelves. Nemadji Pottery crafted from clay deposits left by retreating glaciers is one of the more impressive items in stock. These designs resemble the pottery style of the Native American Indians. Fox, bobcat, and raccoon skin hats add a bit of whimsy to any wardrobe. The Outdoorsman of Tobie's Mill is able to outfit any shopper, sportsman or not.

RESTAURANT COMPLEX

■ TOBIE'S
I-35 and Highway 48
Hinckley, MN 55037
Tel: (612) 384-6175
Hrs: Open daily
AmEx, Visa, and MasterCard are accepted.

Tobie's in Hinckley has become a traditional stop for anyone traveling to the Duluth area. It has maintained this tradition with great food, gift shops, motel, lounge, gas station, and a Christmas tree farm. Mission Creek Theme Park is also connected to Tobie's; quite a stretch from the original restaurant operated by John and Esther Schrade.

The next generation of Schrades now own and operate the Tobie's empire. The caramel rolls baked fresh in the bakery section are reason enough to stop and visit. But then, any of the homecooked meals on the menu are worth the exit off of I-35. The lounge offers a chance for travelers to unwind and socialize, and the AmericInn is just a walk across the parking lot for a good night's sleep.

The Amphitheater in Mission Creek has seen the likes of such talents as the Charlie Daniels Band and Johnny Cash. A trip to the North Shore isn't complete without a stop at Tobie's, which seems to overflow with food, lodging, shopping, entertainment, and fun.

T HEME PARK ATTRACTION

■ MISSION CREEK 1894 THEME PARK
I-35 & Highway 48
Hinckley, MN 55037
Tel: (612) 384-7444 or (800) 228-1894
Hrs: Open Memorial Day - Labor Day 10 a.m. - 6 p.m.
    Sat. & Sun. Only
Visa, MasterCard, and AmEx are accepted.

Mission Creek 1894 takes visitors back to the days of the voyageurs and the steam locomotive. The village of Mission Creek can be reached by a short train ride on a vintage steam powered locomotive. This charming village offers a rustic setting for visitors to experience and enjoy.

Period shops greet visitors strolling along the boardwalk. Bakeries, a candy store, and an ice cream shop beckon those with a sweet tooth. For more substantial indulgence, authentic Mexican and Italian cuisine are offered in the village. For simpler tastes, corn dogs and french fries can be found. Froggy's Saloon serves food and drink in a honky-tonk atmosphere.

The outdoor amphitheater and the Lazy-U-Corral offer musical and comedy entertainment for the whole family. A rodeo and draft horse show add to the authenticity of the western village as well as a shoot-out at the Lazy-U. The Frontier Fort displays wares of artists and craftsmen as well as the village blacksmith. Tours of the Ojibwa Indian Village are offered daily. Additional tours of the Voyageur Camp and Trading Post provide further glimpses into the settlers' way of life. Mission Creek offers a fascinating trip back through time.

International Falls

A s the final outpost on the edge of great boreal forests and lakes stretching to the high Arctic, International Falls offers a rare glimpse of untamed nature. The city was long known as a stopping place on a route traveled by voyageurs in search of beaver furs, but it was not incorporated as a village until 1901. At that time it was named Koochiching, but this was changed to International Falls in 1903 to reflect its location on the Canada border and to celebrate the waterfalls cascading down Rainy River. However, the town might as well have kept its original name because as early as 1905, the falls were dammed to create water power for the paper industry that, today, is still the city's largest employer. As it is, the city's name eventually became the inspiration for "Frostbite Falls," the hometown of itinerant cartoon characters Rocky and Bullwinkle — which is appropriate enough, considering International Falls routinely registers the lowest winter temperatures in the country.

ATTRACTIONS

The city is an excellent starting point for excursions into *Voyageurs National Park* — 219,000 acres of wilderness, islands, and water, which is dominated by four great lakes, three of which form the border with Canada. Unlike the Boundary Waters Canoe Area, motorboating is allowed on the 83,000 acres of water and 2,000 miles of shoreline in Voyageurs National Park, and visitors can rent, or bring their own boats, or take a naturalist tour with *Ride The Pride Boat Tours.* At visitor centers on nearby *Rainy* or *Kabetogama Lakes,* exhibits and orientation films on Voyageurs National Park are available for viewing, along with maps and information on other naturalist programs such as the popular, free *North Canoe Voyages.* In addition, the *Smokey Bear Park* includes a giant 25-foot statue of Smokey and his cubs, the *Koochiching County Historical Museum* shows a pictorial history, and the *Giant Thermometer* (one of the most popular attractions in the town) gives visitors and locals alike a chance to spot a new record-breaking low. At *The Border,* an eclectic shop located downtown just across from the Canadian border, visitors stop for virtually anything from monetary exchange to tackle boxes, snacks, and Native American crafts. Upstairs, there's an impressive art gallery, featuring prints by renowned wildlife artists, and, for fishermen or hunters who bagged a trophy specimen, a professional taxidermy service. For those staying overnight in International Falls or simply looking for a good meal, the *Kettle Falls Motel* — located on the outskirts of town and only accessible by boat — is listed on the National Register of Historic Places and serves homecooked meals in a 1920s atmosphere. Also on the edge of town is the *Grand Mound Interpretive Center,* which includes the largest Indian burial mound in Minnesota and displays Laurel Indian artifacts from 200 B.C. to 800 A.D. For those interested in seeing the papermaking process, *Boise Cascade* offers hour-long tours of the entire process during the summer months. The *Sportsmen's Wildlife Museum* features taxidermic mounts of more than 50 animals and 100 birds — including a 1,500-pound moose — all set in natural-looking displays, along with antiques, artifacts, and logging equipment. Visitors who have been inspired to outdoor deeds by the sportsmen's museum displays can attend *Ice Box Days* in January: 10 days of organized outdoor insanity, including the Freeze Yer Gizzard Blizzard Run, softball, broomball, outdoor chess, and many other events.

For more information on International Falls, contact:
INTERNATIONAL FALLS VISITORS AND CONVENTION BUREAU
P. O. Box 169
International Falls, MN 56649
(218) 283-9400

ACCOMMODATIONS

■ NORTHERN LIGHTS MOTEL
Highway 53
International Falls, MN 56649
Tel: (218) 283-2508
Hrs: Open year-round
MasterCard, Visa, AmEx, and Discover are accepted.

The Northern Lights Motel provides cozy accommodations to visitors and fishermen visiting the International Falls area. "We treat people in so many ways they are bound to like one" is the motto of The Northern Lights.

Pleasing their customers is top priority. Family units and two bedroom units are available.

All of the rooms have portable refrigerators in them, as well as telephones and televisions. Combination tub and showers are in each bathroom; air conditioning and hot water heat are provided for comfort. Laundromat facilities are nearby as well as the Spot Supper Club. Weekly rates are available.

B OAT TOURS

■ VOYAGEURS NATIONAL PARK BOAT TOURS, INC.

P.O. Box 303, R.R. 8
International Falls, MN 56649
Tel: (218) 286-5470
Hrs: Open mid-May to mid-Oct.
MasterCard and Visa are accepted.

The Pride of Rainy Lake and the Sight-Sea-er offer naturalist-guided and other narrated sightseeing tours on the waters of Voyageurs National Park. The Pride is the largest jet-powered passenger boat in the Midwest and is able to move quickly across open expanses or to cruise quietly in shallow bays and coves, allowing passengers to experience the park and its plants and wildlife up close. A 49-passenger vessel, it was custom-built for use on Rainy Lake. The Pride operates from the park's Rainy Lake Visitor Center.

The Sight-Sea-er is a totally different kind of vessel — a 19-passenger covered pontoon boat that offers even more intimate experience of the park. It operates from the Kabetogama Lake Visitor Center. Although the boats operate on different water levels and different routes, the historic Kettle Falls Hotel in the wilderness is a popular destination for both. A cormorant and herring gull rookery is another popular destination of The Pride. Bald eagles and their nests can be seen from both boats.

Special trips such as dinner cruises, buffet supper trips, evening island cruises, and moonlight trips are also scheduled through the summer. These tours are a first class experience in this water-based national park.

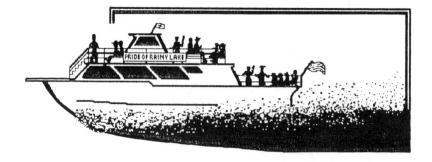

HISTORIC SITE

■ GRAND MOUND
A Minnesota Historical Society Site
Minnesota Highway 11, 17 miles west of International Falls
Mailing Address: R.R. 7, P.O. Box 453, International Falls, MN 56649
Tel: (218) 279-3332
Hrs: (May 1 - Labor Day) 10 a.m. - 5 p.m.
    (Post Labor Day - April 30) Sat. 10 a.m. - 4 p.m., Sun. noon - 4 p.m.

The Grand Mound is the Upper Midwest's largest ancient burial mound, created by the Laurel Indians who lived in this area from 200 B.C. to approximately 800 A.D. Adjacent to the mounds, artifacts are buried at former Indian camps in distinct layers.

Archaeologists have dated the oldest artifacts to the Archaic Indians who camped here some 7,000 years ago. About 4,500 years later, the Laurel Indians moved into the area. They were an adaptable people, fitting their weapons and tools to the environment. They borrowed such weapons as the toggle-headed harpoon from the people of the Sub-Arctic, yet they also took up mound-building — a tradition of the Woodland Indians. A later culture, the Blackduck, added to the mounds until 1250 A.D., although their culture was different from that of the original mound builders. They built fewer and smaller mounds and had adopted the bow and arrow instead of the spear.

The first archaeological excavation of the Grand Mound was in 1933. Research continues today, focusing on the nearby campsite areas, instead of the mound. The nearby history center offers an audio-visual program that covers past Indian cultures and the mounds they built, as well as the nature trails surrounding the area. In winter, cross-country skiing and special programs are offered. There is no admission charge.

Lutsen/Tofte/Little Marais

N estled along the North Shore of Lake Superior, the communities of Lutsen, Tofte, and Little Marais are among the most scenic spots in Minnesota. The towns were originally settled by mineral prospectors, lumbermen, fishermen, and even a few hardy farmers, eking out a living on the rocky land. But the prospectors' dream of sudden wealth was never realized, and after a few boom years, the fishing and logging industries lost their significance. The beauty of the area remained unchanged, however, benefiting a new generation of residents.

ATTRACTIONS

Symbolic of the changes that rocked this area a few decades ago, the superb *Bluefin Bay Resort* was once the home of Norwegian emigrants John and Andrew Tofte, who settled in the quiet bay to make a living as fishermen. The area is also home to a number of other resorts, ranging from rustic to luxurious, including *Lutsen Resort,* which is one of the oldest resorts in Minnesota located on the North Shore. One of the most renowned is the *Village Inn Resort,* conveniently located in *Lutsen Mountain Ski Area* — one of the nation's top ski facilities located amid the beauty of *Superior National Forest,* just next door to the *Boundary Waters Canoe Area.* Lutsen Mountain covers 1,500 acres, features a vertical rise of 800 feet, and encompasses 27 ski hills, including *Moose Mountain,* the largest ski mountain in mid-America. Recently, Lutsen installed a gondola lift system — the only one in the Upper Midwest — which lifts 600 people per hour on 50 gondola cars with a spectacular view of Lake Superior 1,000 feet below.

The Lutsen/Tofte/Little Marais area is also known for its excellent fishing and camping, as well as a proliferation of hiking and skiing trails. These include the well-groomed *North Shore Mountains Ski Trail* (a 215-mile trail system connecting trails in the *Temperance River* and *Cascade River State Parks),* the *Superior Hiking Trail* (125 miles traversing the *Sawtooth Mountains),* the *Sawbill Trail* leading north from Tofte into the Boundary Waters Canoe Area, and the trails along 1,529-foot *Carlton Peak* near Tofte. *Tettegouche State Park,* near Silver Bay, offers camping and spectacular scenery for hiking. In addition to these more rustic outdoor sports attractions, Lutsen features a brand new, challenging golf course, *Lutsen on Lake Superior.*

This magnificent area has also inspired numerous artists, and visitors are invited to the many studios and galleries in Lutsen, Tofte, or Little Marais. During the winter, two very different races buzz through the area: the *John Beargrease Sled Dog Marathon* (the 500-mile, premier dog-sled race in the Lower 48) and the *International 500* snowmobile race, which challenges 250 top drivers on a 520-mile course from Thunder Bay, Canada, to the Twin Cities.

For more information on Lutsen, Tofte, or Little Marais, contact:
LUTSEN/TOFTE TOURISM ASSOCIATION
P. O. Box 2248
Tofte, MN 55615
(218) 663-7804

B ED & BREAKFAST

■THE STONE HEARTH INN
1118 Highway 61 E.
Little Marais, MN 55614
Tel: (218) 226-3020
Hrs: Open year-round
Visa, MasterCard, and AmEx are accepted.

When Benjamin Fenstad homesteaded on the north shore of Lake Superior in 1893, he probably had no idea that a century later his modest cabin would be transformed into a luxury bed and breakfast. Starting in the 1920s, The Stone Hearth Inn — then known as the Lakeside Inn — served travelers making their way along Lake Superior. Originally, they came by stagecoach, or even by dogsled, but today they come to explore scenic Highway 61 as it winds its way along the rugged North Shore.

The ambiance of days past is preserved in each of the five bedrooms and throughout the inn. All rooms are furnished with 1920s-style antiques, including armoires, sitting chairs with reading lamps, fullsize beds and bedside tables. Each also has an attached private bath with ceramic floors, shower and pedestal sink. Mean-while, in the living room, visitors can enjoy the stress-free, warm atmosphere created by the beamed ceiling, hard-wood floors, and fireplace built of rocks from Lake Superior.

The inn also features a 50-foot old-fashioned porch, ideal for stargazing with a loved one or simply enjoying a hearty, homecooked northwoods breakfast. The host's specialties are Norwegian pancakes and stuffed French toast. The menu varies from day to day, which gives visitors the incentive to make The Stone Hearth Inn their headquarters when they explore the Lake Superior region.

R ESORT

■ VILLAGE INN AND RESORT AT LUTSEN MOUNTAIN
County Road 36
Lutsen, MN 55612
Tel: (218) 663-7241 or (800) 642-6036
Hrs: Open year-round
Visa and MasterCard are accepted.

The Village Inn and Resort at Lutsen Mountain holds true to its slogan "A few hours north and a million miles away." The Village is approximately a four-hour drive from the Twin Cities area and only 75 miles from Canada. This four-season resort is in the Sawtooth Mountains, the largest group of mountains in Minnesota and overlooking Lake Superior and the Boundary Waters Canoe Area.

During the summer there are local art fairs, music festivals, and theater. For the outdoors, there is the Superior Hiking Trail, fishing, boating, and the much anticipated championship golf course. The Village offers an indoor pool, whirlpools and a sauna, tennis courts, horseback riding, miniature golf, trout fishing, an alpine slide, children's programs, and volleyball. In the fall the mountains are bursting with reds and oranges of the North Shore's maple stands. In the winter, the Village ski hill boasts the Midwest's highest vertical drop, spread over 27 ski slopes. For the cross-country skier there are nearly 200 kilometers of groomed trails. Once off the slopes, guests may enjoy sleigh rides and dogsled races. Once the snow melts, spring brings a canopy of flowers to the shore.

The Village Inn and Resort offers three types of accommodations. The inn is a new addition presenting the decor of a country bed and breakfast. Each room has cable television, a full bath, and access to the restaurant, lounge, whirlpool, and sauna. The deluxe condominiums range from a one-room efficiency to a one-bedroom loft with a fireplace, kitchen, deck, and two full baths. The townhomes offer spacious two- to four-bedroom units and are equipped with all of the comforts of home.

RESORT & CONDOMINIUMS

■ BLUEFIN BAY

Highway 61
Tofte, MN 55615
Tel: (800) BLUEFIN or (218) 663-7296
Hrs: Open year-round
Visa, MasterCard, and Discover are accepted.

"New England Close to Home" is a valid description of Bluefin Bay Resort on Lake Superior. In the early 1900s Lake Superior provided a bounty of fresh fish which in turn was sent to markets in Duluth, Minneapolis, St. Paul, and Chicago. Lake Superior trout and bluefin gained a reputation for their unique flavor and freshness. The modern day Bluefin follows in that same tradition of good food, cozy accommodations, and friendly service.

The *Twin Cities Reader* named Bluefin Bay " . . . the most romantic resort in Minnesota." Nestled on the shores of Lake Superior, all of the suites, townhomes, and condominiums offer a spectacular view of the shoreline. Fireplaces, private decks, vaulted ceilings, and private whirlpools extend an invitation to guests to relax and enjoy the surroundings. For socializing, Bluefin Bay has a volleyball court, indoor pool, sauna, meeting rooms, tennis court, exercise room, The Bayside Gift Shop, and an 18-hole championship style golf course nearby. Sumptuous meals are the specialty of the Bluefin Restaurant where seafood is naturally the highlight of the menu. The Bridge offers a more casual atmosphere for dining and is saturated with local history and artifacts.

The Bluefin is located in Superior National Forest, which is home to the Superior Hiking Trail. Lutsen Ski Area is just 10 minutes from the resort. Snowmobile and cross-country ski trails permeate the area surrounding Bluefin. There are more than 200 inland lakes within a ten-mile radius of the resort. The Bluefin Bay Resort on Lake Superior possesses excellent accommodations and panoramic surroundings.

Moose Lake

The "Agate Capital of the World," Moose Lake is home to the 108-pound, largest recorded sample of this fine-grained, multicolored stone. But this railroad and farming town has more to offer visitors than *agate hunting.* Nestled in the northwoods, Moose Lake offers campsites, picnic areas, trails, and a refreshing, supervised swimming beach in the conveniently located *Moose Lake City Park and Campground.* Visitors can also hike and camp in the nearby 965-acre *Moose Lake State Park*, with its spectacular view of *Echo Lake.* For bicyclists, the 32-mile *Moose Lake-Hinckley Fire Trail* is one of Minnesota's finest paved biking trails, providing a beautiful view of farm fields, pastures, and wooded areas. Incorporated in 1889, much of the town burned in the great 1918 fire, and a 6.7-mile-long *walking history trail,* complete with markers and a reference map available from the Chamber of Commerce, relates the history of the fire and the settlement of this frontier town by Scandinavian

~R. NEGAARD~

immigrant farmers and loggers. One of the most notable sites is the 27-foot granite monument to the 200 people in and around Moose Lake who perished in the fire. Although a small town, Moose Lake stages a number of events, most notably the unique *Agate Days* during the second weekend after the 4th of July. This event includes the largest gem and mineral show in Minnesota and the agate stampede where tons of gravel are dumped on the main street for rock hounds to sift for agates. During the *Midsommar's Dag Festival* on the third Saturday in June, the residents of Moose Lake let loose to celebrate their heritage with a Scandinavian bake sale and traditional dances.

For more information on Moose Lake, contact:
MOOSE LAKE AREA CHAMBER OF COMMERCE
P. O. Box 110
Moose Lake, MN 55767
(800) 635-3680

RESTAURANT

■ ART'S CAFE
200 N. Arrowhead Lane
P.O. Box 336
Moose Lake, MN 55767
Tel: (218) 485-4602
Hrs: (Summer) Mon. - Sat. 6 a.m. - 9 p.m., Sun. 7 a.m. - 8 p.m.
(Winter) Mon. - Sun. 7 a.m. - 8 p.m.

For a meal as good as Mom's — or maybe better — try Art's Cafe. Located just off the beautiful Hinckley biking and walking trail on old Highway 61, Art's Cafe is a small-town place with tasty home-cooked food, which customers have been driving out of their way to enjoy for almost 50 years.

The menu includes hamburgers and hot beef sandwiches, as well as daily lunch and dinner specials, and mouthwatering breakfasts. Best of all, the cook is flexible, ready and willing to fix your food the way you like it. Half portions for children and light eaters are always available.

While munching their burgers, customers can also contemplate the two colorful murals of moose and deer in a northwoods setting adorning the cafe's interior walls, or get to know some of the other home-cooked-food enthusiasts sharing the cafe with them. As one patron recently claimed, "Eating at Art's Cafe is just like sitting down at your own kitchen table — only more fun."

Mora

A little part of Sweden in Minnesota, Mora has preserved its heritage better than most immigrant communities. Named after a town in Sweden by an erstwhile settler from the old country, this north-central Minnesota city soon grew to become a regional trade and administrative center. Today 3,000 call Mora home, a majority of them putting in their working hours at Fingerhut Corporation, Engineered Polymers Corp., or Country Lakes Foods before enjoying their Swedish meatballs, Swedish crafts, and so thoroughly Swedish-inspired events.

First of all, take the *Mora Vasaloppet,* the country's second largest cross-country ski race, attracting more than 2,000 skiers every February. Patterned after the Swedish Vasaloppet held — of course — in Mora, Sweden, the race brings out the best in Swedish-American hospitality when Mora residents open up their homes in a temporary bed and breakfast program to house the eager skiers from around the world. The race is held in the gentle hills surrounding the town, and when the first skiers approach town across Lake Mora, the 200-pound *Vasaloppet Bell* chimes its greeting. To celebrate the winners, the town recently erected a bronze statue nick-named Ingrid — a representation of the traditional *Swedish Kranskulla,* or wreath girl. And then there's Ole, a statue of a cross-country skier in *Vasaloppet Park* patiently reminding travelers of this race and the other three events in the challenging *Mora Classic: the Snake River Canoe Race, Mora Half Marathon,* and *Mora Bike Race.*

At the *Kanabec County Fairgrounds* next to the Municipal Swimming Pool looms yet another symbol of the town's heritage, the *Dala Horse statue.* Erected by the Mora Jaycees, the 22-foot high, cheerfully painted fiberglass and steel statue is a replica of horses carved in the Mora region of Sweden and has become the city's civic symbol. For deeper insight into Mora's heritage, informed travelers beat a path to the excellent *Kanabec History Center.* In addition to exhibits depicting the history of the county, the center features live craft demonstrations, art shows with local talent, and an exhaustive collection of Kanabec County documents in a professionally staffed research library.

For more information on Mora, please contact:
MORA AREA CHAMBER OF COMMERCE
20 N. Union Street
Mora, MN 55051
(612) 679-5792

Orr

Orr originated as a logging town in 1895, when Captain William Orr set up a trade camp on the shores of scenic Pelican Lake. For a number of years, the erstwhile captain reigned supreme in the small pioneer community, until the logging boom brought the railway and hundreds of lumberjacks to town. Although the fascinating logging days of the turn of the century are over, the town still depends on this traditional industry. However, in later years a modern resort industry has been established to serve travelers to nearby *Voyageurs National Park,* 219,000 acres of wilderness dominated by four great lakes. For those who don't bring their own boats, an intriguing alternative is *Minnesota Voyageurs Houseboats,* which rents houseboats for day- or week-long excursions through Voyageurs National Park.

For more information on Orr, contact:
PELICAN LAKE-ORR AREA RESORT ASSOCIATION
Orr, MN 55771
(218) 757-3479

GENERAL STORE

■ THE ORR GENERAL STORE & MERCANTILE COMPANY
Highway 53 N.
P.O. Box 177
Orr, MN 55771
Tel: (218) 757-3534
Hrs: (Summer) 8 a.m. - 6 p.m. (Winter) 9 a.m. - 5 p.m.
Visa and MasterCard are accepted.

This historic building, originally built in 1905 and known as Pelican Mercantile Company, was restored by owners Eleanor and Phil Anshus in 1983. The transition was a family project and the store now offers a high quality of merchandise.

Old pictures, counter showcases, barrel stove, and other old-time artifacts adorn the walls and interior of this general store. The general flavor of the store's offerings are antique reproduction toys, household articles, old-fashioned candies, upscale crafts, and quality clothing. Eleanor and Phil pride themselves in obtaining unusual gift items. Belts are made by an Amish harness maker, antiques are displayed on consignment, and new sources are continually sought for creative merchandise. Brand names such as Five Brothers, Filson, Lee, Bemidji Woolen Mills, Red Wing shoes, Sorrel, and LaCrosse line the shelves of the general store.

R ESORTS

■ ASH-KA-NAM RESORT
Ash River Trail
Orr, MN 55771
Tel: (218) 374-3181
Visa and MasterCard are accepted.

Ash-Ka-Nam Resort is next to the Ash River Trail, which is the central entrance to Voyageurs National Park, which is the only water-based park in the national park system. With 150 miles of water travel readily available by boat and snowmobiles, Ash-Ka-Nam Resort is a place for all seasons. This beautiful wilderness offers outdoor activity for the whole family, and Ash-Ka-Nam offers comfortable accommodations, boat, motor, canoe, and snowmobile rentals to make visitors' stay a pleasant one.

After the logging business declined, about 1937, the resort site was established. Today, beautiful native log, fully modern, housekeeping cabins are offered for weekly rental as well as a bunkhouse for overnight guests.

A restaurant that seats up to 40 offers a full menu, and the nearby bar overlooks the beautiful Ash River and features a large screen satellite television, fireplace, pool table, and video games. The small store carries groceries, a full line of bait, tackle, gas, and liquor. The docking facilities easily accommodate houseboats and small aircraft. Jon Currie has owned and operated the resort for 19 years. Future plans include deluxe condos with an indoor pool, sauna, fireplace, and hot tub.

■ MELGEORGE'S RESORT AND CEDAR INN
6402 County Road 180, Elephant Lake
Orr, MN 55771
Tel: (218) 374-3621
Hrs: (Summer) May 15 - Nov. 15, 8 a.m. - 10 p.m.
     (Winter) Dec. 1 - Mar. 30, 8 a.m. - 10 p.m.
Visa and MasterCard are accepted.

Established in 1937, Melgeorge's Resort is located on a portion of the old Virginia-Rainey Lake Logging Company's campsite #5. The first fishing and hunting cabins were built by father and son.

In 1969, Ted Melgeorge became the owner and operator of the resort and remodeled the six older cabins he had helped build. New docks were constructed. Business grew and two larger accommodations were built. In 1985, the Cedar Inn Restaurant, seating 85 people, and a seven-room motel unit were completed.

Logging era artifacts found on the site have been appropriately incorporated with the wood and log decor.

"By George, you can't beat Melgeorge's for four-season fun." In the spring, good fishing with guide service and fly-in trips is available. Summer offers family vacation time to explore trails, lakes, and the woods. Fall is excellent for deer hunting, and winter snowmobiling and cross-country skiing areas are plentiful. Located in the true wilderness, Melgeorge's is easily accessible via gravel road and snowmobile trails. They are the only full-time resort on Elephant Lake.

Ted Melgeorge participates and promotes local community activities, such as natural history plays by the local "Pine Town Players" Guests and locals observe and participate in antique snowmobile races.

R ESORT & CAMPGROUND

■ PINE ACRES RESORT AND CAMPGROUND
P.O. Box 25, R.R. 2
Orr, MN 55771
Tel: (218) 757-3144
Hrs: Daily, 7 a.m. - 10 p.m., May 1 - Oct. 5
Visa and MasterCard are accepted.

Pine Acres Resort is ideal for families, located in Voyageur Country on beautiful Pelican Lake, which is a 10,000 acre lake consisting of 54 miles of shoreline and over 50 beautiful islands.

One-, two-, and three-bedroom cabins are completely equipped for light housekeeping. The log siding and knotty pine interiors create a relaxed and simple vacation living. The campground facilities are situated apart from the cabins with hookups for water, sewer, and electricity. Campers can choose from the beautiful wooded and lakeshore sites. Over 30 of the 100 campground sites have adjacent docks. Pelican Lake is noted for its great northern pike, walleye, crappie, sunfish, and bass. Special services include boat, motor, canoe, and pontoon rental; fishing licenses; ice, snack bar, and groceries; fish cleaning and freezer service; complete gas, bait, and tackle shop; and babysitting service.

Kids will enjoy fishing right from the docks, a playground area, safe hiking trails for them to explore, and video game room. There is one-half mile of shoreline with a safe sandy swimming beach for the whole family. During the summer months, planned children activities include movies, marshmallow roasts, volleyball, and many other games and activities. For hunting enthusiasts, in-season hunting for duck, deer, and grouse are good.

Pine Acres Resort is located on the boundary of Voyageurs National Park and the Superior National Forest with its unlimited wilderness, lakes, and abundance of fish and wildlife. Voyageurs National Park has 83,000 acres of wilderness waterways, which today's nature lovers find best explored by boat.

R ESTAURANT & MOTEL

■ OUR FAMILY DEPOT
Orr, MN 55771
Tel: (218) 757-3624
Hrs: (Summer) Mon. - Sat. 5 a.m. - 10 p.m., Sun. 5 a.m. - 8 p.m.
(Winter) Tue. - Sat. 5 a.m. - 8 p.m., Sun. 5 a.m. - 5 p.m., Closed Mon.

This historic depot was previously known as the Orr Depot, originally built in 1923. It stood along Highway 53 in Orr, until May 1979 when it was moved from Ash Lake and then back to its present location, set atop a log basement.

This quaint restaurant marks the site of railroad days gone by. The old pay window and ticket office are still intact. Railroad signs and memorabilia adorn the walls. The original freight room now is the main dining room serving two of the customers' favorite breakfasts; biscuits and gravy, and unbeatable bran muffins. Breakfast, lunch, and dinner specials vary daily, but for a hearty delight, ask for the "Depot Burger."

Motel units are available for travelers. While in the area, stop at the Orr Tourist Information Center for complete vacation information and outdoor recreation activities.

Pine City

L ocated just one hour from both Duluth and the Twin Cities, the friendly small town of Pine City combines the restfulness of a resort with the convenience of a complete, self-supporting community with schools, restaurants, and commercial districts. Set between the serene beauty of *Cross* and *Pokegama lakes,* Pine City boasts no less than 50 miles of uninterrupted waterways within city limits. In addition, there's public access to the pastoral *Snake River* at the Pine City boat landing and to the scenic *St. Croix River* at the historic ferry landing that once provided a shortcut between Minnesota and Wisconsin. The *Chengwatana State Forest*, with its miles of serene hiking and cross-country skiing trails, and well-maintained campsites located just east of the city, provides a welcome respite from the bustle of urban life. Long before the state park was founded, however, fur traders and Indians roamed in the area, and the *North West Company Fur Post* pays tribute to this fascinating chapter in Pine City's history. Located just two miles west of downtown, the authentically reconstructed fur trading post features costumed interpreters reenacting life in the early 1800s.

The fun-filled *Snake River Rendezvous* held at the fur post each September celebrates the annual trade meeting between Indians who trapped animals throughout the winter, voyageurs who bought beaver pelts for the markets in the east, and the fur traders who lived at the post all year. At the *Knap-In* in July, flint knappers demonstrate this ancient art at the North West Company Post. Other events of note include the large flea market held on Wednesday mornings from April to September, free outdoor concerts on Friday evenings in June and July, the *Art Fest* arts and crafts show on the third Saturday of July, and the *Pine County Fair* during the first weekend in August.

For more information on Pine City, contact:
PINE CITY AREA CHAMBER OF COMMERCE
615 W. Third Ave.
Pine City, MN 55063
(612) 629-3861

H ISTORIC SITE

■ NORTH WEST COMPANY FUR POST
A Minnesota Historical Society Site
Highway 7, 1.5 miles west of the I-35 Pine City exit
Mailing Address: P.O. Box 51, Pine City, MN 55063
Tel: (612) 629-6356 or (612) 726-1171 (after Labor Day)
Hrs: May 1 - Labor Day 10 a.m. - 5 p.m.
There is no admission charge.

In the late 1700s, the fur trade was booming in North America and competition between fur trade companies was fierce. The North West Company was one of the biggest players in the fur trade. It ruled over a network of trappers, voyageurs, and fur trading posts that extended from the St. Lawrence River watershed to the Rocky Mountains. In 1804-05, the company sent John Sayer to establish a new post in Wild Rice Country — the area southwest of Lake Superior.

Sayer, his clerk, and several French Canadian voyageurs arrived at the Pine City site in mid-September and proceeded to consult with Ojibwa trappers in the area who were eager to work for them in exchange for tools and materials. They then set about building a wooden post, and obtained winter food stores from the Indians. Once winter set in, the voyageurs kept the post running — cutting firewood, repairing equipment, and trading with the Ojibwa for additional food. In January, the Indians brought the furs they had gathered to the post. Then, when the April thaw came, the voyageurs bound the furs into 90-pound bales and returned with Sayer north to Lake Superior.

Sayer kept a journal of his year at the Pine City post. Using his writings as a guide, the Minnesota Historical Society excavated the original post site and found the charred outlines of the main cabin, fireplaces, food caches, and stockade. In the 1960s, the Society reconstructed the fur post on top of its old foundations. Today, costumed guides act out the lifestyles of the voyageurs, Indians, and fur traders who originally lived there.

Ray/Lake Kabetogama

Two centuries ago, the Lake Kabetogama area was the fur trading voyageurs' kingdom. At that time, the fur trade was the continent's biggest industry, and the daring and cheerful voyageurs tirelessly plied the unchartered wilderness in their quest for beaver pelts to supply the hungry markets in the East. In fact, the 1783 treaty ending the American Revolution established the well-traveled route — dubbed the "Voyageurs Highway" — of these adventuresome French-Canadian canoemen as the international border between the United States and Canada.

Today, canoeists still dot Lake Kabetogama and the other neighboring waterways, but they do not suffer the hardships and dangers of the voyageurs. The 22-mile-long, six-mile-wide Lake Kabetogama is the largest of a chain of 30 lakes in *Voyageurs National Park,* Minnesota's only national park. With 247,000 acres of waterways, naturalist programs and tours, complete boat and canoe rentals, outstanding fishing, excellent trails for hiking, snowmobiling and cross-country skiing, private fly-in trips and quiet camping facilities; Voyageurs National Park provides one of the country's most outstanding wilderness experiences. Naturally, numerous resorts serve the area, with accommodations ranging from luxurious to rustic.

For more information on Ray or Lake Kabetogama, contact:
KABETOGAMA LAKE ASSOCIATION
HC 1, P.O. Box 10
Ray, MN 56669
(800) 777-4540

B ED & BREAKFAST

■BUNT'S BED & BREAKFAST
Lake Kabetogama
Ray, MN 56669
Tel: (218) 875-3904
Hrs: Open year-round
Visa, MasterCard, and AmEx are accepted.

Bunt's Bed and Breakfast is located just one and one-half miles from the Big Walleye at the entrance to Kabetogama Lake. It is Voyageur National Park's new year-round overnight accommodation complete with continental breakfast served each morning. Guests also have the option to order from the breakfast menu at nearby Bunt's Billiards Bar and Grill, which is included in the rates.

Bunt's is a recently completed Lake Kabetogama homestead on 20 wooded acres converted to the area's first bed and breakfast. There are three luxurious sleeping rooms with either king-size beds or double standards, two with private baths. Customers have full use of the sauna, spa, full kitchen, a beamed ceiling living room, loft, double fireplace, and one of Bunt's new custom-built pocket billiard tables. There are two large outside decks for bird watching, reading, barbecuing, or just relaxing. Satellite television is available in the living room area and each private sleeping room has its own regular channel television. Bunt's Bed and Breakfast has miles of marked walking, jogging, snowmobile, and cross-country ski trails to enjoy. The Lake Kabetogama Visitors Center, Voyageurs Park entry point, and Marina with launching facilities are only 1,000 yards due north.

Rest up at this elegant inn. Bunt's Bed and Breakfast brings luxury accommodations to northern Minnesota.

F ISHING SUPPLIES & RESTAURANT

■ BAIT N' BITE
9634 Gamma Road
Ray, MN 55669
Tel: (218) 875-2281
Hrs: (May 1 - Oct. 1) 6 a.m. - 10 p.m.
Visa and MasterCard are accepted.

Bait N' Bite is a family owned and operated restaurant at Lake Kabetogama, serving breakfast, lunch, and dinner. It is also the area's most complete live bait and tackle shop. Lake Kabetogama is one of the four entry points into Voyageurs National Park permitting motorized boats for fishing.

The log building and knotty pine interior provide a warm, friendly, and relaxed visit. The restaurant is proud of its wholesome, home-cooked meals, not to mention the friendly service. Fishing information and licenses are available. The bottle shop offers customers' favorite bottled liquors, wines, wine coolers, beers, and mixers. Monthly or full season boat storage is also available.

Look for the Lake Kabetogama walleye sign and turn on Highway 122, just 1 mile north off Highway 53. The owners, Jim and Marlene Tomczak, pride themselves on the restaurant and fishing services offered to tourists and locals alike.

R ESORT

■ VOYAGEUR PARK LODGE
10436 Waltz Road
Ray, MN 56669
Tel: (800) 331-5694 or (218) 875-2131
Visa and MasterCard are accepted.

There's a wonderful place in Minnesota waiting to be explored. It's a wilderness preserve set aside by the national government to provide safe habitats for thousands of animal and plant species. It's called Voyageurs National Park.

Voyageurs is a water access park (no restrictions on boats or motors) with more than 30 lakes within its boundaries. Several of the larger lakes are dotted with islands inhabited by bald eagle families, blueberry-picking black bears, snowshoe hares, timber wolves, white tail deer, mink, otter, beaver, and so many species of birds even Audubon would be impressed. And then there's Voyageur Park Lodge, a unique vacation site, ready to provide a beautiful and comfortable setting from which guests can explore the surrounding pristine wilderness.

A step above the ordinary, Voyageur Park Lodge and its 11 cottages stand alone on a private, 20-acre peninsula on the shores of Lake Kabetogama, a hard-to-pronounce but otherwise enchanting lake in Voyageurs National Park. Each cottage is tucked in the forest with its sun deck overlooking the lake, offering the private getaway many have been looking for.

Voyageur Park Lodge is a great place to rest and relax and vacation. Plan a week or two with friends and family or a weekend retreat for two. Voyageur Park Lodge has the facilities and services to make a stay carefree and memorable.

R ESORT & RESTAURANT

■ KEC'S KOVE
10428 Gamma Road
Ray, MN 56669
Tel: (218) 875-2841
Hrs: (Summer) Resort - daily
     Restaurant closed Mon.
     Tue. - Sun. 5 a.m. - 9 p.m.
     Lounge 5 p.m. - 1 a.m.
     (Winter) Restaurant
     Fri. - Sun. noon - 9 p.m.
     Lounge Fri. - Sun. noon - 1 a.m.

Kec's Kove is located on beautiful Lake Kabetogama, Minnesota's finest family vacation area. Open year-round, guests enjoy all the seasons for fishing, swimming, deer hunting, ice fishing, snowmobiling, cross-country skiing, or just plain relaxing. Accommodations include two-, three-, and four-bedroom housekeeping cabins, fully equipped and most with cozy fireplaces. Guests can choose from three affordable plans; American, Modified, or Housekeeping. The swimming area is within walking distance from the cabins, and there is plenty of safe playground area for the children. Fishing on Lake Kabetogama is a memorable experience whether for the serious or "just for the fun of it" fisherman, naturalist, photographer, or hiker. The fish are plentiful and the scenery and wildlife are abundant. Boat rental and guide service are available. The lodge has a spacious sitting room and fireplace, great for swapping fish stories and relaxing or just watching television. The recreation room has a pool table, jukebox, and pin ball machines. Kec's Kove offers full bar service, and the restaurant provides an excellent choice of meals and appetizers. If guests are flying in, arrangements can be made for pick-up at International Falls airport.

Kec's Kove has something for the whole family. "Relax and fish in a wilderness wonderland."

Taylors Falls

I ncorporated in 1858, the same year as Minnesota became the 32nd state of the Union, the logging town of Taylors Falls is one of the most fascinating historical towns in the state. With a picturesque setting on beautiful St. Croix River, it was settled mainly by New Englanders, and the many fine examples of Federal and Greek Revival style architecture reflect this heritage. In fact, this quaint town has preserved more than one-third of its original 19th-century buildings. Foremost among these is the *Taylors Falls Public Library,* built in 1854 as a tailor shop and residence. In 1861, the city founders erected the *Methodist Church* in the *Angel Hill Historic District* — an area of fine homes, a schoolhouse, and a jail recreating an eastern village — and the church has been in continuous use ever since. Angel Hill is also site of the imposing *W. H. C. Folsom House.* Built by city founder and logging baron William Folsom in 1854, costumed guides now offer tours of this five-bedroom pine home. But Taylors Falls boasts numerous other attractions, making it one of the most popular tourist destinations in the state. Because of its location on the St. Croix River, the town is an ideal starting point for river excursions on historical riverboats with *Taylors Falls Scenic Boat Tours*, as well as for fishing and for canoe and boat rentals. The river provides an excellent view of the many intriguing rock formations and giant potholes left behind by the grinding glaciers that once dominated the area. *Wild Mountain Water Park and Alpine Slides*, with its water slides, tube rides, and breathtaking ride down the same hill used for downhill skiing in the winter, features the most refreshing fun in the area. Two major parks, the *Wild River State Park* and the *Interstate Park*, complete the outdoor recreational opportunities in Taylors Falls. To celebrate the heritage of the city, which before the advent of tourism revolved around the logging industry, the city arranges the *Wannigan Days* during the third weekend of June and *Log Jam Days* during the last weekend of July.

For more information on Taylors Falls, contact:
TAYLORS FALLS CHAMBER OF COMMERCE
Taylors Falls, MN 55084
(612) 465-6661

A CCOMMODATIONS

■ THE PINES MOTEL
River Street
Taylors Falls, MN 55084
Tel: (612) 465-3422
Hrs: Open year-round
Visa, MasterCard, and AmEx are accepted.

Peace, quiet, and serene atmosphere await guests at The Pines Motel, coming in from both Highways 8 and 95. It is located two blocks from the center of town on the St. Croix River.

Visitors will be pleasantly surprised at the clean, cheerful accommodations this motel has to offer. The eight guest rooms have a comfortable choice of bed combinations, private baths, cable television, air conditioning, in-room phones, and free continental breakfast on Saturday and Sunday. The motel provides a peaceful country setting, yet is just a short walking distance from shops and many fine restaurants. Guests also enjoy the easy access to the area's many sights including the Interstate and Wild River State Parks, the St. Croix River, picnic areas, canoeing, fishing, excursion boats, golfing, museums and historical sites, hiking, snowmobile trails, horseback riding, alpine slides, water slides, downhill and cross-country skiing. On the third weekend in June, visitors come from miles around to celebrate the local festival, Wannigan Days.

For clean, comfortable accommodations at a convenient location and reasonable price, The Pines Motel is the place.

Tower-Soudan

The oldest mining town in Minnesota, Tower-Soudan has been described as "The Cradle of the Iron Mining Industry." The first shipment of iron ore came from the Soudan underground mine, which was considered the richest in the world. The checkered mining communities of Tower and Soudan were composed of members of many nationalities — Finnish, Swedish, Norwegian, Italian, and Slovenian — who often spoke little English and clung to their traditional culture. Nevertheless, the miners and their families eventually forged a close-knit community that through tenacity and determination survived the closing of the Soudan mine in 1962, and went on to create a new future based on cottage industries and tourism. The focus for the resort industry is *Lake Vermilion,* one of the largest unrestricted motor boating lakes in the area, with 365 islands and more than 1,200 miles of tranquil shoreline. In celebration of the town's history, the *Tower-Soudan Underground Mine State Park* offers tours of the Soudan mine, the deepest underground mine in Minnesota. The only tour of its kind in the country, it provides a fascinating glimpse into traditional mining operations from 2,300 feet below the earth's surface. Self-guided tours of open pits, the enginehouse, and crusher building are also available. In addition to the mine, history buffs frequent the *Tower Depot and Train Museum,* a restored depot and steam train, and the *McKinley Monument,* reportedly the first monument to be erected to the memory of President William McKinley.

For more information on Tower-Soudan, contact:
TOWER-SOUDAN CHAMBER OF COMMERCE
P.O.Box 776-B
Tower, MN 55790
(218) 753-2301

■Tours

■SOUDAN UNDERGROUND MINE STATE PARK
P.O. Box 335
Soudan, MN 55782
Tel: (218) 753-2245
Hrs: (Summer) Memorial Day - Labor Day
Daily 9:30 a.m. - 4 p.m.
(Winter) Please call. Reserved groups only.

Be adventurous. Take the tour. The Soudan Mine is one of the few underground iron ore mines in the world that offers tours. A short drive off Highway 169 into Soudan, the mine head frame sits atop a hill. The site, 1,601 feet above sea level, gives a panoramic view of the Iron Range area's forests and is a nice spot for a picnic. An outside display of old mining tools and equipment surround the mine shaft. While inside the "dry" house, a fascinating historic display can be found. The self-guided surface tour includes access to the Drill House, the Engine House, the Crusher, and the Dry House.

However, the real display can be seen only by taking a three-minute elevator ride down into the underground mine descending 2,400 feet below the earth's surface; to the 27th level, from the present to the past. When "down under," visitors are treated to a three-quarter mile train ride to the Montana ore body. From the train, they take a short walk and climb a 32-step spiral staircase into the "stope" — the miner's term for the underground cavity from which the ore was taken. This is the highlight of the tour; where they actually see and experience the methods and lifestyle of the 1960s era underground iron miner.

The Soudan Underground Mine began production in the late 1800s and ended in 1962. It is the first underground mine in Minnesota, and is the birthplace of the state's mining industry. A warm jacket or sweater and sturdy shoes are recommended for the underground tour. The temperature below surface averages 50 degrees. Hiking trails can take visitors back to some of the original and very deep open pit mines.

A CCOMMODATIONS

■ MARJO MOTEL
R.R. 2, P.O. Box 1
Tower, MN 55790
Tel: (218) 753-4851

Tower's only motel has eight rooms, four two-double bed units, and four one-double bed units. It is simple, no frills and has private baths. So what makes this spot special? Its location.

The Marjo Motel is west of the town, just off Highway 169, but located on the channel opening into Lake Vermilion. Lake Vermilion is the most beautiful lake in the area with miles and miles of shoreline to discover. Guests can launch a fishing boat in the summer or trailer and unload their snowmobile in the winter directly from the motel. Also, the motel is situated at a location where guests have direct access to groomed cross-country ski trails and snowmobile trails, most notably the Taconite Trail. Within a few minutes, they can reach Giant's Ridge, a premier downhill and cross-country ski area.

The Marjo Motel may be "just a place to stay overnight," but sometimes that is all that is wanted — to get a good night's rest and start off early in the morning. Prices are reasonable. There is plenty of parking for vehicles and trailers, with good lights for security purposes.

C AMPGROUND

■ HOODOO POINT CAMPGROUND
Lake Vermilion
Tower, MN 55790
Tel: (218) 753-6868 (Summer)
    (218) 753-4241 (Winter, after Oct. 1)

Imagine sitting around a campfire listening to the waves of Lake Vermilion, the wind whispering through the trees, and the Iron Range only minutes away. Hoodoo Point Campground presents a beautiful headquarters for a great northern getaway.

The campground consists of 53 neat campsites situated among the aspen and pine trees on the shoreline. Water and electric hookups are accessible at nearly every site. There are some sites with full hookup, and a dump station is available for sanitation needs. The office building holds a convenience store, laundromat, game room, bathroom, and shower facilities. Boating and fishing are the order of the day. Known for its walleye, northern pike, crappies, and bass, Lake Vermilion is sure to challenge fishing skills. Fishing bait can be found at the campground or in the nearby town of Tower. The gently sloping sandy beach is popular with children for making sand castles or playing a game of horseshoes. In one direction are the many attractions of the Iron Range and in the other direction are Tower and a train museum housed in an old DM&IR railroad coach.

Peaceful evenings contract with energetic days. The perfect way to end the day is to relax by the campfire with quiet conversation and the sunset. Later in the evening, watch the stars and look for the beautiful Northern Lights.

GAMING CASINO

■FORTUNE BAY CASINO
1430 Bois Fort Road
Tower, MN 55790
Tel: (218) 753-6400 or (800) 992-PLAY

Fortune Bay Casino is a state-of-the-art bingo and gaming facility, which opened in August 1986. It is located on the Bois Fort Indian Reservation on Lake Vermilion.

The bingo hall seats 1,000. It is home for local high-stake bingo as well as the Mega Bingo game played via satellite from Arizona. Video poker, pull-tabs, and roulette-style games are also popular. Visitors come from miles around to play. Buses from far away as Winnipeg and Thunder Bay, Canada have been chartered for a trip here. Renovations have added a new wing with a bar and gaming room, including 250 new electronic machines for poker, keno, and slots. A new restaurant overlooks the bingo hall.

MARINA

■J.G. MARINA
2147 Birch Point Road
Tower, MN 55790
Tel: (218) 753-4404
Hrs: Seasonal hours may vary. Call ahead.

J. G. Marina is a full service marina open to the public, which originally began in the 1930s. Located on the shore of Lake Vermilion at Daisy Bay, J.G. Marina has been an authorized dealer since 1936 for Evinrude OMC, Cobra, and Mercruiser. Starcraft and other lines of boats are also available. Lake Vermilion, on north country's western border, has 365 islands and more than 1,200 miles of beautiful shoreline. It is one of the largest unrestricted motor boating lakes in the area, and is renowned for its walleye.

A complete ship store offers maps and complete lake information; O'Brien water skis, kneeboards, tubes, and accessories; Bodyglove wetsuits and clothing; Nike aquasocks; Oakley sunglasses; T-shirts and hats. A convenience store provides all the necessities for groceries and ice. Boat launching, dockage, and gas are also available. There is an extensive parts inventory for new and older motors. Motor maintenance and repair services, and enclosed, secured watercraft storage are available year-round. By special appointment, watercraft are cleaned and waxed at the marina.

Church services are held lakeside the end of June through mid-August by the local area clergy. The Fourth of July Flotilla Parade is also a favorite. The Lake Vermillion experience is an unforgettable adventure, "A Wave Above The Rest."

MINI GOLF, GIFTS & CREAMERY

■ PIER 77 MINI GOLF
County Road 77
Tower, MN 55790
Tel: (218) 753-6004
Hrs: (Summer) May - Sept. 10 a.m. to dusk
   Closed Oct. to May

Pier 77 Mini Golf is an unusual combination of a miniature golf course, gift shop, and creamery. It was built and designed by the owners in 1989, fitting appropriately into its surroundings.

The 18-hole golf course may be miniature in size, but the challenges and enjoyment are not. On the last "shot," if the walleye fish swallows the ball, guests win a free game. It is as much fun for kids as it is for adults. In the gift shop, items are nicely displayed. Allow plenty of time to look around. The nautical gifts and collectibles from northwoods artisans are some of the best to be offered, such as chain saw carvings, metal sculptures, art prints and books, classic T- and pullover shirts. Soft-serve ice creams are dipped in the small ice cream parlor. Specialty flavors are featured weekly in this creamery. Fountain pop, sodas, popcorn, flurries, and specialty desserts are also available.

Pier 77 is approximately 8 miles from Highway 169 on County Road 77. It is easy to find. Just look for the pilings and boats tied up at Pier 77.

R ESORTS

■ BAY VIEW LODGE
2001 Bayview Drive B
Tower, MN 55790
Tel: (218) 753-4825
Hrs: Dining Room (summer)
  Lunch Mon. - Sat. 11 a.m. - 2 p.m.
  Dinner Mon. - Sat. 5:30 p.m. - 9:30 p.m., Sun. 2 p.m. - 8 p.m.
  Bar and Lounge noon - midnight
  (Winter) Fri. 4 p.m .- 11 p.m.
  Sat. noon - 11 p.m.
  Sun. noon - 8 p.m.
Visa, MasterCard, and AmEx are accepted.

Lake Vermilion is considered one of Minnesota's finest angling lakes, well-known for its walleye, bass, panfish, and northern pike. Bay View Lodge overlooks Lake Vermilion just outside of Tower. Established in the late 1920s, this log cabin resort rests in a quiet wooded area near fishing lakes and the Boundary Waters Canoe Area. Michelle and David Beer became the owners in 1987.

Each of the nine cottages and eight furnished housekeeping units offers a view of the lake, as does the dining room of the brand new cedar lodge. The cabins are comfortably equipped with hot and cold running water, private baths, linens, and basic cooking utensils. Several units have fireplaces and all sites have outdoor grills. The restaurant offers a lounge with video games and a pool table. The bar features the "beverage of the week." Boats and outboard motors may be rented through Bay View. Other services available include fishing guides, licenses, gas, oil, bait, boat launching, fish cleaning, and freezer service. Children enjoy fishing from the docks.

At Bay View Lodge resort, guests may take advantage of excellent fishing, swimming from the sandy beach, paddleboats, canoes, kayaks, and shuffleboard. The tranquility of the northwoods, the beautiful blue sky, rippling waters, and breezes off the lake all make for a truly enjoyable visit.

■ WESTHAVEN LODGE

1931G Westhaven Drive
Tower, MN 55790
Tel: (218) 753-3731 ext. 773 or (800) 635-5082 ext. 373
Hrs: (Mid-May to Oct. 1) daily 8 a.m. - 10 p.m.

Westhaven Lodge is an ideal choice for those looking for a retreat into the beautiful northern Minnesota wilderness, yet not wishing to forsake the comforts of modern life. Since 1936, owners of the lodge have provided guests with a casual, relaxed vacation site that combines landscaped grounds, charming cottages, and a host of activities in the midst of unspoiled forest country.

The vacation cottages of Westhaven Lodge all face the bright waters of Lake Vermilion. The lakeside cottages are of split-log construction with knotty pine interiors and are equipped with all the necessary conveniences, including bed linens, microwaves, grills, and time-saving utensils and appliances. Lake Vermilion's 1,200 miles of shoreline contrasts rocky, rugged terrain with sandy beaches, such as the one at Westhaven Lodge. Dotted with more than 300 pine-clad islands, the lake is widely acclaimed as a fisherman's paradise. Relaxing in the large wood-burning sauna, sailing or boating on the lake, exploring the islands, naturalist tours, hiking and biking, picking berries, and canoeing through the adjacent Boundary Waters Wilderness Area are but a few of the pleasures visitors experience at Westhaven Lodge. A children's area has playground equipment, game courts, and a playhouse.

At Westhaven Lodge guests can become immersed in the peace and natural beauty of the northern wilderness, yet be minutes away from paved roads, airports, area attractions, medical care, shopping, and restaurants. Lovers of nature and outdoor activities discover a vacation paradise at Westhaven Lodge.

R ESORT/RV PARK

■ MOCCASIN POINT RESORT AND RV PARK

Highway 77
Tower, MN 55790
Tel: (218) 753-3309
Hrs: May 15-Oct. 1

RV travelers and outdoor buffs enjoy the wooded campsites of Moccasin Point Resort and RV Park, located on one of the prime locations of the Lake Vermilion shores. Campsite docks, a sand beach, electricity and water, and launching facilities as well as a clean, centralized wash house with toilets and hot water showers add to camping pleasures.

A special area with a nice lawn and shade trees adds to the comforts for tent campers. Boats, motors, and canoe rental, off- and on-sale liquors, groceries, bait, licenses, and Boundary Waters Canoe Area permits are also available. Short orders and pizzas are served. The hosts, Jim and Diane Nelson, hold onto their own identity — easy-going, friendly, and accommodating.

When traveling with an RV, many campers make Moccasin Point their base camp while exploring Lake Vermilion and sightseeing on the Iron Range. If the stay is seven days, then one day is free. During the winter, ice fishermen and snowmobilers make Moccasin Point a regular stopping-off spot for warming up, refreshments, and that special camaraderie one encounters in northern Minnesota.

S ERVICE STATION

■ BOB'S STANDARD SERVICE
306 Main Street
Tower, MN 55790
Tel: (218) 753-2125
Hrs: Mon. - Sun. 7 a.m. - 8 p.m.
Visa, MasterCard, and Amoco are accepted.

This is the full service station that gives friendly, competent, honest, and accommodating service and repair for vacationers' cars, truck, or RV. It is located on the east end of Tower's Main Street.

The station's crew is capable and ready to perform general car maintenance and repairs. There is a full line of standard fuels and lubricating oils including Diesel #1 and #2, and kerosene. When emergencies occur, their wrecker and towing service is available 24-hours-a-day with knowledgeable personnel to take charge. Towing service is available for long distance travel, too. A smaller cooler located in the station provides beverages, candy, and some snacks. Bags of ice cubes and block ice await the needy camper. In the winter, snowmobilers are welcome to gas up at the station and obtain the latest snowmobile trail conditions and the area's trail maps. Factory oils and premium gas are available.

Bob and Sheryl Reichensperger, owners, have a great deal of pride in their business and their many happy customers. They may pump gas, check the oil, and clean your windshield but they also brighten your day with a smile, a bit of wit, and a few minutes to relax.

Two Harbors

T he first of Minnesota's iron ports, Two Harbors is still a major shipping center for the Iron Range taconite and iron industry. The city was founded in 1884, when the Duluth and Iron Range Railroad, built to serve the new mine in Soudan, reached Lake Superior in Agate Bay. Nearby Burlington Bay also served as a shipping harbor, and the young community was appropriately named Two Harbors. Once a favored Ojibwa Indian fishing and spearing ground called Kitci Gummi — "a place to spear by midnight" — Two Harbors soon became a bustling industrial town with the largest ore dock in the world. Today, visitors can tour the enormous, 1,388-foot-long *Duluth and Iron Range Railroad Loading Dock* and watch 1,000-foot ore boats glide into port. The *Lighthouse Point and Harbor Museum* located on Agate Bay features exhibits of the history of the shipping of iron ore. Also in Agate Bay is another fascinating maritime history landmark, the retired 1895 tugboat *Edna G.* This was the first steam-powered, coal-burning tugboat on Lake Superior and is included in the National Register of Historic Places. The restored *Duluth Mesabi & Iron Range Railroad Depot,* meanwhile, houses the *Lake County Historical Society Museum* with its intriguing displays of the area's logging, fishing, and railroading heritage. The focus of the exhibition is the history of iron ore mining and shipping, as well as a giant *Mallet locomotive* from 1941 — the largest of its type ever built. Located 20 miles to the north along scenic *North Shore Drive* is *Split Rock Lighthouse,* a restored 1910 landmark open for tours in the summer. Also during the summer, Two Harbors arranges *Summer Band Concerts* in the city park and serves as the starting point for *Grandma's Marathon,* one of the premier running events in Minnesota attracting thousands of athletes from across the country.

For more information on Two Harbors, contact:
TWO HARBORS AREA CHAMBER OF COMMERCE
P. O. Box 39
Two Harbors, MN 55616
(218) 834-2600

H ANDMADE POTTERY & QUILTS

■ THE POTTERY & QUILT SHOP
621 First Ave.
Two Harbors, MN 55616
Tel: (218) 834-4819 (evenings only)
Hrs: (March - Dec.) Mon. - Fri. 10 a.m. - 5 p.m., Sat. 9 a.m. - 1 p.m.
    (July and Aug.) Sun. 11 a.m. - 3 p.m.
    Winter hours vary. Call ahead.
Visa and MasterCard are accepted.

Four years ago, quilt and stoneware artist Dorothy Elder set up a modest workshop on the main street of Two Harbors, an old iron ore port on the north shore of Lake Superior. But soon, news of Elder's skills spread, and today her shop doubles as a popular gallery.

Elder, along with Allan Omarzu, crafts an impressive line of stoneware and porcelain, including vases, pots, dishes, lamps, pitchers, jars, and bowls. Custom-made items are available. They also carry a line of unfinished pottery that they can custom decorate to specifications.

The shop's other specialty is an array of fine quilts. There is a wide selection of Amish quilts for sale in a variety of color schemes and patterns. Customers can bring in color samples and order a custom-made quilt — the perfect addition to a living room or bedroom.

H ISTORIC SITE

■ SPLIT ROCK LIGHTHOUSE HISTORIC SITE & HISTORY CENTER
A Minnesota Historical Society Site
Highway 61
20 miles northeast of Two Harbors
Mailing address: 2010 Highway 61 E., Two Harbors, MN 55616
Tel: (218) 226-4372
Hrs: (May 15 - Oct. 15) daily 9 a.m. - 5 p.m.
    (Oct. 19 - May 10) Fri. - Sun. noon - 4 p.m. History Center only
There is an admission charge.

At the turn of the century, when iron ore shipments on Lake Superior were booming, steamship and iron companies repeatedly requested that a lighthouse be build along the lake's treacherous North Shore. After a disastrous storm in 1905 damaged six ore ships in that vicinity, the U.S. government granted the companies' request and began building Split Rock Lighthouse.

The lighthouse was completed in 1910 and operated for nearly 60 years before it was closed in 1969. By that time, navigational equipment had become so advanced that ships no longer needed the renowned lighthouse to guide them along Superior's rocky shores. The Minnesota Historical Society has restored the lighthouse and its companion building to their pre-1924 appearance. Visitors can tour the brick light tower, a fog-signal building, the keepers' dwellings, and several outbuildings. The ruins of a tramway still are visible. The History Center features a film and exhibit about the lighthouse and the development of the North Shore, as well as a museum shop.

Split Rock Lighthouse's picturesque setting and convenient location just off the North Shore highway have made it one of the most visited lighthouses in the country. Today, the lonely brick building still perches defiantly upon its cliff high above Lake Superior's waters — a stalwart legacy of a bygone era.

R ESORT

■ STAR HARBOR RESORT
1098 Highway 61 E.
Two Harbors, MN 55616
Tel: (218) 834-3796
Hrs: Open year-round
Visa, MasterCard, AmEx, and Discover are accepted.

History and luxury surround guests at Star Harbor Resort. The resort is located 11 miles northeast of Two Harbors in the community of Castle Danger. Built in 1915 and continuing the tradition of North Shore hospitality, Star Harbor was the first cabin resort on the North Shore. New, handcrafted log cabins, built by local craftsmen, complement the 1,300 feet of easily accessible Lake Superior shoreline. They are rustic and traditional, yet modern and comfortable with warm, beautifully furnished interiors. Cabins feature a fireplace, fully equipped kitchen (including microwave), color TV with VCR, bathroom with shower, and windows and deck overlooking the lake.

The area around Star Harbor on Highway 61 between Duluth and Canada is known for its stunning scenery and charming ambiance. The rugged headlands and cliffs alternate with quiet bays, tumbling rivers, and woods of birch, maple, and pine. Every season is a special time to enjoy the North Shore beauty. After spending a day in companionship with nature, nothing can compare to relaxing in a log cabin.

R ESTAURANT

■ BETTY'S PIES
215 Highway 61 E.
Two Harbors, MN 55616
Tel: (218) 834-3367
Hrs: (May through mid-Oct.), daily 8 a.m. - 8 p.m.

At Betty's Pies restaurant near Two Harbors, customers come for the pie and stay for the sandwiches. A North Shore landmark for more than 30 years, Betty's offers a mouth-watering selection of pies, including such temptations as five-layer chocolate and lemon meringue, banana and coconut cream, or fresh raspberry and blueberry in season — all stacked high on handrolled, deliciously thin pie crust.

Conveniently located on Minnesota 61, the major North Shore highway, Betty's also attracts scores of luncheon customers. Try the smoked whitefish platter special — or the wild rice soup and the chicken salad. Homemade chili with onion, cheese, and sour cream is also available, along with a wide variety of sandwiches — including ham, tuna and egg salad, hamburgers, and grilled cheese — all served on fresh rye bread. For dinner, the menu includes a regional specialty: Lake Superior trout. Served with french fries, coleslaw, and homemade rye bread, the trout dinner is far too good to miss.

On sunny days, customers can enjoy their meal on picnic tables set up outside the restaurant. With a view of Lake Superior in the distance, shimmering in the summer heat, what could be better than an outdoor lunch topped off with a delectable pie?

Virginia

S ite of the largest taconite plant in the world, Virginia has burned two times during its turbulent history. After the second fire in 1900, the booming frontier town on the Iron Range was rebuilt entirely with stone, brick, and concrete to ward off further destruction. Only five years later, Virginia boasted a population of 5,000 and had already become the acknowledged center of trade for the Mesabi and Vermilion ranges. Still, lumbering soon became the city's major industry, boosting the population of Virginia to more than 16,000 in the 1920s and earning it a brief status as Minnesota's fifth largest town.

ATTRACTIONS

The *Finntown* neighborhood — the only area of town that escaped destruction in the 1900 fire — has been preserved in the memory of the early Virginians who built the town into a prosperous community. Visitors can take self-guided tours of the neighborhood, absorbing the pioneer spirit of the Iron Range and examining the *Lincoln Building* and *Kaleva Hall,* the 1907 Finnish Temperance Hall. *Virginia Heritage Museum,* a two-room early 20th century log house with its *Peace Flag Exhibit* of the flags of 23 nations pays tribute to the many nationalities that settled Virginia. In the same vein, the annual *Land of the Loon Area Ethnic Arts and Crafts Festival* in July is an extravagant display of the richly varied ethnic arts, crafts, food, and entertainment of the Iron Range. Another site of historic interest is the *Mineview in the Sky,* an observation complex originally built as a vantage point for pit foremen that today permits visitors to view the three-mile-long *Rouchleau Mine,* the deepest pit mine in the area. For those more physically inclined there's the *Laurentian Divide Fitness Trail.* Named after the Laurentian Divide — the point straddled by Virginia from which all water on one side flows south and on the other, north — the trail includes 14 exercise stations with hurdles, chin-up bars, log walks, and a spectacular view of the city and *Superior National Forest.*

For more information on Virginia, contact:
VIRGINIA AREA CHAMBER OF COMMERCE
233 Chestnut Street
Virginia, MN 55792
(218) 741-2717

B AKERY

■ ITALIAN BAKERY
205 S. First Street
Virginia, MN 55792
Tel: (218) 741-3464
Hrs: Mon. - Sat. 5:30 a.m. - 5 p.m. Closed Sunday

The Italian Bakery located in Virginia, the "Queen City" of Minnesota's Iron Range, was founded in 1910. This family-owned business has moved and expanded as its reputation grew.

Using Old World traditional recipes, the Italian Bakery potica and fruitcake gained a national word-of-mouth reputation. In 1965, the Italian Bakery began a mail order business, shipping their delicious potica and fruitcakes all over the world. The potica filling is secret. It requires the finest ingredients: flour, pure creamy butter, whole eggs, honey, lots of walnuts, pure vanilla, and no preservatives. It retains freshness by refrigeration or freezing, and the same integrity is maintained with the fruitcakes.

Try a tradition that people have been raving about since the turn of the century. Send friends a treat. The walnut and walnut raisin potica, fruitcake, and Minnesota wild rice are sent year-round.

B OOKSTORE & NEEDLECRAFT

■ WOODWARDS
Thunderbird Mall
Virginia, MN 55792
Tel: (218) 741-1744
Hrs: Mon. - Fri. 10 a.m. - 9 p.m., Sat. 10 a.m. - 5 p.m., Sun. noon - 5 p.m.
Visa, MasterCard, and Discover are accepted.

Woodwards, your "full-line bookstore and a whole lot more," has an inventory of 36,000 hardcover and paperback books, magazines, and the latest publications. Maps, large print books and books on cassette tapes are available. Customers will find it all — general fiction, children's books, self-help, westerns, business and reference, crafts and hobbies, science fiction, health and diet, inspirational, and cookbooks. They may also find a special bargain, as Woodwards carry a special section of "publisher's closeouts." The regional book section features local authors who occasionally stop by and spend the day to autograph their books. Another feature is the special order service with no charge and no obligation. Especially noteworthy is Woodwards' yarn alcove featuring yarns from baby to bulky weight. Patterns, needles, knitting, and crocheting accessories plus counted cross-stitch materials and supplies are plentiful.

The Woodwards redesigned and redecorated the store's interior, built their own display tables and shelves and added many special touches. With their grand opening in November 1989, this bookstore is one of the most pleasant stores located in the Thunderbird Mall. You can set your packages down on the benches and seat yourself at their reading table, taking your time to look over your potential purchases.

A book is a friend and so are the Woodwards and their staff. These book lovers let customers browse at their leisure.

CANDY STORE

■ CANELAKE'S CANDY
414 Chestnut Street
Virginia, MN 55792
Tel: (218) 741-1557
Hrs: Mon. - Sat. 9 a.m. - 5 p.m.

Here are 40 good reasons to have a sweet tooth — Canelake's old-fashioned homemade candies. Welcome to a real tradition.

Originally started in 1905, the founder of Canelake's Candy Kitchen believed in making his candies with the freshest and best ingredients possible, such as AA butter and real whipped cream. The almonds, cashews, and peanuts were hand-roasted in small batches. The chocolates were tempered and hand-dipped on marble tables. Candies were hand-rolled and hand-decorated and the Canelake boxes were hand-packed. This art and tradition is still carried on at Canelake's Candy using the same wonderful recipes the founder created.

An original Canelake secret candy recipe is known as "Hot Air." Crisp, fluffy, light and airy, this old-time sensation is an all time best seller. Love at first bite! Other selected candies offered include caramels, dipped nuts, toffee, creams, brittles, and bars. At the 1988 St. Paul Technical Institute candy judging contest, Canelake's

Candy was said to be the best assortment of candies in Minnesota. Many times, gift givers like to send a stuffed toy with that special box of candy. Canelake's circus wagon of animals makes selection very easy. The old-time soda fountain offers a choice of many homemade flavors for sodas, malts, and pop. Mail orders are accepted.

F OOTWEAR

■ SHOES AND THINGS
234 Chestnut Street
Virginia, MN 55792
Tel: (218) 741-5717
Hrs: Mon. - Sat. 9 a.m. - 5 p.m. (Thur. 9 a.m. - 8 p.m.)
Visa, MasterCard, AmEx, and Discover are accepted.

Marcie and Mark Speer have teamed up to provide an extraordinary shopping experience at Shoes and Things.

Collaborating their merchandise and architectural expertise, this free-flowing designed shop is also accessible through Rags, as the interiors are connected. An exceptional line of contemporary casual sportswear and footwear can be found at Shoes and Things.

Customers enjoy the charming atmosphere and warm personal attention given as they walk through this delightful store. For just the right clothes and accessories, stop by Shoes and Things. And, don't forget to pass through to Rags, providing a unique selection of contemporary clothing for women.

G IFT SHOP

■ IRMA'S FINLAND HOUSE
Northgate Plaza
Virginia, MN 55792
Tel: (218) 741-0204
Hrs: Mon. - Sat. 9 a.m. - 5 p.m.
Visa and MasterCard are accepted.

It's not necessary to travel overseas to find the most beautiful gifts. Just come to Irma's Finland House. In business for over 20 years, Irma's is located across from the Northgate Plaza Shopping Center and is easily identified by its Scandinavian inspired, multi-colored sail awnings.

Step inside to a cheerful, spacious shop that has gifts from all over the world. As visitors move about the colorful displays, they notice that glass and dinnerware are a highlight of the store, featuring handblown and crystal glassware such as Iittala from Finland, Schott Zwiesel from Germany, and Nybro from Sweden. Arabia of Finland and Noritake highlight the dinnerware, and Hackman and Oneida flatware help complete a table setting. There are linens from ScanAm, jewelry by Aarikka, designer woolen throws and blankets from Finland, and Dickens and Snow Village lighted collector houses.

Other departments feature gourmet foods and cookware, candles and candleholders, wind chimes and mobiles, greeting cards and art prints, men's and children's gifts, and a full line of sauna bath accessories. For new visitors, Irma's offers a nice selection of gifts unique to this area. Stop in for helpful ideas about places to see and things to do while visiting the area. For convenience shopping, Irma's offers orders by telephone, exquisite gift wrapping, direct gift shipping, and a personal touch bridal registry.

GOLF COURSE & PARK

■ VIRGINIA MUNICIPAL GOLF COURSE/PARK
Ninth Street N. and Ninth Ave.
Virginia, MN 55792
Tel: (218) 741-4366
Hrs: (May through Sept.), Mon. - Sun. 7 a.m. to dusk

A "whole" lot in one — no flurry, no hurry, no scurry. The Virginia Municipal Golf Course is located within the city limits, near Highway 53.

Construction began on the first nine holes of the Virginia Municipal Golf Course in September 1930. A nine-hole addition was constructed by the W.P.A. in 1933. The Virginia Park Department took over the management of the 94-acre course in 1947 and today they are still responsible for this beautiful course. The 18-hole golf course is noted for its playability, offering easy and more difficult bunker shots. Beautiful spruce and pine trees have been strategically placed along the fairways, well-groomed greens set against the "iron ore hills" and fresh, clean air add up to an excellent location for rounds of golf.

Green fees are moderate with seasonal rates for single adults, married couples, college students, and children as well as discounted rates for the over 65 age group. The modern clubhouse, constructed in 1983 and overlooking the 1st and 10th holes, houses a fully stocked pro shop and eating area where soft drinks, coffee, snacks, and hot and cold lunches are served. No hard liquors or beer are served. Motorized carts, pull carts, and club rentals are available.

Directly across the south boundary of the golf course is the 25-acre Virginia City Park. Picnic tables, grates, closed-in picnic shelters, children's playground, a baseball field, tennis and basketball courts, a greenhouse, and fountain are additional attractions for area residents and visitors. A special greenhouse show is held during July and August.

RESTAURANTS

■ RAINY LAKE SALOON AND DELI
207 Chestnut Street
Virginia, MN 55792
Tel: (218) 741-6247
Hrs: Sun. - Thur. 11 a.m. - 9 p.m., Fri. - Sat. 11 a.m. - 10 p.m.
Visa, MasterCard, AmEx, and Discover are accepted.

The beauty of white pine dominated the scenery of the Range in the early 1900s as the city of Virginia grew from the lumber and mining industries. The Virginia and Rainy Lake Company boasted the largest white pine lumber mill in the world as it produced 1 million board feet daily. In honor of that rugged, yet serene era, Bob Turja, owner, designed and established the Rainy Lake Saloon and Deli.

Bob's dedication, hard work, ability, and experience are very congenial and evident in this rustic dining establishment. Guests choose from an enticing appetizer selection. The salads are fresh and mounded with meats and vegetables. Those with hearty appetites enjoy the variety of combination dinners featuring tender steaks and fresh fish or chicken. The burgers and specialty sandwiches are smothered with cheeses or topped with sauces and a variety of condiments. Rainy Lake also offers traditional Cajun, Mexican, and Italian selections for those who crave a little more spice.

Because Rainy Lake takes pride in the resources of Minnesota, a special selection of meals includes wild rice grown locally, prepared with a special sauce and just the right seasoning.

■ KOUNTRY KROSSROADS
7010 Highway 169
Virginia, MN 55792
Tel: (218) 749-5355
Hrs: Mon. - Sat. noon - 1 a.m., Sun. noon - midnight

Kountry Krossroads invites patrons to partake in good food, good conversation, and a comfortable environment. The hand-burned and built pine interior adds a rustic element to the atmosphere.

The walls are lined with baseball hats from various customers and their businesses. The walls also hold humorous quotations from customers offering their bit of wisdom. Friday nights bring a tasty fish fry, Saturday offers a shrimp and steak special. Happy hour, or attitude adjustment as it is sometimes called, also takes place on Saturday from 4:30 p.m. to 6 p.m. A fully stocked bar has the makings of almost any drink. For good food in an informal setting, stop by Kountry Krossroads.

S PECIALTY SHOP

■ FUR SPECIALTIES
7637 Hill Road
Virginia, MN 55792
Tel: (218) 749-5326
Hrs: 9 a.m.-9 p.m. daily

Carol Dodds opened Fur Specialties in 1985. She operates from her home on a 40-acre country homestead and is self-taught in tanning and sewing furs.

All furs used are from Minnesota, including wild and ranch furs such as fox, coyote (brush wolf), martin, fishers, muskrat, mink, raccoon, otter, and badger. The tanning process utilized is nondestructive to the fur, allowing it to retain its natural beauty. Dodds carries her theme of "function and beauty" into all the custom pieces she makes: mittens, ear muffs, and four-inch wide hood ruffs. (The ruffs are attached by velcro in order to be removed for cleaning.)

Her specialty is the authentic Eskimo trapper (or musher) hat — a beautiful and very functional item. All of her hats are made individually, and she considers each one a work of art. In addition to original pieces, she makes minor repairs to fur items. Dodds raises, trains, and races sled dogs. Much of her business is customized for fellow mushers.

S PORTING GOODS

■ MESABI RECREATION
1116 Eighth Street S.
Virginia, MN 55792
Tel: (218) 749-6719
Hrs: (Summer) Mon. - Fri. 9 a.m. - 5:30 p.m., Sat. 9:30 a.m. - 4:30 p.m.
        (Winter) Mon. - Fri 9 a.m. - 5:30 p.m., Sat. 9:30 a.m. - 4:30 p.m.
        Sun. noon - 4 p.m.
Visa, MasterCard, AmEx, and Discover are accepted.

Mesabi Recreation was opened in 1979 by Michael Priest to offer a full line of sports equipment. Over the years, the various lines of merchandise have expanded to include bikes, boats, skis, curling, exercise equipment, clothing, and accessories.

Name brands include mountain and road bikes by Giant, Fuji, Timberline, and Diamond Back. Downhill and cross-country skis can be rented and repaired. Ski wear and accessories include Karhu, Marker, Tyrolia, Peltonen, Atomic, Elan, and Head. In sportswear, there are popular name brands by Sport Obermeyer, Serac, Patagonia, Arena, Raisins, Water Rags, and Kaelin. The goal at Mesabi Recreation is to provide quality products and services to customers by a qualified and knowledgeable staff. Customers find the services to be reliable and accommodating. Mesabi Recreation also specializes in wheelchair repair.

W OMENS CLOTHING

■ RAGS
104 Third Ave. S.
Virginia, MN 55792
Tel: (218) 741-5717
Hrs: Mon. - Sat. 9 a.m. - 5 p.m. (Thur. 9 a.m. - 8 p.m.)
Visa, MasterCard, AmEx, and Discover are accepted.

"Shopping is a social experience," quotes Marcie Speer, owner of Rags. This unique, exclusive shop represents women's updated contemporary clothing captured in an amazing environment and atmosphere.

Reinforcing this philosophy, Mark Speer, a local architect, designed Rags as an open, fluid space projecting the merchandise in a pleasing, stimulating environment. The integration of textures, a 12-foot high tin ceiling, brick walls, mirror, soft pink, lavender and white colors, and modular shapes enhance the feminine fashions of Rags. Fashions include a unique market mix from Chicago, New York, and Minneapolis, along with a seemingly endless selection of accessories to complement any outfit. Women from all lifestyles looking for casual to more enduring fashions are pleased with the selection and affordable prices at Rags. The free-flowing space is also accessible through Shoes and Things, as the interiors are connected.

Marcie and Mark invite customers to browse throughout the shop. Rags provides for an individual fashion image and a positive shopping experience.

Canoeing Minnesota's Waters

by John G. Shepard

A height of land between North Lake and South Lake along the Minnesota-Ontario border — one of America's most legendary and ancient canoe routes—was once the site of an unusual ceremony. Northbound French-Canadian fur traders stopped their heavily burdened canoes here to anoint any newcomers in the group with a cedar bough dipped in the northward-flowing headwaters. Then the group toasted each neophyte with a round of high wines as un Homme du Nord, a "Northman," one of a privileged few to travel the vast wilderness that stretched before them.

The historical and geological significance of this site reveals something about Minnesota, for it is indeed a place of watersheds. Minnesota's three continental divides send surface waters flowing toward the Atlantic Ocean, Hudson Bay, and the Gulf of Mexico along a myriad of streams and rivers. And where the water isn't working its way to a distant sea, the glaciers of the last ice age have left a tremendous legacy in fish-filled lakes. In short, *this* is canoe country.

Root River

The Root is a fine quickwater canoeing stream throughout most of its 90-mile run through Minnesota's bluff country to the Mississippi, though the undeveloped stretch from Chatfield to Lanesboro is the most popular for overnight and weekend trips. Many of the river's small tributaries are clear and cool enough to support prime populations of trout. Wildlife abounds and antique and history buffs will enjoy visiting riverside towns like Lanesboro, where artists, fine restaurants, and bed-and-breakfast establishments occupy restored 19th century buildings.

Minnesota River

The silty Minnesota is a great canoeing river, whether or not you have an interest in the rich and sometimes tragic events that have been played out along its banks. The river has cut a wooded valley through the gently rolling prairie south and west of the Twin Cities, where it lazily meanders through the floodplain. Several state parks — Lac Qui Parle, Upper Sioux Agency, Fort Ridgely, and Minneopa — offer good camping upstream of Mankato. It was here that one of the most vicious wars was fought between settlers and Dakota warriors in 1862. Historic sites are found throughout the valley.

Upper Mississippi

The Father of Waters is magnificent throughout its length, but paddlers with a taste for its wilder, unspoiled aspects will do well to explore the upper sections, where the canoe is still the vessel of choice. The river section nearest the headwaters, which may be too low to run many summers, is the most pristine and rich with wildlife. Downstream of Grand Rapids a more powerful Mississippi flows between sandy, heavily wooded banks. Prime canoe country ends at St. Cloud. Camping is possible at established sites all along this Minnesota Department of Natural Resources-designated canoe trail.

Big Fork

The Big Fork River empties into the Rainy River along the Minnesota-Ontario border west of Voyageurs National Park. Once a voyageurs' highway and a channel for millions of board feet of pine that were floated downstream to mills in Ontario, the Big Fork today is a lightly used canoe route that flows for 165 miles from wild rice marshes near its headwaters through dense boreal forests farther downstream. Fishing for walleyes, muskies, northerns, and bass is excellent; and sturgeon at the river's mouth.

The Boundary Waters Canoe Area and Voyageurs National Park

Voyageurs National Park has much the same flavor as the legendary Boundary Waters Canoe Area (BWCA), except that it is smaller (219,000 acres instead of over 1 million) and open to mechanized travel. Canoeists can escape the park's powerboat traffic by disappearing into the interior of Kabetogama Peninsula where good fishing, clear waters, and untrammeled boreal forest await at Locator, War Club, Quill, and Loiten lakes.

The BWCA is America's great wilderness canoeing mecca, with enough pristine lakes, rivers, and forests to wander in for weeks at a time. Canoeists should be experienced in wilderness navigation, camping, and first aid skills. Permits from the U.S. Forest Service are required.

St. Croix River

By the time it completes its 140-mile journey along the Minnesota-Wisconsin border to join the mighty Mississippi, the St. Croix River has taken on such size and flowed through such historically significant terrain that it nearly vies in stature with the Father of Waters. The upper St. Croix flows quickly through pine and hardwood forests with several sections that boast easy rapids in spring and other times of high water. The geologically distinct lower St. Croix is broad and shallow and passes by a number of state parks and some wonderful historic towns: Marine-on-St. Croix, Osceola, Stillwater, Afton. The St. Croix's striking beauty and historical importance earned the river recognition as one of the first national wild and scenic rivers.

©MARTIENA R.
RICHTER

Red
Wing
Cannon Falls
Frontenac
Lake City
Twin Cities

Wabasha
Zumbrota
Kellogg
Mississippi
River
Zumbro Falls
Hwy.
61
Mantorville
Rochester
Winona
Dodge
Center
Kasson
I-90
Racine
Le Crescent
Chatfield
Wykoff
Rushford
Lanesboro
Spring Valley
Caledonia
I-90
Preston
Austin
Spring Grove
Harmony
Mabel

BLUFF COUNTRY

by John G. Shepard

They came north by Mississippi riverboat. At first, just a
trickle; then, a thickening stream — settlers drawn to the
rugged bluff country of southeastern Minnesota. From
Germany, Norway, Poland, Sweden, they laid claim to a
sweeping landscape of clear rivers, hardwood forests, lakes, and
fertile soils.

As the settlers entered the Mississippi's Hiawatha Valley near
Minnesota's southern border, America's mightiest river narrowed
its course and on either bank there gradually emerged, from the
flatlands, parallel ramparts of steep, wooded bluffs rising
hundreds of feet toward the sky. Cliffs stood out above stately
oaks, revealing bands of crumbling sandstone and dolomite
formed millions of years ago when the region was submerged by
a warm and shallow sea.

These imposing bluffs, dissected by deep ravines, were left
intact while the rest of the state was being laid low by ice-age
glaciers 10,000 to 20,000 years ago. In the shadows of the bluffs
were clear-flowing rivers that served the settlers as highways for
traveling into the dense forests and rolling prairies to the west.
Except for the raw beginnings of such river towns as Winona,
Wabasha, and Red Wing, all of whose names derive from regional
Dakota and Ojibwa Indian lore, the river valley was pristine and

untamed — much as it remains today. Then, as now, woods were teeming with deer and wild turkey while the crystalline waters of the Zumbro, Root, Whitewater, and Cannon rivers were ripe with trout.

Today, the descendents of these settlers encourage travelers to discover the richness of this land and to become acquainted with its history. In the Mississippi's quaint river towns, outstanding Victorian architecture and numerous historic sites and museums chronicle a colorful past, while the Father of Waters offers a wealth of recreational possibilities.

There are Mississippi River houseboats to rent for cruising from town to town in the tradition of steamboat pilots such as Mark Twain. Canoeists can explore the backwaters with birdbook and binoculars. Anglers can attempt to lure Mississippi catfish to join them for dinner. The Mississippi's naturally formed Lake Pepin is perfect for sailing or waterskiing — in fact, it was here in 1922 that an adventuresome fellow named Ralph Samuelson made sports history by strapping eight-foot pine boards onto his feet and allowing himself to be pulled behind a motorboat.

Turn westward from the Mississippi's banks, travel up any wooded draw, and the pristine streams and forests of the bluff country will encompass you. The loveliest of state parks — Whitewater, Beaver Creek Valley, Nerstrand Woods — afford outstanding camping, picnicking, and hiking. Tours are given of the underground caverns at Harmony's Niagara Caves and at the Mystery Caves near Forestville State Park, where horseback riders roam miles of wooded trails. New discoveries await around every bend on the canoe routes and bike paths of the Cannon and Root Rivers. And, after coming out of the woods, visitors can partake of civilization's comforts in the quaint river towns steeped in the charm of bygone days.

Austin

A ustin sits on the banks of the Cedar River, proving the settlers' first rule of thumb: Always live near a water supply. The river provided power to the sawmills and flour mills, as well as relief to the settlers and the Sioux Indians native to the area. Austin drew industry to its ranks; the Hormel Company opened in 1887 and has been the primary reason Austin has grown and flourished into the modern era.

Austin is located just 12 miles north of the Iowa border. It provides exquisite beauty while being in close proximity of two major metropolitan areas, the Twin Cities and Rochester. 1991 marked the 100th Anniversary of the Hormel Company and of the Austin Daily Herald, two landmarks in Austin's history. One hundred years ago George Hormel wanted to make his company the largest in southern Minnesota. Today, it is one of the largest in the world. The Weyerhauser Company is another thriving industry in Austin. It has been manufacturing shipping containers since 1954. Austin also is the site of the Miss Minnesota Pageant, held in early June. This is the official preliminary to the Miss America Pageant. (Austin has played host to this event for more than two decades.)

ATTRACTIONS

Cedar River Days are held midsummer with events including a street dance and a community breakfast. The *National Barrow Show* is held in mid-September, attracting people from all over the world to attend the swine exhibition and sale. In February the *Dobbins Creek Ski Run* is scheduled. It is a 10-kilometer ski race at the Hormel Nature Center which allows men and women in various age groups to participate. The *Jay C. Hormel Nature Center* teaches visitors about nature and its creatures. The center is only four years old but has become a very popular attraction.

For more information on Austin, contact:
THE AUSTIN AREA CHAMBER OF COMMERCE
300 N. Main Street
P.O. Box 864
Austin, MN 55912
(507) 437-4563 or (800) 444-5713

A CCOMMODATIONS

■ HOLIDAY INN AUSTIN
HOLIDOME CONFERENCE CENTER
1701 W. Fourth Street N.W.
Austin, MN 55912
Tel: (507) 433-1000
All major credit cards are accepted.

The Holiday Inn Austin is centrally located to Albert Lea and Rochester, and serves northern Iowa and southern Minnesota. It offers accommodations and amenities designed to please both business and pleasure travelers. These range from meeting rooms and shuttle service to swimming pools and a nightclub. Attractive poolside guest rooms have private verandas, and 20 luxury suites offer a whirlpool in every room.

The Holidome was created to provide a year-round tropical paradise. There are three mosaic-lined pools, a whirlpool, sauna, billiard and ping-pong tables, arcade games, putting green, and an extensive Health Club.

The Conference Center is a sophisticated facility, with state-of-the-art audio/visual equipment and trained sales and catering staff. Eight meeting rooms, including an executive boardroom and grand ballroom provide 10,000 square feet that may be partitioned or expanded to accommodate 1,250 people. Four restaurants are available for a variety of dining experiences. Guests may enjoy American/Continental cuisine in the atmosphere of a turn-of-the-century library, or the open-air grill and live entertainment in the high-energy nightclub.

N ATURE CENTER

■ THE J. C. HORMEL NATURE CENTER
1304 N.E. 21st Street
P.O. Box 673
Austin, MN 55912
Tel: (507) 437-7519
Hrs: (Building) Mon. - Sat. 9 a.m. - noon, 1 p.m. - 5 p.m., Sun. 1 p.m. - 5 p.m.
      (Refuge): 6 a.m. - 10 p.m.

Just outside of Austin, a quarter-mile north of I-90, are nearly 300 acres of hardwood forest, pine plantations, and prairie restoration areas, with trails and footbridges over meandering streams. These acres are the home of red squirrel, deer, raccoon, and many species of birds, and is also known as the Hormel Nature Center Refuge. At the Hormel Nature Center, experienced naturalists offer fun and educational ways for children and grown-ups to learn about the natural world.

In 1971, concerned citizens, intent on preserving the natural state of their community, helped to raise the funds that enabled the City of Austin to purchase part of the former estate of J.C. Hormel. Now children and adults can enjoy such programs as spring wildflowers, maple syruping, pioneer crafts, bird watching, nature study, night hikes, cross-country skiing, and cider pressing.

The Hormel Nature Center is a great place to go all year round, with the family for a busy day of fun and learning, or with a friend for a quiet walk along the trails. Hormel Nature Center has something to offer just about everyone.

R ESTAURANT

■ THE OLD MILL
(Two miles north of I-90)
(Exit at Sixth Street N.E.)
Austin, MN 55912
Tel: (507) 437-2076
Hrs: (Lunch) Mon. - Fri. 11:30 a.m. - 2 p.m.
      (Dinner) Mon. - Sat. 5:30 p.m. - 10 p.m. Closed on Sundays
All major credit cards are accepted.

Beautiful antique chairs flank solid wooden tables under hand-hewn beamed ceilings. The scene outside the window is of the historic Ramsey Dam over the Red Cedar River. This rustic scene is the home of The Old Mill restaurant, named after a renovation of the former Ramsey Mill. The Old Mill offers a perfect combination of classic American food in a delightfully historic setting.

Built in 1872 by Mathew Gregson of Lancashire, England, the Ramsey Mill originally produced flour from the grist brought by farmers in horse-drawn wagons. The three-story wooden building housed a wheelpit, grinding floor. The dam was constructed of logs chinked with dirt and stones, later replaced by concrete. A working mill until a few years before Ray and Mary Stromer purchased it, the Ramsey Mill was remodeled and first opened as a restaurant in 1950. Present-day owners Dave and Julie Forland have worked hard to maintain the original atmosphere of the mill.

Enjoy filet mignon, top sirloin steak, broiled filet of pike, or Alaskan king crab, complemented by a wide selection of fine wines. For dessert, choose from a variety of mousse cakes including Chocolate Truffle Mousse Cake or Almond Amaretto. The Old Mill is perfect for an intimate meal for two. With seating for more than 80, The Old Mill can comfortably accommodate private parties.

Caledonia

C aledonia is noted as the Wild Turkey Capital of Minnesota (for the bird, not the bourbon). Located just off of Highway 16 in the extreme southeast corner of the state, the city is in the *Richard J. Dorer Memorial Hardwood Forest*. Caledonia was settled primarily by the Scots. Water melting off of the glaciers in the north carved out deep valleys and left bluffs and hills leading to the Mississippi River. *Schecks Mill* is the only grist mill still in operation and contains original unaltered equipment. Tours are available on request and stone-ground flour can be purchased. The *Historic Village* depicts life as it was for the settlers with people acting out these parts during the county fair. Historic buildings include a settlers church, school, a log home, the *Houston County Historical Society Museum,* and an antique machine shed. *Founders Days* and the *Houston County Fair* provide summer gatherings for the descendants of the early Scots.

For more information on Caledonia, contact:

THE CALEDONIA AREA CHAMBER OF COMMERCE
P.O. Box 24B
Caledonia, MN 55921
(507) 724-2751

B ED & BREAKFAST

■ THE INN ON THE GREEN
Route 1, P.O. Box 205
Caledonia, MN 55921
Tel: (507) 724-2818
Hrs: Open year-round

Just one-half mile south of Caledonia, in beautiful wooded bluff country, the big white colonial home on the edge of Ma Cal Grove Country Club welcomes overnight guests with the warmth of a homecoming. In a sense, visitors to the Inn on the Green are coming home, because in four of the seven bedrooms of this landmark house lives the Jilek family. The remaining three, sunny, individually decorated bedrooms are reserved for visitors to the family's bed-and-breakfast establishment.

Brad and Shelley Jilek purchased the Inn on the Green, which is often mistaken for the golf course's clubhouse, in 1987 when it was still a private family residence. They converted its spacious lower level of the house, which is situated on 10 acres, into three lovely rooms where travelers and vacationers could comfortably stay. A whirlpool and a sauna, as well as central air conditioning, were also installed to enhance the inn's comfort. Each guest bedroom is furnished with french doors that lead to a tranquil garden patio and the surrounding woods, where more than 27 species of birds have been spotted and wild turkeys and deer are frequent visitors. Nearby trout streams attract anglers, hikers can amble through surrounding trails, and in the winter cross-country skiers, snowmobilers, and ice-fishing couples enjoy the beauty and diversity of southern Minnesota. The brilliant spectrum of Mother Nature's autumn extravaganza attracts foliage lovers from all over the Midwest.

Guests also rave about Shelley's gourmet cooking, which rouses them out of bed in the morning with the smells of Bluff Country Apple Pancakes, home-made muffins, hot baked egg dishes, and

fresh-ground coffee. The Jileks offer old-fashioned hospitality at the Inn on the Green while keeping their visitors satisfied with all the modern comforts.

G IFT STORE

■ THE GIFT MILL
114 S. Kingston Street
Caledonia, MN 55921
Tel: (507) 724-5407
Hrs: Mon. - Thurs. 9 a.m. - 5:30 p.m.
    Fri. 9 a.m. - 6 p.m.
    Sat. 9 a.m. - 5 p.m.
    Open Sundays in December 11 a.m. - 4 p.m.
Visa and MasterCard are accepted.

Bath towels, placemats, tablecloths, candles, crystal, Precious Moments figurines and cards are just some of the gifts at the Gift Mill, owned by Jeanne Miller and Florence Frank. The store also features Noritake china and Oneida flatware, as well as Heritage Alpine table lace and curtains imported from Europe. In addition, The Gift Mill carries such men's favorites as carved ducks, brass eagles, and Red Mill animals. After you've made your purchase, ask for free gift wrapping. Brides are also encouraged to register at The Gift Mill, and all who do receive a free gift.

M ILL TOURS

■ SCHECH'S WATER POWERED MILL
R.R. 2, P.O. Box 82
Caledonia, MN 55921
Tel: (507) 896-3481

The only active water-powered mill in Minnesota can be found on a farm six miles north of Caledonia, right off County Trunk Highway No. 10, near Beaver Creek Valley State Park. Schech's Water Powered Mill has been listed in the National Register since 1978. This charming old mill was built in 1876 by John Blinn. He used native limestone for the three-story building, and maple flooring, which can still be seen on the first floor. Michael J. Schech purchased the mill in 1887. He and his sons operated the mill, producing "Schech's Best Flour." They also made cornmeal, rye, buckwheat, and graham flour, as well as whole wheat cereal. These were sold locally in Houston and Caledonia.

When Michael Schech retired in 1913, his son Edward continued the business. In 1922 the wooden dam was replaced with a concrete dam. In 1924 a concrete water wheel pit was constructed. It houses three Leffel water turbines, which operate the mill entirely with water power. When Edward died in 1941, all commercial milling was discontinued. His wife ran the mill business of custom grinding for four more years before retiring. In 1946, her daughter and husband, Eleanor and Ivan Krugmire, moved onto the farm and continued the feed grinding business. Today, the Krugmires grind feed for their own livestock. Corn and wheat are ground and packaged for tourists.

M OTEL & SUPPER CLUB

■ CREST MOTEL & SUPPER CLUB
Highways 44 and 76
Caledonia, MN 55921
Tel: (507) 724-3311
Hrs: (Supper club) Mon. - Sat. 5 p.m. - closing. Closed on Sun.
    (Motel) open year-round
Visa, MasterCard, and Discover are accepted.

A mile southwest of Caledonia in the heart of bluff country, just a short distance from state parks and the Mississippi River, and amidst 400 miles of snowmobile trails is the Crest Motel & Supper Club. Open all year, the Crest Motel and Supper Club combines the convenience of a motel with first-rate dining facilities, making it an ideal stopping place both summer and winter.

Harley and Joanne Meiners welcome visitors and diners to their motel and supper club, built in 1961. The motel features 25 rooms (two-bedroom rooms are available) with air conditioning, telephone, and color television. The supper club with lounge features a full range of meat and seafood dishes served in a rustic, warm atmosphere.

Enjoy barbequed ribs, homemade soups, salad bar; or walleye, lobster, and shrimp entrees. Or, try the nightly Chef's Special. Whether a hearty meal after a day of snowmobiling or turkey hunting sounds attractive (Caledonia is the wild turkey capital of Minnesota), or simply having a cocktail on the patio overlooking the golf course seems refreshing, the Crest Motel and Supper Club is the place to visit. Business meetings, parties, and family reunions are accommodated easily in the private banquet room. Flexible and friendly, the Crest Motel & Supper Club is a special place to stop.

Cannon Falls

C annon Falls earned its name due to a misinterpretation of a French phrase. The French explorers named the area, Riviere aux Canots (River of Canoes). English speaking residents noticed the emphasis on "Canots" and took it to mean Cannon. Thus, the river became the Cannon River and the surrounding area Cannon Falls. The Cannon Falls area was originally inhabited by the Sioux (Dakota) Indian tribe, who later relinquished it through assorted treaties. Today Cannon Falls maintains a population of around 3,000. One of the largest employers in the community is Cannon Valley Woodwork, which employs close to 100 people. Cannon Falls is nestled comfortably between two major metropolitan areas, Minneapolis/St. Paul and Rochester.

ATTRACTIONS

A wide range of outdoor sites and activities dominate the calendar of events of Cannon Falls. *Welch Mill* offers canoeing and tubing down the Cannon River. *Cannon Falls Walking Tours* directs visitors at a leisurely pace to landmark spots throughout the city. Some of the highlights of the walking tour are: *Veterans Minnieska Park,* where artesian water ponds provide smooth glideways for the resident swans and ducks; *Cannon Falls Bandshell and Athletic Field,* built in 1938 as part of the WPA project of the Great Depression; the *William Tanner Home,* named for Cannon Falls' own Civil War hero; the *Trout Rearing Pond,* where the Sportsmen's Club raises more than 3,000 fingerlings each year; and the *Old Creamery/Old Depot* constructed in the early 1800s to serve the railroad. *The Cannon Valley Trail,* one of the most popular attractions, is used for hiking and biking in the summer and for skiing in winter. Annual events include *Cabin Fever Days,* held the first week of February. This event includes a parade, sled dog races, ice and snow games, cross-country skiing, craft fairs, and sleigh rides. The *Cannon Valley Fair* is part of the Fourth of July festivities, with all of the attraction of a small town fair. For those planning on staying in the area, the *Quill and Quilt* is a delightful bed and breakfast.

For more information about Cannon Falls, contact:
CANNON FALLS AREA CHAMBER OF COMMERCE
P.O. Box 2
202 N. Fourth Street
Cannon Falls, MN 55009
(507) 263-2289

Chatfield

T he Chosen Valley" is how Chatfield is described in Margaret Snyder's book, *Chatfield*. Chatfield is located minutes from the Mayo Clinic in Rochester and is at the headwaters of the Root River Canoe Trail that runs through the Minnesota Memorial Hardwood Forest. Gorgeous scenery is found inside and around the town as well as wild game. The fishing opener is greeted with the *Trout Classic Fishing Contest* sponsored by the Fire Department. The *Chatfield Brass Band Free Music Lending Library* is one of a kind: It has all types of music available for lending. Visit the *Old School House,* where there is displayed country art depicting scenes from rural Minnesota. Western Days is celebrated each August with a parade, street dancing, a horse show, and a twilight trail ride.

For more information on Chatfield, contact:
CITY OF CHATFIELD-CLERK'S OFFICE
Thurber Community Center
21 S.E. Second Street
Chatfield, MN 55923
(507) 867-3810

ART GALLERY

■ COUNTRY ART GALLERY
One-fourth mile west of 52 on Highway 30
Chatfield, MN 55923
Tel: (507) 867-4016
Hrs: Mon. - Fri. 8 a.m. - 5 p.m.
　　 Sat. 9 a.m. - 4 p.m. Sun. by appointment
Visa and MasterCard are accepted.

Located in a rural Chatfield schoolhouse originally built in 1892, Country Art Gallery now occupies the one-room, rural school once attended by Harvey Bernard, artist and owner. Bernard's goal to portray the pride and plight of farmers is truly displayed as his works tell the stories of farm life as it once was.

As you visit this restored country school, the original desks and school bell, metal ceiling, hardwood floors, and flag pole bring back memories of heritage that has been preserved. The building itself is a monument to earlier days of farm life. Artworks displayed depict farm life of yesteryear that include threshing time, farmers preparing for the bitter cold winters, country roads of snow and mud, family gatherings, peaceful and rugged nature scenes, barn chores, horse and buggy days, and many more nostalgic farm scenes. These memories come to life in silkscreen prints, pen and ink drawings, oil and watercolor paintings, and other country gifts. The plaques are popular gift items, and limited edition prints are also on display. Additional services include picture framing, shipping, and mail order.

Relive your country school days with a visit to the Country Art Gallery, where art and memories mix.

B ED & BREAKFAST/MUSEUM

■ LUND'S OAKENWALD TERRACE & GUEST HOUSE
218 Winona S.E.
Chatfield, MN 55923
Tel: (507) 867-4003

Lund's Oakenwald Terrace and Guest House takes its guests back in history. Built in 1897, this mansion is exquisitely preserved with beautiful antiques, woodwork, and stained glass depicting the 1920s and 30s period. It is elegantly decorated in dark rich colors, velvet drapes, and lace to set a warm and pleasurable atmosphere. There is a museum in the attic. Each guest room has a private bath, living and dining room, and screened porch. The Guest House can accommodate eight people providing four bedrooms each with a private bath, kitchen and laundry facilities, an electric organ, and living room with a fireplace. A continental or full breakfast is served in the dining room.

The Lund's Oakenwald Terrace and Guest House is a lovely bed-and-breakfast hideaway, personalized to meet any traveler's needs. It's a great trip for antique buyers and "lookers" to see this huge collection of rare and special antiques.

M USIC LENDING LIBRARY

■ CHATFIELD BRASS BAND
81 Library Lane
Chatfield, MN 55923
Tel: (507) 867-3275
Hrs: Mon. - Fri. 8 a.m. - 5 p.m. Evenings and weekends by appointment

The Chatfield Brass Band Free Music Lending Library is the only one of its kind in the world. It was started in 1971, and in 1981 built and dedicated its own building. Built by donations from around the world, it has over 35,000 items for lending in all categories of music. And not just band music! Taking pride in preserving the music heritage, the lending library accumulates, catalogs, repairs, stores, and makes music of all categories available on a free loan basis.

The Chatfield Brass Band Free Music Lending Library has a wide selection of musical holdings. Tunes are in the categories of Dixieland, pop, overtures, waltzes, marches, trombone smears, operettas, serenades, and special music for religious and patriotic occasions, holidays, and many, many more. There is a variety of composer, music history, music studies, and other miscellaneous textbooks to choose from.

A minimal contribution for staff time, postage, and handling is appreciated to cover the cost of selections. Band and library memberships are also available for a minimal annual fee.

The Chatfield Brass Band was formed in 1969 with 16 players and has since grown to 200 players from 25 states. The lending library supplies all the music for its concerts. A monthly newsletter provides information on the activities of the band and library and is available upon request.

Dodge Center

D odge Center began as a railroad town because of the refusal of other cities to pay bonuses to the surveyors who were planning the layout of the train tracks. Rochester is 20 miles to the east of Dodge Center, and Owatonna is 20 miles to the west. In 1870 there was a proposal to change the name of Dodge Center to Silas, the proposal was tabled, however, and remains tabled to this day. *North Park* is the site of the city swimming pool and tennis courts in addition to the 4th of July celebration and the *Miss Dodge Center Pageant.* The Dodge Country Club hosts the *Men's Open Golf Tournament* the weekend after the 4th of July. Father's Day brings a big event each year, the *Annual Fly-In Breakfast.* Planes have flown into the Dodge Center Airport for more than 30 years to bring people to attend the breakfast.

For more information on Dodge Center, contact:
CITY OF DODGE CENTER
23 W. Main
P.O. Box 430
Dodge Center, MN 55927
(507) 374-2575

B ED & BREAKFAST

■EDEN BED & BREAKFAST
R.R. 1, P.O. Box 215
Dodge Center, MN 55927
Tel: (507) 527-2311
Visa and MasterCard are accepted.

The Eden Bed and Breakfast is a quiet serene country home opened in 1986 by Margaret Chapen, who wanted to share her home and "old-fashioned hospitality.," This elegant home with a country setting offers a great escape to country living.

This charming home has four guest rooms: the Green Room has a Spring feeling and shared bath, the Rose Room has a high carved antique black walnut double bed and dresser, the Blue Room has a "Lillian Russell" bedroom suite with blue velvet drapes and private bath, and the light and airy Red Room has a queen-size bed, white wicker furniture, and private bath. There are many old dressers and antique furniture along with heirlooms that have been passed down over the years throughout her home. The dining room has a fireplace to relax by, and the parlor and family room with television are opened to guests to enjoy. Homemade rolls, muffins, and cookies are served to guests, along with a hearty country breakfast in the dining room.

Rice Lake State Park with hiking and cross-country skiing is nearby. A 25-minute drive takes guests to Rochester, MN, the home of the famous Mayo Clinic medical facility. Mantorville is only ten minutes away, featuring the famous Hubbel House

Restaurant, built in 1854. Guests can visit antique shops, the opera house, courthouse, and the famous boardwalk, all of which look much as they did in the 1850s.

Harmony

H armony, one of the better names for a town, earned its title because of bickering taking place over what the name should be. One observer called for harmony to stop the argument, and it stuck. Harmony is yet another river town built by a railroad so it could have access to the abundant wood and water for the steam engines. This town still maintains a vital farming community combined with light industry. Harmony has some of the best trout streams in the state. Endless ski and hiking trails envelope this town, and additional attractions include *Niagara Cave*, which allows visitors to view spectacular rock formations. An Amish community permits tours, and an *Amish Craft Shop* offers unique handcrafted items.

For more information on Harmony, contact:
THE HARMONY TOURISM CENTER
P.O. Box 141, Dept. K
Harmony, MN 55939
(507) 886-2469

A CCOMMODATIONS

■ THE COUNTRY LODGE MOTEL
525 Main Ave.
Harmony, MN 55939
Tel: (507) 886-2515
Visa and MasterCard are accepted.

The Country Lodge Motel is located in Harmony, the heart of Minnesota's largest Amish community and where visitors can expect the unusual.

Each of the nine rooms has two double beds, color television with cable, and telephones. There is one kitchenette suite available. Contemporarily decorated in traditional mauve and teal colors, this motel provides a very relaxing atmosphere. Guests can enjoy a free continental breakfast in the motel lobby, or relax in the lounge and television area. A conference room is available for meetings, parties, or special occasions, with full catering services. While in the area, tour the "old order" Amish community and experience a turn-of-the-century way of farming. Visit Niagara Cave, an underground cavern with a 60-foot waterfall. There are also gift and antique shops offering Amish quilts, dolls, baskets, furniture, and other crafts.

A MISH TOURS

■ MICHEL'S AMISH TOURS

45 Main Ave. N.
Harmony, MN 55939
Tel: (507) 886-5392, Ext. P
Hrs: Mon. - Sat. Call for reservations. No Sunday tours.

Michel's Amish Tours is the one read and heard about in Harmony, the heart of historic bluff country. Visitors to Harmony can tour the largest Amish colony in Minnesota, a life led in strong Christian convictions without many of the conveniences now taken for granted by most Americans. The area is rich in culture, history, and scenic beauty.

Three- and five-hour guided tours are available by car or bus. A trained guide rides in each car to show and tell about the Amish lifestyle and help find traditional Amish wares that visitors may wish to purchase. Bus tours are also available by appointment. The five-hour Amish tour views many Amish farms, and stops now and then at one of their homes where visitors may purchase quilts, baskets, handmade furniture, and many other Amish crafts. Visitors also have the opportunity to watch the Amish working their fields with horses and machinery reminiscent of the late 1800s. On the tour is shown a number of old native limestone houses and barns set in scenic bluff country, the first church built in Fillmore County, and the old stagecoach stop with its hotel accommodations still standing. It passes through the beautiful rolling countryside of the river valley between Preston and Lanesboro and visits the Old Barn Resort, now famous for the restoration of the historic Allis Barn, built in 1884.

Additional to the tours, Michel's Farm Vacations provides unique and fun vacations. Arrangements have been made with approximately 20 farms in the area where guests can stay with one of the host families or in a country vacation home in or near Amish country.

ANTIQUE STORE

■CENTER AND MAIN ANTIQUES
15 W. Center Street
Harmony, MN 55939
Tel: (507) 886-2565
Hrs: Mon. - Sat. 10 a.m. - 4 p.m., Sun. 1 p.m. - 4 p.m.
(Jan. - March), by appointment only, call: (507) 886-4445
Visa and MasterCard are accepted.

Antique lovers know the feeling when they find that perfect piece for their home or office. Whatever kind of antique they are looking for, they'll likely find it at Center and Main Antiques, downtown Harmony.

Whether it be furniture, glassware, primitives, books, coins, pictures, or stoneware, this charming antique shop's selection is endless. The original tin ceiling and hardwood floors of the 90-year-old building add to the warm atmosphere. The shop features oak and walnut furniture from the early 1900s. Although not for sale, the display of cherry wall cabinets is worth seeing. The cabinets, which came from the Royal Confectionary in Winona, are over 90 years old and graced by bevelled glass and stained glass doors. The selection of glassware includes carnival, depression, and German Bavarian and Nippon. Other collectibles displayed are antique dolls and toys, tobacco and tea tins, afghans and linens, and kitchenware found in early kitchens. Furniture restoration and shipping are also available.

CAVE TOURS

■ NIAGARA CAVE
Niagara Cave Road
Harmony, MN 55939
Tel: (507) 886-6606
Hrs: Weekends in May 10 a.m. - 4 p.m.
Memorial Day - Labor Day 10 a.m. - 5 p.m. daily
Weekends in Sept. - Oct. 10 a.m. - 4 p.m.
Closed Nov. - April

Consider taking a trip below ground to an entirely different world than the one of amusement parks, shopping malls, and the usual above-ground sights. Consider Niagara Cave, located just two miles south of Harmony, MN, on Highway 139, then two miles west on Niagara Cave Road.

Niagara Cave was discovered by three farm boys in 1924. The boys were looking for some lost pigs, but what they found was a system of underground caverns — some with ceilings more than 100 feet high — stretching for almost two miles. Over the eons, subterranean streams carved out Niagara Cave, and they are still active today, slowly wearing away the limestone and adding to the cave system. A highlight of the cave is its namesake — a spectacular 60-foot waterfall. Here, visitors can pause on a bridge built across the fall chasm and peer 60 feet down to the foot of the falls, or 70 feet up at the vaulted stone dome of the cavern.

At Niagara Cave, visitors are introduced to the intricate forces that create awesome stalagtites and stalagmites, and take a peak at ancient fossils and crystal formations. A visit here is truly a visit to another world.

Kasson

Kasson is located 13 miles west of Rochester and 70 miles southeast of the Twin Cities. The town was named after Jabez Hyde Kasson, a man of Irish descent who had been one of three to plat the village and secure a railroad depot. Kasson is primarily a farming community displaying all the charm of small town life. The *Kasson Municipal Building* is on The Prairie School National Register of Sites. Built in 1917 this structure served as post office, council chamber, library, fire station, police department, and masonic lodge. The major event in Kasson is the *Festival in the Park* held in August.

For more information on Kasson, contact:
CITY OF KASSON
122 W. Main
Kasson, MN 55944
(507)634-7071

D EPARTMENT STORE

■ LEUTHOLD'S
107-113 W. Main, P.O. Box 278
Kasson, MN 55944
Tel: (507) 634-2261
Hrs: Mon. - Thurs. 9 a.m. - 8 p.m.
      Fri. - Sat. 9 a.m. - 5:30 p.m.
Visa and MasterCard are accepted.

Leuthold's secret to success is having one of the highest qualtiy selections of merchandise in the area. Leuthold's is a "full service" family shopping store.

The birth of the Leuthold stores traces back to Jacob Leuthold, Sr., who migrated from Zurich, Switzerland in 1855, was in business in Mantorville, and later purchased three lots and built a wooden structure 20' x 40' in the same spot where the present Leuthold's Ladies store exists. Ten years later the store burned, and a new building was erected. Mr. Leuthold had five sons, Jacob, Jr., John Henry, Charles, and Rudolph, all of whom followed in their father's footsteps, going into the retail business in various nearby cities as the opportunity presented itself.

The atmosphere is family-oriented. Clothing and shoes include women's, men's, children's, and boy's departments. The basement stores have fabrics, sewing items, towels, blankets, and men's work clothes.

F AMILY RESTAURANT

■ DANIEL'S RESTAURANT
19 W. Main Street
Kasson, MN 55944
Tel: (507) 634-7775
Hrs: Mon. - Thurs. 5:30 a.m. - 9 p.m.
      Fri. - Sat. 5:30 a.m. - 10 p.m., Sun. 6:30 a.m. - 8 p.m.

While passing through the rolling hills of southeastern Minnesota, try stopping in Kasson for a genuine smalltown meal at Daniel's Restaurant. Located on main street, Daniel's is the favorite gathering place for those who appreciate flavorful cooking at a good value.

The menu boasts a mouthwatering selection of soups (36 varieties), sandwiches, dinners and desserts, all made from recipes developed with tender loving care by Daniel and his wife, Marg Ann. Topping the list is the fried cod fish dinner, served every day of the week. If you're lucky enough to be in town Friday night, go for the all-you-can-eat batter-fried fish special. For those who prefer beef or chicken, Daniel's serves juicy hand-patted hamburgers and a chicken fillet to suit every taste. But don't forget to leave room for the made-from-scratch desserts: cheesecakes, each filled with a pound and a half of cream cheese; old style pecan pie; or, if the season is right, fresh strawberry pie.

The Daniels pride themselves on the friendly atmosphere of their restaurant, and they'll go out of their way to make everyone feel at home.

LaCrescent

LaCrescent has been called one of Minnesota's best kept secrets. Known as the "Apple Capital of Minnesota," this town is located 130 miles southeast of Minneapolis/St. Paul. The community draws bicycle enthusiasts from all over the Midwest to tour the Root River State Trail for a scenic ride along the Bluff Country. Hunters have come away with enviable sizes of game including white tail deer and wild turkey. Miles of cross-country ski and snowmobile trails wind throughout the area. Each September the *Annual Applefest* is held to celebrate the apple harvest with a weekend of activities, including a street dance, an arts and crafts fair, and the *King Apple Grand Parade.* The *Apple Blossom Scenic Drive* stretches for eight miles along part of the Hiawatha Trail and presents breathtaking scenery at every turn.

For more information on LaCrescent, contact:
LACRESCENT CHAMBER OF COMMERCE
P.O. Box 132
LaCrescent, MN 55947
(507) 895-2800

G IFT STORE

■ APPLE VALLEY ANTIQUES AND GIFTS
23 S. Walnut
LaCrescent, MN 55947
Tel: (507) 895-4268
Hrs: Mon. - Sat. 11 a.m. - 5 p.m. (Sept.-Dec., Sun. 1 p.m. - 5 p.m.)
Visa and MasterCard are accepted.

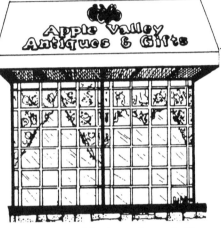

This delightful antique and gift shop, so named because it is nestled in downtown LaCresent — "The Apple Capital of Minnesota," attractively displays antiques, country collectibles, and many other gift ideas.

The "I Love Country" atmosphere invites visitors to select from candles, cards, potpourri, apple items, bath products, baskets, afghans, braided rugs, stoneware, dried flower arrangements, Heritage lace, doilies, cookbooks, cookie molds, and many Minnesota gift items. There is antique furniture such as refinished cupboards, dressers, and tables, along with commodes, rockers, decorating accessories, and much more.

The large selection of gift items and bridal registry makes Apple Valley Antiques and Gifts a great place to shop for any occasion.

R OADSIDE MARKET & GIFTS

■ BAUER'S MARKET AND NURSERY
221 N. Second Street
LaCrescent, MN 55947
Tel: (507) 895-4583
Hrs.: Mon. - Sun. 8 a.m. - 6 p.m.
    (Jan. - March) Mon. - Sun. 9 a.m. - 6 p.m.

The owners of Bauer's Market and Nursery refer to their store as a "growing and friendly business." After a humble beginning almost 30 years ago, Bauer's now occupies more than 10,000 square feet of retail display space.

Although Bauer's began as a roadside business selling apples exclusively, the evidence of that fact is hard to recognize now. Apples still are sold but the varieties seemingly are endless and include the Haralson variety developed by the University of Minnesota, as well as a special hybrid named Regent. A huge selection of other fruits and vegetables, including squash, potatoes, onions, and sweet corn also is available in the produce section. The pleasant, clean country market features all kinds of potted plants, trees, and shrubs. Additional merchandise includes jellies, jams, ciders, Wisconsin cheeses, and sausages, maple syrup and molasses from the northwoods, and an extensive selection of candies and craft items.

Bauer's Market and Nursery also does landscape design as well as commercial and residential landscaping. A mixture of seasonal items provides an ever-changing backdrop for the items sold. On top of everything else a variety of lawn ornaments completes the extensive selection. Stop by Bauer's to receive free samples during apple harvest time.

Lake City

L ake of Tears was the name given to Lake Pepin in 1860 by Father Louis Hennepin after observing Sioux captors weeping as their prisoners were taken up the Mississippi River. Lake City is the gateway to Lake Pepin, only 35 miles north of Rochester. Summer on the lake is a great way to spend your time. Boats move across the lake constantly pulling waterskiers, dropping lines into the water, or just sailing along taking in the scenery and soaking up rays. Waterskiing is said to have been invented by Ralph Samuelson in 1922, here in Lake City. The *Pepin Open Regatta* adds to the 4th of July festivities in the summer. October brings *Johnny Appleseed Days*, and in winter nearby *Mt. Frontenac* offers fabulous skiing with the steepest vertical drop in Minnesota. *Hok-Si-La Park* and *Frontenac State Park* provide outdoor attractions all year-round.

For more information on Lake City, contact:
THE LAKE CITY CHAMBER OF COMMERCE
212 S. Washington Street
Lake City, MN 55041
(612) 345-4123

A CCOMMODATIONS

■ LAKE CITY COUNTRY INN
1401 N. Lakeshore Drive
Lake City, MN 55041
Tel: (612) 345-5351
Hrs: Open year-round
Visa, MasterCard, and AmEx are accepted.

The birthplace of waterskiing, Lake City has everything for the water enthusiast: fishing, canoeing, swimming, windsurfing, and of course, waterskiing. The newly remodeled Lake City Country Inn offers travelers the comfort and relaxation they are looking for after a day on Lake Pepin.

Lake City rests on the shores of Lake Pepin, a particularly wide swath of the Mississippi River running through the Hiawatha Valley. Originally, the city earned distinction as a grain port, but after the river traffic abated in the late 1800s, Lake City became a haven for leisure travelers. Today, many visitors still come to Lake City, either to enjoy the lake or to view the spectacular, towering bluffs surrounding it. After a day of fun, visitors often choose the Lake City Country Inn for its convenient location and for its modern amenities.

There are 26 individually decorated rooms, some complete with jacuzzi. Some are furnished with Victorian-style antiques, while others offer waterbeds and kitchenettes. Visitors may have difficulty choosing between all these different rooms, but one thing is for sure; the area offers spectacular scenery and is known as the gateway to the stunning Hiawatha Valley.

B ED & BREAKFASTS

■ EVERGREEN KNOLL ACRES
R.R. 1, Box 145
Lake City, MN 55041
Tel: (612) 345-2257

Originally built in 1919, this large handsome German-type house has continued to remain in the family. The charming country home is tastefully decorated with a collection of family and local antiques. Each of the three guest rooms is furnished with antique iron beds, country furnishings, and crafts for a truly homey feeling. Guests are welcome to share the main level of the home, relaxing by a cozy fireplace, or enjoying a movie on the television or VCR.

Guests will savor down-home cooking and a hearty country breakfast with homemade breads and preserves. As part of the Michel Farm Vacations Host Farms, guests are also welcome to tour this modern working dairy farm. There are tourist attractions close by, or guests can just enjoy a stroll in the quiet countryside.

■ THE PEPIN HOUSE

120 S. Prairie Street
Lake City, MN 55041
Tel: (612) 345-4454
Visa, MasterCard, and Discover are accepted.

This attractive 1905 Victorian home was built by a man of brewery fame, John C. Schmidt. It is located in the Hiawatha Valley on Lake Pepin, which has the largest marina on the Mississippi River.

Each room has a queen-size canopy bed, fireplace, air conditioning, and comes with a homemade breakfast. The area's attractions and activities include many fine restaurants, river cruises, golf courses, waterskiing, canoeing, downhill and cross-country skiing, biking, hiking, and shopping at many antique stores and gift shops.

Lake City is a place for all seasons, and at The Pepin House guests relax and enjoy a memorable time away. No pets, children, or smoking are allowed.

■ RED GABLES INN

403 N. High Street
Lake City, MN 55041
Tel: (612) 345-2605
Visa and MasterCard are accepted.

Nestled amidst foliage-covered bluffs of the Hiawatha Valley, where the "mighty" Mississippi widens to become Lake Pepin, is Red Gables Inn, an intimate bed and breakfast inn. The inn offers a chance to step back into a quiet unhurried luxury of the Victorian past without sacrificing the comforts of the present.

The Red Gables Inn is a charming mixture of Italianate and Greek Revival, built in 1865 by Helen and Marshall Bessey, a wealthy wheat merchant from Wisconsin. Exquisitely restored, the inn creates an inviting ambience of past splendor and elegance. Each guest room is individually decorated with its own charm and includes twilight wine and hors d'oeuvres. A generous Victorian breakfast buffet of juices, seasonal fruits, cheese platter, home-baked breads and pastries, special egg dishes, and preserves is offered each morning. Guests can enjoy their meal on the screened-in porch or in the fireside dining room. The inn offers gourmet picnic baskets both summer and winter. Bicycles and many "little extras" are provided to make stays memorable. For special occasions, group and whole house renting is also available.

Capture the romantic spirit of the Victorian Era and make a visit to Lake City memorable.

■ THE VICTORIAN BED AND BREAKFAST
620 S. High Street
Lake City, MN 55041
Tel: (612) 345-2167
Hrs: Open year-round

Journey back in time in this 1896 Victorian home where every guest room has a breathtaking view of beautiful Lake Pepin.

The common rooms display carved wood-work, stained glass windows, and antique music boxes. Each of the three guest rooms are decorated with Victorian lace, heirloom quilts, brass, wicker, and other antiques. A continental breakfast is served to guests in the dining room, on the porches, or "breakfast in bed." The Lake City area offers many

amenities to The Victorian Bed and Breakfast guests. Spring and summer provide many outdoor activities such as water sports, golf, fishing, swimming, and antiquing. Sight-seeing in the fall makes for a beautiful drive through the heart of the Hiawatha Valley, where the fall splendor of the Mississippi River bluffs are incredible. Excellent downhill and cross-country skiing areas make Lake City a winter wonderland.

For a quiet and peaceful "getaway," the Victorian Bed and Breakfast offers hospitality in graciously appointed surroundings.

Gift Shop

■Little Brick Jail House
110 E. Marion Street
Lake City, MN 55041
Tel: (612) 345-5343
Hrs: Mon. - Sat. 10 a.m. - 5 p.m., Sun. 11 a.m. - 3 p.m.
    (Hours may vary seasonally. If closed, please feel free to call for an appointment anytime.)

The Lake City Jail, no longer incarcerating criminals, serves as a much more friendly place to visit than it did in 1900. It has since been given new life. Now a historic gift shop, it offers a friendly atmosphere to shop for Victorian treasures.

The old city jail was built by L.S. Lutz for approximately $1,000 and contained only two cells with two bunks each. The entire building was lined with boiler iron and had a cement floor. Bringing the bars back to the windows and remodeling the little

jail, Mark and Denise Peters turned it into a cozy store full of Victorian collectibles.

Visitors can smell the soft scent of baskets of bath soap, potpourri, and hand-dipped candles. Homemade fruit jams and syrup made from wild berries, handmade lace and linen, bears, and dolls are displayed in a creative fashion. Lithophanes, a revival of a porcelain art form which vanished 100 years ago, are made by a local Lake City artist and are just some of the gifts available in this charming shop.

GOLF COURSE & SKI AREA

■ MOUNT FRONTENAC GOLF COURSE
Highway 61
Frontenac, MN 55026
Tel: (612) 388-5826 or 612) 345-3504
Hrs: Daily, sunrise to sunset
Visa and MasterCard are accepted.

Just up the road from Lake City, in the heart of Minnesota's Hiawatha Valley, the town of Old Frontenac is one of the earliest settlements in Minnesota. It was established along the Mississippi River bluffs by French fur traders in the 1700s. The Mount Frontenac Ski Area has been in operation since 1968, and the golf course since 1985, at this splendid site. It provides a great opportunity of recreation for golfers and skiers alike.

This 18-hole golf course is very challenging, but playable for the average golfer. Located on 400 acres of land, it has a spectacular view of the Mississippi and scenic Lake Pepin and is surrounded by beautiful pine, spruce, and oak trees. Skiers are challenged by the slopes of Mount Frontenac with beginner, intermediate, and expert runs. A 420-foot vertical drop is the ultimate for the experienced skier. Family ski programs and lessons are available. A new full-service clubhouse and pro shop have been added to the facilities. Special tournaments for both sports can be arranged.

Visitors can enjoy a challenging and scenic round of golf, or ski the Mount Frontenac slopes on top of the Mississippi River bluffs here at "one of Minnesota's best-kept secrets."

R ESTAURANT & CRAFT MALL

■ THE ROOT BEER STAND AND CRAFT MALL
805 N. Lakeshore Drive
Lake City, MN 55041
Tel: (612) 345-2124
Hrs: Root Beer Stand - April through August
  Craft Mall - May through Christmas
Visa and MasterCard are accepted.

Built in 1948, The Root Beer Stand is one of the oldest existing businesses in Lake City, where root beer remains the specialty of the house and is pleasantly delivered by tray-carrying car hops to each car window!

The Root Beer Stand drive-in is a tradition in Lake City, located across from scenic Lake Pepin. Visitors to the area's largest marina on the Mississippi and other attractions can enjoy their favorite sandwich along with a malt or root beer like it was years ago. For outdoor enjoyment, picnic tables are available overlooking beautiful Lake Pepin. Dutch elm carvings of an eagle and bear, along with other carvings, surround The Root Beer Stand.

Conveniently located next door in the "Craft Mall," visitors can stroll through the Country Woodshed, once a small motel. This inviting gift shop includes miniatures to pine furniture, quilted items to dried floral arrangements.

Thirsty travelers stop by for a frosty mug of homemade root beer and a freshly made cheeseburger at The Root Beer Stand, "A Lake City tradition for 42 years."

R ESTAURANT & LOUNGE

■ WATERMAN'S RESTAURANT & LOUNGE
1702 N. Lakeshore Drive
Lake City, MN 55041
Tel: (612) 345-5353
Hrs: (Dining) Mon. - Sun. 11 a.m. - 10:30 p.m.
  Winter hours may differ.
  (Lounge) Mon. - Sun. 11 a.m. - closing
Visa and MasterCard are accepted.

With beautiful Lake Pepin just outside the door, diners can relax and enjoy the lake and view of the surrounding bluffs while dining or having a quiet drink at the bar or on the outside deck.

Waterman's offers fine food and drink in a casual but luxurious atmosphere. Boaters have access to deepwater docks, a bait shop, boat rentals, and launching ramp. The restaurant is constructed primarily of cedar and oak throughout. The dining room is warmed by a large brick fireplace. Open air dining is available on the deck just off the lounge. Lunchtime selections are numerous with fresh garden salads served with any of the homemade house dressings, a variety of sandwiches and chef choices of citrus chicken, beef burgundy, North Atlantic cod, and much more. Dinner selections are extensive, with appetizers and entrees such as walleye pike, rib-eye steak, char-broiled chicken breast topped with lemon sauce, shrimp or scallops, or ham steak topped with a pineapple glaze. Every day the chef prepares unique offerings using the finest and freshest ingredients and herbs available. A perfect conclusion to a dinner is New York cheesecake, fudge-topped peanut butter pie, or chocolate Amaretto cheesecake.

Whether in town for waterskiing, fishing, snowmobiling, taking a scenic drive, or participating in any of the local festivals, guests find Waterman's an outstanding choice.

R IVER CRUISES

■ SPIRIT OF LAKE CITY
310 S. Washington Street
Lake City, MN 55041
Tel: (612) 345-5432
Hrs: Daily - 2 p.m. Scenic Cruise. Call for reservations. May - Oct.
Visa and MasterCard are accepted.

For a more leisurely pace, travelers come aboard the paddlewheeler "Spirit of Lake City" and listen to the tales of past riverboat days and see the beauty of the Hiawatha Valley.

The "Spirit of Lake City" is the perfect setting for any occasion. Relax on the Scenic Cruise and enjoy the beauty of the Mississippi River. Hear stories and legends of Mark Twain and Laura Ingalls Wilder. For an evening to remember, the Sunset Dinner Cruise will provide an elegant evening cruise and delectable dinner on beautiful Lake Pepin. The Riverboat Buffet and Sunday Brunch also are popular cruises for families and friends. Guests enjoy the historic narration as they relax and indulge in the fine food provided on their river cruise. All cruises are available for groups and charters. Advanced reservations are required.

Summer in Lake City means waterskiing. Locals and tourists join in the fun at the annual Water Ski Days three-day festival or the Pepin Open Regatta during the July 4th weekend. Fall beckons the harvest and celebrates Johnny Appleseed Days in October.

This is an excellent choice for a special meeting, wedding, class reunion, prom, anniversary or birthday party, or any other social event. Lake City is just 65 miles south of Minneapolis-St. Paul on Highway 61 or 35 miles north of Rochester on Highway 63.

WILDLIFE ART & COLLECTIBLES

■WILD WINGS GALLERY
South Highway 61
Lake City, MN 55041
Tel: (612) 345-3663
Hrs: Mon. - Sat. 9 a.m. - 6 p.m.
    Sun. 11 a.m. - 5 p.m.
All major credit cards are accepted.

Art collectors yearning for the wild side of life stop by Wild Wings Gallery in Lake City. The gallery is actually an offshoot of Wild Wings, one of the nation's leading publishers of wildlife art, and it offers prints by some of the finest wildlife artists in the United States.

Originating in Frontenac, MN, Wild Wings is more than 20 years old, and today operates ten galleries and seven franchises, as well as selling wholesale to more than 700 galleries across the country. Bill Webster, the founder of the company, was an avid duck stamp print collector before most people knew what duck stamp prints were. In the late 1960s, as a favor to his hunting partners David Maass and David Hagerbaumer — who were also wildlife artists — he agreed to try marketing some of their work. Working out of his kitchen and loft, Bill offered a few prints for sale at first before creating a catalog in 1971. He opened his first gallery in 1974 in Edina, MN.

At Wild Wings Gallery in Lake City, collectors will find work by such artists as Robert Abbett, David Maass, Michael Sieve, Rosemary Millette, Lee Kromschroeder, Ron Van Gilder, and Nancy Glazier. Along with original artwork and limited edition prints, the store carries collectibles, home furnishings, and gifts for the home or office. Those wild about limited edition prints or simply looking for a unique gift on the fly should stop by Wild Wings Gallery.

Lanesboro

The Lanesboro Townsite Company, originally formed in New England, gave birth to the town of Lanesboro, which is situated neatly alongside the tracks of the Southern Minnesota Railroad. This village is on the National Register of Historic Places, a tribute to the preservation of its original state over the decades. The scenery around Lanesboro is intoxicating and is accentuated by the Root River, which runs through the center of town. The *Forest Resource Center* can help with selecting a ski or a hiking trail, or workshops to give insight to the surroundings. *Sylvan Park* is one of the nicest city parks in southeastern Minnesota with two spring-fed trout ponds that provide a fresh catch for an enjoyable meal. *Brewster's Outfitters* provide visitors with quality rental equipment to make the most of the outdoors. *Michael's Adventure Outfitters* offers horseback riding to cover the bluff area, and *Duke Addicks Tours and Tales* will give the imagination a healthy workout. The *Scenic Valley Winery* downtown offers temptations for the palate. A great way to spend a summer day is to follow the *Root River bike trail,* which stretches over 20 miles along the spectacular scenery of the Root River. Summer festivals include *Art in the Park* and *Buffalo Bill Days.* *Oktoberfest* bids farewell to the warm autumn days and offers to those attending a taste of Germany.

For more information on Lanesboro, contact:
THE LANESBORO COMMUNITY CLUB
P.O. Box 20
Lanesboro, MN 55949
(507) 467-3722

ANTIQUE SHOP

◼ MERCHANT OF LANESBORO
103 Parkway N.
Lanesboro, MN 55949
Tel: (507) 467-2666
Hrs: (Summer) Wed. - Mon. 11 a.m. - 7 p.m.
     (Winter) Sun., Mon., and Wed. - Fri. 11 a.m. - 5 p.m.,
     Sat. 11 a.m. - 7 p.m.
     Closed on Tuesdays all year

Nestled in the heart of Lanesboro, which is listed on the National Register of Historic Places, Merchant of Lanesboro is a fascinating antique store. David and Marlys Goodsell, owners, have housed their shop in a 19th century brick building that was once a general mercantile store.

At Merchant of Lanesboro, there is a wide selection of antique furniture items such as dressers, tables, and stoves — all museum quality. David and Marlys also restore antiques for customers, and their shop features hand-sewn quilts, art by local artists, linen, rugs, glasswear dishes, and antique tools. Vintage clothes as well as new sportswear are available in the store's loft area.

A visit to Merchant of Lanesboro also opens up the possibility of spending the whole afternoon in Lanesboro, sampling the locally made delicacies downtown or sipping the fruit wines produced at the local vineyard.

B ED & BREAKFASTS

■ CARROLTON COUNTRY INN
R.R. 2, P.O. Box 139
Lanesboro, MN 55949
Tel: (507) 467-2257
Hrs: 8 a.m. - 10 p.m.
Visa and MasterCard are accepted.

Carrolton Country Inn, near historic Lanesboro, is an 1880s farmhouse which was formerly in one family for over 100 years. Charles and Gloria Ruen, owners, renovated the home and now provide accommodations for bed and breakfast, whole house rental, and family reunions.

The inn is nestled among hills in an open valley in southeast Minnesota's historic bluff country. Located on the Root River and Root River State Trail, hiking, biking, cross-country skiing, fishing, and canoeing can be enjoyed year-round. The Ox Cart Road Drive takes guests directly to the inn. It is the first roadway in the area and was once used by the stagecoach lines. The home is completely restored. Victorian overtones run through the inn, with antique furnishings, dumb waiter in the butler's pantry, original milk paint on the woodwork, and a beautiful open staircase. Within walking distance, visitors can view the original three-story log home built in 1856. The inn is also located in one of the most heavily pop-

ulated deer areas in the state. Hunters are offered hunting accommodations on the whole house rental or house-keeping plan. Bed-and-breakfast guests can choose from four private bedrooms. A full, country breakfast is provided, but prepared by the guest, thus ensuring complete privacy.

Guests will also enjoy the many area attractions of historic Lanesboro. The entire downtown area has been listed on the National Register of Historic Places. The Amish community south of town is the largest in the Midwest. Many fine restaurants, two caves, a winery, museums, and much more are available to visit in the area.

Carrolton Country Inn is a hideaway where time has preserved a century home for your enjoyment. It's "country and comfortable."

■ SCANLAN HOUSE BED & BREAKFAST

708 Parkway Ave. S.
Lanesboro, MN 55949
Tel: (507) 467-2158
Visa, MasterCard, and AmEx are accepted.

At Scanlan House Bed & Breakfast, travelers enter a time of quiet romance. Built in 1889 by the son of Lanesboro's founder and listed on the National Registry of Historic Places, the house epitomizes an elegant but unpretentious Victorian home. Owners and hosts, Gene, Mary and daughter Kirsten Mensing, who restored the inn, pride themselves on offering uncommon, yet comfortable lodgings.

The Queen Anne style Scanlan House is highlighted by a circular tower with a balcony and a sheltered drive where horsedrawn vehicles once stopped so that guests could disembark. The interior is adorned throughout with the elegant woodwork, stained glass, and the ornate built-in furnishings typical of a fine turn-of-the-century residence. Five bedrooms are available to guests, each furnished with stunning antiques. Modern amenities include TV, air conditioning, and bike and ski rentals. The communal parlor offers a cozy loveseat in the tower circle and a computer that guests may challenge in a game of chess. Overnight guests enjoy a breakfast/brunch in a whimsical dining room in which each table sports a different color of linen and a different style of tableware. The changing menu features such delectables as homemade muffins and breads, German sausages, Belgian waffles, pumpkin pancakes, and cinnamon coffee. Champagne is served on special occasions.

During the summer months, antique car tours through the historic Lanesboro residential district and points of interest are available. Located a short distance from antique shops, bluffs, and hiking trails, Scanlan House can provide a simple, but unforgettable getaway or a lavish package for a honeymoon, birthday, or other special occasion.

F RENCH RESTAURANT

■ THE VICTORIAN HOUSE OF LANESBORO
709 S. Parkway
Lanesboro, MN 55949
Tel: (507) 467-3457
Hrs: Wed. - Sun. 5:30 p.m.
By reservation only.

There is nothing more romantic than a tale that begins on the high seas and today is a celebration of a love affair with fine food. Jean Claude and Sonja Venant bring their international culinary talent to the Midwest by way of the "Song of Norway," a Royal Caribbean Cruise Line where Jean Claude worked as executive chef and Sonja as hair stylist. The Victorian House of Lanesboro is their successful joint venture.

Patrons come regularly from Iowa and the Twin Cities to enjoy authentic French cooking in a Victorian setting. Guests sip wine in the formal parlor and select from several entrees such as Care D'agneau Provencale (lamb breaded with parsley and garlic) or Filet Mignon "Auxpoivres Vert" (tenderloin beef in brandy with peppercorn sauce). Sonja boasts of "the best escargot in Lanesboro" (steaming snails in garlic butter), and of her famous Chocolate Sin dessert (chocolate crepe with ice cream and chocolate syrup, topped with whipped cream, strawberries and candied violets).

The Victorian House of Lanesboro was built for Senator Samuel Nelson of Lanesboro around 1870. Inside, the original white oak is accented by stained glass windows. Antiques from all over the world include an ornate Chinese wedding chest, a cherry wood grandfather clock from Holland, and a square grand piano.

Dinners are served Wednesdays through Sundays starting at 5:30 p.m., and are by reservation only. The Victorian House at Lanesboro accommodates dinner parties of up to 32.

$\boxed{\text{H}}$ISTORIC INN

■ MRS. B's HISTORIC LANESBORO INN
103 Parkway
Lanesboro, MN 55949
Tel: (507) 467-2154

On a bank of the Middle Fork of the Root River, in one of the most ancient valleys in Minnesota, stands Mrs. B's Historic Lanesboro Inn. Located in one of the 25 late 19th century buildings downtown, this building and the entire district are listed on the National Register of Historic Places.

Remodeled and restored from an 1872 building, each of Mrs. B's nine rooms is different: each has its own character, private bath; some have access to a balcony, some have fireplaces, and some have breathtaking views of the river. Breakfast is served daily with dinner offered most evenings by reservation. Menu selections change daily and are prepared with only the freshest of meats and fish supplied by local merchants. County gardeners provide fresh produce, and herbs used to prepare Mrs. B's fine cuisine are grown on-site. After a meal, diners can relax in the lobby where they will find a library, a reed organ, a baby grand piano, and fireplace. For small business groups, Mrs. B's provides meeting facilities and whole house rental rates.

Diners often stroll down Lanesboro's main street, which presents a storybook setting of quaint historic buildings framed by the Root River's wooded bluffs. The Root River Recreational Trail provides biking, cross-country skiing, and hiking trails. The State Trout Hatchery, one of the state's largest, is located southwest of town. Trout fishing, hunting, and canoeing are excellent. Special annual events include Buffalo Bill Days, Father's Day Art in the Park, and Oktoberfest. The history of the valley is shown in exhibits at the Lanesboro Historical Museum.

Owners Nancy and Jack Bratrud and their sons proudly invite visitors to relax and be pampered at Mrs. B's in this historic "hidden town" at Lanesboro.

ATURAL RESOURCE CENTER

■ FOREST RESOURCE CENTER
R. R. 2, P.O. Box 156A
Lanesboro, MN 55949
Tel: (507) 467-2437

The Forest Resource Center (FRC) is a private, non-profit corporation promoting the wise use of natural resources. It is located six miles from historic Lanesboro, surrounded by 900 acres of state forest land. Graded hiking and skiing trails wind through wooded bluffs abundant with wildlife and birdwatching.

The FRC seeks to increase public awareness of the importance of wise forest management. Hardwood forests can provide commercial forest products, help control soil erosion, maintain water quality, improve wildlife habitat, and provide recreational opportunities. Land owners can learn these management practices through programs which offer financial incentives. The commercial-size Shiitake mushroom cultivation project at the FRC has shown to be profitable as well as showing long-term benefits to the woodlands.

The FRC publishes "Shiitake News" which offers information on every aspect of these mushrooms. It has also published a guide for those interested in growing Shiitake mushrooms.

THEATRE

■ COMMONWEAL THEATRE COMPANY
206 Parkway Ave. N.
P.O. Box 15
Lanesboro, MN 55949
Tel: (507) 467-2525
Hrs: Wed. - Sun. evenings, May - Sept.
Please call for further information.

High-quality professional theater can be enjoyed in Lanesboro thanks to the enterprising efforts of three very talented individuals and the cooperation of the Lanesboro Arts Council.

Eric Lorentz, Scott Putman, and Scott Olson are the "Director's Collective" of the Commonweal Theatre Company. Together with the Lanesboro Arts Council they have transformed the 1930s era St. Mane Theatre into a 140-seat, air conditioned venue for the best in live theater entertainment.

The Commonweal season typically includes romance and action, such as "Tom Jones" and Harvey Schmidt's musical "The Fantastics," Gardner McKay's award-winning "Sea Marks," and "The Taming of the Shrew", in addition to a traveling puppet show for children. Commonweal also produced, in cooperation with Lutheran Hospital of LaCrosse, "On Tidy Endings," a moving one-act play about the AIDS crisis. Matinee performances, booked in advance, are available to large groups and include lunch. Celebrate summer with Lanesboro and southeastern Minnesota's newest and most exciting artistic attraction.

Mantorville

M antorville is an exceptionally well preserved city, a true window to the past. This town is on the National Register of Historic Places, a rare honor. (Other sites on this list are Williamsburg, Gettysburg, and Freedom Square in Philadelphia.) The citizens of Mantorville have painstakingly preserved the history of the state and the nation. Mantorville limestone has been the constant in the economy of this charming town. This stone was soft and easily worked into buildings; over the years it became harder with weathering, enabling many buildings to maintain their original form. The *Grand Old Mansion* truly is a must-see sight. Built in 1899, this Victorian mansion now is a bed and breakfast with tours available. Additional sights are the

Hubbel House, the *1850s Original Log Cabin,* and the *Mantorville Mercantile Company.* Located just 14 miles west of Rochester, Mantorville must be visited to be appreciated.

For more information on Mantorville, contact:
MANTORVILLE CHAMBER OF COMMERCE
P.O. Box 358
Mantorville, MN 55955
(507)635-3231 or 635-2481

B ED & BREAKFAST/TOURS

■ THE GRAND OLD MANSION
501 Clay Street
Mantorville, MN 55955
Tel: (507) 635-3231
Hrs: Call ahead

The best place to see Mantorville is from the second floor balcony of the Grand Old Mansion. From the white and brown frame houses decorated with gingerbread to quaint stores recreating the setting of Old Mantorville, you can see it all. This Victorian mansion was originally built in 1899 by Teunis Slingerland. Knowledgeable in restoration, the present owner, Irene Stussy Felker, has restored the mansion to its original design.

The Grand Old Mansion is a beautiful Victorian home with the original woodwork, prism cut glass, handcarved staircase, and a wide assortment of Irene's antiques which she has collected on her travels around the world, not to mentioned the 200-year-old Viennese setter from Austria. It is open for tours and for bed and breakfast. Each of the three bedrooms is furnished with antiques and has its own period style; they are available to tourists and travelers for overnight accommodation and include a full breakfast. Tours, individual or by the bus load, are also available for a nominal fee.

Begin by relaxing and enjoying real hospitality at the Grand Old Mansion. Mantorville's tour guide, Irene, takes visitors through the sites of the town, which is listed on the National Register of Historic Places. The historic charm will enlighten the entire family.

F URNITURE & GIFTS

■ THE MERCANTILE STORE
Highway 57
Mantorville, MN 55955
Tel: (507) 635-5132
Hrs: Daily. Closed Mondays (call first)
Most major credit cards are accepted.

In this small town established in 1854, visitors can find handmade and fine crafted oak furniture in the best styles of today and yesteryear at The Mercantile Store.

The family-owned business started with antique telephones and added furniture to its inventory, creating quality handcrafted products. There are over 1,000 different oak items including dining room sets, hutches, rolltop desks, curio cabinets, wooden lazy susans, bookcases, entertainment centers, rocking chairs, many styles of tables, and for any item not found, they will make it! There are also many interesting accessories and antique telephones displayed throughout the store. If interested in an oak heirloom for the future, visitors find that this is the place to have it special made.

While in Mantorville, visit some historic sites. Information is available at the Mantorville Tour Center on Main Street. Self-guided tours include the Hubbell House, a hotel built in 1854, and the Dodge County Historical Museum.

R ESTAURANT

■ HUBBELL HOUSE RESTAURANT AND LOUNGE
Main Street
Mantorville, MN 55955
Tel: (507) 635-2331
Hrs: Tue. - Sat:
   (Lunch)11:30 a.m. - 2 p.m.
   (Dinner) 5 p.m. - 10 p.m.
   Sun. 11:30 a.m. - 9:30 p.m. Closed Monday
   Closed Thanksgiving, Christmas, and New Year's Day
Visa, MasterCard, AmEx, Discover, and Diners Club are accepted.

Civil War decor, superb food, and a rich history have made the Hubbell House Restaurant and Lounge a favorite of connoisseurs from all over the country. Though its guest book reads like a "who's who" of the famous of both past and present, this old country inn retains its hospitality, grace, and charm.

Casual dining in an atmosphere of 19th century opulence awaits visitors at the Hubbell House Restaurant and Lounge; Civil War antiques, glowing table lamps, and historical displays set the tone. The inn's history is reflected in rooms filled with treasures from the past and named for such celebrities as Horace Greeley and Senator Ramsey. A highlight among the many documents and Civil War momentos on display is a land grant signed by Abraham Lincoln himself. Visited by such notables as W. W. Mayo and U. S. Grant, the restaurant has been serving fine cuisine since the 1850s when John Hubbell built the original log hotel and added the three-story limestone structure that exists today.

At the Hubbell House Restaurant and Lounge, diners may feast on prime and choice beef selections such as Chateaubriand, properly aged steaks, and many chef specialties, or on such midwestern favorites as broiled jumbo shrimp, cold-water lobster, and Minnesota's own walleye pike.

The Hubbel House Restaurant and Lounge is located 65 miles south of the Mendota Bridge and 20 minutes west of Rochester in Mantorville. Mantorville is a National Registered Historic site with museums and shops, plus many historic buildings.

Preston

P reston is a small town tucked in the heart of the bluffs which offers a large variety of wildlife and natural beauty in the surrounding area. Preston is located at the entrance to the *Forestville State Park* and is also near the *Root River State Trail System* which offers biking, hiking, and cross-country skiing all set in a beautiful valley surrounded by Minnesota's hardwood forests. *Mystery Cave* is the longest cave in Minnesota with more than 12 miles of natural passages. Research conducted in Mystery Cave has given insight to understanding ground water flow, bat populations, timing of formal glacial advances and retreats, and the deposition of cave sediment. The Old Fillmore County Jail has been transformed into the *Jail House Bed and Breakfast* and is on the National Register of Historic Places. *Preston Trout Days* puts the best of Preston on display.

For more information on Preston, contact:
PRESTON TOURISM COMMISSION
109 St. Paul 2SW
P.O. Box 657
Preston, MN 55965
(507) 765-4541

C OUNTRY BED & BREAKFAST

■SUNNYSIDE COTTAGE OF FORESTVILLE
R. R. 2, P.O. Box 119
Preston, MN 55965
Tel: (507) 765-3357

Sunnyside Farm is a 720-acre farm overlooking the Root River Valley next to Forestville State Park. Originally built in the 1940s as a summer retreat, the cottage had been the home to farmhands and renters for over 30 years. Today, Darrell and Lois Ray have returned it to what it really was — a quiet, peaceful retreat.

The Cottage is designed for one family or one party of guests at a time. It is offered on a whole house rental plan. It is a delightful little three-bedroom, air-conditioned house, furnished in country-style modern furnishings. The kitchen offers full appliances and utensils for cooking needs. The dining room and living room with fireplace are combined to offer cozy eating and relaxing. A screened porch offers a relaxed ambience from early morning coffee to the sounds of wildlife at evening dusk. Other amenities include microwave, television, playpen, crib, highchair, gas grill, picnic table, screened patio, sandbox and games for the children, and a rustic swing to relax and enjoy the peaceful retreat in the Forestville woods. A generous breakfast is provided. A wooden fruit basket is also provided with all the utensils necessary for guests to enjoy a picnic in the woods.

Pick berries, fish for trout on the Root River, or just hike through the countryside. Don't miss the farm tour where guests will experience farm life and children will enjoy petting and feeding the farm animals. When life is a little too hectic, Sunnyside Cottage provides the setting for a relaxed and enjoyable retreat.

F RUIT & VEGETABLE ORCHARD

■PRESTON APPLE AND BERRY FARM
Highways 52 and 16
Preston, MN 55965
Tel: (507) 765-4486
Hrs: 9 a.m. - 7 p.m.
    Closed in April

Preston Apple and Berry Farm is the culmination of years of hard work and perseverance by Joe Gosi and his family. Born in Hungary, Joe fled his homeland in 1956 to begin a new life in the United States. The first few years he worked at a variety of jobs,

intermittently working at an orchard near Minneapolis-St. Paul. He knew, even in Hungary, that he enjoyed growing fruits and so in 1964 he began his career in earnest at an orchard, where he was a manager for 21 years. In 1985, he left to begin his own orchard and vegetable business on 17 acres along Highway 52 in Preston. Now, he and his family have 800 apple trees on five acres, four acres of strawberries, a half acre of raspberries, and a large garden patch that includes corn, tomatoes, green beans, pumpkins and squash, peppers and gourds.

Along with fresh fruits and vegetables, their small store has jams and jellies, honey, maple syrup, cheese, popcorn, and frozen apple pies. There is always an abundance of apples from August through February with many varieties for any taste or dish. In early spring, their greenhouse offers bedding plants, hanging flowering baskets, potted plants, and seeds. During the fall and holiday season, Christmas trees and poinsettias are offered. Other seasonal items include apple turnovers and muffins, caramel apples, applesauce, and fresh apple cider. Fresh fruit baskets and boxes are always available and make an excellent choice for gift giving.

HISTORIC INN

■ THE JAIL HOUSE
109 Houston St.
Preston, MN 55965
Tel: (507) 765-2504
Visa and MasterCard are accepted.

The Jail House is located in the Old Fillmore County Jail and is listed on the National Register of Historic Places. Built in 1869 in a Victorian Italianate style architecture, this building served as a jail house from 1869 to 1971. Purchased in 1987, the Jail House has been restored to its original Victorian splendor offering bed and breakfast accommodations.

An open staircase with a curved walnut bannister invites guests to the upper bedrooms. Each of the 12 "cells" has been tastefully furnished in a Victorian motif. All have private baths and queen-sized beds. There are seven fireplaces throughout the inn, four of which are in the individual guest rooms, along with jacuzzis and unique bath fixtures. Two large stone fireplaces in the common areas invite guests to relax, make new friends, and maybe hear an interesting tale or two of past "cell mates." A complete breakfast is served weekend mornings in the dining area and sun-space. Weekday breakfast can be pre-arranged. Group accommodations are available for business meetings and seminars, private dinners and parties, and other special occasions with complete catering services available. Mystery weekends, sleigh rides, and other special packages are offered during the winter months. Guests also enjoy the area's historic bluff country. The Root River Trail offers endless activities for biking, hiking, and cross-country skiing. There are many antique, craft, and gift shops to browse, along with many other historic sites and museums to discover.

R ESORT & CAMPGROUND

■ THE OLD BARN RESORT
R. R. 3, P.O. Box 57P
Preston, MN 55965
Tel: (507) 467-2512
Visa and MasterCard are accepted.

Located in one of the most scenic valleys in historic bluff country, the Old Barn Resort is at the top of the camp vacation experience. The Root River meandering through the valley makes the location of the Old Barn Resort stunningly beautiful.

The historic barn sets the theme. Built in 1884, it has found new life as the restaurant, hostel, gift shop, and campground headquarters for the Old Barn Resort. The careful restoration and unique blend of old and new are exceptional. The lower level of the Barn contains a 56-bed hostel, which is ideal for individuals and groups. Four dormitories house guests in bunk beds with ample bathroom facilities, director's quarters, kitchenette, and game room. Two meeting rooms are available for seminars or other special occasions to accommodate up to 200 people, with complete catering services. The Old Barn also offers the best "home cooking" in the area with a complete menu. In addition to the Barn, The Old Barn Resort offers one of the newest, most up-to-date campgrounds in the upper Midwest. There are 80 developed campsites, with water and electrical hook-ups, and more than half with sewer connections. For campers who like to "rough it" more, wooded tent sites are also available. Complete bath and shower facilities are convenient to all sites. A solar-heated building with a heated swimming pool provides swimming from April to November 1. Bikes, canoes, roller blades, and tubes are also available for rent. The Old Barn Amish Craft Store offers the finest in beautiful Amish quilts, baskets, dolls, furniture, and other crafts. Guests can also schedule an Amish Tour, where a trained guide will take them through Minnesota's largest Amish colony.

Red Wing

L ocated in the beautiful Hiawatha Valley along the spectacular
bluffs and the mighty Mississippi River lies the town of Red
Wing, originally the site of a Dakota Sioux farming village. Two
missionaries with the Evangelical Missionary Society of Lausanne,
Switzerland were the first European settlers in this region.
Although French Voyageurs first named the area Barn Bluff, the
name permanently chosen was Red Wing, in honor of Chief Red
Wing of the Dakotah tribe, who first greeted them.

From its origins as a missionary outpost, Red Wing became a
busy riverfront trade center. It prospered into the 19th century as
an industrial center specializing in leather processing, lime
quarries, and clay-related industries. The Red Wing boot
manufactured by the Red Wing Shoe Company since 1905 helped
make the name well-known. The City Beautiful movement in the
early 20th century prompted grand homes and government
buildings still majestic today. Red Wing is 50 miles southeast of
the Twin Cities on the Mississippi River.

ATTRACTIONS

The *American Museum of Wildlife Art* displays a regional
wildlife perspective, and the *Goodhue County Historical Museum*
provides a visual history of the community. The *T.B. Sheldon
Auditorium Theatre* presents various events and an ongoing
multi-media presentation of Mr. Sheldon's work since opening
night in 1904. Among several apple orchards located in the Red
Wing area are *Hay Creek Apple Farm* and *Flower Valley Orchards.*
For more outdoor activity are the *Welch Village Ski Area* and, for
bicyclists, the 18-mile wooded *Cannon Valley Trail.* The *Princess
Red Wing Excursion Boat* offers two- and a half-hour dinner
cruises. Annual events include *Shiver River Days* in January,
which bring mutt races, wine tasting, and a figure skating show to
the city. *River City Days* in August, the *Red Wing Festival of Arts*
in mid-October, and *The Craft Fair* in November round out each
year's festivities.

For more information on Red Wing, contact:

RED WING AREA CHAMBER OF COMMERCE
P.O. Box 133B
Red Wing, MN 55066
(612) 388-4719

A CCOMMODATIONS

■ STERLING MOTEL
Junction of Highway 61 and Highway 63 S.
Red Wing, MN 55066
Tel: (612) 388-3568 or (800) 341-8000
Hrs: Open year-round
Visa, MasterCard, AmEx, and Diners Club are accepted.

Good grooming, quaint styling, and an excellent location are the hallmark of the Sterling Motel. With its tidy rooms and friendly, accommodating service, this lodging establishment offers a welcome haven to the many boaters, skiers, golfers, and hikers who annually visit the region.

The Sterling Motel's regular and queen-size rooms feature in-room coffee, HBO/cable television, tubs and showers, direct dial telephones, and customer-controlled air conditioning and heating. Each room has a sense of spaciousness and neatness. Located just one and a quarter miles from historic downtown Red Wing, the Sterling Motel is within easy walking distance of Colvill Park's large outdoor swimming pool and picnic area as well as tennis courts, two marines, and boat launches on the Mississippi River. In winter, guests can explore nearby Frontenac State Park on cross-country skis or ski downhill at the Welch Village Ski Area. Golfers will enjoy the 18-hole Mississippi National Golf Course.

A NTIQUES

■ TEAHOUSE ANTIQUES
927 W. Third Street
Red Wing, MN 55066
Tel: (612) 388-3669
Hrs: Open daily
No credit cards are accepted.

Teahouse Antiques is a quaint little shop off the beaten path, but certainly on the right track for the antique collector. The shop is located in the rear of an historic, octagonally-shaped home built in 1857. The building itself is worth a look, having been constructed in an innovative style for the era. Hosts Morris and Delores Callstrom offer at the rear of this unusual home a full range of antique items, including china, fine glass, silver, Red Wing pottery, furniture, linens, and hard-to-find vintage clothes. Teahouse Antiques is celebrating over 25 years in business.

B ED & BREAKFASTS

■ CANDLE LIGHT INN

818 W. Third Street
Red Wing, MN 55066
Tel: (612) 388-8034
Hrs: Open daily.
    Check-in at 4 p.m. and check-out at 11 a.m.
Visa and MasterCard are accepted.

The Candle Light Inn is a graceful bed and breakfast establishment that remains true to its historic roots. The original stained glass, light fixtures, and polished wooden mantles reflect not only light, but their owners' attention to detail in preserving the quality of their beautiful Victorian residence, which is listed on the Minnesota Historic Register.

The Candle Light Inn is comprised of seven bedrooms, two living rooms, a library, kitchen, six bathrooms, two screened porches, and five fireplaces. Four bedrooms are available for guests, some with fireplaces and whirlpools. Each bedroom reflects the period in which the home was built. A brass bed, bow windows, and original in-laid linoleum accent the bright colors of the Rose Garden Room. "Renaissance revival" best describes the mood of Margaret's Room. The Queen Victoria Room highlights the East Lake era, and the Heritage Room is a cheerful blend of homey comforts: a hand-crocheted bedspread, candlewick wallpaper, and curtains, all in rich, warm colors. Each of the five fireplaces is a masterpiece: one is solid marble; one brass-trimmed; and three display wooden mantles with marble trim. The cabinetry, trim, and staircases throughout the house are a carefully polished and preserved blend of cherry, butternut, oak, and walnut.

Ruth and John Lane, owners of the Candle Light Inn, welcome guests to their beautiful home. Homemade cooking and other goodies await guests at this authentic and charming bed and breakfast in Red Wing.

■PRATT-TABER INN

706 W. Fourth Street
Red Wing, MN 55066
Tel: (612) 388-5945
Hrs: Check-in at 4 p.m. and check-out at 11 a.m.
Visa and MasterCard are accepted.

"When I search for a peaceful moment, I will think of sitting on the porch of the Pratt-Taber Inn," so says Garrison Keillor of this gracious historic home in Red Wing. Built in 1876 by A.W. Pratt, one of Red Wing's first bankers, the red brick inn, now on the National Registry of Historic Places, is within walking distance of churches, historic downtown Red Wing, and the Mississippi River.

The furnishings of the Pratt-Taber Inn reflect the Italianate, Renaissance Revival, and Country Victorian styles. Fine details include feather-painted slate fireplaces and gingerbread woodwork. An original Tiffany lamp illuminates one room, and lead-glass windows sparkle throughout the house. The Pratt-Taber Inn provides six beautifully decorated rooms for guests. One to three-room suites also are available, and the home boasts old fashioned tubs, as well as showers.

Guests will love the Pratt-Taber Inn's breakfasts. Coffee, tea, lemonade, apple cider, and homemade goodies are guaranteed to tempt the palate, and are served in bed, if guests wish. Or, they may want to breakfast in the dining room or on the charming screened porch. Hostess and owner Jane Molander exudes friendliness and hospitality, making a stay at the Inn a pleasant and memorable experience. Guests arriving by boat, train, or bus may be met and toured along Red Wing's scenic skyline bluff drive.

■SWANSON-JOHNSON INN
R. R. 2, P.O. Box 77
Red Wing, MN 55066
Tel: (612) 388-FARM or (800) 657-4740
Hrs: Daily
Visa and MasterCard are accepted.

Just one hour from the Twin Cities, Swanson-Johnson Inn offers an intimate and unforgettable country vacation experience. The Inn is located in Vasa, MN, one of Minnesota's oldest Swedish communities. Situated on land first settled in 1861, the owners can proudly show guests a copy of the deed signed by Abraham Lincoln. Accommodating up to ten guests, the Swanson-Johnson Inn offers a taste of genuine country life complete with hearty meals, farm animals, and wide-open spaces.

Guests are served a full country breakfast and the large kitchen is open to guests throughout their stay. Bedrooms are decorated country style with authentic dry sinks and wash basins. Hands-on experience caring for the farm animals — horses, chickens, rabbits, calves, pigs, ducks, and more — gives children and adults rich memories of their visit. Relax at the pond, or hike the four-mile trail through meadows and woods in summer and cross-country ski the trail in winter. Alpine ski paths and the Welch Ski Village are minutes from the farm. After a vigorous day on the slopes, the family room's eight-person hot tub is blissfully relaxing.

The Swanson-Johnson Inn is a cozy spot nestled in the Minnesota countryside. Summer or winter, its many charms beckon to families or solitary travelers looking for a chance to enjoy "the real America."

G ALLERY AND FRAME SHOP

■RIVERFRONT GALLERY
Riverfront Centre
320 Main Street
Red Wing, MN 55066
Tel: (612) 388-3103
Hrs: Mon. - Sat. 9 a.m. - 5 p.m., Sun. noon - 5 p.m.
Visa, MasterCard, and Discover are accepted.

Located in the Riverfront Centre in downtown Red Wing, the Riverfront Gallery is ready to welcome lovers and collectors of all kinds of art. Spacious and well-lit, the Riverfront Gallery offers a wide selection of original and limited edition prints and distributes the works of such publishers as Greenwich Workshop, Mill Pond Press, and Hadley House. Collectors of portraits,

Americana, wildlife, and Western art will love the prints by such sought-after artists as Redlin, Terpning, Bateman, Parker, Killen, McCarthy, and Doolittle and Olson.

The Riverfront Gallery, owned and managed by Tom Dwelle, has been in business since 1985. Recently, the Riverfront Art and Frame Shop opened in nearby Lake City. Operating as an "open shop," the new, larger space allows customers to observe work in progress.   A recent visit was paid by award-winning Minnesota artist Jerry Raedeke to remarque and personalize prints. Professional framing is offered on-site, as well as at the Riverfront Art and Frame Shop in Lake City, and there is interest-free, 90-day financing.

G OLF COURSE

■ MISSISSIPPI NATIONAL GOLF LINKS
409 Golf Links Drive
Red Wing, MN 55066
Tel: (612) 388-1874
Hrs: Daily from dawn to dusk, April - Oct.
Visa and MasterCard are accepted.

Mississippi National Golf Links is located just one hour southeast of the Twin Cities along the Mississippi River in Red Wing. This scenic course features nineteenth-century charm and twentieth-century convenience. The first 18 holes of this 27-hole public golf course are nestled among the Mississippi River bluffs. The newest nine holes are built on top of the bluffs and offer additional quality play and unparalleled views of the river valley. The course, opened in 1985, has quickly become a favorite of golf enthusiasts from throughout the Midwest.

The white colonial-style clubhouse features a lovely bar/grill and banquet room. It also houses a full-line pro shop. Power carts, pull carts, rental clubs, a driving range, and group and private lessons by PGA professionals are all part of the scene at Mississippi National.

H ISTORIC HOTEL

■ ST. JAMES HOTEL
406 Main Street
Red Wing, MN 55066
Tel: (612) 388-2846 or (800) 252-1875
Visa, MasterCard, AmEx, Carte Blanche, and Discover are accepted.

Located on Main Street and the centerpiece of Red Wing, this Victorian hotel was purchased in 1977 and carefully restored to its original elegance. Built in 1875 by 11 proud businessmen, the St. James Hotel is now listed on the National Register for Historic Places. The 60 guest rooms have been elegantly decorated with authentic period handmade quilts and filled with antiques and reproductions.

Each room is named after a Mississippi Riverboat and most offer breathtaking views of the "mighty" Mississippi and the Red Wing bluffs. Winterlude, Victorian Holiday, and Applause packages are available including theatre, dinner and breakfast, complimentary champagne, turndown service, and morning coffee in the privacy of your room. Meeting and banquet facilities are complete and accommodate 10 to 300 people. The St. James Hotel is an elegant setting for weddings or any other special occasion. Dining and entertainment in the Port of Red Wing restaurant, bar, and lounge are among the finest in the area.

Overlooking the Mississippi River is the Veranda Cafe, open for breakfast, lunch, or dinner. Outdoor dining is available, weather permitting. Located on the fifth floor and overlooking the city, guests can relax at Jimmy's, a pub in the English tradition. Guests can also enjoy the peaceful atmosphere and fireplace warmth in the Library. The enclosed Shopping Court offers a variety of specialty and gift shops, and there is free parking for hotel guests and shoppers.

H ISTORIC THEATRE

■ THE SHELDON PERFORMING ARTS THEATRE

Third Street at East Ave.
Red Wing, MN 55066
Tel: (612) 388-2806
Hrs: Box office: Mon. - Sat. noon - 5 p.m.
    Call for performance times.
Visa, MasterCard, and Discover are accepted.

A "jewelbox"! That was the newspaper description of the T.B. Sheldon Performing Arts Theatre when it opened in 1904. Now, almost 90 years later, the theatre has been restored to its approximate original appearance and once again is serving as an exquisite performing arts hall that delights artist and patrons alike.

The Sheldon, the nation's first municipal theatre, offers classic and contemporary fare. Visual art exhibits, theatre productions, concerts, family programs, and classic films — all have their place at the Sheldon. Indeed, the theatre's stated mission is to provide the highest quality and variety in the performing arts, as well as to educate students about program production. Artists such as Leo Kottke, and groups such as the Budapest Chamber Orchestra and the Minneapolis Children's Theatre Company have performed here in the past, and the roster of illustrious artists and events at the Sheldon continues to grow. Not enough time to attend a major show? Then stop by the theatre on a Saturday morning and attend the weekly "Echoes of the Sheldon" tour. This introduction to the theatre combines film with live guides who will explain the history and restoration of the building. They will point out the

many beautiful details within it, ranging from the mosaic tile floor in the entryway to the Austrian crystal chandeliers in the intimate 471-seat auditorium.

Through its restoration and revitalization, the Sheldon continues to contribute to Red Wing's cultural life.

M|USEUM

■THE AMERICAN MUSEUM OF WILDLIFE ART
3303 N. Service Drive
U.S. Highway 61
P.O. Box 26
Red Wing, MN 55066-0026
Tel: (612) 388-0755
Hrs: Mon.-Sat. 10 a.m. - 5 p.m., Sun. noon - 4 p.m. Closed holidays

Founded in 1987 in the village of Old Frontenac — the American Museum of Wildlife Art houses wonderful, original works of art by recognized living and deceased wildlife artists. It was founded in response to burgeoning interest in the heritage of wildlife art.

Red Wing is the perfect setting for the Museum, which was recently relocated from the village of Old Frontenac to a town that offers a larger, more central location. At the head of the Hiawatha Valley overlooking the Mississippi River and Lake Pepin, it has been described as one of North America's most picturesque settings. Wildlife abounds in the area, and the paintings in the galleries seem to mirror their surroundings.

Its director, Byron G. Webster, recognizes wildlife art as the oldest, most enduring art form known to humanity and that American wildlife artists have made significant contributions to the American art scene. Collected and maintained by the Museum, a reference library of books, magazines, limited edition prints, photographs, and audiovisual tapes of wildlife and wildlife art are available to the public. The new facility offers ample parking, handicap accessibility, and a gift shop. Workshops, seminars, and educational programs are held regularly.

P|OTTERY & GIFT STORE

■RED WING POTTERY SALESROOM
1995 W. Main
Red Wing, MN 55066
Tel: (612) 388-3562 or (800) 228-0174
Hrs: Mon. - Thur. 8 a.m. - 6 p.m., Fri. - Sat. 8 a.m. - 7 p.m.
     Sun. 9 a.m. - 6 p.m.
Visa, MasterCard, AmEx, Diners Club, and Discover are accepted.

"We're the white building," the staff likes to say. Sure enough, just west of Highway 61, a distinctively large, white structure with cheerful geranium-lined windows awaits shoppers.

The staff offers Minnesota-style hospitality, inviting shoppers to browse at their own pace through the bright rooms of attractively arranged merchandise.

Where to start? There are several rooms from which to choose. The Dining Room displays pottery dinnerware, glassware, china, and crystal from around the world, with names such as Lenox, Mikasa, and Noritake. The Homestead Room displays gifts and accessories with a country flair, and many patterns of Christmas dinnerware. The Gallery features fine collectibles from around the world. Bargain hunters will be especially pleased with the Annex, where discontinued items sell for 50 percent off. Be sure to visit the Garden Shop with its garden pottery and old-fashioned crockery items. Last but not least, the Candy Store makes and sells fudge and candy the old-fashioned way—from scratch, by the pound or by the piece. Next door is Loons and Ladyslippers, featuring the work of local artists and special Minnesota items.

Richard Gillmer, then President of Red Wing Potteries, opened the Red Wing Pottery Salesroom to sell merchandise after a worker's strike closed the factory in 1967. Today, the Salesroom offers the Midwest's largest selection of quality dinnerware and pottery. Gift wrapping, shipping, and a wedding registry also are offered.

P OTTERY SALES & TOURS

■ RED WING STONEWARE CO.
4909 Moundview Drive
Red Wing, MN 55066
Tel: (612) 388-4610
Hrs: 10 a.m. - 5 p.m.
Visa and MasterCard are accepted.

When John Falconer opened his pottery manufacturing and sales business in Red Wing, in 1984, he continued a 130-year tradition that had made the town famous. Collected by people across the country, Red Wing's hand-made, early American pottery with its distinctive bird-wing, numbers, and birch leaves designs were rapidly becoming even more popular than when they were made. Red Wing's last original pottery producer had closed years ago, so when visitors came to see the famous pottery works, they were disappointed.

That was until John Falconer moved into town. Falconer has revived the old pottery designs and added some new ones of his own, and in 1990, he opened a brand-new pottery studio and showroom where visitors can watch the pottery actually being made.The new facilities have enough space for Falconer's expanding pottery works and allow customers to browse through his full line of pottery items including crocs, jugs, butterchurns, lamps, dinnerware, cups, mugs, beanpots, and bowls. The pottery reflects its traditional roots in reproductions of original motifs, and in contemporary designs that fit well with the traditional line. Falconer's company also does custom logo work for companies and individuals, and offers special wildlife designs.

Red Wing Stoneware Co. prides itself on the superior quality of its hand-made items. Once visitors see the company's showroom, they know why.

▮R ESTAURANT

▮ LIBERTY RESTAURANT & LOUNGE
303 W. Third Street
Red Wing, MN 55066
Tel: (612) 388-8877
Hrs: Sun. - Thu. 8 a.m. - midnight, Fri. - Sat. 8 a.m. - 1 a.m.
Visa, MasterCard, AmEx, Discover, and Carte Blanche are accepted.

Mouthwatering pizza and a unique antique setting are the hallmarks of Liberty Restaurant & Lounge in downtown Red Wing. Housed in a century-old building, Liberty's decor gives patrons a nostalgic trip back to yesteryear. However, the restaurant's renowned pizza creations are thoroughly modern and downright tasty.

Pizza isn't all that's to be found at Liberty's. The restaurant also offers American, Mexican, and Italian dishes; a popular Sunday brunch; and a chicken, fish and shrimp buffet on Fridays. The diet menu is well-liked—it's not often that Canadian walleye pike and broiled shrimp in the shell are listed under light entrées.

For those staying in nearby motels or visiting the Marina, Liberty's offers a complimentary shuttle to and from the restaurant. How's that for service? Along with the scrumptious dinners, it all adds up to genuine, old-fashioned hospitality.

S CANDINAVIAN GIFTS

■ UFFDA SHOP

Corner of Main and Bush (across from St. James Hotel)
Red Wing, MN 55066
Tel: (612) 388-8436 or (800) 488-3332
Hrs: Mon. - Sat. 9 a.m. - 6 p.m. (Jan. - Apr. , 9 a.m. - 5 p.m.)
   Thur. 9 a.m. - 9 p.m., Sun. noon - 5 p.m.
   Open until 9 p.m. Thanksgiving through Christmas
Visa, MasterCard, Discover, and AmEx are accepted.

Enjoy a visit to the Uffda Shop, one of the most delightful import shops in the Midwest. The Uffda Shop rings true to its name, for "Uffda" it is—overflowing with Norwegian treasures and beautiful gifts from throughout Scandinavia. A year-round Christmas corner features ornaments from around the world, German nutcrackers and pyramids, and a wide selection of nativity scenes. Gnomes, trolls, nisse, and tomtes watch as visitors look over fine Scandinavian crystal, porcelain, and a wide variety of jewelry, including Swedish pewter and lacy Norwegian Sølje.

The "true blue" Scandinavian will enjoy jokebooks, flags, stickers, and windsocks, as well as sweaters from Dale of Norway, supplies for hardanger embroidery, and hard-to-find gourmet gadgets.

The Uffda Shop hosts a variety of special events throughout the year, including a Christmas Open House, rosemaling demonstrations, lefse making, and trunk shows. UPS shipping and free gift wrapping are available. Write or call for a copy of the free Christmas catalogue.

S HOPPING

■ POTTERY PLACE

2000 W. Main Street
Red Wing, MN 55066
Tel: (612) 388-1428
Hrs: May 1 - Dec. 23, Mon. - Fri. 9 a.m. - 8 p.m.,
   Sat. 9 a.m. - 6 p.m., and Sun. 11 a.m. - 6 p.m.
All major credit cards are accepted.

Pottery Place is Minnesota's first factory outlet center, complemented by specialty shops, 20 antique dealers and restaurants. The outlet stores are owned and operated by the factories they represent. Their direct link to the factories, the special buys from other manufacturers, bulk shipping, and no dependence on middle distributors are a few reasons they offer quality merchandise at bargain prices.

Many national brands are displayed as one strolls the tile and wooden walkways of this National Historic Building, which housed Red Wing Pottery until 1964. One can also observe turn-of-the-century pottery-making in Red Wing, preserved in the form of photographs, molds, kilns, and a cast iron boiler.

Pottery Place offers a wide variety of quality merchandise and provides a fun and unique shopping experience.

■ST. JAMES HOTEL SHOPPING COURT

406 Main Street
Red Wing, MN 55066
Hrs: Mon. - Sat. 9 a.m. - 6 p.m., Thur. 9 a.m. - 9 p.m., Sun. noon - 5 p.m.
Most major credit cards are accepted.

The Shopping Court is located in the St. James Hotel complex, a Victorian hotel built in 1875 and restored in 1979. There are 12 specialty shops surrounding the lobby in the hotel, offering a wide variety of merchandise. A large central court with tables and chairs is excellent for art shows, convention meeting headquarters, and style shows.

Shops consist of four women's apparel including the Dahl House, Permans, M'Dona's/Wedding Dreams, and The Levee. The Yankee Peddler offers quality men's wear and accessories, formal wear, and rental for weddings. Visitors also can check out the Red Wing Book Company; Steamboat Park art gallery, Shear Perfection salon, Uniquely Yours fashion accessories, River Peddler antiques, and Marita's handmade Victorian gifts. Gift wrapping is available at all stores. Quality selection surrounded by the Victorian ambience provides an exciting experience for hotel guests and browsers.

Rochester

R ochester, the largest city in southern Minnesota, is only 36 miles west of the Wisconsin border and 41 miles north of the Iowa border. The terrain is rolling farmland laid across the Zumbro River Valley. In 1863 Dr. William Worall Mayo settled in the city with his sons William Jr. and Charles and gave this place worldwide notoriety with the Mayo Medical Center. Rochester has many cosmopolitan attractions, accommodations, and restaurants to entertain its bustling population. The Mayo Complex and IBM are the two largest employers in the surrounding area and have a profound economic impact on the Rochester community. Rochester has the world's largest winter concentration of giant Canadian geese. A former Mayo Clinic patient donated 12 of the geese to the area in 1947. These geese are thought to have attracted the few remaining giant Canadian geese at that time to also make their home on Silver Lake. These geese were at one time believed to be extinct until biologists discovered the flock on a routine visit to Rochester. These birds are considered to be an integral part of Silver Lake and the Rochester community, adding to the splendor of the city.

ATTRACTIONS

The Mayo Clinic, the largest medical complex in the world, treats nearly 300,000 patients annually coming from all over to receive the highest quality treatment available today. Group tours are available of up to 50. *St. Mary's Hospital* is a Mayo Foundation hospital started by the Franciscan Sisters that has and still does work in conjunction with the Mayo Clinic. Tours are conducted Tuesdays and Thursdays at 3:10 p.m., departing from the Mary Brigh Information Desk. The third member in the trio of medical meccas is the *Rochester Methodist Hospital* offering tours on Wednesdays at 2 p.m with advance reservations required. Additional attractions are *Mayowood,* the former home of the Mayo family that was declared a Minnesota Historic Site in 1967 and named to the National Register of Historic Places in 1970; the *Plummer House,* home to one of the first physicians at the Mayo Clinic; *The Rochester Art Center; The Quarry Hill Nature Center* and the *Heritage House. The Peace Fountain* was created by local sculptor Charles Eugene Gagnon and dedicated to world peace. Located in downtown Rochester, it is a tranquil place to contemplate peace. Annual events for the summer include the *Rochester Festival of the Arts* in June, *The Rochesterfest* in June, and the *Threshing Show* in late July. A *Greek Festival* is held by Silver Lake in August with dancing and authentic Greek food.

For more information on Rochester, contact:
ROCHESTER CONVENTION AND VISITORS BUREAU
150 S. Broadway, Suite A
Rochester, MN 55904
(507) 288-4331 or (800) 634-8277

A CCOMMODATIONS

■ KAHLER LODGING
20 Second Ave. S.W.
Rochester, MN 55902
Tel: (507) 282-2581 or (800) 533-1655
Visa, MasterCard, AmEx, Discover, and Diners Club are accepted.

Kahler Lodging started in Rochester in 1912 when John Kahler built the Zumbro Hotel to provide lodging for Mayo Clinic patients and their families. Today, Kahler Lodging consists of the Kahler Hotel, with 700 guest rooms; Clinic View Inn, with 142 rooms; Holiday Inn Downtown, with 172 rooms owned and operated under the Holiday Inn franchise; and the Kahler Plaza Hotel, with 194 rooms.

All Kahler accommodations have excellent sites in the heart of downtown Rochester. The Kahler Hotel, which covers a full city block, is said to be the largest hotel in the Midwest. In addition to serving medical guests, this hotel provides a full complement of modern meeting and banquet facilities, and 55 specialty shops and boutiques grace the lower floor. Recently renovated, Clinic View Inn provides modern amenities and a New England-style restaurant. For convenience, a pedestrian subway connects the inn with the Mayo medical complex, Rochester Methodist Hospital, and Kahler Hotel. Holiday Inn Downtown, renovated in 1983, primarily serves business travelers and medical guests. The AAA 4-diamond-rated Kahler Plaza Hotel offers luxury accommodations to medical guests and corporate travelers, as well as excellent downtown service to leisure and business travelers.

All Kahler Lodging hotels are within walking distance of Rochester's Mayo Civic Center and only minutes from Soldiers Field Golf Course, Apache Mall, and the well-known Silver Lake, which is an annual haven for thousands of Canada geese.

© MARTIENA R. RICHTER

■ RADISSON HOTEL CENTERPLACE

150 S. Broadway
Rochester, MN 55904
Tel: (507) 281-8000
Fax: (507) 281-4280
All major credit cards are accepted.

The Radisson Hotel Centerplace in downtown Rochester is a paragon of convenience, beauty and comfort: minutes away from the airport, and IBM, and accessible by skyway from the world famous Mayo Clinic. An elegant cherry wood interior with brass and imported Italian marble graces the hotel, and more than 200 rooms and private suites, some with whirlpools, are available. Two restaurants offer a choice of unique evening or casual dining. Enjoy homemade pastas, poultry, and seafood at The Meadows restaurant; or homemade soups, sandwiches, and daily specials at McCormick's Restaurant and Bar. Everything is conveniently connected to shopping areas and theaters via skyway. The Radisson Hotel Centerplace was recently ranked 77 out of 100 for city center property by *Lodging Hospitality* magazine.

Meeting space for up to 550 is available, including a ballroom, a boardroom, and the Centerplace Room for private parties. All events are attended by the services of a personal meeting planner, an on-site audiovisual coordinator, and catering staff. Extensive recreational facilities are available, including a lap swimming pool, a whirlpool, and state-of-the-art exercise equipment for recreation and relaxation.

A recipient of AAA's Four Diamond award, the Radisson Hotel Centerplace is the perfect place for individuals, families, and business groups; a world class hotel successfully blending modern efficiency with Old World charm.

■ SOLDIERS FIELD BEST WESTERN SUITES

401 Sixth Street S.W.
Rochester, MN 55902
Tel: (507) 288-2677 or (800) 366-2067 (reservations only)
All major credit cards are accepted.

Within a quiet Rochester residential area just four blocks from downtown and one-and-a-half blocks from the world-famous Mayo Clinic subway lies Soldiers Field Best Western Suites, a motel with 128 units and 90 popular kitchen suites on eight floors. Completed in 1988 by owners Rod and Patty Younge, the decor in this innovative lodging and entertainment complex is both upbeat and modern. The Younges designed the lobby in comfortable southwestern style, and, with a remarkable attention to detail, furnished the rooms with upholstered roller chairs, designer-look king and queen-size beds, brass cabinetry, and drawer space.

Among the Younges' most unique offerings is summertime rooftop dining, where drinks, light grilled entrées and salads are offered — weather permitting. The motel's first class restaurant's "singing waiters" are perhaps the complex's most enjoyable and famous amenity. The waiters and waitresses, mostly local college and amateur singers, many with remarkable talent, sing at various times during the night both solo and in concert directed by pianist John Devaal. The music and food all combine to make this dining experience both memorable and a great value.

The complex also offers a bar, pool with jacuzzi and wading pool, sauna, excercise room, playroom, meeting rooms, laundry, billiard, and video game rooms. In addition to the tourist and local entertainment trade, the complex caters to Mayo medical clientele. To accommodate the needs of the long-term customers who reside in an adjoining apartment building, Soldier's Field also features a gift shop, beauty shop, bakery, and mini-grocery.

ANTIQUES

■ JOHN KRUESEL'S GENERAL MERCHANDISE
22 Third Street S.W.
Rochester, MN 55902
Tel: (507) 289-8049
Hrs: Closed Sun. and Mon.
   Tue. - Fri. 11 a.m. - 5:30 p.m.
   Sat. 1 p.m. - 5 p.m.
Visa and MasterCard are accepted.

John Kruesel's General Merchandise, located downtown Rochester, along with tourists and locals alike, has been frequented by the rich and famous visiting the Mayo Clinic each year.

Specializing in the unusual, this store has one of the largest 18th to 20th century American antiques and lighting collections. Included in this extraordinary merchandise, customers will find jewelry, military vehicles, precious metals, and many other items that have an elegant museum quality. John Kruesel, the store's owner, is a licensed auctioneer and also specializes in consulting and restoration, estate sales, and business liquidations.

For quality merchandise far above any others, John Kruesel's General Merchandise has outstanding and unusual collectibles.

ART CENTER

■ ROCHESTER ART CENTER
320 E. Center Street
Rochester, MN 55904
Tel: (507) 282-8629
Hrs: Tue. - Sat. 10 a.m. - 5 p.m., Sun. noon - 5 p.m.

Rochester Art Center offers, for the art lover in all of us, a cornucopia of events and programs ranging from rotating exhibitions to "hands-on" workshops, classes, lectures, and videos. Every June, Rochester Art Center sponsors the Festival of the Arts. More than 100 craftspeople and visual artists from the region as well as musicians, jugglers and mime artists, converge to provide a spectacular and unforgettable event. Rochester Art Center, part of the Mayo Park Cultural Complex since 1953, also provides special educational programs for children, adults, families, and all other segments of the community. Free admission is provided to all gallery exhibitions.

COFFEE & TEA SHOP

■ COFFEE & TEA, LTD., INC.
Zumbro Market
11 - 15 Fourth Street S.E.
Rochester, MN 55904
Tel: (507) 228-9224
Hrs: Mon. - Fri. 10 a.m. - 8 p.m., Sat. 10 a.m. - 6 p.m., Sun. noon - 5 p.m.

Tanzania Peaberry, Ethiopian Harrari, Sumatra Dark. No, these are not species of exotic birds but gourmet coffees. Coffee has come a long way since the days of preground cans purchased at the supermarket. Coffee and Tea, Ltd., Inc., Rochester, located in Zumbro Market, celebrates coffee's maturation by catering to gourmet coffee lovers, offering freshly roasted coffees and blends. More than 65 kinds of coffees and more than 100 varieties of teas are displayed in bright antique jars filled with chocolate-hued coffee beans and pastel-colored teas. Order a cup of the coffee of the day and sit at a table, or pick up some Russian or Apricot Orange tea for a friend. The tea is always fresh, and the water is always hot at the Rochester Coffee and Tea, Ltd., Inc.

GIFT SHOPS

■ CARLA'S
201 14th Ave. S.W.
Rochester, MN 55902
Tel: (507) 288-7791
Hrs: Mon. - Thur. 8:30 a.m. - 9 p.m., Fri. 9 a.m. - 6 p.m.
Sat. 9 a.m. - 4 p.m., closed Sun.
Visa and MasterCard are accepted.

The charming gift shop called Carla's is located downtown Rochester in the Blondell's Crown Square Hotel, across from St. Mary's Hospital. Rochester is known world-wide as the home of the Mayo Clinic and two of the nation's most outstanding private hospitals.

Visitors will have no trouble finding that special gift for someone, whether for a special occasion or a "pick-me-up" for a friend in the hospital. The popular gift items include Raikes Collectible Bears, original Cabbage Patch dolls, helium balloons, Fannie May candy, sweatshirts and T-shirts, jewelry, stuffed animals, posters, candles, fragrances, and seasonal gifts. There's something for everyone at Carla's, and gifts can be found at all price ranges. The Rochester area offers many other attractions. Schedule a tour of Mayowood, or visit the Art Center, Public Library, Heritage House, and the many other shopping facilities and restaurants. There's plenty to see and do for a weekend!

Enjoy browing through Carla's; the gift items are limitless and the staff friendly and helpful.

■THE CHRISTMAS SHOPPE
18 S. Broadway
Rochester, MN 55904
Tel: (507) 282-1626
Hrs: Mon. - Fri. 10 a.m. - 5:30 p.m.
    Sat. 10 a.m. - 5 p.m.
    (Nov. and Dec.)
    Thur. 10 a.m. - 8 p.m.
    Sun. noon - 4 p.m.
Visa and MasterCard are accepted.

Many people who have discovered The Christmas Shoppe on their visit to Rochester come back every year. People quite often are looking for special and original one-of-a-kind gifts. At The Christmas Shoppe they find exactly that.

This delightful gift shop is very attractive and inviting. The unusual and beautiful displays demonstrate the quality and creativity found here. The shop carries all Department 56 Villages, including Dickens Village, and displays one of the largest assortment of hand-blown glass Old World Ornaments in the United States. There is a variety of seasonal gifts for Halloween, Thanksgiving, and Easter. Nancy Duxbury, the store's owner, and Terri Anderson, a valued employee, "create and sell" one-of-a-kind wreaths, centerpieces, and wall arrangements. The array of gifts and collectibles offered make this shop exceptionally unique, as the Christmas items displayed make wonderful gifts year-round for birthdays, weddings, showers, or any other special occasion. Repeat customers look forward to the annual Christmas Open House, which attracts many visitors from miles away. Phone orders are always welcomed, and shipping of selections can be arranged.

The Christmas Shoppe is more than just a place to buy Christmas gifts and decorations, it's a place to go and have good feelings about Christmas and the holidays all year long.

▋RESTAURANTS

■BROADSTREET CAFE AND BAR
300 First Ave. N.W.
Rochester, MN 55901
(507) 281-2451
Hrs: Open Mon. - Sun.
    Hours vary
All major credit cards accepted.

The Broadstreet Cafe and Bar in Rochester is a very charming American bistro housed in a renovated historic warehouse. The

Redwood Room, located in the downstairs of The Broadstreet, serves Mediterranean food.

Two dining settings in one location presents a no lose situation. The Broadstreet serves lunch, dinner, and Sunday brunch. The menu changes weekly. An omelette with fresh asparagus and white cheddar is one of the favorite brunch selections. If your brunch tastes turn toward a lunch time flavor, the grilled pork tenderloin is a choice selection. Dinner specialties include grilled fresh swordfish, broiled duck breast, or seafood pasta. For a more ethnic flavor, the Redwood Room offers a unique pizza with toppings of lamb sausage, chevre and red onion, shrimp, marinara and monterey jack cheese.

Enjoy the casual atmosphere with live music Wednesday through Saturday along with a cup of espresso. With so many choices in one place, guests will never need to leave!

■GIUSEPPI'S RESTAURANT
220 S. Broadway
Rochester, MN 55904
Tel: (507) 288-3231
Fax: (507) 288-6602
Hrs: Daily 6:30 a.m. - 10 p.m.
All major credit cards accepted.

Located on the second floor of the Holiday Inn, Giuseppi's has a unique American/Italian menu that is sure to leave diners pleasantly surprised. The secret to Giuseppi's authentic Italian cuisine and innovative dishes is Chef Bill Meyer. An experienced chef, Meyer takes pride in his wide range of Italian sauces that step outside the boundaries of traditional marinara and Alfredo sauces.

Stop by Giuseppi's for lunch, and try the basil cream chicken, salmon and sweet pea linguine or salads served in black pepper pasta shells. A wide variety of sandwiches are also available, including the local favorite, plum turkey. For dinner, sample some of the outstanding appetizers such as Vienna bacon-wrapped bread sticks, prosciutto and melon plate and lobster dill tortellini. For the main dish, how about broiled salmon fan fillets, petite tenderloin filet, or plum brandy chicken? Of course, no Italian restaurant would be complete without pasta, and Giuseppi's has the variety one would expect — from herb linguine fresca to linguine bolognese, from garlic beef and Madeira fettuccine to fettuccine marinara primavera.

Special dietary needs are accommodated. And for dessert, try Chef Meyer's classic: Baileys and dark chocolate cheesecake. It's a bit of heaven.

■HENRY WELLINGTON

216 First Ave. S.W.
Rochester, MN 55902
Tel: (507) 289-1949
Hrs: Mon. - Sat. 11 a.m. - midnight
    Sun. 11 a.m. - 11 p.m.
Visa, MasterCard, Diners Club, and AmEx are accepted.

In a building that dates back to the turn-of-the-century, in rooms filled with antiques and memorabilia, Henry Wellington is a restaurant to be remembered. There are several intimate rooms where diners may order from the extensive menu and children's menu.

Well known for the best New England Clam chowder in the region, Henry Wellington serves all homemade soups and salad dressings. Newt's Bar & Grill upstairs is available for sandwiches and lighter fare. Henry Wellington first opened in 1978, building a reputation for having the largest menu selection in Rochester.

■MICHAELS RESTAURANT

15 S. Broadway
Rochester, MN 55904
Tel: (507) 288-2020
Hrs: Mon. - Sat. Open 11 a.m.
    Call for information and dinner reservations
    Closed Sun.
Visa, MasterCard, AmEx, and Discover are accepted.

Located in downtown Rochester, Michaels is among the town's premier restaurants. Since 1951, Michaels has become well known for its old country charm atmosphere and world famous food and service. The restaurant seats 400 people and is certainly one of the largest restaurants in Minnesota.

The nearly block-long interior is divided into five unique rooms, like "The Library," which has a fireplace and book-lined walls, and "The Hutch," another popular room with the restaurant's only booth seating. From midwestern favorites to native Greek specialities, customers will enjoy an exquisite cuisine of traditional American steaks and seafood, Greek foods, roast duck, and fresh fish. After a meal, relax in the lounge with live piano music. For special occasions, the beautiful Greek Haraka Dining Rooms are available evenings for private parties or meetings.

People know what to expect at Michaels — casual, elegant surroundings and impeccable service.

■ SANDY POINT SUPPER CLUB
R.R. 4
Rochester, MN 55901
Tel: (507) 367-4983
Hrs: Mon. - Fri. 4:30 p.m. - 10 p.m.
      Sat. - Sun. noon - 11 p.m.
Visa, MasterCard, AmEx, and Discover are accepted.

Gerry Strandemo's Sandy Point Supper Club has been a Rochester favorite for more than 40 years. Well known for its beautiful river location, friendly service, and fine fare, "The Out of Town Place" makes guests feel right at home and eager to return.

One of the largest menus to be found in Minnesota offers a full range of well-prepared, hearty dinners, from tasty hors d'oeuvres to refreshing desserts. An excellent senior citizen's menu is also featured for guests 62 and over. Diners may select from an extensive list of seafood, beef, and midwestern-style entrees, and even have the luxury of mix-and-matching their favorite combinations. Avalon Stuffed Shrimp is a tasty blend of bay shrimp, snow crab, and Monterey Jack cheese on a bed of wild rice or potato. African broiled lobster tail comes in both king- and queen-size portions, as does the restaurant's tender, juicy prime rib. Succulent steaks, cooked to perfection, include prime filet mignon, New York strip, and teriyaki. Tangy barbecued pork ribs, Chicken Kiev, Cornish game hens, and baked duck are among the Midwest favorites featured.

Banquets for all occasions are easily accommodated at the club, and a very picturesque setting overlooking the river makes dining here a special treat year-round. Plenty of parking, nearby boat docking, a friendly open atmosphere, and delicious food make Sandy Point Supper Club a favorite of people from all over.

■ THE 7TH RIB
Highway 63
(15 miles south of Rochester)
Rochester, MN 55967
Tel: (507) 378-7427 (RIBS) or (800) 658-2553
Hrs: Closed Monday
      (Lunch) Tues. - Sat. 11 a.m. - 2 p.m.
      (Dinner) Tues. - Sat. 4:30 p.m. - 10:30 p.m.
      Sun. 11 a.m. - 10 p.m.
All major credit cards are accepted.

The 7th Rib is seventh heaven for diners and dancers alike. Just 15 miles south of Rochester on U.S. Highway 63 sits the oldest southeastern Minnesota family-owned restaurant. People from around the world have made the short drive since 1933.

The rustic, but contemporary restaurant boasts a very plentiful menu and seating capacity of 250 people. Guests can enjoy a selection of steaks, ribs and chops, fish and broiled seafood. All-you-can-eat ribs, steak and fish specials are served Tuesday through Thursday, which also includes the salad bar, held by a hundred-year old bobsled. The 7th Rib is also the home of "The Challenger," a 72-ounce New York strip steak; any guest who believes he can finish it in 45 minutes eats free! The Sunday Brunch Buffet offers a variety of tempting items to please the entire family. Banquet facilties are available to accommodate up to 100 people with complete catering services. Take-out orders are also welcomed.

Specializing in 50s and 60s music, the new Cabaret Lounge provides fun and exciting entertaining on the weekends. This 3,000 square foot music room perhaps has the most sophisticated lighting system in the area. Lounge specials are offered daily and a big screen TV draws in the sporting events enthusiasts.

The cordial atmosphere of The 7th Rib provides the perfect relaxed setting for lunch, dinner, or any special occasion. The food is superb and the entertainment exhilarating. It has become very popular locally and to many guests visiting the Rochester area.

■ WONG'S CAFE

4 S.W. Third Street
Rochester, MN 55902
Tel: (507) 282-7545
Hrs: Mon. - Fri. 6 a.m. - 9:30 p.m.
    Sat. 11 a.m. - 9:30 p.m.
    Sun. 11 a.m. - 9 p.m.
Visa, MasterCard, and Diner's Club are accepted.

Imperial chicken. Steamed cod fillets, Chinese style. Just the words make one hungry! Wong's Cafe has been serving these and many other sumptuous entrees for more than 40 years in downtown Rochester. Located in a former bank on historic Third Street, Wong's Cafe offers extensive Chinese and American fare at very reasonable prices.

Opened by Ben and Neil Wong in 1952, Wong's Cafe offers top-notch service in the family tradition, in pleasant, contemporary surroundings. Very popular are the combination plates such as Chicken Subgum Chow Mein complete with cashews, water chestnuts, and mild peppers. Other dishes are equally tempting. Wong's also offers a delicious lunch menu.

One reason for the success of Wong's Cafe lies in their "made to order" service — meeting the special dietary needs of their customers, upon request. Another reason is the brothers' insistence upon cooking with the very finest and freshest ingredients. The Wongs even grow their own bean sprouts! Be sure to visit Wong's Cafe for Rochester's finest Chinese and American cuisine and impeccable service. Takeout and delivery are available.

T HEATRE

■ THE ROCHESTER CIVIC THEATRE
Mayo Park
Rochester, MN 55904
Tel: (507) 282-8481
Hrs: Box office open Mon. - Fri. 8:30 a.m. - 1 p.m., 2 p.m. - 5:30 p.m.

The Rochester Civic Theatre is a nonprofit arts organization dedicated to professional-quality productions. Staffed by professionals and dedicated volunteers serving Rochester and southeastern Minnesota, the Rochester Civic Theatre annually serves up a lively season of American classics, musicals, dramas, comedies, and young people's productions from August through June.

Recent performances have included "Fiddler on the Roof," "Broadway Bound", and "Dracula." Young people's plays have included "Cinderella" and "A Christmas Carol." The curtain rises at 8 p.m. for Thursday through Saturday performances. Sunday matinees start at 2 p.m., with Saturday matinees at 4 p.m. A performance at the Rochester Civic Theatre is a great way to entertain the family and support this community project at the same time. Gift certificates also are available.

T OURS

■ ASSISI COMMUNITY CENTER
1001 14th Street N.W.
Rochester, MN 55903
Tel: (507) 289-0821
Hrs: Mon., Wed., and Fri. 2 p.m.
    Reservations required

Assisi Heights is the home of the Sisters of St. Francis of Rochester, Minnesota. It is located on the highest hill in Olmsted County and overlooks the city. The building itself, Italian

Romanesque in architectural design, was built similar to the Basilica of St. Francis in Assisi, Italy. The chapel of Our Lady of Lourdes with its tall campanile containing bronze bells cast in Holland, beautiful stained glass windows, and mosaics and marble from around the world, is a focal point of interest in this complex.

Not only do Sisters come here to retire, but their administrative offices are located at this site. The Sisters in active ministry today perform a variety of services in the fields of education, social work, and healthcare, as well as spiritual direction and retreat work. They work in many parts of the United States and some foreign countries. Assisi Heights houses a Synod office of the Evangelical Lutheran Church in America, the Rochester Montessori School, and Assisi Community Center.

Assisi Community Center is one of the largest conference/retreat centers in Minnesota, and is a part of the Assisi Heights complex. ACC has over 130 individual bedrooms and has meeting rooms of various sizes to accommodate the needs of many groups. Spiritual, educational, and cultural groups of all religious traditions are welcomed throughout the year for various lengths of time. ACC also sponsors over 40 of its own programs in the areas of personal growth, spirituality and social justice, publishing its calendar of events in September and January. Personal time to "get away" individually, private days of retreat, as well as spiritual direction, massage, and/or counseling can be arranged through Assisi Community Center. Tours are conducted three times a week and may be arranged at other times to accommodate large groups. Reservations are required a few days in advance.

■OLMSTEAD COUNTY HISTORY CENTER AND MAYOWOOD MANSION

County Road 22 S.W.
P.O. Box 6411
Rochester, MN 55903
Tel: (507) 282-9447
Hrs: Call for information and Mayowood tour reservations.

A must when visiting southeastern Minnesota is a stop at the Olmsted County History Center in Rochester where visitors can learn about the area's history and visit fabulous Mayowood Mansion.

The Olmsted County History Center is more than a museum filled with relics of the past. It is a 17,000 square foot educational facility interpreting the history of the area from geological formation through contemporary times. The gallery was totally renovated in 1990 and features exhibits dealing with Indian inhabitants, white settlement, immigrants, the Mayo family and the development of the Mayo Clinic, International Business Machines Corporation, and area agriculture and industry. The facility also includes an extensive genealogical and research library and a museum shop offering unique gifts and historical reproductions.

Mayowood Mansion, the 55-room former country home of Mayo Clinic founders Doctors C.H. and C.W. Mayo, is also open to the public for professionally guided tours. The mansion was once the center of a self-contained 3,000-acre estate and is now listed on the National Register of Historic Places. The home is furnished with antiques, artwork, and decorative items collected by the Mayo family. Tours depart from the History Center on a regular schedule. A nominal admission fee includes bus transportation to the mansion.

WILDLIFE ART & COLLECTIBLES

■ WILD WINGS GALLERY
Centerplace Galleria
111 S. Broadway
Rochester, MN 55904
Tel: (507) 281-3022
Hrs: Mon. -Fri. 9:30 a.m. - 8:30 p.m., Sat. 9:30 a.m. - 5:50 p.m.,
 Sun. noon - 5 p.m.
All major credit cards are accepted.

Wild Wings Gallery originated in Frontenac, MN, when its founder, Bill Webster, agreed to market duck stamp prints created by his hunting partners David Maass and David Hagerbaumer in the late 1960s. Webster was an avid duck stamp print collector and his hunting partners were wildlife artists. It was a fruitful combination — Wild Wings is now more than 20 years old and operates ten galleries and seven franchises, as well as selling wholesale to more than 700 galleries nationwide.

Wild Wings in Rochester exhibits work by artists such as Robert Abbett, David Maass, Michael Sieve, Rosemary Millette, Lee Kromschroeder, Ron Van Gilder, and Nancy Glazier. Along with original artwork and limited edition prints by these renowned artists, the gallery has collectibles, home furnishings, and gifts for purchase.

Webster has succeeded in selecting wildlife art that is enjoyable to view and is interesting and worthwile as an investment. His knowledgeable staff willingly explains background information about individual artwork and prints.

Rushford

Located in the heart of Bluff Country along the scenic Root River lies the small town of Rushford. Sometimes called the Trail City because of the crossing of old Indian trails, Rushford offers a wide range of recreational activities in the warm and friendly atmosphere of a small community. Downtown lies the historic *Rushford Depot* which was built in 1867 and today serves as both a tourist information center and the start (or end) of the Root River trail system. The *Root River Trail* is a 35-mile multiple use trail that winds along the Root River and was developed on an abondoned railroad grade. This trail is great for canoeing, bicycling, rollerskating, cross-country skiing and walking. The *Mill Street Inn* offers home-cooked meals and pies in a renovated

1870 building and there are several nice parks within the city that offer picnic shelters and dramatic views of the area from the top of the bluffs. The largest employer is *Rush Products Company,* which manufactures auto switches.

For more information on Rushford, contact:
TOURISM COMMITTEE
P.O. Box 338B
Rushford, MN 55971
(507) 864-2444

Spring Grove

S pring Grove has the honor of being the first Norwegian settlement in Minnesota. Located just 155 miles southeast of the Twin Cities, many of its citizens can trace their roots back to Norway. Rosemaling is still an art form that is practiced in Spring Grove. Residents perform the folk painting on wood to keep the art of rosemaling current. The original settlers were looking for wooded land with an abundant water supply. This hamlet possesses an inviting outdoor life, with skiing and snowmobiling in the winter, and fishing and hiking in the summer. During the summer there also are outdoor concerts, plays, and musicals. Autumn brings the *Fall Foliage Fest*, which provides exceptional tours of the "Trolltown, USA."

For more information on Spring Grove, contact:
SPRING GROVE AREA
Past, Present and Future
P.O. Box 241
Spring Grove, MN 55974
(507) 498-5221

COLLECTIBLE GIFTS & ANTIQUES

■ COUNTRY LACE
Main Street
Spring Grove, MN 55974
Tel: (507) 498-5779
Hrs: Mon. - Sat. 10 a.m. - 5 p.m. Open on selected Sundays
Visa and MasterCard are accepted.

Tucked away in Spring Grove, Country Lace beckons visitors and shoppers who have a soft spot for dried flowers, lace curtains, and delectable, old-fashioned sweets.

Owned by Pam Geving and Lori Morken, the collectibles and handicrafts found at Country Lace now occupy the space that was once reserved for pews and the pious. The shop is located in a converted town church, resplendent with beautiful, original, stained-glass windows, vaulted ceilings, wooden floors, and hand-painted wall and ceiling murals. Filling the space of the old church's roomy interior now are seven individually decorated rooms that are brimming with baskets, dried flowers, linens and heritage laces, collectible dolls and antiques, specialty books, hand-made quilts, unusual gift cards, Christmas items from around the word and much, much more. The shop is a wonderful detour for those passing through on their way to nearby campgrounds, bike trails, Beaver Creek Valley State Park, and hunting and fishing spots.

R ESTAURANT & BAKERY

■ THE BAKE SHOPPE CAFE
131 Main Street
Spring Grove, MN 55974
Tel: (507) 498-5482
Hrs: Mon.-Thur. 6 a.m.-5 p.m., Fri.-Sat. 6 a.m.-9:30 p.m.,
    Sun. 4 a.m.-9 p.m.

Citizens of Spring Grove have operated businesses on this lot since 1880. Groceries, general merchandise, books, furniture, and videos are some of the items that have been vended on the site located in the heart of Spring Grove. In 1982 the store became The Bake Shoppe Cafe and offers lovingly baked, homemade muffins, breads, soups, sauces, and much more.

Currently owned and operated by Sharon Danielson, the cafe boasts a loyal following. Consistent with the area's Norwegian influence, the chefs and bakers at the cafe present hungry diners with such specialties as the Ole Burger, Lena Burger, the Viking Conquest, and the Oslo. Sandwiches arrive on baked-daily homemade bread and many are complemented and made unique by the cafe's famous homemade sauces. On weekends the cafe's famed fish dinner features deep-fried, blackened or pan-fried fish served with the chef's special sauces and made-from-scratch pizzas. Visitors can sip bottomless cups of coffee or order newly baked muffins, a generous slice of savory pie, or Norwegian-style lunches.

Daily specials promise something new even to the most regular customers of The Bake Shoppe Cafe. The cafe also fulfills custom cake and bakery orders.

Spring Valley

S pring Valley is another small historic city located in the bluff country only 30 miles south of Rochester, and there are good roads in all directions. The population hovers around 2,500 with many historic buildings scattered throughout the town. The *Methodist Church Museum* is a Laura Ingalls Wilder Historic Site. The famed author of the Little House series of books lived here with her husband Almanzo Wilder in the 1890s and attended the Methodist Church. This church is on the National Register of Historic Sites. Additional suggested historic sites to see are the *Pioneer Home Museum* and the *Carnegie Library*. The *Mystery Cave* is the state's largest natural limestone cave and is open to the public. Annual events include: the *Forestville Festival* in the Forestville State Park in early June; the *Ag Days Festival* in late August; and the *Christmas Open House* in December.

For more information on Spring Valley, contact:
SPRING VALLEY AREA CHAMBER OF COMMERCE
209 N. Broadway Ave.
Spring Valley, MN 55975
(507) 346-7365

DISPLAY GARDENS

■ THE TREEHOUSE
Highway 63 S.
Spring Valley, MN 55951
Tel: (507) 561-3785
Hrs: (April - June)
 Mon. - Sat. 9:30 a.m. - 5:30 p.m.
 Sun. 1 p.m. - 5:30 p.m.
 (July and Aug.)
 Mon. - Sat. 9 a.m. - 4 p.m.
 Closed Sunday
 (Sept. and Oct.)
 Mon. - Sat. 9 a.m. - 5 p.m.
 Sun. 1 p.m. - 5 p.m.
 Closed winter

This beautiful garden spot of historic bluff country is located 12 miles south of Spring Valley on Highway 63. The 80-acre farm has been painstakingly and masterfully built into a successful garden center. The gardens at The Treehouse were originally designed to give retail customers landscaping ideas. Over the years, quite a number have been planted. Now, two acres of display gardens are open for the public to enjoy walking through. Visitors can enjoy the array of colorful plants featuring perennials, annuals, small shrubs, evergreens, shade trees, water fountains, and statuary. The nursery supplies 250 varieties of perennials, spring annuals, vegetable plants, and a wide selection of trees, shrubs, roses, and evergreens.

There are free self-guided tours of the gardens, and a playground is available for children. All the plant material is well labeled. Advance arrangements for guided tours for groups are suggested.

Wabasha

Wabasha was named in honor of a Sioux Indian Chief, Wa-pa-shaw. It is one of the oldest towns on the upper Mississippi River and has been occupied continuously over the years. The early settlers were fur traders. The economy later switched to lumbering, milling, and boat building. Windows to the past are seen all over Wabasha; one need only look. The *Wabasha County Museum at Reads Landing* has much of this history preserved. Formerly a school house, this building currently keeps the history of the town from the pioneer days through World War II. The *Arrowhead Bluffs Museum* has kept the history of the native Indians alive for all to see, including many artifacts and wildlife exhibits. The *Anderson House*, built in 1856, is Minnesota's oldest operating hotel. *Coffee Mill Ski Area* beckons skiers to explore the slopes carved by the water melting from the glaciers during the ice age.

For more information on Wabasha, contact:
WABASHA CHAMBER OF COMMERCE
P.O. Box 105
Wabasha, MN 55981
(612) 565-4158

GALLERY & FRAME SHOP

■ DICK'S FRAME AND UPTOWN GALLERY
164 Pembroke
Wabasha, MN 55981
Tel: (612) 565-4793
Hrs: Mon. - Sat. 9 a.m. - 5 p.m.
    Sun. 11 a.m. - 3 p.m.
Visa and MasterCard are accepted.

One of the finest collections of limited edition prints by local Minnesota artists can be found here at Dick's Frame and Uptown Gallery. Wildlife prints by Redlin and Maas are also on display.

What started as a hobby by Dick and Sally Schurhammer in 1982, expanded to a full-time business in 1986. Astonishing is the number of artists in this area that demonstrate their talents and carry on the heritage of Minnesota through their artwork. The gallery displays many woodworks and carvings, handcrafted collectibles, paintings, and sculptures on consignment from local artists. Specializing in custom framing, people travel from miles around to have Dick do their framing. Gift wrapping is available upon request.

For lovers of artwork, a trip to Dick's Frame and Uptown Gallery can give them an idea of how a painting or sculpture might fit in their home.

GIFT OUTLET

■ COUNTRY BOUQUET OUTLET
317 Main Street W.
Wabasha, MN 55981
Tel: (612) 565-3808
    (612) 388-3530 - Red Wing Store
Hrs: Mon. - Sun. 9 a.m. - 5 p.m.
    Hours may vary
Visa and MasterCard are accepted.

Country Bouquet was born on a Minnesota prairie near Wabasha, by two artisans eager to market their handcrafted folk art pieces. With their commitment to producing a quality product with competitive pricing, they soon discovered they would have to hire additional artisans to meet the demands for orders. Along with this came the necessity of moving from their small backyard shed to larger quarters. They found this new home near Wabasha, but more importantly, it was here they found people who are committed to their artwork. That care shows in the product. The customer in turn recognizes that care as being a distinctive quality of Country Bouquet, and so they grew. Today their products are found in shops and stores nationwide, but they have not forgotten their humble beginnings, nor their desire to give their customer the best product they can produce.

Visitors to the outlets in Wabasha — and their new store in the Red Wing pottery location — savor the delight of life as it used to be; peaceful and uncluttered. They discover the treasures in Country Bouquet stores. In these shops, they find carved Santas and birds, collector dolls, furniture, and miniature villages all made right here near the river, plus gifts from other artisans across the United States.

And if, by the end of the day, they're just too tired to drive home, they spend the night in Wabasha and start all over again the next morning.

Historic Inn

■ THE ANDERSON HOUSE
333 W. Main Street
Wabasha, MN 55981
Tel: (612) 565-4524 or (in MN) (800) 862-9702 and (outstate) (800) 325-2270
All major credit cards are accepted.

In beautiful Hiawatha Valley, hugging the Mississippi River is Wabasha, one of the original rivertowns. Tourists and vacationers come year-round for the limitless sights, events, tours, and shops. One most notable of these is The Anderson House, a country inn set in the residential part of town. The Anderson House opened in 1856, and has been run by four generations of the Anderson family since 1896. The rooms are filled with antiques and furniture dating back to the inn's early days. Present-day innkeepers John, Gayla, and Jean Hall keep Grandma Anderson's popular recipes a part of the daily menus. These recipes are a large part of what made the inn a success over the years, and now may be found in two popular cookbooks. The Anderson House offers "special happenings" coinciding with holidays and special services, including their famous cat rentals. Families with children are welcome, and special package plans are available for individuals traveling alone.

MUSEUM

■ ARROWHEAD BLUFFS MUSEUM
Highway 60
R.R. 2, P.O. Box 7
Wabasha, MN 55981
Tel: (612) 565-3829
Hrs: Open daily from May 1 to Jan. 1.
  10 a.m. - 6 p.m.
  Open by appointment only from Jan. 2 to April 30

Located 1 1/2 miles west of Wabasha on Highway 60, Arrowhead Bluffs Museum is the life's work of Les Behrns and his son, John. For 30 years the Behrnses collected objects from around the country for their unique exhibit of old firearms, Indian and pioneer artifacts, and mounted specimens of North American wildlife.

Highlights of the collection include every Winchester gun made from 1866 to 1982, complete with all commemoratives made before 1982. The solid oak museum cases also contain many other unique firearms from the past made by such famous names as Henry Rifle, Colt, and Smith & Wesson. Visitors can also peruse the Behrnses' considerable collection of early American Indian artifacts and pioneer tools and eye the beautiful mounted wildlife specimens. A main attraction at the museum is a flock of mounted wild sheep posed in a realistic mountain setting.

A gift shop connected with the museum offers a wide assortment of art and handicrafts such as afghans, jewelry, belt buckles, pottery, and furniture. The Behrnses also operate a hunting and fishing consulting service. For a fascinating peek at America's wild and wooly heritage, stop by the Arrowhead Bluffs Museum.

◨ESTAURANT

◼ VELVET ROOSTER
P.O. Box 301
Hiawatha Drive S.
Wabasha, MN 55981
Tel: (612) 565-4698
Hrs: (April - Dec.)
    Tue. - Sat. lunch 11 a.m. - 2 p.m.
    Tue. - Thu. dinner 5 p.m. - 9 p.m.
    Fri. - Sat. dinner 5 p.m. - 9 p.m.
    Sun. 9 a.m. - 8 p.m. Closed Mon.
    Call for Jan. - March hours.

Homemade foods and generous buffets are the contemporary claim to fame of the Velvet Rooster. Listed on the National Register of Historic Places, this former County Facility landmark, established in 1884, is one of the few left in the state. Now in its second generation, this family owned and operated eatery blends modern comfort with old-fashioned charm.

At the Velvet Rooster, wholesome, ample meals are served for modest prices. Homemade cheesecake, freshly baked pies, and shortcake tempt the most dessert- resistant diners to indulge, and

the all-you-can-eat buffets attract patrons from miles around. The Luncheon Buffet includes three main meat entrees. Friday features a Seafood Buffet, and Saturday and Sunday buffets offer a combination buffet including six main meats. Vegetables, dressings, potatoes, homemade soups, and dinner rolls add to the abundance. The extensive, 27-item salad bar offers both garden fresh and pickled vegetables and salad dressings made from the families' favorite recipes. Farm fresh eggs and honey-laced pancakes head the roster of delights of a seasonal Sunday breakfast buffet along with mouth-watering selections of freshly baked pastries.

The Velvet Rooster also offers complete catering services for banquets, and meeting rooms are available upon request. It can easily accommodate groups who are planning weddings, anniversaries, family reunions, and conventions. Bus groups are also welcome. The restaurant offers special menu selections and a carry-out service.

Affordable, satisfying meals in pleasant surroundings make the Velvet Rooster one of Wabasha's most popular restaurants. Nestled along the banks of the rural Mississippi River Valley area, 1-1/2 miles south of town, the Velvet Rooster offers diners a taste of Minnesota's southern hospitality.

TOY & CHRISTMAS SHOPS & MFG.

■ L.A.R.K. TOYS INC.
Lark Lane
Kellogg, MN 55945
Tel: (507) 767-3387
Fax: (507) 767-4565
Hrs: Mon. - Fri. 8:30 a.m. to 4:30 p.m.
    Sat. - Sun. 10 a.m. to 5 p.m.
    For winter hours, please call first.
Visa and Mastercard are accepted.

Located on Lark Lane off Highway 61 and County Road 18 just south of Wabasha across from the town of Kellogg is L.A.R.K. Toys. Imagine storybook dreams of handcarved rocking horses, full-size carousel animals, and original wooden pull toys like green-shelled turtles, grasshoppers, and teddy bears that ride bikes! In the L.A.R.K. workshops, woodworkers are crafting these treasures for today and tomorrow.

In 1983, Donn Kreofsky, former art and photography teacher, began making a few toys in his garage, and sold them locally. Today his business, L.A.R.K. (Lost Arts Revival by Kreofsky) Toys, Inc., designs and manufactures wooden toys sold across the United States.

L.A.R.K.'s pull toys are crafted by hand of pine with no metal parts, and range in size from six inches to more than three feet high. Handcolored with warm, childsafe stains, the toys have captivating cam-action movements that make bears pedal, grasshoppers and bunnies hop, and stegos lumber along.

In 1990, L.A.R.K. added a year-round Christmas Shop in the middle of the carving studio and woodshop. Visitors can browse and watch the progress of the animals being made for the "largest handcarved original carousel to be built in the last 65 years." A hippo, giant goldfish, pig and troll, mother ostrich with hatchlings, sea turtle, 900-pound life-size moose, and the Four Seasons horses share a large room with other animals and the carver as he works. See how raw pine and basswood are transformed into handstained, all-wood action toys or carved into beautiful carousel animals.

Toy lovers of all ages are able to view the toy workshops and the carousel carving operation, and enjoy the playful possibilities in the toy and Christmas Shop.

Specialty toys to be enjoyed in the toy shop include over 100 different tin wind-ups, wonderful hand puppets from the United States, shiny marbles from England, handpainted animals from Germany, and nesting eggs from Europe and the USSR.

Winona

W inona was named after Chief Wah-Pah-Sha's daughter, Wenonah, who plunged to her death after leaping from a high bluff when she was not allowed to marry the man she loved. The bluffs loom over the Mississippi river like a frame around a picture. The limestone bluffs wind throughout the Hiawatha Valley gracing it with a rare beauty. In the early days Winona was an important rivertown, frequented by fur traders, lumbermen, and railroad men. It also was rich in soil, which lead to wheat becoming the most profitable crop in the Midwest. The railroad took away some of the importance of the steamboat, but there still was a respectable amount of river traffic because of lumbermills in the area.

Winona is the eastern gateway to Minnesota, as it is one of the first cities to be encountered on the southeast border of the state. Winona was largely settled by German and Polish immigrants. Much of their culture and history has been preserved by the historical societies in the area. Winona places great importance on education and is home to four institutions of higher learning: Winona State University, St. Mary's College, The College of St. Teresa, and Winona Technical Institute.

ATTRACTIONS

Winona is a paradise for outdoor activity. It combines the advantages of a major waterway — the Mississippi River — with the captivating bluffs surrounding the area. *Sugar Loaf Mountain* is said to be the cap of Chief Wah-Pah-Sha transformed into stone.

The *Upper Mississippi National Wildlife and Fish Refuge* is more than 260 miles long and up to three miles wide. In the spring and fall this refuge is a haven for some of the nation's largest concentrations of canvas back duck, tundra swans, and bald eagles. The *Julius C. Wilke Steamboat Center* contains an actual size replica of a steamboat. The center displays artifacts from the river's history and from the Victorian era. The *Polish Cultural Institute of Winona* preserves the rich culture of the city with heirlooms and folk art. The *C.A. Rohrer Rose Garden* is one of the largest rose gardens in the midwest. It features more than 2000 plants and is located at the east end of the bandshell on the north shore of Lake Winona.

The *Winter Carnival* kicks off the new year each January with three days of contests, tournaments, and entertainment. The *Wildwood Mountain Climb Bike Race* is held in mid-June and consists of a three mile loop race through the bluffs above Winona. *Steamboat Days at Lake Park* usher in the 4th of July with a parade and the Rivertown Renaissance Open Air Art Show and Food Fair. The Sugar Loaf Classic Bicycle Tour winds down summer at the end of August with a 27-, 62-, or 100-mile loop of the bluffs. *Winona Wildlife Weekend* greets fall with a show of noted wildlife painters and artists displaying their work. The first Sunday of December celebrates the Victorian era with a *Victorian Christmas*, offering tours of Victorian homes, refreshments, and nostalgic activities.

For more information on Winona contact:
THE WINONA AREA CHAMBER OF COMMERCE
P.O. Box 870
168 W. Second Street
Winona, MN 55987
(507) 452-2272

B ED & BREAKFAST

■ CARRIAGE HOUSE BED & BREAKFAST
420 Main Street
Winona, MN 55987
Tel: (507) 452-8256
Hrs: Open year-round
Visa and MasterCard are accepted.

More than a century ago, lumber baron Conrad Böhn built his grand Victorian home in the old river town of Winona. Along with the house, he erected an extravagant three-story carriage house large enough to fit six carriages, several horses, a hay loft, and sleeping rooms for the stable boys.

Today, the carriage house has found new purpose as a luxurious, charming bed and breakfast. The current owners of the Böhn mansion, Deb and Don Salyards, have decorated each room with an elegant, unique theme reminiscent of a bygone era. Guests sleep in full-size four-poster canopy beds, and most rooms come with private baths. The tariff also includes complimentary beverages and breakfast, and visitors will have a chance to learn more about the history of one of Winona's — and the state's — oldest homes.

The Carriage House Bed & Breakfast is conveniently located in the heart of the city, within easy walking distance to the Mississippi River and the many sights of historic downtown Winona. Guests can also take the Carriage House tandem bike for a trip around scenic Lake Winona.

ECONOMY LODGING

■ STERLING MOTEL
Junction Highways 64 & 14
Winona, MN 55987
Tel: (507) 454-1120
All major credit cards are accepted.

Located along the Mississippi River Valley Bluff, the Sterling Motel has been established in Winona since 1958.

This full-service motor inn is just a short walk from shopping, a golf course, a variety of fine restaurants, and five minutes from the local colleges. Each of the 32 modern units has a double bed, a telephone, cable television, and air-conditioning. Queen-size waterbeds and free cribs are also available. The setting is perfect for the overnight traveler and family visiting the Winona area. There are many bike and ski trails to enjoy, along with a visit to the Winona Historical Museum, the historic displays at the Wilkie Steamboat Center, or a riverboat ride on the Mississippi. Pets are allowed, and a 24-hour restaurant is just a few steps from the motel.

For exceptionally clean and comfortable guest rooms, the Sterling Motel provides a quality service at very affordable rates.

G IFT STORE

■ THE OAKS GALLERY AND COUNTRY STORE
425 Cottonwood Drive
Winona, MN 55987
Tel: (507) 454 - 3603
Hrs: Mon. - Sat. 10 a.m. - 6 p.m.
    Sun. noon - 6 p.m.
Visa and MasterCard are accepted.

A shopping bonanza awaits customers at The Oaks Gallery and Country Store. The largest shop of its kind in Minnesota and in surrounding states, the store offers customers the quaintness of a turn-of-the-century general store along with the sophistication of a fine-arts gallery and everything in between.

The Country Store section offers apple butter, spiced teas, and candy. It also contains Victorian books and paper dolls, with antique reproduction Coca-Cola and Nestlé tins. Handmade wooden furniture, ceramics, wreaths, floral arrangements, and more make up the Oaks Gallery. There's even a fine arts section that includes original oil paintings, watercolors, wildlife prints, and calligraphy. All items in the store are sold on a direct-sale basis from the artist to the customer, eliminating high markups.

H ISTORIC HOTEL

■ THE HOTEL
Third and Johnson
Winona, MN 55987
Tel: (507) 452-5460
Hrs: Open year-round

Victorian charm and modern convenience meet and blend at The Hotel in downtown Winona. As its name implies, The Hotel was once the most important hotel in Winona — an exclusive businessman's establishment where Victorian age entrepreneurs met and mingled.

Built in 1892, today The Hotel is totally renovated yet preserves its original architectural highlights, such as interior brick walls and hardwood banisters in the staircase. All 24 rooms are tastefully decorated in Victorian style. Each room is also equipped with a private bath, color TV, telephone, and individually set comfort controles. The Hotel also boasts a dining room with a dinner and lunch menu featuring beef, seafood, and poultry dishes. For lunch, try a Schinkentaschen, The Hotel's ham and cheese sandwich specialty.

The Hotel also offers special packages for one- and two-night stays complete with a bottle of chilled champagne upon arrival and continental breakfast.

H ISTORICAL MUSEUM

■ WINONA COUNTY HISTORICAL SOCIETY
160 Johnson Street
Winona, MN 55987
(507) 454-2723
Hrs: Mon. - Fri. 10 a.m. - 5 p.m., Sat. - Sun. 1 - 5 p.m.
Visa and MasterCard are accepted in gift shop.

The Winona County Historical Society, founded in 1935 in a Mississippi River county rich with life and history, boasts the largest county membership of any county historical society in Minnesota. It was established for the purpose of preserving, documenting, and interpreting the human history of Winona county. In addition to operating a nationally registered historic site and two museums, it maintains a large collection of artifacts that represent daily life from 1850 to the present. It sponsors several educational programs that bring history alive to Winona county citizens and visitors.

The Armory Museum located at 160 Johnson Street in Winona, is open year-round,

Mon-Fri. 10 a.m. -5 p.m., and Sat-Sun. 1 p.m.-5 p.m. There is a small admission fee. Presenting slices of turn-of-the-century life, exhibits are laid out like the sections of an old town. A Main Street, blacksmith shop, pharmacy, and robbery-proof Security State Bank are some of the exhibits filled with interesting artifacts.

Arches Museum of Pioneer Life is located on U.S. Highway 14, midway between Stockton and Lewiston, 11 miles west of Winona. It's open May 1 - Oct. 30, Wed.-Sun. There is a small admission fee. Named for the stone railroad arches nearby, the museum houses early agricultural equipment, tools, and household items. An authentic one-room schoolhouse, log house, and barn harken back to a bygone era.

Historic Bunnell House is located just off U.S. Highways 14 and 61 in Homer. It's open Memorial Day through Labor Day and on weekends through mid-Oct., Wed.-Sat. 10 a.m.-5 p.m. and Sun. 1 p.m.-5 p.m. The old house overlooks the Mississippi River, and a ramble through its hallways transports visitors back in time to the days when the river valley was just being settled.

The society also runs several historical libraries and bookstores: the Laird Lucas Memorial Library, located in the Armory Museum, is recognized for having one of the finest local archives in the state. Several special events, such as the September Harvest of Quilts — an exhibit featuring over 100 different old and new quilts — and the Victorian Fair in October, continuously present the area's fascinating history and rich heritage to visitors.

R ESTAURANT & LOUNGE

■ ZACH'S ON THE TRACKS
Front and Center Streets
Winona, MN 55987
Tel: (507) 454-6939
Hrs: (Lunch)
    Mon. - Sat. 11:30 a.m. - 2:30 p.m.
    (Sunday brunch)
    10:30 a.m. - 2 p.m.
    (Dinner)
    Mon. - Thur. 5 p.m. - 9:30 p.m.
    Fri - Sat. 5 p.m. - 10 p.m.
All major credit cards are accepted.

The Winona and St. Peter Freight House originally built in 1883 is now the home of Zach's on the Tracks and the Side Track Tap Restaurant and Lounge. There is a great deal of nostalgia to enjoy, including railroad memorabilia, local photomurals, and a gigantic salad bar served from an antique freight cargo-wagon. The building is a significant remnant of Winona's railroad history and is listed on the National Register of Historic Places.

Bare brick walls, authentic railroad memorabilia, and wood and glass chandeliers complete the scene at Zach's where dining guests will enjoy a unique brand of hospitality. Luncheon items feature a varied menu. Popular salads include the Western Pacific Taco Salad and Pioneer Limited mounded with fresh spinach leaves, tossed with fresh vegetables and topped with a delicious hot bacon dressing. House specialties include the Roundhouse, crab meat topped with tomato and cheese on a toasted English muffin, and the Great Northern Reuben, along with several other tempting "freighthouse" delectables. Dinner presents an exceptional array of entrees, including prime rib, filet mignon, pork medallions, chicken divan, and Canadian walleye pike. To enhance the dining pleasure, a complete bar service is available. Accommodations for business meetings, banquets, wedding reception, and other special occasions can be arranged with complete catering services.

For an enjoyable dining experience, visit Zach's on the Tracks, a sophisticated casual restaurant with a bit of railroad nostalgia.

S WEATER OUTLET

■ WINONA KNITS SWEATERS
1200 Storr's Pond Road
P.O. Box 400
Winona, MN 55987
Tel: (507) 454-3240 or (800) 888-2007

Among the industrial founders of Winona is Winona Knitting Mills. Since 1943, three generations of the Woodworth family have owned and operated the mill. In the mid-1970s, Pat Woodworth became president of the newly incorporated sweater retail company now known as Winona Knits. The first store was originally located adjacent to the knitting mill and served as a retail outlet for sweater overruns and production irregulars from the factory.

The overwhelming popularity of being able to "buy sweaters direct from the factory" enabled the company to expand. It wasn't long before the store's inventory included first-quality garments and select items from other U.S. knitting mills. Today, Winona Knits stores can be found throughout the Midwest, with new stores opening in eastern and western states. In 1989 Winona Knits moved to a new location at the shore of Lake Winona. Special attention was given to the exterior design and landscaping to make it "a natural part of the setting." Winona Knits supports the community through corporate sponsorship of events such as the American Birkebeiner Cross Country Ski Race and the Sugar Loaf Classic Bicycle Tour.

The company is also committed to wildlife and habitat preservation. The Common Loon appears as a part of the corporate logo. Winona Knits sponsors the Minnesota Loon Festival and works to support LoonWatch, a preservation and education program of the Sigurd Olsen Environmental Institute.

Wykoff

Wykoff, located just southeast of Rochester, is a small town created, in essence, by the Southern Minnesota Railroad Company. In the late 1800s three separate fires destroyed the majority of the buildings that made up Wykoff. The resilience of this town was apparent then, just as it is now. The citizens constantly are looking to improve their quiet town for themselves, as well as for visitors. Historic buildings line the streets of Wykoff.

Favorites are the *Historic Wykoff Jail, Ed's Museum, Doh's House,* and *The Hour Shop.* The Annual Fall Festival is held in September, with the locals providing entertainment as well as sponsored tournaments for volleyball, softball, and a dance. December brings *"Christmas in Wykoff,"* consisting of a large craft show in the Community Hall, a visit from Santa, and a Christmas Ball held in the old high school gym. Wykoff offers pleasant surroundings as the "gateway to Forestville State Park."

For more information on Wykoff contact:
WYKOFF
c/o Lila Eickhoff
101 Centennial Street E.
R.R. 1, P.O. Box 6
Wykoff, MN 55990
(507) 352-4011

CLOCK & SCULPTURE STUDIO

■ HOUR SHOP
138 N. Silver
Wykoff, MN 55990
Tel: (507) 352-4070 or 352-4043
Hrs: Open by appointment only

Time is a concept dealing with the order and duration of events. Most have wished for that particular moment when "time could stand still," and as we busy ourselves day-to-day we don't seem to have time for anything. Jim Borden, sculptor and designer, hopes that his work will make people reflect on this concept of time.

Time for Jim Borden is universal motion; the seasonal cycles and flow of change. "I want to communicate something about time that speaks to our lives," Borden said. "If my sculptures give people a chance to reflect on life and how much time we have to live our lives, then it's saying something worth saying." Borden's Timeshapes are abstract time-keeping mechanisms made entirely out of wood using black walnut, oak, cherry, maple, or other beautiful hardwoods. They are clocks and also moving sculptures. Timeshapes move majestically, yet whimsically, providing an almost hypnotic effect on people who stop to watch it. They keep time like any clock, yet they invite the observer to step out of the rat race of time; to pause and enjoy the present moment. The clock is run by a spring or weight and can be self-winding. Other unusual timekeepers designed by Borden are ornate wooden mantelpieces and staid grandfather clocks. Among Borden's custom-designed Timeshapes, as they are called, are 19th century German clocks, cuckoo clocks, and other antique clocks. Other kinds of wood scuptures as well as unusual pieces designed for churches are also created at Hour Shop.

Patterns and blueprints are not used to design these magnificent clocks. Genuine woodworking talents and imagination for mechanical motion and movement are demonstrated in these unique timekeepers.

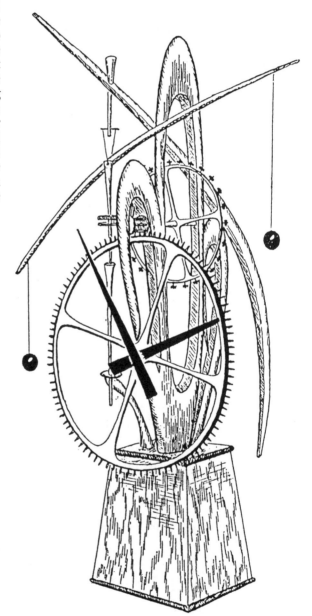

Zumbrota

Z umbrota, located in the Zumbro Valley, is the hub of Goodhue County. The residents of Zumbrota have worked hard over the years to develop a warm, traditional, and prosperous community. Zumbrota sits between the cities of Minneapolis/St. Paul and Rochester on Highway 52. This location makes it ideal for residents and businesses. The *Old Covered Bridge* is the only original of its kind still standing in the state and is a popular attraction. This bridge was built in 1869 from white oak and wooden pegs. The residents efforts paid off in 1970 with the creation of the *Covered Bridge Park* so the bridge could be moved and preserved for all. *Sherwood Forest* is another scenic attraction in Zumbrota, complete with walking trails, hayrides, live music on Saturday nights, and fossil hunting in the *Zumbrota Clay Pits*. The Goodhue county fair is held every year the first week of August.

For more information on Zumbrota, contact:
CITY OF ZUMBROTA
P.O. Box 158
Zumbrota, MN 55992
(507)732-7318

R ESTAURANT & MOTEL

■ THE COVERED BRIDGE RESTAURANT, LOUNGE & MOTEL
1439 North Star Drive (Just off Highway 52)
Zumbrota, MN 55992
Tel: (507) 732-7321 (restaurant)
    (507) 732-7852 or (800) 848-8888 (motel)
Restaurant Hrs: Daily 11 a.m. until closing (Hours may vary)
All major credit cards are accepted.

Located 20 miles north of Rochester, the AAA-rated Covered Bridge Restaurant is named after Minnesota's only remaining covered bridge, located only a mile away. The restaurant is a family business owned and operated by Corky and Joan Falk, and their daughter Shari — all actively involved in daily operations.

In the restaurant is a collection of antique light fixtures, historical pictures of the Zumbrota area, wildlife plates and prints, and old guns. Tastefully displayed, they combine to create an intriguing and unusual decor. But there's more than decorations, there's food — and plenty of it. The house specialties are batter fried cheese curd appetizers, a large salad bar, prime rib and barbequed ribs. Live dinner music is provided by Gene Chermey on piano Friday or Saturday nights. A lunch menu is also available and features two daily specials, including homemade soups and desserts.

Son Allan operates the new Super 8 Motel next door to the restaurant. The motel opened in 1990, and features 30 guest rooms, all with telephones and remote control cable TV. A waterbed is available, along with two large king-size rooms. The remaining rooms feature either a queen-size bed or two extra long double-size beds. Non-smoking rooms are also available upon request, and pets are allowed with special permission. Each morning, guests wake up to fresh coffee and complimentary breakfast with toast or English muffins served in the lobby.

Minnesota History Afield

by John G. Shepard

F irst came the bonanza of the fur trade. Then came logging and farming. By the time the mineral rush hit northern Minnesota at the end of the nineteenth century, there was a pattern established in the way these enterprises worked themselves out on the land.

The early fur traders encountered boreal forests, lakes, and rivers that spread northward, it seemed, to infinity. The trading empire established by the North West and Hudson Bay Companies was equally extensive, stretching from Montreal in the east to the Pacific and Arctic Oceans in the west and north. To fulfill their contracts, thousands of French-Canadian voyageurs labored under excruciating conditions, often carrying loads of more than 180 pounds over difficult portages and paddling their bark canoes 16 hours each day. And for their trouble, these laborers earned enough money in a year's time to be able to purchase one or two of the fur hats produced by the beaver pelts they struggled to transport halfway around the world.

The annual voyageurs' rendezvous that took place during the height of the fur trade on Lake Superior's shore at the Grand Portage log fort is brought back to life each summer. Reenactments of the trading and celebrations at the Grand Portage

National Monument often coincide with an annual pow-wow on the adjacent Grand Portage Indian Reservation in late August. The reconstructed North West Company wintering post at Pine City is Minnesota's second outstanding historic fur trade site. A North West Company partner and a small group of voyageurs spent the winter of 1804-5 in this rough-hewn log post trading with local Ojibwa bands. Today, entertaining and informative costumed guides with a full assortment of artifacts convincingly transport visitors back to the early 19th century.

Europe's seemingly insatiable appetite for furs finally declined by the mid-19th century. In the fur trade's aftermath came an onrush of homesteading settlers that coincided with a clear-cut logging boom to forever transfigure the face of Minnesota's forests. In half a century, millions of acres of towering red and white pine in the North and hardwood species in the central part of the state fell to the sawers' blade.

The best learning opportunities on Minnesota's logging history are found at two sites — one related to the northern pineries, the other in the heart of what was called the Big Woods.

The Minnesota Historical Society-run Forest History Center in Grand Rapids combines a modern interpretive center with an exactingly recreated logging camp, circa 1900. Displays at the interpretive center focus on the history of the relationships that Minnesotans — both Native American and of European descent — maintained with their forests over the centuries. The coarse and bawdy lifestyles of the men and women (there were a few) who made a living bringing down the big pine are brought to life in the nearby Northwoods Logging Company camp.

Typically, when a homesteading settler staked out a plot in the wilderness, the first trees cleared were used to build a log house. Then, as time passed and civilization made sufficient inroads, someone would set up a sawmill and the old log dwellings slowly gave way to "stick built," or wood-frame, constructions.

This process has been well preserved at the Geldner Sawmill — a steam-powered mill that has been scrupulously maintained at its original location a few miles southeast of Cleveland in central Minnesota. The second Sunday each month, June through August, you'll find smoke billowing out of the mill's tall stack as interpretive guides get the big circular saw whirring.

Iron ore mining in Minnesota followed a similar path to those blazed by preceding industries. And it is a path that can be traced by visiting two historic sites along one of the world's greatest iron ranges: the Mesabi. Minnesota's first, deepest, and richest iron mine was established in 1898 by a couple of local entrepreneurs who discovered chunks of ore so pure that in their raw state they could be welded together.

Tours of the Soudan mine, just east of Tower, involve a three-minute ride in a rattling elevator down to the mine's lowest level, 2,341 feet below the surface. Here a small train takes visitors down a horizontal tunnel, or "drift," to arrive at a recreated work site. Mannequins are posed ready to operate deafening carbide-tipped air-powered drills, their work illuminated only by the headlamps they wore.

As the iron ore industry grew in Minnesota, the underground mining techniques used at the Soudan mine and the hard hematite ore that it yielded proved to be the exception. Most Minnesota ore was of a rare powdery consistency that baffled early prospectors. It quickly became apparent that the most efficient way to gather this ore was to use strip mining techniques that have dramatically altered the appearance of the landscape.

At the western end of the Mesabi near Calumet, the Department of Natural Resources has preserved the Hill Annex open pit mine as an historic site. Tours include a visit to an interpretive center — where exhibits illuminate the changing technologies and lifestyles of the miners who labored from 1903 until 1978 — and a bus tour into the gaping maw of the now inactive pit. Like the industries that preceded it, open pit iron mining's boom eventually led to bust as the extractable resource was finally depleted.

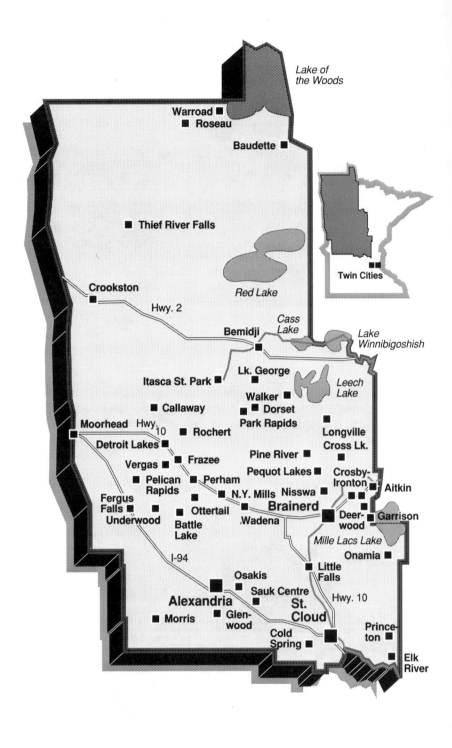

Lake of
the Woods

Warroad ■
■ Roseau

Baudette ■

Thief River Falls ■

Twin Cities

Crookston ■
Hwy. 2

Red Lake

Cass
Lake

Bemidji ■

Lake
Winnibigoshish

Lk. George ■
Itasca St. Park ■

Leech
Lake

Walker ■
■ Dorset
Park Rapids

Callaway ■

Moorhead Hwy.
10 ■ Rochert

Longville ■
Cross Lk. ■

Detroit Lakes ■
Vergas ■ ■ Frazee

Pine River ■

■ Pelican
Rapids

■ Perham

Pequot Lakes ■

Crosby-
Ironton

■ ■ Aitkin

■ N.Y. Mills

Nisswa ■

Fergus
Falls ■   ■
Underwood

■ Ottertail
Battle
Lake

Brainerd

Deer-
wood

■ Garrison

.Wadena

Mille Lacs Lake

I-94

Onamia ■

Osakis ■

■ Little
Falls

Alexandria

■ Sauk Centre

Hwy. 10

■ Morris

■ Glen-
wood

St.
Cloud

Princeton ■

Cold
Spring

Elk
River

HEARTLAND

by John G. Shepard

I f there is one geographic fact that argues for Minnesota's prominence in the heartland of the nation, it is that the greatest river in the land rises from its soil. And Itasca State Park, which since 1891 has sheltered the Mississippi's source from encroaching civilization, is a setting that delivers even more than what you might hope for from such a place.

The Father of Waters begins its epic southern journey by flowing northward out of Lake Itasca as a humble little creek. Dense forests contain stands of virgin pine (the park boasts the state's largest white and red pines on record) that emanate as much serenity and grandeur as a cathedral. Even the park's buildings, built of huge pine logs, have a larger-than-life quality about them, and the bracing air itself seems thick with the site's historical and geographic significance.

Historically inclined travelers will also be intrigued by the region's strong relationship to Viking tradition. In Alexandria, ethnic pride has given rise to the prominent display of a mysterious stone chiselled with an archaic runic script that has been embroiled in controversy since it was brought into public view in 1898.

It was in that year that a Swedish farmer, Olaf Ohman, claimed to have discovered the Kensington Runestone entwined in the roots of a tree on his land. A Viking historian, Hjalmar Holand, translated the script as being an account of a group of Viking adventurers traveling through the region in 1362. You can decide for yourself whether or not this story is plausible — and whether Alexandria thus deserves the self-proclaimed title, "Birthplace of America" — by examining the Runestone firsthand at the Alexandria Chamber of Commerce's historical museum.

Travelers of a literary bent will find much to explore at the birthplace of America's first Nobel laureate for literature, Sinclair Lewis. Sauk Centre was the site of what biographers have called an "unhappy boyhood" for Lewis. The town was also the fictionalized setting for several of the author's best-known novels, in which he put forth a lively critique of America's small town, middle-class values. Landmarks that occupy the pages of *Main Street* and other Lewis books can be seen much as they were described by Lewis early in this century. Other things in Sauk Centre have changed, however. Today, signs on I-94 point the way to the Sinclair Lewis Interpretive Center, and what was once the intersection of Third Avenue and Main Street is now the junction of The Original Main Street and Sinclair Lewis Avenue. Lewis's boyhood home is also open for tours.

Finally, before you leave Minnesota's heartland, be sure to pay a visit to the birthplace of one of this country's greatest aviators and most intriguing citizens — Charles A. Lindbergh Jr. This reserved Minnesota Swede was an explorer, inventor, and a champion of the technology that carried him, solo, across the Atlantic to world fame in 1927. At the same time, he worked as a devoted humanitarian and prophetic advocate of the natural environment. His restored family home and an excellent museum are found along the banks of the Mississippi in the town of Little Falls.

Aitkin

F or half a century, Aitkin was the gateway to the northwestern Minnesota frontier. From the 1870s to the early 1920s, eager travelers and settlers would arrive in Aitkin by the newly built railway, or by coach, and board a riverboat to venture further north along the Mississippi. Eventually, the riverboat traffic ground to a halt and the logging industry, which depended on the river to float timber downstream, fell into leaner times. Still, the town wasn't abandoned to suffer the fate of so many other river towns, but instead matured to become the self-supporting city it is today. In addition to the travel and lumber industries, smaller manufacturing companies such as Woodland Container, Aitkin Iron Works, and Mille Lacs Wild Rice provide the city with a diverse economic base.

ATTRACTIONS

Production of wild rice — the tasty seeds of an aquatic grass — is a natural in a city surrounded by no less than *365 lakes,* all within half an hour's drive from downtown. The lakes are also the main attractions for travelers, who flock to the town to enjoy the many fine resorts in the area. Those who make it to town on fishing season opener in May can participate in the *wackiest fishing hat competition,* when a prize is awarded to the person wearing the strangest and most imaginatively decorated fishing hat. When the bass season opens a few weeks later, the town puts on the *Bass Super Angling Saturday* — an event featuring celebrities and, of course, a bass fishing contest. Apart from fishing, the fascinating heritage of the town is celebrated in a variety of ways, including the annual *Riverboat Heritage Days* in July. During three days of family fun, the festival features a parade, pancake breakfast, stock car races, chainsaw demonstrations, and other events. Historic or traditional shops such as the art deco-style *Rialto Theatre,* the gift shop *The Green Bough,* the new and used book seller *Booktowne* and the country art shop *Northern Images Gallery* also contribute to keeping the river town spirit alive.

For more information on Aitkin, contact:
AITKIN AREA CHAMBER OF COMMERCE
P.O. Box 127
Aitkin, MN 56431-0127
(218) 927-2316

A CCOMMODATIONS & RESTAURANT

■ 40 CLUB INN AND RESTAURANT
Highway 210 W.
Aitkin, MN 56431
Tel: (218)927-2903
Hrs: Open year-round
Visa, MasterCard, and Discover Card are accepted.

The 40 Club Inn and Restaurant was built in 1940 on 40 acres of property one mile west of downtown Aitkin. The inn addition is new, just opening in the spring of 1991. The food in the restaurant attracts visitors from all over the area. Combined with the new inn, patrons can now make a weekend of a pleasant dining experience.

The Sunday and Thursday buffets feature several different entrees with all of the trimmings. The broasted chicken and prime rib dinners are very popular on Saturday evenings. For a visit during the week, diners enjoy the daily noon lunch buffet, which includes the salad bar. Each Valentines Day the lobster feed attracts couples from all over the county. Other menu favorites are the famous 40 Club Chicken, the king-size T-bone, and the Canadian walleye.

The 40 Club Inn has 27 rooms featuring remote cable television, hot tub, sauna, and double-, queen- or king-size beds. The inn also has a fabulous bridal suite with a jacuzzi in the room. The rooms are decorated with a Southwestern theme. Meeting and banquet rooms are also available at The 40 Club Inn and a continental breakfast is served each morning in the lobby.

D EPARTMENT STORE

■ BUTLER'S
301 Minnesota Ave. N.
Aitkin, MN 56431
Tel: (218) 927-2185
Hrs: Mon. - Fri. 9 a.m. - 5:30 p.m., Sat. 9 a.m. - 5 p.m.
Discover, Visa, and MasterCard are accepted.

Butler's Department Store in Aitkin is located in the former Aitkin Opera House. Built in 1903, this building was home to the opera house, general store, buggy warehouse, barber shop, hardware store, and a bank. The original one-stop shop. The Aitkin Opera House hosted vaudeville acts and traveling theatre troupes, as well as hometown groups. Judy Garland performed on its stage as a child.

Butler's is a store with a museum-like quality. Historical and Victorian artifacts are on display throughout its interior. Established in 1947 by the Butler family, it is still a pillar of the community as a retail dry goods store. Butler's attracts customers from all over the state because of the low prices featured on merchandise. Butler's carries a full line of men's, women's, and children's clothing. There are also three fabric departments carrying upholstery, drapery, and quilting fabric. A camera department with full accessories and a bargain basement are also featured in the store.

The friendly atmosphere and helpful employees enhance the small town shopping experience. Relics and antiques displayed in the store offer an extra added attraction that preserves the history of Aitkin. Competitive pricing and good quality have kept Butler's in the retail business for more than 40 years.

GIFT STORE

■THE GREEN BOUGH
22nd Street N.E.
Aitkin, MN 56431
Tel: (218) 927-3419 or (800) 845-ROSE
Hrs: Mon. - Fri. 9:30 a.m. - 5:30 p.m.
    Sat. 8 a.m. - 5:30 p.m., Sun. 11 a.m. - 3 p.m.
Visa, MasterCard, and AmEx are accepted.

The Green Bough in Aitkin started out in a garage when owner Trudy Gross decided to expand on what she had learned in a night class. Currently The Green Bough manufactures up to 3,000 wreaths each year, which are shipped throughout the country. This store caters to corporate customers as well as tourists that

stop to shop. Every item in the store is discounted, allowing shoppers to leave with an armful of merchandise for what a bag full would cost.

The Green Bough built its reputation on the beautiful wreaths created in the store, but there are many other items available as well. A complete line of dolls from all over the world is found on the shelves. Dolls ranging from basic to collectors items and priced all the way up to $2,000 offer an expansive selection. "Antique Corner" features fine antique items and furniture pieces for the novice or the collector. Custom flower arrangements are designed daily with the customers able to contribute their ideas on the design. A year-round Christmas display features ornaments and original holiday arrangements.

Hunting season is an especially busy time for the store, followed by the bustle of Christmas shoppers. The Green Bough has expanded Aitkin-made articles to a national level. The World Trade Center in Dallas, TX carries American-made crafts offered by some of the 15,000 distributors. In Dallas, The Green Bough emphasizes freeze-dried flowers and arrangements shipped to other stores throughout the country.

Alexandria

I n 1889, an Alexandria farmer discovered a flat stone with strange markings locked within the roots of an aspen. The markings turned out to be runic inscriptions, later translated as a record of a Viking expedition through Hudson Bay and down the Red River in 1362. Although controversy still rages surrounding the authenticity of the runestone, true Alexandria patriots have no doubts. To them, Alexandria was the birthplace of America, visited by Europeans more than a century before Columbus set his foot on what he believed was India.

ATTRACTIONS

The strange legend of the Viking expedition has been immortalized in a giant 28-foot-tall statue of a Viking — *"Big Ole"* — standing next to the **Kensington Runestone Museum,** which houses the runestone along with displays of Indian artifacts and antique guns. Nearby is the fascinating **Fort Alexandria Agricultural Museum,** complete with a 1917 fire engine, antique cars and farm machinery, log cabins, an 1885 school house, and a general store filled with old tools and implements. But Alexandria is not only for history buffs. It's a city of 8,000, with the services and opportunities offered by a middle-sized community, such as large employers (3M Company, Douglas Machines, and Fingerhut Manufacturing Co., among others), and arts and entertainment. In Alexandria, visitors find everything from the professional theater company **Theatre L'Homme Dieu** to a modern shopping mall. Recreational possibilities center on the many lakes in the area, serviced by a number of small and friendly "Ma and Pa" resorts. Foremost in the city's resort community, however, is the great **Andes Tower Hills,** a ski area with two triple chairlifts, 11 downhill runs and 20 kilometers of groomed cross-country trails located 15 miles west of the city. Golfers will not want to forget the **Resorters Golf Tournament** held annually in July at the **Alexandria Golf Club.**

For more information on Alexandria, contact:
ALEXANDRIA LAKES AREA RESORT & VISITORS BUREAU
206 Broadway
Alexandria, MN 56308
(218) 763-3161 or (800) 235-9441

A NTIQUES

■BUD'S BARN ANTIQUES
(15 miles north of Alexandria on Hwy 29)
Parkers Prairie, MN 56361
Tel: (218) 338-6166
Hrs: Open daily 9 a.m. - 5 p.m.
Visa and MasterCard are accepted.

A love of antiques built this business near Alexandria. Shirley Loveland and her sons, Richard and Steven, sell an extensive line of antiques and collectibles to people from all over the country. Bud's Barn Antiques was opened in 1971. Shirley started in the antique business by attending auctions with her father while still a young girl. As her experience, knowledge, and appreciation for antiques grew, so did a profitable business.

Red Wing Stoneware is a speciality of Bud's Barn, carrying one of the best collections in the state. Richard Loveland is an expert on the stoneware as well as duck decoys and antique fishing lures and gear. An ample selection of furniture items is available, finished or unfinished, for those interested in handcrafting their own furniture. Antique jewelry, cast iron toys, glassware, Norwegian collectibles, and antique clocks offer further intrigue to the collector.

If Shirley doesn't have it in stock, she often knows where to find it. Living in the area all her life has given Shirley valuable insight on who has what, its authenticity, and how much it's worth. The two barns that comprise Bud's Barn enhance the antique shoppers' experience by lending a rustic environment — this is evidenced by the many customers that return year after year.

B ED & BREAKFASTS

■ THE CARRINGTON HOUSE
R.R. 5, P.O. Box 88
Alexandria, MN 56308
Tel: (612) 846-7400
Hrs: Open year-round
Visa and MasterCard are accepted.

The Carrington House Bed and Breakfast Inn is a stately mansion on the shores of Lake Carlos. First built in 1911 as a summer home, The Carrington House opened as a bed and breakfast in 1988. There are four rooms in the main house and a seasonal cottage available May through October, which features a double whirlpool.

Antiques and family heirlooms adorn the interior of this mansion. Ceilings reaching 12 feet add to the spacious and elegant feel in the living room. A four-season porch overlooking Lake Carlos features a spectacular view of the area. Wood floors run throughout the house, and the friendly atmosphere and personal attention fill every room.

Right outside is a private lakeshore with a sand bottom for swimming and fishing. Lake Carlos is a clean, clear spring-fed lake in the Alexandria Chain of Lakes. The surrounding bluffs around Lake Carlos offer hiking and cross-country ski and snowmobile trails. The Alexandria Golf Club is located just a mile and a half down the road and Theatre L'Homme Dieu is also nearby. A full breakfast is served each morning with juice, fresh fruit, coffee or tea, various egg dishes, fresh rolls or muffins, and cereal. Breakfasts are served in the dining room or can be served on the lakeside porch.

■ THE ROBARDS HOUSE
518 Lincoln Ave. W.
Alexandria, MN 56308
Tel: (612) 763-4073
Hrs: Open year-round
Visa and MasterCard are accepted.

The Robards House on Lake Winona in Alexandria is a Victorian bed and breakfast that opened for business in April of 1990. Originally this 101-year-old home belonged to Oscar Robards, a man who stopped in Minnesota on the way to California in search of gold. Accompanied by his brother George, the two stopped in Fergus Falls and decided to settle in the northland, altering their original plan to pan for gold in the West. The brothers moved on to Alexandria to open and manage a hardware store, and there they stayed.

Each of the four rooms in The Robards House is named after families of historical significance to Alexandria. The LeRoy Room has a private bath, dressing room, and small porch with a view of Lake Winona. Pederson's Room is the bridal chamber, offering an exquisite view of the grounds as well as the lake. This room also has a handcrafted king-size bed and private bath. The Cowing Room has a view of the grounds, private bath, and full-size bed. The Kinkead Room has twin beds and is furnished with antiques. The Penthouse Suite on the third floor is truly fashioned for romance. It has a private patio with a view of the surrounding scenery, a sunken living room, dining area, mini-library, and a private bathroom.

Fresh ground coffee, homemade rolls, breads, and orange juice are served for breakfast each morning. A cookbook from the early 1900s was found in the house, and some of the original recipes are still used. The Robards House is located near downtown Alexandria, several golf courses, and any number of lakes in the area that provide activity for summer and winter.

$\boxed{\text{E}}$CONOMY LODGING

■ANDRIA MOTEL
312 Spruce Street
Alexandria, MN 56308
Tel: (612)763-6651
Hrs: Open year-round
Visa, MasterCard, and Discover are accepted.

The Andria Motel was originally built in the 1950s and named after the original owner's daughter, Andria. This motel offers economy lodging with a personal touch. A favorite with the visiting fisherman and snowmobilers, The Andria has 12 rooms available with a continental breakfast served each morning directly to each room.

Family rooms are available for families or couples; outdoor barbecue grills and picnic tables are also available on the floral-covered grounds. Color cable TV including HBO and Midwest Sports Channel is also provided in each room. The Andria is a member of Encore and Travel Sense Travel Clubs and is also a member of the Minnesota Motel Association. It is conveniently located on Highway 27, only 11 blocks from downtown Alexandria. The owners and employees are always willing to lend a helping hand or some helpful advice on sight-seeing.

GIFT SHOPS

■ FROM THE HEART
522 Broadway
Alexandria, MN 56308
Tel: (612) 762-1754
Hrs: Mon. - Sat. 9 a.m. - 5:30 p.m. (Thurs. 9 a.m. - 9 p.m.)
Discover, Visa, and MasterCard are accepted.

From the Heart occupies what was once, at the turn of the century, an opera house. The store opened 16 years ago, moving to its current downtown location in 1989. The goal of the owners, Nan and Gary Folsom, is to carry as many diverse and unusual items as possible. From the Heart stocks many items that no other outlet in the area carries.

Hummel figurines and imported Anri woodcarvings of Italy are extra special items carried in the store. Fine gifts and collectibles from Swarovski, Lladro, Dept 56, Jan Hagara, David Winters, Cairn Gnomes, and Crabtree & Evelyn are also stocked. Alternative greeting cards, candies, and gift baskets appeal to the lighter side. From the Heart maintains a bridal registry as well as offering selections of china, glassware, linens, candles, and potpourri. Souvenirs abound for the summer traveler with items such as T-shirts and Minnesota gifts featuring the ever popular loon.

Custom orders, free gift wrapping, and shipping services are available. From miniature figurines to full-size furniture, treasures are everywhere in all sizes. Wonderful items for everyone are housed under the roof of this former opera house that is From the Heart.

■ MY FAVORITE THINGS
515 Broadway
Alexandria, MN 56308
Tel: (612) 762-8750
Hrs: Mon. - Fri. 9 a.m. - 7 p.m., Sat. 9 a.m. - 5:30 p.m.
(Memorial Day to Labor Day, Sun. 11 a.m. - 3 p.m.)
Visa and MasterCard are accepted.

Imagine finding a shop where visitors felt they could take a step back in time just by entering the store; a place that carried a wide assortment of gift items in a blend of Victorian and country tradition. There they would find My Favorite Things.

Two artistic women opened the shop in October of 1989 and developed the inventory around their own talents. Vicki Johnston

creates hand-poured, hand-painted porcelain collector dolls, which are found on the shelves. Ginny Kluver does folk art painting and makes Santa Clauses in every style, shape, and size imaginable. The artists combined their skills in making a Victorian carousel. My Favorite Things is home to the largest doll house in central Minnesota. There is also an ample assortment of Teddy Bears and other stuffed animals to choose from, including those by Steiff and Raikes. Each person working at My Favorite Things is involved in craft making of some sort. The lower level of the store, "My Favorite Dungeon," features artistic crafts and a complete line of craft supplies. Other delights to be found include gourmet foods and a candy case displaying a variety of truffles, assorted chocolates, hard candies, gourmet jelly beans, and sugar-free candy.

My Favorite Things staff can help assemble custom-designed gift baskets, and offer gift wrapping and shipping services. Visitors to this charming shop may find it to be a place "where the romance of Valentine's Day lingers all year long."

◼ GIFTS & HOME DECOR

■ THE FARMHOUSE
609 N. Nokomis
Alexandria, MN 56308
Tel: (612)762-2243
Hrs: Mon. - Sat 10 a.m. - 5 p.m., Sun. 1 p.m. - 4 p.m.
All major credit cards are accepted.

The Farmhouse Country Store was created by Kay Pring after she and her husband Orleigh purchased the Clarno homestead, which had been an actual working farm. The city of Alexandria sprouted up around this homestead, providing a central location to the heart of the city. Kay was one of the first to create a store within a house. This concept has become quite common in the area, and Kay has offered her consulting advice on several ventures.

The Farmhouse is designed and accessorized like a real home with nine rooms, giving a real perspective of how things fit into a home. Holiday seasons, particularly Christmas and Easter, reflect the spirit and beauty of special themes. Featured themes for Christmas are Victorian, country, and traditional. In addition to the particular holiday features, The Farmhouse also carries a large doll selection, quilts, wall shelves, and pictures. Decorating ideas abound throughout the interior with authentic hand-crafted Amish furniture and unique floral arrangements for both tabletops and walls.

Gift ideas permeate the mind with a selection of brass and pewter accessories. Baskets in all shapes and sizes as well as collector plates, dishes, placemats, and tablerunners for the home are on display. For the children an array of books, toys, and ornaments are available. Interior designers Gail and Kardy are ready with creative suggestions for all interiors. Fourteen years' worth of experience and ideas are infectious within The Farmhouse.

R ESORT

■ ARROWWOOD-A RADISSON RESORT
2100 Arrowwood Lane
Alexandria, MN 56308
Tel: (612) 762-1124 or (800) 333-3333
Hrs: Open year-round
All major credit cards are accepted.

Halfway between the Twin Cities and Moorhead on I-94, nestled into 450 acres of rolling grasslands and lakeshore, is Arrowwood-A Radisson Resort. The only Minnesota resort to receive AAA's Four Diamond rating, the Arrowwood-Radisson offers more activities in a week than some resorts offer in a year. Couples, families, and business groups will find this the perfect place on Lake Darling to play, work, or both. Elegant, comfortable rooms, restaurants, ample conference-banquet space, pool, sauna, and whirlpool are just some of the indoor amenities. Outdoor lovers will find plenty to do all year-round, including but not limited to horseback riding, fishing, boating, hiking, tennis, archery, skiing, snowmobiling, and sleigh rides, not to mention the 18-hole golf course. Full-time activities coordinators stay busy running Camp Arrowwood, which provides a day of activities for children four through 12 and daily activities for all guests.

Arrowwood-A Radisson Resort, originally known as Darling Dude Ranch, opened as Arrowwood Lodge in 1971. Five years later the Radisson began to manage the property. It is apparent that management is in tip-top shape, judging by the beautifully tended lawns, the well-equipped conference rooms, and the courteous staff. Arrowwood-A Radisson Resort received the Radisson's Presidents Award for 1990.

"One of the prettiest dining rooms in Minnesota" is the Lake Cafe, according to *Mpls./St. Paul* magazine. Sumptuous American and Swedish cuisine, served as an entree to Lake Darling's gorgeous sunsets, might in itself just be worth a trip to Arrowwood-A Radisson Resort.

R ESTAURANTS

■ BRONC'S ON BROADWAY

319 Broadway
Alexandria, MN 56308
Tel: (612) 763-3999
Hrs: Tues. - Sat. (lunch) 11 a.m. - 2 p.m. (dinner) 5 p.m. - 10 p.m.
All major credit cards are accepted.

From the day Bronc's on Broadway opened its doors to the public in 1986, it's lived up to its motto: "Good food done good." The restaurant's owners and operators, Richard and Janet Wiles, share a love for quality food and quality dining, and they want their customers to have nothing but the best.

Richard and Janet find the freshest meats and poultry available, and cut it themselves to prepare their sandwiches and dinners. Whenever possible, they purchase organically grown produce from local farms. They even make their own salad dressings, bake their own dinner rolls and salt sticks, and prepare their own desserts. They will also accommodate special dietary needs by sauteeing entrees in olive oil rather than in butter, or by using skim rather than whole milk. In their salads, they use only cholesterol-free mayonnaise; and for vegetarians, they'll prepare a medley of seasonal fresh vegetables. Richard and Janet will do all they can to prepare your meal to fit your specifications.

But food is not the only attraction at Bronc's. While guests dine, for example, on Miltona Bay Clam Chowder, Bronc's Burger,

Seafood Fettucini (made with fresh seafood), or other mouthwatering entrees, they enjoy the comfortable surroundings. The restaurant is a renovated home from the 1900s, furnished with antiques from across the country. The bar is imported from England, while the classic fireplace mantlepiece hails from Colorado. Built around the turn of the century, the piano is as old as it looks. And the light fixtures are restored antiques, rewired to fit today's electrical standards. Indeed, Bronc's on Broadway offers "good food done good" — with an ambiance that makes it taste even better.

■**INTERLACHEN INN**
County Road 42 N.
Alexandria, MN 56308
Tel: (612) 846-1051
Hrs: Open daily 5 p.m. til close
Visa and MasterCard are accepted.

The Interlachen Inn is tucked away in the pine trees just north of Alexandria between Lake Carlos and Lake L'homme Dieu. It is a cozy cottage that features a full dining menu at reasonable prices. Jim Pennie is the owner as well as the chef and pays close attention to each entree as it is prepared. The customers at Interlachen receive the finest food and service. Traditional entrees such as prime rib of beef and a full assortment of steaks are favorites with the customers. Fresh walleye pike is served either batter-fried or broiled. For light eaters there are special selections to accommodate their appetites. For heartier appetites, the jumbo shrimp or delicious barbeque ribs are just the ticket. For a quiet, intimate atmosphere and scrumptious food, the trip through the woods is well worth it.

Baudette

Once a major link in the fur trade route, Baudette is today known for another natural resource: walleyes. Every year thousands of eager fishermen flock to this quiet northwoods outpost to try their luck with the fighting fish in the one-million-acre Lake of the Woods, generally regarded as the best walleye lake in Minnesota. A wilderness paradise with 14,000 islands and 65,000 miles of beaches and rocky shoreline located on Baudette's doorstep, *Lake of the Woods* boasts the longest walleye season in the state, the largest bag limit and, most importantly, the largest average size of walleye of any large lake in the state. To serve visitors to the area, a host of resorts offer services ranging from guided charter boats, motor boat rental, fish cleaning and packing, to fly-in services to remote spots or shuttle service to heated ice fishing houses. An interesting spot is the *Northwest Angle,* a peninsula in the northwestern part of the lake cut off from the rest of the United States by the Canadian province of Manitoba. The northernmost point in the lower 48, the Northwest Angle features several resorts. In addition to the many varied parks in the Baudette area — including *Zippel Bay State Park, Williams Community Park,* and *Bay Front Park* — the *Lake of the Woods Historical Museum* has a large display of local historical artifacts, and the restored *Fort St. Charles* offers a tantalizing glimpse into the pioneer days. For the children — or those young of heart — there's the *Williams Children's Theater.* Events in the area are numerous and varied, including the *Lake of the Woods County Fair, Old Blueberry Fest, Fall Fest, Back Home Days,* and the fascinating *Days Threshing Show,* where visitors can observe the time-honored art of grain threshing.

For more information on Baudette, contact:
LAKE OF THE WOODS AREA TOURISM BUREAU
P.O. Box 518
Baudette, MN 56623
(800) 382-FISH (in Minnesota)
(800) 351-FISH (outside Minnesota)

R ESORT

■SCHUSTER'S RED CARPET LODGE
R.R. 1, P.O. Box 165
Baudette, MN 56623
Tel: (218) 634-2412 or (800) 243-2412
Hrs: 7 a.m. - 10 p.m. daily

Near Lake of the Woods, along 400 feet of shoreline on the Rainy River, lies Schuster's Red Carpet Lodge for summer and winter fishing. When Betty and Tom Schuster bought the lodge in 1974, their goal was to make it "a home away from home any time of the year."

One-, two-, and three-bedroom housekeeping cabins and fourplexes are settled among birch and pine trees. All are fully carpeted, completely modern, with fully-equipped kitchens and cable TV. The lodge itself has white siding with red trim and a deck, as well as private loading docks. Meals are served family-style in the dining area, which overlooks the river. American Plan meals and pack lunches are available by reservation. A short order menu and liquor bar are also available. Services include fully-equipped charter boats, package plans for two-day trips Sunday through Thursday, angling and reef fishing, bombardier service, private dock slips, RV hookups, and launch trips.

Bemidji

L egend has it that the giant lumberjack Paul Bunyan once roamed the Bemidji area. Already at birth, he was larger than most babies, demanding the milk from an entire dairy herd for every bottle meal. Later on in life, he made a spectacular lumberjack team with his giant ox, Babe, who inadvertently formed a lake everywhere he stepped. Today, geologists claim that the lakes were formed by retreating glaciers, but in the late 1800s when logging was the main industry, the legend of Paul Bunyan was often recited in the many camps dotting the dense woods surrounding Lake Bemidji. Although the logging industry eventually faltered, Bemidji went on to become a regional retail and manufacturing center of 11,000 residents.

ATTRACTIONS

Whether Paul Bunyan's ox Babe created the lakes in the Bemidji area, or not, they still form the nucleus of an attractive park system. Including no less than 11 parks — foremost among these the 100-year-old *Lake Itasca State Park,* site of the headwaters of the Mississippi — the city is another excellent springboard for a lake-related getaway. Public beaches abound, as well, both in *Diamond Point, Nymore,* and *Cameron parks.* For those visiting in the winter, the *Buena Vista Ski Area* offers excellent skiing opportunities on 14 ski runs and 25 kilometers of cross-country trails. To ensure that visitors don't miss the city's connection with the Bunyan legend, the local theater company — Minnesota's oldest professional summer theater — bears the name *Paul Bunyan Playhouse,* two giant *statues of Paul and his ox* loom above the shore of Lake Bemidji near the *Paul Bunyan Amusement Park,* and the city's tourist information center is located (where else?) in the *Paul Bunyan House.* The Paul Bunyan House also features the intriguing *Fireplace of the States* built with stones from every state in the country. Also in the same building, visitors can frequent the *Historical and Wildlife Museum* with its displays of Ojibwa Indian crafts and artifacts, logging mementoes, and pioneer artifacts. In the same vein, *Pioneer Park* in nearby Solway is an authentic working museum of pioneer life. In addition to settler history, the city is also an excellent vantage point from which to explore the fascinating local Native American culture. Often, *pow wows* — traditional Indian dance gatherings —are arranged in the area. A number of craft stores, such as *The Old Schoolhouse, Bemidji Woolen Mills,* and especially *Lady Slippers Designs* feature locally made American or native crafts, while the homey shop *Christmas Fantasy* specializes in gifts and crafts of another kind: Christmas ornaments.

For more information on Bemidji, contact:
BEMIDJI VISITORS & CONVENTION BUREAU
P. O. Box 66
Bemidji, MN 56601
(800) 292-2223

A CCOMMODATIONS

■ SUPER 8 MOTEL
1815 Paul Bunyan Drive
Bemidji, MN 56601
Tel: (218) 751-8481 or (800) 800-8000
Hrs: Open year-round, 24-hours-a-day
All major credit cards are accepted.

The Super 8 Motel specializes in service of the highest quality for its customers. One-hundred-and-one newly renovated rooms offer clean, comfortable, and economic lodging. The English tudor style of the motel provides an air of elegance to the surroundings without the extra cost. The interior offers the invitation to relax in a whirlpool and sauna.

Two luxury suites with a wet bar and a fireplace are available. Both suites serve nicely as conference rooms.

Located on the edge of the northwoods, the Super 8 Motel is only a mile away from downtown Bemidji and popular Bemidji attractions. Lake Bemidji is also nearby, offering a public beach for summer enjoyment. As part of the morning hospitality, complimentary coffee, orange juice, and fresh fruit are provided throughout the week.

CANDY STORE

■ CHOCOLATES PLUS
102 First Street
Union Square
Bemidji, MN 56601
Tel: (218) 759-1175
Hrs: Mon. - Sat. 10 a.m. - 9 p.m., Sun. noon - 5 p.m.
Visa, MasterCard, AmEx, and Discover are accepted.

"Experience truffles the way they were meant to be, fresh from the kettle with no preservatives . . ." suggest the owners of Chocolates Plus. Mouth-watering butter toffee. . . candied orange peel . . . caramel corn with real butter . . . licorice . . . the list goes on. Hungry yet? Now imagine the aroma of freshly ground coffee mixed with the luscious smell of dark chocolate.

A trip to Chocolates Plus is a treat to all the senses. Try a fresh homemade truffle, smell the flavorful coffee, and delight in displays of unique chocolate novelties — spotted cows, pizzas, and chocolate bags filled with treasures.

Chocolates Plus offers something for everyone to indulge in without guilt. Fat- and cholesterol-free yogurt and sugar-free candy are also available. Chocolates Plus is also a great place to purchase coffee and tea brewing equipment. Mail order and shipping are available, as well as special orders.

F ACTORY OUTLET

■ BEMIDJI WOOLEN MILLS
P.O. Box 277
Bemidji, MN 56601
Tel: (218) 751-5166
Hrs: Mon. - Sat. 8 a.m. - 5:30 p.m.
Visa and MasterCard are accepted.

The Bemidji Woolen Mills was created in 1918 because of the foresight of its original owner, Ira Batchelder. He saw the impending demise of the general store and the trend toward speciality stores. The far-sighted Batchelder started his speciality store with merchandise that was sure to sell in the cold winter climate of Minnesota — wool.

An overwhelming selection of woolen items are available today through Bemidji Woolen Mills: blankets, coats, socks, long underwear, slippers, mittens, caps, pillows, yarn, and batting. The finest assortment of ready-made garments or wool to fashion quality garments can also be found at Bemidji Woolen Mills.

J EWELRY & GIFTS

■ BUSBY'S COUNTRY CHARM
(Two and a half miles west of Bemidji)
1726 Jefferson Ave. S.W.
Bemidji, MN 56601
Tel: (218) 751-6163
Hrs: Mon. - Fri. 10 a.m. - 5 a.m., Sat. 10 a.m. - 4 p.m.
    Sun. noon - 4 p.m. after May 15
Visa and MasterCard are accepted.

Busby's Country Charm is exactly that — a charming store right out in the country. Set back among the pines and back in time — or at least in prices — the store offers affordable quality jewelry and merchandise with a country flavor. Fine jewelry such as diamonds and precious gems, gold and sterling silver rings, necklaces, bracelets, earrings, as well as household items including stained glass, copper, brass, lace, crystal, china, and a full selection of hand-thrown pottery are just some of the items sold at Busby's Country Charm. "You have to see it to believe it," says owner Martha Busby about her treasure-trove in the pines.

Gifts are available for almost every taste from Amish hand-carved oak hay forks to three-carat diamonds. Select a gift from an array of rings and jewelry items, or browse through the fine lace and linen displays.

R ESORTS

■ A PLACE IN THE WOODS
11380 Turtle River Lake Road N.E.
Bemidji, MN 56601
Tel: (218) 586-2345 or (800) 676-4547
Hrs: Open year-round
Visa and MasterCard are accepted.

A Place in the Woods is newly developed by a family of friends to provide an authentic log cabin setting in which guests can enjoy the beauty of the northwoods. Although A Place in the Woods offers the beauty of the pristine northwoods area and Turtle River Lake, the bustling city of Bemidji is just a few short miles away. The log cabins — named after birds native to the area — offer fireplaces, well-furnished kitchens, grills, bathtubs, and in some, jacuzzis.

A Place in the Woods occupies 45 acres of land, with 1,800 feet of those acres running along the shoreline of Turtle River Lake and one-eighth of a mile along Moose Creek. Nature trails wind throughout the woods, inviting explorers to discover its wonders. Turtle River Lake is a natural walleye lake that also has a respectable bass population. Waterskiing and boating are other popular activities on the lake.

Aside from the abundance of outdoor activities, there is Eagles Nest Lodge, which contains grocery items, a meeting area, sun deck, and hot tub as well as a library loft that has books and games of all kinds available. In the lower level of the lodge is the Hatchlings Hideout, a unique area that provides arcade entertainment. It is the belief that if the kids are having fun, the parents will have fun as well. Especially for Kids is a program that provides supervised activities such as craft time, nature hikes, fishing seminars, and a treasure hunt to name a few. For a resort that covers all of the bases, there is A Place in the Woods.

■ RUTTGER'S – BIRCHMONT LODGE
530 Birchmont Beach Road N.E.
Bemidji, MN 56601
Tel: (218)751-1630 or (800)726-3866
Hrs: Open year-round
Visa, MasterCard, Amex, and Discover are accepted.

Ruttger's Lodge is located along 1,700 feet of beautiful sandy beach along Lake Bemidji. Sailing, fishing, waterskiing, or leisurely sunbathing make a summer vacation at Ruttger's complete, but that isn't all this lodge has to offer. This lodge is also home to the Paul Bunyan Playhouse, which is the area's oldest professional summer theater. Youngsters are continuously entertained with supervised children's programs, available through the lodge, as well as indoor and outdoor pools and outdoor tennis courts.

Accommodations include lakeside lodge rooms, deluxe cottages, or modern townhomes. Lakeside dining and cocktails complete an enticing vacation plan no matter what the season. Ruttger's has something for everyone.

■ WOLF LAKE RESORT
12150P Walleye Lane
Bemidji, MN 56601
Tel: (218) 751-5749 or (800) 322-0281 (Ext. 10)
Hrs: Call for reservations 8 a.m. - 10 p.m.
   (Closes after deer hunting season; reopens in May)
Visa and MasterCard are accepted.

Wolf Lake Resort is a modern housekeeping resort located along a quarter-mile of shoreline on Big Wolf Lake. It is easily accessible, yet away from it all on 90 acres of forest land. Spacious grounds provide space for peace and privacy for the entire family.

Wolf Lake Resort has something for the entire family; swimming in a large outdoor heated pool, fishing, skiing, paddleboats, canoeing, game room, laundry facilities, sauna, whirlpool, and playground equipment. Sailing and windsurfing lessons are also available for guests. Boat and motor rental and other amenities are available at very reasonable rates. There are a few limited campsites, some with full hook-up. Accommodations offer 16 cottages complete with kitchens and bathrooms. A 14-foot aluminum boat is provided with each cottage, or free dock space for those guests furnishing their own boat. A sheltered harbor eases the handling of boats. Picnic tables and barbecue grills are also provided. Big Wolf Lake is a spring- and river-fed lake.

Although a smaller lake — 1,053 acres — it is part of the Mississippi River chain of lakes with easy passage to at least five other lakes, including Lake Andrusia and Cass Lake. This chain has some of the finest fishing in northern Minnesota for panfish, walleye, northern, and muskie. A three- to five-hour canoe trip starting upstream on the Mississippi to Big Wolf Lake is very popular. For those guests who like to take time out from fishing and swimming, the surrounding area is abundant with shopping, museums, fine dining and restaurants, amusement parks, golf courses, and the popular Itasca State Park. Kermit and Mary Bjerke are proud of the fact that so many of their guests are Wolf Lake Resort regulars.

Brainerd Lakes Area

L ocated at the geographical center of the state, Brainerd was born in 1870 when the Northern Pacific Railroad company crossed the river at this site to create the first transcontinental railroad. Early county leaders wanted to name the city Smithville after the president of Northern Pacific, John Gregory Smith, but the gallant railroad man chose, instead, "Brainerd," his wife's maiden name. The name "Gregory" would do for the city center square, he decided. Also, in this burgeoning time of settlers and railroading, the legend of Paul Bunyan — the giant lumberjack — originated, and to this day this prosperous trade and manufacturing city calls itself "the hometown of Paul Bunyan" in defiance of neighboring Bemidji's similar claim to this legendary figure.

ATTRACTIONS

But Bunyan is big enough to be claimed by two cities, and popular enough of a legend to sustain a number of attractions both in Brainerd as well as in rival Bemidji. Foremost among these in Brainerd is *Paul Bunyan Fun Center,* an amusement park with a plethora of rides, miniature golf, and bowling lanes dominated by a 26-foot-tall animated Paul Bunyan figure. Another place of interest dedicated to the friendly lumberjack is the *Paul Bunyan Arboretum,* with over 3,000 different species of plants filling 120 acres of land, and 12 miles of hiking or cross-country trails. Those who find themselves hankering for more lumber lore can choose to visit the *Crow Wing County Historical Museum,* an authentically restored home decorated with primitive paintings of the early logging and railroading days, and *Lumbertown USA,* a recreated lumber town from the early 1870s. Another point of historical interest is the *Brainerd water tower,* the first municipal, concrete tower in the United States built during the years 1919 to 1922. But Brainerd isn't all history, it's a resort center particularly known for the fishing opportunities in the nearby 450 lakes and the excellent camping and hiking facilities in *Crow Wing State Park.* It's also the headquarters of *In-Fisherman's Communications,* publisher of the *In-Fisherman* Magazine, and *Babe Winkelman Productions* with its television series and instructional fishing videos. Other sports attractions of note include the renowned *Brainerd International Raceway* — which each summer hosts major national competitions in drag, Classic and Formula 1 racing — the *Ski Gull* ski area, and the *Granny's Softball on Ice* and *Annual Snow Golf* tournaments.

For more information on the Brainerd Lakes Area, contact:
BRAINERD LAKES AREA CHAMBER OF COMMERCE
Sixth and Washington Streets
Brainerd, MN 56401
(218) 829-2838 or (800) 432-3775, ext. 89

A CCOMMODATIONS

■ PAUL BUNYAN MOTEL
1800 Fairview Drive N.
Brainerd, MN 56401
Tel: (218) 829-3571 or (800) 553-3609
Hrs: Open year-round
All major credit cards are accepted.

The Paul Bunyan Motel sits among giant Norway pines and
spruce trees, the perfect environment for a place with the name of
a legendary lumberjack. The gazebo in the landscaped courtyard
gives guests an opportunity to enjoy the
beauty of the outdoors around them.
The motel has an indoor pool, sauna,
whirlpool, and gameroom. The
rooms offer color cable television
with free Showtime and touch-
tone phones. There are 34 units
available, 24 are standard rooms
and ten are suites. The suites
provide a wet bar, microwave,
refrigerator, two televisions, and
two phones. Some of the suites have
private jacuzzis to relax tired muscles.
Paul Bunyan Amusement Park is right next
door, and the Brainerd International Raceway is just down the
road six miles.

F ISH, SEAFOOD & GIFTS

■ MOREY'S FISH HOUSE
Highway 371 N.
Brainerd, MN 56401
Tel: (218) 829-8248 (Brainerd) or (800) 548-9630 (Motley)
Hrs: Open year-round
Visa, MasterCard, Discover, and AmEx are accepted.

Morey's Fish House is a Minnesota original. In the mid-1930s
Ed Morey was the owner of a small smokehouse in northern

Minnesota. Ed was looking for a perfect fish smoking procedure, and after two years of attempts, he developed it and founded the Morey Fish Co. in Motley. In 1947 the company burned down, but it was immediately rebuilt and maintained a strong following. A second retail outlet was built in Brainerd in 1970, and the company developed into one of the finest smoked fish operations in the state.

Morey's Fish House carries a wide selection of smoked fish, fresh fish, and seafood. Special features are the New England clam chowder and the wild rice soup. The Salmon Sampler Pak is packaged with several types of salmon: the BBQ, the classic, cajun style, peppered and dill. Other favorites include the whitefish combo and the fresh chinook fillets.

Morey's also carries a selection of cookbooks and Minnesota-related gift items. The staff is very helpful and will share recipes and cooking tips for the fish. Morey's will also design, pack, and ship custom gift boxes just about anywhere. Dry ice insures the freshness of the selections during shipping. The commitment to quality can be seen in the service at Morey's and tasted in the food.

GALLERY & FRAME SHOP

■IRON OWL FRAMING SHOP AND GALLERY
601 W. Washington
Brainerd, MN 56401
Tel: (218) 829-0342
Hrs: Mon. - Fri. 10 a.m. - 5 p.m.
     Sat. 10 a.m. - 4 p.m.
     Closed Sun. (Open evenings near Christmas)
Visa, MasterCard, AmEx, and Discover are accepted.

Located in the vacationland area of Brainerd, Iron Owl Framing Shop and Gallery is a complete gallery providing art consultation, framing, and stained glass overlay services, along with a wide array of prints, paintings, and posters.

The gallery area is nicely decorated with soft, modern colors with exquisite stained glass overlay windows in the front of the store. The selection to be found in the gallery mostly includes prints and decorator art such as wildlife, florals, paper art, abstracts, botanical prints, and decorative posters. Original artwork and posters are also available. Artists represented include Larry Anderson, Terry Redlin, Les Kouba, Brian Jarvi, and many more. The owner, Jim Hoff, is an artist himself. His drawings can be found on numerous paper products such as notecards, stationery, and memo pads. The gallery also specializes in stained glass overlay and sandblasted art glass. Leasing of art has become very popular to area businesses. Custom picture framing, delivery, and installation are also available.

The Iron Owl Framing Shop and Gallery makes a continued effort to provide outstanding service and quality artwork.

GALLERY & GIFT SHOP

■ CHRISTMAS POINT WILD RICE COMPANY
Westgate Mall, Highway 371
Brainerd-Baxter, MN 56401
Tel: (218) 828-0603
Hrs: Mon. - Sat. 10 a.m. - 9 p.m., Sun. noon - 5 p.m.
Visa, MasterCard, AmEx, and Discover cards are accepted.

Christmas Point Wild Rice Company was established in 1975 to process and distribute Native American hand-picked wild rice. It blossomed into a gift shop and art gallery featuring a wide variety of gifts and the largest selection in northern Minnesota of wildlife art by local and national artists. This rustic shop is a large log cabin with wood-beam floors situated in the middle of a modern shopping center. Sue and Larry Olin have filled their shop with the best of Minnesota. The gourmet food section has fancy Native American hand-picked rice, spices, and Minnesota jellies from the White Earth and Leech Lake Indian Reservations. Coffee, assorted teas, and rice cookbooks round out the selection.

There is a Minnesota Loon section and a duck section where collectors can find loon crafts, souvenirs, and carved wooden ducks by Minnesota artisans. Other specialty items on display include hand-loomed rugs, jewelry, pressed flowers, T-shirts, and music by Minnesota artists.

GIFTS & HOME DECOR

■ SOMEONE'S HOUSE – INTERIORS AND GIFTS
4995 Highway 371 N.
Brainerd, MN 56401
Tel: (218) 829-7984
Hrs: Open year-round Mon. - Sat. 10 a.m. - 5 p.m.
　　　Call for extended hours during the summer and holidays.
Visa and MasterCard are accepted.

Located on Highway 371, just six miles north of Brainerd, a charming two-story home provides a shopping experience to guests and residents that truly connotes "Someone's House."

A myriad of home furnishings and accessories is attractively displayed in a warm and inviting atmosphere that encourages home decorating. There are many elegant and unique items to choose from, such as lamps, hand-hooked rugs, wallpapers, drapes, pictures, pillows, dried statice wreaths and arrangements, and other specialty items to decorate a home. Name brand, quality-crafted furniture is also available. A warm and friendly staff assists customers with suggestions for their home decor. Someone's House has two open house events each year. "Spring is in the Air" is held each spring concurrent with the opening of fishing season, offering a "fresh air" of spring design. Dazzling, summery glassware, along with specialty trays and linens, unique baskets, and potted flowers, will brighten a picnic or patio. Charming children's and baby gifts are classic Winnie the Pooh frames, bookends, collectible teapots, and infant to toddler clothing lines. Held each fall during the hunting season, "Christmas is in the Air" provides traditional and unique gifts and accessories. "Make a Wish" selection and gift wrapping are also available.

For something distinctively different and very special, Someone's House is the place to shop. The beautiful array of items found at this quaint store is worth a visit.

HISTORIC VILLAGE & MUSEUM

■ LUMBERTOWN U.S.A.
8001 Pine Beach Peninsula
Brainerd, MN 56401
Tel: (218) 829-8872
Hrs: (May - mid-Sept.) 9:30 a.m. - 5:30 p.m.
Visa and MasterCard are accepted.

Lumbertown U.S.A. is an authentic 1870s logging village, established in the heart of Madden Resorts. Jack Madden originally built the town as a historic museum, preserving the bustling lumber town village and lifestyle of the 1870s. Restoration of the town began in 1954 with 11 buildings, growing to the present 30 buildings. Many of these are original structures that have been moved to the Lumbertown site.

Take a walk through history down the streets of the town. Visit the "Last Turn" Saloon, Town Hall, and the Old Red School. Come face-to-face with Buffalo Bill Cody, Annie Oakley, and other turn-of-the-century celebrities in the Lumbertown Wax Museum. Walk on and see the Sugar Bush syrup mill and the saw mill. Relive the lumber days in the general store, tonsorial parlor, blacksmith shop, and the oldest print shop in Minnesota. The Old Ice Cream Parlor serves lunch as well as a selection of ice cream specialties. Children will enjoy going to the levee on the Blueberry River. There they can ride on the riverboat Blue Berry Belle or take a scenic ride on a genuine replica of the first Northern Pacific locomotive.

Lumbertown U.S.A. can be a fun and educational experience. Group and school tours are available. A picnic area, nine-hole miniature golf course, and a gift and souvenir shop ensure a good time for the whole family.

M USEUM

■ THIS OLD FARM

7344 Highway 18 E.
Brainerd, MN 56401
Tel: (218) 764-2915
Hrs: (Memorial weekend - Labor Day) Sat. - Sun. 9 a.m. - 5 p.m.
No credit cards are accepted.

Richard Rademacher has turned his lifetime hobby of collecting antiques into an old-time village and museum called This Old Farm, located just seven miles east of Brainerd on Highway 18.

This Old Farm has thousands of unusual antiques. Many of them are displayed in their setting as they were used years ago.

An original log house from a nearby homestead stands today completely furnished with all that was needed in those days. A kitchen, parlor, dining room, and bedroom are filled with irreplaceable antiques from toys to glassware. Stop at the saloon fully decorated with an authentic player piano, one arm bandit, nickelodeon, and the brass rail bar.

Visit the old schoolhouse from the early 1900s, old-time store, barber shop, dentist office, post office, and filling station where the gas pump rings up only pennies for a gallon of gas. See the line of antique cars, trucks, tractors, gas and steam engines, horsedrawn buggies, sleighs, and farm machinery. Don't miss the annual Steam Threshing Show. It is two exciting days when steam engines run the thresher, horses work the fields, and children can ride the stage coach.

Don't miss the chance to re-live the "good ol' days," for both the young and old to enjoy.

R ESORT

■ MADDEN'S ON GULL LAKE
8001 Pine Beach Peninsula
Brainerd, MN 56401
Tel: (218) 829-2811 or (800) 247-1040 (in Minnesota)
      or (800) 233-2934 (outside Minnesota)
Hrs: Mid-April - late Oct.
Visa and MasterCard are accepted.

This expansive resort was built on land that was owned by the Northern Pacific Railroad in the 1860s and was developed from the modest beginnings of a small golf course with a single clubhouse. Today, Madden's on Gull Lake offers three separate resort facilities, each with its own style and conference facilities, excellent dining, and endless recreational possibilities.

On scenic Pine Beach Peninsula of Gull Lake, 130 miles northwest of Minneapolis/St. Paul, the three resorts include the colonial-style Madden Lodge, the rustic Madden's Pine Portage, and the Madden Inn and Golf Club. These combine to provide 285 air-conditioned cottages and luxury units as well as modern lodge and hotel rooms. The three resort centers have individual dining facilities, a central banquet facility, and an informal coffee shop. Groups may plan special indoor or outdoor meal functions, from elaborate banquets to casual cookouts. Theme buffets and table service are available for traditional meals. Madden's also provides versatility in planning meetings. All details, from room set-up to scheduling and catering, can be coordinated by Madden's staff.

Thirty meetings rooms of varying size and seating capacity, including the Town Hall Conference Center, allow personalized meeting support services.

Visitors may enjoy 45 holes of golf on three courses, the Croquet & Tennis Center, volleyball, shuffleboard, game rooms, cycling, jogging, and trapshooting. Two fully-equipped marinas, three sandy beaches, six pools - three indoor with spa and sauna - provide facilities for water sports activities. In the evening, relax with friends at the 19th Hole Lounge, or enjoy live entertainment in the O'Madden Pub. Madden's offers many special services, from business to party planning. Holiday and special value package plans are also available.

■ R ESORTS & RESTAURANTS

■ KAVANAUGH'S ON SYLVAN LAKE
2300 Kavanaugh Drive S.W.
Brainerd, MN 56401
Tel: (218) 829-5226 or (800) 562-7061
Hrs: (Resort) Year-round
      (Restaurant) Sunday Brunch Memorial Day to Labor Day

Kavanaugh's is located in Brainerd's famous Pine Beach Area, approximately 120 miles north of the Minneapolis-St. Paul metro area. It is the only resort on Upper Sylvan Lake, which is one of the cleanest and clearest lakes in Minnesota.

This 15-acre resort features 1,200 feet of shoreline, including two sandy beaches. Accommodations offer one-, two-, and three-bedroom deluxe lake villas and cottages with either a lakeside deck or patio, fully equipped kitchens, cable television, telephone, and typical amenities. There are several accommodation packages to choose from to suit individual needs at affordable rates. Kavanaugh's offers a wide range of activities from hiking, boating, swimming, fishing, skiing, golfing, tennis, to just plain relaxing. Guests also enjoy the beautiful indoor heated pool, sauna, and whirlpool. Summer vacation is traditional; however, spring, fall, and winter promise unique opportunities for nature lovers and photo buffs in the serenity of the hardwood forests. The warm elegance of Kavanaugh's Restaurant is only surpassed by the excellent meals expertly prepared. Kavanaugh's features gourmet seafood, prime steaks, and vintage veal. Guests can also enjoy cocktails on Kavanaugh's lakeside deck, adorned by a panoramic view of Sylvan Lake. Kavanaugh's has been honored with a Silver Spoon Award and AAA's Three Diamond rating. The Pine Bough Gift Shop offers specialty art and hand-crafted gifts.

■ QUARTERDECK RESORT AND RESTAURANT

1588 Quarterdeck R. W.
County Road 77
Brainerd, MN 56401
Tel: (218) 963-2482
Hrs: Sun. - Thur. 11 a.m. - 10 p.m.
   Fri. - Sat. 9 a.m. - 11 p.m.
Visa, MasterCard, and AmEx are accepted.

Nestled in the heartland of Minnesota and along beautiful Gull Lake's shorelines is an incredible family resort and restaurant with vacation pleasures for adults and children — The Quarterdeck Resort and Restaurant.

The Quarterdeck Resort offers two-, three-, and four-bedroom lakeside vacation homes complete with living and dining room areas, fully equipped kitchens, and some with fireplaces. The luxury villas all have fireplaces attractively furnished and designed for couples. All homes have breathtaking views of Gull Lake. The sandy beaches are excellent for swimming. There is a planned and supervised recreational program for children, and other outdoor activities include tennis, basketball, shuffleboard, badminton, horseshoes, and volleyball. A short walk from the resort lies Birch Bay Golf Club, with several other golf courses nearby. The fishing is excellent, and special packages for boat and motor rentals are available. Children enjoy panfishing right off the docks. For leisure tours, pontoon boats are also available.

The renowned Quarterdeck Restaurant and Supper Club overlooks Gull Lake, offering over 100 menu items, with nightly entertainment in the lounge. The Quarterdeck offers outstanding facilities for groups, conventions, and family reunions. The Quarterdeck staff will design packages to accommodate the desired menu and lodging desired for individual groups. Winter enthusiasts enjoy the 1,000+ miles of groomed snowmobile and cross-country ski trails. The Quarterdeck is situated on the trail between the Pillsbury State Forest and Minnesota's only lighted lake trail on Gull Lake. Downhill skiing is less than a mile away, and ice houses are available for ice fishing.

RESTAURANT

■IVEN'S ON THE BAY

5195 N. Highway 371
Brainerd, MN 56401
Tel: (218) 829-9872
Hrs: Open daily (dinner) 5 p.m. till close
     Sunday Brunch 10 a.m. - 1 p.m.
All major credit cards are accepted.

Iven's On The Bay is a quality seafood house overlooking the west bay of North Long Lake; it was established in 1984. An exceptional dining experience, in a very pleasant and relaxed atmosphere, awaits all guests.

Only the highest quality, nutritionally prepared food is served. Most entrees are broiled, charbroiled or steamed, and many menu items meet the American Heart Association's "Dining Ala Heart" serving standards. Special attention is given to details, cleanliness, and professionalism; this reflects the entire staff's commitment to "excellence in hospitality." Wonderful choices pervade Iven's prize-winning menu. Though seafood is the primary emphasis, meat, meat/seafood combos and vegetarian items are offered. Fresh fish and/or shellfish flown in is always available as the "chef's feature of the day." The specialty of the house, Golden Pan-Fried Walleye, is the most popular menu item. A nice variety of chicken and steaks includes Chicken Oscar, made with asparagus and crab meat. A Roasted Nut Cassolet is one of five vegetarian offerings.

For an evening of fine dining or an indulgence in a great Sunday brunch, a visit to Iven's is memorable. Consider Iven's for a small group function or private party — it's a perfect place.

Crosslake

A quiet village of only 1,000 people, Crosslake is one of those quaint northwoods towns that visitors always want to return to. Visiting the town is convenient enough since it is home to a number of lakeside resorts, motels, and campgrounds located on the fabled *Ossawinnamakee Lake Chain* — otherwise known as the *Whitefish Chain* — 14 island-studded lakes that feed into the Pine River at the historic *Crosslake Dam,* with the nearby *Crosslake Super Waterslides.* In addition to the dam, the town also boasts other points of historic interest, including the Old *Town Hall Museum* and an *1895 Log Home.* This tiny community is also renowned in antique circles for its multitude of antique and gift stores. If antique hounds time their arrival well, they may be able to attend the annual, delectable *Chili Cook-off* in August, the annual *Art Show,* also in August, and the fun-filled *St. Patrick's Day Parade and Celebration.*

For more information on Crosslake, contact:
CROSSLAKE AREA CHAMBER OF COMMERCE
P.O. Box 315
Crosslake, MN 56442
(218) 692-4027

B ED & BREAKFAST

■ LO-KIANDY INN
P.O. Box 33, S. Landing Road
Crosslake, MN 56442
Tel: (218) 692-2714 or (612) 560-3847 (Metro area)
Hrs: (Summer) daily (Fall and winter) Fri. - Sun.
Visa, MasterCard, ÁmEx, and Discover are accepted.

Located on Loon and Island lakes, Lo-Kiandy Inn is known as "The Castle on Two Lakes," only 145 miles north of the Twin Cities.This elegant bed and breakfast inn has five contemporary guest rooms, each with its own personal decor and private bath. Each room overlooks the centerpiece of the two-story house, a large indoor swimming pool and spa area. A scrumptious breakfast is served on the balcony overlooking the inn. Lo-Kiandy's prime location offers easy accessibility to the lakes. A dock is available at the inn for guests to launch their boats. The inn also has bikes for guests to explore the wooded roads surrounding the area. There are four golf courses within ten miles of the inn and there is plenty of night life, restaurants, gift and antique shops to enjoy. Arrangements can also be made for airport pick-up; there are two within the area.

G ALLERY & GIFT SHOP

■ DUBOIS WOODCARVING
County Road 6
Crosslake, MN 56442
Tel: (218) 692-4258
Hrs: (Summer) daily 10 a.m.- 5 p.m. (Winter) Hours by appointment
Visa, AmEx, and MasterCard are accepted.

Cy DuBois is the woodcarver-in-residence at DuBois Woodcarving. While recuperating from back surgery in 1975, he began painting some unfinished wood duck decoys and decided to start carving them himself. The Shoppe and Gallery opened in June of 1984, selling wood carvings and limited edition prints. Cy and his wife, Jane Anne, later expanded the shop to include gifts and wood signs.

DuBois first studies the birds in their natural habitat and then devotes as many as 100 hours to each carving. The store has an abundance of offerings, including custom framing, Adirondack furniture, bird houses and feeders, and custom-routed signs. Of course, the wide selection of one-of-a-kind handcarved waterfowl is its signature item. The shop is also known as "loon headquarters in Northern Minnesota." Paintings by Minnesota artists may be seen in the Gallery. Wooden whirligigs and Madonna shrines are two of the more unusual items to be found at DuBois Woodcarving.

Gift buyers can select among books, notecards, calendars, and T-shirts from DuBois. For the hard-to-please, one of the many windsocks might fit the bill. The shoppe and gallery are located in Midtown across from the Dairy Queen.

GIFT SHOP

■ JUDY'S HOUSE OF GIFTS
(One block east of the park)
Crosslake, MN 56442
Tel: (218) 692-3123
Hrs: (Memorial Day - Labor Day) Mon. - Sat. 9:30 a.m. to 5 p.m.
   Sun. 10 a.m. to 3 p.m.
   Closed Mon. and Tues. in the winter
Discover, Visa, and MasterCard are accepted.

Judy's House of Gifts makes its home just off of Crosslake's main street. The impressive cedar log building looks like a cabin tucked away in the northwoods of Minnesota. The smell of candles, potpourri, and eucalyptus greets each visitor upon entering. Dried flowers and customized floral arrangements create a homey feeling. A full array of baskets, spiced tea, jewelry, and dolls can be purchased as gifts or as a personal treat. Red Wing Stoneware and Blueberry Pottery are favorite brands featured in the shop.

Collectibles from Dept 56 Villages are featured among a wide selection of revered pieces. Duck decoys, weather stations, and a range of men's gift items make Judy's House of Gifts a one stop gift shop. The friendly service keeps customers coming back.

R ESORT

■ BOYD LODGE
(on Whitefish Lake) HC 83, P.O. Box 667
Crosslake, MN 56442
Tel: (218) 543-4125 or (800) 247-1058
Hrs: Open year-round

Boyd Lodge on Whitefish Lake provides an opportunity for a getaway or the constant activity of a thrill-seeking vacation. Relaxation can be found in the warmth of the sauna or the coziness of one of the 19 cabins.

The cabins include a redwood deck, carpeting, kitchen, and all of the comforts of home. During the winter months, the fireplace provides a warm haven after a satisfying day of skiing. One-thousand feet of white sand stretches out along Boyd Lodge. Whitefish Lake is clean, clear, and most important of all - safe. It is weed-free with no sudden drop-offs for little ones who may venture out. Reduced rates at nearby Whitefish Golf Club are available for the avid golfer.

S UPPER CLUB

■ ECHO RIDGE SUPPER CLUB
HC83, P.O. Box 117
Crosslake, MN 56442
Tel: (218) 692-4800
Hrs: (Summer) open daily 4 p.m. (Winter) open Wed. - Sun. 4 p.m.
Visa, MasterCard, and AmEx are accepted.

Perched on the shores of picturesque Cross Lake — a glimmering link in the beautiful Whitefish chain of lakes — Chuck

Thompson's Echo Ridge Supper Club welcomes patrons with scenic fine dining and top-notch entertainment. Thompson's guests, some zooming up to Echo Ridge by boat and docking in the slips provided along the restaurant's lake front, come to savor succulent beef and seafood entrees, relaxing musical performances and the view outside the large picture windows. The comfortable interior soothes with mauve and gray tones and the dark wood of the restaurant's structure. While feasting on such menu selections as Walleye Almondine, Filet Mignon, lobster tails, or Polynesian chicken, diners are entertained by local acts. Depending on the night of the week, crowd-pleasing, request-taking pianists, big-band-sounding trios, or easy-listening rock-and-roll dance music livens the ambiance. No matter what season or night of the week, fine dining and entertainment are at the Echo Ridge Supper Club.

Nisswa

Nisswa isn't a large city, but it is unique. Located 13 miles north of Brainerd on Highway 371, the town features a shopping street lined with Bavarian-style buildings — the shops carrying the spectrum from porcelain gifts to fishing tackle. An excellent selection of antiques has also made the town a popular destination, in addition to the requisite nearby lakes and resorts. There is always the popular *Sherwood Forest Lodge* on the west side of *Gull Lake.* Constructed out of huge logs, it features one of the largest stone fireplaces in northern Minnesota. It offers bed-and-breakfast accommodations along with a coffee and gift shop serving breakfast and lunch. For a special gourmet meal, the *Lost Lake Lodge* promises to be a culinary experience. Shopping and scenery aren't all that make Nisswa stand out from the rest; there are annual events to satisfy the most eccentric of tastes. In July, the *Minnesota Loon Festival* brings out the best in competitors struggling to make the best loon call, and Wednesdays in the summer the residents crown the fastest turtles in the town during the *Turtle Races,* held downtown at 2 p.m. Other yearly festivals such as *Crazy Days,* a two-day affair with a Nisswa Lions Corn Feed, and the German-inspired Bierstube festival *Iowegian Days* — both in August — seem quite tame in comparison.

For more information on Nisswa, contact:
Nisswa Area Chamber of Commerce
P.O. Box 185
Nisswa, MN 56468
(218) 963-2620 or (800) 950-9610

ACCOMMODATIONS

■ NISSWA MOTEL
Downtown Nisswa
P.O. Box 45
Nisswa, MN 56468
Tel: (218) 963-7611
Hrs: Open year-round
Visa and MasterCard are accepted.

Nisswa Motel can be found among the tall pines and fresh air of downtown Nisswa. Seventeen units feature spacious, comfortable rooms with modern accommodations including air conditioning, direct-dial telephone, color cable TV, and in-room coffee. Other conveniences include parking right outside the door to each room and ample parking for boats, snowmobiles, and trailers.

Russ and Myrna King are gracious hosts who are happy to direct guests to the local sights, like nearby lakes and the Brainerd lakes area snowmobile trails. Their many repeat customers return to the area to enjoy the recreation and lakes, as well the shops and restaurants of the Nisswa area.

ANTIQUES & GIFTS

■ WINDSONG GALLERY AND ANTIQUES
Nisswa Square
Nisswa, MN 56468
Tel: (218) 963-7596 or (218) 568-4947 (winter)
Hrs: (Summer) Mon. - Sat. 10 a.m. - 8 p.m.
   Sun. 11 a.m. - 4 p.m.
   Off season: By appointment
Visa and MasterCard are accepted.

Windsong Gallery and Antiques is a quaint, friendly shop located in the courtyard of Nisswa Square in downtown Nisswa. In 1977 the store was established as a gallery and gift shop, and in 1984 antiques were added.

The gallery exhibits paintings and prints by Minnesota artists. The work of Minnesota artisans is represented in pottery, jewelry, and metal sculpture. Antiques and collectibles that are reflective of the lakes are the specialty here. There is an interesting selection of American Indian artifacts and beadwork, Red Wing Stoneware, wood primitives, and unusual antique hand tools. A general line of antiques with a sporting and outdoor theme includes old knives, hunting and fishing related gear, and investment grade duck and fish spearing decoys. Antique pine and oak furniture is also available. Windsong actively buys, sells, and trades antiques; and owners Bonnie and Erick Erickson encourage people to bring their antiques in for evaluation.

"Windsong is a place dedicated to the earth, the outdoors, and the beauty of nature." The antiques and gifts in this shop complement each other and satisfy a wide variety of interests. Shipping can be arranged for most purchases.

B OOK & TOY STORE

■ RAINY DAYS
County Road 18
Nisswa, MN 56468
Tel: (218) 963-4891 or (800) 635-7809
Hrs: Open year-round (extended summer hours)
Visa and MasterCard are accepted.

For the past ten years, Rainy Days Bookstore and Toy Store has been a fixture in downtown Nisswa. This store offers a charming selection of books and toys for all ages. New owner Suzy Turcotte treasures the opportunity to own this shop; after all, hasn't everyone dreamed of owning a toy store when they were young?

The bookstore carries an impressive selection of special children's books along with a nice array of regional books and magazine choices. The toy store offers a wide selection of toys, imported games, puzzles, and stuffed animals. The doll collection has one of the widest selections available in the state. Some of the brands carried include Lego, Playmobil, Corolle, and Gotz dolls. Rainy Days Bookstore and Toy Store has a great selection of toys and books for any day.

G IFT SHOPS

■ CARRIAGE GALLERY & GIFTS
544 Main Street
Nisswa, MN 56468
Tel: (218) 963-4963
Hrs: (May 14 - Oct. 21) Mon. - Sat. 10 a.m. - 5 p.m.
     Sun. 11 a.m. - 3 p.m.
Visa, MasterCard, and Discover are accepted.

Carriage Gallery & Gifts, on Main Street in Nisswa, is actually two shops in an old carriage house and gallery connected by a front porch. The Country House is full of original collector gifts, such as handmade stuffed animals, woodenware, framed pressed flowers, and a wide assortment of cards. Pine and oak furniture can be found here and there throughout the shop.

The Gallery displays original art, prints, carvings, pottery, and glassware, and features custom framing. Pat Hardy, co-owner of this charming gallery, travels to local and national gift shows across the country to bring back art and handmade country crafts. Each item is a design by the artist. Browsers are encouraged to comb the many small rooms of homespun treasures for that special gift to take home.

■WOODEN WINGS AND THINGS

Nisswa Square
Nisswa, MN 56468
Tel: (218) 963-3969
Hrs: (May 1 - Sept. 30) 9 a.m. - 9 p.m.

Additional Location:
Crosslake, MN 56442
Tel: (218) 692-3491
Hrs: (May 1 - Sept. 30) 10 a.m. - 6 p.m.
Discover, Visa, and MasterCard are accepted.

Wooden Wings and Things in Nisswa Square displays many unique Minnesota items. The featured merchandise is of the

highest quality at affordable prices. The owners have had such great response to their shop that they have opened a second in Crosslake and, during the holidays, display their items in the Twin Cities area malls.

One of the truly unique items available are the shellscapes. These are handpainted half-shells depicting wildlife scenes. The shells used are some of the largest freshwater shells in the world today. A description of where each shell originated accompanies the shellscape. Jim Harpole has received much acclaim for his original shellscapes. Harlan Zieske is another featured artist who specializes in outdoor art using various media.

Susan Renae Sampson limited edition prints are also available. These prints are a reflection of Midwestern life. Handcarved loons, ducks, eagles, and fish can be found throughout the store. All are hand-painted by the artist. For leisurely shopping, Wooden Wings and Things has much to offer.

R ESORT

■ GRAND VIEW LODGE
South 134 Nokomis
Nisswa, MN 56468
Tel: (218) 963-2234 or (800) 432-3788 (in Minnesota)
    or (800) 345-9625 (outside Minnesota)
Hrs: Open May - Sept.

Listed on the National Register of Historic Places, the Grand View Lodge in Nisswa offers a wealth of options for vacationers. Whether it's for the opportunity to stay in the original 1919 lodge or the lake view across the beach, three generations of guests have returned year after year.

First of all, there is golf, and lots of it. The original Gardens Course, a nine-hole, par 35 course well-known for its spectacular scenery, has been followed by The Pines, a championship 18-hole, par 72 course, one of the state's most challenging. The Pines was designed by Joel Golstrand, former PGA touring pro. Both courses are situated to maximize views of the natural environment and provide outstanding golfing. Related to the two are professional golf instruction and school, a large driving range, putting greens, and clubhouse. Tennis enthusiasts take advantage of seven LayKold tennis courts, with tennis pro and lessons. There is an incredible 1,500-foot sandy beach, which provides enough space to launch a variety of rental boats and all kinds of water sports. Indoor workouts can take place in the heated swimming pool, sauna, and exercise room. Families will enjoy learning and

adventure programs for youngsters, organized activities for teenagers, shopping, biking and hiking tours. Accommodations for approximately 220 vacationers are provided by 14 rooms in the Grand View Lodge, and over 60 luxurious lake townhomes and cottages. There is a wide range of plans available at individual and family rates. Choose from two dining atmospheres. A lounge with live music and regular dances are evening entertainment.

Over 15,000 flowers and shrubs influenced *House and Garden* Magazine to call the resort "a floral masterpiece of the northland." Mesaba-Northwest Airlink offers daily flights to Brainerd. Private planes may also use the airport and be met by lodge staff.

RESTAURANT & PUB

■ THE CHANNEL INN AND GRANNY'S PUB
401 Lost Lake Road
Nisswa, MN 56468
Tel: (218)963-4790
Hrs: (Dinner) Sun. - Thur. 5 p.m. - 10:30 p.m., Fri. - Sat. 5 p.m. - 11 p.m.
    Open daily for lunch
Visa and MasterCard are accepted.

Located on the Gull Lake Narrows, The Channel Inn and Granny's Pub provides great food, quenching drinks, and entertainment for all who visit. The lunch menu consists of burgers, speciality sandwiches, and tempting salads. Daily specials range from all-you-can-eat crab on Monday to sirloin for two on Sunday. The dinner menu contains some tasty house specialities such as Long Island duck, steak McMann, and prime rib of beef. Additional suggestions are the lobster and the peppered ribeye.

Granny's Pub and Outdoor Patio presents live music throughout the year. Sandwiches, appetizers, and subs are featured on the menu in the full service pub.

S CANDINAVIAN GIFT SHOP

■ THE SWEDISH TIMBER HOUSE
7678 Interlachen Road
Lakeshore
Nisswa, MN 56468
Tel: (218) 963-7897
Hrs: Open daily 10 a.m. - 5 p.m. from early May to late Oct.
    (Fri., Sat., Sun. in Dec.)

The Swedish Timber House was hewn of spruce, constructed and erected in Leksand, Sweden, Brainerd's sister city in Dalarna. The building was dismantled, numbered, and shipped to Minnesota where it was reconstructed on the western shore of Gull Lake in 1970. It is a Scandinavian store filled with merchandise from Sweden, Norway, Denmark, and Finland. The store is located 12 miles north of Brainerd on Highway 371 and left five miles on County Road 77 (Interlachen Road).

The scenery surrounding the store is worth a visit in itself, where wildflowers cover the five acres on which the store is built.

Maple and oak trees surround a trail from the store down to the lake. In the fall the trees are a sight to behold. The Swedish Timber House carries clothing from Swedish weavers, and clogs and woolen sweaters from Norwegian knitters. Jewelry of silver amber and lapis and the famous Solje designs of Norway are featured. Home accessories of wrought iron forged in Sweden and Denmark display the traditional patterns of these countries. The crystal selection includes pieces from all over the world

Collectors' treasures and gifts line the shelves. There are 20 different sizes of Swedish Dala horses from Nusnas in Dalarna as well as Dala roosters and pigs. Unique Christmas decorations are extra special items of Old World charm. Each year owners Lloyd and Ingrid Anderson go to Sweden to personally choose the best items the Scandinavian countries have to offer and bring them back to the store for their customers.

■S UPPER CLUB

■ BAR HARBOR
6512 Interlachen Road
Lakeshore
Nisswa, MN 56468
Tel: (218) 963-2568
Hrs: Daily noon - 1 a.m.
Visa, AmEx, Diners Club, and Bar Harbor are accepted.

For over 30 years, Bar Harbor was known as the "fun spot of Northern Minnesota." People came from miles around to hear all the famous big bands and to take in the action of legalized gambling. It was a great loss when Big Bar Harbor Pavilion burned to the ground in 1968. Constructed on the same location are the new Bar Harbor Townhouses. Across the street is the Bar Harbor Supper Club on beautiful Gull Lake, combining gracious living with fine dining in a lovely natural setting.

Hungry travelers would be advised to try the renowned broiled giant lobster tails and charbroiled steaks. The open grill allows customers to see their steaks being cooked from the dining area. In the winter, diners may bring their own steaks. For those not as hungry, there is a

varied selection of light and a la carte items. To get an extra lift, try the espresso and cappuccino drinks. Choose from the Barefoot Bar menu for al fresco dining on the outdoor patio. The casual ambience pervades at happy hour 3:30 - 6 p.m. Sun. through Fri.

In the summer, 24 boat slips allow access to the restaurant by water, and when the lake freezes over in the winter, snowmobiles are welcome. Special events at Bar Harbor keep the restaurant jumping year-round. One such celebrated event in the winter is the weekend nine-hole golf course on the ice, followed by a fantastic cocktail party and dinner. Live entertainment, excellent dining, and proud service are the hallmark of the Bar Harbor experience. The club is considered a local landmark and attracts a following from residents as well as vacationers.

Pequot Lakes

A s the name implies, the town of Pequot Lakes is a find for the active sportsfisherman. In fact, the town's landmark is its *water tower,* a huge replica of the legendary, giant lumberjack Paul Bunyan's fishing bobber. Pequot Lakes is a hub for an area that includes the *Whitefish, Ossawinnamakee, Gull, Pelican,* and numerous other scenic lakes. Visitors can pick from a wide variety of resorts to enjoy their northwoods getaway. For those who eventually tire of fishing, this town of only 681 offers 72 holes of golf on four courses, and a surprising variety of shops. In particular, *antique* and *gift shops* proliferate, in addition to a fine selection of *art galleries* where local artists display their creations. There's even a live theater in town, in addition to a series of unique festivals that offer some theatrics of their own. Foremost among these are the annual *Bean Hole Days* in July, where 150 gallons of beans are cooked in the ground, and the eccentric *Fourth of July Celebration* featuring a liar's contest, bed race, pie-eating contests, and other antics.

For more information on Pequot Lakes, contact:
PEQUOT LAKES AREA CHAMBER OF COMMERCE
P.O. Box 208
Pequot Lakes, MN 56472
(218) 568-8911

A RT GALLERY

■ PINE CONE GALLERY
130 W. Front Street
Pequot Lakes, MN 56472
Tel: (218) 568-8239
Hrs: Daily 9:30 a.m. - 5:30 p.m.
   Hours vary in the winter
All major credit cards are accepted.

The first impression of Pine Cone Gallery may well be the scent of pine upon stepping through the door. The next impression is the fine quality of merchandise in the store. Located in the resort community of Pequot Lakes for over nine years, the gallery inventory carries a myriad of original pieces. Duck, fish, and bird carvings, limited edition prints, and custom greetings cards are popular items.

Artwork ranges from paintings to sculpture, pottery, and stained glass. Handblown Philabaum Glass perfume bottles are a line collected by the Smithsonian Institute and available to the patrons of Pine Cone Gallery. All paperweights are custom-made and very beautiful. Other pieces include jewelry, crystal figurines, brass decor items, and children's books. Shipping arrangements can be made for any purchase.

B ED & BREAKFAST

■ STONEHOUSE BED & BREAKFAST
HCR 2, P.O. Box 9
Pequot Lakes, MN 56472
Tel: (218) 568-4255
Hrs: Open year-round.
Visa and MasterCard accepted.

Stonehouse Bed and Breakfast is a cozy, private, stone cottage in the woods near Pequot Lakes. Designed and built by hosts Craig and Claire Nagel, Stonehouse offers a scenic and peaceful retreat for its guests. Constructed of local materials and situated several hundred feet from the main residence, Stonehouse provides uncommon beauty and privacy.

Stonehouse has comfortable beds, a split-stone fireplace, private bath, electric heat, a kitchen, a screened porch, and a beautiful terrace complete with a barbeque and a fountain. Two stained glass windows, designed by Claire Nagel, enhance the beauty of the sunrises and sunsets at Stonehouse. The cut stones in the fireplace were chosen by Craig to show the variety of the rock in

the area. The wood used to make up the interior was cut from the local woods.

Breakfast is served each morning up at the Nagel kitchen with a different menu each day of the week. The Nagels offer pleasant conversation and a hearty country breakfast with fresh eggs from the chicken coop outside. There are nature trails winding throughout the surrounding woods. Photo opportunities abound. Stonehouse is located in the heart of the Brainerd Lakes Area, with access to countless recreational opportunities as well as tranquil surroundings for the ultimate experience in relaxation; good for the body as well as the soul.

DINING & SHOPPING

■ JACK PINE CENTER
(One block east of stoplights)
P.O. Box 225
Pequot Lakes, MN 56472
Tel: (218) 568-4901
Hrs: (May - Oct.) daily 9 a.m. - 5 p.m.
Visa and MasterCard are accepted.

Jack Pine Center is an unusual shopping complex in downtown Pequot Lakes. Built in 1981, the center is a beautiful building of rustic design, highlighted with exposed beams, skylights, and

wood panels through-
out. Occupants com-
prise an ice cream
shop, seven quality
gift shops, and
Beverly's Restaurant
and Pub. The rest-
aurant serves break-
fast, lunch, and
Sunday brunch from
an appealing menu.
Selections feature
several salads, sand-
wiches, and house
specialties. Desserts
include homemade
pies, which are fresh-
baked daily. Beverly's
has a screened-in
porch for summer
dining under the
towering pines.

GAME FARM & TOURS

■ WILD ACRES GAME FARM

HC 83, P.O. Box 108
Pequot Lakes, MN 56472
Tel: (218) 568-5024
Hrs: Open Sept. - March
Shooting hours 8 a.m. to sundown

Wild Acres Game Farm is owned and operated by Mary Ebnet,
who has worked within the game bird industry for the past 20
years. Wild Acres provides game birds to restaurants throughout
the state as well as individuals. Wild Acres is fully licensed by the
Minnesota Department of Natural Resources to operate as a
private hunting area. Game birds available for hunting are
mallard ducks, pheasants, wild turkeys, bobwhite and crazy quail,
and partridge. Dogs and handlers are provided or, if guests
choose, kennel facilities for their own dog. Wild Acres has a rustic
lodge to retire to after the hunt; meals and accommodations can be
arranged for in advance. Guided tours of the farm are conducted
daily. Call ahead for groups.

Gift shop & attraction

■WORLD OF CHRISTMAS
Highway 371
Pequot Lakes, MN 56472
Tel: (218) 568-5509
Hrs: Open daily May 1 - Christmas Season
   Hours vary, call ahead.
Visa, MasterCard, and Discover are accepted.

Christmas isn't just for December anymore. At World of Christmas, the season of joy, peace, and goodwill lives on all year. Here are all the decorations everyone loves: Christmas trees, santas, reindeer, and Nativity sets to name just a few. But that's not all. Gifts for all seasons and all reasons can also be found at this magical and fun shop.

In 1974, Neal and Carol Holter opened a gift shop in Grand Rapids, ND, and put some Christmas merchandise on display in the summer. The idea was such a hit with customers that they expanded the concept and created the World of Christmas stores in Minnesota in 1978. Today, they have four individual shops located in various northern Minnesota towns: Park Rapids, Pequot Lakes, Detroit Lakes, and Walker. At each World of Christmas store, customers will find such old holiday favorites as nutcrackers, wood carvings, lighted Christmas villages, and ornaments. But the shelves are brimming with non-holiday gifts as well.

The Pequot Lakes store includes a jewelry, accessory, and clothing boutique next door that is well worth the short stroll on the newly built wooden walkway. And just a stone's throw away is the Bump & Putt where adults and children alike can have the time of their lives. Or visitors can pick up some mouthwatering cream or butter fudge from the in-house Nutcracker Sweet.

Resort

■BREEZY POINT RESORT
HCR-2, P.O. Box 70
Breezy Point, MN 56472
Tel: (218) 562-7811 or (800) 432-3777 (in Minnesota)
   or (800) 328-2284 (outside Minnesota)
Hrs: Open year-round
All major credit cards are accepted.

Breezy Point Resort sparkles on the edge of magnificent Big Pelican Lake, offering an unparalleled choice of vacation options.

Inhabiting 3,000 acres of glorious woods and water in central Minnesota's famed Brainerd Lakes Area, Breezy Point is a complete four- season vacation resort.

More than 200 luxurious accommodation choices include townhomes complete with indoor spas overlooking the lake to apartments, chalets, and tastefully decorated individual resort rooms. The "gemstone" of the resort is the original home of Captain Billy Fawcett, founder of Breezy Point. This ten-bedroom mansion is available for rent and continues to provide a very special haven as it did once for the likes of Carol Lombard and Clark Gable. Breezy Point's indoor recreation complex, Breezy Center, hosts a heated pool, children's pool, sauna, whirlpool, tanning booths, game room, poolside eatery, and lounge. Popular dance bands fill the Marina Lounge, and fine dining in the Marina Restaurant provides Breezy's guests with a view as delightful as the menu selections. Plus, Charlie's Restaurant features smoked barbecued ribs and chicken as well as pasta selections and special "Just For the Health of It" entrees.

Walleye, bass, pike, and panfish abound in the clear lake, making Breezy a superb selection for fishing enthusiasts. Fishing boats are available for rent as well as ski boats, pontoons, and paddleboats. A 57-foot cruiser — The Paddlin' Pelican — makes daily tours around the lake while guests soak up the sun and lush scenery. Two 18-hole golf courses offer amateurs and professionals alike a challenging as well as beautiful golf experience. All this is but a start to all the recreational activities at Breezy Point. Four Laykold tennis courts, indoor and outdoor pools, biking, hiking, trail rides as well as scheduled recreation programs are just a sampling.

Cold Spring

L ocated in a classic Minnesota lakes area, Cold Spring is a small town with a future. In 1874, before the city was even platted, the first of Cold Spring's continuing, successful businesses established its headquarters. This pioneer was *Cold Spring Brewing Company,* which today remains one of only three major beer breweries in the state. The brewery, which relies on the cold spring water that originally gave the city its name, has recently expanded to produce North Star Sparkling Water said to be purer than Perrier. Also in the food industry, Gold'N Plump Poultry processes its chicken products in Cold Spring, while the *Cold Spring Bakery* — recognized as one of the state's finest — offers tours of its operations. Aside from these mouthwatering products, Cold Spring is also home to the world's largest producer of building granite, the *Cold Spring Granite Company*, which employs more than 1,700 people and maintains offices in nearby St. Cloud as well as in Minneapolis, Texas, California, New York, and Canada. A video presentation of the operation is available every Wednesday at the Cold Spring City Hall. Despite successful industries such as these, Cold Spring is still a quiet town with a good selection of outdoor recreation opportunities, including canoeing on the *Sauk River;* snowmobiling on the *Kegle Brau Trail* and skiing in the nearby *Powder Ridge* and *Mount Notch* ski and resort areas. There's even a *Blue Heron Rookery* in town, established by the Nature Conservancy to help preserve the bird. In the spring nesting season, visitors congregate at a viewing area for a rare look at the nesting herons.

For more information on Cold Spring, contact:
COLD SPRING AREA CHAMBER OF COMMERCE
P.O. Box 328
Cold Spring, MN 56320
(612) 685-4186

B ED & BREAKFAST

■ PILLOW, PILLAR AND PINE
419 Main Street
Cold Spring, MN 56320
Tel: (612) 685-3828 or (800) 332-6774

This charming 1908 three-story mansion is located in downtown historic Cold Spring, just 15 miles west of St. Cloud. The mansion was built by businessman Marcus Maurin, in a Greek revival architecture, as a wedding gift for his daughter. Considered a perfect haven for quiet getaways and romantic rendezvous, business meetings, reunions, and other special occasions; guests can also enjoy year-round community events during their stay. For outdoor enthusiasts, golfing, boating, hiking, and biking are available close by.

The home has warmth and charm highlighted by stained and leaded glass, original wood oak and maple floors, fireplaces, antique light fixtures, and a wrap-around porch. There are three cozy rooms to choose from. The Hearts and Doves Suite offers a large four-poster queen bed, whirlpool for two and private bath; or guests may choose the Sun Flower Room or the Green Room, each including a continental breakfast served in the privacy of the room or in the dining room.

Enjoy a restful weekend at this charming mansion. Pillow, Pillar and Pine welcomes guests to discover hospitality at its best.

■ S UPPER CLUB

■ BLUE HERON SUPPER CLUB

305 Fifth Ave. S.
Cold Spring, MN 56320
Tel: (612) 685-3831
Hrs: Tue. - Sun. 5 p.m. - 10 p.m.
Visa and MasterCard are accepted.

The Blue Heron Supper Club invites guests for a truly elegant fine dining experience of traditional fine American cuisine. It is an appropriate name by all means, for the Blue Heron Rookery outside Cold Spring is the home of thousands of great Blue Herons, where visitors are encouraged to visit.

Much acclaim has been bestowed upon the cuisine at the Blue Heron Supper Club, which was built in 1972. Owners, Mike and Marlene Dols, have ensured an atmosphere that is elegantly modern and provides a warm ambience. The loyal customers and variety of enticing entrees reflects their success. Prime meats and fresh seafoods as well as creatively original dishes and nightly specials are prepared and presented with a personal touch. Such favorites include prime rib, combination steak dinners that are charcoal broiled, and barbecued pork ribs that are hickory and mesquite-smoked daily. Delectable fish and chicken dinners are carefully hand-breaded with a special German beer batter. All entrees include the famous Blue Heron soup and salad bar. All dressings and soups are homemade and served using the freshest ingredients. The staff will be happy to recommend the perfect wine to enhance any dinner selection. Friday evenings guests are entertained by a strolling violinist. Enjoy the cocktail lounge and live entertainment to end the perfect evening. Complete banquet facilities and service for private parties and receptions are available.

Crookston

F arming is king in Crookston. Located on the eastern edge of the flat and fertile Red River Valley, the city became a major farming and agricultural processing center early in its development. It was predominately settled by immigrants of

Scandinavian heritage, until the Great Northern Railway reached the fledging village in 1872 and a shantytown of tents and tarpaper shacks grew up around the railway crossing at the Red River. Today, the modern city of Crookston with its 8,000 inhabitants is a far cry from this early settlement. In fact, Crookston's home county of Polk has become the state's largest producer of wheat, barley, sugar beets, and potatoes. The city is home to a number of major agriculture-related employers, including the sugar beet processing plant American Crystal Sugar Company and the sunflower seed processor Dahlgren and Company, as well as the Northwest Agricultural Research Station of the University of Minnesota.

ATTRACTIONS

Most of Crookston's attractions are, not surprisingly, agriculture-related. On the top of the list reigns the *Polk County Historical Museum,* which includes several rooms depicting the lives of early settlers, as well as a log house built by a Norwegian settler in 1872, an 1890 schoolhouse, and a truly fascinating collection of antique machinery. The annual *Red River Valley Winter Show* — a major, week-long festival in February attracting more than 40,000 visitors — includes livestock and crop exhibits, pet shows, and a children's barnyard. Later on during the winter and spring, the Winter Show building becomes the venue for more farm-related family fun, including horse-pulling contests, rodeos, and a series of horse shows.

For more information on Crookston, contact:
CROOKSTON AREA CHAMBER OF COMMERCE
114 S. Main Street
Suite A
Crookston, MN 56716
(218) 281-4320

Crosby/Deerwood/Ironton

Collectively known as the Cuyuna Range, these towns have a long and checkered history as rough-and-tumble mining communities. The range, which was named both after Cuyler Adams who discovered the iron ore in the 1890s and his dog, Una, eventually produced 100 million tons of ore before the resource was depleted. Today, many of the vast open iron pits have turned into lakes. These lakes — arguably the state's newest — have been stocked with more than 40,000 trout and now provide some of the hottest *fishing* around. Steering clear of the fishing lines, *scuba divers* are also eagerly exploring the crystal clear waters of the former iron mines. This mining heritage is the focus of most of the historic attractions in the area, including the *Croft Mine and Historical Park* in Crosby, which offers a truly fascinating trip back into the past. The highlight of the visit is a tour with a rattling elevator down into the mine itself, where recordings of ore drills reverberate along the tunnel walls and dioramas and illustrations bring the mining days to life. Above ground, visitors can explore restored mining buildings and mining artifacts. Also in Crosby, the *Cuyuna Range Historical Museum* presents yet more mining memorabilia, including tools, vintage clothing, and displays illustrating the broad ethnic diversity of the iron miners. Deerwood, the oldest city on the range, greets visitors with a statue of a leaping deer and the landmark 1936 *Deerwood Auditorium* — the site of events as varied as *country music shows,* the *Great River Rabbit Show,* and an inevitable, Scandinavian-inspired *lutefisk and meatball supper* each November. In addition, the city is home to one of the oldest resorts in Minnesota, the *Ruttger's Bay Lake Lodge* from 1898. Ironton, meanwhile, is the most restful of the three Cuyuna Range towns, home to a public library and a quiet, landscaped city park complete with picnic tables and grills.

For more information on Crosby, Deerwood, and Ironton, contact:
Crosby Area Chamber of Commerce
P.O. Box 23
Crosby, MN 56441
(218) 546-6990 or (800) 545-2841

Detroit Lakes Area

The list of communities making up the Detroit Lakes area reads "vacation paradise" to informed Minnesota travelers: Callaway, Frazee, Perham, New York Mills, Rochert, Ottertail, Pelican Rapids. All are quaint, interesting communities, and all are conveniently located in the midst of an area dotted with hundreds of walleye lakes. An experienced and friendly travel industry makes up the bulk of the area's income, although Detroit Lakes, boasts a few major manufacturing industries including Swift Eckrich's meat processing plant and Snappy Air Distribution Productions' sheet metal factory.

ATTRACTIONS

It's also in Detroit Lakes where most of the area's major attractions are located — apart from the fishing lakes and resorts, which crop up around every bend. Vacation fun is guaranteed at the bustling, one-mile-long public sandy beach located within city limits, complete with a full-service marina, lifeguards, a fishing pier, walkways, benches and playground facilities. Other fun-filled diversions include *The Human Maze* (a large-scale labyrinth), the *Go, Putt 'N' Bump* (an amusement park with Go-Karts and bumper boats), *Wet 'N' Wild Minnesota* (which includes a speed slide and the state's longest waterslide) and *Lakeside Putter* (18 holes of mini golf located on the city beach). Also in the light-hearted vein, Detroit Lakes is home to some of the state's most entertaining events. Take, for instance, the *We Fest* country music festival in August that attracts more than 80,000 fans and stars the like of Johnny Cash and Alabama; the *Northwest Water Carnival* in July with ten days of more than 50 fun family events; and the *Dairy Days* in June featuring a 600-foot-long banana split. Those who enjoy a few moments of calm often choose to take a romantic dinner cruise on the *Island Girl*, exploring the Detroit Lakes shoreline; or play a few rounds of golf at the *Detroit Country Club* (site of the nationally known men's amateur *Pine to Palm Golf Tournament* each August). Then, for history buffs, there's the *Becker County Historical Museum*, as well as *Buggy Wheel Antiques*, with its excellent antique selection. In the winter, the hills and resorts at *Detroit Mountain* come alive with downhill skiers, and cross-country skiers find their way to the 200 groomed, cross-country trails in the area. For most travelers, however, a visit to Detroit Lakes isn't complete without an excursion to some of the smaller communities surrounding the town. In Perham, for instance, visitors can cheer on their favorite turtle at the races each Wednesday, and in New York Mills the *Finn Creek Museum* features a log house and a sauna built by early Finnish settlers. Eight miles northeast of Detroit Lakes reigns the outstanding *Tamarac National Wildlife Refuge*, with miles of trails and nesting bald eagles, and in Frazee the *Turkey Days* in August is not at all a turkey of an event, but instead finds the town enjoying a log rolling show, street dance, turkey crawl, and other eclectic entertainment.

For more information on the Detroit Lakes Area, contact:
DETROIT LAKES REGIONAL CHAMBER OF COMMERCE
P.O. Box 348
Detroit Lakes, MN 56501
(800) 542-3992

ACCOMMODATIONS

■ HOLIDAY INN - DETROIT LAKES
Highway 10 E.
Detroit Lakes, MN 56501
Tel: (218) 847-2121 or (800) HOLIDAY
Hrs: Open year-round
All major credit cards are accepted.

The Holiday Inn is located on 500 feet of sandy shoreline on Big Detroit Lake. In addition to the beach attraction there is an indoor heated pool, sauna, hot tub, video games, and ping-pong all in the Holidome Fun Center.

Free cable television and Home Box Office premium cable channel are provided in each comfortable room. Docking facilities are available as well as the services of Island Girl Cruise Liner for charters and sight-seeing tours.

■ OAK MANOR MOTEL
895 Highway 10 E.
Detroit Lakes, MN 56501
Tel: (218) 847-4454 or (800) 888-2124
Hrs: Open year-round
All major credit cards are accepted.

For nearly 50 years the Oak Manor Motel has offered "rates you can sleep with." Owned and operated by Ed and Joyce White, the Oak Manor Motel is AAA approved and affiliated with the Budget Host chain of motels. The Oak Manor Motel is a family-operated business that puts an emphasis on comfort and reasonable rates. The two acres of wooded terrain are decorated with 100-year-old oak trees and picnic areas on the grounds.

Twenty-four modern units range in size from single to family units. All units are individually heated and air conditioned. Cable television and free HBO are also included. Some units are equipped with small refrigerators and there is a cottage available with two beds and a complete kitchen. Plug-ins for cars are available in the winter months.

Located on Highway 10, the Oak Manor Motel is near popular restaurants and recreation sights in Detroit Lakes. It offers clean and modern accommodations in a friendly atmosphere.

CROSS-COUNTRY SKI RESORT

■ MAPLELAG
R.R. 1
Callaway, MN 56521
Tel: (218) 375-4466 or (800) 654-7711
Hrs: (Labor Day - Memorial Day)
Visa, MasterCard, and AmEx are accepted.

There's no need to leave the state to stay at one of the nation's top ten cross-country ski resorts. *USA Today* rated Maplelag near Detroit Lakes one of the top ten cross-country ski resorts in the United States. Maplelag offers 35 miles (53 kilometers) of groomed trails for excellent winter enjoyment. Jim and Mary Richards first built Maplelag to make maple syrup from the abundant maple trees, but it soon became apparent that cross-country skiing was really the main attraction of Maplelag. The cabins are original restored Finnish and Norwegian structures brought to Maplelag from all areas of northern Minnesota as well as newly constructed cabins.

"Skiing is something you do to pass the time between meals" has been the slogan for Maplelag for 17 years. In addition to the tremendous meals including the Scandinavian smorgasbord on Sundays and the bottomless cookie jars, there are a few other diversions between meals besides skiing. Minnesota's largest hot tub sits outside able to hold up to 25 visiting skiers. Maplelag also has two saunas and a steam room to warm those chilly bones. With two choices of saunas, there is a choice to suit or not to suit. Moonlight skiing, skating, snowshoeing, and ice fishing number among the various outdoor activities. Then Saturday night presents a chance to dance. Disc jockey Jimmie Anderson hosts the party at the main lodge.

Maplelag boasts the largest collection of antique skis as well as antique advertising signs in the area. They also have built in more than 60 stained glass windows in the main lodge and at least one in every cabin. In 1992 Maplelag plans to open the world's largest fish decoy museum. In the summer months Concordia College of Moorhead hosts a language camp at the resort offering Swedish and Russian for children seven to 18 years old. In September the Northern Lakes Decoy Show is held at Maplelag.

G IFT SHOP

■WORLD OF CHRISTMAS
Highway 10 W.
Detroit Lakes, MN 56501
Tel: (218) 847-1334
Hrs: (May 1 - Christmas Season) Open daily.
    Hours vary, call ahead.
Visa, MasterCard, and Discover are accepted.

No longer is Christmas just for December. At World of Christmas, the season of joy, peace, and goodwill lives on all year. Visitors see all the decorations everyone loves: Christmas trees, santas, reindeer, and Nativity sets to name just a few.

Neal and Carol Holter opened a gift shop in Grand Rapids, ND, in 1974, and put some Christmas merchandise on display in the summer. The idea was such a hit with customers that the Holters expanded the concept and in 1978 established the World of Christmas stores in Minnesota. Today, they have four individual shops located in northern Minnesota in: Park Rapids, Pequot Lakes, Detroit Lakes, and Walker. At each World of Christmas store, customers will find such old holiday favorites as nutcrackers, wood carvings, lighted Christmas villages, and ornaments.

At the Detroit Lakes store, children and adults alike will enjoy the beauty of the northern forest and the lake country. Nestled within these idyllic surroundings, World of Christmas keeps the magic of nature and the holidays forever alive. Take a refreshing stroll among the trees on the store's grounds, and then step inside and see the unique gift items that evoke the spirit of these northwoods. Guests might want to take one or more home as a momento of their trip, along with some mouthwatering cream or butter fudge from the Nutcracker Sweet.

G IFTS & FURNITURE

■THE RED WILLOW/WHITEHOUSE INTERIORS
1160 S. Washington Ave.
Detroit Lakes, MN 56501
Tel: (218) 847-6297
Hrs: Hours vary. Open daily
All major credit cards are accepted.

A stone's throw away from the beach at Detroit Lake sits The Red Willow, which offers gifts, furniture, and interior design. The space the shop now occupies was originally a nine-room house

built at the turn of the century. Open since 1984, The Red Willow charts the change of the seasons in the charming displays arranged throughout the year. The Red Willow maintains a high quality of selection and an everchanging display of inventory.

There is something for every taste. Hand-crafted solid wood, upholstered and wicker furniture, as well as the Bob Timberlake furniture collection are featured. Brass and ceramic furnishings, baskets, and an extensive selection of pictures offer endless choices to enhance the interior of any home. Collectors will enjoy the vast array of Precious Moments, Heritage Village, and original Snow Village pieces available. A year-round Christmas section carries many one-of-a kind items and a vast array of Santas to please children as well as adults. Be sure not to miss the Italian Fish Room.

Each room in The Red Willow has a different theme: a primitive and a country room, a children's room, a northwoods cabin section, a holiday theme room, and the Waverly Boutique, which carries in-stock fabrics and wallpaper. The Red Willow prides itself on offering the most unique and up-to-date gift items and furnishings available. The store captures the charm and warmth of northwestern Minnesota in its merchandise as well as its friendly sales associates.

R ESORT

■ FAIR HILLS RESORT
R.R. 1, P.O. Box 128
Detroit Lakes, MN 56501
Tel: (218) 847-7638 or (800) 323-2849
Hrs: May 1 - Oct. 1
Visa, MasterCard, and AmEx are accepted.

Fair Hills has been open since 1906, when the Ashelman brothers (Hud, Frank, and George) decided to devote all of their time to the resort business. The Ashelmans built their farmhouse on an abandoned stone foundation in 1902 and began to take in boarders. This venture was profitable, resulting in what is still Fair Hills today. In 1918 Fair Hills was sold, and continued to be sold every two years until 1925 when Ed and Bessie Kaldahl purchased it from a St. Cloud bank that had repossessed the property. The resort is now run by grandson Dave Kaldahl and his family.

Fair Hills is a seasonal resort located on the eastern end of Pelican Lake. This lake is one of the cleanest and safest lakes in the area. Several types of boats are available at the resort: speedboats, sailboats, fishing boats, paddleboats, canoes, and kayaks. Windsurfing instruction videos are available for viewing before taking the boards out for a spin. There is also a nine-hole golf course at the resort, and Detroit Lakes Country Club is only five miles away with a 36-hole course. Six tennis courts, a swimming pool, wading pool, and whirlpool offer further outdoor enjoyment.

There are 88 units at Fair Hills, able to serve up to 250 guests. Individual cabins or motel-type rooms offer a choice in lodging. The cabins offer either the American Plan (where meals are included in the price of the stay) or the Housekeeping Plan (where a kitchen is provided with the lodging). Fair Hills emphasizes family vacations, there is no lounge or liquor served on the premises, but there are activities throughout the week to keep guests entertained every moment. A full-service restaurant with a new menu each day is located in the resort. For a family vacation that will suit every member, make reservations early for Fair Hills.

■R ESTAURANTS

■ THE FIRESIDE
East Shore Drive
P.O. Box 346
Detroit Lakes, MN 56502
Tel: (218) 847-8192
Hrs: Open daily 5:30 p.m. - close Apr. - Nov.
No credit cards are accepted.

The Fireside overlooking Detroit Lake has maintained its reputation for great food and great service for more 30 years. Although it has changed owners over time, the customers return year after year for the consistently good food. Current owners Tom and Jennifer Graham have added a patio on which to fully enjoy the beautiful sunsets on the lake. Some of the highlights on the menu include: swordfish fillet, lobster tail, filet mignon, and tempura vegetables. Hungry patrons can expect a wait on summer weekends, allowing time for a relaxing cocktail by the lake.

■LAKESIDE 1891

200 W. Lake Drive
Detroit Lakes, MN 56502
Tel: (218) 847-7887
Hrs: Hours vary with season
Visa and MasterCard are accepted.

One-hundred years ago a German immigrant named August Guethling built the Lakeside Lodge to replace the old Pioneer Resort. To commemorate the opening, a dance was held on May 28th, 1891 and the doors have remained open ever since. Several owners have operated the Lakeside Lodge, adding their own unique improvements to accommodate the growing population and increase in tourism over the years in Detroit Lakes. In the spring of 1986 the lodge was purchased by TFG, Inc. which constructed a whole new building on the site but retained the name of Lakeside in honor of the building's long history.

This building offers fine dining and the exquisite scenery of Detroit Lake. Lakeside 1891 is renowned for steaks of the highest quality and a nightly chef's special. A century of history is still retained in the restaurant with memorabilia gracing the interior. Outdoor dining is available on the patio overlooking the beach of Detroit Lake, and in the winter a spectacular view of the frosty northland can be seen from the numerous windows overlooking the lake.

Current owners Dan and Erika Tigges suggest three highlights on the menu: grilled marinated chicken, prime rib carved to order in three different cuts, and the filet mignon available in two cuts. Lakeside 1891 uses fresh poultry, beef, fish, vegetables, and daily baked bread for the enjoyment of its guests. Banquet facilities are available as well as a bar menu specializing in short orders. Lakeside 1891 offers historical surroundings combined with fine dining.

■ SEDONA'S ON THE LAKE

1375 W. Lake Drive
Detroit Lakes, MN 56501
Tel: (218) 847-8828
Hrs: (Summer) 11 a.m. - 11 p.m.
    (Winter) 4:30 p.m. - 9 p.m.
Visa, MasterCard, and Discover are accepted.

Sedona's is named after the beautiful town just north of Phoenix, AZ. The Southwestern touch is apparent in the food as well as the interior at Sedona's in Detroit Lakes. New owner Don Ludovissie recently purchased this spacious restaurant on the west side of Detroit Lake that offers a comfortable atmosphere, great food, and a fantastic view overlooking the lake.

Sedona's serves quality fresh food at reasonable prices. Specialties are American and Mexican entrees with a full line of sandwiches and appetizers. Exceptional appetizers include: Wings of Fire — chicken wings breaded and fried then dipped in hot-hot-hot sauce and baked. Waffle Fries are a unique menu item, they are criss-cut whole potatoes deep-fried and served with Sedona's Secret Sauce. For dinner the world-famous BBQ ribs are outstanding, and of course the freshwater walleye couldn't be any fresher since the lakes are so nearby. For the lighter side Sedona's offers the Sedona burger with guacamole, tomato, and onion; or a rib sandwich.

There are boat docking facilities at Sedona's and a Beach Bar in the summer, which offers a great view of the beach volleyball matches. Live entertainment and dancing help to wear off dinner in the bar and lounge area. Next door to Sedona's is the Voyager Bowling Alley where patrons can damage a few pins before or after dinner. For a touch of the Southwest in the north, Sedona's is on the Lake.

R ESTAURANT & MOTEL

■ THE OTTER SUPPER CLUB AND MOTEL

Highway 78
P.O. Box 86
Ottertail, MN 56571
Tel: (218) 367-2525
Hrs: Open year-round
All major credit cards are accepted.

In 1870, Otter Tail City was a bustling frontier town in northwestern Minnesota with five hotels, 27 saloons and no fewer than five lawyers. By 1885, however, most of Otter Tail City's 1,200 inhabitants had left town. The new Northern Pacific

Railroad had bypassed Otter Tail, leaving it with few commercial ties to the rest of the state.

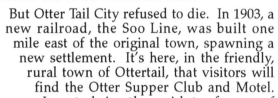

But Otter Tail City refused to die. In 1903, a new railroad, the Soo Line, was built one mile east of the original town, spawning a new settlement. It's here, in the friendly, rural town of Ottertail, that visitors will find the Otter Supper Club and Motel. Located in the midst of one of Minnesota's most renowned lake and recreation areas, the Otter Supper Club offers dining at its finest. On Wednesday nights, owner and operator Dennis Dahl roasts 300 pounds of beef on the spit for an all-you-can-eat extrava-ganza; on Friday nights, he tempts visitors with an oriental special. The Sunday buffet from 11 a.m. to 4 p.m. features broasted chicken, barbecued ribs, broiled cod, and beef plus more items too numerous to mention. Many dinner guests, however, opt for his specialty: USDA choice sirloin steaks charcoal-grilled to perfection and served with sauteed whole button mushrooms. There is also a friendly lounge area to take in some of the local characters and conversation. In addition, off-sale package liquor is available.

The Otter Supper Club features live entertainment in the summer and year-round Polkafests on Sundays from 2-6 p.m. featuring polka music and dancing. Dahl offers a second high-quality dining alternative at D. Dahl's Char House in Detroit Lakes, where U.S.D.A choice steaks and seafood are featured.

W ILDLIFE REFUGE

■ TAMARAC NATIONAL WILDLIFE REFUGE
HC 10, P.O. Box 145
Rochert, MN 56578
Tel: (218)847-2641
Hrs: Mon. - Fri. 7:30 a.m. to 4 p.m.
    (Memorial Day - Labor Day) Sat. - Sun. noon to 5

Tamarac National Wildlife Refuge was created by executive order in 1938 by Franklin Roosevelt to provide a breeding ground for migratory birds and other wildlife. This refuge also provides a

©MARTIENA R. RICHTER

safe haven for endangered species such as the bald eagle. Currently Tamarac has one of the highest nesting densities of bald eagles on a national wildlife refuge with 16 active bald eagle nests. This refuge is also home to timber wolves, bear, moose, deer, and beaver.

Run by the U.S. Fish and Wildlife Service, total acreage of Tamarac is 42,724 acres consisting of half wetlands and half timberland. In the fall the White Earth Indians harvest the wild rice while the fall colors envelope the refuge in earthy beauty. There is an interpretive center open to the public with regularly scheduled presentations. There are over 200 species of birds found in Tamarac, making it the perfect bird-watchers' retreat in addition to being a hospitable environment in which to study nature. Hunting and fishing are permitted in designated areas. Tamarac Lake is one of the spots that is open to fishing during all state fishing seasons. A wildlife film series and interpretive program are scheduled each weekend during the summer months.

For cross-country skiing, the Pine Lake-Tamarac Lake area has nearly eight miles of trails. Average snowfall for the area is around four feet so there is always a good snow base. Leaflets available at the visitor center provide direction for a ten-mile self-guided auto tour May through October. Group presentations are available by calling in advance. Tamarac National Wildlife Refuge gives access to a view of wildlife in its own environment.

Elk River

E arly Indians knew this place well. They called it "Wich a wan" — where two rivers join, and often camped by the green-tinted waters of the Elk River where it joined the mighty Mississippi. Today, the rivers still meet in present-day Elk River, although the elks that inspired the river's name are long gone. Instead, a bustling, rapidly growing city of 11,000 has taken their place. Elk River is benefiting from its proximity to Minneapolis, regularly adding new businesses to its stable of 400 locally based companies while inexorably becoming absorbed into the fringe of the Twin Cities metropolitan area, 30 miles to the southeast. Still, the city maintains a small-town atmosphere with a first-class, genuine bakery and butcher shop, and boasts a number of parks including *Lake Orono*, with a public beach, and the *Lions Community Park*. Most importantly, Elk River is the gateway to *Sherburne National Wildlife Refuge* with miles of trails and excellent wildlife observation opportunities. It is also a cultural haven, home to a *Community Theater, Community Band & Chorus, Land of Lakes Choirboys*, and an annual *Fine Arts Festival*. The agricultural heritage of the city is celebrated in annual summer festivals, such as the *Sherburne County Fair, Antique Engine Show*, and *Pioneer Threshing Weekend*, and at the excellent *Oliver H. Kelley Farm,* a living history farm from the mid-19th century complete with old-fashioned farm animals.

For more information on Elk River, contact:
ELK RIVER AREA CHAMBER OF COMMERCE
729 Main Street
Elk River, MN 55330
(612) 441-3110

H ISTORIC SITE

■ OLIVER H. KELLEY FARM
A Minnesota Historical Society Site
U.S. Highway 10
(2.5 miles southeast of Elk River, MN)
Mailing Address: 15788 Kelley Farm Road, Elk River, MN 55330
Tel: (612) 441-6896
Hrs: May 1 - Oct. 31 (farm and visitors' center): Daily 10 a.m. - 5 p.m.
　　Nov. 2 - April 26 (visitors' center only):
　　Sat. 10 a.m. - 4 p.m.
　　Sun. noon - 4 p.m.

From the very beginning, Oliver H. Kelley was clearly a progressive thinker and an ambitious farmer. He and his wife, Lucy, purchased their farm in 1949, and soon Kelley had mortgaged it to purchase modern implements, turning his farm from a labor intensive operation into a mechanized business. In 1867, he founded the Patrons of Husbandry — better known as the Grange — farmers' organization that demanded reduced railroad rates and better social and economic conditions for farmers.

The fascinating lives of Kelley, his family, and other Minnesota farm families are depicted at the Oliver H. Kelley farm — a "living history" farm where interpreters in period clothing perform the tasks and chores of a typical mid-nineteenth century farm family. Visitors can participate in the work with hands-on activities designed to teach them about the changes that were occurring in agriculture at that time. The farm also has historic varieties of plants that have not been hybridized, and old breeds of farm animals seldom seen today, including lineback cattle and Berkshire hogs. Forty acres are farmed with horses and oxen, and visitors may see horse-powered threshing and plowing by oxen. In the house, interpreters perform such domestic chores as churning butter, cooking farm produce over a wood stove, and scrubbing laundry on an old washboard.

After touring the farmstead and nature trail, visitors also can view a video and exhibit about the Grange and about the changing nature of farming during the mid-nineteenth century. In addition, the Interpretive Center houses a bookstore featuring books about agricultural history, women's history, and gardening.

Fergus Falls Area

H istory awaits on the doorstep in Fergus Falls, a park- and lake-studded city located just off Interstate 94 a couple of hours east of Moorhead. Established in 1856 by a young explorer and named in honor of the man who financed the expedition, James Fergus, the city has maintained an amazing variety of old buildings in the *historic downtown district.* Informed visitors are quick to embark on a *historic walking tour* to observe the profusion of Italianate-style buildings, popular around the turn of the century for their decorative trim, arches, and brickwork. As time wore on and fires and tornadoes ran their course, alterations were made to some of the buildings, but there's still a hundred years of history in the *Lower Newman Block,* the *Fergus Falls National Bank building,* the *Otter Tail Power Company,* and numerous others. (Visitors are advised to obtain a walking guide published by the Fergus Falls Heritage Preservation Commission.) In addition to the walking tour of downtown, the *Otter Tail County Museum* is also highly recommended, boasting a professionally designed Indian dwelling and a Main Street complete with a general store, doctor's office and — of course — a saloon. The museum also rents cassettes describing driving tours to historic sites throughout the Fergus Falls area, including to the nearby, lovingly restored *Phelps Mill.* During the second week of July, the mill is the site of the *Phelps Mill Summer Festival,* a two-day extravaganza of arts and crafts displays, stage shows, a puppet theater, and music performances ranging from Appalachian clogging to German brass. Other events of interest to arts fans take place regularly in *A Center for the Arts,* an eclectic theater presenting a variety of quality performances in music, dance, comedy, and drama.

For more information on the Fergus Falls Area, contact:
FERGUS FALLS AREA CHAMBER OF COMMERCE
202 S. Court Street
Fergus Falls, MN 56537
(218) 736-6951

A NTIQUES & COUNTRY GIFTS

■ COUNTRY FANCIES

426 W. Lincoln Ave.
(One mile east of Westridge Mall)
Fergus Falls, MN 56537
Tel: (218) 739-4828
Hrs: Mon. - Fri. 10 a.m. - 9 p.m.
Sat. 10 a.m. - 6 p.m., Sun. noon - 5 p.m.
Visa and MasterCard are accepted.

The spicy fragrance of potpourri greets customers as they walk through the front door of this charming old home built in 1890. This is Country Fancies, "a Country-Victorian storehouse of decorating ideas." A peek inside the antique leaded-glass windows reveals tasteful arrangements of antique and wicker furniture, collectibles, brass, wood shelves, graceful candles, window lace, jewelry, crystal and china, and year-round Christmas decorations. Most striking, however, are the floral arrangements. Wreaths, centerpieces, and one-of-a-kind silk flower bouquets are displayed on tabletops and shelves.

Country Fancies was opened in 1986 by Jim and Karen Selken, who also own Wahpeton Floral and Gift in Wahpeton, ND. Evidence of their love of flowers is everywhere. Designing floral arrangements is a store specialty, says manager Norma Hallisey. Customers are encouraged to bring samples of fabric or wallpaper to have arrangements custom-designed to match their homes.

Several color-coordinated rooms display Country-Victorian style decor to its best advantage, so customers get a realistic view of how items might look. An experienced interior decorator, Hallisey offers her expertise to customers who wish to consult with her about decorating. The store also features a bridal registry and a two-day approval service, especially popular with customers who may want to see items displayed in their home before purchasing.

A RT GALLERY

■ FORER CORNERS

715 Pebble Lake Road
Fergus Falls, MN 56537
Tel: (218) 739-3423
Hrs: Tue. - Fri. 9 a.m. - 5:30 p.m., Sat. 9 a.m. - 3 p.m. Closed Sun. - Mon.
Visa and MasterCard are accepted.

Forer Corners custom framing gallery specializes in custom frames with a special touch. The results truly are beautiful. Owner and custom framer Brad Forer carefully mats and frames each signed print. A painting of a Minnesota scene by Minnesota artist Terry Redlin, for example, might be accented with a feather or design in the matting to bring out a particular color or detail.

Drop by the friendly Forer Corners and pick up a signed print by a Minnesota artist, a collector's plate, or a gift. Look for examples of Forer Corners' award-winning technique called French matting. Forer Corners is located on Highway 59, in southern Fergus Falls.

$\boxed{B}$ ED & BREAKFAST

■ BAKKETOPP HUS BED & BREAKFAST
R.R. 2, P.O. Box 187 A
Fergus Falls, MN 56537
Tel: (218) 739-2915

On a hilltop eight-and-a-half miles north of Fergus Falls, overlooking a lake and surrounded by serene woods, lies the graceful home of Judy and Dennis Nims. Doubling as a luxurious bed and breakfast under the name Bakketopp Hus — "hilltop house" in Norwegian — the Nims' home is becoming a favored destination for more and more visitors to northwestern Minnesota.

As the name suggests, the owners of Bakketopp Hus — located on Long Lake a half mile east of County Road 27 — pride themselves on Norwegian foods and themes, an irresistible combination to many Norwegian-American travelers. In addition to Norwegian items, the Nims' attractive decorating scheme includes an impressive assortment of antiques and American

Country furnishings. Two decks overlooking the lake, high, vaulted ceilings, a fireplace, and natural woodwork complete the rustic, yet sophisticated, surroundings.

The Nims have three guest rooms available, each with its own unique decor and amenities. The master suite comes with a bay patio door opening out to garden patio, a king-size waterbed, full bath, hot spa with natural cedar walls, and a skylight. Those looking for the ultimate in relaxation are quick to sample the six-person jacuzzi. The lower level guest room also includes a king-size waterbed, and a pool table, and player piano for entertainment. Finally, the upper level guest room features a deck, a smaller bed, and quaint country furnishings for those traveling alone. Whichever room guests choose, they can look forward to a different full breakfast daily, beautiful scenery, and nearby nature trails and picnic area — and a night spent in Norwegian style and comfort at Bakketopp Hus.

B OOKSTORE & GIFTS

■ VICTOR LUNDEEN COMPANY
126-128 W. Lincoln
Fergus Falls, MN 56537
Tel: (218) 736-5433
Hrs: Mon. - Sat. 9 a.m. - 5:30 p.m.
Visa, Discover, and MasterCard are accepted.

Visitors experience a piece of history when they step into Victor Lundeen Company, the oldest family operated business in Fergus Falls. Still doing business from the original store front, Victor Lundeen Company specializes in printing services, as it has for 77 years. Today, Victor Lundeen Company also positions itself as a bookseller and stationer. The store displays giftware, stationery, office products, artist supplies, drafting tools, and a wide variety of books — bestsellers and classics, regional books, children's, cookbooks, and how-to books.

Generations of shoppers have found their way to Victor Lundeen Company since Lundeen first opened the print shop in 1914. Years later, he was joined by his sons and nephew. In 1981, the Victor Lundeen Company expanded into the adjacent bank building. Today's store is large and can take several hours to browse through.

The printshop markets its products throughout the Upper Midwest and offers a complete spectrum of printing services, including an in-house design and layout department that can deliver finished products, if needed, in 24 hours. Such specialty advertising items as name-imprinted pens are typical orders for the Victor Lundeen Company. Whether customers want to update business cards, promote their business, or pick up a gift item, Victor Lundeen Company is there to meet their needs.

GIFT SHOP

■ THE PHELPS MILL STORE
R.R. 2, P.O. Box 47
Underwood, MN 56586
Tel: (218) 826-6158
Hrs: (Memorial Day - Labor Day)
   Mon. - Sat. 10 a.m. - 6 p.m., Sun. noon - 6 p.m.
   (May, Sept., Oct.) Sat. - Sun. only noon - 5 p.m.

For a hundred years, The Phelps Mill Store has stood guard on County Road 45 across from the old Phelps Mill. Stepping into this designated National Historic Place is stepping back into American history and the simple quiet of country life. Traditions have been maintained and the store kept well stocked with old-fashioned pleasures and treasures.

Most popular with passersby are the shop's ice cream counter and its abundance of stick candies in modern as well as traditional flavors. Shelves of these sentimental sweets separate the two main

rooms of the store, which are filled with handmade country gift items, country decorating accessories, sweatshirts, T-shirts, baskets, cookbooks, candles, cotton handloomed rugs, braided rugs, and souvenir items of Minnesota.

Visitors are welcome to shop, then purchase dishes or cones of ice cream to take out and enjoy on a park bench on the sweeping front porch. They can sit and listen to birds sing and water cascade down the falls at the old mill site across the street. The store's exterior has been immaculately maintained; a fresh coat of gray paint is trimmed in white and set off by black shutters. The porch is weighted down with old planted whiskey barrels and overhung with plants and windsocks. The Phelps Mill Store has put history to good use, offering for more than two decades a gift shop that includes rural warmth.

L LAMA FARM

■ HORSESHOE VALLEY LLAMAS
R.R. 5
Fergus Falls, MN 56537
Tel: (218) 736-4707
Tours by appointment

Horseshoe Valley Llamas offers an opportunity to learn more about these native South American animals. Horseshoe Valley began in 1984 with three bred females and has expanded into a herd of 30. All of the animals are registered with the International Llama Registry.

The llamas maintained at Horseshoe Valley contain some well-known bloodlines such as Doolittle, Poncho Via, and Chilean. Tours are free to individuals; groups are $10. Horseshoe Valley Llama Tours are an interesting way to become acquainted with this intriguing animal.

M OTEL

■ THE LAKELAND MOTEL
Highway 59
Fergus Falls, MN 56537
Tel: (218) 736-6938
Hrs: 8 a.m. - 10 p.m.
Visa and MasterCard are accepted.

The Lakeland Motel in beautiful Fergus Falls has comfortable, quiet rooms just minutes away from five lakes, 21 parks, supervised swimming beaches, tennis courts, horseshoe courts, and a public golf course. Sound interesting? That's not all. For the outdoor lover, Fergus Falls (named after James Fergus, an expedition financier in 1856) is the perfect place to relax or to recreate an expedition to the area's some 1,000 lakes less than an hour's drive away.

History lovers will enjoy the Otter Tail County Historical Museum, as well as the Center for the Arts and the Fergus Falls Concert Association. Nearby restaurants, stores, and the enclosed Westridge Mall also invite shoppers and diners. Whether visitors are a fan of the outdoors or the indoors, Fergus Falls can keep them busy, and the Lakeland Motel is conveniently close to it all. Rooms also include cable TV.

▌M USEUM

■OTTERTAIL COUNTY HISTORICAL MUSEUM
1110 W. Lincoln
Fergus Falls, MN 56537
Tel: (218) 736-6038
Hrs: Mon. - Fri. 9 a.m. - 5 p.m., Sat. - Sun./Holidays 1 p.m. - 4 p.m.

The Ottertail County Historical Society was founded in July of 1927 and opened its first Historical Museum in May of 1934. The museum was established to preserve and display the history of Ottertail County throughout the years, tracing the history of northern Minnesota from the glaciers to the Ojibwa Indians to the Mormons up through today. As history was compiled the need for expansion grew, with the most recent addition in 1983 giving the museum over 15,000 square feet of exhibit space.

Currently there are 107 different displays viewed by nearly 15,000 visitors annually. It is one of the top five museums in the state and the surrounding regions. The E.T. Barnard Library gives easy access to maps, census records, platbooks, newspapers, photographs, and various history records. There is an extensive research and archives department in the museum.

The Ottertail Historical Society is supported by 1,152 members and 125 active volunteers. Guided tours are available upon request. Always concerned with the enrichment of the younger citizens, there is constant development of educational programs. In the Educational Center are museum tours, slide/tape shows, traveling kits, programs, traveling exhibits, and a historical sites tour. Currently the Historical Society publishes a booklet entitled "Educational Programs for Teachers and Groups" for the benefit of area educators.

Q UILT SHOP

■ THE QUILTER'S COTTAGE

715 Pebble Lake Road
Fergus Falls, MN 56537
Tel: (218) 739-9652
Hrs: Tue. - Fri. 10 a.m. - 5 p.m.
    Sat. 10 a.m. - 3 p.m. Closed on Sun. and Mon.

Cheri Steenbock, owner of The Quilter's Cottage located on the southern edge of Fergus Falls, is proud of the personalized service she offers regardless of the size of the quilting project. Quilting is enjoying a modern-day renaissance, having come a long way from the days when it was simply a practical way to make quilts out of old clothing. Cheri's store caters to lovers of this old but newly popular art form.

The Quilter's Cottage sells 100 percent cotton fabrics and all the equipment, patterns, and books one might need to finish a project. A teaching staff of up to eight offers classes in all types of quilting and is ready to help with customers' quilting needs. Come and enjoy seeing and making this beautiful art form.

R ESORT

■ WOODLAWN RESORT

Blanche Creek Road
Battle Lake, MN 56515
Tel: (218) 864-5389
Hrs: June 1 to Sept. 1

Owned and operated by one family since 1948, Woodlawn Resort offers a lot for vacationers to do, which probably accounts for the many guest families returning every year. Owners Bud and Phyllis Narveson provide enough activities to keep even the busiest person occupied. Windsurfing and sailing lessons are available, as are a tennis court, fishing boats and canoes, a shallow water volleyball net, a library full of games and books, and golf courses and riding trails nearby.

Nine carpeted, fully equipped cottages are located right on the lakeshore. The cabins have from two to four comfortably furnished bedrooms and completely outfitted kitchens. All the cottages have spectacular views.

The resort is situated in secluded wilderness, which is perfect for watching wildlife. A guide is provided for those who want to wander off and explore the territory.

RESTAURANTS

■ BAO CUISINE
108 E. Lincoln
Fergus Falls, MN 56537
Tel: (218) 739-2106
Hrs: Mon. - Thur. 6:30 a.m. - 8 p.m., Fri. 6:30 a.m. - 9 p.m.
      Sat. 7 a.m. - 9 p.m., Sun. 8 a.m. - 2 p.m.

Fergus Falls has the fortune of being host to a restaurant specializing in some of the tastiest food on earth. Chinese cuisine long has been regarded as one of the world's greatest cuisines, and Chef Bao Do and family certainly do justice to this reputation. Bao Cuisine Chinese restaurant presents daily a culinary cornucopia of such entrees as pork marinated in oriental herbs; shrimp and chicken sauteed with fresh pea pods, onions, mushrooms, and water chestnuts;, and boneless chicken breast sauteed with apple and ameretto sauce. Fresh ingredients are the key to the success of Bao Cuisine, and are featured daily in the popular luncheon buffets, which include sweet-and-sour pork, teriyaki chicken, or shrimp and beef sauteed in a variety of delicious sauces. Classic American sandwiches, hamburgers, and seafood dishes also are served.

Bao Cuisine is located in a spacious historic building in the heart of downtown Fergus Falls. Charming wooden floors retain the historic character of the building, and the decor sports a modern country touch. Capacity seating, at 110, provides plenty of space for banquets.

Be sure to stop in for lunch or dinner at Bao Cuisine, conveniently located on East Lincoln Street. One small taste is worth a fortune.

■ MABEL MURPHY'S
I-94 and Highway 210 W.
Fergus Falls, MN 56537
Tel: (218) 739-4406
Hrs: Open daily 11 a.m. - 1:30 a.m.
Visa, MasterCard, and AmEx are accepted.

Mabel Murphy's Restaurant is as original as the story behind the name. Said to be an "Irish import," Mabel fled Ireland to escape the potato famine. The sailing ship headed for America sank, and after two months in the water Mabel emerged as one of the few survivors. Captured by renegades, she later escaped disguised as a wagon wheel. Thankfully she was the possessor of excellent cooking skills, which can still be enjoyed today.

Some of the featured dishes are Alaskan king crab, Long Island duckling, and homemade Irish stew. Since 1977 Mabel Murphy's eating and drinking establishment has attracted the hungriest of visitors and has turned them into satisfied customers.

■ THE VIKING CAFE

203 W. Lincoln Ave.
Fergus Falls, MN 56537
Tel: (218) 736-6660
Hrs: Mon. - Sat. 5:30 a.m. to 7 p.m., Sun. 7 a.m. to 2 p.m.

Since 1946 The Viking Cafe has provided good home-style cooking to downtown Fergus Falls. Family-owned and operated for over 30 years, the Viking Cafe features a daily smorgasbord with fresh vegetables, oven-baked chicken, homemade potatoes and gravy, ribs, and homemade cookies.

Since the cafe is known throughout the area for great breakfasts, people will drive 100 miles out of their way just to visit it. This restaurant is famous for its coffee, homemade rolls, hand-cut bacon, ham, and meats, and the chef's

homemade specials under $5, all made from scratch. The cafe has a loyal following, which includes the employees. Known as "the meeting place in Fergus Falls," the atmosphere provides a special ambiance to its patrons combined with friendly service. The menu is printed daily, and the cafe has been noted to have the cleanest bathrooms in northwestern Minnesota.

Glenwood

A s legend has it, the Glenwood area was once home to beautiful Minnewaska, daughter of a Dakota Indian chief. Unbecoming the daughter of a chief, she had fallen in love with a young warrior, Pazekee. When she wanted to marry him, her parents predictably refused, and in her anger and frustration she fled from home with Pazekee. Then, tragedy struck, and she drowned in the great lake that lapped at the shores by the tribe's camp. Today, the lake still bears the name Lake Minnewaska in her memory, although the sky-tinted waters are plied by a scattering of waterskiers, pontoons, and sailboats rather than birchbark canoes. In fact, quiet Glenwood calls itself the "best-kept secret in Minnesota" with its excellent resorts, two *golf courses*, top-of-the-line dining, bingo and bowling opportunities, and hiking, swimming, and camping in *Glacial Lake State Park*. Other spots of natural beauty include *Morning Glory Gardens* — an old chapel surrounded by more than 30 varieties of flowers — and the *Indian Burial Grounds* three miles west of the city, with their view of Lake Minnewaska and Lake Pelican. After visiting the burial grounds, those with a taste for more history can tour the grand interior of the 1913 Craftsman-style *Ann Bickle Heritage House.* The *Polk County Historical Museum* features excellent

© MARTIENA R. RICHTER

displays of a country store and a pioneer kitchen, as well as a gallery of Indian arts and crafts, while the 1903 *Terrace Mill* located 12 miles south of town provides an intriguing insight into the early days of flour milling. Among local events, the *Waterama Festival* is the city's greatest extravaganza. Held every July, the festival includes a pontoon parade, waterskiing shows, theatre productions, and a host of other fun-filled events.

For more information on Glenwood, contact:
GLENWOOD CHAMBER OF COMMERCE
137 E. Minnesota Ave.
Glenwood, MN 56334
(612) 634-3636

R ESORT

■PETERS SUNSET BEACH
2500 S. Lakeshore
Glenwood, MN 56334
Tel: (612) 634-4501 or (800) 356-8654
Hrs: May 1 - Oct. 15

Peters Sunset Beach vacation resort on Lake Minnewaska is listed on the National Register of Historic Sites but provides timeless vacation enjoyment. In 1990 Peters Sunset Beach celebrated its 75th anniversary of providing enjoyment to visitors from all over. The Peters family treated their guests as family and that tradition still lives on today.

Lake Minnewaska provides activities for everyone. The sandy shallow beach area provides a safe swimming area for kids as well as adults. Fishing, boating, sailing, and waterskiing number among the additional activities for the utmost enjoyment. The Pezhekee golf course is a top quality 18-hole course that invites golfers to display their skill playing to a total of 6,500 yards. Some of the unique features of the golf course are a suspension bridge — a 180-foot walking bridge spanning a ravine — and the fairways that cut through a beautiful oak and maple forest. Tennis courts, bicycle rental, racquetball, and biking and jogging trails round out the list of sporting choices. The Duck Room in the main lodge provides arcade challenges.

Cottages, townhouses, and hotel-style rooms make up the 175-person capacity of lodging alternatives. Cottages offer complete furnishings including a kitchen and linens. Air conditioning, fresh towels, maid service, color television, outdoor grill, and, in most units, fireplaces. Townhouses have all of the features of the cottages plus laundry facilities and a dishwasher. Private hotel rooms have small refrigerators and private bathrooms. Peters Sunset Beach provides a beautiful vacation retreat for all tastes.

S UPPER CLUB

■ MINNEWASKA HOUSE
Highway 28 & 29
(Between Glenwood and Starbuck)
Glenwood, MN 56334
Tel: (612) 634-4566 or (800) 828-0882
Hrs: Open daily 11 a.m. - 2 p.m. , 5 p.m. - 10:30 p.m.
All major credit cards are accepted.

The Minnewaska House supper club and lounge has been satisfying the appetites of customers for 26 years. This supper club is a traditional steak, chop, and seafood house with an excellent menu. An open hearth grill is on full display in the dining room allowing guests to savor the char-broiled aroma of their meal before it reaches the table.

The seafood selection is the largest in central Minnesota with such mouthwatering treats as crab, shrimp, walleye, swordfish, and lobster. All of the meat is handcut on the premises with specialities including ribs, steak, teriyaki, pork chops, and lamb chops. Thirteen popular cuts give steak lovers the opportunity to get exactly what they want. The lounge area specializes in sandwiches and a short order menu. Live music is presented on Fridays and Saturdays. For a meal that will always meet the highest expectations, the Minnewaska House provides excellence in dining.

Lake George

I t's not easy to get lost in Lake George, goes the local proverb, but it's easy to lose your heart. Indeed, this tiny community is a restful haven that's hard to leave behind, a town complete with small family-run industries, restaurants, bait shops, and resorts. One of the main attractions for first-time visitors to Lake George, however, is not the small-town ambiance but rather its location just seven miles east of *Lake Itasca State Park.* The second largest state park in Minnesota, Lake Itasca — which celebrated its centennial in 1990 — forms a protective shield of lakes, marshes, and dense woods around the famed headwaters of the Mississippi. Lake George visitors who time their arrival well can also attend the annual *Blueberry Festival* in July and pick their winter supply of this northwoods treat, which is particularly plentiful in this area.

For more information on Lake George, contact:
LAKE GEORGE AREA ASSOCIATION
P.O. Box 1635 B
Lake George, MN 56458
(218) 266-3468

GALLERY

■ THE SCHOOLCRAFT GALLERY COLLECTION
Highway 71
Lake George, MN 56458
Tel: (218) 266-3977
Hrs: (Memorial Day - Sept.) Mon. - Sat. 10 a.m. - 6 p.m.
        Sun. 11 a.m. - 5 p.m.
        (Winter - By appointment only)
Visa, MasterCard, and Discover are accepted.

This unique log schoolhouse was built in 1905 and was previously known as the Trout Creek School in Schoolcraft Township, and in 1958 as the Log School Museum. In 1977 the

contents of the school were given to the Hubbard County Historical Society, and in 1981 was restored by Gregory and Paulette Giese and opened as the Schoolcraft Gallery, offering the finest in northwoods gifts.

The log school is still the main gallery of original art in many forms. This rustic log building features a collection of Ojibwa crafts. The handmade quilts are decorative and appropriately considered heirlooms. The stoneware pottery by the Hamiltons is recognized for its distinctive character, and decorative art pottery by Pat Shannon is featured.

The Schoolcraft Trading Post is rustic, with a decor reminiscent of the 1800s fur trading and pioneer era. It is filled with intriguing gifts of old-fashioned candies, fine imported chocolates, along with many gourmet items with a northwoods flavor, such as wild rice, preserves, and maple syrup. Traditional Post items include genuine pelts, Ojibwa jewelry and basket-work, hand-crafted buckles, a wide selection of knives, and coonskin caps.

The Teddy Bear House is a children's delight. There are shelves of cuddly teddy bears in all sizes and colors, along with other "bear" items such as stickers, cups, notes, greeting cards, and other collectibles. The Books 'n' Print Shop gives visitors a wide selection of nature books, works of local authors, and photographers, plus a carefully chosen collection of children's books. There is a large variety of greeting cards, custom-designed stationery, notes, announcements, and bookplates.

Little Falls

O n October, 1805, the itinerant explorer Zebulon Pike stood, exhausted, by a series of rapids while a violent snowstorm raged around him. The fight to forge the rapids upstream had been too much. He retreated downstream, only to return a few weeks later with sleds to continue his fruitless search for the headwaters of the Mississippi. With subtle irony, the rapids that thwarted his original expedition were named Little Falls, and in the years that followed a settlement grew up by the frothy river, each generation of woodsmen and pioneers trying to harness its potential for electricity and the booming logging industry. It was in this spirit of exploration and pioneering that Little Falls most famous citizen, Charles Lindberg, Jr., was raised. His exploits are no secret, since he became the first to cross the Atlantic by air in a plane he helped build in May 1927. Today, visitors to Little Falls can enjoy a guided tour through *Charles A. Lindbergh's Home and Interpretive Center* and relive the flight that changed aviation history. Fortunately for Little Falls, many other buildings of historic interest also remain, including the distinctive, Victorian-style *Dewey-Radke home;* the Polish, ornate *Our Lady of Lourdes Church;* the Romanesque, sturdy *Morrison County Courthouse,* and the Northern Pacific Railway *Depot* designed by famed architect Cass Gilbert, better known as the designer of the U.S. Supreme Court and the Minnesota State Capitol. Other historical sites of particular significance are the *Charles A. Weyerhauser Memorial Museum* — featuring a display of lumber pioneer Weyerhauser's contributions to Little Falls history — and the *Camp Ripley Military Museum* located within the nation's largest year-round National Guard camp. Impressively enough for a city of only 7,000, Little Falls also offers a vast selection of recreational activities, parks, and campgrounds, as well as the *Hole-in-the-Day-Players Community Theater,* the *Heartland Symphony Orchestra, Stroia Ballet Company,* and a fine collection of nightclubs. Other culture-related activities include the two-day *arts and crafts fair* — the Upper Midwest's largest, featuring over 750 exhibitors — a popular *Antique Auto Show* (both held in September), and fine arts exhibitions throughout the year.

For more information on Little Falls, contact:
LITTLE FALLS AREA CHAMBER OF COMMERCE
202 S.E. First Ave.
Little Falls, MN 56345
(612) 632-5155 or (800) 325-5916

HISTORIC SITE

■ **LINDBERGH HOUSE**
A Minnesota Historical Society Site
Charles A. Lindbergh State Park
(Two miles south of Little Falls, MN, on Lindbergh Drive)
Mailing Address: R.R. 3, P.O. Box 245, Little Falls, MN 56345
Tel: (612) 632-3154
Hrs: (May 1 - Labor Day) daily 10 a.m. - 5 p.m.
     (Sept. 7 - April 26) Sat. 10 a.m. - 4 p.m., Sun. noon - 4 p.m.
There is an admission charge.

Charles A. Lindbergh, Jr., who was famous for his solo, nonstop airplane flight from New York to Paris in 1927, spent a happy childhood on his parents' farm in Little Falls. His father, Charles A. Lindbergh, Sr. was elected to Congress in 1906, and the family moved to Washington, D.C. Charles, Jr., and his mother, however, returned to the farm every summer, and it was here that the young boy spent hours gazing up at the drifting clouds, dreaming of flying.

The present Lindbergh House is the second home built by the Lindberghs on their 110-acre farm. The first, a three-story, 13-room frame house, burned down in 1905, when Charles, Jr., was only three years old. The second house was constructed in a simpler style and was never completely finished inside since the family used it only as a summer house. After Charles, Jr., became famous, souvenir hunters converged on the house, which was standing empty, and stripped it of everything they could find. Eventually, the conservation-minded Lindberghs gave the house and farm to the State of Minnesota as a memorial to Charles, Sr. The former farm is now a state park.

Recently, the Minnesota Historical Society restored the house to its original turn-of-the-century appearance, and added a visitor's center nearby wherein there is detailed the life and times of three generations of Lindberghs.

Longville

This tiny northwoods community of 200 is located in the midst of the awesome natural splendor of *Chippewa National Forest,* just next door to the *Deep Portage Conservation Reserve.* The reserve is an outstanding wildlife area of 6,000 acres of woods and marshes, miles of trails, and excellent opportunities for close observation of Minnesota wildlife. Considering the natural bounty surrounding Longville, it might not come as a surprise that the city is known to support more racing turtles than people. In fact, the residents of Longville take their favorite sport so seriously that the state legislature has proclaimed the town "The Turtle Racing Capitol of the World" — a distinction that's reaffirmed every Wednesday afternoon when Main Street is closed off to allow the *turtle races* to proceed. After the blistering pace set by the sporty reptiles, Longville residents don't settle down into a sleepy calm as one would expect, but instead start planning the next on their surprisingly long list of events. In the spring, it's *Easter Egg Hunt, Spring Fashion Show* and *Smelt Fry and Bake Sales;* in the summer, *street dances, Music Jamboree, bazaars,* and *flea markets* take over this friendly little town. Fall finds Longville enjoying the annual *Musky Tournament, Fall Fashion Show, Crazy Days* and *Kids' Halloween Party;* and come winter, the town puts on an *Old-Fashioned Christmas Celebration* with a tree-lighting ceremony and hay rides with Santa Claus.

For more information on Longville, contact:
LONGVILLE LAKES AREA CHAMBER OF COMMERCE
P.O. Box 33
Longville, MN 56655
(218) 363-2630

GALLERY & GIFT SHOP

■ KING GALLERY
Main Street
Longville, MN 56655
Tel: (218) 363-2646
Hrs: (Memorial Weekend - Labor Day) Mon. - Sat. 10 a.m. - 5 p.m.
    Sun. 10 a.m. - 2 p.m.
    (Labor Day - Oct.) Mon. - Sat. 10 a.m. - 5 p.m. Closed Sun.
Visa and MasterCard are accepted.

The King Gallery is located at the intersection of the main streets in Longville, "turtle racing capitol of the world."

The shop invites the browser and shopper to spend time enjoying the wide selection offered by King Gallery. The gallery features more than 100 artisans and crafts people with an emphasis on work produced in Minnesota. King Gallery is most noted for the copper enamel metal sculptures by Hanson, Brumm, and Hudovernik; and a fine selection of porcelain and stoneware by well-known potters, such as David and Jo Hamilton, Susan Davy, David Karaksoulis, Cherie Platter, and Karen Howell. Custom framing of limited edition and decorator prints is also available. There is an assortment of gifts to choose from that include sterling silver, bronze, and enameled jewelry; hand-painted necklaces, earrings, and pins; glassware; hand-carved birds; wild rice, and greeting cards. A unique selection of loon items is featured in both sculpture and framed prints. Hand-painted pillows and wearing apparel by Judith Norberg are some other popular items.

King Gallery offers quality artwork, represented by Minnesota's finest.

GOLF COURSE

■ ERWIN HILLS GOLF COURSE
Highway 200
Longville, MN 56655
Tel: (218) 363-2552
Hrs: Daily 7:30 a.m. - 8 p.m.
Visa and MasterCard are accepted.

Completed in 1987, Erwin Hills is a nine-hole, par 36 golf course. It is located just six and one-half miles north of Longville on Highway 200, or just 19 miles east of Walker on Highway 200.

The fairways wind through rolling hills and quiet woods, giving players a sense of peace and relaxation. Course architect, Robert Weston, designed Erwin Hills in the true "Links" tradition with no adjacent fairways, adding to the character of the course. The picturesque fifth hole plays across a shimmering ten-acre pond. Memberships are available and other services include private and group lessons, men's and women's leagues, cart rentals, and driving range.

RESTAURANT & GOLF COURSE

■ PATRICK'S FINE DINING AND RIDGEWOOD GOLF COURSE
P.O. Box 295
Longville, MN 56655
Tel: (218) 363-2995
Hrs: (Summer) Mon. - Sun. 8:30 a.m. - 10 p.m.
        (Winter) Mon.-Fri. 11:30 a.m. - 2 p.m. , 4:30 p.m. - 9 p.m.
        Sat. - Sun. 11:30 a.m. - 9 p.m.
Visa, MasterCard, AmEx, and Discover are accepted.

In 1986 Patrick's Fine Dining opened in Longville. Its founders and owners, Pat and Maralyn Tabaka, felt it was high time that the town housed its own high-quality supper club. Then in 1988, the couple added to their community once again, this time building a championship 18-hole golf course two miles to the southeast for the recreation of Longville residents and visitors.

Set on an island in beautiful Girl Lake, the Patrick's Fine Dining features delectable cuisine and quality local entertainment in a tranquil, remote location. A three-season porch overlooks the lake, and the bright, country-style dining room makes guests feel at home in the rustic dining room, bar, lounge, or small private dining room. Wednesday through Saturday nights during the summer and Friday and Saturday nights during the winter, patrons twirl and spin around the lounge's dance floor to the lively strains of local musical acts. Customers who dine at Patrick's choose from a menu that includes walleye fillets, barbequed loin-back ribs, roast duck a l'orange, and Chateaubriand—a tenderloin for two served with steamed fresh vegetables, special potatoes, and Patrick's own Chateau Sauce. For those who want to work off the results of their indulgence, the Tabaka's Ridgewood par 72 golf course offers 6,535 yards and 18 holes of challenging golf, as well as a practice driving range, putting green, pitching area, and sand bunker. Soon it will also boast a smaller, 1,080-yard course. Private and group lessons are available, and golfers can take a mid-course meal break at the Ridgewood picnic area.

Both recreation and fine dining make Longville an attractive stopover for rest and relaxation.

Mille Lacs Lake Area

M ille Lacs Lake is as close to a fisherman's paradise as they come. Every summer, 175,000 anglers try their luck on Minnesota's second largest lake. During the winter, diehards congregate in a veritable town of 5,000 ice fishing shacks to tempt the 40 different species of fish in the icy waters below. The lake's most popular species — walleye — has an estimated population of more than one million, and each year, more than 200,000 of this fighting fish are caught and turned into 500,000 pounds of delectable eating. Visitors to the area can choose between a profusion of lake resorts, located in the small communities ringing the lake from Isle in the southeast to Garrison in the northwest. An added incentive to superb fishing for many of those who flock to Mille Lacs is the strong Native American heritage of the area, maintained among the *Mille Lacs Band of Chippewa* on their reservation on the west shore of the lake. Each summer, the tribe organizes a *pow wow* — a fascinating gathering with traditional dances, songs, food and games. Also on the reservation (near Vineland just off Highway 169) is the *Mille Lacs Indian Museum,* an excellent opportunity to explore the arts, crafts, and history of the region's Chippewa people. (On an entirely different note, the reservation is also site of the newly opened *Grand Casino Mille Lacs,* featuring slots, poker, blackjack, and other games.) In addition, the museum maintains a well-stocked *gift shop* where visitors will find Indian beadwork, birchbark crafts, prints, paintings, and books published by the Minnesota Historical Society, which owns and operates the museum. Those still searching for that something special can venture north of Garrison to the *Stone House* and its selection of various gift items as well as wild rice, honey, and other Minnesota products. Mille Lacs Lake is also ringed by three recreational areas that offer hiking, swimming, camping, and cross-country skiing opportunities: *Father Hennepin State Park* near Isle, *Mille Lacs Kathio State Park* near Vineland, and *Wealthwood State Forest* on the north side of the lake. One of the most popular special events in the area is the *Crystal Carnival* in February, featuring hot air balloon lifts, UpSkiing across the ice, snow sculpting — and a uniquely challenging nine-hole golf course. For those who prefer to golf in the summer, *Mille Lacs Lake Golf Resort* in Garrison offers a par-71, 18-hole course with watered fairways.

For more information on Mille Lacs, contact:
MILLE LACS AREA TOURISM ASSOCIATION
P.O. Box 692
Isle, MN 56342
(612) 676-3634 or (800) 346-9375

B AIT & TACKLE SHOP

■ TUTT'S BAIT AND TACKLE
Highway 18 W.
Garrison, MN 56450
Tel: (612) 692-4341
Hrs: Open year-round 6 a.m. - 9 p.m.

Tutt's Bait and Tackle has been dealing out the bait for the last 50 years in Garrison. A shop with fish and big game mounted on the walls, Tutt's is located only one-quarter mile from Lake Mille Lacs, also known as "the walleye factory." Proprietors Joan and Orrin Tutt can serve anyone's fishing needs to a "T." In addition to the extensive selection of live bait, tackle, and lures; Tutt's has hunting

and fishing licenses and supplies, clothing, and sunglasses. There is even LP gas available for cooking those prized fish fillets after a long day on the lake. If the fish aren't biting, Tutt's will be happy to console visitors with the selection of a movie rental to enjoy back at camp.

HISTORIC SITE

■ MILLE LACS INDIAN MUSEUM
A Minnesota Historical Society Site
(On U.S. Highway 169, 12 miles north of Onamia)
Mailing Address: HCR 67, P.O. Box 195, Onamia, MN 56359
Tel: (612) 532-3632
Hrs: (May 1 - Labor Day) Daily 10 a.m. - 5 p.m.
There is an admission charge.

A great battle, fought in 1745, changed the history of northern Minnesota. Bands of Ojibwa Indians, retreating from their original homeland near Lake Superior, confronted the Dakota in the area of Mille Lacs Lake. Faced with defeat, the Dakota moved from their ancient lands surrounding "Mde wakan" — spirit lake — south to the Minnesota River in the southern part of the state. Today, the Ojibwa still live along the shores of Mille Lacs Lake on the reservation of the same name.

Once the center of Dakota Territory, the Mille Lacs Lake region is now home to one of the greatest Ojibwa historical museums in the country. The Mille Lacs Indian Museum, located just off highway 169, features exhibits of Ojibwa historical items and Ojibwa crafts. In a series of interpretive collections, the museum brings to life the ancient woodland traditions of canoe building, weaving, hidework, fishing, and trapping. The most outstanding aspect of the museum, however, is the life-size dioramas. These portray Ojibwe life in each of the four seasons: trapping and hunting in the winter; processing maple syrup in the spring; gardening in the summer; and harvesting wild rice in the fall.

After visitors tour the museum, they browse through the Trading Post — a craft shop brimming with traditional Ojibwa hand-crafted items. Here visitors can find baskets, fiberwork, beadwork, and textile products made by Ojibwa Indians who specialize in the ancient art forms.

RESORT

■ IZATYS GOLF & YACHT CLUB
Lake Mille Lacs
Onamia, MN 56359
Tel: (800) 533-1728
Hrs: Open year-round
Visa, MasterCard, and AmEx are accepted.

Izatys Golf and Yacht Club provides one of the greatest resort experiences on Lake Mille Lacs. In 1987 an extensive renovation project began, which involved replacing the old cabins and lodge with a new clubhouse, guest accommodations, and an enclosed boat harbor. A challenging 18-hole golf course was also added as part of the improvements. It is the only course in Minnesota designed by the Dye family of golf course architects. Located only 90 miles north of Minneapolis, Izatys is an hour closer to the metro area than the other large resorts in the state.

Lake Mille Lacs is the second largest lake in Minnesota and offers a variety of recreational choices. The enclosed harbor was cited by *Boating* Magazine in the January 1990 issue as one of the eight best places in the United States to run out of gas. Rental boats and a 48-foot fishing launch are available to explore the waters of the lake. Parasailing is a special attraction at Izatys, which is one of the few commercial parasailing operations in Minnesota. Izatys also has a tennis center, indoor and outdoor pool, and a spa. For the winter there is cross-country skiing, snowmobiling, ice fishing, and a supervised children's program year-round.

The Club XIX Lounge offers a great view of the harbor and light entertainment. The Sand Bar on the shore allows guests to relax and lounge near the water. The beautiful townhomes each have a private patio, fireplace, and a fully equipped kitchen. The Grand Casino Mille Lacs is a Vegas style casino near the resort. The casino features 350 video slot machines, mega-bingo, and blackjack among other games. A shuttle service is available to guests at Izatys. For a great resort vacation, make plans to visit Izatys.

R ESTAURANT & LOUNGE

■ HEADQUARTERS LODGE
(One mile south of Garrison on 169)
Garrison, MN 56450
Tel: (612) 692-4346
Hrs: (Lunch) Sat. and Sun. 11 a.m.
     (Dinner) Year-round 4 p.m. - closing

After a day of sightseeing or fishing, Headquarters Lodge is a great place to go for a great dinner. Owner-operated for more than ten years, the restaurant is located on scenic St. Alban's Bay of Lake Mille Lacs.

Loyal patrons and newcomers alike appreciate the casual lakeside atmosphere of Headquarters Lodge. It has evolved into a favorite Mille Lacs dining spot by adapting to the changing tastes of its customers. John and Mary Stenback and Bill Malone have all

brought their own cooking expertise to the partnership that produced this restaurant. John, Mary, and Bill's extensive restaurant experience is seen in some of the famous ethnic buffets. Entrees on the extensive menu are made using only the freshest ingredients. Even the meat is cut to order on the premises. Exotic spices and unusual sauces flavor shrimp, walleye, fresh seafood, and locally produced rainbow trout. A nightly dinner special is offered in addition to the regular menu, all of which include the popular soup and salad bar. Parents will appreciate the special "Minnow Menu" for children, designed to make the evening an enjoyable experience for the whole family. A lovely outdoor screened porch has a fabulous view of the lake, where food and cocktails may be savored in the sunshine or by moonlight.

The reputation for excellent food at Headquarters Lodge is accompanied by its additional menus and services. Look for the daily happy hour, late night menu, and senior citizen discounts. Catering for banquets and private parties is an irresistible way to entertain friends. Individuals and charters may take advantage of the 55-foot pontoon launch for walleye fishing, or stay closer to shore on the lighted dock, convenient for boating, fishing, skiing, or a quiet stroll after dining.

Moorhead

Moorhead and its sister city across the North Dakota border, Fargo, are the cultural capitals of the heartland region. With a population topping 30,000, Moorhead is a vibrant city with three colleges, excellent shopping centers, plentiful restaurants hotels,

hotels, and a lively entertainment scene. But like many other communities in the region, the city had an inauspicious beginning as a riverbank settlement. In its search for a navigable route between St. Paul and Fort Gary near present-day Winnipeg, Manitoba, the St. Paul Chamber of Commerce offered a reward to the first person to propel a steamboat up the Red River. In June 1859, the Anson Northrup became the first to make the trip, and two decades of river traffic continued while Moorhead grew to accommodate the travelers. When the Northern Pacific Railroad entered the city in 1871, Moorhead's future was secure, and it eventually became the leading farm processing center for the booming agriculture of the Red River Valley.

ATTRACTIONS

Historical attractions abound in Moorhead, including *Clay County Museum* with its frontier exhibits; *Comstock Historic House* — home of Ada Comstock, the first president of prestigious Radcliffe College — and, last but not the least, the *Heritage-Hjemkomst Interpretive Center* complete with changing historic and science exhibits and the fascinating 76-foot Viking ship replica that sailed from Duluth to Bergen, Norway. Still in the international vein, the *Concordia Language Village* is a nationally recognized language program for seven- to 18-year-olds sponsored by Concordia College of Moorhead. Cultural attractions in Moorhead include the *Fargo-Moorhead Symphony Orchestra,* the *Fargo-Moorhead Civic Opera, Red River Dance & Performing Company, Mahkahta Dance Theatre* and the *Plains Art Museum,* featuring Native American and West African art. As far as special events go, the list is long, including such varied fare as ethnic dancing, food, and entertainment at the *Scandinavian Hjemkomst Festival* in June; the German heritage celebration *Valley Fest/VolksTanz* later in the summer; and the unique *A Merry Prairie Christmas,* a three-week extravaganza starting the first Saturday after Thanksgiving with parades, a costume ball, and a host of other special events.

For more information on Moorhead, contact:
MOORHEAD-FARGO CONVENTION AND VISITORS BUREAU
P.O. Box 2164
Fargo, ND 58107
(701) 237-6134 or (800) 362-3145 ext. 155

H ISTORIC SITE

■ COMSTOCK HOUSE

A Minnesota Historical Society Site
Fifth Ave. S. and Eighth Street (Highway 75)
Mailing Address: 506 Eighth Street S., Moorhead, MN 56560
Tel: (218) 233-0848
Hrs: (May 25 - Labor Day) Sat. - Sun. 1 p.m. - 5 p.m.
There is an admission charge.

In 1871, a young man arrived in "wild and lawless" Moorhead, a frontier town in western Minnesota. His name was Solomon Comstock, and he shaped the development of Moorhead — indeed, the length of the Red River Valley — as few others have.

For more than 60 years, Comstock served as county attorney for Clay County, and during much of his life he served in the state legislature. In 1888 he was elected to Congress. He also served on the board of regents for the University of Minnesota and became one of the founders of Moorhead State College, built upon land he donated. His oldest daughter, Ada, shared his belief in the importance of higher education, becoming one of Minnesota's greatest historical figures. She was the first dean of women at the University of Minnesota; she was president of Radcliffe College from 1923 until 1943; and she served on a series of educational and governmental commissions.

Today, visitors to Moorhead can relive the era of the young immigrant family from Maine. The Comstock home is maintained as a historic site by the Minnesota Historical Society and is open to visitors in the summer. Built in 1881, the 11-room, two-story woodframe structure is resplendent with Queen Anne and Eastlake designs so popular in Victorian architecture and has been faithfully renovated to its original appearance.

M USEUM

■ HERITAGE HJEMKOMST INTERPRETIVE CENTER

202 First Ave. N.
Moorhead, MN 56560
Tel: (218) 233-5604
Hrs: Mon. - Sat. 9 a.m. - 5 p.m., Thur. 9 a.m. - 9 p.m., Sun. noon - 5 p.m.
Visa and MasterCard are accepted.

Along the shores of the winding Red River on 11 acres of wooded park land is the Heritage Hjemkomst Interpretive Center, a large double-masted building built in 1986. Located in the heart of downtown Fargo/Moorhead, the Center was developed through a joint venture of the Clay County Historical Society and the Red River Valley Heritage Society.

The Clay County Museum and Historical Society occupy the lower level of the building. Heritage Hall has 7,000 square feet devoted to traveling exhibits. Every four months a new program is offered. Major exhibits from regional, national, and international museums are featured, including those of the Smithsonian Institution. Presented in the past have been programs on holograms, space, dinosaurs, Native Americans, and Norwegian immigration. Hjemkomst Hall is the main level of the Interpretive Center. The theme "Dare to Dream" is encompassed by the authentic replica Viking ship "Hjemkomst," for which the center is named. Through photographs, recordings, and a fascinating 28-minute videotape, visitors can witness the dramatic story of how Robert Asp had a dream to build a Viking ship and sail to Norway. He began building his ship in 1971. The ship was christened "Hjemkomst," which means "homecoming" in Norwegian. The hand-built ship is 76 feet long, weighs 16 tons, and has a mast that climbs to 70 feet.

The handicapped-accessible Heritage Hjemkomst Interpretive Center also houses the Heritage Gift Shop, which offers souvenirs and gifts. Meeting rooms and an auditorium are available for rental. Tours may be arranged, and there are special group rates.

RESTAURANT

■SPEAK EASY RESTAURANT & LOUNGE
1001 30th Ave. S.
Moorhead, MN 56560
Tel: (218) 233-1326
Hrs: Mon. - Sat. 11 a.m. - 1 a.m., Sun. 4 p.m. - 1 a.m.
All major credit cards are accepted.

The Speak Easy has a prevalent 1930s gangster theme throughout the menu and the decor. A 1931 Auburn automobile sits in the lobby surrounded by a wood and brick interior enhanced by crystal chandeliers and etched glass.

Some of the categories on the menu include The Boss's Specialties, Killer Kent's Nightly Specials, and the Baby Face Menu. Tasty Italian dishes make up a big part of the menu. The Sting is a combination dinner of spaghetti, lasagna, and eggplant chips; The Blind Date consists of ribs, Italian sausage lasagna, and shrimp; The Big Cheese is fettuccine and two cannelloni served with deep-fried eggplant and battered mushroom pieces. Good service is guaranteed as the consequences would be disastrous!

Osakis

The origin of the name Osakis is shrouded in mystery, although the residents of this lakeside town have many different legends to choose from. One story claims that a party of Chippewa and Dakota Indians once fought a pitched battle in this area. The Chippewa lost, and the lone survivor swam across the lake to the safety of an early settler's cabin, shouting "Oh-sa-kis" — "save us" — as he rose from the water. Another tale relates that early Chippewa, inexorably moving westward and displacing local tribes in the 18th century, named the lake "oh-za-kees" ("place of the Sauks") after the tribe that occupied the area at the time. Regardless of the origin of the name, the lake remains as attractive as in those early days, its 53 miles of shoreline rimmed by *resorts* and frequented by vacationers who never quite want to leave this *fishing* paradise. In fact, the lake — which ranks among the top ten Minnesota fishing lakes — is known for its outstanding walleye production, and is the source of walleye eggs for a five-county stocking program. Aside from fishing, Osakis hosts the annual *Osakis Festival* each June — a ten-day extravaganza of carnivals, floater plane rides, bingos, a Miss Osakis pageant, live music, pie eating contests, horse shows, and street dances.

For more information on Osakis, contact:
LAKE OSAKIS RESORT ASSOCIATION
Dept. Q
Osakis, MN 56360
(612) 859-4794 or (800) 422-0785 ext. 17

GIFT SHOP & LODGING

■JUST LIKE GRANDMA'S
113 W. Main
Osakis, MN 56360
Tel: (612) 859-4504
Hrs: (Memorial Day - Labor Day) 10 a.m. - 5 p.m. Weekends in Sept.
Visa and MasterCard are accepted.

Just Like Grandma's offers as many things to do as a real trip to Grandma's. The house was originally built in 1903 and had been privately owned until 1984. Never having any intention of buying a house in Osakis, Carol Mihalchick took a look at the home with a friend and two weeks later she and her husband Steve were property owners in Osakis.

With a great deal of help, Carol and Steve worked frantically to open Memorial Day weekend 1985. Just Like Grandma's is currently a bed and breakfast, tea room, and gift shop. The abundance of antiques and gifts led to the expansion of Osakis Antiques on Main Street. In 1989 the School House, Summer Kitchen, and Tea Room were incorporated into the business.

Just Like Grandma's also sponsors a 5K Race toward the end of June and Grammafest, which is a two-day summer celebration in mid-August. A gazebo for outdoor meals from the Summer Kitchen is also available. The barn area offers more gifts and an ice cream counter to enjoy sweet treats. In mid-October the Twelve Days of Christmas Boutique invites patrons to get a jump on the holiday season by offering unique gift items. Just Like Grandma's provides a variety of activities with a cozy atmosphere.

R ESORT

■ IDLEWILDE RESORT & LODGE
(On Lake Osakis)
P.O. Box 299
Osakis, MN 56360
Tel: (612) 859-2135
Hrs: Open year-round
Visa, MasterCard, and AmEx are accepted.

Lake Osakis boasts as excellent a population of walleye, northern, and bass as can be found in Minnesota. Best known for sunfish and crappie fishing, Lake Osakis is a fisherman's paradise as well as offering a variety of water sport activities.

Idlewilde Resort provides the perfect resort in which to enjoy a great vacation anytime of year. Ten cabins with two to four bedrooms are available as well as five housekeeping units in the lodge. A store, laundry facilities, and sporting equipment provide for visitors' vacationing needs. An indoor pool and sauna can be enjoyed in the event of temperamental weather. A sand volleyball court provides a great opportunity for a friendly game with the neighbors.

Park Rapids

F ew other towns in Minnesota have a longer history of catering
to travelers than Park Rapids, a community of 3,000
surrounded by quaint villages, 400 lakes, and more than 200
resorts. Originally settled by farmers in the late 1800s, the town
began to be a favored vacation spot only a few decades later. Early
in the 20th century, vacationers were already arriving by train at
the Park Rapids station where they were met by resort owners
with teams and wagons. Other tourists rented launches to
venture up the rivers to camps located on one of the numerous
lakes. Through the ensuing decades, the Park Rapids area has had
ample opportunity to develop fascinating attractions and events
for visitors, while at the same time maintaining its small-town
atmosphere.

ATTRACTIONS

Park Rapids is known as the gateway to *Itasca Park* at the
source of the Mississippi River. The area is also known for its
superb selection of arts and crafts shops highly popular with
vacationers who flock here in the summer. *Summerhill Farm,*
open only from May through September, features the work of
artisans and crafts people from all across the country displayed in
four quaint farm buildings. Formerly a barn, stable, carriage
house and cottage, these buildings now serve as unique backdrops
to this excellent craft collection. *Silver Star City* is a wild west
family entertainment theme park with an atmosphere of
yesteryear. In addition, there's *Granny Annie's,* a fascinating shop
filled to the brim with quality crafts, antiques, and local delicacies
such as honey and maple syrup. One might want to time their
arrival to coincide with one of the three Park Rapids *craft fairs*
held in July, August, and mid-November. More traditional crafts
are the center of attention at the *Hubbard County Historical
Society Museum,* which includes a display of a frontier
schoolroom and early farm implements. Meanwhile, the *North
Country Museum of Art*, upstairs in the Historical Society
building, features an ongoing exhibit of 15th-19th century
European paintings — the only one of its type and quality outside
the Twin Cities area. A more modern attraction is the *Aqua Park,*
a wildlife museum, aquarium and park with a cougar, foxes, deer,
Arctic wolves, and other wild animals. The list of events in the
Park Rapids area begins during the 4th of July weekend with the
Minnesota State Logging Championships and *National Bow
Sawing Championships,* a fascinating display of physical strength

attracting competitors from all over the world. Then the *Park Rapids Rodeo* bursts on the scene, followed by the annual *Taste of Dorset* — a fun-filled day hosted by the tiny village of Dorset east of Park Rapids, where visitors can sample the local cooking, listen to piano players, and ride a hay rack right on Main Street.

For more information on Park Rapids, contact:
PARK RAPIDS CHAMBER OF COMMERCE
P.O. Box 249 G
Park Rapids, MN 56470
(218) 732-4111 or (800) 247-0054

B ED & BREAKFAST

■ DORSET SCHOOLHOUSE BED & BREAKFAST

P.O. Box 201
Park Rapids, MN 56470
Tel: (218) 732-1377
Hrs: Open year-round
Visa and Mastercard are accepted.

Echoes of school bells and laughing children's voices fill the history of the Dorset Schoolhouse, built in 1920. Closed to the bustle of books and learning in 1970, today the refurbished schoolhouse offers a comfortable country break from the hustle of life in the '90s. The hospitality of northern Minnesota is evident in all of the services of this schoolhouse-turned-bed-and-breakfast.

Adorned with antiques and country furnishings, the schoolhouse boasts six cozy guest rooms, each with a patio door to the deck. Here guests can bask in the morning sun, wallow in the cool afternoon shade, or count the evening stars. Visitors relax, read, and socialize in the enlarged old schoolhouse cloakroom, and bathe luxuriantly in what was once the nurse's office and library. Original maple floors and the authentic old lights remain to remind visitors of the days-gone-by when reading, 'riting and 'rithmatic were the primary occupations of the schoolhouse's occupants.

The building is adjacent to the 30-mile paved Heartland Trail. Summer biking and winter snowmobiling are just a stone's throw away, while nearby Itasca State Park, the Chippewa National Forest, and Long Pine offer groomed cross-country trails for novice and expert skiers. It's a place to unwind and partake in a bit of history, while enjoying the convenient proximity of the many fine shops, restaurants, and natural attractions that have made Dorset famous over the years.

Each morning guests awaken to the savory smells of a complimentary continental breakfast, which includes home-baked muffins, seasonal fruits, cereals, cookies, juice, coffee, and tea. Extensive renovations haven't dulled the charm of this quaint country schoolhouse, only shifted the target of their appeal. Laughter and good smells still fill its redwood-sided walls, but today the pace within is decidedly slower and the occupants more peaceful than they were in bygone days.

G IFT SHOP & ATTRACTION

■ WORLD OF CHRISTMAS
Highway 71 N.
Park Rapids, MN 56470
Tel: (218) 732-9609
Hrs: (May 1 - Christmas Season) Open daily. Hours vary, call ahead
Visa, MasterCard, and Discover are accepted.

Christmas isn't just for December any more. At World of Christmas, the season of joy, peace and goodwill lives on all year. Visitors see all the decorations they've always loved. But that's not all. Gifts for all seasons and all reasons can also be found.

In 1974, Neal and Carol Holter opened a gift shop in Grand Rapids, ND, and put some Christmas merchandise on display in the summer. Today, they have four individual shops located in Park Rapids, Pequot Lakes, Detroit Lakes, and Walker. At each World of Christmas store, customers will find such old holiday favorites as nutcrackers, wood carvings, lighted Christmas villages, and ornaments. But the shelves are brimming with nonholiday gifts as well. Wicker, stuffed animals, T-shirts, Scandinavian souvenirs, and Precious Moments figurines are just some of the items that are perfect for special occasions all year.

At the Park Rapids store, children and adults alike can enjoy bumper boats, water wars, an 18-hole miniature golf course, and nine holes of frisbee golf. The Evergreen Express narrated train ride will teach guests about the plants and trees of Minnesota, and the batting cages will help kids improve their batting skills. In addition, the delicious fudge that is one of the hallmarks of World of Christmas stores is made right here on the premises. Visit the Nutcracker Sweet and try some. Or how about a sandwich and drink at the snack bar? At World of Christmas, find loads of family fun and food; and the magic of holiday.

G IFT SHOP & RESTAURANT

■ SUMMERHILL FARM
Highway 71 N.
Park Rapids, MN 56470
Tel: (218) 732-3865
Hrs: (May 11 - Sept. 30) Mon. - Sat. 10 a.m. - 6 p.m., Sun. noon - 4 p.m.
Visa, MasterCard, and AmEx are accepted.

Located just seven miles north of Park Rapids and on the way to Itasca State Park, the Summerhill Farm shops are built into the hillside overlooking Summerhill Pond. The farm was built in 1937 and the original exteriors are painted in slate blue with white trim and railings to exhibit a warm country charm. The brick walkways are bordered with beautiful flower beds and baskets, adding to the area's enchantment. Each of the five gift shops provide a unique display of the finest arts and crafts from around the country. "The Barn" displays charming country products, folk art, greeting cards, and an exceptional variety of hand-crafted items. "The Stable" features pottery by Mary Melancon and calligraphy by Mary Mittlestadt, both Minnesota artists. A fine selection of Minnesota photography is also available. Children will be delighted with "The Carriage House" displaying toys and miniatures, Minnesota jams and jellies, and candy. Women's apparel, jewelry, afghans, decorator pillows, baby items and books, and many other unique hand-crafted American gifts can be found at "The Cottage." Visitors looking for a perfect gift or souvenir in "The Second Story" will find a nice selection of quality designer T-shirts to choose from. The "Sun Porch Restaurant" offers a restful setting in which to savor a light lunch or homemade dessert. Specializing in strawberry-rhubarb pie and wild rice soup, other popular menu items include "The Sun Porch," a light lunch including soup, french bread, cheese, and fresh fruit; or enjoy "The Summerhill Sub," served on a french roll with a cup of homemade soup.

Summerhill Farm is highly recommended by area resorts for its incredible selection of quality and unique gifts. The beautiful surroundings and pleasant staff make for enjoyable browsing and a memorable shopping experience.

R ESORT

■ THE TIMBERLANE LODGE
R.R. 3
Park Rapids, MN 56470
Tel: (218) 732-8489
Hrs: Open year-round
Visa and MasterCard are accepted.

Located approximately four miles east of Park Rapids on Long Lake, The Timberlane Lodge is set amid 150 acres of Norway pine, spruce, ash, maple and birch, and has a half mile of lake frontage. It's a northwoods paradise that's easy to get to, but hard to leave. Guests soon find themselves becoming spoiled by the lodge's hospitable service, superb food, and relaxing atmosphere.

Built in 1948, The Timberlane Lodge boasts knotty pine interiors throughout the lodge and in its cottages and cabana guest houses.

Grand fireplaces of stone grace the lodge's lounges and the cabanas, which can sleep up to ten guests. The cottages and cabanas have full housekeeping and come with all the amenities such as microwaves, coffee makers, pullman or full kitchens, carpeting, and full baths. Each faces the lake, assuring complete privacy. Guests have complete access to all the lodge's facilities, which range from an enclosed three-season pool, a sauna, and whirlpool to an outdoor ice-skating rink, cross-country ski and walking trails, and snowmobiling in the winter. Long Lake is one of the top walleye lakes in the state, and fishing is especially encouraged. The lodge has ample beach frontage, and there are special children's programs to keep the kids busy too. And after a day of fun, don't miss the lodge's excellent dinner offerings. In summer, outside dining overlooking Long Lake is particularly popular.

R ESORTS & RESTAURANTS

■ NORTH BEACH AND SHIPWRECK RESTAURANT
Northern Pine Road
Park Rapids, MN 56470
Tel: (218) 732-9708
Hrs: Open year-round
All major credit cards are accepted.

Located six miles north of Park Rapids off Highway 71, North Beach offers townhouse accommodations where guests can expect seclusion and luxury living and the delectable option of eating at the nearby Shipwreck Restaurant.

From the outside deck just off each townhouse's living room, guests can look out over lovely Potato Lake. Every two-floor unit includes two bedrooms that sleep six, one and a half baths, full housekeeping, a kitchen, and dining area. Maid service is also available for a nominal fee. There are many outdoor activities available at North Beach. Try hiking, volleyball, fishing, or swimming along with many other summer recreation possibilities. In the winter, strap on a pair of skis and put in some cross-country mileage, or take advantage of the cold weather to skate, slide, sled, or snowmobile. Whatever guests' outdoor interests are, they'll have a chance to indulge them here. And after playing hard, how about relaxing at the lovely heated indoor swimming pool?

Enjoy some terrific food and drink at the Shipwreck Restaurant. With a variety of seating arrangements and a menu featuring such specialties as sirloin steak, barbecued ribs, and all-you-can-eat crab legs, dinner at the Shipwreck Restaurant is sure to be a memorable event.

North Beach and Shipwreck Restaurant meld fine living and dining with the idyllic beauty of the northwoods — an unbeatable combination.

■ VACATIONAIRE
Island Lake Drive
Park Rapids, MN 56470
Tel: (218) 732-5270
Hrs: Open year-round
All major credit cards are accepted.

Vacationaire combines, for its guests, the beauty of northwoods nature with all the amenities of resort living. Located on Island Lake, it offers so many activities it may take a bit of time to decide just what to do.

In the spring and summer, guests can try fishing, waterskiing, horse shoes, tennis, or shuffleboard. In the fall and winter, the options shift to grouse, deer, or duck hunting; snowmobiling, cross-country skiing, ice fishing, or swimming in the indoor pool and sauna. Or do nothing!

The hosts at Vacationaire, Mary and Jim Grewe, are dedicated to making the stay of their guests memorable. Guests stay in deluxe accommodations either in lodge rooms, suites, cabins, or condominiums. The knotty-pine cabins come with fireplaces and kitchens, and Vacationaire's full-service restaurant offers breakfast, lunch, and dinner. The house specialties are prime rib and barbecued ribs. Or try a cocktail at Ye Ol' Minnow Bucket cocktail lounge in the main lodge.

R ESTAURANTS

■ COMPADRE'S DEL NORTE
R.R. 3, P.O. Box 30
Dorset, MN 56470
Tel: (218) 732-7624
Hrs: (Summer) 12 - at least 8:30 p.m. Open later Fri. - Sat.
   (Spring and Fall) Thur. - Sat., 5 p.m. - 8:30 p.m., Sun. noon - 8:30 p.m.
Personal checks, but not credit cards, are accepted.

Deep in the heart of Scandinavian country, way up north in Hubbard County, the once-sleepy town of Dorset draws caravans of tourists to its boardwalk to sample the authentic Mexican food at Compadre's del Norte. The restaurant was built in 1985 from the town's old post office and an adjacent retail building. Set in a legendary land of lakes and loons, Campadre's has become a legend in itself.

The restaurant is owned by Rick Kempnich and his father, Mike, and it features deliciously authentic Mexican cuisine in a casual and lively atmosphere. Compadre's patrons rave about many of its dishes: chimichangas, taco burritos, seafood enchiladas, and Mexican pizza receive top reviews. In fact, many customers are so enamored with the restaurant's special enchiladas that they can't bear the thought of a winter without them. Each fall, before the restaurant closes for the winter, patrons commission the Kempnichs to prepare dozens and dozens of enchiladas for home freezing. Compadre's also serves American fare for those who

©MARTIENA R. RICHTER

prefer it. Margaritas are the drink of choice here. Customers sip the seven- or 17-ounce specialties on the restaurant's patio while waiting for tables, or sample the Margaritas Especial, Compadre's own version of this tropical thirst-quencher. Delicious, alcohol-free margaritas are also a specialty of the house. Comfortable in hot and cool weather, Compadre's boasts a breezy deck with umbrella tables overlooking the boardwalk, and features a fireplace and bar area indoors for cozy winter retreats. A party room is available for large groups who visit on special occasions.

Lively Mexican music played indoors and out sets the restaurant's festive atmosphere. Compadre's close proximity to beautiful northern Minnesota wilderness areas usually lures visitors the first time, but the delicious authentic cuisine and the friendly, festive experience keep them coming back for more.

■ LONG VAN RESTAURANT

703 E. First Street
Park Rapids, MN 56470
Tel: (218) 732-5491
Hrs: Closed Sun. Tue. - Fri. 11 a.m. - 2 p.m. and 5 p.m. - 9 p.m.
    Sat., Mon. 5 p.m. - 9 p.m.
Visa and MasterCard are accepted.

Drawing on the expertise of other family members who have been in the food business for a number of years, the Doans developed Long Vans into the quality establishment it is today.

Pagoda-style oriental architecture makes it a Park Rapids area showpiece. In keeping with the genuine oriental design, the interior features authentic decor in its dining rooms and banquet facilities. A comfortable, relaxed atmosphere that is family oriented prevails at Long Vans. Oriental music along with the decor sets the mood. All food is prepared daily from only the

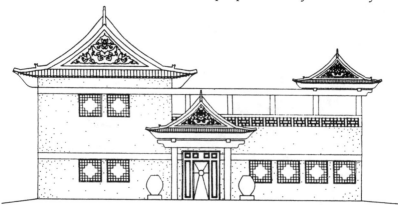

freshest ingredients. Natural sauces, family recipes exclusive to Long Vans, are used to enhance the flavor of fresh vegetables and entrees. This Cantonese style of food preparation should appeal to health-conscious individuals looking for fare that is low in fat and high in flavor. Popular menu items include Lo Mein, Chow Mein, lemon chicken, sweet and sour pork, pepper steak, and beef with black bean sauce. Daily lunch specials are served as well as a combination special of the day.

The Doan family invites guests to enjoy some of the best authentic oriental cuisine in northern Minnesota.

■ THE RED LANTERN

600 N. Park
Park Rapids, MN 56470
Tel: (218) 732-9377
Hrs: (Summer) Daily 11 a.m. - 10 p.m.
    (Winter) Sun. 11 a.m. - 8 p.m., Tue. - Thurs. 11 a.m. - 9 p.m.
    Fri. - Sat. 11 a.m. - 10 p.m.
Visa, MasterCard, and AmEx are accepted.

The Red Lantern, a full-service restaurant with a surprising variety of food and drink, is located on the outskirts of Park Rapids.

Everything from Mexican, to Chinese, to down-home heartland cooking is offered, along with a tantalizing array of low-fat, low-sodium, and low-cholesterol dishes. These "heart-smart" entrees range from teriyaki chicken breast to broiled walleye fillets. In addition, there are such all-time favorites as prime rib, slow-cooked pork ribs, and New Zealand lobster, and for more ethnic food, try a chimichanga — deep-fried and stuffed with roast beef, cheese, and taco sauce — or enjoy one of many fine Chinese dishes. At the Red Lantern, steaks are hand-cut and beef is ground on the premises, and their daily and nightly "chef specials" satisfy even the most discriminating palate. The Red Lantern also is well known for its drink specialties. A mai tai, fuzzy navel, grasshopper, or piña colada is a perfect accompaniment to prime rib. Then there is always the king of mixed-drinks; the Red Lantern Hurricane. Made with a blend of three Bacardi rums and fruit juices, the hurricane packs quite a punch, and the house rules allow only two per person.

Along with the great food, guests enjoy the stained-glass lights and the rustic decor of the Red Lantern. Intimate booths allow for quiet conversation, while tables are widely scattered and never packed closely together. From food to atmosphere, The Red Lantern offers a quality dining experience at an affordable price.

S TATE PARK

■ ITASCA STATE PARK

(28 miles north of Park Rapids on Highway 71)
Mailing address: Division of Parks and Recreation
Interpretive Services
Itasca State Park
Lake Itasca, MN 56460
Tel: (general state park information): (612) 296-6157, or (800) 652-9747
    (Itasca State Park Headquarters): (218) 266-3654

As the source of the mighty Mississippi River, Itasca State Park is one of the most famous state parks in the nation. Here, where a little brook emerges from Lake Itasca, are the fabled headwaters — so small and shallow that visitors can actually wade across to the other side. More than half a million visitors come to Itasca State Park each year just to see this tiny beginning to such a legendary river. They come, too, for a look at the awesome 250-year-old red pine stand known as Preacher's Grove, a remnant of the soaring pine forests that once covered northern Minnesota, and to enjoy Itasca's other outdoor attractions.

The park, which celebrated its 100th birthday in 1991, is known for its extensive hiking trails — 33 miles' worth — set amid splendid northwoods scenery. In addition, the park holds a seven-mile bike trail, a scenic, ten-mile wilderness drive, an historic log lodge, and an excursion boat trip that follows the route explorer Henry Rowe Schoolcraft took across Lake Itasca when he "discovered" the Mississippi's headwaters. (Actually, Schoolcraft's Ojibwa guide, Ozawindib, knew that Lake Itasca was the river's source, and lead the explorer there.) Within the park's 50 square miles, visitors have the chance to see an abundance of Minnesota flora and fauna, including trumpeter swans, bald eagles, 27 different species of orchids, and rare carniverous peatlands plants. They can also choose to visit two prehistoric sites: the Nicollet Creek area, where 8,000-year-old Indian artifacts have been found preserved in lake sediment; and Itasca Indian Mounds, 500- to 900-year-old burial mounds.

Since Itasca State Park is so vast and offers so much, a good bet is to stop first at the Forest Inn Visitor Center located in the South Itasca Center. During the summer, a park naturalist is on hand to answer questions seven days a week. Interpretive programs are conducted all year, with additional outings offered during the summer months. The park also has a variety of lodging from rustic to plain-but-modern; however, room is limited so call ahead.

Pine River

A s its name implies, the small town of Pine River is the site of some of the state's finest pine forests. In fact, when early settlers arrived in the area, they so marveled at the sight of the soaring, 125-foot-tall white pines that they believed it to be the richest land of timber in the Northwest. A century of farming and extensive logging later, most of the original white pine stands are gone, but the area is still home to vast forests, a small but stable timber industry, and a network of quality resorts. Apart from excellent fishing and hunting, many travelers to the area are attracted to the canoeing opportunities on the *Pine River.* The town is located on a newly designated *canoe waterway route* starting in upper Cass County and continuing down through the scenic *Whitefish chain of lakes.* In the winter, the *Foothills Snowmobile Trail* offers 11 miles of prime snowmobiling. The town is a gateway to *Itasca State Park,* with the headwaters of the Mississippi, as well as *Deep Portage,* an excellent forest reserve complete with an interpretive center and guided hikes. For more genteel sports, Pine River boasts the new *Pine River Golf Course,* free *tennis courts,* and escorted *horseback riding tours.* Annual events range the spectrum from an *eelpout feed* in February to the huge *Summerfest* in late June featuring a boisterous parade, a popular craft fair, and a fun-filled horseshoe tournament.

For more information on Pine River, contact:
PINE RIVER CHAMBER OF COMMERCE
Box 131
Pine River, MN 56474
(218) 587-4000

R ESORT & MUSEUM

■ DRIFTWOOD FAMILY RESORT & MUSEUM
R.R. 1, P.O. Box 404
Pine River, MN 56474
Tel: (218) 568-4221 or (800)950-3540
Hrs: Open year-round
AmEx is accepted.

Driftwood resort is located on the Whitefish chain of lakes and has provided families with summer vacation fun for 25 years. This family-oriented resort is made up of 25 cabins which have one to four bedrooms, carpeting, a refrigerator, private bath, and some are equipped with kitchenettes. There is also a golf course, pool, whirlpool, racquetball, pony rides, and any number of water activities to wile away those hot summer days.

The Minnesota Resort Museum is also located here featuring chronological displays from the Ice Age through the Industrial Age. This is the only museum in the world devoted to presenting all aspects of resorting throughout the last 100 years. The 8,400-square-foot museum covers two floors and is open to the general public with a gift shop and dining room of its own. Driftwood provides resort living with an educational trip back through time all in one place.

Princeton

F or visitors to the Twin Cities who only have limited time, Princeton is an excellent choice for a glimpse of the state's undisturbed wilderness. Located nearly one-and-a-half-hours northwest of Minneapolis, the town is a bustling community of 3,400 with a high school, modern hospital, and a number of large industries, including Crystal Cabinet Works and the school supplies manufacturing firm Smith System. Still, Princeton maintains an appropriately quiet atmosphere considering its role as gateway to some of the premier wilderness areas in the state.

ATTRACTIONS

On the top of the list of Princeton's nature areas reigns *Sherburne National Wildlife Refuge.* Encompassing 30,665 acres of pristine oak woods, marshes, and grasslands; this outstanding refuge is home to more than 250 species of birds at different times throughout the year. A 12-mile drive and hiking trails provide excellent opportunities to view these and other animal species. Bordering the refuge is the unique *Sand Dunes State Forest* with its strange, continually forming sand dunes, and its trails, campgrounds, and beach on tiny *Ann Lake.* In addition, Princeton is situated on the shores of the excellent canoeing river Rum River, which allows canoeists to float 100 miles downstream. After spending all this time with nature, visitors can wind down with a visit to the *Mille Lacs County Historical Museum* located in the vintage, 1903 *Princeton Railway Depot;* a game at the *Rum River Golf Club* with its modern, comfortable clubhouse; or just a stroll down the quaint Main Street for a bite to eat in one of the local restaurants. For something completely different, some may want to pay a visit to the stock car races at *Princeton Speedway.* If the noise and excitement at the races aren't enough, visitors can enjoy the tug-of-war, carnivals or street dances at the *Rum River Festival* in early June; share the fun of the demolition derby and tractor pull during the *Mille Lacs County Fair* in August, or cheer on their favorites during the world's largest invitational *cross-country race* in September.

For more information on Princeton, contact:
PRINCETON CHAMBER OF COMMERCE
909 East LaGrande
P.O. Box 381
Princeton, MN 55371
(612) 389-1764

GAME BIRD HATCHERY & GIFTS

■ OAKWOOD GAME FARM
30703 Highway 169
Princeton, MN 55371
Tel: (612) 389-2031 or (800) 328-6647
Hrs: Mon. - Sat. 8 a.m. - 5 p.m., Sun. by appointment
All major credit cards are accepted.

Oakwood Game Farm in Princeton has come a long way since its humble beginnings in 1967. That year, Jim and Betty Meyer raised 50 pheasant chicks as a hobby. Today, they hatch 400,000 pheasant chicks annually on their 100-acre spread, making their family-owned game farm one of the largest producers of wild game birds in the United States. But even though the numbers have changed, the Meyers' dedication to producing the best birds in the industry remains intact.

Indeed, Oakwood Game Farm enjoys a widespread reputation for quality products, and the Meyers ship day-old pheasant chicks and hatching eggs to customers all around the world. In addition to pheasants, chukar partridges and wild turkeys are also available both as hatching eggs, chicks, or adult birds. The Meyers also provide adult pheasants for dog-training and to hunting preserves for releasing, an attractive option for hunters nationwide.

For those who want their birds without the hassle of hunting them, Oakwood has another alternative. By calling the farm's toll-free number, they can request a brochure that describes a succulent selection of fresh or smoked wild turkey, pheasant, chukar partridge, bobwhite quail, and mallard duck, in addition to genuine wild rice. Harvested by hand with canoe and thrashing pole in the lakes of northern Minnesota, rice — actually the seeds from an aquatic grass — is a perfect accompaniment to a game bird dinner. For those who are driving through Princeton, all these products are available in Oakwood's retail store as well as wildlife prints, taxidermy-mounted game birds, maple syrup, and much more.

Roseau

The farming community of Roseau, which alone produces 80 percent of the country's timothy grass seeds, was once part of the fur trading voyageurs route across northern Minnesota. Today, the city's name — a French translation from Chippewa for "reed river" — is the only memory of the intrepid Frenchmen's influence in this area. Although canoeists still follow the path of the voyageurs along the Roseau, and fishermen try their luck in nearby *Lake of the Woods,* the city is best known as the headquarters of *Polaris Industries.* The largest producer of snowmobiles and all-terrain vehicles, Polaris offers tours of its operations at 2 p.m. every afternoon from Monday to Friday. Good locations to try out a brand new Polaris are *Hayes Lake State Park* — 3,000 acres of lakes and pine woods with abundant camping, picnicking, and hiking opportunities — or *Roseau River Wildlife Area,* an excellent spot to view waterfowl, deer, or moose. In celebration of its farming heritage, the town operates the *Pioneer Farm & Village* — an impressive seven acres of farm buildings, including an early post office, country store, church, pioneer home, and a rare cigar factory. Another point of historic interest is the *Roseau County Historical Museum* with its 10,000 items, including the state's largest collection of bird eggs. The rural heritage is also the focus of the town's largest events — the annual *county fair* and frequent *horse shows,* both held in the summer.

For more information on Roseau, contact:
ROSEAU CIVIC AND COMMERCE ASSOCIATION
302 Second Ave. S.E.
Roseau, MN 56751
(218) 463-1542

Sauk Centre

The small farming town of Sauk Centre was just 22 years old in 1885 when the city's most famous son, novelist Sinclair Lewis, was born. The solitary Lewis' boyhood in Sauk Centre was not a happy one, which helps to explain the bitterness in his landmark novel Main Street, a candid and not entirely kind exposé of life in Sauk Centre. The novel made Lewis the first American winner of the Nobel Prize for literature and provided the reluctant Sauk Centre with lasting, national fame. Today, Lewis's barbs against his hometown are forgotten, and a series of historical attractions celebrate this great literary genius. At his restored boyhood home, there's guided tours by members of the Sinclair Lewis Foundation, while at the *Sinclair Lewis Interpretive Center* visitors can learn the fascinating story of his life. Informed literary fans will also make sure not to miss the *Palmer House,* a restaurant and hotel since 1901 where Lewis worked as a young man; and *Main Street Drug,* a building from 1903 with a decorative cornice where Lewis's father, a doctor, had his office. Other sites of historical interest include the *Old Mill* that has loomed above the Sauk River since the 1860s; the *Old First National Bank;* the *Caughren House* (now the Marc'ette Place Floral & Gifts) and the *Bryant Public Library,* one of the few Carnegie libraries left in Minnesota. The memory of Sinclair Lewis is the focus of one of Sauk Centre's major annual events — *Sinclair Lewis Days* — featuring a huge flea market, a craft show, and a parade that marches, fittingly, down Main Street and Sinclair Lewis Avenue.

For more information on Sauke Centre, contact:
SAUK CENTRE CHAMBER OF COMMERCE
P.O. Box 222
Sauk Centre, MN 56378
(612) 352-5201

G IFT SHOP

■ COBBLESTONE COURT GIFT SHOP
328 Main Street
Sauk Centre, MN 56378
Tel: (612) 352-6897
Hrs: Mon. - Thurs. 9 a.m.- 5 p.m.
      Fri. 9 a.m.- 8 p.m., Sat. 9 a.m. - 5 p.m.
      (Extended Christmas hours)
Discover, Visa, and MasterCard are accepted.

A visit to Sauk Centre would not be complete without a stop at Cobblestone Court Gift Shop. Originally constructed as the First National Bank in 1884, the building still maintains its stately facade and lavish interior of marble, granite, and oak. Owners Kathy and Tom Oschwald opened Cobblestone Court in 1982 after months of careful restoration had uncovered the riches of this precious gem.

Today, this historically encased gift shop is a showcase dealer for the Dept 56 Village Collection. Other collectibles include Swarovski Crystal, Precious Moments Collection, Jan Hagara Victorian Figurines, and the David Winter Cottages. Many decorative accessories, prints, lamps, and Howard Miller clocks are also on display. Customers enjoy the year-round Christmas room on the lower level where the original bank vault is still intact. Unique and creative greeting cards can also be found to accompany gift selections.

Open house events are hosted twice a year, at Easter and again at Christmas. Shipping, mail order, and free gift wrapping service are available. Cobblestone Court Gift Shop offers a relaxing atmosphere in which to browse. This spacious shop offers many temptations for the serious collector or the spontaneous shopper.

H ISTORIC HOTEL

■ PALMER HOUSE HOTEL AND RESTAURANT

Sinclair Lewis Ave. and Main Street
Sauk Centre, MN 56378
Tel: (612) 352-3431
Hrs: Open year-round

The Palmer House Hotel and Restaurant was built in 1901 by R.L. Palmer. Sinclair Lewis, famous citizen and author, worked there for a short time. In his book Main Street, Lewis refers to the hotel as the "Minnimashie House" and later as the "American House" in Work of Art. Traveling salesmen were the major patrons in the early years. As these salesmen began to switch their lodging preference to motels, the boom era for the early Palmer House came to a close.

In 1974 Dick Schwartz and Al Tingley purchased the structure and set out to restore the hotel so it could become what it once was. More than $200,000 later, The Palmer House is on the National Register of Historic Places and is run as a full-service restaurant with 37 rooms available for lodging. Many of the rooms were restored to their original state right down to the stained-glass windows imported from Vienna, Austria in 1901. Antiques are scattered throughout to bring the past to life.

Homecooked style is the speciality of the restaurant at reasonable rates. The dinner theatre is a monthly feature during the summer, and with advance notice, owner Al Tingley will prepare a nine-course meal for groups up to 20. The American Dream can be seen all around with a visit to the Palmer House Hotel and Restaurant.

St. Cloud

A fter years of relative obscurity as a heartland trade center, a modern, progressive St. Cloud is bursting on the scene. The St. Cloud metropolitan area is growing faster than any other in the state, and predictions place St. Cloud's population at no less than a quarter of a million people by 2010. These are heady statistics for a city located in the midst of a farming region that has suffered for years in one of the worst farm crises of the century. Fortunately for St. Cloud, however, the city has grown to reach the critical mass needed to become a regional center, absorbing new business from a wide area and forming a self-sufficient community of colleges, service businesses, and industry. The city's manufacturing industry, in particular, is highly diverse, shielding it from a fatal reliance on a single economic base. Originally founded on the granite industry, St. Cloud's largest employer is still Cold Spring Granite, the leading producer of granite in the world. But St. Cloud is also a national center for optics, producing nearly half of all lenses made in the U.S.; and for paper products and printing. The city's 19 local print shops make it the largest center for commercial printing between the Twin Cities and the West Coast, while Champion International in nearby Sartell produces the paper for 20 of the 25 largest-circulation newspapers in the country.

ATTRACTIONS

For a small glimpse of the industries that have helped make St. Cloud a 1990s boomtown, stop by *Champion International* for the summer tours of its paper mill. Other tours of interest include *Golden Shoe Tours,* covering the greater St. Cloud area by horse-drawn carriages, trolleys, or motorcoach; and *Pirates Cove Paddle Boat Tours,* which follow the Mississippi River as it winds its way slowly through St. Cloud's historic downtown district and on to rolling farm areas dotted with many well-kept *century farms.* Walking, not sailing, provides the best view of the historic buildings in the downtown area, however. The landmark *Stearn's County Courthouse* with its six, 36-foot-high granite pillars earns the highest accolades from most visitors, but history buffs also

find their way to some of the many other historic buildings (most of which are listed on the National Register of Historic Places): the *Fifth Avenue Commercial Buildings* which are designated an historic district; *St. Mary's Cathedral;* the *Paramont Building;* the *Stearns County Heritage Center* housing local history collections; and the *County Stearns Theatrical Building* built with pillared grandeur. The latter serves as the venue for the performances of the *County Stearns Theatrical Company,* but St. Cloud is also home to a number of other performing arts companies, including the *St. Cloud Symphony* and the *Stephen B. Humphrey Theater* featuring nationally known actors. A performance of another kind is the focus of attention at *Radio City Music Hall,* a shopping center with a balcony view of the disc jockeys of KCLD Radio at work. For even more shopping, make tracks to *Mall Germain,* a pedestrian walkway bordered by three blocks of unique shops and home to the graceful sculpture *The Granite Trio,* a tribute to the city's heritage.

A city of St. Cloud's size comes alive with events virtually every week. Some of the largest, however, include the tradition-bound *Sleigh and Cutter Parade* in February; the colorful *Upper Mississippi Hot Air Balloon Rally* in May; the lively *Mississippi River Music Fest* and the community-oriented *Wheel, Wings and Water Festival* in July; featuring a fascinating air show, formula powerboat races, a parade, variety shows; and more.

For more information on St. Cloud, contact:
ST. CLOUD AREA CHAMBER OF COMMERCE
P.O. Box 487
St. Cloud, MN 56302
(612) 251-2940

ACCOMMODATIONS

■ RADISSON SUITE HOTEL
404 W. Street Germain
St. Cloud, MN 56302
Tel: (612) 654-1661 or (800) 333-3333

The Radisson Suite Hotel is the only Four Diamond Hotel in St. Cloud and is an impressive addition to the expanding St. Cloud skyline. Located in the rejuvenated downtown area, this hotel offers the finest of everything. The beautiful glass-encased elevator provides a spectacular view of the city. Each guest room is tastefully decorated and has a wet bar, refrigerator, and microwave. Some suites are available with a jacuzzi and a VCR. The award-winning Chanticleer Restaurant serves enticing meals with all of the freshest ingredients. A complimentary hot breakfast buffet is served each morning, and two complimentary cocktails are provided each evening in the Fox Lounge.

C OLLECTIBLES & GIFTS

■ A LITTLE BIT COUNTRY
3333 W. Division
St. Cloud, MN 56301
Tel: (612) 259-7923
Hrs: Mon. - Fri 10 a.m. - 9 p.m., Sat. 10 a.m. - 5 p.m., Sun. noon - 5 p.m.
    Extended holiday hours
Visa, MasterCard, and Discover are accepted.

Located in Midtown Square shopping center in St. Cloud is one of central Minnesota's largest and most exciting country stores.

The owners, Trish and Les Cheney, have searched the countryside to bring customers the highest quality in country. There is a unique selection of primitive signs from Tennessee, lace curtains from Iowa, rag dolls from Oklahoma, and old-fashioned candy from Pennsylvania. The Minnesota room is enriched and trimmed with an endless variety of Minnesota loons and ducks, recipe books, mugs, Minnesota food favorites such as Honey Hot Fudge, wild rice, and Mint-e-sota Hot Chocolate mix. Other country pleasures include painted crocks, wind socks, potpourri, country lamps and baskets, pottery, Yankee candles, bird houses, old-fashioned children's toys, country afghans, and other fine country knick-knacks and collectibles. The Victorian porch room offers an enchanting selection of romantic treasures trimmed with ivory lace and laden with pearl pebbles. For the Christmas holiday season, A Little Bit Country displays exceptional old-fashioned country decorations, Christmas collectibles, and other treasures.

C OMMUNITY THEATRE

■ COUNTY STEARNS THEATRICAL COMPANY
22 S. Fifth Ave.
St. Cloud, MN 56301
Tel: (612) 253-8242
Hrs: Non-production days 11 a.m. - 5 p.m.
    Days are extended during production
Visa and MasterCard are accepted.

Listed on the National Register of Historic Places, the building was purchased by the County Stearns Theatrical Company and with extensive renovation was restored into an exciting and vibrant community theatre with a 170-seating capacity.

Productions include classics to contemporary dramas and "doo wop," all chosen to make the audience laugh, cry, smile, and think. Audiences have enjoyed musicals such as "Oklahoma," "Fiddler on the Roof," "Hello Dolly," and "Kiss Me Kate." Children have been entertained with "Snow White," "Cinderella," and "Sleeping Beauty." Other popular productions include "Taming of the Shrew," "Rainmaker," along with comedies such as "Brighton Beach Memoirs" and "The Odd Couple." Most of the performances for the past years have been sold out with another hit season anticipated. Early reservations for select productions are encouraged. Group rates, and season and contributing memberships are available.

Over the past 16 years, County Stearns Theatrical Company has become a vital, viable part of the area community due to the selfless devotion of hundreds of volunteers through their acting, set construction, promotion, ushering, ticket sales, and business-office assistance. Their extraordinary efforts truly make this a community theatre. Audiences can be assured of an exciting and phenomenal entertaining evening to remember.

◼D ECORATIVE DUCK DECOYS

◼ JENNINGS DECOY COMPANY
601 Franklin Ave. N.E.
St. Cloud, MN 56304
Tel: (612) 253-2253 or (800) 331-5613
Hrs: Mon. - Fri. 8 a.m. - 5 p.m., Sat. 9 a.m. - 2 p.m. Closed Sun.
Visa and MasterCard are accepted.

Located along Highway 1, just north of Highway 23 in St. Cloud, is Jennings Decoy Company, a unique wildlife gift gallery.

Specializing in loon carvings, nature's beauty is recreated in these Jennings exquisite artpieces. Each reproduction is skillfully hand-painted, finished, and signed by the artist. Old-time hunting decoys are captured in the working decoy reproductions of a mallard drake, Canada goose, canvasback, and black duck. A wide variety of species are available, ranging from inexpensive miniatures to limited editions and one-of-a-kind carvings. Each artpiece is hand-painted and finished for years of lasting beauty. Wildfowl reproductions make excellent gifts. Other gift products include cedar clothes protectors, pen sets, bookends, ornaments, and magnets.

Jennings offers a variety of kits for hunters and do-it-yourselfers, complete with paint, instructions, brushes, and glass eyes. There is a complete line of carving tools, supplies, and "How To" books for the beginner and advanced carver. Jennings will also custom cut from customers' patterns. Over 200 cutouts are available cut from kiln-dried basswood.

Jennings Decoy Company brings the finest of blank decoys, cutouts, and tools to the St. Cloud area; and they are offered nationwide. A detailed supply catalog and price list is available just by calling. The owners, Steve Ree and Mark Johnson, welcome the opportunity to be of service and will custom design a carving.

G ALLERY & FRAME SHOP

■ NATURE'S STUDIO
419 W. Street Germain
St. Cloud, MN 56301
Tel: (612) 259-6484
Hrs: Tue. - Sat. 10 a.m. - 5:30 p.m.
Visa and MasterCard are accepted.

Judy Smoley, studio owner, is a true lover of art. Impressionistic art styles, American folk art, wildlife, and western florals are colorful, warm, and sensitively displayed around her.

Judy encourages customers to select artwork that makes them feel happy when they look at it. At Nature's Studio, customers can browse through quality selections of original artwork by Midwest artists. Artists include Doolittle, Bateman, Olson, Brenders, Kennedy, Barnes, and Wysocki. Various popular cartoon character prints such as Donald Duck, Bugs Bunny, the Flintstones, Winnie the Pooh, Garfield, and many more come to life on the gallery walls. A fine selection of bronze sculptures, limited edition plates, posters, and a variety of woodcarvings are also displayed. Customer framework is available in a variety of wood and metal.

At Nature's Studio is a complete collection of prominent works at reasonable prices. Judy prides herself in extending a personalized service that customers come back for.

M USEUM

■ STEARNS COUNTY HISTORICAL SOCIETY
235 S. 33rd Ave.
St. Cloud, MN 56302
Tel: (612) 253-8424
Hrs: (June 1 - Aug. 31) Mon. - Sat. 10 a.m. - 4 p.m., Sun. noon - 4 p.m.
    (Spring, fall, winter)Tue. - Sat. 10 a.m. - 4 p.m., Sun. noon - 4 p.m.
    Closed Mon.

The Stearns County Historical Society was organized in 1936, dedicated to preserving the history of Stearns County. The seed of the Society was planted much earlier, on January 1, 1873, when a group established itself as "The Old Settler's Association." Gradually the association declined and evolved into the Historical Society, with both groups interested in preserving local history from early inhabitants to present time.

The Stearns County Historical Society is one of the largest history museums in Minnesota, located in the Heritage Center, a new historical and cultural center in central Minnesota. It has over 9,000 historical valuable items in addition to 200,000 photographs and images, 10,000 biographies of individuals, and 500+ linear feet of historical documents in its archival collection. The Heritage Center helps visitors discover and experience what life was like in Stearns County in the 1850s. Experience the recreations of Indian dwellings of the Dakota and Ojibwa tribes. Walk through the granite quarry replica, depicting the granite industry from prehistoric time through present day. The exhibit, "Bringing Home the Cows," features one of the largest collections of dairy farming artifacts in the Midwest. The "Lifewaters" exhibit guides visitors through the days of fur trading, steamboats, Indian canoes, logging and mills. After browsing the pioneer history of Stearns County, stop by the museum store where there are unique and distinctive gifts, reflecting Stearns County and Minnesota history.

Visit the Stearns County Heritage Center and re-live great moments of the past. It's "A lifetime of experience under one roof."

R ESTAURANTS

■ CHARLIE'S
102 Sixth Ave. S.
St. Cloud, MN 56301
Tel: (612) 252-4538
Hrs: Daily 10:30 a.m. - 1 a.m.
Visa, MasterCard, and AmEx are accepted.

Located in the historic district of downtown St. Cloud in a 100-year-old building is Charlie's, a restaurant with a casual atmosphere and great food. The original bar is still intact, along with a variety of other antiques such as an old barber chair, soapbox derby car, musical instruments, old bicycles, sleds, and skates that complement the years that have gone by.

Charlie's menu features a variety of appetizers, sandwiches, salads, and popular pasta dishes. Enjoy a fine selection of steaks, barbecued ribs, chicken, and a "warm" selection of cajun style menu items. Seafood specials such as swordfish, broiled scallops, lobster, salmon, shrimp, and Minnesota's finest walleye pike are also available. Choose a fine wine to complement your dinner. Sunday brunch at Charlie's is unlike others. Meals are served tableside along with an enticing variety of hors d'oeuvres, caramel rolls, desserts, champagne, and fruit juices. Complete the evening by visiting the Comedy Gallery, upstairs, featuring local and national acts every Friday and Saturday with live music following the comedy entertainment.

■ D.B. Searle's

18 S. Fifth Ave.
St. Cloud, MN 56301
Tel: (612) 253-0655
Hrs: (Restaurant) Sun. - Thurs. 11 a.m. - 10 p.m., Fri., Sat. 11 a.m. - 11 p.m.
    (Bar) 11 a.m. - 1 a.m.
All major credit cards are accepted.

D. B. Searle's is a most innovative restaurant in the St. Cloud area. The restaurant was originally established in 1861, known as "The African Saloon and Barbershop." Owners, Jeff and Holly Celusta, pride themselves on the unique brand of hospitality and creativity provided to customers.

The menu presents an exceptional selection of entrees, and daily luncheon and dinner specials. Top sirloin, teriyaki, filet mignon, and rib eye steaks are grilled over mesquite wood. A fine selection of seafood and favorites such as barbecue ribs and chicken is also available. Specialty burgers include "The 5th Avenue" and can be topped with mushrooms, bacon, and cheese, Italian sauce and mozzarella, or grilled onions and cheddar cheese, all complemented with the "5th Avenue" candy bar. Other entrées include house specialties such as sliced breast of turkey with asparagus spears, chunks of seafood with broccoli, or diced ham with fresh mushrooms and broccoli, all served with a crowning of Hollandaise sauce over a popover shell. Begin your meal with a superb choice of appetizers. Sip a savory cup of espresso or cappuccino and enjoy Searle's most popular dessert, Le Beignet Souffles, a deep-fried pastry rolled in confectioner's sugar and served with hot fudge and strawberries. Before or after dinner there is a full bar offering nightly bar drink specials to enjoy in the lounge or to complement the meal. Banquet facilities are available to make a memorable experience for any occasion.

D. B. Searle's is the perfect place for enjoying an intimate atmosphere in the "lover's booth," and as they say, "Hang your hat on Searle's hospitality."

S PECIALTY CARDS & GIFTS

■ TOOTSIE'S
22 S. Fifth Ave.
St. Cloud, MN 56301
Tel: (612) 252-7075
Hrs: Mon. - Wed., Fri., 10 a.m. - 5:30 p.m., Thur. 10 a.m. - 8 p.m.
   Sat. 10. a.m. - 5. p.m.
   (Extended holiday hours)
   Closed Sun.
Visa and MasterCard are accepted.

Imagine a shop filled with whimsical gift ideas. From casual and unique to humorous and outrageous, Tootsie's can imagine it!

Pam McIntosh, the store's owner, views her retail business in much the same way she views life — she likes to have a good time. The store has a wonderful selection of greeting cards for the timid and sensitive to the bold and uncanny. There are a variety of popular gift items such as T-shirts, key chains, jewelry, neon signs, stationery items, buttons, books, and much more. For "tricksters," they won't need to shop anywhere else, rubber chickens, strap-on noses, and many other gag gifts are plentiful.

The shop is attractive and accented with high ceilings, fireplace, and stained glass windows located in the County Stearns Theatrical Building. "Put a grin on your chin." Tootsie's can be a very entertaining place to shop.

Thief River Falls

For years, visitors to this bustling northwoods farming and trade center have been asking how the city acquired its peculiar name. Legend has it that a Dakota Indian warrior once lived in the area where the Red Lake empties into a frothy river. Since he was known to rob those passing through, the Dakota named the river "Robber River." When an Army major later made a survey of the area, he found the name Thief River more phonetically pleasing, and so the revised name stuck. The "falls" was an afterthought, added when a dam was built at the mouth of the Red Lake and the rapids were converted to a waterfall. The beauty of the surrounding nature didn't suffer when the Thief River was tamed, however, and today the outstanding wilderness areas on the town's footsteps are its major attractions. The most remarkable of these is *Agazzis National Wildlife Refuge* — a 61,000-acre haven of wilderness unequaled in Minnesota in wildlife diversity; where timber wolves, moose, deer, waterfowl, and golden and bald eagles range. Other nature areas with excellent birding and wildlife-viewing opportunities within a short driving distance include the *Thief Lake Wildlife Management Area, Beltrami Island State Forest, Roseau Bog Owl Management Unit,* and *Pembina Wildlife Management Area.* The city's location at the juncture of three major ecosystems — tall grass prairie, boreal forest, and aspen parklands — provided the inspiration for the Audubon Society's native plant management area *Wetland, Pines and Prairie Sanctuary.* Also of interest for nature lovers, the landscaped *Friendship Garden* pays tribute to the friendship between nearby Canada and the United States. In addition to quiet contemplation of nature, Thief River Falls also offers more raucous activities, such as *river tubing* for a straight two hours or — in a different season — snowmobiling along the 50-mile *Wapiti Trail* on a former railroad bed or on other wilderness trails. In fact, snowmobiling is the main winter sport in town thanks to *Artco Industries,* which offers tours of the plant that for decades has manufactured one of the top-selling snowmobiles in the country, Arctic Cat. If this has given vacationers a taste for more history, they may choose to visit the *Pennington County Pioneer Village,* a living history museum with log houses, stores, rail depot, and other buildings filled with historical artifacts. The main event of the year, the *Pennington County Fair,* also celebrates the agricultural heritage of this community with farm-related exhibits in addition to popular rides, demolition derbies, and concerts.

For more information on Thief River Falls, contact:
THIEF RIVER FALLS CHAMBER OF COMMERCE
2017 Highway 59 S.E.
Thief River Falls, MN 56701
(218) 681-3720

Wadena

Wadena was once a small trading post on the Red River Trail, a path built in the 1840s for oxcarts carrying goods between St. Paul and Winnipeg, Manitoba. In 1874, Northern Pacific Railroad took over from the lumbering oxen, and the modern Wadena was born. Today, the only reminder of this early Red River Trail and the hardships of the settlers is an historical marker in *Sunnybrook Park* — a cozy community area with picnic grounds, duck pond; and animal park with peacocks, buffalo, and deer. (This animal park isn't the city's only one; the *Animal Acres*

Zoo north of town features lions, bears, and jaguars.) From its beginnings as a trading post, Wadena has grown into a prosperous trade and manufacturing center of 5,000, complete with its own theater company, *Madhatters Community Theater Group;* a nine-hole *golf course; tennis courts; ice rinks,* and a modern, 35,000-square-foot *community center* with racquetball courts, sauna, whirlpool, and well-equipped exercise room. Local artisans, crafts people, and entertainers are the center of attention during the two main events of the year, the *Wadena Area Christmas festival* and the *Art in the Park Show* during the annual *June Jubilee* festival.

For more information on Wadena, contact:
WADENA CHAMBER OF COMMERCE
222 Second Street S.E.
Wadena, MN 56482
(218) 631-1345

Walker

Nestled in the southwest corner of vast Leech Lake, this tiny resort community revels in an abundance of water and woods. Originally a fur trade post, then a lumber town before finally becoming a resort community, the history of Walker mirrors the development of northern Minnesota as a whole. In fact, thousands of visitors will take the analogy one step further, noting that the town is Minnesota distilled to its essence: an unpretentious fishing, boating, canoeing, and hiking paradise, populated by generous, friendly, and almost annoyingly healthy descendants of Scandinavian and German settlers.

ATTRACTIONS

The natural beauty of the area is, not surprisingly, the town's greatest draw. It's located in *Chippewa National Forest,* renowned for its lakes, trails, and camping opportunities; near the fabulous *Deep Portage Conservation Reserve,* boasting 6,000 acres of pristine woods and marshes; and right next door to *Lake Itasca State Park,* site of the headwaters of the Mississippi with excellent nature trails, picnic areas, excursion boat, and a wildlife museum. Of particular interest to bikers, hikers, and snowmobilers is the *Heartland Trail* — a 50-mile path on an abandoned railway line from Cass Lake to Park Rapids — offering beautiful views of the changing nature and topography in the area. For visitors who haven't been tired out by the Heartland Trail, the *Tianna Country*

Club golf course (unabashedly billed as northern Minnesota's most beautiful) maintains an excellent 18-hole championship course, complete with power cart rentals and even golf lessons for beginners. In addition to sports, Walker also offers plenty of history. The *Cass County Historical Museum* displays artifacts used by early settlers, while the *Old Pioneer School House* evokes a bygone era with old school books, student desks, and oil lamps. Last, but not least, an intriguing collection of Indian artifacts and mounted animals attracts hundreds to the *Walker Wildlife and Indian Artifacts Museum* each year. The fascinating displays include ceremonial drums, beadwork, and medicine bags, as well as an exceptional collection of butterflies and protected birds such as loons, owls, and bald eagles. Annual events in Walker focus, naturally, on water-related outdoor activities. In February, the *International Eelpout Festival* heats up the town as fishing enthusiasts try to catch trophy-sized specimens of the state's ugliest fish. Come June, it's time for the *Mariner Walleye Open Classic Tournament,* and in August the town hosts one of the largest sailing regattas in the Midwest, the *Leech Lake Regatta.*

For more information on Leech Lake, contact:
LEECH LAKE AREA CHAMBER OF COMMERCE
P.O. Box G
Walker, MN 56484
(218) 547-1313 or (800) 833-1118

A CCOMMODATIONS

■ LAKEVIEW INN
Highway 371
Walker, MN 56484
Tel: (218) 547-1212
Visa and MasterCard are accepted.

Lakeview Inn is conveniently located on the eastern edge of downtown Walker, overlooking Walker Bay of Leech Lake and lying within the boundaries of the Chippewa National Forest. Minnesota travelers and area guests enjoy the quality comfort and a location that is convenient to Walker's many recreational attractions.

The Lakeview Inn is newly remodeled and extensively refurnished, creating an inviting ambience. Accommodations feature single rooms, two-bedroom suites, or two-bedroom kitchenettes fully equipped with all the modern conveniences for cooking and just relaxing. The picnic area is complete with gas grills, providing the finishing touch for vacation feasts.

Walker's community recreational facilities near Lakeview Inn include a supervised sandy beach and swimming area, a community boat landing with docks, tennis courts, an outdoor basketball court, volleyball area, and a children's playground.

In addition to being the gateway to one of Minnesota's premier lakes, the Walker area is also central to three area golf courses, pleasurable dining, and convenient shopping. Outstanding fishing and hunting opportunities further accent the area's vacation-land flavor. Cross-country ski areas and trails abound.

ACCOMMODATIONS & RESTAURANTS

■ AMERICINN MOTEL AND JIMMY'S FAMILY RESTAURANT
Highway 371 North Walker
Walker, MN 56484
Tel: (218) 547-2200 or (800) 634-3444
Hrs: Motel (Summer and Winter) daily 24-hours-a-day
    Restaurant (Summer) 7 a.m. - 10 p.m.
    (Winter) 7 a.m. - 8 p.m.
All major credit cards are accepted.

The spacious lobby of AmericInn Motel and Jimmy's Family Restaurant is enriched with an oak check-in desk and staircase, vaulted ceilings, clear story windows, and a split rock fireplace. It is tastefully decorated with huge foliage and a touch of country charm, all to create a home-away-from-home atmosphere. There are 29 deluxe unit accommodations and mini suites which include microwave, refrigerator and wet bar, queen-size bed and queen sofa sleeper. The motel also features an indoor heated pool, sauna and spa, and game room. Guests receive a free continental breakfast, which includes pastries, juice, and coffee.

Jimmy's Family Restaurant serves breakfast all day long. Lunch and dinner menu items offer the finest selection in steaks, fresh Canadian walleye, broasted chicken, and ribs. Homemade desserts are available daily. Complete catering services are also available. There is ample space for RV and boat parking, with auto plugs for winter guests. Summer guests participate in activities on Leech Lake, fine shopping in downtown Walker, and the many trails for nature lovers in the state and national forests. Winter guests enjoy over 300 miles of groomed snowmobile trails, endless kilometers of groomed cross-country ski trails, and ice fishing.

AmericInn Motel and Jimmy's Family Restaurant is located across from Cochran's Marina on beautiful Leech Lake. It's just three blocks from downtown shopping and two blocks from the start of the Heartland Trail, a 30-mile paved bike trail. The Kellogg Family, owners and operators, have been in the hospitality business for more than 37 years.

■ CHASE ON THE LAKE LODGE
Sixth and Cleveland
Walker, MN 56484
Tel: (218) 547-1531 or (800) 533-2083
Hrs. Daily
Visa, MasterCard, AmEx, and Discover are accepted.

When visitors enter the town of Walker, one of the prime muskie and pike lakes of Minnesota comes into view — Leech Lake. They then turn north at sixth street, go one block, and there they arrive at Chase on the Lake Lodge, a hotel and restaurant built by Mr. and Mrs. L.H. Chase in 1921 to serve the summer tourist and the timber industry trade. This authentic and comfortable bed and breakfast inn is now listed on the National Register of Historic Places.

Though the hotel has since been refurbished for year-round occupancy, it still retains much of its original feeling of Old World courtliness. The rooms are of modest size, with a pleasant warmth that is a product of the beautiful woodwork and many original

furnishings. The gracious atmosphere is the work of Jim Aletto and his family, who operate the hotel. A colorful marine dining room overlooks Walker Bay, serving a choice menu of seafoods, chicken, steaks, and fresh pastries. A fine selection of liquors and wines are available to complement meals. End the evening in the lounge where entertainment is offered nightly during the summer.

Also in the summer, guests enjoy fishing, sailing, muskie derbies, and much more. Autumn brings hunting enthusiasts and winter provides ice fishing, snowmobiling, sled-dog races, stock car races on ice, and some of the finest cross-country skiing around. All the services and facilities of the Chase are available for group meetings and other special occasions.

The Chase is the "hub" of activity in the area. Guests will like the Aletto family, their beautiful historic hotel, and the serene countryside that surrounds it.

ANTIQUES & GIFT SHOP

■ SHOREBIRD ANTIQUES AND GIFTS
Shorebird Hair Company
Fifth Street
Walker, MN 56484
Tel: (218) 547-2212
Hrs: (Mid-May through Labor Day) daily 9:30 a.m.
　　　(Winter) Tue. - Sat. 10 a.m. - 5 p.m.
Visa and MasterCard are accepted.

Shorebird Antiques and Gifts and Old Time Photos is located in one of Walker's oldest buildings. Just a half block north of Main Street toward City Dock, it is located near ample free parking for campers or boats. Visitors can also come by boat and anchor at City Dock.

Shorebird features the area's largest collection of antique hand-carved duck decoys, fishing lures, ice spearing decoys and, of course, shorebirds. In addition to a wide variety of antique glassware and country collectibles, Shorebird also specializes in beautiful made-in-Minnesota pottery including mugs, rice, jars, canisters, pitchers, and much more. Along with antique jewelry, Shorebird also has unique, locally handmade, one-of-a-kind spoon jewelry made from antique silverware. Handloomed, all cotton afghans, scented handmade candles, signed and dated cloth dolls, Leanin' Tree cards, baseball cards, windsocks, tea, camel bells, and a variety of wood and wire items are just a few of the many offerings displayed in a rustically decorated setting. Old-time photos allows guests to dress in authentic-look costumes and capture memories of their visit to the area with a sepia-toned old-time photo. The newest addition to Shorebird is Hair Company. Hair Company's manager trained in Canada and worked with members of the Canadian National Hair Styling team. Hair Company is authentically decorated in the style of the 1890s, but the hair styling is strictly now.

B OOKSTORE

■ IMAGINATION STATION
Main Street
Walker, MN 56484
Tel: (218) 547-2111
     (218) 547-3118 (Evenings fall and winter)
Hrs: (Memorial Day - Labor Day) Mon. - Sat. 10 a.m. - 5 p.m.
     (Mid-May - Memorial Day and Sept. - Dec.) Sat. only
Visa and MasterCard are accepted.

Upon entering this bookstore, customers are transported back in time by the relaxed, rustic atmosphere. Barnboard paneled walls surround a potbellied stove and a railroad baggage cart. An oak church pew will invite browsers to relax as they page through an old favorite or newly discovered book. Imagination Station satisfies the senses, including one of the most important;the imagination.

Imagination Station was created by Joe and Bev Jorland to provide literature and picture books for discriminating readers of all ages. Drawing on 20 years of experience as educators, Joe and Bev select books that encourage the love of reading and challenge the creativity of developing minds. Included are books that reflect not only the rich diversity of our global community, but also the unique poetry, fiction, history, and nature writing by regional authors. Because space is limited, only top quality books find their way to the shelves of Imagination Station.

This bookstore is a haven for booklovers, where browsing and sampling are encouraged. Customers can take time to discover that distinctive book that will delight a special friend or grandchild, or remain a cherished keepsake for themselves. Personalized assistance and special orders are available, and at times there are readings by one of the region's many published authors. Imagination Station is truly an "Adventure in Reading."

G IFT SHOP

■ WORLD OF CHRISTMAS
Shingobee Island on Highway 371
Walker, MN 56484
Tel: (218) 547-3993
Hrs: (May 1 - Christmas Season) open daily. Hours vary, call ahead
Visa, MasterCard, and Discover are accepted.

Christmas isn't just for December any more. At World of Christmas, the season of joy, peace, and goodwill lives on all year.

Visitors will see all the decorations they've always loved: Christmas trees, santas, reindeer, and Nativity sets to name just a few. But that's not all. Gifts for all seasons and all reasons can also be found at this magical and fun shop.

In 1974, Neal and Carol Holter opened a gift shop in Grand Rapids, ND, and put Christmas merchandise on display in the summer. The idea was such a hit with customers that they expanded the concept and created the World of Christmas stores in Minnesota in 1978. Today, they have four individual shops located in the northern Minnesota towns of Park Rapids, Pequot Lakes, Detroit Lakes, and Walker. At each World of Christmas store, customers will find such old holiday favorites as nutcrackers, wood carvings, lighted Christmas villages, and ornaments. But the shelves are brimming with nonholiday gifts as well. Wicker, stuffed animals, T-shirts, Scandinavian souvenirs, and Precious Moments figurines are just some of the items that are perfect for special occasions all year long.

The Walker store on Leech Lake features a nearby bungalow that houses overflow merchandise and is connected to the main store by a lovely wooden deck. The deck has outdoor furniture and Christmas decorations and is often full of customers relaxing and enjoying the beautiful scenery. Fishermen have been known to throw out a line while waiting for family members, and a resident flock of geese provide entertainment for all. When customers are through enjoying the outdoors, they can stop by World of Christmas' Nutcracker Sweet and pick up some fudge to top off the day. At World of Christmas there is family fun and the magic of holiday cheer all year-round.

GIFT & CHOCOLATE SHOP

■ TIGER LILY'S AND CHOCOLATE MOUSE
P.O. Box 178
Walker, MN 56484
Tel: (218) 547-3727
Hrs: (Summer) Mon. - Sat. 9 a.m. - 6 p.m., Sun. 10 a.m. - 4 p.m.
(Winter: Jan. - Apr.) Fri. - Sat. 9 a.m. - 6 p.m.
Visa and MasterCard are accepted.

Tiger Lily's is a quaint French country boutique in a building originally built in the 1940s by a local artist Austin Sarff. It served as a private home for over 40 years before becoming Tiger Lily's. To complement the shop's name, the large sloping lawns are filled with flower beds of tiger lilies. A delicate fragrance of potpourri fills the rooms as visitors enter Tiger Lily's. The shop creates an ambiance that is attractive and inviting to both the shopper and browser. The main level is divided into a number of interesting rooms. The front entry and living room feature greeting cards, rugs, limited edition prints, and collectible glassware. The bedrooms are filled with hand-crafted Victorian goods, luxurious bed and bath linens, designer fragrances and jewelry, Christian gifts, exceptional toys and accessories for babies and children, and a complete line of Crabtree and Evelyn toiletries.

Customers will also find a wonderful display of crafts by local artisans. The heavenly aroma of chocolate catches their attention as they walk to the lower level of Tiger Lily's. Fresh homemade fudge and other fine gourmet chocolates at the Chocolate Mouse make it a haven for the most discriminating sweet tooth. Gourmet coffee and tea are also available. Tiger Lily's and Chocolate Mouse is a delightful Victorian boutique and gourmet shop.

GOURMET FOODS

■ TIANNA FARMS KITCHEN
P.O. Box 629
Walker, MN 56484
Tel: (218) 547-1306
Hrs: (Mid-May - Christmas) Mon. - Fri. 10 a.m. - 4 p.m., Sat. 11 a.m. - 4 p.m.

Tianna Farms Kitchen is located just outside the city of Walker, in north-central Minnesota. It was originally operated as a showcase dairy farm and creamery, until World War II made it difficult to continue and it ceased to exist. In the spring of 1981, the "jelly queen," Betty Hawkins, envisioned a new innovation for the dairy buildings and created Tianna Farms Kitchen. She enjoyed cooking, and the farm's gardens yielded an abundance of fruits, vegetables, and berries.

The old farm office building was remodeled and converted to a modern commercial kitchen and showroom for jams, jellies, and pickles. The many wild berries are found abundantly in the nearby forests or along roadsides. To preserve the full strength and true flavor of the preserves, they are not diluted. Some of the most popular and favorite jellies and vegetables are raspberry jam, dilly beans, and the exquisite wild berry jellies. Other exceptional items include mint jelly, crabapple jelly, blueberry jelly, apricot jam, strawberry jam, bread and butter pickles, beet pickles, and sweet dill. Together with the homemade goodies prepared in the kitchen, customers will also find an assortment of products which are either made or grown in Minnesota, such as Minnesota wild rice, honey, and 100 percent pure maple syrup. Tianna Farms

Kitchen offers a mail order service and any product can be made on a special order basis.

The quality and origin of the products, the care and expertise in their preparation, and the varieties available make Tianna Farm Kitchen popular among its customers. Specializing in homemade jams and jellies made from wild and homegrown fruits, it's "As Homemade As Made At Home."

❚S❚ PECIALTY SHOP

■ LITEN HUS
Fifth Street
Walker, MN 56484
Tel: (218) 547-3919
Hrs: (Mid-May - mid-Oct.) open daily
     (Summer) open evenings
Visa, MasterCard, and Discover are accepted.

According to its owner, Susan Nyhusmoen, Liten Hus was created as a result of a personal interest in Scandinavian heritage and a strong belief that people in the area need the opportunity to gain an understanding of ethnic background and heritage.

Liten Hus is located in an old brick building built in the mid-1920s, elegantly decorated in Scandinavian blue with hand stenciling around lace-trimmed windows. The atmosphere is cheerful and relaxed. Much of the merchandise displayed throughout the store is shipped directly from the Scandinavian countries. Included among the selections are Norwegian and Icelandic cotton and wool sweaters; distinctive sterling jewelry from Scandinavia; Iittala crystal; George Jensen of Denmark silver; porcelain by Royal Copenhagen and Porsgrund; books that draw on Scandinavian heritage; cassette tapes; Tom Clark gnomes collection series; Scandinavian food items; a unique card selection and much more. Each visit to Liten Hus yields a new discovery, a piece of crystal, a new sweater, or a wonderful card that may have escaped the shopper's eye on previous visits.

Stop by Liten Hus, "Little House," where the flags fly in downtown Walker and see why it's one of the busiest corners in northern Minnesota.

Warroad

I n 1820, French fur traders founded a trading post on Lake of the Woods, just east of a long, brooding ridge. At this time, Indians used this ridge as a warpath; the Chippewa venturing south from their stronghold at the great lakes of the north, the Dakotas trekking north from their land by the Red River in the south. The French began to call this small outpost on their fur trade route "chemin de guerre" — road of war — and when a small logging and farming town grew up around the abandoned trading post a century later, the fledgling community was named "War Road."

ATTRACTIONS

When visitors today gaze upon the vast waters of Lake of the Woods, they instantly grasp why the native people of the area fought for this land. Just like then, the opportunities for *hunting, fishing, hiking, camping,* and *wildlife viewing* are outstanding. Many *resorts* line the lake, and a road — or air transportation, for those who prefer the quicker route — leads to the quaint community and friendly resorts of the *Northwest Angle*, the northernmost point in the Lower 48. For those who are intrigued by the history of the area, the Warroad Historical Society has established the *Ka-beck-a-nung Trail* (road of war trail) that makes a beeline through the community and its history. Selected spots along the route include the *Canadian National Railway Depot,* listed on the National Register of Historic Places; *Father Aulneau Memorial Church,* said to be the largest log church in the world; and the *American Fur Company Historical Marker,* which marks the location of an 1820 trading post. However, a tour of the Warroad area isn't complete without a visit to *Marvin Windows,* a leading international manufacturer of custom windows; and *Christian Brothers,* the only hockey stick manufacturer in the United States. Both firms offer tours of their facilities. When it comes to events, the town's largest focus is on Lake of the Woods. During the first weekend after Fourth of July, the town hosts the *ESCAPE (Exciting Scenic Canadian American Powerboat Excursion),* where 100 powerboats participate in a four-day cruise around the lake. A similar informal cruise — except with sailboats — is sponsored by the *LOWISA (Lake of the Woods International Sailing Association)* during the last week of July. Following the sailing cruise is a full week of challenging, popular sailing regattas.

For more information on Warroad, contact:
WARROAD AREA CHAMBER OF COMMERCE
P.O. Box 7
Warroad, MN 56763
(218) 386-3543 or (800) 328-4455

F ISHING GUIDES & SERVICES

■ REED'S FISHING FACILITY
1201 E. Lake Street
Warroad, MN 56763
Tel: (218) 386-1124
Hrs: Daily 6 a.m. - 10 p.m.
     Summer fishing (May 15 - Sep. 15)
     Winter fishing (Dec. 20 - Apr.)
Visa, MasterCard, and Discover are accepted.

Lake of the Woods offers the best walleye fishing in North America, and fishing headquarters for this area is at Reed's Fishing Facility in Warroad.

Baithouse, summer launch fishing with guides, boat and motor rentals, bait and tackle, fishing licenses, winter fishing, and ice houses are all available here. Conveniently located across from Warroad Airways, fly-in fishing and hunting in the United States and Canada are also offered. Launches include three 26-foot boats with canopy tops, accommodating fishing groups up to six people. The boats can fish both Minnesota and Manitoba waters.

There are limited docking facilities and no charge for boat launching. No region in Minnesota can offer the diversified fishing of this area.

M OTELS & RESTAURANTS

■ THE PATCH MOTEL AND RESTAURANT
Highway 11 W.
Warroad, MN 56763
Tel: (218) 386-2723
Hrs: Motel: Daily 24-hours-a-day
     Restaurant:
     (Summer) Daily 6 a.m. - 11 p.m.
     (Winter) Daily 6 a.m. - 9:30 p.m.
Visa, MasterCard, and AmEx are accepted.

The Patch Motel and Restaurant is located on Highway 11, the "Fisherman's Freeway," just six miles from a 24-hour US/Canada customs port of entry. It is Highway 11 that delivers anglers to the

© MARTIENA F. RICHTER

famous walleye waters of Lake of the Woods. The Patch was built on what was formerly a strawberry patch; therefore the name.

The Patch Restaurant offers three dining areas with a combined seating of 156, a complete menu, and excellent food and service. The Orchard Room is excellent for banquets, meetings, weddings, and other special parties. Hosting such groups, along with many charter and tour groups and athletic teams, is a priority.

Because Warroad is known as Hockeytown USA, the Patch Restaurant is proud of the many hockey celebrities whose pictures are hanging on the walls. The restaurant is famous for its pan-fried walleye and homemade apple, rhubarb, and berry pies.

The Patch Motel offers single, double, quad, and waterbed rooms. The registration desk is an eyestopper. The desk is handcarved oak and the glass in the desk is etched strawberries. Amenities provided include indoor swimming pool, jacuzzi, exercise room, color television, air conditioning, VCR and movie rental, babysitting service, gift shop, and conference facilities.

The landscaping includes a playground for the kids, picnic area, and a path that leads to "The Patch." Whether pausing for a snack or an overnight stay, visitors are urged to "Pick Our Patch."

■ REED'S MOTEL AND RESTAURANT

1201 E. Lake Street
Warroad, MN 56763
Tel: (218) 386-1124
Hrs: Daily 6 a.m. - 10 p.m.
Visa, MasterCard, and Discover are accepted.

Reed's Motel and Restaurant is located on Minnesota's beautiful Lake of the Woods, where family and friends can relax northern Minnesota style.

The restaurant offers lakeside dining with a complete menu including seafood, steaks, chicken, and daily specials, complemented by a salad bar and soup, and homemade desserts. With prior arrangements, fishermen can enjoy and have prepared their own "catch of the day." Local artists display their works throughout the restaurant and are offered for sale to the public. The motel complex offers spacious comfortable rooms with the seventh night's stay free and housekeeping units that are fully stocked. Camping facilities, golf course, and a souvenir shop are close by for guests. Group and senior citizen rates are also offered.

The courtesy and warm friendly service of the hosts at Reed's Motel and Restaurant will make the visitors' stay enjoyable.

TOURS

■ CHRISTIAN BROTHERS HOCKEY EQUIPMENT

Warroad, MN 56763
Tel: (218) 386-1111
Hrs: (20-minute tours Mon. - Fri.) 8 a.m. - 10 a.m., 10:30 a.m. - noon
    12:30 p.m. - 2:30 p.m., 3 p.m. - 4 p.m.

The name "Christian" has been associated with the game of hockey since 1960. Roger Christian and brother Billy were key players in securing the first Olympic gold medal for the United States in hockey. After performing with the 1964 U.S. Olympic hockey team and several U.S. national teams, the brothers returned home to Warroad. They formed a partnership with Hal Bakke, Roger Christian's brother-in-law, and built Christian Brothers Hockey Equipment.

The Christian brothers combined their knowledge of hockey with that of carpentry to develop a line of hockey sticks. The company offers more than ten stick models with over 250 styles and patterns. This impressive selection includes shafts made with combinations of unidirectional glass and solid or laminated wood core of poplar, aspen, white ash, or birch. The blades are rock elm reinforced with graphite or fiberglass mesh wrap. In the 1980s Christian Brothers introduced its aluminum shaft to the American and Canadian markets. "This," Hal Bakke says, "really put us on the map." The company's most recent innovation is its design utilizing a special blend of braided fibers. Visitors are welcome to see the Christian Brothers operation; a 20-minute tour of the factory is offered year-round.

The ever-increasing popularity of hockey has brought Christian Brothers from its modest beginnings to the booming business it is today. Come and see how state-of-the-art technology and advanced materials and design have brought Christian Brothers hockey sticks international acclaim.

Minnesota's Literary Legacy

by John G. Shepard

Mark Twain got to know Minnesota from the pilot house of a steamboat, then wrote about it in *Life on the Mississippi*. As a teenager in 1929, Minneapolis-born journalist Eric Sevareid undertook a 2,000-mile canoe trip from Ft. Snelling in the Twin Cities to Hudson Bay, publishing *Canoeing with the Cree* in 1935.

There is no better guide to the North Star State's distinctive character than reading the works of these and other writers who have been inspired by Minnesota muses. Also, Minnesota's literary legacy has created some travel destinations that are most interesting in their own right.

Henry David Thoreau was advised by a doctor to travel to the northwestern frontier for medicinal purposes in 1861, the year before his death. The journal of his adventure (Thoreau's *Minnesota Journey: Two Documents*, Thoreau Society, 1962) reflects the eye of a keen naturalist, though one who apparently was not in the best of health. Thoreau's notes are filled with detailed observations of dozens of indigenous plants, trees, and animals and of the people he met on his travels.

During the same era, the experiences of a homesteading family on the Minnesota prairie left a deep impression on the young Laura Ingalls Wilder, whose beloved children's books eventually gave birth to the "Little House on the Prairie" television series. Her family's first prairie dwelling, a dugout built in 1874, was constructed against a hillside near the banks of Plum Creek a few miles from Walnut Grove in southwestern Minnesota. Today, the Laura Ingalls Wilder museum nearby, and an outdoor pageant based on anecdotes drawn from the Little House books, attract visitors each summer.

In the 1920s, Sinclair Lewis drew on his boyhood experiences in Sauk Centre to write compelling fiction that is critical of small town American life. His novel, *Main Street* (Harcourt, Brace & Howe, 1920), secured the author's world-wide reputation and was partly responsible for his winning America's first Nobel Prize in literature. *Main Street* is the tale of Carol Kennicott, a hopeful, cultured young woman from Minneapolis who marries a doctor and comes with him to live in his intellectually stifling home town, Gopher Prairie, which she quickly grows to hate. Sites relating to Lewis' boyhood are preserved in Sauk Centre today.

The novels of jazz-age legend F. Scott Fitzgerald were influenced by his upbringing at the fringes of St. Paul's high society. Fitzgerald's glitzy world was rooted in many St. Paul haunts, including the apartment of his birth (481 Laurel Ave.), the apartment at 599 Summit in which he was living upon the publication of his first novel, *This Side of Paradise* (Charles Scribner's Sons, 1920), and the Commodore Hotel, where his daughter, Scottie, was born to the notorious Zelda. Fitzgerald's most famous book, *The Great Gatsby* (Charles Scribner's Sons, 1925), describes the experiences of a young man who, like the author, was sent east for an education at a prestigious school only to be drawn into New York's frantic jazz-era social life.

Other parts of Minnesota society have been eloquently captured in the writings of Meridel Le Sueur, a poet, novelist and essayist whose work represents voices not widely heard. *Ripening* (Feminist Press, 1982), a selection of Le Sueur's writing, chronicles the experiences of Native Americans, populist farmers, and women from the 1920s to the present.

Those who hear the call of the wild will want to spend some time with the books of Sigurd Olson, whose life was dedicated to celebrating and preserving the wilderness along the Minnesota-Ontario border. Simple, evocative line drawings punctuate anecdotes and musings about Olson's many adventures in canoe country. *Listening Point* (Alfred A. Knopf, 1958) describes the process of building a log cabin along the shore of Burntside Lake near Ely. Sigurd F. Olson's *Wilderness Days* (Alfred A. Knopf, 1972) is a collection of the author's favorite writings.

As you travel Minnesota's highways, keep your eyes open for the elusive town of Lake Wobegon. Though not yet identified on any map, the day-to-day occurrences in "the little town that time forgot and the decades cannot improve" are familiar to more than two million listeners of National Public Radio and readers of Garrison Keillor's popular books. Pick up a copy of *Lake Wobegon Days* (Viking Penguin Books, 1985) and you'll be immersed in a town more essentially Minnesotan than any you're likely to encounter in the flesh.

© MARTHENA R. RICHTER

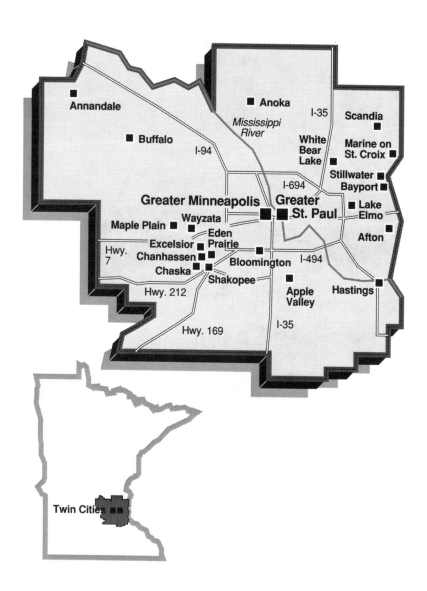

Annandale

Anoka

Mississippi River

I-35

Scandia

Buffalo

I-94

White Bear Lake

Marine on St. Croix

I-694

Stillwater

Bayport

Greater Minneapolis

Greater St. Paul

Lake Elmo

Maple Plain

Wayzata

Afton

Eden Prairie

Excelsior

Hwy. 7

Chanhassen

Chaska

Bloomington

I-494

Shakopee

Hastings

Hwy. 212

Apple Valley

Hwy. 169

I-35

Twin Cities

METROLAND

by John G. Shepard

Who would have guessed that a ragged little settlement clustered about a saloon run by a colorful ex-furtrader named Pierre "Pigs Eye" Parrant would someday become a world-class travel destination? Well, someday is now, and what was once a remote wilderness outpost has become a cultural center sharing the stage with some of America's greatest cities.

For lifelong residents who regard Minneapolis and St. Paul with the sort of easy familiarity common to small-town life, the Twin Cities' notoriety comes as something of a shock. But in the spotlight's glare at events like the 10th U.S. Olympic Festival and Superbowl XXVI, and in the wake of accolades from international travel authority Arthur Frommer and publications like *Newsweek*, it's hard to deny that the world has indeed taken notice.

Fortunately, for visitors and residents alike, Minneapolis and St. Paul retain their friendly, folksy appeal amidst the many cultural events and attractions that draw people from the world over to these two Mississippi River towns. Minneapolis and St. Paul are eminently livable cities. Streets are safe and clean, architecturally intriguing buildings dot the landscape, and getting about town is relatively easy. Also, the rivers, lakes, rolling hills, and forests that have nurtured the growth of these cities are ever close at hand.

To get a feeling for whence these cities have arisen, a visit to the Mississippi River is essential. Several replica paddlewheelers, whose predecessors carried waves of settlers to the region, regularly make the trip from Harriet Island near downtown St. Paul upstream through a heavily wooded gorge toward Minneapolis. En route, the boats pass beneath the ramparts of Historic Fort Snelling — another "must-visit" site. Summer tours of the reconstructed fort, which in 1821 was the region's first permanent structure, include informative films and exhibits as well as opportunities to hobnob with role-playing soldiers in authentic period dress.

The dazzling variety of cultural events happening in the Twin Cities runs the gamut from world-class to delightfully provincial. Theatre buffs can choose from a variety of small stages in the acclaimed West Bank theatre district or the Tony-award winning Guthrie Theatre in Minneapolis. Music lovers can take in concerts by the world-renowned St. Paul Chamber Orchestra, the Minnesota Opera, and the Minnesota Orchestra at Orchestra Hall and at the fabulous Ordway Theatre. The civic calendar is filled to overflowing with music festivals and night club events. The Walker Art Center, the Minneapolis Institute of Arts, and St. Paul's Minnesota Museum of Art complement a number of other smaller museums appealing to a variety of artistic and historic tastes.

Sports enthusiasts have plenty to keep them busy, too. Year-round professional action is non-stop with Twins baseball, Vikings football, North Stars ice hockey, and Timber Wolves basketball. The Minnesota Gophers compete at the collegiate level. The Twin Cities have also been home to recent major events like the World Series, the U.S. Open Golf Championship, the Stanley Cup Playoffs in ice hockey, the U.S. Figure Skating Championships, the International Special Olympic Games, and the SuperBowl in January 1992.

Then there are the special events that can be found nowhere else but here. Join the locals for annual gala celebrations like the Renaissance Festival, Minneapolis's summer Aquatennial celebration, and St. Paul's Winter Carnival. You just may not want to leave.

Afton

T his historical town on the St. Croix began as a three-acre field of corn and potatoes in 1893 and quickly became a progressive agricultural community. Residents built the state's first flour mill in 1843, and 18 years later tested the first, belching, steam-powered threshing machine. At that time, the village had just been platted, and immigrants from New England — who originally settled the city — began to arrive in force. Many of the original buildings from the community they formed still remain. Today known as the "old village," the ten-block by four-block area, complete with small, clapboard-side homes, gas lights, picket fences, and narrow, uncurbed streets, presents an almost irresistible attraction for area residents who long for the genteel touch of New England.

ATTRACTIONS

The "old village," with its unique gift shops and restaurants, including *The Afton Toy Shop, The Little Red House,* and *Selma's Ice Cream Parlor,* is Afton's foremost attraction. But the town's location on the scenic, protected *St. Croix River* provides excellent opportunities for boating and fishing. *Afton State Park,* with its hiking and cross-country trails, swimming and picnic areas, and camping grounds, is the premier choice for an exploration of the hilly, tree-covered St. Croix River valley. In proper Victorian style, *Afton Cruise Lines* offers river cruises each Sunday from June through October. (Group charters are also available.) The cruises are a service of the historic *Afton House Inn,* a hotel catering to those who love old-fashioned service, traditional lodging, and fine dining. The Afton House is particularly popular with ski enthusiasts in the winter since the town is home to *Afton Alps,* an alpine and cross-country ski area with 36 groomed trails and 18 chair lifts. In fact, the peak ski season sees most of the activity in Afton — annual events such as the *June Strawberry Festival,* the *Fourth of July Parade,* and the *Art in the Park* festival in October are suitably peaceful entertainment for this tradition-bound community.

For more information on Afton, contact:
CITY OF AFTON
P.O. Box 386
Afton, MN 55001
(612) 436-5090

Annandale

L ocated less than an hour northwest of Minneapolis, Annandale may well be the most convenient choice for a fishing excursion when time is limited in Minnesota. The city is surrounded by a host of lakes and rivers fairly teeming with sizeable fish, and numerous resorts catering to out-of-town visitors. But despite its attraction for the fishing set, Annandale isn't simply a resort town erected to serve the tourism industry. It's a small town that's preserved its rural heritage better than most. The main street, lined with false-fronted brick buildings huddled beneath a spindly watertower, is about the most Midwestern sight Minnesota has to offer.

ATTRACTIONS

The city's historical landmark is the 1895 *Thayer Hotel,* a national historic site that now welcomes visitors to its 14 rooms with period furnishings. (A quite different but equally attractive lodging alternative is *Maple Hill Resort,* a resort offering luxury accommodations in condos in addition to all conceivable resort activities.) Just off highway 55 on the outskirts of town, a grain elevator decorated with murals in flaming colors commemorates the historical roots of the area. The ultimate celebration of Annandale's pioneer heritage, however, is *Pioneer Park,* a marvelous history center of 28 buildings and five museums with 10,000 artifacts. In the homestead section, visitors can marvel at a fully-furnished log cabin from 1850 and a sod house; the farm machinery building houses a covered wagon and a threshing machine; and the frontier village is crowded with a barbershop, a blacksmith's shop, dentist's office, buggy shop, and numerous other buildings. Pioneer Park is also the venue for some of the city's top events, most notably the *Maple Syrup Festival* on the second Sunday in April when park staff dish up pancake meals accompanied by genuine maple syrup made on the premises. During the *Fourth of July Celebration,* which features the state's oldest continuous running parade, Pioneer Village comes alive with games and entertainment; and on the third Sunday of August, old-time music fills the air during the *Fiddler's Contest.*

For more information on Annandale, contact:
ANNANDALE CHAMBER OF COMMERCE
R.R. 3, P.O. Box 233
Annandale, MN 55302
(612) 274-5365

ANTIQUES

■ COUNTRY SQUARE ANTIQUES
Highway 55 and Oak Ave.
Annandale, MN 55302
Tel: (612) 274-5848
Hrs: Daily 10 a.m. - 5 p.m.

Treasures from the past stock the shelves of Country Square Antiques, bringing the past into the present. This is a multi-dealer shop working with approximately 12 area dealers. Affordable prices can be found on items such as glassware, stoneware, and graniteware. An intriguing collection of furniture can also be found here, ranging from primitive to fine hand-crafted furniture. Antique toys and linens are also available.

Look for Country Square Antiques on Highway 55 across from the grain elevator mural, which was painted in honor of the 100th anniversary of Annandale. Country Square Antiques is like a visit to the past.

HISTORIC HOTEL

■ THAYER INN AND RESTAURANT
Highway 55 and Maple Street
Annandale, MN 55302
Tel: (612) 274-3371
Hrs: Open year-round
MasterCard and Visa are accepted.

The Thayer Inn and Restaurant listed on the National Historic Register offers fine meals and cozy getaways. Originally a private home, the inn has been in operation since 1895. It features eight regular size rooms, four suites, and two bridal suites. The motto is "we don't kill you with our prices, we kill you with kindness."

There is at least one piece of furniture from the original hotel in each room. All of the furniture and decor are authentic for the period, from claw-footed bath tubs to restored Victorian woodwork throughout the inn. There is also a sauna and a full bar and lounge as well. Albert's Tavern occupies a cozy corner of the lobby, which is open all day and evening.

Current owner Al Lovejoy is painstakingly restoring and redecorating each room in time for the inn's 100th anniversary celebration in 1995. Grandma's Dining Room features a family-style menu with complete breakfasts, lunches, and dinners. Prime rib is the speciality of the house in the evening. In conjunction with Cobblestone Carriage Service, the inn offers a carriage ride and picnic basket package to tour downtown Annandale and enjoy the beauty of Pleasant Lake. The Thayer Inn and Restaurant provides comfortable yet elegant surroundings with a scrumptious dining experience.

Anoka

A t first glance, Anoka may seem like a rather quiet Minnesota town, with a typical history of fur trading, farming, and saw and flour milling powered by a century-old dam. But appearances are deceiving. In fact, Anoka was a booming city a century ago, coming heartbreakingly close to upstaging Minneapolis as the leading metropolitan center of the state. Anoka lost that race, but it has seen more than its share of characters and events that are humorous, odd — or maybe a little of both. First of all, the city is comedian and master storyteller Garrison Keillor's hometown and is the inspiration for his fictional Lake Wobegon. It was also the home of the late Jonathan Emerson, a settler who inscribed 2,500 words from the Bible along with his personal philosophy on a monument, erected it in the city cemetery, and died only a year later. And finally, Anoka is the distinguished "Halloween Capital of the World."

ATTRACTIONS

Each year, Anoka stages a giant *Halloween Celebration* complete with a football game, card parties, bingo, horseshoe tournament, kiddie parade and, of course, a costume contest. Originating in 1920, Anoka's Halloween Celebration may well have been the first of its kind in the nation. On a more subdued note, the *Anoka County Historical Museum,* housed in a 1904 mansion, contains local artifacts dating back to before the Civil War. History buffs also seek out the *Father Hennepin Stone* near the mouth of the Rum River. The stone carries the inscription "Father Louis Hennepin," which may have been carved by the itinerant Franciscan explorer himself. Finally, free weekly *Concerts in the Park* are held in George Green Park during the summer.

For more information on Anoka, contact:
ANOKA AREA CHAMBER OF COMMERCE
222 E. Main Street
Suite 108
Anoka, MN 55303
(612) 421-7130

Bloomington

M ost visitors to Bloomington wouldn't guess this is the state's third largest city, covering almost 40 square miles with a population of 90,000. Located just minutes from the Minneapolis-St. Paul International Airport, Bloomington appears more as a suburb of Minneapolis than a city in its own right. The truth is, Bloomington has become a major Midwestern city, attracting leading corporations such as Control Data, Ellerbe, Inc., Thermo King, and Donaldson Company with its convenient location and excellent communications and infrastructure. The city is dissected by Interstates 35 and 494, which has made it a favorite location for many visitors to the Twin Cities through the years. Instead of braving the traffic and parking rates in downtown Minneapolis or St. Paul, they choose to stay overnight in one of the two dozen Bloomington hotels — one-third of the area's top hotels — and make the city a springboard for exploring attractions and events throughout the entire metropolitan area.

ATTRACTIONS

Not that Bloomington doesn't have attractions of its own. One of the most surprising features of this booming city is its emphasis on environmental protection. One-third of the city has been set aside for recreation and conservation, including 8,000 acres of beautifully landscaped parks such as *Hyland Park Reserve* and the *Minnesota Valley National Wildlife Refuge*, a magnificent area embracing the river, swamps, and woods and offering miles of trails for biking, hiking, and skiing. Another nature-related attraction is the *Normandale Japanese Gardens*, a quiet retreat of bridges, lagoons, waterfalls, and trees maintained in traditional, meticulous Japanese fashion. Other sights conducive to introspection are the *Bloomington Historical Museum* with its pioneer artifacts; and *Bloomington Art Center*, a gallery featuring artists from a five-state region. The action is not so quiet at the *Met Center*, however, the cavernous home to the Minnesota North Stars professional hockey team, and venue for a variety of concerts and sporting and family events. The long-awaited *Mall of America*, the nation's largest shopping and entertainment complex scheduled to open in the fall of 1992, also should prove to be a popular Bloomington attraction. This 4.2 million-square-foot, fully-enclosed mall will feature some of the country's top retailers, including Bloomingdale's, Macy's, and Nordstrom, 400 specialty shops, 1,000 hotel rooms, dozens of nightclubs and restaurants, and *Undersea World America* — a 1.2 million-gallon aquarium.

EVENTS

Bloomington hosts a number of arts-related events throughout the year. The most notable of these is the *Minnesota Midsummer Music Festival,* a bi-annual extravaganza featuring top-name performers and a different international theme each year. The last festival was held in 1990 with German music as the theme. *Summerfete,* meanwhile, is an annual event, held each Fourth of July in Hyland Hills Ski Area. The star performers are the members of the Minnesota Orchestra, and in the evening, the sky lights up with traditional Independence Day fireworks. *Arts in the Park* is a city-wide program held during the summer months, featuring band concerts, festivals, puppet shows, dance, and theater performances. Also arts-related is the unique *Bastille Day,* a celebration of the French Independence Day complete with champagne, mouthwatering French pastries and desserts, and live entertainment and dancing held at the Hotel Sofitel in July. *Minnesota Prairie Day* held statewide on August 10 makes its appearance in Bloomington at the Minnesota Valley National Wildlife Refuge where visitors can view a prairie in full bloom. During the winter, *Winterrific* heats up the town with sporting events, an ice fishing contest, skiing competitions, and more.

For more information on Bloomington, contact:
BLOOMINGTON CONVENTIONS AND VISITORS BUREAU
9801 Dupont Ave. S.
Suite 120
Bloomington, MN 55431-3180
(800) 346-4289

ACCOMMODATIONS

■CROWN STERLING SUITES
7901 34th Ave. S.
Bloomington, MN 55425
Tel: (612) 854-1000
All major credit cards are accepted.

Crown Sterling Suites combines extraordinary comfort and value simultaneously by offering guests spacious two-room suites for the price of a standard hotel room. This rare combination makes Crown Sterling a popular choice near the Minneapolis/St. Paul International Airport. A separate living room and bedroom area make up each suite along with a kitchenette, wet-bar, refrigerator, freezer, and microwave. A full bathroom and extra vanity area add even more comfort for guests. In the morning they are greeted with a complementary full cooked-to-order breakfast served in the scenic garden atrium and each evening a two-hour complementary cocktail gathering is provided. For additional dining, Woolley's restaurant serves lunch and dinner and a terrific Sunday brunch. Woolley's lounge has a hot hors d'oeuvres happy hour Monday through Friday for tasty snacking and a chance to unwind with a favorite drink.

An indoor pool, whirlpool, sauna, and steamroom offer an additional opportunity to relax. Discount privileges and free transportation to a local health club are also available upon request. Crown Sterling also has comfortably designed meeting and banquet rooms for business or pleasure. The largest ballroom can accommodate up to 225 people, and catering can be arranged through Woolley's Restaurant.

■RADISSON HOTEL SOUTH AND PLAZA TOWER
7800 Normandale Blvd.
Bloomington, MN 55435
Tel: (612) 835-7800 or (800) 893-8419
All major credit cards are accepted.

The Radisson Hotel South and Plaza Tower provide the type of quality lodgings customers expect from a hotel bearing the Radisson name. Nearly 600 guest rooms display the quality and care this chain has come to be known for. Fifty of these lavish rooms are deluxe cabanas overlooking the indoor Garden Court pool area.

The Plaza Tower contains 170 rooms designed with the traveling executive in mind. A work area, conversation area, alarm clock, writing desk, sofa, easy chair, and spacious sleeping quarters make business trips easier to bear. When meal time arrives, several choices are available — the Aurora dining room has an extensive American menu with seasonal specialities and monthly regional dishes; The Shipside restaurant has scrumptious grilled swordfish and broiled mixed grill in a gracious wharf-side atmosphere; Kaffestuga is a Scandinavian-style coffee shop with an authentic smorgasbord from which to choose or a full service menu if guests prefer. The Spectator's lounge is a great place to kick back and unwind while enjoying the setting of the Garden Court. The Plaza Club provides personalized concierge service.

Complimentary continental breakfasts, newspapers, and hors d'oeuvres are just a few of the extra amenities available at the Plaza Club. The Great Hall can accommodate up to 2,500 people for any type gathering, and 20 additional meeting rooms can provide for meetings or conferences.

■THE REGISTRY HOTEL
7901 24th Ave. S.
Bloomington, MN 55420
Tel: (612) 854-2244 or (800) 247-9810
All major credit cards are accepted.

The Registry Hotel provides the ultimate in elegant accommodations in the Twin Cities area. Guests' every wish will be attended to by the gracious staff whose attention to detail is remarkable. Over 300 luxurious guest rooms and suites are available. Every room features individually controlled air conditioning, an alarm clock, color television with HBO, ESPN, and in-room movies.

The Executive floor and the Concierge floor offer extra special amenities for guests such as soft terry bath robes, mineral water, and fresh flowers. Breakfast is ready and waiting for guests when they place their breakfast menu on the doorknob before 3 a.m. that morning. Cafe Gazebo also has a delicious breakfast menu along with lunch and dinner selections available later in the day. This cafe offers a French setting with a view of the enclosed pool atrium. Latour offers a more formal dining experience with its Continental and American regional cuisine; brunch on Sunday is a genuine treat. Le Gourmet serves as an intimate setting for parties of ten or less. Cocktails and dancing can be enjoyed in Ravels lounge, which has a complimentary buffet during happy hour.

The athletic and health facilities are a great way to relieve stress, as well as soaking in the whirlpool. Banquet and conference rooms are also available for social or business gatherings.

MEGAMALL

■MALL OF AMERICA
Bloomington, MN 55425
Tel: (612) 851-3500 (Public Relations)

Picture a shopping mall with four major anchor stores, 400 specialty shops, dozens of restaurants and cafes, and a family amusement center theme park all enclosed in a building of 4.2 million square feet. What is it? Melvin Simon & Associates calls it "Mall of America." The Indianapolis-based company chose the 78-acre site of the former Metropolitan Stadium in Bloomington to build the nation's largest enclosed retail/entertainment facility, which will open August 7, 1992.

Mall of America aspires to be the most exciting American shopping experience, attracting people from all over the world.

Just five minutes from the Minneapolis/St. Paul International Airport, its location affords direct access via Interstate 494. Bloomingdale's, Macy's, Nordstrom, and Sears are the four anchor department stores, together for the first time in one location. Shopping environments from cosmopolitan and trendy to a European marketplace are created on three levels in the four mall corridors, which have been developed into separate streets. Level Four is devoted to entertainment, featuring restaurants, nightclubs, and a cinema complex with 14 movie screens. In the midst of all this, covering seven acres in the center of the mall is Knott's Camp Snoopy. This will be the nation's largest enclosed family theme park, designed and run by Knott's Berry Farm of Buena Vista, CA. Scattered among a northwoods environment will be 26 rides and attractions. A roller coaster, water flume ride, craft demonstrations, and educational exhibits, as well as restaurants, gift shops, and the whole Peanuts Gang will make the theme park an ideal place to spend the day. There is no admission charge to Knott's Camp Snoopy. Each ride has a separate fee.

Other exciting features at Mall of America are Underwater World, a 1.2 million-gallon walk-through aquarium, an 18-hole miniature golf course, and a 5,000-square-foot Lego factory as seen through a child's eyes. Special services offered will include coat checks, nearly 13,000 free parking spaces, and child care facilities.

N ATIONAL WILDLIFE REFUGE

■ MINNESOTA VALLEY NATIONAL WILDLIFE REFUGE
(At the 34th Ave. exit off Interstate 494)
Mailing address: 3815 E. 80th St.
Bloomington, MN 55425
Tel: (612) 854-5900
Hrs: (Visitor Center) daily 9 a.m. - 9 p.m.
(Refuge) Open daily, daylight hours only

Stretching for 34 miles along the Minnesota River from Fort Snelling to Jordan, MN, the Minnesota Valley National Wildlife Refuge is unique in the nation. Located within the Twin Cities metropolitan area, the refuge is home to over 300 wildlife species, some roaming the blufflands comprised of oak savannas and prairie grass, others wandering the valley woodland dominated by giant cottonwoods, basswoods, and silver maples, or the extensive wetlands where cattails and bulrush flourish.

The refuge Visitor Center and Headquarters is located in Bloomington, MN. Within this leading center of the U.S. Fish and Wildlife Service, visitors can browse through exhibits about

© MARTIENA R. RICHTER

wildlife management and view a 12-minute, 12-projector slide program that provides orientation to the area. The exhibits are interactive and feature photos, computers, and other displays sure to enthrall the whole family.

A bookshop and a resource library are also located in the Visitor Center — offering brochures and information, including maps of the extensive hiking trails and visitor guides to the four management units offering facilities: Louisville Swamp, Wilkie, Black Dog, and Long Meadow Lake.

The wildlife refuge exists to preserve and protect wildlife habitat and to encourage environmental education and nature-oriented recreation where it is compatible with wildlife. Refuge personnel encourage visitors to take advantage of this unparalleled urban preserve by participating in some of the many activities allowed there. Hiking is permitted anywhere on the refuge except in biologically sensitive or "closed" areas, and there are established bicycle trails. In addition, other activities such as horseback riding, fishing, and cross-country skiing are permitted in designated areas.

R ESTAURANTS

■ DA AFGHAN

929 W. 80th Street
Bloomington, MN 55420
Tel: (612) 888-5824
Hrs: Hours vary, call ahead
All major credit cards are accepted.

Although it's a bit of a challenge to find this cul-de-sac cafe, aficionados have found the way and beat a path to its unassuming doors. Within, the stage is set for a Middle Eastern feast at tables spread with Persian carpets, gleaming mirrors, and artworks from the owner's homeland. He has enrolled his gracious family to prepare and serve treasured recipes.

The food is fit for the kind he once served, ranging from unique Afghani pizzas and pastas to lamb especially selected for the restaurant. Char-broiled kebabs over rice pilaf, homemade yogurt and chutneys, and desserts that range from baklava to cinnamon-scented rice pudding complete the exotic palette. Sampler and family-style platters are also featured on the menu.

■ GREGORY'S

7956 Lyndale Ave. S.
Bloomington, MN 55420
Tel: (612) 881-8611
Hrs: Hours vary, call ahead
All major credit cards are accepted.

Hospitality is a tradition in the Long family. A third-generation restaurant, Gregory's was originally established in 1952 as The Ranch House. Four dining rooms, three cocktail lounges, and two party rooms carry decor from the 1980s. Harriet Long, owner, says it is restaurant policy that everything at Gregory's is made from scratch. Choose from the extensive appetizer list before ordering from the selection of hand-cut steaks, prime rib, seafood, chicken, and ribs. Sandwiches and salads are lighter fare for those not ready for a full dinner. Save room for the inventive desserts that augment the wonderful old standards on the menu. The lunch menu is just as delectable as that for dinner — offering sandwiches, salads, burgers, and some slightly scaled-down versions of dinner entrees. All items on both menus are available for take-out. In 1991 Gregory's was honored by the Academy Awards of the restaurant industry when it received the Best of the Best Award in two categories, naming Gregory's in the nation's top 50 restaurants in general excellence and banquet facilities.

■KINCAID'S

8400 Normandale Lake Blvd.
Bloomington, MN 55437
Tel: (612) 921-2255
Hrs: Hours vary, call ahead.
All major credit cards are accepted.

If this isn't the hottest spot in the suburbs, no one has told the crowd that pounds the doors down day and night. A sheet of window walls capture the drama of Hyland Park Nature Preserve that borders this restaurant, which anchors an ultra-modern office tower. Inside, a wall of plants continues the nature theme, borne out by clubby, masculine trappings of hunting and fishing pursuits. Kincaid's routinely captures top honors in area popularity polls, not only for its agreeable, informed service, stand-out lineup of international beers, and generous portions, but for what counts even more: skillfully prepared food.

Kincaid's chophouse menu goes beyond great steaks and prime rib. Equally quick to disappear are imaginative pastas and seafood from the fresh catch sheet. Entrees include the now-legendary herbed pan bread, and salads topped with Maytag blue cheese. Those who can still dream of dessert won't be disappointed with the smooth-as-satin creme brulee.

Buffalo

Beautifully located amidst rolling farmland just to the west of Minneapolis, this city of 6,000 is an excellent vantage point from which to enjoy the lakes of central Minnesota. Resorts abound in the area, offering an excellent option for those who want a taste of Minnesota nature — but still wish to remain within convenient driving distance of the Twin Cities. Not that Buffalo itself is without interest; the city is the county seat of Wright County and offers a wide variety of services in addition to an excellent public park system. The parks surrounding *Lake Pulaski* and *Buffalo Lake,* both located within the city limits, include playground equipment, boat launching sites, fishing piers, swimming beaches, and picnic areas. The city also sponsors an impressive array of events, starting with *Buffalo Days* in early June, a week-long extravaganza with a banquet, parade, variety show, street dance, Miss Buffalo Coronation, and more. Later in the month, the annual *Buffalo Championship Rodeo* takes over town. Its barbecues, pony and wagon rides, rodeo dance, chuckwagon breakfast and, of course, thrilling rodeo performances, make this event an excellent choice for those interested in Western fare. In a similar vein, the *Pork Chop Feed* in mid-July features volumes of sizzling pork chops as well as a water ski show; while in late August, an *Antique Car Run* is the featured event. The *Sidewalk Art Festival* and the *Fall Business Expo,* both held in the second half of September, cap the events.

For more information on Buffalo, contact:
BUFFALO AREA CHAMBER OF COMMERCE
P.O. Box 94
Buffalo, MN 55313
(612) 682-4902

◼A NTIQUES & COLLECTIBLES

◼ BUFFALO NICKEL
Highway 55 and Third Street
Buffalo, MN 55313
Tel: (612) 682-4735
Hrs: Daily 10 a.m. - 6 p.m.
MasterCard and Visa are accepted.

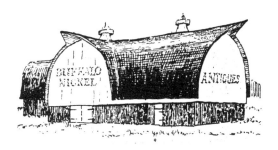

Buffalo Nickel was originally a dairy barn when it was first built. After chasing the pigeons out, Mert and Bonnie Thompson transformed the barn into a homey and intriguing antique store. The Buffalo Nickel is a multi-dealer store working with an average of 40 dealers. Because of each dealer's different style, Buffalo Nickel is like 40 different stores.

Buffalo Nickel attracts nearly everyone passing by, from young couples who find the antiques charming and quaint to older couples who can recall a bit of their history. There are special treasures for all who enter. The dealers create a "room" complete with backgrounds and accessories. Sometimes entire estates are displayed, a complete home in room-like settings. Buffalo Nickel specializes in furniture — primitives in pine and oak as well as wardrobes, cupboards, and desks. Harvest and round oak tables are always in stock. The inventory as well as the displays are constantly changing. Upon entering through the barn doors, seasonal smells and items offer a greeting. In the fall there is the spicy smell of wreaths and dried flowers. Christmas brings the aroma of pine and holiday trim. The structure itself is worth a visit. The refurbished barn with treasures galore offers something for everyone.

Chanhassen

B y choosing the name Chanhassen ("sugar maple" in the Dakota language) the city's founders underscored the most important features of this area — the woods, lakes, and rolling hills of the Minnesota River Valley. Today a growing community only a short drive from Minneapolis, Chanhassen has retained much of its natural beauty. In all, there are 11 lakes within the city limits, protected from excessive development by a foresighted city administration. Because of its progressive policies, some of the newer developments that hug the bluffs along the Minnesota River have become highly attractive to Twin Citians — as well as to corporations such as Rosemount, Inc., McGlynn Bakeries, and Data Serv — who are looking for the flavor of the country with the convenience of the city.

ATTRACTIONS

The wealth of nature in Chanhassen makes it an appropriate choice for the location of the *University of Minnesota Landscape Arboretum.* The arboretum houses more than 4,000 species and cultivars sprawled across a 900-acre area. Devoted to developing plant cultivars suitable for life in Minnesota, the arboretum welcomes visitors, who can browse along more than six miles of hiking trails or drive three miles of paved roads through the grounds. Another major attraction is the top-notch *Chanhassen Dinner Theatres,* a 600-seat, four-stage theatre that has offered 90 productions since it opened in 1968 as one of the first of its kind in the nation. Presenting such Broadway musicals as "Me and My Girl" and "Oklahoma" as well as comedies like "Greater Tuna" and "Groucho: A Life in Revue," each week the theatre attracts nearly as many people as reside in the town.

For more information on Chanhassen, contact:
CHANHASSEN CHAMBER OF COMMERCE
80 W. 78th Street
Chanhassen, MN 55317
(612) 934-3903

ACCOMMODATIONS

■CHANHASSEN COUNTRY SUITES BY CARLSON

591 W. 78th Street
Chanhassen, MN 55317
Tel: (612) 937-2424
All major credit cards are accepted.

Located just west of I-494 near the intersections of Highways 5 and 101, Chanhassen Country Suites is adjacent to the Chanhassen Dinner Theatres, and only a short jaunt from such attractions as the Old Log Theatre, Valley Fair Amusement Park, and Canterbury Downs Race Track. Although it's an ideal location for those looking for a day — or night — full of fun and entertainment, Chanhassen Country Suites is also a quiet retreat of lovely country furnishings and subdued luxury.

As the name suggests, Chanhassen Country Suites offers suites, rather than rooms, for the discriminating traveler. All suites feature king- or queen-size beds with country comforters, microwave, refrigerator, sofa sleeper, and a full, built-in wet bar. Every suite features a large, well-lit work area and two telephones equipped with computer hook-ups. Some suites are equipped with private whirlpool.

Visitors will especially enjoy the historic decorations in the lobby and other common areas. The centerpiece of the vaulted, two-story lobby is a unique fireplace with a hood from "Charlie's Cafe Exceptionale," a renowned Minneapolis restaurant. The old desk in another corner was once a school master's desk. Today it's still riddled with carvings of dates and initials. An antique cupboard, reconditioned sleigh seats, rugs, and other antiques complete the sense of grace and warmth from an era gone by. Those who are looking for a home away from home in the Chanhassen area, coupled with the added comforts of continental "plus" breakfast, exercise room, free coffee and newspapers, and indoor pool, have been quick to find their way here.

A RT GALLERY

■ LAKESHORE WILDLIFE GALLERY
7851 Park Drive
Chanhassen, MN 55317
Tel: (612) 474-3625
Hrs: Mon. - Sat. 9 a.m. - 5 p.m.
    Closed Sun.
Visa, MasterCard, and Discover are accepted.

Lakeshore Wildlife Gallery is perfect for displaying the unique works of wildlife art seen not just in Minnesota.

Lakeshore promotes a wide selection of talented artists specializing in original and limited edition prints of wildlife art. The gallery includes works by Robert Abbett, Art Cook, William Koelpin, and William Turner. It is the only gallery that carries Turner bronze sculptures. Collectors can also meet artists in person at the fall show, which takes place annually at the end of August. Lakeshore brings in artists from around the country with originals and prints for display. Some federal duck stamp award winners also attend. Most works are framed; however, custom framing and shipping are available.

For wildlife art and custom framing, stop by at Lakeshore Wildlife Gallery. Customers are pleased and delighted by the diversity and quality of the wildlife art collections.

D INNER THEATRE

■ CHANHASSEN DINNER THEATRES
501 W. 78th Street
Chanhassen, MN 55317
Tel: (612) 934-1525 or (800) 362-3515
Hrs: Open Tues. - Sun.
All major credit cards are accepted.

The Chanhassen Dinner Theatres have entertained local theatregoers as well as visitors to the state for more than 20 years. Since 1968 The Chanhassen has presented Broadway quality plays along with delicious dinners to its 5,000 weekly patrons.

The L.A. Times call Chanhassen Dinner Theatres "...the best dinner theatre in the country." and *Gourmet Magazine* calls it "...one of the very best." As the largest professional dinner theatre complex in the nation, Chanhassen presents top Broadway productions such as "Camelot," "Oklahoma," and "Hello Dolly!" In addition, Chanhassen is proud to feature "I Do! Do!" now in its 20th year starring the original cast, a world record-breaking accomplishment. The sprawling complex encompasses three separate dinner theatres, two cocktail lounges, nightclub, meeting and banquet rooms, and a ballroom.

The full service dining room offers meals ranging from Chicken Marengo to Seafood Tortellini. Group rates are available and pre-theatre cocktail parties are one way to add a special touch to an evening at the theatre. The exclusive Director's Room overlooks the main dinner theatre and can accommodate up to 32 guests in this exclusive private dining area. Tickets for productions are available with and without dinner. For a special night of entertainment and dining, the Chanhassen Dinner Theatres are just the ticket.

P UBLIC GARDEN

■ MINNESOTA LANDSCAPE ARBORETUM
3675 Arboretum Drive
Chanhassen, MN 55317
Tel: (612) 443-2460
Hrs: Grounds: Mon. - Sun. 8 a.m. - sunset
    Building & Library: Mon.- Fri. 8 a.m. - 4 p.m.
    Sat. - Sun. 11 a.m. - 4:30 p.m.
    Closed most major holidays.

The Arboretum calls itself "a resource for northern gardeners," but it's also an exquisite setting for any visitor who enjoys beauty and the outdoors. Lavish gardens, extensive natural areas, and plant collections grace its 905 acres of rolling hills and woods.

Visitors may walk paths through rose gardens, herb gardens, a Japanese garden, and many others. Hikers will discover trails through woods, restored prairie, and marshes. The Three-Mile Drive — which visitors may follow by hiking, driving, or taking a narrated tram tour — winds through lovely collections of shrubs, pines, firs, balsams, miniature trees for smaller yards, flowering and fruit trees, and the hardy Northern Lights azaleas developed especially for northern climates. In the Leon Snyder Building, visitors can stroll through the Meyer-Deats Conservatory; shop in the gift shop for books, jewelry, gardening items, or stop for lunch at the Tea Room. The Andersen Horticulture Library is a nationally recognized resource for professional and home gardeners, featuring over 9,500 volumes on gardening and horticulture.

The Arboretum itself was established in 1958 by the University of Minnesota's Department of Horticultural Science, while the adjacent Horticultural Research Center was founded at the turn of the century. Since then, the Center has introduced more than 70 cold-hardy fruit varieties, and the Arboretum's Research Department has developed special cold-climate landscape varieties of azaleas, dogwood, honeysuckle, and red maple.

The Arboretum is open year-round so that visitors can enjoy the beauty and promise of all the seasons. The delights of summer gardens, gorgeous fall colors, cross-country skiing in the winter, and maple syruping in the spring — plus the seasonal special events — make the Minnesota Landscape Arboretum a treasure for all its visitors.

MINNESOTA STATE FLOWER — SHOWY LADY SLIPPER

R ESTAURANT

■ THE RIVIERA RESTAURANT
560 W. 78th Street
Chanhassen, MN 55317
Tel: (612) 934-9340
Hrs: (Lunch) 11:30 a.m. - 2 p.m.
  (Dinner) Tue. - Thur. 5 - 10 p.m.
  Fri. - Sat. 5 - 11 p.m., Sun. 4 - 10 p.m.
Visa, MasterCard, AmEx, and Diners Club are accepted.

There is something special about a family-run restaurant. Maybe it's the atmosphere of quiet elegance, run by those who know exactly what families want on a special night out. Or maybe it's the evidence of a smoothly operated long-standing family tradition. Or, perhaps it's the special camaraderie among staff, some of whom have been a part of the team for 20 years. Better yet, maybe it's the wonderful food, expertly prepared by a skilled chef. The Riviera Restaurant is a combination of all of these. Tom and Lou Krueger, with son Steve and a dedicated staff, together operate one of Chanhassen's top notch family restaurants. One can't beat this combination of impeccable service and great food.

The Riviera has operated as a family-owned business since 1938, serving at first as a private restaurant. The current Riviera, opened to the public in 1972, has not lost the feel of a private restaurant, having been remodeled to preserve the quiet ambiance and special service that customers appreciate.

Homemade soups, steak and seafood entrees, succulent seafood (shrimp, walleyed pike, lobster), Beef Stroganoff and Chicken Kiev, a well-stocked salad bar, and selections bearing the approval of the American Heart Association make dinner at the Riviera worth a special trip. Reservations are not required for small groups, but are recommended for weekend evenings.

Chaska

N estled on the banks of the Minnesota River in the southwestern Twin Cities metropolitan area, Chaska combines an intriguing history and a well-preserved natural environment with the conveniences of a modern city. With only 11,000 inhabitants, Chaska is one of Minneapolis' smaller suburbs, yet still home to leading companies such as Fluoroware, Inc., Lake Region Manufacturing and PSI Nordic Track. These companies are building on a manufacturing tradition that started as early as the 1880s, when the clay resources in the Chaska area made the young town a thriving brick manufacturing center. This industry earned Chaska the nickname "Brick City," and today the many *brick buildings* in the historic downtown area showcase this fine Chaska product, which still forms part of the town's economic life. Another unique aspect of Chaska is *Jonathan,* one of the country's first planned communities dating from the late 1960s. Jonathan was a federally funded experiment in residential, industrial, and recreational planning; and the community's development set the scene for Chaska's current high standard of living. Contributing to Chaska's quiet atmosphere is the natural beauty of the surrounding Minnesota River area, particularly the nearby *Carver Park Reserve* with its waterfowl sanctuary, paved bike trails, hiking trails, and nature center. The residents of Chaska also frequent the city's two excellent golf courses, the public *Par 30* and the *Hazeltine National Golf Club,* designed by Robert Trent Jones and site of the 1991 U.S. Open Golf Championship. In addition to golfing events, *River City Days* take over the downtown city square the last full weekend of July with a community picnic, art fair, kids' games, water fights, and more; and on Friday evenings during the summer, downtown streets echo to the sounds of popular *band concerts.*

For more information on Chaska, contact:
CHASKA CHAMBER OF COMMERCE
203 Chestnut Street
Chaska, MN 55318
(612) 448-5000

Eden Prairie

C ity and country meet in Eden Prairie, a town of 39,000 located in the wooded hill country southwest of Minneapolis along the bluffs of the Minnesota River. Although Eden Prairie has all the modern conveniences and infrastructure typical for a city its size, including a variety of large shopping malls, it still maintains a rural flair with a substantial acreage of protected forest and wetlands. Still, considering how the city earned its name, community leaders could hardly have allowed wholesale development; in 1853, the eastern journalist Elizabeth Eliot arrived in the area and promptly called it a "Garden of Eden," and the name Eden Prairie has stuck ever since.

ATTRACTIONS

R esidents of Eden Prairie often turn to the city's extensive park system for recreation. At the 20 developed neighborhood parks, such as those surrounding *Round Lake, Staring Lake,* and *Riley Lake,* residents and visitors alike can enjoy swimming beaches, tennis courts, and playgrounds. The two regional parks in town, *Anderson Lakes Regional Park* and *Bryant Lake Regional Park,* encompass several hundred acres of marsh and woodlands with excellent opportunities for fishing, boating, and hiking — all within a 45-minute drive of downtown Minneapolis. Another intriguing attraction in Eden Prairie is the *Air Museum Planes of Fame,* with its collection of World War II aircraft lovingly restored to flying condition. The major events in town include *outdoor concerts* every Wednesday, Friday, and Sunday at 7 p.m. during the summer months, the *Fourth of July celebration* at Round Lake Park, and the *Schooner Days Celebration,* also during the summer — an old-fashioned ice-cream social where residents mingle and visitors can get a sense of the strong community feeling in this Midwestern town.

For more information on Eden Prairie, contact:
EDEN PRAIRIE CHAMBER OF COMMERCE
250 Prairie Center Drive
Suite 130
Eden Prairie, MN 55344
(612) 944-2830

A IR MUSEUM

■ PLANES OF FAME AIR MUSEUM
14771 Pioneer Trail
Eden Prairie, MN 55344
Tel: (612) 941-2633
Hrs: Memorial Day Weekend through Labor Day weekend
    Sat. and Sun. 10 a.m. - 5 p.m.
    Call for appointment to visit weekdays.

The Planes of Fame Air Museum is dedicated to preserving our American aviation history and to educating the public about the contribution air power made to the Allies' victory during World War II. It is one of the only two flying museums in North America, comprised of predominantly World War II Fighter Planes. All of the museum's pristine aircraft are flown on a regular basis. The museum's aircraft have also been featured in numerous flying-related publications, and several aircraft have appeared in both television and movie productions.

Visitors will see informative exhibits, aerial combat films, and some of the most famous aircraft of the war, all authentically restored to flying condition. This superb flying collection includes a P-38 Lightning, P-40 Warhawk, P-47 Thunderbolt, F4U Corsair, F4F Wildcat, F6F Hellcat, P-51 Mustang, Gruman F8F Bearcat, TBM Avenger, YAK-11, British Mk XIV Spitfire, B-25, A-26, C-47, T-28, SNJ, Stearnman N2S, and J-3 Cub. The museum also has recently acquired the rare German-designed, Swiss-built, Schlepp target tug. Air rides are available so visitors can experience the thrill of an open cockpit flight in the Army or Navy Stearman N2S. Gift certificates are also available.

The Planes of Fame Air Museum is located near the northwest gate of Flying Cloud Airport in Eden Prairie. The Air Museum and Gift Shop can be a truly exciting experience in American history.

ANOE EXPEDITION

■ THE MUSKRAT, INC.
9561 Woodridge Circle
Eden Prairie, MN 55347
Tel: (612) 943-2460
Hrs: Summer only (July to Oct.)

Canoe trips no longer need to involve only the rigors of wilderness camping. Now one can enjoy a canoe trip on scenic Minnesota rivers in luxurious comfort. The Muskrat, Inc., specializes in arranging weekend expeditions combining river trips and bed-and-breakfast lodgings.

A two-day "River Ramble" consists of six to ten people, or Ramblers, with a guide. The guides are experienced, veteran canoe campers, and the canoes and gear are first-rate. Ramblers meet at a selected bed and breakfast on Friday evening and after breakfast Saturday, the Ramblers are transported to the chosen river for the canoe tour. Ramblers enjoy a river bank picnic lunch and return to the inn for the night. The second day follows the same procedure. The four selected bed-and-breakfasts have a delightful ambience of an earlier time, all built in the 1800s and listed on the National

Register of Historic Places. Each inn has its own way to pamper its guests to make their stay a memorable one. Rambles include canoeing on the Root River, Cannon River, and Zumbro River, through southeastern Minnesota known as the Hiawatha Valley Area. The countryside is serene and beautiful, and the area offers a wide variety of quaint shops with hand-crafted gifts and historical collections.

A Muskrat River Ramble is a Minnesota "must" for the outdoor adventure of river canoeing and the pampered comfort at night of a gracious, historic house. It is an elegant, out of the ordinary experience not to be missed.

RESTAURANT

■ LIONS TAP FAMILY RESTAURANT
16180 Flying Cloud Drive
Eden Prairie, MN 55347
Tel: (612) 934-5299
Hrs: Mon. - Thurs. 11 a.m. - 11 p.m.,
    Fri. and Sat. 11 a.m. - midnight
    Sun. 11:30 a.m. - 11 p.m.
Handicap accessibility

Originally a roadside vegetable stand, this Eden Prairie landmark became Lions Tap Family Restaurant in 1977. It has been cited in local and national restaurant surveys for its tasty hamburgers. Lions Tap combines a comfortable atmosphere with reasonable prices making it popular with all types of people, including families with children, travelers, locals, business people, and students.

Owners and managers Bert and Bonnie Notermann take special care when making their hamburgers. Initially as an experiment, they made up a special seasoning. As customers gave their applause, the seasoning became a part of the business. Made up at home, the "secret seasoning" is added to fresh ground beef. The burgers are patted individually and cooked on a specially seasoned grill. French fries added make up the Lions Tap specialty at a great price.

Two large dining rooms and a friendly bar provide comfortable seating for small or large groups. Bert Notermann was the 1989 Small-Business Person of the Year of Eden Prairie. He attributes his award and successful business to hard work and his efforts to keep employees happy, who in turn keep the customers happy.

Excelsior

For a glorious 40 years, from the late 1800s to the 1920s, Excelsior was one of the nation's premier resort towns. Arriving by steam railway, visitors were whisked off to the many grand hotels, or ferried across the lake by steamboats bearing such unmistakably Victorian names as "The Belle of Minnetonka." Beautifully located on the south side of Lake Minnetonka, Excelsior was a highly prestigious address for well-heeled Minnesotans, who erected mansions and extravagant summer homes along the lakeshore. Today, Excelsior retains much of the flavor of this romantic history in the many small and intriguing *antique* and *specialty shops* — including *Antiquity Rose, D. B. & Company,* and *The Sign of the Eagle* — housed in the century-old buildings lining *Water Street.* The *Wyer-Pearce House,* a large Victorian summer house listed on the National Register of Historic Sites, has been restored and is open for tours. Another of the more than 50 historical buildings and sites in the Excelsior area is the *Old Train Depot,* which houses the collections of the *Historical Society* and is open Saturday mornings during the summer. As in the early days of Excelsior, the paddlewheeler, *Lady of the Lake,* is waiting to take visitors on a scenic excursion of Lake Minnetonka as the sun sets above the undulating, tree-lined horizon. Even today, citizens and visitors to Excelsior still enjoy the picnic grounds, swimming beaches, and softball fields in *Excelsior Commons,* an area set aside in 1853 to be used by the "common" public. Another favored meeting ground in Excelsior is *Old Log Theater,* a dinner theater offering farce and drama for half a century. On Thursday evenings during the summer, Old Log Theater performances are accompanied by outdoor band concerts in the Commons; the third Saturday of June, meanwhile, features an *Art Fair;* and the last weekend in July Excelsior stores slash their prices during *Krazy Days.* Excelsior celebrates fall with an antique market, parade, and good food during *Apple Days* on the first Saturday after Labor Day. In the winter, residents flock to the steaming pots of chili crowding the sidewalks during the annual February *Chili Open.*

For more information on Excelsior, contact:
GREATER EXCELSIOR AREA CHAMBER OF COMMERCE
P.O. Box 32
Excelsior, MN 55331
(612) 474-6461

A NTIQUES & COLLECTIBLES

■ AN ELEGANT PLACE
New location:
1250 E. Wayzata Blvd.
Wayzata, MN 55391
Tel: (612) 449-9505
Hrs: Mon. - Sat. 10 a.m. - 5 p.m.

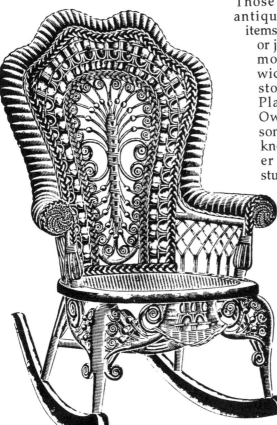

Those looking for antique wicker, have items in need of repair, or just want to know more about the wicker craft, should stop in An Elegant Place for a chat. Owner Gert Patterson has an excellent knowledge of wicker developed by study and hands-on experience. She also can help appraise and authenticate the age.

The shop is run by Patterson and her partner, Kathleen Stevenson. While Patterson enjoys repairing and restoring wicker pieces to their original condition, Stevenson shows antique linen and jewelry from Europe. Some date back to 1880, but are as beautiful as when new. The selection includes furniture, gifts and accessories, linens and laces. The shop staff will special order wicker and hard-to-find fine linens. Patterson and Stevenson are full of ideas for curtains and window treatments, using today's and yesterday's linens.

NTIQUES & DINING ROOM

■ANTIQUITY ROSE
429 Second Street
Excelsior, MN 55331
Tel: (612) 474-2661
Hrs: (Antiques) Mon. - Sat. 10:30 a.m. - 4:30 p.m.
　　　(Lunch) Mon. - Sat. 11 a.m. - 2:30 p.m.
Visa and MasterCard are accepted.

This two-story turn-of-the-century house holds an antique shop where visitors can browse through treasures and collectibles with the aroma of fresh-baked muffins and bread wafting from room to room. Antiquity Rose holds many delights waiting to be discovered, including Rose's Dining Room, a popular spot for lunch.

Owner Bernadine welcomes visitors to spend hours perusing the jewelry, pictures, clothing, china, glassware, and furniture that can be found throughout the ten-room house, then to relax in the dining room and enjoy creations cooked by Rona and Martha. Homemade soups, breadsticks, and desserts from Grandma's treasured old recipes, as well as flavorful teas are only some of the offerings on the menu. Customers will enjoy hearing the history of the items they purchase.

Bernadine and her longtime employees, including Emmy, attempt to gather as much information as possible about each item for sale in the shop. They have created a shop in which the serenity and geniality of a bygone era have been recaptured.

■B OOKSTORE

■FROG ISLAND BOOKSTORE
50 Water Street
Excelsior, MN 55331
Tel: (612)474-7612
Hrs: Daily
Visa, MasterCard, and AmEx are accepted.

A visit to Frog Island Bookstore in Excelsior is a rare experience. Named after an island in Gideon's Bay in Lake Minnetonka, Frog Island was home to many frogs and many children taking refuge from daily household chores. The shelves are overflowing to the ceiling with books and other eclectic treats for the mind. Frog Island Bookstore specializes in children's books and limited press releases along with a collection of rare books that many other bookstores don't normally carry.

A complete collection of mystery, biography, fiction, reference, sports, regional and international travel, crafts, and cooking books fill the shelves along with books dealing with current events and social issues. Maps, posters, games, hand puppets, and puzzles can be found in Frog Island. Out-of-print searches and special order services are available. There is always someone available to help with selection and history on local publications.

Book Fairs are a popular service provided by Frog Island. Books are brought to schools with a portion of the proceeds contributed to aid the school libraries. Story hours are regularly scheduled on Saturdays at 10 a.m. and often feature local guest storytellers. Authors' appearances are scheduled throughout the year with an opportunity for autographs.

HISTORIC SHOPPING MALL

■ EXCELSIOR MILL
310-320 Water Street
Excelsior, MN 55331

Excelsior Mill, originally a lumber mill, now houses a collection of quality specialty shops. The building itself retains much of its original architecture, which lends a quaint atmosphere to the mill. Dormers have been added and the massive ceiling beams exposed. The corridor between the shops is paved with brick, giving the feeling of a small country village, with here and there a park bench, plants, and pictures of the town of Excelsior in bygone days. The shop windows are packed with charming, country-look items, inviting customers to come on in and take a look around.

And during the holidays, the mill brings a touch of old-fashioned cheer to the modern world with special entertainment and fantastic decorations. With so many shops to choose from, customers are sure to find the items they need, whether they be furnishings, decorations, or hand-made specialties. Here are just some of the shops at Excelsior Mill:

■ D.B. AND COMPANY

310 Water Street
Excelsior, MN 55331
Tel: (612) 474-7428
Hrs: Mon. - Wed. & Fri. 9:30 a.m. - 7 p.m.
   Thur. 9:30 a.m. - 8:30 p.m.
   Sat. 9:30 a.m. - 5:30 p.m.
   Sun. noon - 4:30 p.m.
Visa and MasterCard are accepted.

At D.B. and Company visitors will find "gatherings for heart and home," a wide collection of fine handicrafts, gifts, and decorative accessories. From down-home country to elegant contemporary, this store features the work of Minnesota artists and artisans.

Step inside and immediately customers will be charmed by the delights displayed everywhere. The shelves are full of nostalgic accessories, wall decor, pillows, holiday and collectible ornaments, and dolls of all kinds. In one corner find baskets brimming with flowers, treasures and treats, while on the wall nearby hang dried and natural arrangements, wreaths of pine cones or grape vines, and framed prints. Visitors can also indulge their creativity by purchasing ribbons and bows, wreath or wall hanging components, and many other gatherings. D. B. and Company offers a wide range of ideas for making the heart a little happier and the home a little cozier.

■ PROVISIONS

320 Water Street
Excelsior, MN 55331
Tel: (612) 474-6953
Hrs: Mon. - Wed., Fri. - Sat. 9:30 a.m. - 5:30 a.m.
   Thur. 9:30 a.m. - 8:30 p.m., Sun. noon - 4:30 p.m.
Visa, MasterCard, and AmEx are accepted.

Provisions makes dinner parties and entertaining fun again. Offering a myriad of interesting and useful items for the kitchen and table, this shop has everything to make meals truly memorable.

Provisions carries tableware, porcelain dinnerware, and exquisite serving pieces. The shop also carries the little touches that add so much — serving bowls, teapots, canisters, aprons, towels, placemats, even candles, and an extremely varied collection of greeting cards and paper products. Hundreds of satisfied and loyal customers attest to the popularity of Provisions' merchandise. Many out-of-state customers even call in to order special gifts or just stock up on their favorite kitchenware.

■ THE SAMPLER

314 Water Street
Excelsior, MN 55331
Tel: (612) 474-6953
Hrs: Mon. - Fri. 9:30 a.m. - 6:30 p.m.
    Sat. 9 a.m. - 5:30 p.m.
    Sun. noon - 4:30 p.m.
Visa and MasterCard are accepted.

Specializing in quilting and needlework, The Sampler calls to mind the wonders of Grandma's attic stuffed with stitchery, pillows, lace doilies, and loads of other beautiful creations. Along with finished products, visitors will also find here the basic supplies for quilting, needlework, lace making, rug braiding, and related crafts.

In addition to a wide variety of inventory, The Sampler offers classes for children and adults in quilting, quilted clothing, needlework, battenburg lace, window shades, basic stenciling, braided rugs, heirloom sewing, smocking, and lampshades. The Sampler can give advice on how to make crafts of all kinds. The shop also specializes in handmade gifts, custom orders, quilt finishing and services, framing, pillow making, doll making, and most other decorative services such as window treatments and lampshade making. Now everyone can enjoy the beauty of homemade wares, just like Grandma.

■ THE SIGN OF THE EAGLE

312 Water Street
Excelsior, MN 55331
Tel: (612) 474-2315
Hrs: Mon. - Wed. & Fri. - Sat. 9:30 a.m. - 5:30 p.m.
    Thur. 9:30 a.m. - 8:30 p.m., Sun. noon - 4:30 p.m.
All major credit cards are accepted.

Imagine a house done in early American or country decor. Visitors can find everything they need at Sign of the Eagle.

This store specializes in all the Americana items such as Shaker-style tables, chairs and trunks, New England furniture and upholstery, and country items and cupboards. Of course, no house is complete without lamps, and Sign of the Eagle carries a very large selection of Early American and country lighting fixtures. The store also has quality pewter and brass, and copper accessories by Michael Bonnie. There are genuine folk art, replica antique toys, and country afghans in Williamsburg patterns. The list of items goes on and on. The staff also will special order items. Sign of the Eagle brings Americana charm to customers' homes.

RESTAURANT

■ LORD FLETCHER'S ON LAKE MINNETONKA
3746 Sunset Drive
Spring Park, MN 55384
Tel: (612) 471-8513
Hrs: (Lunch) Mon. - Sat. 11:30 a.m. - 2 p.m.
    (Dinner) Mon. - Thur. 5:30 - 10 p.m.
    (Dinner) Fri. - Sat. 5:30 - 10:30 p.m.
    Sun. (Brunch) - 11 a.m. - 2 p.m.
    (Dinner) 4:30 p.m. - 9:30 p.m.
Visa, MasterCard, and AmEx are accepted.

Located on beautiful Lake Minnetonka, Lord Fletcher's is one of the most popular gathering spots for food and beverage in the Twin Cities area. Lake Minnetonka is the largest lake in the metropolitan area with over 100 miles of shoreline.

What makes this the favorite of visitors and area residents is its notability for food and lakeview dining, seasonal activities, and relaxed surroundings. Summertime provides for superior outdoor dinning and beverages, three volleyball courts, and docking for boats. Boaters of all types, who are interesting to watch, frequent Lord Fletcher's marina. The lake is excellent for fishing, swimming, and waterskiing. Snowmobiling, broomball, and cross-country skiing are popular for the winter enthusiasts at Lord Fletcher's. The menu changes seasonally, along with the house specialties, which include walleye pike, prime rib, roast lamb, and pasta dishes. The Beanery Restaurant and Grandaddy's Sports Bar offer a more casual dining atmosphere. Lord Fletcher's is an excellent choice for private parties, with complete banquet facilities.

Lord Fletcher's on Lake Minnetonka plays a major role in luring visitors and locals alike for boat- and people-watching.

T HEATER

■ OLD LOG THEATER
P.O. Box 250
Excelsior, MN 55331
Tel: (612) 474-5951
Hrs: Box office 9 a.m. - 9:30 p.m. daily

Near the shores of Lake Minnetonka, on ten acres of wooded grounds, is the Old Log Theater. It became the Northwest's first professional theater company when it opened in 1940. It is known as the "oldest continuously running professional theater in the United States."

The Old Log Theater began as a summer stock company, performing 13 shows in 13 weeks in a converted log stable. In 1960, a new theater was built and operation became year-round. The wooden benches and earthen floor were exchanged for comfortable, widely spaced opera seats and sloping, carpeted aisles. Seating capacity is now 655. Dining facilities for a luncheon or dinner before the show accommodate up to 400 people. It is possible to provide chuck wagon dinners on the lawn by special arrangement. The resident company of actors and actresses are members of Actors Equity, and come from all over the country. There is also a resident staff of designers and technicians who provide the quality work seen in each production. Productions include classic American drama, Broadway comedy, English farce, and children's shows. Alumni of the Old Log Theater include such well-known actors and actresses as Lois Nettleton, Loni Anderson, Nick Nolte, and Julia Duffy.

Don Stolz was hired as the director in 1941, and in 1946 he purchased the Old Log Theater. Since then, the Stolz family has been intimately involved in every aspect of the theater. Don and his wife, Joan, and their five sons have done everything from working the box office and parking cars to acting, directing, and leading in the active management of this successful theater. Each of their five sons shows outstanding talent in various aspects of the theater. Tom, Dony, Jon, and Tim are actively involved at the Old Log Theater.

Hastings

A scenic rivertown steeped in tradition, Hastings is fast becoming one of Minnesota's greatest attractions. This city of 15,000 features rugged and colorful scenery along the Mississippi River, a downtown area studded with historical buildings, and the shopping facilities, restaurants, and other trappings of a modern city. Even the city's early beginning is a story worth telling visitors. The founding fathers of Hastings were land speculators, who settled at the confluence of the St. Croix and the Mississippi rivers when the area still belonged to the Dakota Indians. At that time, the city carried the somewhat incongruous name Olive Grove, and in 1853 the founding fathers finally decided that each of them should suggest a name and throw his choice into a hat. Hastings, the middle name of Henry Sibley, one of the speculators, was the lucky draw. The rest of Hastings' history, however, was not based on luck. Located on the "Great Mississippi River Highway," the city became a teeming gateway for explorers, traders, and businessmen, and finally settlers, searching for their American dream beyond the sunset in the West. While Hastings never grew to the size of Minneapolis and St. Paul, it eventually attracted major companies such as Smead Manufacturing (a leading national manufacturer of filing systems), Con Agra mill (the longest continuously operating mill in the state), Tom Thumb, and Koch Refinery.

ATTRACTIONS

History is the focus for most visitors to Hastings, and an excellent starting point is the colorful *wall mural* on the west wall of the Maco-B bar on Second Street downtown, depicting scenes from Hastings' past. Another stop is the Hudson River Gothic revival *LeDuc-Simmons Mansion,* located at 17th and Vermillion Street. Erected by General William LeDuc, once secretary of agriculture under President Rutherford B. Hayes, the mansion is now being restored to its former grandeur, complete with nine fireplaces, servants' quarters, and a chapel. Having had a taste of Hastings' history, visitors often choose the walking tour of 30 historic sites and buildings. Guided by a map available from the Chamber of Commerce, the tour includes such landmarks as the Greek Revival *Olson House,* the Italianate *Pringle-Judge House,* and the *Thorne Lowell House* built of beautifully cut limestone. A final must is the *Lock and Dam No. 2,* completed in 1931 as a way to provide sufficient depth for river traffic. Located one mile north of the city, the dam includes an observation platform for visitors to view the great barges passing on their way from St. Louis to St. Paul. But all is not history in Hastings. Just to the south of the city is one of the country's most unique vineyards, *Alexis Bailly Vineyard*, where the Baillys bury their French-adapted grapevines during the winter to help them survive Minnesota's frigid winter temperatures. The Hastings area also features a variety of parks and nature areas. The *Carpenter St. Croix Valley Nature Center* offers daily access to a self-guided trail, featuring a diverse landscape of wooded ravines, oak savanna, orchards and a spectacular view of the lower St. Croix River. In addition, the Center hosts regular programs, including releases of raptors rehabilitated at the Minnesota Raptor Center. The *Spring Lake Park Reserve*, meanwhile, features hiking and cross-country ski trails along with the scenic *Schaar's Bluff Picnic Area;* while *Welch Village Ski Area* is a popular winter attraction.

EVENTS

Major annual events celebrate the city's heritage and its historical ties to the mighty Mississippi. *Rivertown Days* in July is one of the premier summer festivals in the Twin Cities metropolitan area, featuring five days of music, waterskiing shows, and other events. The *Front Porch Festival* in mid-May focuses on the architectural heritage of the city and includes tours of historic Hastings homes, theater performances, and traditional entertainment such as a maypole dance and arduous rocking chair marathons. Finally, the *Main Street Festival* in late September features a number of events with an old-fashioned theme.

For more information on Hastings, contact:
HASTINGS AREA CHAMBER OF COMMERCE
1304 Vermillion Street
Hastings, MN 55033
(612) 437-6775

ACCOMMODATIONS

■ AMERIC-INN MOTEL
2400 Vermillion Street
Hastings, MN 55033
Tel: (612) 437-8877
Hrs: Daily 24-hours-a-day
All major credit cards are accepted.

Americ-Inn Motel features modern elegance at an affordable price. This modern two-story brick and wood lodging serves up generous portions of both hospitality and restfulness. The free continental breakfast and the fireplace in the lobby are just representative of the many things that set this motel apart from the pack.

The 20 rooms at Americ-Inn Motel come equipped with extra-long beds, color televisions, ceramic baths, personal phones, individual thermostats, and comfortable furniture. Guests may arrange for a bridal, king-size, executive, or regular suite. In addition, the motel provides nonsmoking and handicapped accommodations. Meeting and banquet rooms are available, as are laundry services and refrigerators. Animal lovers will be glad to hear that Americ-Inn Motel allows pets on the premises.

In addition to the extensive facilities, the motel's owners provide free coffee, orange juice, and danish, and a ready supply of helpful services for guests. Owner Ron Sheetz is a golf enthusiast and would be happy to help arrange a game for interested guests. The Americ-Inn also offers corporate rates, and shuttle service is available to and from the marina and airport.

A PPAREL SHOP

■ CLAIRE'S
116 E. Second Street
Hastings, MN 55033
Tel: (612) 437-3100
Hrs: Mon. - Fri. 10 a.m. - 5:30 p.m.
    Thur. 10 a.m. - 8 p.m.
    Sat. 9:30 a.m. - 5 p.m.
Visa, MasterCard, and Discover are accepted.

Claire's is not just another little clothing store. Located in one of several historic buildings listed on the National Register of Historic Places in downtown Hastings, Claire's offers the finest selection in sportswear from teens to moms and grandmothers.

Claire's is locally owned and operated by Claire Mathews and her family, bringing the latest of fashions to the Hastings area, while providing a warm and friendly service. Great lines such as Ocean Pacific, Cherokee, Lee, California Ivy, and L.A. Seat Covers are some of the many popular brands featured at Claire's. Customers can choose smart stylish fashions from designer jeans and other well-cut slacks to sweaters, shirts and blouses, and fresh, professional styles in dresses and skirts. They will also find an excellent selection in wardrobe accessories to choose from.

At Claire's, families will find the quality and fashion in the name brands they have come to trust, at affordable prices.

B AKERY & DELI

■EMILY'S BAKERY AND DELI
1212 Vermillion Street
Hastings, MN 55033
Tel: (612) 437-3338 (bakery) or (612) 437-2491 (deli)
Hrs: Mon. - Fri. 5 a.m. - 7 p.m.
  Sat. 5 a.m. - 5 p.m., Sun. 7 a.m. - 2 p.m.

More than 40 years ago, Elmer and Emily Walker opened a bakery in the old river town of Hastings. Now located in the Midtown Shopping Center on Highway 61, Emily's Bakery and Deli is still a part of the city scene — and it is still owned and operated by the same family. Elmer and Emily's grandchildren, Norine Kippels and Steve Fox, have proudly maintained the family tradition of top quality, made-from-scratch bakery items and have added a scrumptious line of deli items.

In the bakery section, visitors are faced with a tempting array of breads, buns, rolls, doughnuts, and muffins. For those with a sweet tooth, homemade pies are also available, along with a wide variety of cakes decorated to order for all occasions, including weddings. In the deli, which includes tables for dine-in customers, patrons can choose from an astonishing array of more than 30 different types of salads, ranging from fresh fruit salad to Szechwan pasta and old-fashioned potato salad. Sandwiches are also available, made from top-quality deli meats and the bakery's own bread.

Emily's box lunch is a tasty and wholesome alternative to a fast-food meal. How about a smoked ham sandwich with homemade cheese bread, potato salad, and a bakery treat to cure those highway blues?

B EAUTY SALON

■LE SALON
1110 Highway 55
Hastings, MN 55033
Tel: (612) 437-5505 or (612) 438-3820
Hrs: Mon. - Fri. 8 a.m. - 9 p.m.
  Sat. 8 a.m. - 5 p.m.
  Sun. 10 a.m. - 5 p.m.

Le Salon is located in a charming red brick building on Highway 55, just 30 miles south of Minneapolis and St. Paul in Hastings. The owners and operators have won many state, local, and national awards.

Sisters and Le Salon owners, Ruth Ann and Elizabeth Houle also own and operate the Minnesota Cosmetology College in South St. Paul, which serves as a training center for beauticians. With over 20 years of experience, they also operate beauty shops in Stillwater and West St. Paul. Each staff person is highly trained with the skills needed for his or her particular job. Le Salon is a high quality beauty salon specializing in body waves and design hair cutting for men and women. Special services such as tanning, manicures and pedicures, cosmetic application and massage, customized highlighting and glazings, eyebrow arching and waxing, and facials, are all available. The men and women areas are private, and consultations are provided with highly trained beauty operators. Gifts and swimwear are also available.

Le Salon provides services in its salon to "make people feel good about themselves."

B ED & BREAKFAST

■ THORWOOD
Fourth and Pine
Hastings, MN 55033
Tel: (612) 437-3297
Visa, MasterCard, and AmEx are accepted.

Romance, luxury, privacy, and resounding Victorian elegance — The Thorwood is a French Second Empire in style. Thorwood is one of three Victorian bed-and-breakfast inns located in Hastings and is on the National Register of Historic Sites. The River Rose and Hazelwood are two of the 17 rooms from which to choose.

In 1880, Thorwood was originally built by William and Sarah Thompson who at that time had a lumber business on the Mississippi River. In 1929, it was used as a hospital and care center, until the 1950s. Dick and Pam Thorson purchased the building in 1979 and with extensive renovation and redecorating opened the first Bed and Breakfast in Hastings.

The seven impeccably designed rooms are complete with feather-filled comforters, old-time working radios, fireplaces viewable from double pearl whirlpools; and warmly decorated with Victorian antiques. During the summer, trays of pillar candles are used in the fireplaces for ambience. There are musical wedding dolls for honeymooners. Victorian picnics are also available. Each room is a perfect setting for an intimate breakfast of oven omelets, hot pastries, sausage, muffins, fresh fruit, and fruit-filled croissants — a true Thorson trademark.

A walking tour of nearby historic Hastings is a real delight. Take in the natural beauty; the Mississippi, St. Croix, and Vermillion rivers converge here. Thorwood has an outstanding reputation for pampering its guests.

F LORISTS

■ OLSON'S FLOWERS AND GREENHOUSE
809 W. 11th Street
Hastings, MN 55033
Tel: (612) 437-3718
Hrs: Mon. - Fri. 9 a.m. - 5:30 p.m.
    Sat. 8 a.m. - noon
    Closed Sun.
Visa, MasterCard, and Discover are accepted.

The flower children have all grown up now, but flowers will never go out of style. Olson's Flowers and Greenhouse proves the point by marketing beautiful flowers, plants, and accessories at its family owned and operated business.

Olson's Flowers and Greenhouse invites customers to browse in its large greenhouse and gift areas. Visitors are awed by the sheer abundance of greenery and by the explosion of color. Silk and dried flowers, bedding plants, cut flowers, hanging baskets, figurines, wreaths, storybook dolls, and country gifts add variety to the wonderful selection of healthy plants and flowers. The shop prides itself on its attention to customer's needs and can provide flowers for every occasion, including weddings, funerals, birthdays, and anniversaries.

The store is also a member of the wire service Teleflora, so customers can send flowers to loved ones, even those far away.

G IFTS & INTERIOR DESIGN

■ BRIDGEPORT INTERIORS
1204 Vermillion Street
Hastings, MN 55033
Tel: (612) 437-3092
Hrs: Mon. - Thurs. 9 a.m. - 7 p.m.
    Fri. 9 a.m. - 5 p.m., Sat. 10 a.m. - 4 p.m.
Visa and MasterCard are accepted.

The owner of Bridgeport Interiors, Darlene Bohlken, has been in the interior decorating field since 1964 and has earned a reputation for both high-quality workmanship and fine taste.

Bohlken travels around the country to find the special items that fill her attractive shop.

Bohlken is most proud of her custom drapery work, but Bridgeport Interiors also carries wall coverings, upholstery, bedspreads, pine furniture, and many other gifts and accessories for the home. Pictures, mirrors, wreaths, towels, rugs, lamps, hats, folding screens, bath and kitchen accessories, clocks, and flower arrangements all provide an inviting assortment of home decorating ideas. The large display area makes browsing a pleasurable pastime.

An ideal shop for those with major redecorating in mind as well as for those who just want to add a little spice to their living room, Bridgeport Interiors offers something for everyone. The imaginative window displays beckon passersby to stop and experience the magic of this complete home decorating establishment, and a gracious and friendly staff make shopping for home accessories a pleasure.

GIFT SHOP

■ FANCY THAT!
110 E. Second
Hastings, MN 55033
Tel: (612) 437-6851
Hrs: Mon. - Sat. 10 a.m. - 6 p.m.
    Thur. 10 a.m. - 8 p.m.
    Sun. noon - 5 p.m.
Visa, MasterCard and AmEx are accepted.

Rebuilt after a fire in the 1920s, the Fancy That! gallery is the youngest building in historic, downtown Hastings. It nestles among neighbors that date to the 1850s. Partaking in the history of the town, the gallery houses a variety of unusual gifts and displays them among antiques and collectibles with Victorian country charm.

Owner Jan Ostberg, who has more than 20 years of experience in the gift shop business and has been running Fancy That! since 1989, maintains that people come from miles around to browse through the most wonderfully unusual gift cards in the area. Many are handmade. Also making the shop unusual are its separate display areas for different gift categories. A Kid's Korner, Kitchen Nook, Bath Shop, and permanent Christmas Room are stocked with gifts of fine art, pottery, books, listening/feeling tapes, note cards, Hastings souvenirs and guide books, hand-painted T-shirts, tennis shoes, and baby things. Stepping off the streets of century-old Hastings, visitors feel the 1890s charm carried on within the walls of the shop as well. The antique display units, check-out counter, cash register, and more date back to the 1890s. A tin ceiling and pot-bellied stove, old trunks, and quaint tables add additional charm.

Fancy That! boasts gifts and novelties for all seasons, ages, and interests. Walking through its displays is walking through history, but its offerings are sure to please those stuck in the present.

R ESTAURANT

■MISSISSIPPI BELLE
101 Second Street
Hastings, MN 55033
Tel: (612) 437-5694
Hrs: (Lunch) Tue. - Sat. 11 a.m. - 2:30 p.m.
    (Dinner) Tue. - Thur. 5 - 9 p.m.
    Fri. and Sat. 5 p.m. - 10 p.m.
    Sun. 11 a.m. - 6 p.m.
Visa, MasterCard, AmEx, Discover, and Diners Club are accepted.

Diners can have the fun of eating aboard a riverboat that is as stable as the earth itself at Mississippi Belle, the well-known restaurant in a boat-shaped building. A local architect designed the building to look like a riverboat with a paddle wheel, instantly making the place famous.

Mississippi Belle seats 70 in a dining room highlighted by red and white Victorian furnishings; the upper deck seats 40 for private meetings, parties, and other special occasions. Lovely gold leaf mirrors and steel engravings of an 1883 riverboat adorn the walls. The interior also boasts stained glass windows and crystal chandeliers; an intimate bar lies tucked to one side.

The only thing that tops the decor is the food; the luscious Canadian Walleye Pike has become quite popular, and the Seafood Au Gratin is excellent. Escargots and homemade soup make for tasty appetizers, and the orange rolls served with dinner are a treat. Diners should also save room for a piece of one of the heavenly dessert pies.

Mississippi Belle earned its superlative reputation by serving great food in a warm, friendly atmosphere. Excellent service adds the perfect touch to this rare dining experience.

WINERY

■ ALEXIS BAILLY VINEYARD
18200 Kirby Ave.
Hastings, MN 55033
Tel: (612) 437-1413
Hrs: (June - Oct) Fri. - Sun. noon - 5 p.m.
    Open house the first two weekends in June
    Harvest celebration first weekend in Nov.

Wine could never be made from Minnesota-grown grapes, skeptics told David A. Bailly, but he proved them wrong. In 1973, Bailly bought 20 acres of land in the Hiawatha Valley of the Upper Mississippi and planted French hybrid vines. Four years later, the Alexis Bailly winery produced its first bottle of wine, and David Bailly has never looked back.

Today, the winery is managed by David's daughter, Nan, and produces eight different wines. The Leon Millot, considered the winery's finest, is a full-bodied red wine that needs two to three years of aging to develop its flavor and soften its tannins. Alexis Bailly's most popular wine is Maréchal Foch. Similar to wines from the Beaujolais region in France, the Maréchal Foch should be drunk young, while its fruit is still fresh. For dessert, the winery offers the Hastings Reserve, a rich, sweet, and intense wine made in the style of port.

Alexis Bailly's wines are made through a laborious, time-consuming process. To protect the vines from Minnesota's winters, they are buried under six inches of soil and a thick blanket of snow. Harsh conditions, however, often produce wine with character. Marketed under the slogan, "Where the grapes can suffer," every vintage of Alexis Bailly wines has won medals in national competition and received critical acclaim. Visit the vineyard on a summer weekend and taste its award-winning wines for free. The vineyard is located one mile south of Hastings off Highway 61. Turn right at 170th Street.

Maple Plain

A quiet community located 35 minutes west of downtown Minneapolis, Maple Plain has avoided the large-scale industrial development of other towns in the greater metropolitan area. It is still largely an agricultural center, with a smattering of industry and a downtown business district that serves local needs. Once, however, the city was a booming railroad town, with a growing lumber industry based on the abundant hardwood forests in the area. An alternative, curious source of income in those early days was ginseng, a prolific native plant whose roots were shipped to eager buyers in China. Today, ginseng is no longer a major cash crop, but visitors to Maple Plain can still experience the native plants of the area in a host of local parks. Among the finest are *Baker Park* and *Rebecca Park,* 2,000-acre swathes of woods, lakes, and open fields complete with picnic and camping grounds, beaches, play areas, trails, and boating and fishing access to *Lake Independence, Half Moon Lake,* and *Spurzem Lake.* Also in Baker Park is the fine *Baker Golf Course* with its 18 regular holes and nine-hole executive course, while Rebecca Park features fascinating nature trails. For those looking for even more extensive trails, the scenic *Luce Line Recreational Trail* from Plymouth to Glueck runs past Maple Plain one and a half miles south of town. The trail is a fine-grade, abandoned railroad line, and offers excellent opportunities for jogging, hiking, biking, or horseback riding past shimmering lakes and through marshes, pastures, and farm fields. On a slightly smaller scale, the city of Maple Plain maintains four city parks — *Rainbow,*

Northside, Bryantwood, and *Pioneer* — with picnic grounds, playgrounds, and ball courts.

For more information on Maple Plain, contact:
CITY OF MAPLE PLAIN
1620 Maple Ave.
Maple Plain, MN 55359
(612) 479-3205

ANTIQUES

■COUNTRY SCHOOL HOUSE SHOPS
5300 Highway 12
Maple Plain, MN 55359
Tel: (612) 479-6353
Hrs: Mon. - Fri. 10 a.m. - 7 p.m.
    Sat. - Sun. 10 a.m. - 6 p.m.
Visa and MasterCard are accepted.

The Country School House Shops offers the special collections of over 100 area antique dealers. The three-story, brick schoolhouse was built in the 1920s and has been restored to its present state as an antique mall, located just 25 miles west of Minneapolis and 12 miles west of I-494 on Highway 12.

Customers will enjoy browsing through three floors of individual displays of antiques, collectibles, and "one-of-a-kind" handmade items by local artists and craftsmen. The owners have carefully compiled an incredible selection of quality furniture — primarily oak and primitive pine pieces in "home-ready" condition. There are entire rooms filled with old toys and dolls, sporting and decoy collectibles, advertising memorabilia, turn-of-the-century china and glassware, handmade baskets, old books and rare prints, plants and dried-floral arrangements, candles and linens, original artwork, and handmade jewelry. There is even a room with refinishing supplies, reproduction hardware, and price guides covering all categories of antiques and collectibles.

Other related services include interior design, furniture refinishing and restoration, upholstering, appraisals, auctions, and custom-designed furniture. The Shops also hold monthly events such as flea markets, special antique exhibits, and holiday shows.

Greater Minneapolis

M inneapolis was founded in 1867, almost 13 years after St. Paul, the city's rival settlement across the Mississippi River. From the very beginning, competition between the two was fierce. In 1872, Minneapolis incorporated the smaller village of St. Anthony into its city limits, and thus obtained the sawmills and flour mills that would eventually turn little Minneapolis into an industrial powerhouse. By 1890, the city had surpassed St. Paul in population as well as in the number of agricultural processing plants, and warehouses. Minneapolis's industrial infrastructure soon sprawled up and down the Mississippi. The city never looked back.

Today, Minneapolis is one of the fastest growing cities in the country and — together with its sister city of St. Paul — has gained recognition as an ideal location for high-tech, service-oriented businesses. Indeed, the Twin Cities boast more than their share of Fortune 500 businesses — 29 in all, including General Mills, Pillsbury, and Dayton-Hudson.

Minneapolis also ranks high on quality-of-life scales, offering residents a wide variety of cultural entertainment, as well as outstanding outdoor recreational opportunities. The city has 22 lakes within its limits, most with parks and trails along their shores. Jogging, biking, walking, and fishing are just some of the park activities Minneapolis citizens enjoy during the balmy summer months. In winter, they turn to cross-country skiing and ice skating.

And no matter the season, they can always be found shopping — sometimes at high-class stores like Saks Fifth Avenue, other times at more down-to-earth establishments. When they aren't perusing the latest fashions, they're attending premier art exhibits, musical performances, or theater shows. One thing is for sure, Minneapolis residents know how to enjoy life.

ATTRACTIONS

Minneapolis is known for its thriving theater scene. Visitors will want to check out the wide range of playhouses offering everything from Shakespeare to avant-garde farce. The *Guthrie Theatre* — one of the top-ranked theaters in the country — is located here, as well as the nationally renowned *Children's Theatre Company,* which offers professional adaptations of classical children's literature, with an occasional new production thrown in for good measure. Then there are the less well-known venues such as *Mixed Blood Theatre,* specializing in multi-cultural productions, *Cricket Theatre,* offering audiences the work of contemporary, area playwrights, and *Theatre de la Jeune Lune,* whose French and American theatre company performs whimsical productions rooted in mime and farce. The *West Bank Theater District* near the University of Minnesota campus is also a hotbed for theater companies, and for comedy there's always *Dudley Riggs' Brave New Workshop and ETC Theatre,* specializing in side-splitting skits and stand-up comedy.

Minneapolis also offers a varied music scene that will appeal to all tastes and ages. The *Minnesota Orchestra,* lead by music director Edo de Waart, features high-calibre performances by guest conductors, soloists, and ensembles from around the world, while the *Minnesota Opera* concentrates on the finest in both traditional and contemporary works. In addition, Minneapolis has fine, *live music cafes* scattered throughout the city, offering *jazz, blues, folk,* and *rock* music.

When it comes to museums, Minneapolis can hold its own with bigger cities like Chicago or Houston. The *Minneapolis Museum of Art,* housed in a neo-classic building, has a fine collection of European work, as well as American and non-European art. The nationally renowned *Walker Art Center,* on the other hand, specializes in modern art and sculpture. Adjacent to the Walker is the *Minneapolis Sculpture Garden,* hailed by critics as one of the nation's finest outdoor sculpture gardens. For a taste of local immigrant history, on the other hand, visitors should stop by the *American Swedish Institute* where hundreds of Swedish artifacts are displayed in the lovely surroundings of a turn-of-the-century mansion once owned by a prominent Swedish-American businessman. For nature buffs, there's always the *Bell Museum of Natural History* located at the University of Minnesota, featuring mounted animal displays and other nature-related exhibits.

Nature of a different sort is the focus of the *Minneapolis Planetarium* where the night sky takes center stage every day, and the latest discoveries in space science are also highlighted. After the planetarium, visitors can admire a more down-to-earth view at *Foshay Tower,* the first skyscraper in Minneapolis. Built in 1929, the Foshay Tower was the tallest building in the city until the 1970s when the critically acclaimed glass-and-steel *IDS Tower* was built. Since then, other towers have taken their place on the Minneapolis skyline, including the art-deco *Norwest Tower* designed by the respected architect Cesar Pelli.

The Norwest Tower is connected to *Gaviidae Common,* Minneapolis's newest, upscale shopping venue, where Saks Fifth Avenue and 60 other high-class *specialty stores* shamelessly tempt shoppers to spend a dime or two. Gaviidae is actually located on *Nicollet Mall*, the center of the downtown shopping district, just a few blocks from the IDS Tower's *Crystal Court* shopping complex and *The Conservatory*, another haven for sophisticated shoppers. All the shopping fun isn't confined to Nicollet Mall, however; Minneapolis also boasts some creatively renovated warehouses-cum-shopping-centers located on the banks of the Mississippi River. Known as *St. Anthony Main Shopping and Entertainment Center* and *Riverplace*, the two complexes offer quaint, unique shops with innovative display areas and a sense of history.

After the shopping, there's always time to relax and take in a game or two at one of Minneapolis's many professional sports venues. The *Hubert H. Humphrey Metrodome* is the world's largest air-supported multiple-use stadium and is the home of the *Minnesota Vikings* professional football team and the *Minnesota Twins* professional baseball team. Tours of the metrodome are popular with visitors. Then there's always the new *Target Center*, headquarters for the *Minnesota Timberwolves* basketball team.

Quieter times can be had by visitors to *Minnehaha Falls*, a lovely waterfall hidden in its own park and said to be the inspiration for Henry Wadsworth Longfellow's poem *Song of Hiawatha*. Beaver and deer may be spotted by the falls, but for some real animal-watching most people head for the *Minnesota Zoo* in nearby Apple Valley. Located just 20 minutes south of Minneapolis, the zoo is considered one of the ten best in the country and features 450 different species of animals. For those who are interested in Midwestern farm culture but don't have the time to venture into outstate Minnesota, the *Brooklyn Park Historical Farm*, a ten-acre living history farm in Brooklyn Park, offers a fascinating insight into late 1800s settler life.

EVENTS

Minneapolis's events center around the outdoors. Things begin to warm up in early summer with *Concerts in the Parks,* a series of outdoor music concerts held in various Minneapolis parks throughout the summer. In the same vein, the Minnesota Zoo offers live music concerts every Sunday evening June through August. The Minnesota Orchestra also offers a special summertime concert series called *Viennese Sommerfest* where guest conductors and soloists join the orchestra to showcase some of the best classical music. A festive *Marketplatz* is part of the fun, set up outside Orchestra Hall and offering food, drink, entertainment, and live music.

In mid-July it's time for high spirits and light-hearted competition as the *Minneapolis Aquatennial* makes its annual appearance. A salute to Minneapolis' lakes, the aquatennial features 250 events, including two parades that are rated in the national top ten and many water-related competitions. Then, at the beginning of August, artisans and artists from across the country converge on Minneapolis for the *Uptown Art Fair*, a weekend filled with art, art, and more art sold under the warm, sunny skies of summer.

The sports-minded side of Minneapolis' personality comes out during the *Twin Cities Marathon* in mid-October. This annual run from downtown Minneapolis to the State Capitol in St. Paul attracts 6,000 runners from across the nation and is considered one of the most beautiful urban marathons in the country. As autumn gives way to winter, Minneapolis residents gear up for the holiday season with a *Thanksgiving Day Parade*. Then it's on to a *Victorian Christmas* at Riverplace where old-time Christmas decorations and Victorian-era holiday entertainment recall the spirit of Christmas past.

For more information on Minneapolis, contact:
MINNEAPOLIS CONVENTIONS & VISITORS ASSOCIATION
1219 Marquette Ave.
Minneapolis, MN 55403
(612) 348-4313 or (800) 445-7412

ACCOMMODATIONS

■ BEST WESTERN NORMANDY INN
405 S. Eighth Street
Minneapolis, MN 55404
Tel: (612) 370-1400 or (800) 362-3131 (in Minnesota)
    or (800) 372-3131 (outside Minnesota)
Visa, MasterCard, AmEx, Diners Club, Carte Blanc, En Route, and Eurocard are accepted.

The Normandy is a quaint 16th century Norman French inn located in the heart of Minneapolis, the Upper Midwest's most vibrant business center. It is very accessible from all major roads and is within walking distance to the Metrodome, New Convention Center, Orchestra Hall, Nicollet Mall, City Center, all government and business centers, and the city's best downtown shopping. It is within minutes of the Guthrie Theatre and Walker Arts Center, and many fine restaurants. The 16th century French influence can be found throughout the hotel. An old European blend of dark oak, slate floors, stained glass, and lead chandeliers elegantly define the hotel's warmth, charm, and hospitality. It houses the well-known Normandy Village Dining Room and Lounge, which for more than 40 years has served charcoal steaks and chops, seafood, and all-you-can-eat prime rib. Each dinner is complemented by steaming Village hot popovers and the house caesar salad. Guests can enjoy an indoor swimming pool, sauna, and whirlpool in the garden atrium. A wide variety of comfortable and tastefully decorated rooms at very affordable prices will attract the most discriminating guest.

The Normandy is also known for its meeting and banquet facilities. Corporate rates are the best offered in town and all guests enjoy a complimentary welcome cocktail party on Friday nights. Parking is free and complimentary limousine service is offered in the downtown Minneapolis area.

For elegant dining and attentive service, the Normandy Inn has everything to make a meeting, conference, or banquet enjoyable and complete.

■HOTEL SOFITEL
5601 W. 78th Street
Minneapolis, MN 55439
Tel: (612) 835-1900 or (800) 763-4835
All major credit cards are accepted.

Hotel Sofitel brings the romance and ambiance of France to each guest who visits. Upon entering and witnessing the beauty of the airy atrium, a sense of European style can be felt. All of the 287 rooms maintain that feeling with fresh-cut flowers, imported bath amenities, fluffy towels, and crisp bed linens. Meals also follow this same pattern.

Le Cafe Royal offers traditional French cuisine with all of the details to enhance the meal such as white linen, china, and silver. Chez Colette provides French provincial dining, and La Terasse is designed in the style of a bistro. This sidewalk cafe style setting serves casual lunches, dinners, and snacks. Breads and pastries are baked fresh each day and served in each of the eateries. These scrumptious creations from the oven have earned a reputation of their own and bring people in to purchase these mouthwatering selections alone.

The whirlpool, sauna, and swimming pool relax tired muscles. Nautilus and therapeutic massage are also offered. Hotel Sofitel provides the atmosphere of France while only ten minutes from the airport.

■RADISSON PLAZA HOTEL MINNEAPOLIS

35 S. Seventh Street
Minneapolis, MN 55402
Tel: (612) 339-4900
All major credit cards are accepted.

On the site of the original Radisson Hotel in the heart of Minneapolis, yesterday's grand tradition of comfort, elegance, and impeccable service is recaptured in the new Radisson Plaza Hotel Minneapolis. Each of the 357 well-designed rooms feature a combination of warmth, classic luxury, and modern convenience that includes all the amenities one would expect in a five-star hotel. The Radisson Plaza's two superb restaurants offer a winning variety of dining selections and ambience. The Festival features grilled entrees, a delightful dessert table, and live entertainment. The Cafe is a casual atrium restaurant offering authentic international cuisine. A full array of conference and banquet facilities cater to specific needs. The Scandinavian Ballroom provides a grand, majestic setting for groups up to 500 people or can be divided into two sections for smaller groups. There are three boardrooms for private meetings, featuring executive amenities such as high-backed leather chairs, viewing screens, and television monitors with VCRs.

The Radisson Plaza is conveniently located in downtown Minneapolis with just a short walk to all major business centers, the city's finest retail shops, restaurants, and the Hubert H. Humphrey Metrodome.

■THE WHITNEY HOTEL

150 Portland
Minneapolis, MN 55401
Tel: (612) 339-9300 or (800) 248-1879
All major credit cards are accepted.

Located in the old milling district of downtown Minneapolis, The Whitney Hotel recalls an era when splendor was prominent throughout the hotel.

From lobby to penthouse, it's an atmosphere that exudes the quiet sophistication of an 18th century European hotel. The lobby and guest rooms feature mid-18th century English decor and furnishings from marble flooring, rich mahogany and cherry woods to brass chandeliers, door handles, and bath fixtures. Accommodations offer a choice of luxurious flats or bi-level suites with spiral staircases. Most important, there is more than one staff member for each of the 97 guest rooms to ensure a memorable stay. The penthouse features three bedrooms, two living rooms, a grand piano, fireplaces, whirlpools, and deck with a breathtaking view of the Mississippi River. Amenities provided in each room include plush monogrammed towels and robes, imported soap, refrigerator, bed turndown service, 24-hour room service, and complimentary newspaper. Limousine and valet parking service are also available.

Gourmet dining of classic American cuisine is the norm at the Whitney Grille. Exquisite entrees include sauteed or grilled seafood prepared in a special sauce; or grilled pheasant, duck, and chicken served with wild mushrooms and Minnesota wild rice, all served with seasonal vegetables. A superb selection of fine pastries and desserts is also available. An adjacent lounge provides for a comfortable setting for cocktails, before or after dinner. For a more casual aura, weather permitting, dine on the outdoor Garden Plaza toward the river. The meeting rooms offer an excellent setting for corporate parties or conferences, weddings, or any other occasion.

The Whitney Hotel is truly the ultimate in accommodations. It is perfect for a quiet getaway weekend providing all the riches and warmth of a luxury hotel. Be prepared to be pampered and receive attentive, yet discreet, service.

A NTIQUES

■ ANTIQUES MINNESOTA
1516 E. Lake Street
Minneapolis, MN 55407
Tel: (612) 722-6000

Additional Location:
1197 University Ave.
West St. Paul, MN 55104
Tel: (612) 646-0037
Hrs: Mon., Wed. - Sat. 10 a.m. - 5 p.m.
        Sun. noon - 5 p.m. Closed Tues.
Visa and MasterCard are accepted.

Antiques Minnesota is clearly the leader in multi-dealer antique shops. Originally opened in 1979, it is the first multi-dealer mall in the State of Minnesota with over 100 dealers represented in the showrooms. Located in South Minneapolis, Antiques Minnesota is just five minutes from the downtown metro area, accessible from both the I-94 and 35W interstate exits.

Antiques Minnesota is arranged as a mini-mall on four levels of what used to be a Masonic Temple in the 1920s. It has the largest, most diverse collection of vintage merchandise in the five-state area. "Experience the past" browsing through 40,000 square feet of antiques and collectibles including furniture, textiles, pictures, glassware, linens, paper goods, china, jewelry, silver, toys and dolls, primitives, and much more. The dealers will answer questions and help customers locate the particular item they are looking for. Free parking, no admission fees, educational displays, two repair shops—Carhon Clock Repairs and Lamp Mender — are just some of the other advantages at Antiques Minnesota. For something really special in any price range, Antiques Minnesota is the place to shop for real old-fashioned values.

A NTIQUE MALL

■ COBBLESTONE ANTIQUES, INC.
1010 W. Lake Street
Minneapolis, MN 55408
Tel: (612) 338-2258
Hrs: Tue. - Sat. 10 a.m. - 5 p.m.
Sun. 11 a.m. - 5 p.m.
Visa, MasterCard, and AmEx are accepted.

Cobblestone Antiques isn't the only business operating in Minneapolis' renowned warehouse district, but few others are more suited to their historic surroundings. This five-year-old antique mall is housed in a large, century-old renovated brick building, and features a 17,000-square-foot showroom floor bursting with top-quality items.

Representing more than 50 professional antique dealers, Cobblestone Antiques offers genuine silver and porcelain knicknacks, valuable estate jewelry, and traditional pottery. Visitors should check out the wide selection of quality furniture. Ranging from American Country style via Classic and Period to the finest Victorian, Cobblestone has something for everyone. For those in the decorating mood, the mall also features an abundance of classic artwork, prints, and lighting articles. In addition, don't miss the stained glass windows, art glass, and cut glass for that unique touch that will set any home apart from the rest.

Located only four blocks from Nicollet Mall — the city's showcase of modern fashions and furnishings — Cobblestone Antiques presents an attractive alternative for those in the mood to reflect on the beauty of the past, when cocktail tables were always wood and reading lamps never plastic.

A PPAREL & SADDLE SHOP

■SCHATZLEIN SADDLE SHOP, INC.

413 W. Lake Street
Minneapolis, MN 55408
Tel: (612) 825-2459
Hrs: Mon. - Sat. 9:30 a.m. - 6 p.m.
All major credit cards are accepted.

Horse owners and urban cowboys alike will find something to interest them in this 84-year-old Western and English tack and apparel store.

The shop traces its beginnings to 1907, the year Emil Schatzlein immigrated to Minneapolis and opened a saddle and harness shop to continue practicing the trade he learned in Germany. His son, Jerry, took over the reins in 1958, and today, six of Jerry's children run the store. Their expertise and the quality merchandise they sell is well-known in horse circles. Customers come from around the country to visit or have specialty items mailed to them. The custom repair shop in the basement continues a long tradition of tack making, and equipment from the past still can be found there. Along with tack for horses, Schatzlein also has a wide variety of apparel for the English or Western rider, as well as for those who'd rather walk. Here customers will find such country staples as boots, jeans, shirts, dresses, belts, and jewelry.

Browse through the shelves of fascinating merchandise and maybe try on some Levi 501s to round out the cowboy look. The store's old-fashioned display cases, solid wood flooring, and down-home atmosphere are reminiscent of a bygone era — a time when carriages and wagons were part of everyday life and the horse reigned supreme.

ART GALLERIES

■ ELAYNE GALLERIES
Gaviidae Common
651 Nicollet Mall
Minneapolis, MN 55402
Tel: (612) 338-1092
Hrs: Mon. - Fri. 9:30 a.m. - 8:30 p.m., Sat. 9:30 a.m. - 6 p.m., Sun. noon - 5 p.m.
Visa, MasterCard, AmEx, and Discover are accepted.

This delightful, contemporary art gallery is owned and operated by Elayne Lindberg, founder, and husband, Ross and daughter, Bonnie. Elayne Galleries is one of the most respected and popular art dealers in the Twin Cities area. Whether customers are interested in original oils, watercolors, wildlife art, reproductions, collector limited-edition graphics, posters, or paper sculptures, Elayne has what they are looking for. If a choice is not available, Elayne will special order a selection.

Elayne "is" the gallery and often called a Renaissance woman. She is listed in *Who's Who in America* and *Who's Who in the Midwest*. She is best known for her art inventory and handwriting analysis. She also wrote the book *The Power of Positive Handwriting*. Exhibitions and one-man shows are a specialty at Elayne Galleries, bringing the artist and the public together. The gallery carries most popular artists as well as local artists. Exclusive artists featured are Erte, Thomas McKnight, Leroy Neiman, Norman Rockwell, Bill Mack, and Harold Altman. A variety of media is displayed by local artists such as Terry Redland, Kevin Daniels, Mario Fernandez, Darryl Wiikkula, and Robert Olsen. The gallery also offers special services such as appraisals, restorations, custom framing, corporate leasing, delivery and installation, including home, office, and investment consultations.

Elayne's philosophy is that art is foremost for the buyer's enjoyment. The inventory, personalized customer service, and affordable prices were confirmed by the industry when Elayne Galleries received *Decor* Magazine's 1989 Award of Excellence and Award of Merit — the only gallery to receive both awards.

■ JAVIER PUIG DECORATIVE ARTS
118 N. Fourth Street
Tel: (612) 332-6001
Hrs: Tue. - Sat. 10 a.m. - 5:30 p.m. Closed Sun. and Mon.
    Closed last two weeks in Aug.
Visa and MasterCard are accepted.

Bill Puig, former curator of decorative arts at the Minneapolis Institute of Arts, opened the Javier Puig Gallery in the heart of downtown Minneapolis. The gallery features artists of national and international reputation, as well as local artists.

The gallery is divided into two distinct spaces, the back, or gallery space, where the exhibits are held; and the front area, which houses a large selection of artworks, very reasonably priced. Pieces can be made to order by a number of world-known artists. Javier Puig Gallery specializes in beautiful and unique objects of art that all have a functional purpose in the home. Every piece is handcrafted and exquisitely designed. Glass bowls and vases threaded with brilliant colors or painted in layers of molten glass will hold flowers and fruit, or stand alone as sculptural works of art. A brightly polished pewter and wood tea set sits elegantly on its tray or serves a beautiful afternoon tea. Brightly painted and glazed tableware, from large serving platters to mugs, make a fantastic table setting. One-of-a-kind pieces of jewelry, crafted in various materials, can be found, along with unusual clocks and mirrors. Handcrafted furniture, from tables and chairs to standing table lamps, are available.

There is something to accommodate all tastes and budgets. One could actually come to a gallery of this kind and fully furnish a home. The gallery is unlike any other in Minneapolis, in its scope and practice. None other offers the selection and quality or consistently held exhibitions of decorative arts. The Javier Puig Gallery represents excellence, expertise, and quality.

■ THE RAVEN GALLERY
3827 W. 50th Street
Minneapolis, MN 55410
Tel: (612) 925-4474
Hrs: Tues. - Sat. 10 a.m. - 5:30 p.m.
      Thur. 10 a.m. - 8 p.m.
      Holiday hours may vary; call ahead
Visa, MasterCard, and AmEx are accepted.

The Raven Gallery is Minnesota's center for contemporary Native American art. Offering only the finest in prints, paintings, sculpture, and crafts created by the indigenous peoples of North America, The Raven Gallery provides a colorful and personal insight into Native American cultures.

Visitors will experience first-hand the unique artwork and fine crafts produced by the people of many tribes. Each tribe's crafts were formed by the environment in which they lived, and today, modern Native American artists share the world of their ancestors through their artwork. From the deserts of the Southwest comes Pueblo pottery, silver and stone jewelry, and fine basketry. The

Northwest Coast and Central Woodlands are represented by fine prints and carvings. The Arctic comes alive through the spare, near-surreal sculptures and prints created by the Inuit.

The 18-year-old gallery has earned a widespread reputation for the quality and variety of its unique offerings. It particularly emphasizes fine works created by outstanding artists of this region as well as by artists of national and international repute. Works by masters such as Amy Cordova, Carl Gawboy, Gerard Tsonakwa, Lillian Pitt, and R.C. Gorman grace the warm, comfortable display areas. Well-trained staff members are more than willing to share their extensive knowledge about the lives and work of these and other artists. But the Raven Gallery has more than paintings and sculptures. Its collection of masks, pipes, jewelry, baskets, and musical instruments makes the gallery a must for anyone interested in the rich and fascinating cultural heritage of the first Americans.

■THE WOODEN BIRD
Ridgedale Center
12663 Wayzata Blvd.
Minnetonka, MN 55343
Tel: (612) 542-1926
Hrs: Mon. - Fri. 10 a.m. - 9 p.m.
    Sat. 9:30 a.m. - 6 p.m.
    Sun. noon - 5 p.m.
Additional locations: Northtown Center, Rosedale Center, Brookdale Center, Eden Prairie Center, Southdale Center, and Burnhaven Mall.
Visa, MasterCard, Discover, and AmEx are accepted.

From its humble beginnings in 1975 as a manufacturer of hand-crafted wooden decoys in St. Bonifacius, MN, The Wooden Bird has developed a fine reputation as an art gallery specializing in quality representations of North American wildlife, Americana, Western, figure, and landscape art. In addition to offering more than 50 finished wood-carved products, The Wooden Bird galleries feature premium limited edition art graphics and collector plates of artists such as Terry Redlin, Jerry Raedeke, Clark Hulings, Steve Hanks, Ozz Franca, Ted Blaylock, Les Didier, Bryan Moor, Kenneth Riley, Olaf Wieghorst, and Bev Doolittle.

Ray E. Johnson founded The Wooden Bird with the help of two friends. Their original intent was to create wooden bird decoys on a lathe that replicated Wisconsin antiques. The showroom next to the small factory in St. Bonifacius proved so popular that in 1976, the first retail store was opened in Rosedale.

Today The Wooden Bird has 20 galleries in the Midwest and California, specializing in custom framing and representational art from Hadley House and other leading publishers. Unique design using only acid-free materials, has established The Wooden Bird as trusted framers. Outdoor and Western theme gifts, some exclusive to The Wooden Bird, have made the galleries prime sources for gift buyers seeking the beautiful and unusual.

■B ED & BREAKFASTS

■EVELO'S BED AND BREAKFAST
2301 Bryant Ave. S.
Minneapolis, MN 55405
Tel: (612) 374-9656
Hrs: By appointment only
Visa, MasterCard, and AmEx are accepted.

What does one do with a turn-of-the-century house, a love of entertaining, and a passion for Victorian and Art Nouveau design?

David and Sheryl Evelo knew just what they were doing when they started Evelo's Bed and Breakfast from their home in 1979. Originally known as the "Bell House," it was built in Minneapolis's historic East Lowry Hill area in 1897 by architect William Kenyon. Inside, stunning hand-crafted millwork, polished wood, and intricate Art Nouveau wall designs invite one into a quiet oasis of beauty and taste.

Bedrooms, tucked away on the third floor, are furnished with original period furniture. A refrigerator, a coffeemaker, and a telephone are available in the guest area. Breakfast is an artistic and culinary triumph, as David and Sheryl serve their own healthful and unique recipes on colorful Fiestaware dishes in the dining room. Homemade pastries and berry conserves, cantaloupe with blueberries, yogurt, and edible nasturtiums from the garden have been some of their breakfast offerings.

It is a charming experience to meet David and Sheryl, and to stay at Evelo's Bed and Breakfast. Their love for entertaining is apparent, both in their hospitality and in every detail of their beautiful home.

■ THE INN ON THE FARM

6150 Summit Drive N.
Brooklyn Center, MN 55430
Tel: (612) 569-6330
Hrs: Open year-round
All major credit cards are accepted.

The Inn on the Farm is part of the Earle Brown Heritage Center. This bed and breakfast is truly an original due to the location alone. Nestled in the heart of Brooklyn Center, The Inn on the Farm offers the best of both a city and country setting. A real retreat from the city can be found without ever leaving the metro area.

Eleven rooms are featured in four separate houses on the farm. The Earle Brown House contains the original bedroom of the estate's owner, Earle Brown. This room offers an extensive view of the grounds and the warmth of overstuffed chairs and rich woodwork. The Gwen Brown Room is an authentic portrayal of the Victorian era with an inviting brass bed and exquisite light fixtures. The Carriage House and Foreman House provided lodging to employees of the estate. These rooms boast features such as a private deck and a window seat alcove.

The Farmhouse contains five rooms that were occupied by family and friends of the Browns. The John and Jane Martin Suite served as quarters for the grandparents and contains two rooms with a bay window overlooking the garden. Each room contains a private whirlpool bath with period decor surrounding guests in the comfort of a past era. Breakfast is an added bonus to their stay and is served each morning in the dining room. The Heritage Center and Carriage Hall and Exhibit Complex are fascinating.

⬛B OOKSTORES

Editor's Note: In the Twin City metro area, there are many fine bookstores — both independent outlets and chains — from Odegards on France Avenue in Edina to conglomerates such as B. Dalton, Waldenbooks, and Barnes & Noble. All have a great selction of titles to satisfy a variety of tastes, which a strong literary market like the Twin Cities demands.

■BAXTER'S BOOKS
608 Second Ave. S.
Minneapolis, MN 55402
Tel: (612) 339-4922
Hrs: Mon. - Thurs. 7:30 a.m. - 5:30 p.m., Fri. 7:30 a.m - 6:30 p.m.
 Sat. - Sun. 10 a.m. - 4 p.m.
Visa, MasterCard, and Discover are accepted.

Baxter's Books is more than just a bookstore. With its highly personal service, comfortable tables and chairs, frequent book signings, and author breakfasts, Baxter's is no less than the vibrant center of an extended book lover family.

Located in the heart of downtown Minneapolis a few blocks from the IDS Center, Baxter's specializes in business-related publications. To better serve its busy downtown readers, the store maintains a highly efficient book ordering service, and a delivery service that can have books on any Twin Cities doorstep within 24 hours of ordering. But Baxter's is not only for business readers; in fact, the relatively new bookstore boasts the widest selection of books in Minneapolis. Headed by Arlene Kase, a former children's librarian, the extensive children's department maintains the most eclectic, high-quality collection of juvenile literature in the Twin Cities area. In addition, Baxter's selection of philosophy and fiction is impressive, befitting the discriminating literary taste of its customers.

With its focus on personal customer service, Baxter's is attracting more and more lovers of good literature from an ever wider area. To keep in touch with its readers, the store distributes a newsletter; and the owner, Brian Baxter, participates in a WCCO radio show with Charlie Boone and narrates bedtime stories for listeners to Radio US. Opening this store was a dream-come-true for Baxter — and for Twin Cities book lovers.

■ BORDERS BOOK SHOP
3001 Hennepin Ave S.
Minneapolis, MN 55408
Tel: (612) 825-0336
Hrs: Mon. - Thurs. 10 a.m. - 10 p.m.
    Fri. - Sat. 10 a.m. - 11 p.m.
    Sun. noon - 6 p.m.
Visa, MasterCard, and Discover are accepted.

Borders Book Shop is part of an expansion of a small chain of bookstores anchored in Ann Arbor, MI. After 20 years of experience in the bookselling business, Borders knows what the public wants in a bookstore. Over 75,000 titles are available with another expansion planned in 1992 to encompass 90,000 titles. These titles include subjects such as history, social sciences, computers, cookbooks, local interest, and books on gardening and nature. The children's section alone contains 10,000 imagination-provoking choices.

Each month highlights of noteworthy non-bestsellers are featured at a 30 percent discount, *New York Times* bestsellers in hardcover are also featured at a 30 percent discount. Most of the additional hardcover titles (including children's) are sold at a discount of 10 percent. The staff members have diverse interests, each able to provide a wide range of information to customers who may ask for assistance with their book choices. Art posters, domestic and international newspapers, and periodicals are also available to complete the vast number of enticing items at Borders.

B OUTIQUE

■ LARUE'S
3952 Lyndale Ave. S.
Minneapolis, MN 55409
Tel: (612) 827-7317
Hrs: Mon. - Fri. 11 a.m. - 8 p.m., Sat. 10 a.m. - 6 p.m.
    Sun. noon - 6 p.m.
Visa, MasterCard, and AmEx are accepted.

Located in a quiet residential neighborhood, just minutes from shopping and retail areas, a jewel of a store waits for those looking for just the perfect complement to their wardrobe. Award-winning

Larue's clothing and accessory shop has the finest selection of custom-designed clothing and accessories in the Twin Cities. At Larue's one can find accessories designed by more than 100 local and regional artists and jewelers, and designer clothing from all over the country. Larue's selections are modern yet timeless, eclectic yet classic, a tasteful blend of vintage-influenced and funky modern apparel.

Kathleen Lawrow has owned and managed Larue's for 14 years. Many of her customers appreciate her fashion expertise and consult with her regularly for advice on wardrobe and accessories. They also appreciate such special touches as personalized service, spring water, and complementary gift wrapping. Inside Larue's is a cozy yet spacious interior with incense wafting over colorful displays of clothing and jewelry, staffed by congenial, well-informed sales people.

In addition to clothing and accessories, Larue's also sells gift items, elegant soaps, and refillable lotions for the environmentally conscious consumer.

CONTEMPORARY CRAFT GALLERY

■ROOMERS
Calhoun Square
3001 S. Hennepin Ave.
Minneapolis, MN 55408
Tel: (612) 822-9490
Hrs: Mon. - Sat. 10 a.m. - 9 p.m., Sun. noon - 6 p.m.
Visa, MasterCard, and AmEx are accepted.

This craft gallery opened in August 1989 and has represented over 150 different artists. Mixed media from recycled plastic bag palm trees to glass, pottery, and wood can be found.

Roomers features unique and very unusual pieces for the home, which could be called serious whimsy. They range from handcrafted jewelry to functional porcelain saxophones, to fine wall art. Picture frames made of bottle caps; clocks of all shapes, sizes, and colors; blown and fused glass; functional and nonfunctional pottery in matte finish or high glaze; unusual mirrors; and tableware represent only a few of the fine hand-crafted collection displayed. The inventory changes frequently and so Julie Landa, the store owner, makes the look of the store change frequently, too. Julie constantly shows new artists and goes out of her way to represent a broad cross-section of artists from around the country and Europe. Julie does not overstock items that sell well; this way there are only a few pieces available and customers won't see it everywhere. Picture framing services are also available.

Roomers is inviting and visitors want to walk in and see everything. The atmosphere is fun and whimsical and the service is friendly and cheerful. A variety of merchandise with a wide appeal and range of prices makes it easy to find something for every home and taste.

$\boxed{C}$ OFFEEHOUSE

■ THE WELL
2415 Hennepin Ave. S.
Minneapolis, MN 55405
Tel: (612) 377-8027
Hrs: Mon. - Thurs. 8 a.m. - 11 p.m., Fri. - Sat. 8 a.m. - 12 a.m.
    Sun. 8 a.m. - 11 p.m.

Minutes from Uptown, in the quiet of a restored Victorian mansion, enjoy homemade goodies and a reprieve from busy Hennepin Avenue. The Well is a casual place. As the name suggests, it is a meeting place, a catch-up-with-friends place, a snack, lunch, or just a people-watching place. Enjoy dessert (cheesecake, pie, cakes, muffins), choose from 13 kinds of espresso, or have lunch: fresh salad, soup, and sandwich specials are offered daily.

"Good food at a cheap price" is the motto of the folks at The Well. Listen to local performers, chat, or just plain watch the action from a table on the porch.

$\boxed{C}$ OFFEE & TEA SHOP

■ COFFEE & TEA, LTD., INC.
Linden Hills
2728 W. 43rd Street
Minneapolis, MN 55410
(612) 926-1216

Chowens Corner
18336 Minnetonka Blvd.
Wayzata (Deephaven), MN 55391
(612) 475-3014

Victoria Crossing Mall
867 Grand Ave.
St. Paul, MN 55105
(612) 291-7847

Dinkytown
402 14th Ave. S.E.
Minneapolis, MN 55414
(612) 378-1410

Hrs: Hours vary at each location.

There is nothing like the smell of freshly roasted coffee. Heady, aromatic, and pungent, the tantalizing aroma fills the air at Coffee & Tea Ltd., Inc., Linden Hills, where a museum piece 1910 Royal Coffee Roaster roasts coffee ten hours a day. Attracted as much by the pungent aroma as by the taste of yet another rich blend, customers drop in for their regular supply of bulk coffee, and stay to sample a new blend and to chat with owner Jim Cone.

Jim owns five stores, four in the Twin Cities area. Coffee & Tea, Ltd., Inc., at Linden Hills is among just a handful of shops in the Midwest that roasts its own coffee and the only one in the Midwest to offer its variety — 65 kinds of coffee and 150 kinds of tea, to be exact. Consumption of gourmet coffee continues to increase, and Jim ships ever-greater amounts of mail order coffee to each state every month.

The Coffee & Tea, Ltd., Inc. shops also sell accessories. Shiny plunge pots and top-rated Espresso and Cappuccino machines promise delicious home-brewed treats, along with tea pots, strainers, mugs, and infusers. In warm weather, tables and chairs are set up outside for sampling and socializing. Now, how about that cup of coffee?

E NTERTAINMENT

■ DUDLEY RIGGS' THEATRES
Brave New Workshop
2605 Hennepin Ave. S.
Minneapolis, MN 55454
Tel: (612) 332-6620
Hrs: Call for showtime hours
Visa and MasterCard are accepted.

Dudley Rigg's Brave New Workshop is a veritable institution in the Twin Cities. For more than 30 years, the actor/writers at Brave New Workshop have combined their flair for improvisation with an unflinching eye for social commentary, serving up show after show of razor-sharp, cutting-edge satire.

These folks are funny! So funny, in fact, that alumni from Brave New Workshop have gone on to write for such shows as Saturday Night Live, Night Court, and the new Carol Burnett Show. Louie Anderson, Susan Vass, Franken and Davis, and the Flying Karamozov Brothers all owe their start to the Brave New Workshop and its goal of producing comedy theatre for thinking people. Founder Dudley Riggs himself declares that it's the audience that makes each performance unique. "Involving audiences keeps us energized, informed, and honest," says Riggs.

The Workshop is handicap-accessible, is on a bus line, and has parking available. Group rates and catering are also offered.

F INE JEWELRY

■ SCHEHERAZADE JEWELERS
In the Galleria
3525 W. 69th Street
Edina, MN 55435
Tel: (612) 926-2455
Hrs: Mon. - Fri. 10 a.m. - 9 p.m., Sat. 10 a.m. - 6 p.m.
　　　Sun. noon - 5 p.m.
Visa, MasterCard, and AmEx are accepted.

American and international designs in fine jewelry are the specialty at Scheherazade — exquisite pieces of wearable art created by top designers from around the world.

Because it buys from sources worldwide, Scheherazade features a wide variety of prices, but no compromise in design or workmanship. Named after the fabled Arabian princess of "The Thousand and One Nights" fame, Scheherazade was founded in 1971 by Scott and Marilyn Rudd. Today, the Rudds continue their tradition of seeking out the boldest jewelry creations representing the cutting edge of jewelry design. They also feature a display of Minnesota's leading designers and an in-house goldsmith and gem setter who can work to customers' specifications.

Even Scheherazade's location is a cut above the rest. The store is part of the Galleria — a collection of distinctive, non-commercial shops specializing in personalized service. Like the Arabian princess of old, Scheherazade is truly unique and captivating.

G ALLERY & STUDIO

■ ZYLLA GALLERY
3900 Vinewood Lane
Plymouth, MN 55441
Tel: (612) 553-7982
Hrs: Mon. - Sat. 10 a.m. - 2 p.m.
All major credit cards are accepted.

Since 1968, Ken Zylla has been a full-time painter, creating with pallet and brush wildlife scenes that reflect his unique point of view. Ken is one of a few artists whose style instantly is recognizable, being full of bold color and fine detail. His multi-point-of-view paintings have earned him more than 20 awards, including three "Best of Show," two "Popular Choice" and three "Overall Best Exhibit".

A visit to Ken's gallery in Plymouth, MN, is a fascinating introduction to the artist and his art. Here, customers will find a broad array of prints and oil paintings. Much of Ken's work focuses on Minnesota wildlife, particularly game birds in flight or foraging for food. Other popular prints feature moose and deer in a northwoods setting. The subject matter reflects Ken's hobby of raising game birds, and his love of the outdoors fostered by his boyhood in northcentral Minnesota. As an active member of several conservation organizations, Ken also has donated limited edition prints to Ducks Unlimited, and to other organizations across the country. Recently, he won the Palette and Chisel Award from Ducks Unlimited for donating more than a half-million dollars' worth of artwork toward the organization's fund-raiser.

Whether customers come to Ken's gallery to browse through his finished artwork or to view work in progress, they are sure to enjoy their visit and learn about wilderness at the same time. The gallery also provides framing services, and prints can be shipped to friends and family.

GIFT SHOPS

■ GENERAL STORE OF MINNETONKA

14401 Highway 7
Minnetonka, MN 55345
Tel: (612) 935-2215
Hrs: Tue. - Wed., Fri. - Sat. 9:30 a.m. - 6 p.m.
　　　Mon. and Thur. 9:30 a.m. - 9 p.m., Sun. noon - 5 p.m.
Visa, MasterCard, and Discover are accepted.

The general stores of the past always had something for everyone, and that's why the name "General Store" was chosen for this unique shop specializing in the gifts of yesteryear. Located a quarter mile west of Highway 494 on Highway 7 in Minnetonka, The General Store of Minnetonka has quality, handmade merchandise sure to please the whole family.

In a rustic atmosphere of vaulted ceilings and barn siding, General Store of Minnetonka displays the work of 250 talented artists and crafts people. Peek into the antique iron cribs, and see handmade pillows or perhaps an exquisite quilt. In the Country Primitive area, the shelves are filled with traditional salt-glaze Rowe pottery, pitchers, crocks, hand-dipped candles, tin accessories, and so much more. In the Country Kitchen section, the cupboards hold cookbooks, gourmet food items, wreaths, and country collectibles. There's also a children's room full of old-fashioned toys, a Victorian courtyard decorated with romantic lace and dainty miniatures, and a Minnesota Wildlife area featuring original watercolors and wood-carvings of the state's flora and fauna. At Christmas, the store is especially magical, glittering with decorations and items from Christmases past, and brimming with the scent of spicy pot-pourri and flowers.

In this busy, high-tech era, it seems that homemade beauty, pride in workmanship, and attention to detail was a thing of the past. But every season, all year-round, Country Store of Minnetonka offers items made by craftspeople and artists whose expertise is a living link to the country artisans of old. A trip to the General Store of Minnetonka is like a day in the country.

■ MADE IN MINNESOTA
12575 Wayzata Blvd.
Minnetonka, MN 55343
Tel: (612) 541-0427
Hrs: Mon. - Fri. 10 a.m. - 9:30 p.m.,Sat. 9:30 a.m. - 6 p.m.
    Sun. noon - 5 p.m.
Visa, MasterCard, and AmEx are accepted.

Made In Minnesota specializes, logically enough, in handmade products from Minnesota. But it is not just a souvenir shop, rather; it is a fascinating cornucopia of quality food, crafts, and books guaranteed not to be found anywhere else.

With its convenient location in Ridgedale Shopping Center on I-394 just 12 miles west of downtown Minneapolis, Made In Minnesota has for seven years made its unique products for visitors and locals alike. Take the specialty food for example: one highly popular item is wild rice, hand-harvested from the lakes of northern Minnesota. Actually the seeds of an aquatic grass, wild rice is a perfect accompaniment to a variety of entrees. Made In Minnesota also has wild rice recipe books for sale. Another favorite item is maple syrup which, along with the pure honey, blueberry and strawberry jam, and caramel is sure to satisfy any sweet tooth. Prepackaged sample baskets of these and other food items are available for sale at the store, or for home delivery. Ask for the shop's catalog to order by phone.

Take the time also to explore the literature, pottery, and wood- and woven-items displayed on shelves and in nooks throughout the shop. What Minnesota keepsake could be more appropriate than a loon letter opener, or a book — including an audio cassette — on how to speak proper "Minnesotan"? And for baseball fans, there is (who else?) Kirby Puckett pancake mix.

■ MINNESOTA MEMORIES

40 S. Seventh Street,
Suite 216
Minneapolis, MN 55402
Tel: (612) 333-3528
Hrs: Mon. - Fri. 9:30 a.m. - 9 p.m.
 Sat. 9 a.m. - 6 p.m.
 Sun. noon - 5 p.m.
 Extended Christmas hours

Minnesota Memories has something for anyone who has visited, lives, or ever lived in Minnesota. This souvenir and gift shop is located downtown Minneapolis in "City Center," a shopping center that offers three levels of more than 80 retail shops, services, and restaurants.

Minneapolis is a site for many national conventions, and visitors from all over the country want something to remember their stay in Minnesota. Minnesota Memories offers an array of postcards, Minnesota books, and assorted calendars. The large selection of T-shirts, sweatshirts, visors, coffee mugs, wind chimes and bells, and Minneapple design merchandise makes it quite easy to choose the perfect souvenir or gift. Hand-carved Minnesota loons and an attractive choice of Minnesota wilderness stuffed animals make an exceptional gift from Minnesota. Reproductions of Minnesota's renowned Red Wing pottery and many other American and Minnesota-made items can also be found. Prices are moderate and shipping is available within the United States.

For the best choice of souvenirs and gifts, customers can't go wrong at Minnesota Memories.

G OLF & CLUBHOUSE

■ EDINBURGH, USA
8700 Edinburgh Crossing
Brooklyn Park, MN 55443
Tel: (612)424-9444
Hrs: Open daily 6 a.m. to 1 p.m.
Visa, MasterCard, and AmEx are accepted.

Golf originated in Scotland, but in Brooklyn Park a piece of Scotland can be found at Edinburgh, USA. Designed by the firm of Robert Trent Jones II, this golf course is one of the most challenging Minnesota has to offer. With nearly 70 bunkers and 12 acres of water, the golfer comes face to face with such features as an island fairway, a peninsula green, and one of the world's largest putting surfaces — combining the 9th green, the 18th green, and the practice putting area.

In 1987, Edinburgh, USA earned the First Runner Up Award as Best New Public Golf Course by *Golf Digest*. In 1990 *Golf Digest* rated it in the Top 50 Public Courses in the Country and also was named one of the Top 100 Golf Shop Operations in the Country. In 1990 and 1991 Edinburgh hosted The Northgate LPGA event.

The Clubhouse at Edinburgh, USA is a public facility with a First Class Membership Club called The St. Andrews Club. The St. Andrews Club offers five different memberships: individual social; individual golf; joint golf; corporate social; or corporate golf. The elegant dining and locker areas are the finest of any club and are part of the beautiful 40,000 square feet of the Clubhouse. The Clubhouse hosts events such as wedding receptions, golf outings, holiday parties, and business and social meetings. An extensive catering brochure lists choices for the menu of preference. Fashioned after a classic Scottish Manor, the Clubhouse can provide a unique touch to any gathering.

G RAIN EXCHANGE TOURS

■ THE MINNEAPOLIS GRAIN EXCHANGE
400 S. Fourth Street
Minneapolis, MN 55415
Tel: (612) 338-6212
Tours: Tue. - Thur. 8:30 a.m., 10:15 a.m. Call for appointments.
Trading Floor Observation Balcony open Mon. - Fri. 9:30 a.m. - 1:15 p.m.

A massive room stands three stories high and a third of an acre long. Light pours through arched windows onto mahogany tables displaying grain samples. The time is 9:25 a.m. The place is the Minneapolis Grain Exchange's Trading Floor.

As men and women prepare grain samples or cluster near the futures pit, they prepare for something as awesome as the room — international commodities trading. As 9:30 a.m. strikes, a bell rings, people shout, and trading begins. For the next four hours, the Minneapolis Grain Exchange is a hub of activity: 10 million bushels of grain contracts change hands in the futures market and 1 million bushels pass through the cash market — the world's largest. The purpose of it all — price discovery and risk transfer.

The Grain Exchange was founded in 1881. The current building was completed in 1902 and is listed on the National Register of Historic places. Of 11 active commodities exchanges nationally, the Minneapolis Grain Exchange is the only authorized futures market for Hard Red Spring Wheat futures and options and White Wheat futures. Free tours, led by informed guides, include a video summary, discussion with a long-time trader, and a trip to the Trading Floor.

L IMOUSINE SERVICE

■ TWIN STAR LIMOUSINE

P.O. Box 581967
Minneapolis, MN 55458-1967
Tel: (612) 641-1385 or (800) 999-8333
Hrs: Daily 24-hours-a-day
Visa, MasterCard, AmEx, and Discover are accepted.

Chauffeured transportation offers many options for business and pleasure. Twin Star Limousine offers the largest variety of chauffeured vehicles in Minnesota and is committed to being the finest limousine service in this market.

Twin Star Limousine features Lincoln Town Car sedans, presidential stretch limousines, 14 passenger vans, and cargo vans. Vehicles are lavishly complete with color television, deluxe stereo sound system, cellular telephone, privacy partition and intercom, complimentary newspaper and beverage service, with ultra plush leather interior, and custom lighting. Customers can expect a discreetly attired and courteous chauffeur that will take them carefully and promptly to their destination. Whether riding in a sedan or luxurious stretched limousine, Twin Star chauffeurs will add that special feeling of excellence. Corporate accounts are invited and champagne, floral service, and gift certificates are available upon request.

Twin Star Limousine is the choice of the finest hotels and many of the major corporations in the metropolitan area, as well as those Fortune 500 companies visiting Minnesota. This dimension in luxury transportation is perfect for business meetings, corporate seminars and promotional tours, sporting events, airport transportation, weddings, birthday and anniversary specials, and just for the fun of it. Whether planning a special evening out on-the-town or entertaining a business client, with Twin Star Limousine, customers are always "Driven with Distinction."

M AP & TRAVEL STORE

■LATITUDES MAP AND TRAVEL STORE

Calhoun Square
3001 Hennepin Ave. S.
Minneapolis, MN 55409
Tel: (612) 823-3742
Hrs: Mon. - Sat. 10 a.m. - 9 p.m.
       Sun. noon - 6 p.m.
Visa, MasterCard, AmEx, and Discover are accepted.

Latitudes Map and Travel Store truly is a first: a store that specializes in travel. All travelers will find something of interest, whether it's traveling to the lake cabin for the weekend, to Europe on business, or to remote and exotic places. Latitudes Map offers a full selection of Minnesota county maps, U.S.G.S. topographical maps of Minnesota and surrounding states, topographical maps of Canada, Mexico, Europe, and just about all places for which there are maps available. And Latitudes' maps are not confined only to Earth. One can find a globe of the moon, of Mars, and even maps of the stars.

Selling maps makes a lot of sense in an increasingly international world, reasons owner Tom Hedberg, and his love of maps is beginning to be shared in greater numbers by others. Latitudes has recently moved to its present location which offers more store space, a larger inventory, and longer hours.

In addition to the most complete set of maps and globes this side of the universe, Latitudes has travel supplies such as packs, bags, language and travel books, games, and even electrical outlet adapters specific to each country. All ages can find something useful or just plain fun at Latitudes Map and Travel Store.

MUSEUMS

■ THE AMERICAN SWEDISH INSTITUTE

2600 Park Ave. S.
Minneapolis, MN 55407
Tel: (612) 871-4907
Hrs: Hours vary. Closed on Mon. and holidays
Visa and MasterCard are accepted.

The American Swedish Institute is an historical and artistic chronicle of American-Swedish immigrant history and culture. Inside the castle-like mansion is arrayed an impressive collection of historical artifacts, traditional and modern Swedish and American art, and many personal possessions of the family of Swedish immigrant, Swan J. Turnblad.

Swan Johan Turnblad was publisher of one of the largest Swedish language newspapers in the country. He donated his mansion to the Swedish-American community in 1929 to "foster and preserve Swedish culture in America." The 33-room mansion, finished in 1908, took five years to build, and employed 18 skilled craftsmen to carve and sculpt the ornate interior ceilings and woodwork. Of particular distinction are the 11 Kakelugnar imported porcelainized tile stoves designed to be extremely fuel-efficient. It is the largest collection of its kind outside of Sweden.

Browse through the museum, the bookstore, and the gift shop, which features fine imported Scandinavian glass, crystalware, and other items. Stop in the coffeeshop for pastries and coffee, and enjoy a concert of traditional Swedish songs. On-going classes in Swedish language, genealogy, and crafts also are offered. Special annual events are the celebration of Santa Lucia Day (December 13), and Midsommar (third Saturday in June).

■ MINNEAPOLIS INSTITUTE OF ARTS
2400 Third Ave. S.
Minneapolis, MN 55404
Tel: (612) 870-3131
Hrs: Tues. - Weds., Fri. - Sat. 10 a.m. - 5 p.m.
    Thur. 10 a.m. - 9 p.m.
    Sun. noon - 5 p.m.

The Minneapolis Institute of Arts houses more than 80,000 works of art spanning all cultures and all time periods, including paintings, sculptures, decorative arts, prints and drawings, photographs, period rooms, and textiles from Europe, Asia, Africa, and the Americas. The Minnesota Artist's Exhibition Program shows the work of local artists.

Highlights of the permanent collection include an Egyptian mummy and works by Rembrandt, Monet, Picasso, and Van Gogh. The museum also owns the Purcell-Cutts House, a beautifully restored Arts and Crafts-style home on Lake of the Isles in Minneapolis. Special exhibitions have been masterpieces of French Impressionism, splashy Caribbean festival costumes, and unforgettable images captured by the world's foremost photojournalists. The popular "Art in Bloom" and "Rose Fete" annual events feature food, entertainment, stunning floral arrangements, and a sale of hand-crafted art objects. As part of its commitment to make art available to everyone, the Institute eliminated the general admission charge in 1988. Some special exhibitions have a small entry fee, and all exhibitions are free on Thursday evenings.

The Institute offers numerous public programs, such as films, concerts, lectures, and monthly family days with children's activities. Tours are offered for adults and school groups. Special tours for hearing impaired and visually impaired visitors are also available. The Studio Restaurant and the Coffee Shop are open for lunch or a quick snack. Posters, prints, cards, books, jewelry, and children's toys are some of the art-related gifts for sale at the Museum Shop.

■ THE POTOMAC MUSEUM GROUP
Calhoun Square
3001 Hennepin Ave. S.
Minneapolis, MN 55408
Tel: (612) 824-7077
Hrs: Mon. - Sat. 10 a.m. - 9 p.m., Sun. 11 a.m. - 6 p.m.
Visa, MasterCard, and Discover are accepted.

Ever wonder what lived on Earth 300 million years ago? Take a walk into the distant past at Potomac Museum Group in Calhoun

Square. As the name "museum" implies, things normally seen only in a museum can be found there. Dinosaur bones, shark teeth, and leaf imprints are just a few of the fossils available. Children love this store. They'll find dinosaur books, life-like dinosaur sculptures, posters, and polished rocks. Adults like this store, too. For sale are such beautiful home-decorating items as shimmering crystal clusters, multi-colored onyx goblets, and stone table-tops — all created from natural rocks, minerals, and crystals from the earth.

Owned by co-directors Jon Kramer and Hal Halverson, the Potomac Museum Group began in 1975 as a student interest group at the University of Maryland. Both Kramer and Halverson take great efforts to prepare their materials carefully, resulting in beautiful specimens that can be both objects of beauty and educational tools.

Sales staff at the Potomac Museum Group are very knowledgeable, and happy to answer questions. Everyone is welcome to browse and touch. This natural art gallery is a true gem of a store.

■WALKER ART CENTER AND MINNEAPOLIS SCULPTURE GARDEN
Vineland Place
Minneapolis, MN 55403
Tel: (612) 375-7622
Hrs: Tue. - Sat. 10 a.m. - 8 p.m.
    Sun. 11 a.m. - 5 p.m.
    Closed Mon.
    (Sculpture Garden) 6 a.m. - midnight

The Walker Art Center is internationally recognized for its exhibitions of 20th-century art, and for its innovative presentations of music, theater, dance, and film. Adjacent to the Walker is the Minneapolis Sculpture Garden, seven-plus acres of gardens, walkways, and plazas containing more 40 sculptures ranging from human-scale pieces to large structures. Focal points are the Spoonbridge and Cherry fountain — visible from all parts of the Garden and now a symbol of Minneapolis, Frank Gehry's Standing Glass Fish — a 25-foot towering glass-scaled fish, the Whitney Bridge — a double-arched footbridge connecting the Garden to Loring Park and downtown Minneapolis, and Cowles Conservatory.

The Walker Art Center, founded in 1879 by Thomas Barlow Walker, opened at its present location in 1927. The award-winning building, designed by Edward Larrabee Barnes, opened in 1971 and expanded in 1984. The Minneapolis Sculpture Garden opened in 1988, a joint project of the Walker Art Center and the Minneapolis Park and Recreation Board.

Exhibitions at the Walker Art Center have included Picasso: From the Musee Picasso, Tokyo: Form and Spirit, and the first large-scale exhibition of Russian Constructivist art. John Cage, Philip Glass, and Laurie Anderson are among those who have performed at the Walker. A remarkable showcase of contemporary artistic expression, the Walker Art Center will keep museum-goers busy for at least one trip, if not two or three.

NIGHTCLUBS

■ FINE LINE MUSIC CAFE

318 First Ave. N.
Minneapolis, MN 55401
Tel: (612) 338-8100
Hrs: Mon. - Fri. 5 p.m. Music starts 8:30 p.m.
    Sun. 12:30 p.m. for brunch
Visa, MasterCard, and AmEx are accepted.

The Fine Line Music Cafe features some of the nation's finest live entertainment combined with sumptuous cuisine. "Come for the food, stay for the music" is truly a slogan that best describes the mission of the Fine Line. Cradled in the heart of the warehouse district, the Fine Line features entertainers running the entire musical spectrum. Blues, jazz, reggae, folk, and rock music provide the ambience in an intimate cafe setting that places the audience right up to the stage.

Since 1988, an assortment of rising national acts perform throughout the year in addition to several top local bands that perform on a weekly basis. Sundays bring a Gospel Brunch to the cafe. This unique event has become a favorite in the area; various gospel choirs offer their chorus for an inspirational Sunday afternoon. Sunday evenings feature supper with Pop Wagner and Ann Reed and Friends.

The food at the Fine Line has been praised on its own accord. Appetizers of spicy chicken wings and calamari are among the best. Antipasto, spinach and pasta salads, and entrees of blackened fish and beef tenderloin medallions are particularly good choices from the menu. Desserts are as varied as the entrees. The unique diplomatico is an espresso-soaked sponge cake filled with chocolate mousse and covered with ganache. The wine list features choices to enhance the meals as well as the palate.

■GLAM SLAM
110 Fifth Street N.
Minneapolis, MN 55401
Tel: (612) 338-3383
Hrs: Tues. - Sat. 8 p.m. - 1 a.m.

Glam Slam is a completely new concept in nightclub entertainment. This Minneapolis club, which opened in October 1990, features elaborate, live performances by internationally known artists on a theater-size stage, while guests dance the night away on a sweeping 1,300-square-foot dance floor below.

Located in the fashionable warehouse district just one block north of the Timberwolf Arena, Glam Slam enjoys the exclusive support of Paisley Park Studios, the famed recording center of Minneapolis-born artist Prince. To the delight of his many local fans, the nightclub — which can accommodate as many as 1,200 guests — features Prince himself and other Paisley Park groups at regular intervals.

But top-name performers are not the only attractions at Glam Slam. The sound and light system is state-of-the-art, and the interior skillfully incorporates the original look of the renovated textile building to produce a bold, airy effect. From the balcony, where the seating is intimately arranged in lounge-type fashion with tables, chairs, and couches; patrons enjoy an unrestricted view of the dance floor. The 26-foot ceiling, meanwhile, makes the Glam Slam dance floor one of the most attractive in the city. And after dancing to the accompaniment of the hottest dance music of the day and the best disc jockeys in Minnesota, remember to check out the selection of Helen Horatio Design clothes bearing the Prince insignia, which are a fitting souvenir from a truly innovative nightclub.

OPERA

■THE MINNESOTA OPERA
620 N. First Street
Minneapolis, MN 55401
Tel: (612) 333-6669
Call for performance schedule.
Visa, MasterCard, AmEx, and Discover are accepted.

The Minnesota Opera is recognized nationally and internationally for its leadership in the interpretation of both contemporary music theater and as standard opera repertoire. The Minnesota Opera offers to its audiences a varied selection, which includes experimental music theater works, traditional European and American operas with internationally acclaimed artists, and American musical theater. The Minnesota Opera also is committed to training musicians and developing new audiences via educational programs.

The Minnesota Opera was established in 1963 under the name Center Opera as a performance venue of the Walker Art Center . Early on, the Company gained a national reputation for performing original pieces by American composers. After becoming independent in 1969 and changing its name, the Minnesota Opera today enjoys wide community support. Three warehouses on the banks of the Mississippi River are home to the Company since September of 1990, accommodating rehearsal facilities, scenery and costume shops, and administrative offices.

Under the direction of Kevin Smith, the Minnesota Opera remains committed to its goal of offering performances that are musically strong and theatrically engaging. The Company performs primarily at the Ordway Music Theatre, with additional performances at the World Theater and, beginning in late 1991, at the State Theater. The chance to catch a performance by the Minnesota Opera is an opportunity not to be missed.

$\boxed{Q}$UILT SHOP

■EYDIE'S COUNTRY QUILTING
3020 W. 50th Street
Minneapolis, MN 55410
Tel: (612) 929-0645
Hrs: Mon. 10 a.m. - 3: p.m., Tue. - Sat. 10 a.m. - 5 p.m., Sun. noon - 4 p.m.
Visa and MasterCard are accepted.

Fifteen minutes from the airport and close to several antique shops is Eydie's Country Quilting shop. Step into Eydie's Country Quilting and be enveloped by the past — a past in which time was measured in tiny, patient stitches. There is something cozy and familiar about Eydie's Country Quilting. Perhaps it is the dry goods feel of the store, with its wooden floors, wicker bins filled with colorful fabrics and the quilts adorning the walls with their familiar patterns.

Eydie's carries both modern quilts and reproductions of traditional quilts, quilting supplies, and books. In addition to offering classes, Eydie's Country Quilting takes orders for custom-made quilts and ships them when they are finished. The staff at Eydie's Country Quilting will even finish an uncompleted quilt top. Drop by Eydie's Country Quilting to see the art of quilt-making at its finest.

R ESTAURANTS

Editor's Note: The dining scene in the Twin Cities has come of age. Toss out that image of lutefisk and lefse, for the days of dull dinner tables are over. Today it's possible to enjoy a whole spectrum of restaurants, ranging from elegant preparations of haute cuisine to creative, cutting-edge cuisine of the 90s, as well as steakhouses, supper clubs, and a panoply of fun and informal bistros and cafes offering ethnic delights. To mention every dining spot of excellence is impossible, or we'd have to double the size of the guidebook. Here is a listing of some favorite people-pleasers - a sampling of the tried-and-true that promises to provide exciting dining dimensions for every palate.

■ AZUR

Fifth Floor
Gaviidae Common
651 Nicollet Mall
Minneapolis, MN 55402
Tel: (612) 342-2500
Hrs: Call ahead
All major credit cards are accepted.

Here on the top floor of Gaviidae Common, flush with boutiques and designer shops, Azur draws a hip and classy crowd to dine on southern fare - south, as in the sunny shores of France, Spain, and Italy. The D'Amico brothers have devised a dining room with faux-wood, real marble, concrete floors streaked with neon, and a fireplace stolen from some Olympic festival. The ad crowd loves the place. So do knowing diners from the ex-urbs, who dote on the deceptively simple Mediterranean fare such as osso buco, snapper with artichokes, platters of scampi to be shared, and a dessert sampler — just some of the lusty temptations to waft from the kitchen. These are agreeably enhanced by a one-of-a-kind wine list that celebrates the fruit of the sun.

■ BLACK FOREST

1 E. 26th Street
Minneapolis, MN 55404
Tel: (612) 872-0812
Hrs: Call ahead
All major credit cards are accepted.

The Student Prince is alive and well and living in Minneapolis. His present-day cronies wander over from the nearby College of Art and Design to lift frosty steins of beer aside Bohemian alums who still appreciate a good strudel when they see one. Other locals gather in the Bavarian-style bar and restaurant to trade bites of wienerschnitzel and the kitchen's famous sauerkraut balls (tasting is believing). In summer, diners mingle under the outdoor arbor. Here bratwurst and burgers reign, served with gemütlichkeit by waitresses in dirndls. Owners Erich and JoAnn Christ revisit the homeland regularly to incorporate new German specialties on the Old World list.

■ COCOLEZZONE
5410 Wayzata Blvd.
Golden Valley, MN 55416
Tel: (612) 544-4014
Hrs: Call ahead
Visa, MasterCard, and AmEx are accepted.

Milan, eat your heart out: this is where the action is. Pastel marble (true and false) line the walls, dividing the high ceiling from the polished floor. And just as true to the Old Country as its Italian chef, Rosanna, are the rows of closely packed tables laden with breadsticks and vials of olive oil.

Pizza is spun before diners' eyes in the open kitchen — a prelude to a score of inventive pastas, lush salads, and straightforward entrees that tout the natural flavors of fish, fowl, and beef. The dessert cart, laden with everything from chocolate mousse to tiramisu, spells caloric trouble but culinary bliss.

■ THE EGG AND I
2704 Lyndale Ave. S.
Minneapolis, MN 55408
Tel: (612) 872-7282
Hrs: Mon. - Fri. 6 a.m. - 3 p.m.
     Sat. - Sun. 8 a.m. - 3 p.m.
Tel: (612) 647-1292
Visa, MasterCard, and AmEx are accepted.

Imagine the sound of clinking cups, the aroma of a stack of kamikazi pancakes, and the friendly banter of staff and customers. This is a typical morning at The Egg and I restaurant, where loitering is welcome, the coffee hot, and the staff cheerful and efficient.

The Egg and I restaurant has been in operation for ten years, having recently relocated and expanded. Located in the heart of south Minneapolis, The Egg and I is committed to reflecting the nature of the community, and features a gallery of pieces by local artists along one wall. Clientele also reflect the nature of the area — business people wearing suits, weight lifters in sweats, artists and shoppers. The interior is sunny, framed in front by a large picture window, and the food is fresh, featuring daily omelette specials, homemade clam chowder, sandwiches, and gargantuan muffins. The Egg and I is conveniently located on Lyndale Avenue, close to bus lines, with parking in the back. There is also a second location on University Avenue in St. Paul.

If the idea of lingering over breakfast and people-watching by a sunny window sounds enticing, The Egg and I is the perfect place — alone, with a friend, or with the family.

■ D'AMICO CUCINA
Butler Square
100 N. 6th Street
Minneapolis, MN 55403
Tel: (612) 338-2401
Hrs: Call ahead
All major credit cards are accepted.

The century-old bricks and beams of the landmark Butler Building have been historically preserved — but there's nothing dated about the first-class restaurant it harbors. The slick interior was designed by Richard D'Amico, complete with leather chairs and frosted lighting from Milan.

The equally stylish California-meets-Italy menu came from the imagination of his brother Larry, culinary whiz kid of the family. The seasonally changing list segues from soup to nuts, with stopovers for inventively sauced pastas, individual pizzas with designer toppings, entrees that pair fish, veal, prime beef, and even venison with inspired sauces. The dessert tray, on a lucky night, includes a chocolate-chianti bread pudding and homemade ice creams. Servers marry an informed, professional air with a sunny will to please. A great in-depth Italian wine list complements the stellar food.

■ FIGILIO
Calhoun Square
3001 Hennepin Ave.
Minneapolis, MN 55408
Tel: (612) 822-1688
Hrs: Call ahead
Visa, MasterCard, and AmEx are accepted.

When it's hot, it's hot — and that's Figilio, the five-year-old bar cafe and restaurant that's the hit of Uptown. Singles make it their mecca for downing trendy starters like spicy chicken wings and calamari. Neighborhood folks looking for creative pastas have also adopted it, filling tables for the floor show in the open kitchen, where pizzas whisk through the air like flying saucers.

The wood-fired ovens also turn out fish, steaks, burgers, and chicken with a distinctive smoky aroma, served with peasant bread and olive oil. For dessert the morte nel cioccolato — death by chocolate — is as good a way to go as any.

■510 RESTAURANT
510 Groveland
Minneapolis, MN 55403
Tel: (612) 874-6440
Hrs: Call ahead
All major credit cards are accepted.

The grande dame of fine dining has set the standard for elegance in Minneapolis ever since it opened its pretty, patrician doors over a dozen years ago. A silver-gray backdrop and gracious portieres framing tall windows under crystal chandeliers set the tone for an intimate evening, where the dining is relaxed.

Tuxedoed servers explain chef Scott Bergstrom's menu, based on careful French-style preparations of universal favorites. Soups are superior here, whether a delicate game consomme or puree of rich root vegetables. Sweetbreads, herb-crusted lamb, and the fish of the day make fine choices, followed by homemade ice creams, berry tarts, and wickedness personified in a dense chocolate torte.

■GOODFELLOW'S
The Conservatory
Fourth Floor
800 Nicollet Mall
Minneapolis, MN 55402
Tel: (612) 332-4800
Hrs: Call ahead
All major credit cards are accepted.

Food doesn't come any finer. Chef Tim Anderson, a protege of Texas culinary prodigy (and part owner) Stephan Pyles, has crafted an award-winning menu that melds Texas and Minnesota with a hand that isn't shy about its spices.

Wisconsin veal, Minnesota wild rice, local trout, and northwoods berries gain a new lease on life when paired with chipotles, papaya, avocados, and whatever else Tim has up his sleeve. The elegantly understated dining room in soft pink tones features modern art that would be the envy of many a collector. A voluminous wine list of 450-plus entries is offered by one of the best waitstaffs in town.

◼ LORING CAFE
1624 Harmon Place
Minneapolis, MN 55403
Tel: (612) 332-1617
Hrs: Call ahead
Visa and Mastercard are accepted.

This could be Soho. This could be San Francisco. But it's Minneapolis, where a bit of Bohemia blooms aside an urban park. Diners watch strollers silhouetted against the cityscape, and they watch each other at this hit of the see-and-be-seen scene. Owner Jason McLean parades his theatrical background through a series of rooms that move from an artsy bar with stage for local musicians, to a playhouse echoing insightful drama.

A bakery feeds the other senses, and a restaurant has a hidden courtyard where a lone sax player sits atop the roof and tweedles his magic into the night. The food is as eclectic and the service as informal as the setting. Best bets: shrimp with green peppercorns, barbecued ribs with black beans, Jason's creative pizzas, and wild mushroom salad.

◼ LUCIA'S
1432 W. 31st Street
Minneapolis, MN 55408
Tel: (612) 825-1572
Hrs: Call ahead
Visa and MasterCard are accepted.

The welcome sign "ouvert" is the first clue that chef/owner Lucia Watson learned her love of food in France. The second is her menu, crafted with the finesse of a food fanatic. Her small and cheery Uptown restaurant and adjoining wine bar, where flowers bloom and low candles light the tables, provides respite from the fast lane. So does the relaxed cuisine, drawn from a short list of daily specials.

Soups are special here, as are the country salads, home-baked wheat bread, and entrees favoring chicken, pasta, or beef with herb-laced sauces. The dessert tray of homemade pies, tarts, and layered tortes is every bit as good as it looks.

■ MARKET BAR-B-QUE

1414 Nicollet Ave.
Minneapolis, MN 55403
Tel: (612) 872-1111
Hrs: Call ahead
All major credit cards are accepted.

The Market has been smoking the best ribs in town since the '30s, when the Polski brothers opened their famous pork palace on Glenwood Avenue. Urban renewal took that original site, but the brothers' sons made a successful move to another downtown site, where business is booming. The original high wooden booths made the junket, too, complete with the little brass plaques that name their famous occupants — everybody from jazz greats, to stage stars, to football heroes.

The classic jukebox with its in-booth selectors stayed on, too, as did the down-home, honky tonk tone of the joint and the wood-fired pit. It produces dry, racy-tasting bones to slather with your choice of sauces, from mild to hellfire, as well as chicken and char-broiled steaks sided with tangy slaw and fries.

■ MURRAY'S

26 S. Sixth Street
Minneapolis, MN 55402
Tel: (612) 339-0909
Hrs: Call ahead
All major credit cards are accepted.

Murray's invented steak — at least, as far as Minneapolis is concerned. Pat Murray follows in the footsteps of his father and mother, who opened the landmark restaurant in the '40s. He is proudest of what he calls his Silver Butterknife Steak, named for the delicate tool he claims is all you'll need to carve it.

Pat's list of diners includes celebrities of showbiz, big names in sports, and junketing politicos; who know enough to ask for Murray's famous bread basket and ice box pie. Locals love to celebrate in this room, done in pink, wrought iron, and mirrors reflecting strolling violinists.

■ SRI LANKA CURRY HOUSE

2821 Hennepin Ave.
Minneapolis, MN 55408
Tel: (612) 871-2400
Hrs: Call ahead
Visa, MasterCard, and Diners Club are accepted.

There's only one Ceylonese restaurant in all the country, and it's right here in Minneapolis, serving the Uptown district and aficionados from afar with what is reputed to be the spiciest food around. Sri Lanka — once Ceylon — is an exotic island off the southern tip of India, and from there owners Evan and Heather Baliysuriya have brought their families' favorite recipes.

Dine on curries of vegetables, seafood, chicken, lamb or beef, served mild to as hot as you fancy, with sides of chutney and warm, crusty naan. To squelch the flames, there are cooling shakes of exotic fruits like mango and starapple. And when time allows, Heather picks up her guitar to sing for lucky diners.

■ TEJAS
The Conservatory
800 Nicollet Mall
Minneapolis, MN 55402
Tel: (612) 375-0800
Hrs: Call ahead
All major credit cards are accepted.

Deep in the heart of The Conservatory — that mecca of unique boutiques that also houses Goodfellow's, lies Tejas. Named for the home state of co-owner Stephan Pyles, it boasts a menu as hip as its decor, where coyotes howl at life-size cactus and strings of red chili pepper lights loop over the walls of adobe white.

The flavors from the open kitchen blend the best of northwoods and southwest cuisines in creations such as venison chili, rabbit tostadas, sweet corn aside peppers in a fiery salsa, a Caesar salad with cayenne croutons, and for dessert, a chocolate-cayenne torte. Margaritas made the old-fashioned way and a list of longnecks that would impress most Texans are on hand to quench the fire.

■ WINDOWS ON MINNESOTA
5000 IDS Center
Minneapolis, MN 55402
Tel: (612) 349-6250
Hrs: Call ahead
All major credit cards are accepted.

Come for the view, stay for the food. Here on the pinnacle of the ultramodern IDS skyscraper designed by the renowned Philip Johnson, all tables command sightlines of the city spread below and stars that twinkle almost within reach. Subdued elegance is the byword here, from waiters in tuxedos that create flaming specialties at tableside to a menu that highlights both beef and seafood (including the classic Minnesota walleye) in a choice of preparation styles. Austrian chef Ernst Konrad shows off his native talents in dishes such as an ethereal mushroom strudel as well as show-stopping desserts.

S HOPPING COMPLEX

■ RIVERPLACE
Corner of Hennepin and Historic Main Street
Minneapolis, MN 55414
Tel: (612) 378-1969 - Information Line
Hrs: Mon. - Thur. 10 a.m. - 9 p.m.
    Fri. - Sat. 10 a.m. - 10 p.m.
    Sun. noon - 5 p.m.
All major credit cards are accepted. May vary at each store.

Located on the beautiful and historic Mississippi riverfront, just a bridge away from thriving downtown Minneapolis, is Riverplace. It is a village within the city that stands where the city's pioneers originally settled in the 1850s. Riverplace, Inc., a subsidiary of Kajima Corporation, owns and operates the Riverplace complex. Kajima Corporation, founded in 1839, is one of the oldest and largest general contracting, architectural, engineering, and development companies in the world.

Riverplace is an exquisite shopping, dining, and entertainment experience. This complex also features luxury condominiums and apartments. Shopping in the restored historic buildings offers a wide variety of merchandise from name brand fashions and accessories to original art, handcrafts, books, and furniture. Formal and informal dining features a variety of cuisines from Greek to Mexican specialties, to Gulf coast seafood, European, Japanese, and other ethnic foods. Stroll the cobblestone courts and enjoy the open air cinema and street theater. Take the family for a ride in a horse-drawn carriage down historic Main Street and around Nicollet Island. To top the evening, enjoy live comedy, music, and dance at Riverplace. Special events and seasonal festivals are scheduled throughout the year. Riverplace is an exciting and affordable event for young and old.

S PECIALTY GIFT & CARD SHOP

■ THE REINDEER HOUSE
3409 44th Street W.
Minneapolis, MN 55410
Tel: (612) 920-4741 or (800) 328-3894
Hrs: Mon. - Wed. and Fri. - Sat. 10 a.m. - 6 p.m., Thur. 10 a.m. - 8 p.m.
    Holiday hours may vary; please call ahead
Visa, MasterCard, and AmEx are accepted.

Two decades after it first opened its doors to the public, The Reindeer House gift and card shop has become a Minneapolis institution. Located in a cheerful, renovated home near Lake Harriet in the southern part of the city, the gift shop is brimming with wreaths, dolls, cut design shades, figurines, potpourri, and other hand-crafted items, all artistically displayed in a friendly, aromatic atmosphere.

Although it offers an astounding variety of craft items, The Reindeer House was originally founded by the late, renowned greeting-card designer Anita Beck to display her work, and the shop remains the home store for cards designed in her name. These are available via mail-order or for purchase directly at this store, as well as others around the country. But The Reindeer House has also always been a center for local craftspeople to display their creations, and today, nearly 100 artists participate in this cooperative venture.

Among those artists, one of the best known is Mary Thiele, a highly imaginative teddy-bear creator. Her artistic teddy bears have become many a child's favorite toy, and a wide selection of her work is on display in The Reindeer House's children's room — a true treasure-trove for those who are looking for just the right gift for their toddlers. But fanciful teddy bears, cards, and crafts are not the only reason people keep coming back to The Reindeer House. They have come to enjoy the personal service of one of Minneapolis's oldest and most authentic gift shops, maintaining the quality and artistic flair that Anita Beck stood for all her life.

▌S▐ PECIALTY SHOP

■ GARDEN OF EDEN

Burnsville Center
Promenade Level
Burnsville, MN
Tel: (612) 892-7770

Uptown
1418 W. Lake Street
at Hennepin
Minneapolis, MN
Tel: (612) 824-3715

Bandana Square
Energy Park
St. Paul, MN
Tel: (612) 644-2944

Victorian Crossing
867 Grand Ave.
St. Paul, MN
Tel: (612) 293-1300

Garden of Eden opened its first store in 1971 with a private label line of naturally based bath and body-care products and perfume oils. Other product lines were added, and these shops now stock product lines such as Crabtree and Evelyn, Scarborough, Kama Sutra, Avigal Henna, Bellmira Baths, Kappus Soaps, as well as products carried in health food stores, such as Nature's Gate, Aloegen, Kiss My Face, Rachel Perry, Reviva, and Tom's.

Private label products such as bubble bath, shower gel, moisturizers, lotions, massage and bath oils are dispensed right at the store in refillable bottles and can be scented from a choice of about 90 fragrance oils. Glycerine soaps, facial care products, and makeup round out the Garden of Eden product line.

Potpourris, sachets, room scenters, incenses, drawer liners, and related products are available for the increasingly popular home fragrances, now called the desirable "fourth dimension" by interior decorators.

Garden of Eden takes pride in being a wonderful source for gifts — and gift bags, boxes, and baskets to help create customized and personalized gifts. Trained, helpful salespeople add to the delightful experience of shopping at Garden of Eden stores.

S YMPHONY ORCHESTRA

■ MINNESOTA ORCHESTRA
Orchestra Hall
1111 Nicollet Mall
Minneapolis, MN 55403
Tel: (612) 371-5656 or (800) 292-4141
Hrs: Call for performance times
All major credit cards are accepted.

The Minnesota Orchestra enjoys a prominent place as one of the nation's leading symphony orchestras. Nationally and internationally acclaimed, the Minnesota Orchestra brings season after season of excellent performances to Minneapolis' Orchestra Hall, its home base, and regularly performs in St. Paul and other parts of the state.

The Minnesota Orchestra was founded in 1903 as the Minneapolis Symphony. From the start, it earned a reputation as the "orchestra on wheels" from its extensive tours throughout the United States. It also has visited such places as Mexico, Australia, and Hong Kong, and it is heard by millions throughout the world on recordings and radio broadcasts.

Under the dynamic leadership of Edo de Waart, Music Director for the past five years, the Minnesota Orchestra continues its commitment to provide enjoyable concerts for everyone. Enjoy Beethoven or Mozart in the acoustically acclaimed Orchestra Hall, stop by on a Thursday or Friday morning for a Coffee Concert, be entertained at a Weekender Pops concert; or bring the whole family to a special children's event. Orchestra Hall is accessible via several bus lines, and ramp parking is available.

T HEATER

■ THE GUTHRIE THEATER
Vineland Place
Minneapolis, MN 55403
Tel: (612) 377-2224
Hrs: Call for performance schedules
Visa, MasterCard, AmEx, Discover, and Diners Club are accepted.

"If you are in the vicinity, it's a must...," quoted New York's *Village Voice* recently about the Guthrie Theater's current repertory season. Twenty-seven critically acclaimed seasons have passed since its founding, and the Tony Award-winning Guthrie Theater still has the power to grip audiences. Since its inception in 1963 as a repertory theater with an outstanding company, few other theaters have produced such a broad range of plays. Exploring the great classical plays with contemporary interpretations, the Guthrie has become the flagship of the American theater movement. Today, the Guthrie is the largest regional theater in the United States, with more than a thousand seats, not one of which is more than 52 feet from the stage.

Internationally known British director Sir Tyrone Guthrie founded the Guthrie after a national search for a good location. His travels led him to Minneapolis, whose civic and arts communities embraced the concept of a repertory theater. In its very first season, the Guthrie set a precedent for excellence.

Highly respected today as one of America's leading theater directors, Guthrie director, Garland Wright, continues to stretch both actors and audiences, collaborating with writers and scholars to develop new performance techniques and working to maintain community outreach through education and touring. Pick from two or three plays on an extended weekend and enjoy one of the finest performances the Twin Cities has to offer. Backstage tours are available Saturdays; groups by appointment.

Z OO

■ MINNESOTA ZOO
13000 Zoo Blvd.
Apple Valley, MN 55124
Tel: (612) 432-9000
Hrs: Open daily except Christmas Day (Summer) Apr. - Sept. 10 a.m. - 6 p.m.
(Winter) Oct. - Mar. 10 a.m. - 4 p.m.
Visa, MasterCard, and AmEx are accepted.

As sensitivity toward and appreciation for the earth's non-human inhabitants grows, so does the Minnesota Zoo. Situated

©MARTIENA R. RICHTER

just ten minutes south of the Twin Cities in Apple Valley on 480 acres, the zoo has been dubbed one of the country's ten best by wildlife experts. Committed to strengthening the bond between people and the living earth; the zoo, its exhibits, and its animals and habitats provide a fascinating window into the natural world. Families who explore this Apple Valley sanctuary will come away rich with knowledge about the inhabitants of the oceans, jungles, lakes, forests, and plains. They learn about increasingly important conservation issues. Entertainment abounds as well in the form of shows, special exhibits, animal feedings, and animal antics.

The zoo, like nature itself, continuously alters and fluctuates. Six trails amble around nationally acclaimed habitats that more than 1,700 mammals, birds, fish, reptiles, and amphibians call home. The habitats, a great number of them staged in beautiful outdoor spaces, are carefully composed to ensure that animals reside in a place similar to their environments in the wild. Reflective of the changing seasons, visits at various times of the year reveal different wonders. In winter, the trails open to cross-country skiers who glide by camels, caribou, Japanese snow monkeys, and native wildlife. During the summer, special shows are frequent; visitors marvel at the choreography of dolphin shows, see wildlife close up during live animal demonstrations, and float over the zoo's Northern Trail aboard the Skytrail Monorail. A Children's Zoo offers demonstrations such as wool spinning and an exploratory view of wildlife. Special presentations focus on such animals as llamas and reindeer. Camel rides also are offered at the Children's Zoo, and puppet shows entertain youngsters year-round. Also, the zoo features a program called the Zoo Ark, a traveling mini-zoo that can be scheduled to present wildlife programs at schools, community events, and meetings. Different programs are targeted to interest grades K-12.

Any time of year, the Minnesota Zoo has something exciting happening. A recently added koala exhibit draws hundreds of thousands of curious visitors who yearn to see the furry, round Australian marsupial for themselves. There's never a routine day at the Minnesota Zoo; surprises pop up around every corner.

Greater St. Paul

S t. Paul began its existence in the early 1800s as a French Voyageur village with the rather unbecoming name of Pig's Eye. The strange name was bestowed on the settlement in honor — or dishonor, as the case may have been — of Pierre "Pig's Eye" Parrant, infamous retired fur trader and saloon owner extraordinaire. Respectability came to the village in 1841 when Father Lucien Galtier arrived and proceeded to build a log-cabin chapel dedicated to St. Paul. He petitioned to change the settlement's name accordingly, and so St. Paul came into being.

Built on the Mississippi River, St. Paul has 29 miles of shoreline and many lovely parks and smaller European-like squares. It is a more urbane city than its rival twin Minneapolis, preferring to emphasize its gracious architecture and rich history rather than its industrial capabilities and high-tech companies. Not that St. Paul lacks modern, state-of-the-art innovation. Together with Minneapolis, St. Paul has a solid track record as a home of Fortune 500 companies, including the huge conglomerate 3M and the respected H.B. Fuller Company.

Like Minneapolis, St. Paul also offers its residents plenty of outdoor activities all year-round, from roller skating and outdoor picnicking, to ice-skating and ice fishing.

ATTRACTIONS

St. Paul offers visitors a wide range of entertainment beginning with its many historical sites. *Summit Avenue,* the country's longest stretch of residential Victorian architecture, should be the first stop on any itinerary of historical places. This beautiful street in the heart of St. Paul was once home to F. Scott Fitzgerald, Sinclair Lewis, and Amelia Earhart, among others. At the top of Summit stands the exquisite *St. Paul Cathedral,* modeled after St. Peter's in Rome, but filled with its own unique interior flourishes. Just a block away, the *James J. Hill House* continues to impress visitors more than 100 years after it was built. Owned by the Minnesota Historical Society and open for tours, the mansion cost an estimated $280,000 in 1887 when it was built by railroad baron James J. Hill.

Just a few streets away, visitors will find another historical residence, the *Alexander Ramsey House,* originally home to the first governor of the Minnesota territory. And then there's always *Grand Avenue,* another historic street lined with small specialty shops and cozy restaurants — the warm heart of St. Paul's *Historic Hill District,* an area of vintage Victorian era homes.

To catch a glimpse of life in the Minnesota Territory before St. Paul or Minneapolis were cities, visitors should drop by *Historic Fort Snelling,* a living history site where costumed guides act out the day-to-day life of early fort dwellers. From Fort Snelling it's a small jaunt to the *Minnesota State Capitol Building,* designed by Cass Gilbert — the architect of the U.S. Supreme Court Building — and considered one of the most beautiful state capitols in the country. Guided tours of the capitol are free of charge.

More history is evident in downtown St. Paul, mixed with contemporary architecture and '90s style. The restored *Landmark Center* was once a federal courthouse where gangster trials were held; today it is a center for performing and visual arts. Nearby is *Galtier Plaza,* a shopping center with a tropical twist, boasting its own atrium-like architecture. But it is the modern *St. Paul Center* mall that earns the greatest praise for housing the country's largest indoor commercial park, the tropical *Town Square Park.* Nestled near the park, visitors will also discover *Cafesjian's Carousel,* built in 1914 and just recently saved by a St. Paul couple from being broken up and auctioned off, horse by horse. The carousel is now open for rides, and volunteers are in the process of restoring each horse to its original splendor.

Connected to St. Paul Center is the tallest building in St. Paul, *The World Trade Center,* a clearinghouse for international trade. Also located downtown is the *Science Museum of Minnesota* and the *William McKnight Omnitheater.* Housed in the same modernistic building, the museum and omnitheater delight children and adults — the museum with hands-on science exhibits and the omnitheater with stunning science- and nature-related movies projected onto a huge, wrap-around screen. Not far away is the equally fascinating *Minnesota Museum of Art,* which blends science, technology, and natural history.

St. Paul also offers plenty of arts-related entertainment. First on the list is the world-renowned *St. Paul Chamber Orchestra,* which treats audiences to high-calibre performances of chamber music in the elegant *Ordway Music Theatre,* a glass and brass European-style theatre. Then there are the theater companies that call St. Paul home, including the excellent all-black *Penumbra Theatre,* the classically inclined *Park Square Theater,* and the decidedly different *Great North American History Theatre,* which specializes in plays that relate to a particular event or character in history. Last but not least, the restored turn-of-the-century *World Theater,* once the venue for Garrison Keillor's *A Prairie Home Companion,* now offers a wide mix of entertainment.

A more relaxing outing might include a visit to *Harriet Island,* across the Mississippi from St. Paul, or an afternoon at *Como Park Zoo and Conservatory.* The zoo is free to the public and the conservatory features changing flower exhibits geared to the seasons. Flowers also make an appearance at the seasonal *St. Paul Farmer's Market* along with table after table of tempting home-grown fruit and vegetables. Farming at the turn-of-the-century is the focus of *Gibbs Farm Museum,* a national historic site complete with costumed guides who depict the lifestyles of farmers from that period.

Another glimpse of the past can be had on the *Jonathan Padelford* and *Josiah Snelling,* two riverboats offering historically narrated cruises between downtown St. Paul and Fort Snelling. After the riverboats, a visit to *Bandana Square* is entirely appropriate. This renovated shopping complex was once a railroad-car repair station and still retains the original railroad tracks imbedded in its floor. At Bandana Square there's something for everyone; children can visit the hands-on *Children's Museum,* while their parents admire the model railroad displays at the *Twin City Model Railroad Club, Inc.* — or vice versa.

EVENTS

St. Paul's events are as varied as the city itself. The fun begins in January with the largest winter celebration in the country, the *St. Paul Winter Carnival,* a tribute to the die-hard spirit of the early voyageurs who founded St. Paul. The voyageurs would have a yearly winter rendezvous full of spirited competition and comradery, and the Winter Carnival today continues that tradition with hundreds of events, contests, and games.

After a few months' lull, St. Paul again comes alive in May with the *Festival of Nations*, celebrating the city's cultural heritage with more than 80 different ethnic groups represented. In June, it's time for *Grand Old Day*, the largest one-day street festival in the Midwest, held on historic Grand Avenue. And just a few weeks later comes *Taste of Minnesota*. Held on the doorstep of the state capitol, Taste of Minnesota features four days of feasting and entertainment culminating, on July 4, in a free performance by the Minnesota Orchestra accompanied by fireworks over the capitol building.

Later in July, Harriet Island becomes the venue for *River Fest*, a ten-day music festival featuring big-name performers, and at the end of the month the Minnesota Historical Society hosts the *Gilded Age Festival*, a celebration of the Victorian era held at the James J. Hill House and the Alexander Ramsey House. As the summer wears on, Minnesotans wait anxiously for their favorite event, the *Minnesota State Fair*, held in late August at the country's largest state fairgrounds in St. Paul. The Minnesota State Fair is everything a state fair should be and more — as befitting one of the largest fairs in the United States.

In October, St. Paul joins Minneapolis in hosting the highly regarded *Twin Cities Marathon*, which covers the miles from downtown Minneapolis to the state capitol building in St Paul. And during the holiday season, old-fashioned cheer takes center stage when *A Victorian Christmas and Gala Ball* is held at the Alexander Ramsey House.

For more information on St. Paul, contact:
St. Paul Convention Bureau
600 NCL Tower
445 Minnesota Street
St. Paul, MN 55101-2108
(612) 297-6985 or (800) 627-6101

■ A CCOMMODATIONS

■ DOUBLETREE CLUB HOTEL
Minneapolis/St. Paul Airport
2700 Pilot Knob Road
Eagan, MN 55121
Tel: (612) 454-3434
All major credit cards are accepted.

Doubletree Hotels have locations across the United States and Canada. These are very reasonably priced, attractive hotels with a strong emphasis on comfort. The Minnesota Doubletree is a Club Hotel, therefore, in addition to the standard amenities, guests are treated to complimentary airport transportation, a full cooked-to-order breakfast, morning newspaper, and a hosted evening reception. Frequent flyer miles may also be available.

Club facilities available to guests include exercise facilities, pool, sauna, a reading room/library, and well-appointed meeting rooms. Seven comfortable, versatile conference rooms accommodate meetings for five to 125, complete with professional attention to details by experienced staff. Guest rooms are spacious quarters with full work desk, two phones, cable television, and sitting area. Featuring 24-hour coffee service, late night snacks, and large screen television in the Club, Doubletree Club Hotels are an exceptional value, perfect for a weekend getaway or long-awaited vacation.

■ THE SAINT PAUL HOTEL
350 Market Street
St. Paul, MN 55102
Tel: (612) 292-9292
All major credit cards are accepted.

When The Saint Paul opened in 1910, it was the ultimate in hotels. Built on the corner of Fifth and St. Peter Streets in downtown St. Paul at the whopping cost of $1 million, the Italian Renaissance Style edifice boasted a roof garden, a grand ballroom, a fine dining room, and no less than 284 porcelain bathtubs.

Seventy years later, after years of neglect, The Saint Paul was renovated to regain its position as the city's grandest and finest hotel. Today, its 254 guest rooms and suites overlooking the fashionable Rice Park area and the Ordway Theater once again are attracting the discriminating visitor. Arriving via the circular driveway, visitors are treated to a unique lobby dominated by a five-and-a-half-foot-wide fireplace with a custom-built, gold-trimmed mantle, a genuine 1925 Italian black and gold neoclassic design concierge desk, and ten-foot columns stenciled with a classic art nouveau pattern. The rooms feature plush carpeting, all new furniture, upholstery, and wallcoverings, remote control televisions, and computer-compatible telephone lines.

The Saint Paul offers four-star dining in its acclaimed St. Paul Grill. For those looking for something more casual, there's the Cafe. Open daily for lunch and dinner, the St. Paul Grill specializes in grilled meats and fish, including such favorites as fresh Minnesota walleye, dry-aged steaks, and homemade roast beef hash with fried eggs. But in addition to offering a first class dining and hotel experience, The Saint Paul has yet another benefit for visitors to the city. Its location on the skyway system puts it within easy walking distance of all the downtown major attractions and makes it a favored destination for an increasing number of travelers to the Upper Midwest.

ART GALLERIES

■ KRAMER GALLERY

229 E. Sixth Street
St. Paul, MN 55101
Tel: (612) 228-1301
Hrs: Tue. - Fri. 9 a.m. - 5 p.m.
     Sat. 10:30 a.m. - 2:30 p.m.
     Closed Sun. and Mon.
Visa, MasterCard, and AmEx are accepted.

Across Mears Park from Galtier Plaza and in the heart of St. Paul's artistic Lowertown district, the Kramer Gallery specializes in American and European paintings of the late 19th and early 20th centuries. Featuring the works of professional artists of the time, Kramer Gallery's collection includes American Western, still life, landscape, and impressionistic works in oil and watercolor, as well as sculpture. A regional focus is featured as well. Minnesota artists and subjects of the same period include works by Fournier, Heldner, and Brewer. For those wishing to locate fine American Indian art, Kramer Gallery specializes in artifacts from the nineteenth century with Southwest, Plains, and Woodlands origins. Colorful textiles, basketry, beadwork, jewelry, and stone items form a part of this extensive collection.

The Kramer Gallery also offers a research library and professional restoration and conservation services for corporations, museums, and private collectors. A member of the Appraisers Association of America, the Gallery provides written appraisals for insurance, estate, or donation purposes.

Kramer Gallery is run by knowledgeable art dealers in the business for more than 20 years. Whether for personal or business use, Kramer Gallery offers high quality traditional looking artwork in a modern setting.

■RAYMOND AVENUE GALLERY
761 Raymond Ave.
St. Paul, MN 55114
Tel: (612) 644-9200
Hrs: Mon. - Fri. 10 a.m. - 4 p.m.

The Raymond Avenue Gallery was established to fill a gap in the art community of St. Paul and Minneapolis. Here is a place for area artists working in the crafts to exhibit in a gallery setting. All of the artists represented are among the finest in their fields, and their works encompass a diversity of approach as well as media.

The gallery is also a place for people to savor the experience of being surrounded by beautiful objects and to add to their collections. Among the artists represented are Joseph Brown, the director of the gallery and a nationally exhibited potter, and the internationally recognized potter Warren MacKenzie. Also exhibited are nationally recognized artists who create scarves, clothing, jewelry, metalwork, paper, and other crafts. The Raymond Avenue Gallery has a reputation of being a gallery well worth visiting to see carefully selected and displayed area crafts.

B ED & BREAKFAST

■CHATSWORTH BED AND BREAKFAST
984 Ashland Ave.
St. Paul, MN 55104
Tel: (612) 227-4288
Hrs: Open year-round

Looking for a quiet respite from the city, yet one that is still accessible and in a convenient location? Chatsworth Bed and Breakfast is the perfect combination: a beautiful, 1900-vintage Victorian house tucked into a large tree-lined residential lot and close to the airport, both downtowns, 35E, and I-94.

Donna Gustafson, owner of Chatsworth Bed and Breakfast, welcomes guests to her St. Paul home. There are five elegantly decorated bedrooms to chose from. Guests may wish to stay in the Four Poster Bedroom with the canopied poster bed and private double whirlpool bath, the African-Asian Room with a double whirlpool bath, the Oriental Room, the Scandinavian room with antique decor, or the Victorian Room, also with private bath. Enjoy a leisurely breakfast in the paneled dining room and relax by the fireplace. Walk to the Governor's Mansion on Summit Avenue or stroll by Grand Avenue's unique shops and restaurants, just a few minutes' walking distance from Chatsworth Bed and Breakfast.

Donna serves hearty muffins, fresh fruit, and a special treat: homemade cranberry bread. She is an excellent source of information for visitors from out-of-town. Business travelers, entertainers, writers, workshop and conference participants, and relatives attending weddings or family reunions are some of the interesting guests Donna has hosted. Enjoy Chatsworth Bed and Breakfast for a special respite with a personal touch.

BOOKSTORES

■ HUNGRY MIND
1648 Grand Ave.
St. Paul, MN 55105
Tel: (612) 699-0587
Hrs: Mon. - Thurs. 9 a.m. - 10 p.m.
    Fri. - Sat. 9 a.m. - 11:30 p.m. , Sun. 10 a.m. - 6 p.m.
Visa, MasterCard, and Discover are accepted.

The Hungry Mind Bookstore on Grand Avenue opened in 1970 and has appealed to customers from a varied cross-section of the city — patrons that enjoy books without being pretentious or grim about it.

The environment is very casual with overstuffed furniture on which the customers can sit back and decide which selections to take home. The 20-foot ceiling and large skylight enhance the atmosphere and make it look as though it could be the loft home of anyone — that is anyone who really enjoys reading.

Various authors have held signings and readings: Garrison Keillor, Carol Bly, Angela Davis, Rod Carew, and Louis Anderson are just a sample of the many who have stopped by.

The Hungry Mind has featured a reading series since 1975 and has expanded to include the critically acclaimed restaurant Table of Contents.

■ODEGARD BOOKS SAINT PAUL
857 & 867 Grand Ave.
at Victoria Crossing
St. Paul, MN 55105
Tel: (612) 222-2711 or (800) 247-0635
Hrs: Mon. - Thurs. 10 a.m. - 10 p.m.
    Fri. - Sat. 10 a.m. - 11 p.m.
    Sun. 11 a.m. - 5 p.m.
Visa, MasterCard, Discover, and AmEx are accepted.

Odegard Books Saint Paul has brought a bookselling tradition to the City of St. Paul. The original Odegard's opened in 1978 and has led to the creation of Odegard Encore Books in 1980 and Books for Travel in 1990 with an in-store travel agency. The triumverate is located at the intersection of Victoria and Grand Avenues, which offers a very neighborhood-like atmosphere.

The knowledgeable staff is always available to assist customers with that hard to find title or to suggest a popular item. In addition to the various hardcover and paperback selections, Odegard's also carries audio cassettes of fiction, non-fiction, and selected music as well as magazines and newspapers. All of the books at Odegard's Encore are sold at a reduced price.

Books for Travel offers an immense range of items to help plan that long-awaited trip. Maps, travel guides, books, and accessories serve as invaluable resources. Travel Associates is a travel agency located within the bookshop ready to assist with all travel arrangements. Author readings and signings are additional attractions of this store. Odegards Books Saint Paul provides a wide range of service and selection for the Twin Cities area.

C ANDY STORE

■ MAUD BORUP CANDIES
20 W. Fifth Street
St. Paul, MN 55102
Tel: (612) 293-0530
Hrs: Mon. - Fri. 9:30 a.m. - 5 p.m.
    Sat. 10 a.m. - 3 p.m.
    Closed Sun.
Visa and MasterCard are accepted.

Maud Borup Candies has been famous since 1907 for delectable handmade chocolates. The chocolates are masterpieces, and the secret of this quality is a combination of the careful preparation of small batches and the use of only the best ingredients. Using the original recipes and formulas, copper kettle cooking assures smooth creams and chewy caramels.

The intoxicating chocolate aroma draws customers inside where they must decide from over 100 varieties of hand-dipped chocolates. Succulent cherries with the stems in are coated in a dark bittersweet chocolate. Chewy nougats are made with real honey and imported cashews. Fondant-dipped nuts are a specialty. The hand-blanched Jordanola almonds can't be beat, nor can the roasted salted nuts. Eggshell glazed fruits, such as apricots, prunes, ginger, and pineapple can't be resisted. Chocolate, maple, rum, and nut caramels are all made with dairy-fresh cream. Decorated hand-dipped bon-bons have a variety of tempting centers, each with its own special sensational taste. No need to punch the bottom of the chocolate to find out what is inside. The curlicues on top of each chocolate tell what is inside each piece. There is a wonderful selection of solid milk chocolate novelties, and any selection can be mailed or delivered as a gift.

National and international in reputation, Maud Borup chocolates are mailed all over the world to kings and queens and discriminating people who want the very best. For the chocolate lover, Maud Borup Candies "Is Worth Its Weight In Gold," and made the good old-fashioned way.

◤C HILDREN'S BOOKSTORE

■ THE RED BALLOON BOOKSHOP
891 Grand Ave.
St. Paul, MN 55105
Tel: (612) 224-8320
Hrs: Mon. - Fri. 10 a.m. - 9 p.m., Sat. 10 a.m. - 6 p.m., Sun. noon - 5 p.m.
AmEx, Discover, Visa, and MasterCard are accepted.

The Red Balloon Bookshop is geared toward enhancing a child's imagination. Specializing in children's books from tots to teens, The Red Balloon has a full staff of professional booksellers to assist customers.

Games and toys are also available; these items feature popular storybook characters such as Paddington Bear and Babar. Children's music fills the air as customers choose their favorite stories from the shelves. The stained glass windows and high ceilings create a warm, open atmosphere in which to shop. Special ordering and author events can be found as well as story hours on Wednesdays and Saturdays at 10:30 a.m. The Red Balloon offers the finest in children's favorites.

C OFFEEHOUSES

■ BAD HABIT CAFE
418 St. Peter Street
St. Paul, MN 55102
Tel: (612)224-8545
Hrs: Mon. - Thur. 7 a.m.- 11 p.m.
    Fri. 7 a.m. - 3 a.m.
    Sat. noon - 3 a.m.
    Sun. noon - 6 p.m.

The Bad Habit Cafe serves a full line of espresso drinks and fresh fruit juices, and naturally, coffee. What would a coffeehouse be without this feature? Along with a full line of beverages, The Bad Habit features an award-winning cheesecake as well as muffins, scones, bagels, cookies, soups, and daily sandwich specials. Weekends bring live music, with no cover charge. The music ranges from jazz to blues and folk music. Local artists' work is displayed along the walls, and upstairs a wall of books collected at various auctions and antique shows line the shelves.

The Bad Habit Cafe has become popular with the local theatre crowd and younger crowd that occupies the late night hours. For an atmosphere like no other, visit The Bad Habit Cafe.

■ DUNN BROS. COFFEE
1569 Grand Ave.
St. Paul, MN 55105
Tel: (612) 698-0618
Hrs: Daily 7:30 a.m. - 11 p.m.
Visa and MasterCard are accepted.

Chosen "best coffee" by the readers of *City Pages* in March 1989, here at Dunn Brothers Coffee customers will only get "Great Java, No Jive."

Originally from Portland, where he learned his coffee-roasting skills, owner Ed Dunn opened Dunn Brothers Coffee in January 1987. When entering the coffeehouse, the delicious aroma of coffee is truly enticing. Only a small selection of the best coffee beans available at harvest time are purchased throughout the year. Coffee beans are roasted daily in small batches so that customers consistently taste the full flavor potential of every coffee that is sold. Among the favorites are coffee beans selected from Kenya in East Africa and Hawaiian Kona beans. Customers can relax with coffee and a fresh pastry while reading a book or the newspaper, talking to friends, or listening to local musicians who supply acoustic music three to four times at night during the week.

Everyone is welcome and coffee is the only thing Dunn Brothers Coffee takes seriously.

CONSERVATORY

■ COMO PARK CONSERVATORY
Midway Park and Kaufman Drive
St. Paul, MN 55103
Tel: (612) 489-1740
Hrs: Year-round 10 a.m. - 6 p.m.

The Como Park Conservatory has offered a relief from winter for Minnesotans since 1915. This greenhouse has beckoned visitors throughout the years in all seasons. The Conservatory is housed in a Victorian building that was placed on the National Register of Historic Places in 1976. Approximately three acres of plants and flowers fill the building. Admission is charged November through April, .50 for adults, .25 for seniors and youth, free for children 10 and under. Volunteers support the staff with their time and knowledge.

The Conservatory plays host to several shows throughout the year. The Chrysanthemum Show takes place in November for three weeks. Original stock plants from the 1915 show and new varieties are propagated annually to be included in the 40,000-plus display. The Winter Flower Show displays poinsettias, cyclamens, primroses, cineraria, and azaleas. The show takes place the first week in December and continues until the end of February with various additions and changes. The Spring Flower Show features Easter lilies, calla lilies, tulips, hydrangeas, hyacinths, narcissus, snapdragons, and many tropical plants and flowering shrubs. This celebration of spring runs from the end of March through April. The Summer Display features gloxinias, coleus, petunias, geraniums, and border plants. This display can be viewed all through the summer until after state fair time. It is a must see for the home gardener. The Conservatory is a popular place for wedding photos as well.

Additional gardens have been established throughout Como Park by The Como Conservatory. The Gates Ajar is planted each year by the staff and symbolizes the gates of heaven, which are left open for those who have earned their way. The McKnight Formal Gardens focus on the Paul Manship sculpture "Indian Boy and Dog," surrounding it with crabapple trees.

The Ordway Memorial Japanese Garden captures the tranquility and artistry of the Orient. The Palm House, North House, Fern Room, and Sunken Garden make up the public display areas. Service areas and production greenhouses are further attractions at the park. The Como Park Conservatory is just the place to rejuvenate the senses.

GALLERY

■ FILM IN THE CITIES
2388 University Ave.
St. Paul, MN 55114
Tel: (612) 646-6104
      (612) 291-0801 Jerome Hill Theater
Hrs: (Gallery) Mon. - Fri. 9 a.m. - 5 p.m.
      Sat. noon - 4 p.m.

Film in the Cities is a "media arts and education center that fosters the creation, appreciation and understanding of film, photography, video and audio as forms of art and communication..." Named as the "best film programming in the Twin Cities" by *Mpls/St. Paul Magazine*, Film in the Cities selections include independent and foreign films, as well as productions by regional artists with premieres of independent, foreign, experimental, and restored classic films, along with festivals focusing on specific cultures.

The Photography Gallery, located at 2388 University Avenue in St. Paul, displays works by emerging and established Minnesota and nationally recognized photographers, in a range from traditional to experimental. Books and periodicals relating to photography are available for purchase.

The site also houses the Education Center, where classes in film, video, photography, audio, and screenwriting are offered. Don't miss the chance to catch an exciting film presentation by this innovative Twin Cities arts organization. Movies are shown at the Jerome Hill Theater, First Trust Center (5th Street and Jackson), in St. Paul.

GIFT & CLOTHING STORE

■ THE BIBELOT SHOP
1082 Grand Ave.
St. Paul, MN 55105-3001
Tel: (612) 222-0321

Additional location:
2276 Como Ave.
St. Paul, MN 55108-1795
Tel: (612) 646-5631
Hrs: Mon. - Fri. 9:30 a.m. - 8 p.m.
    Sat. 9:30 a.m. - 5:30 p.m.
    Sun. noon - 5 p.m.

One of the more adventurous stores on St. Paul's Grand Avenue, The Bibelot Shop (pronounced "bee-be-lo") has a lively collection of gifts, clothing, and jewelry. Roxana Freese and her staff travel extensively to find remarkable and unusual gift items to add to their already eclectic collection. This intriguing shop features jewelry made by local and national artisans and contemporary, casual clothing made of all natural fibers.

For the young and young-at-heart, there is a wonderful selection of toys - stuffed animals, handmade games, and puzzles are only a few waiting on the shelves. To wrap it all up, the Bibelot Shop has artistic gift wrap and greeting cards for every occasion. The original store on Como Avenue, which celebrated its 25th anniversary in September 1991, carries a similar selection of everything. "Bibelot" is French for "small precious gift," and certainly describes much of what is to be found at these stores.

HISTORIC SITES

■ ALEXANDER RAMSEY HOUSE
A Minnesota Historical Society Site
Exchange and Walnut Streets
(two blocks south of the St. Paul Civic Center)
Mailing Address: 265 S. Exchange Street
                St. Paul, MN 55102
Tel: (612) 296-0100
Hrs: (April - Dec.) Tue. - Fri. 10 a.m. - 4 p.m.
    Sat. 1 p.m. - 4:30 p.m.
    Closed on major holidays
There is an admission charge.

In 1849, President Zachary Taylor appointed a Pennsylvania man named Alexander Ramsey as Minnesota's first territorial governor.

Ramsey was enamored by the frontier state, took it as his adopted home, and only ten years after his arrival was elected the young state's second governor. A staunch Republican, he served two terms in the United States Senate and was appointed secretary of war by President Rutherford B. Hayes in 1879.

When Ramsey returned from Washington seven years later as Minnesota's most eminent elder statesman, he retired to his French Second Empire style limestone mansion. Built in 1872, his home was a testament to his political ambitions — an extravagant, 15-room architectural gem set in the fashionable Irvine Park district west of downtown St. Paul. Ramsey purchased only the finest decorations and materials for his mansion, including black walnut woodwork, marble fireplaces, crystal chandeliers, ornate brass door fittings, fashionable rugs, furniture, and china. Even his carriage house was ornately decorated, befitting a man who entertained such eminent visitors as President Hayes, himself.

Today, the carriage house is the starting point for guided tours of Ramsey's mansion, which was willed to the Minnesota Historical Society by Ramsey's last descendants in 1964. Instead of sheltering horses and carriages, the carriage house now contains a television monitor where visitors can see a program about Ramsey's life and career, and a Victorian gift shop operated by Society staff. A costumed guide takes visitors on tours of the house, even allowing them to peek into the kitchen where Annie, the cook, is busy baking Victorian-era goodies. Special holiday programs make December a particularly popular month to visit the mansion, which is still furnished with the original family pieces — silent witnesses to the success of Minnesota's first prominent statesman.

■ HISTORIC FORT SNELLING
A Minnesota Historical Society Site
(At Highways 5 and 55, St. Paul)
Mailing Address: Fort Snelling History Center
St. Paul, MN 55111
Tel: (612) 726-9430
Hrs: May 1 - Oct. 31 (fort and visitors center)
Daily 10 a.m. - 5 p.m.
Visitors center hours vary in winter. Call ahead
There is an admission charge.

As the most remote United States fort in the northwest, Fort Snelling was a bustling center of law and commerce when it was built in 1820 upon the bluffs overlooking the Mississippi and Minnesota rivers. From behind the Fort's thick, limestone walls, the 5th Regiment of Infantry guarded U.S. interests, kept the peace, and protected the valuable fur trade. At the same time, representatives of the United States administered government policy to the Dakota and Ojibwa Indian tribes.

Now Fort Snelling has been restored to its original appearance and invites visitors to explore the history enacted within its walls. Historically dressed interpreters go about the everyday life of early 19th century fort inhabitants. Officers put the soldiers through their drills, while the blacksmith fashions and repairs tools in his nearby shop. Army wives complain about the living conditions, and the post surgeon mixes medicines in the hospital. Visitors, too, can participate in fort duties and chores such as shouldering muskets, patching clothes, or scraping hides. And after a tour of the fort, they can stop in the sutler's store to stock up on any frontier supplies they may be needing.

Skits and demonstrations are held regularly at the fort, as are special events. With its living history and restored buildings, Fort Snelling truly is a gateway to the past.

■JAMES J. HILL HOUSE
A Minnesota Historical Society Site
(On Summit Avenue, one-half block west of the St. Paul Cathedral)
Mailing Address: 240 Summit Ave.
St. Paul, MN 55102
Tel: (612) 297-2555
Hrs: Wed., Thur., Sat. 10 a.m. - 3:30 p.m.
There is an admission charge.

The Great Northern Railway was one of the keys to the early expansion of the United States and the settlement of the west. Its long, gleaming tracks tied the scattered towns together and bridged their isolation. And the man behind the success of the Great Northern was James J. Hill, the great "Empire Builder." Hill saw to it that his railroad had the flattest grades, the straightest track, the most powerful locomotives, and the longest trains. He was a man of superlatives, and when it came to building his mansion in St. Paul, he demanded the same degree of perfection and quality that he required from his railroad.

The James J. Hill House has 36,000 square feet, including 32 rooms, 13 bathrooms, 22 fireplaces, and a 100-foot reception hall. Built of sandstone in the Richardsonian Romanesque style, the house was constructed in 1891 from the plans of Boston architects Peabody and Stearns. With its carved woodwork, stained glass, and skylit art gallery; the house is a testimony to Hill's success, as well as being one of the most impressive residences ever constructed in the Midwest.

Visitors to the James J. Hill House can learn how the Hills lived and gain insight into the Victorian era in the Midwest — a time when fierce individualists like Hill made their fortunes from the shrinking frontier.

■ MINNESOTA STATE CAPITOL
A Minnesota Historical Society Site
(North of downtown St. Paul, off I-94 and 35E)
Mailing Address: Aurora and Constitution Avenues
          St. Paul, MN 55155
Tel: (612) 297-3521
     (612) 296-2881 (Group Tours)
Hrs: Mon. - Fri. 8:30 a.m. - 5 p.m.
     Sat. 10 a.m. - 4 p.m.
     Sun. 1 - 4 p.m.
There is no admission charge.

The Minnesota State Capitol, more than anything else, symbolized the start of a new age for the great Northwest. When construction of the massive granite and marble edifice began in 1896, Minnesota no longer was a frontier, but a growing, ambitious state eager to make its mark in the nation. It went without saying that the new capitol should be grander than any other of its kind.

Incorporating classical elements with Minnesota symbols and materials, St. Paul architect Cass Gilbert based the capitol structure on Italian Renaissance style, complete with terraces, balustrades, and steps made with grey granite from St. Cloud, MN, and a 223-foot marble dome. Adorning the building are works of nationally recognized artists of the time, such as Daniel

Chester French and Edward Potter. Their magnificent steel and copper sculpture group of a charioteer and two women leading a group of horses sits at the base of the dome, above the main entrance. Inside the capitol, the rotunda, the governor's reception room, the senate, and house and state supreme court chambers are decorated by commissioned paintings, sculptures, historic flags, gold leaf, and chandeliers.

Today, the capitol is open for visitors, who marvel at the art and soak up the atmosphere of the important political processes underway in its chambers. Guided tours are also available hourly.

H ISTORY CENTER

■ MINNESOTA HISTORICAL SOCIETY'S HISTORY CENTER
Capitol Complex Area
160 John Ireland Blvd.
St. Paul, MN 55102
Tel: (612) 296-6126 or (800) 657-3773

When it comes to state history, Minnesota is looking to the future. As in other states, there are many county and local organizations that provide information on the state's history through various programs and materials. What Minnesota has that other states do not, is a huge new History Center. Roughly equivalent in size to the State Capitol, the L-shaped building encompasses 420,000 gross square feet; the first level of the east-west leg is approximately the length of two football fields. The Minnesota History Center is located on the south edge of the State Capitol complex, across John Ireland Boulevard from the Cathedral of St. Paul, and overlooks downtown St. Paul.

The History Center is set to open its libraries and reference collections in summer of 1992, with autumn of 1992 marking the grand opening. The Minnesota Historical Society will have its new home here. The State Archives as well as the society's extensive library, manuscript, art, and artifact collections will be available to visitors through a centralized reference service. Easy access is also provided to audio-visual materials, newspaper, map, and book collections. More than 50 self-serve microfilm readers will be available for public use. Museum and exhibit space account for 40,000 square feet; the education wing is devoted to classrooms, lecture spaces, laboratories, and studios, including a hands-on area for children. One of the most exciting benefits for the public will be the opportunity to see state historical treasures which have been in storage for years. Three galleries on the upper floors of the

History Center are spacious enough to hold the larger artifacts from the society's collection.

The History Center will have an outdoor plaza for outdoor performances and programs, its own restaurant, and greatly-expanded museum shops. Please note that the opening dates are tentative, and that further information is available by calling the phone numbers listed above.

M USEUM

■ MINNESOTA MUSEUM OF ART
Landmark Center, Fifth at Market
Saint Paul, MN 55102-1486
Tel: (612) 292-4355 Tours (612) 292-4369
Hrs: (Gallery)
> Tue. - Fri. 10:30 a.m. - 4:30 p.m.
> Thur. 10:30 a.m. - 7:30 p.m.
> Sat., Sun. 1 p.m. - 4:30 p.m.
> (Jemne Building Galleries)
> Same as above, plus Sun. 11:30 a.m. - 4:30 p.m.

Minnesota Museum of Art (MMA) occupies two historic buildings in downtown St. Paul. The Art Deco-period Jemne Building, an example itself of fine American Art, is home to the museum's collections. The Museum School, MMA administrative offices, and additional galleries occupy the largest part of the Landmark Center, a Romanesque structure which used to be the old Federal Courts Building.

Beginning as an art school, this institution was incorporated in 1927 and began exhibiting works of art in 1939. In the 1940s the museum began its collection, which now numbers over 9,800 objects of art. The museum's primary focus is its commitment to American art, particularly artists of this region. Artwork of all media and all regions of the United States is featured in the permanent collection as well as special exhibitions, interpretive and educational programs. Featured in the Jemne Building are exhibitions of American art and that of selected non-Western cultures. Films and theater productions are held in the Jemne Building auditorium.

The Museum School in Landmark is where MMA carries out its original objective of art education. The staff consists primarily of working artists, who instruct adults and children in a variety of art programs. These include adult and youth weekend, after school, and summer workshops and programs. The Landmark Center Galleries feature special exhibitions and the Gallery 208 program — contemporary artists of the upper Midwest. The Minnesota Museum of Art offers its visitors an intimate atmosphere in which to enjoy art.

Admission to all MMA galleries is free, as are tours of galleries and special exhibitions. MMA visitors may also enjoy the Deco Restaurant in the Jemne Building — open for lunch and Sunday champagne brunch —and Landmarket: The Museum Store in Landmark Center.

M USEUM & THEATER

■ THE SCIENCE MUSEUM OF MINNESOTA AND THE WILLIAM L. MCKNIGHT OMNITHEATER
30 East Tenth Street
St. Paul, MN 55101
Tel: (612) 221-9488
Hrs: Tue. - Sat. 9:30 a.m. - 9 p.m.
       Sun. 11 a.m. - 9 p.m.
       Open Mon. Easter through Labor Day
Advance ticket sales are available
Visa and MasterCard are accepted.

The Science Museum of Minnesota has something of interest for each member of the family to see. With 40,000 square feet of exhibits, the museum is always fascinating, educational, and often surprising to visitors of all ages.

The almost one million visitors per year come to see such core exhibits as dinosaur skeletons in the Paleontology Hall; highlights of the landscape, flora, and fauna of Minnesota; interactive technology exhibits; and an exhibit on Hmong culture. The museum also offers changing special exhibits. Some of these have included "Across Antarctica," which covered the International Trans-Antarctic Expedition, co-headed by Minnesotan Will Steger; "Bears: Imagination and Reality," which featured 23 taxidermic mounts of grizzly and black bears; and "Gold!" which allowed visitors to pan for gold at a working sluice (and keep any gold flakes they found). The Science Museum also houses the spectacular Omnitheater, with its five-story domed screen. By surrounding visitors with both sight and sound, the Omnitheater gives special impact to its breathtaking and beautiful movies — movies such as "The Great Barrier Reef," "Tropical Rainforest," and "Ring of Fire."

In addition, the Science Museum of Minnesota is the oldest museum/live theater company in the country. Visitors have the chance to attend original one-act plays that highlight the history and science behind everyday life. Along with science demonstrations, such "hands-on" activities are the crowning touch to this museum that offers so many things to see and do. Visitors who come for an hour find themselves staying for the day.

NIGHTCLUB

■ BLUES SALOON
601 Western Ave.
St. Paul, MN 55103
Tel: (612) 228-9959

The Blues Saloon near downtown St. Paul has been called the best in the country by *Rolling Stone* Magazine. It is one of the five largest blues clubs in the United States and Europe. It has been in existence as a bar since 1890 and has seen a lot of talent and satisfied patrons pass through its doors over the years. Patrons are very loyal and return often just as the artists who perform are inclined to do. The Blues Saloon is located five minutes from downtown St. Paul and only 15 minutes from Minneapolis.

The Blues Saloon has gained a national reputation but is still a comfortable place for anyone to enjoy the entertainment. Customers of all types keep coming back, from professional to blue collar, young and old alike. The music is the common denominator for the varied crowd. *Working Woman* Magazine endorsed it as "One of the best blues places for professional women and for women to come alone." Not an easy reputation to earn in this day and age.

Artists such as James Cotton, Buddy Guy, Junior Walker, Junior Lockwood, and Etta James return again and again to entertain. The Blues Saloon is a favorite hangout for national artists when traveling through the area.

PERFORMING ARTS CENTER

■ ORDWAY MUSIC THEATRE
345 Washington Street
St. Paul, MN 55102
Tel: (612) 224-4222
Hrs: (Box office) Mon. - Sat 10 a.m. - 5:30 p.m., Sun. 11 a.m. - 3 p.m.
Visa, MasterCard, and AmEx are accepted.

When the Ordway Music Theatre opened its doors in January 1985, critics, concert-goers, and performers alike greeted the new building with unanimous acclaim. A graceful, yet vibrant structure of glass framed by bands of copper, the Ordway promised to become a respected, nationally renowned performing arts center.

Five years later, the Ordway hasn't disappointed anyone. The unusually intimate and elegant theater, located in the heart of downtown St. Paul, has featured such major Broadway performances as "West Side Story," "Les Miserables," "The Heidi Chronicles" (winner of the 1989 Tony Award for Best Play) and the whimsical, exceedingly popular musical "Cats" — winner of no less than seven Tony Awards, including Best Musical. But the Ordway doesn't limit itself to plays and musicals. The "Dance International" series presents an eclectic selection of top international dance talents, ranging from the world-renowned, classical Royal Winnipeg Ballet to the legendary Shanghai Acrobats, spellbinding the audience with their athletic skills. For Christmas, the Ordway presents traditional holiday specials, including The Dale Warland Singers, which has long enjoyed renown as America's top choir.

The Ordway prides itself on being accessible to all age groups. Children, in particular, are encouraged to attend. The theatre brings in more than 10,000 students grades 3-12 to view selected performances during the season and to absorb the world of performing arts. Architect Benjamin Thompson wanted the Ordway to be a "people place," and he appears to have succeeded.

R APTOR CENTER

■ THE RAPTOR CENTER
1920 Fitch Ave.
St. Paul, MN 55108
Tel: (612) 624-4745

The Raptor Center at the University of Minnesota is the largest medical facility in the world for the care and treatment of birds of prey (raptors) and other species of rare or endangered birds. The Raptor Center has recently moved into its new building, which features exhibits of live birds, educational displays, indoor flight pens, and medical facilities in which to treat the raptors. The treatment techniques used at the center have spread throughout the world to veterinarians. The objectives of the center are scientific investigation, rehabilitation, veterinary education, and public education.

Many of the raptors are brought to the center for treatment after injuries from migration and hunting seasons. Many others are injured by cars or by ingesting poisonous chemicals in their environment. Many of the trumpeter swans that developed lead poisoning were treated at the center. The center is part of the veterinary hospital at the University of Minnesota but has been able to incorporate exhibits, public events, and education into its mission. One of the more popular events is the release of raptors that have recovered. This event takes place each spring at the Minnesota Landscape Arboretum.

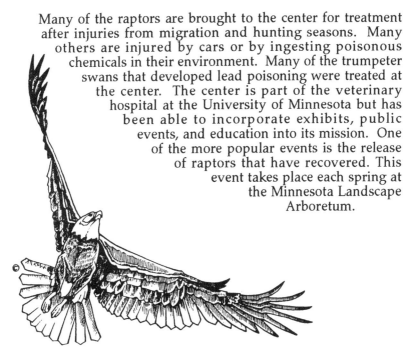

The Raptor Center is funded almost entirely by private contributions and grants from foundations. Donations combined with volunteers help in accomplishing the commitment of this center. Tours for large groups may be scheduled ahead of time or visitors may stop during the week and view the exhibits at their own pace. Donations of $1 per child or $2 per adult are requested, and a gift shop is available to purchase souvenirs.

∎R ESTAURANTS

∎ BOCA CHICA
11 S. Concord Street
St. Paul, MN 55107
Tel: (612) 222-8499
Hrs: Call ahead
All major credit cards are accepted.

For over a quarter of a century Boca Chica, "the little mouth," has been the dining pillar of St. Paul's Mexican community, centered on colorful Concord Street just across the Robert Street Bridge from downtown. Amidst the sounds of mariachi music and adobe-style decor, the casual neighborhood cafe serves the tacos, enchiladas, burritos, and tostadas — ala carte or on combination plates — that are the standby of border cooking. But their forte is the sampling of authentic dishes from the owners' heritage, such as green chile and nopales (cactus) specialties. Mexican beers and margaritas add to the fiesta atmosphere.

■ CAFE LATTE
850 Grand Ave.
St. Paul, MN 55105
Tel: (612) 224-5687
Hrs: Call ahead
AmEx is accepted.

Peter and Linda Quinn were furniture restorers whose fascination with things Victorian led them to undertake home renovations in this historic Crocus Hill neighborhood of St. Paul. Soon they found themselves in a mid-life career change and proud owners of Grand Avenue's most popular cafe. Cafe Latte is a San Francisco-style coffeehouse-cum-cafeteria whose tables are perpetually packed with everyone from couples courting on a budget, to socialites straining to see and be seen, to would-be poets composing their next sonnet over a caffe latte. That specialty coffee drink is *the* best seller, followed closely by espresso and flavored cappuccinos.

But the cafe's fame has been won with its line of delicious homemade desserts that range from a mile-high chocolate turtle cake to cheesecakes rich with fruit and berries. Rustic breads from the Quinns' bakery form the basis of Cafe Latte's sandwiches, augmented by pan-ethnic soups and salads. Scones fresh from the oven are another signature attraction.

■ CHEROKEE SIRLOIN ROOM
886 S. Smith Ave.
St. Paul, MN 55118
Tel: (612) 457-2729
Hrs: Call ahead
All major credit cards are accepted.

Here's where taxi drivers deliver their favorite customers when they beg these pros, "Take me where I can get a great steak." Three generations of Caspers oversee this casual supperclub, just across the High Bridge from the lights of downtown. To satisfy popular demand, the establishment has grown over the years from the original dark and cozy bar to a series of sprawling dining rooms featuring photos of old St. Paul. The decor is as homey as the service. Rick Casper, abetted by father, brothers, son and wife, greets and seats his patrons. He then, often as not, sends over an order of their tire-sized onion rings as a surprise to the birthday party or a bottle of wine for anniversary guests.

Rick recommends his unique 16 oz. top sirloin, but the filet and prime rib find their share of takers, too — as well as doggie bags to recycle the huge slab of beef in the morning. These days the heart-healthy salmon proves popular as well.

■ COSSETTA'S
211 W. Seventh Street
St. Paul, MN 55102
Tel: (612) 222-3476
Hrs: Call ahead

This mecca of Italian cooking grew from a hole-in-the-wall deli to its present location, just across the street, where striped awnings, Neapolitan ballads, and heroic aromas lure diners to the door. Once inside, it's a cafeteria set-up, showcasing everything from pepper salad to homemade lasagne and meatballs in Cossetta's lusty red sauce.

The other side of the grand staircase features a deli-grocery. Families live it up here, gazing at the vintage photos of old St. Paul as they line up at the pizza station, where the visuals get even better as pizza crusts fly like frisbees through the air. Fans also make a beeline after a concert at the nearby Civic Center when nothing but a fix of spaghetti will do.

■ DAKOTA BAR & GRILL
Bandana Square
1021 E. Bandana Blvd.
St. Paul, MN 55108
Tel: (612) 642-1442
Hrs: Call ahead
All major credit cards are accepted.

The turn-of-the-century bricks and beams of Bandana Square once framed a railroad roundhouse. Today people make tracks to the Dakota Bar & Grill within those historic quarters. But dated it's not: The Dakota boasts not only the best of local and national jazz musicians performing in the bar — often personal friends of owner/jazz buff Lowell Pickett — but also a nifty new flip on farm kitchen cooking.

Chef Ken Goff has won national acclaim for his celebration of Midwestern cooking (no lobster, no kiwifruit), showcased in creative combinations. Diners seek the courtyard's umbrella tables in the heat of summer, then migrate to the candlelit, tiered dining room once the air turns crisp. Goff's specialties include a

Minnesota Brie and apple soup, spinach salad topped with new potatoes and local goat cheese, and corn cakes gilded with wild mushrooms, among the appetizers. Entrees hit a new high with the likes of river trout with dill and crayfish, barbecued rabbit in plum sauce, and free-range chicken over homemade noodles.

■ FOREPAUGH'S
276 S. Exchange Street
St. Paul, MN 55102
Tel: (612) 224-5606
Hrs: Call ahead
Visa, MasterCard, and AmEx are accepted.

When Minnesota was a brand-new state back in the mid-1800s and its first governor, Alexander Ramsey, lived across the street, this elegant Victorian mansion was the belle of the neighborhood. Today the clapboard queen flaunts lacy curtains, gingerbread trimming, and period furnishings from its cozy, firelit lounge to a series of dining rooms.

This destination restaurant, complete with distinguished French chef and costumed staff, prides itself on its buttery escargot as well as a special way with fish and veal. Enjoy a libation on the open-air veranda facing Irvine Park with its vintage gazebo during the height of summer, or gaze on its Christmas card vista as winter rolls around.

■ LEEANN CHIN RESTAURANTS
Union Depot Place, Suite 120
214 E. Fourth Street
Saint Paul, MN 55101
Tel: (612) 224-1616

Leeann Chin grew up in a family in the grocery and restaurant business. When she immigrated to the United States in 1956, she brought with her the unique cooking techniques she learned in her native Canton, China. Beginning as a homemaker operating a sewing business from her home, she progressed to teaching cooking classes for friends and then at community schools. From there she began a catering business.

In 1980, Leeann opened her first restaurant in the Bonaventure Shopping Mall in Minnetonka. This restaurant and two others, located in the St. Paul Union Depot and Minneapolis International Centre, offer elegant dining in a contemporary, museum-like setting. The decor, made up of soft earth tones and natural textures, was chosen to highlight the Chinese artwork displayed in each restaurant. It also calls attention to the delicious food arranged on the marble-top buffet. Leeann Chin specializes in Cantonese and Szechuan cuisine, using fresh vegetables, lean meats, and seafood. The buffet-style presentation gives customers the opportunity to try several appetizers and entrees. In addition to the lunch and dinner buffet, Leeann Chin Carryout Chinese Cuisine offers the convenience of healthy carryout food for home or the office. There are ten carryout/eat-in locations in the Twin Cities area, many of which offer delivery service. In the summer, the sidewalk cafes at the Kenwood and Milton Mall locations are quite popular.

Leeann Chin Restaurants came to be known as the Twin Cities' premier Chinese restaurants by serving excellent Chinese cuisine at affordable prices. As well as the restaurants and carryout locations, Leeann Chin's famous appetizers are available in Party Starters portions. For large-scale occasions, the Leeann Chin Catering and Conference Center is located at Union Depot Place in St. Paul.

■ MUFFULETTA
2260 Como Ave.
St. Paul, MN 55108
Tel: (612) 644-9116
Hrs: Call ahead
Visa, MasterCard, and AmEx are accepted.

Muffuletta is the kind of dining find every neighborhood deserves, but few are lucky enough to achieve. A dowager house in the St. Anthony Park neighborhood favored by the University's faculty has been converted into a series of clean, bright dining nooks that boast an equally fresh and sunny menu.

Homemade pasta is the specialty here, along with a bounteous spinach salad, fresh catch of the day, and its namesake, the foot-long Muffuletta sandwich. Summertime the umbrella-clad deck is standing room only, as is the line at Sunday brunch.

■ TABLE OF CONTENTS
1648 Grand Ave.
St. Paul, MN 55105
Tel: (612) 699-6595
Hrs: Call ahead

Table of Contents sits in front of the Hungry Mind, a popular bookstore on the Macalester College campus. The hankie-size restaurant, whose stark white walls are hung with avant--garde works by local artists, boasts a menu as sophisticated as its setting. Talented young chef Scot Johnson's trick is to keep his list short and sweet — pork, chicken, and seafood that gain their verve from inspired sauces with an international flavor. His wafer-crust pizza is always in demand, as are the homemade ice creams and sorbets. No reservations are taken, but that doesn't daunt the long line-up of campus professors and socialites from nearby Summit Avenue.

S PECIALTY SHOP

■ COAT OF MANY COLORS
1666 Grand Ave.
St. Paul, MN 55105
Tel: (612) 690-5255
Hrs: Mon. - Fri. 10 a.m. - 8 p.m., Sat. 10 a.m. - 5:30 p.m., Sun. noon - 5 p.m.
Visa, MasterCard, and AmEx are accepted.

Providing a feast for the eyes and food for thought, Coat of Many Colors ethnic store turns shopping into something out of the ordinary. Proprietors Terry and Mabel Nichols founded the store after a trip to Guatemala where they admired the beautiful handiwork. They vowed to market Guatemalan and other Third World hand-crafts in the United States and donate a portion of the profits to Third World development.

Coat of Many Colors specializes in apparel made from natural fabrics such as all-cotton clothing from Ecuador, Guatemala, and India. It also offers rayon clothing from Indonesia and a large selection of ethnic style jewelry and unusual hand-made gift items such as baskets from Africa, and masks and bells from Sri Lanka.

The Nichols pride themselves on the store's peaceful atmosphere. Whether customers have come to buy or just to browse, they'll find a visit to Coat of Many Colors is a fascinating and relaxing way to pass the time.

Z OO & GIFT SHOP

■ COMO ZOO
Midway Park and Kaufman Drive
St. Paul, MN 55103
Tel: (612) 488-5571
Hrs: (Apr. 1 - Sept. 30) 8 a.m. - 8 p.m. grounds
        10 a.m. - 6 p.m. buildings
        Oct. 1 - March 31) 8 a.m. - 5 p.m. grounds
        10 a.m. - 4 p.m. Buildings

Como Park Zoo has been the pride of St. Paul since 1897 with its winding graveled paths and beautiful gardens. It is currently one of the only zoos in the nation located in the center of a major metropolitan area. Much of the construction done at the zoo was part of a Works Progress Administration (WPA) project of the 1930s. The bear grotto, monkey island, barn, and main zoo were built due to the WPA. This zoo is a favorite of the metro area as well as visitors from around the state. The goals of the zoo are to recreate the animals' environment; educate visitors on and off the grounds; aid in conservation measures; and conduct ongoing scientific studies to better serve the animal kingdom. Como Zoo is also one of the few zoos that does not charge an admission or parking fee.

The first major exhibit building to open was the Large Cat Building. The building has four major exhibits: Siberian tigers; African lions, cougars, and snow leopards. Due to the weather in Minnesota, the cats are housed indoors during the cooler months but are at home in outdoor exhibits during the summer. The Aquatic Animal Building opened in 1982 and consists of polar bears, harbor seals, penguins, sea lions, alligators, sea birds, and freshwater fish. Sparky, the resident sea lion, entertains visitors with performances throughout the summer. Sparky's show has been a tradition for more than 30 years. Seal Island and the Land and Water Bird Exhibit are also major attractions to the zoo.

The Primate Building is entertaining with its array of gorillas, orangutans, and various other primates. During the warm weather the apes can be observed in their own community where they climb, swing, and play. The African Hoofed Stock Facility houses even more exotic animals. The Como Zoological Society raised funds to obtain three reticulated giraffes, three sable antelope, and three greater kudu antelope. The Como Zoo holds fun and entertainment for all who visit.

Scandia

Not surprisingly, this community of 3,200 is known for its Scandinavian — specifically Swedish — heritage. It was home to the first Swedish settlers in Minnesota, who carved out a piece of land in 1850 on the shores of Hay Lake. This scenic town on the rugged St. Croix River still proudly maintains the memory of those early pioneers. The impressive outdoor museum *Gammelgården* boasts a 22-foot *monument* commemorating the Swedes' arrival, along with a selection of log buildings, handmade tools, and treasured items brought from Sweden in the late 1800s.

The focal point of the fascinating collection of buildings is the *gammelkyrkan* (old church) from 1856, the oldest Lutheran church building in Minnesota. Nearby stands the former *Hay Lake School,* now a one-room school museum, along with the 1868 *Johannes Erickson Log House Museum* with a complete reconstruction of a Swedish immigrant home. Gammelgården museum also features a gift shop with Swedish imports, local handicrafts, and Minnesota products, and is open to the public for guided tours on Saturdays and Sundays from May through November. A lesser-known historical attraction is a nearby, old *Swedish farm* lovingly restored and open for tours.

For more information on Scandia, contact:
WASHINGTON COUNTY HISTORICAL SOCIETY
P.O. Box 123
Scandia, MN 55073
(612) 433-5972

R ESTAURANT

■ MEISTERS BAR & GRILL
Downtown
14808 Oakhill Road
Scandia, MN 55073
Tel: (612) 433-5230
Hrs: Mon. - Sat. 9 a.m. - 1 a.m.
Sun. noon - 9 p.m.
Closed Sundays from Nov. through May

Meisters Bar & Grill in Scandia forms the heart of the local community in more ways than one. For more than 30 years, the locals have gathered every morning at Meisters for a quiet cup of coffee and a bite to eat, or for a drink on a warm summer night. But the Meister family also started the annual event that transforms sleepy Scandia: "Taco Daze" — a day of parades, games, and dances held on the Saturday after Labor Day

For most of the year, however, Meisters Bar & Grill simply serves some of the best homemade cooking around. The restaurant is known for its Meisterburgers — hefty, juicy portions of hamburger on sesame seed buns or with colby cheese — and for its vast selection of sandwiches. How about chopped steak or breaded veal and cheese on a toasted bun, or liver and onion on rye bread for something different? The restaurant serves a complete dinner menu of smoked pork ribs, choice T-bone steaks, chopped sirloin, hamburger steak, grilled ham, breaded cod, or shrimp served with homemade tartar sauce. Pints of homemade dressings are also available for take-out. The restaurant is located in the midst of scenic Minnesota farm country, so on a sunny day visitors at Meisters can eat their meals on the tables set up outside — and even take a walk in the nearby woods after dinner.

Shakopee

The entertainment center of Minnesota, Shakopee attracts more than three and a half million visitors each year eager to explore the popular amusement parks, horse racing, and family events. But Shakopee has not lost its soul to the entertainment industry, instead maintaining a strong, small-town community feeling, as well as an industrial area with companies such as Anchor Glass Container, Toro Company, and Conklin Company; and nature areas and historical sites. Residents cherish their heritage as a Minnesota River frontier town, once the site of a Dakota Indian village. In fact, the city was named after the chief of the Dakota band that originally lived in the area southwest of current-day Minneapolis, although the Indians eventually moved a few miles up the river following a treaty between the tribe and the U.S. government. In August 1862, the young town became the site of the last great Indian War in the state, when the U.S. government neglected its treaty obligations and delayed the distribution of supplies and payments to the Dakota Tribe. In succeeding years, Shakopee experienced the ups and downs of a frontier community, including grasshopper plagues and droughts decimating the crops, and the distinction of building the first bridge across the Minnesota River. Eventually, a railroad connected the city with nearby Mendota.

ATTRACTIONS

Today, people no longer arrive in Shakopee by way of the railroad, but rather by car on one of the major freeways intersecting the city. A large portion of these visitors heads for one of the major attractions in the Twin Cities area — the thoroughbred, quarterhorse, and standardbred harness racing at *Canterbury Downs Race Track.* Minnesota's only horse racing track, Canterbury Downs features paramutuel betting, food, and drinks in a crowded, fun-filled atmosphere. Racing of a different caliber takes place at *Raceway Park,* an asphalt, quarter-mile track with figure-eight and Nascar late model stock cars. Another attraction filled with speed and excitement is *Valleyfair Family Amusement Park,* an old-fashioned entertainment park with stomach-wrenching rides, an abundance of food, an authentic 1925 carousel, water rides, antique trolley, and arcade games to suit any taste and budget. For those looking for a more quiet outing, *Creative River Tours* offer relaxing cruises along the Minnesota River. During most of the 45-minute cruise, the boat Emma Lee chugs lazily through the beauty of the *Minnesota Valley National Wildlife Refuge* while the crew provides a narrative of the area's history and wildlife. The cruise originates at *Murphy's Landing,* an outstanding 19th century living history museum featuring original log buildings, costumed interpreters performing the daily activities of a settler village, horse-drawn trolleys, and a well-stocked gift shop.

EVENTS

Murphy's Landing is the site of one of the city's first major events, the *Annual Eagle Creek Rendezvous* on Memorial Day Weekend, reenacting the annual meeting between fur traders and Indians with an encampment of tents and tepees, games, and contests. Later in the summer, the *Storytelling Festival* features historical tales and stories. Some of the other annual events held at Murphy's Landing include the *Laura Ingalls Wilder Day* in July, the *Festival of Herbs* in early August and *Candlelight Evening* in October, featuring the usual evening activities performed by pioneers at night. Entertainment of a more modern style takes place at Valleyfair, where bands perform every day during the summer in the *Amphitheater* or on one of the other stages. The most popular event in Shakopee, however, is the *Minnesota Renaissance Festival,* held seven weekends and Labor Day from late August through the end of September. The festival venue is an entire reconstructed medieval village, complete with shops selling crafts, souvenirs, and foods; hundreds of costumed interpreters roaming the streets recreating the somewhat rowdy atmosphere of 16th-century England; seven stages offering continuous song, dance, pantomime, and other entertainment; and thrilling, swashbuckling equestrian events, including a spirited jousting competition.

For more information on Shakopee, contact:
SHAKOPEE CONVENTION AND VISITORS BUREAU
P.O. Box 203
Shakopee, MN 55379
(612) 445-1660

FESTIVAL

■ MINNESOTA RENAISSANCE FESTIVAL
3525 145th Street W.
Shakopee, MN 56379
Tel: (612) 445-7361
Hrs: Weekends mid-August - September and on Labor Day
Visa and MasterCard are accepted for advance telephone orders.

Every year for a delightful one-and-a-half months, the Renaissance comes alive in this small town. A 22-acre wooded lot four miles south of Shakopee on Highway 169 is transformed into an entire village evoking the 1600s, complete with craft shops and cafés. Performers dressed in time-authentic garb mingle with visitors, providing a unique look into life in Europe 400 years ago.

When visitors enter the Renaissance Festival grounds, they can take their pick among the seven stages offering continuous entertainment. Here they see performances popular in the 1600s, such as juggling and magic acts. On other stages comedians, jesters, mimes, and dancers perform. In addition to stage acts, the festival has a specific entertainment theme each weekend, such as "A Royal Family Affair" when a new queen is crowned. Another weekend is dubbed a "Sporting Holiday" and features such events as elephant races and a tug of war. Don't miss the armored jousting event — for many, it is the highlight of the visit. For the kids, meanwhile, the Festival offers a children's area where children can build a sand castle, color, or do mixed media artwork. The older and more adventurous can even ride an elephant; or take the animal carousel, round-abouts, or "kids-in-a-boat" ride.

After watching the entertainment, browse through the craft shops displaying the wares of more than 240 artisans. Here, chances are, visitors will find just the right gift. And then, finally, there's the food. After all the walking on the festival grounds, visitors can eat their way through more than 120 uncommon foods, such as spinach pie, turkey drumsticks, and Scotch eggs.

GOLF COURSE

■ STONEBROOKE
2693 County Road 79
Shakopee, MN 55379
Tel: (612) 496-3171
Hrs: 7 a.m. to dark
Visa and MasterCard are accepted.

"Before there was golf, nature was creating Stonebrooke." Stonebrooke was literally built around the existing landscape. The layout of the land was preserved when designing and building this course. The trees that line the course are very old and majestic and the most spectacular feature is Lake O'Dowd. This lake was incorporated right into the golf course on the seventh and eighth holes.

A ferry boat carries golfing parties across the lake to their second shot on the eighth hole. The skipper and his first mate load up the golf carts and clubs while golfers sit back and enjoy a leisurely cruise across the lake with a favorite beverage. Another interesting feature of the course is the cattail marsh that creates both an interesting enhancement to the course as well as a test of the golfer's ingenuity. The course itself is in immaculate condition, the "bent grass" greens are large and very undulated. The staff is proud of the surroundings and genuinely enjoys working with visitors. All of these factors work together to make Stonebrooke one of the finest courses in the state. Challenging and breathtakingly beautiful, Stonebrooke must be played to be fully appreciated.

L IVING HISTORY MUSEUM

■ HISTORIC MURPHY'S LANDING
2187 Highway 101 E.
Shakopee, MN 55379
Tel: (612) 220-3988
Hrs: Hours vary according to season and events. Call ahead for information
Visa is accepted.

Murphy's Landing was once a haven for travelers; a place of rest for weary settlers, a stepping stone to the great and unchartered frontier for explorers and fur traders. It was a modest little inn along the Minnesota River Valley from which R.G. Murphy operated a ferry boat crossing.

Today, Murphy's Landing is once again alive with the sights and sounds of the 19th century. The Landing, now a living history museum, portrays settlers' lives from 1840 to 1890 for the enjoyment of a new generation of travelers. Along the streets and in the homes, costumed interpreters recreate the everyday life of townspeople busily going about their chores, yet they all have time to stop and chat with visitors and share anecdotes about life in a riverfront community.

Along with family homes, visitors will also find community-oriented buildings scattered throughout the town. Visit the one-room school house, which depicts education in the late 19th century. Or stop by the church and imagine the sound of reverent voices raised in song. Outside, the mouth-watering smell of traditional food cooking on wood stoves tempts visitors to enjoy a snack or a leisurely meal at Murphy's Fine Foods Restaurant. Chances are by then they have lost track of time and have become immersed in the daily life of the settlers — a time and place when life was simple, yet demanding and uncompromising.

Stillwater

The residents of Stillwater don't feel a great need to visit Europe to see the Old World; they already live in their own little piece of it. The state's first town and the birthplace of Minnesota Territory in 1849, Stillwater climbs the hills above scenic St. Croix River in much the way a German town would perch above the Rhine. The city landscape is dotted with old-fashioned church spires and Victorian and Greek Revival homes, transversed by narrow streets that wind their way from the riverfront to the tree-studded hillcrest above. Along with the neighboring St. Croix River communities of Marine on St. Croix, Oak Park Heights, Bayport and Lake Elmo, Stillwater has scrupulously maintained its historical roots, celebrating its heritage as a lumber boom town while at the same time developing into the vibrant, modern city of 13,000 it is today. The Andersen Corporation is one of the area's largest employers, producing windows and patio doors.

ATTRACTIONS

Once, thousands of logs were floated down the St. Croix to the mills of Stillwater, but today fishermen and canoeists frequent the river instead, either on a short jaunt or on a challenging excursion along the *St. Croix River Canoe Route* from *William O'Brien State Park* north of town all the way south to the St. Croix's junction with the mighty Mississippi. Another craft that makes its home on the St. Croix is the *Andiamo Showboat*, which offers dinner cruises accompanied by music and entertainment. Other historical excursions are offered through the fascinating *Joseph Wolf Brewery Caves* — beer-storage caves hand-dug in the early 1840s — and by the *Minnesota Zephyr*, an elegant dining train from the 1940s that makes a romantic three-hour journey north along the St. Croix River Valley. (Visitors who can't get enough of dining in a traditional railway environment are known to pick the *Freighthouse Restaurant*, located in the historic rail depot, for their next meal.) Fine dining and unique shopping are, in fact, two of the main attractions of Stillwater, and the ideal places to start hunting for that special gift or dinner are in the shops and restaurants of *The Brick Alley* building in downtown Stillwater or the *Grand Garage* on Main Street. Among the profusion of shops and restaurants, however, some stand out particularly. *Brine's*, housed in an historic 124-year-old building on Main Street, is a family-operated meat market, deli, bakery, restaurant, and bar — all on three different floors in the same building, and all excellent. *Sherstad Woods*, also on Main Street, specializes in custom woodwork and in unique, handmade wooden fruits, cypress clocks, plant stands, and more. Finally, *Northern Vineyard* on Main Street, three blocks north of the bridge, sells wines produced and bottled by Minnesota wineries. In downtown Stillwater, a majority of the stores are located in historical buildings; but there are other, notable historic sites, including the *Washington County Historic Courthouse* — an imposing Italianate structure from 1867, and the *Warden's House Museum* — the 1853 home of 11 wardens who administered the first territorial prison in the Northwest. Today, the warden's house features a large collection of pioneer artifacts. Visitors can explore other historical buildings on a *Rivertown Restoration Walking Tour* of downtown Stillwater, either by following the *Stillwater Walking Tour* Brochure or participating in a guided tour held each September.

EVENTS

The area's heritage is celebrated during *Lumberjack Days*, Stillwater's largest community festival featuring log rolling, a waterski show, and music during the last week of July. At the *Rivertown Art Fair* during the third weekend in May and the *Fall Colors Art Fair* during the first weekend in October, visitors and residents can browse in a wide selection of arts and crafts booths in Lowell Park. Also in Lowell Park, area restaurants offer samples of their finest concoctions during the *Taste of the St. Croix Valley*, held the second weekend in June. In August, Twin Cities musicians occupy the park every Wednesday evening during the popular *Music on the Waterfront* series. The year's events are capped by the *Victorian Christmas* celebration, when residents decorate the downtown area and carolers and horse-drawn cutters frequent the streets.

For more information on Stillwater, contact:
STILLWATER AREA CHAMBER OF COMMERCE
423 S. Main Street
Stillwater, MN 55082
(612) 439-7700

ANTIQUES

■ THE MILL ANTIQUES
410 N. Main Street
Stillwater, MN 55082
Tel: (612) 430-1816
Hrs: Mon. - Thur. 10 a.m. - 5 p.m., Fri. 10 a.m. - 7 p.m.
      Sat. 10 a.m. - 5 p.m., Sun. 11 a.m. - 5 p.m.
Visa and MasterCard are accepted.

A towering 80-foot stone smokestack identifies the home of The Mill Antiques and leads visitors to investigate. The building was constructed in 1869 by pioneer Isaac Staples as a sawmill and manufacturing company, and is one of the oldest structures in the community. Inside are massive stone walls, high ceilings, and rough sawed lumber. The antique store is the largest of three buildings located within the Isaac Staples Sawmill Complex, which is listed on the National Register of Historic Places.

Established in 1982 as an antique sales and showroom, the multi-level building now boasts over 18,000 square feet of space with 80 dealers displaying their antiques in this historic setting. It contains quality period furniture and collectibles such as glassware, lamps, dinnerware, silver, and jewelry of the highest quality; all reasonably priced. Other merchandise includes vintage clothing, linens, textiles, and kitchenware. A wide assortment of collector's plates, stoneware, toys, fine prints, advertising, and paper Americana are featured. A country store inside the building offers both old and new collectible merchandise and gift items. A new addition to the building features refinished and "as is" condition furniture items, including a wide selection of primitive and Victorian to Scandinavian pine furniture. A complete furniture and lamp restoration shop with replacement parts, refinishing supplies, and rewiring is available; along with appraisals, estate sales, and other related services.

For one of the largest antique selections in the St. Croix Valley, don't miss The Mill Antiques.

■ MORE ANTIQUES
312 N. Main Street
Stillwater, MN 55082
Tel: (612) 439-1110
Hrs: Mon. - Sat. 10 a.m. - 5 p.m., Sun. 11 a.m. - 5 p.m.

For an excellent choice of fine furniture and functional antiques and memorabilia, More Antiques is the place to visit. Owner Everist Speltz has been in the antique business for 35 years, representing more than 15 of Stillwater's finest dealers. This is a browser's and collector's paradise.

Located on the north end of Main Street, downtown historic Stillwater, this spacious antique shop has over 6,000 square feet of phenomenal antiques and collectibles very well displayed, all on one floor. The wide aisles are exceptionally appealing for the handicapped and elderly for a more relaxed shopping experience. One can find large selections of primitive, country, folk art, Hummels, Scandinavian pieces, posters, cards, antique jewelry, and old magazines all in neat categories and appropriately labeled. A player piano, country store coffee grinder, double hoosier counter cabinet, Victorian lamps, 1894 bicycle, marble-top dressers, Victorian living room sets, turn-of-the-century oak, and other fine furniture are just a few of the many items that can be found. Pottery, depression glass, cut glass, Red Wing stoneware, beer steins, 1840 and 1890 porcelain china, sterling silver and silverplated pieces, and many more items make More Antiques a one-stop store. Packing and shipping services are available.

■ MULBERRY POINT ANTIQUES
270 N. Main Street
Stillwater, MN 55082
Tel: (612) 430-3630
Hrs: Daily, extended hours in summer
Visa, MasterCard, and Discover are accepted.

A 1929 warehouse is the home of Mulberry Point Antiques — and more than 16,000 square feet and four levels of 60 reputable antique dealers. Special care is taken to make sure that customers enjoy the unique store displays, each cleverly sectioned off by attractive functional furniture arrangements.

All pieces are authentic and no reproductions are accepted for display. There is a wonderful selection of crocheted and woven bedspreads, handmade rugs, an Indian quilt, and other linens. There are wicker baskets, hanging chandeliers, glass lamp shades, Red Wing crocks, early china pieces, and many other household items. The selection of beautiful collectibles, silver, flatware, vintage clothing, children's toys, and antique jewelry is endless.

The "Rough Room" offers furniture and other items to be refinished at very good bargains for someone with a knack in restoring. There is something for everyone here and something that will fit every budget. There are several dealers in the shop to assist customers, and shipping arrangements can be made.

It is a visual and textural delight to walk through the floors of yesterday at Mulberry Point Antiques. Allow plenty of time to browse and enjoy strolling through one floor to another.

■ SOUTH MAIN MERCANTILE
125 S. Main Street
Stillwater, MN 55082
Tel: (612) 439-1223
Hrs: Mon. - Sat. 10 a.m. - 5 p.m., Sun. noon - 5 p.m.
Visa, MasterCard, AmEx, and Discover are accepted.

South Main Mercantile has brought an unusual array of antiques to downtown historic Stillwater. Located in a building originally built in 1887, this charming antique shop is filled with an unbelievable selection.

The shop specializes in Victorian, primitive, and oak furniture. Local dealers obtain merchandise that is unique and unusual. Architectural antiques include doors, frames, and mantles. Other individual items include 1849 and 1902 quilts, 19th century Italian game table, Victorian corner chair, marble top Victorian tables, Haviland china, a beautiful oriental teak woodcarved jewelry box, vintage clothing, and new and old hardware. The shop also carries a fine selection of chandeliers and lamps, linens, dishes, stoneware, old trunks and clocks, tapestry, old and new rag rugs, outdoor wrought-iron furniture, postcards, and many old books and magazines. Customers will be impressed by the clear markings on the merchandise providing a history of the item, dates, and price.

A RABIAN HORSE FACILITY

■ HORSESHOE LAKE ARABIANS
13600 Hudson Blvd.
Stillwater, MN 55082
Tel: (612) 436-7551
Hrs: Mon. - Sat. 10 a.m. - 3 p.m., Sun. by appointment

Close to the St. Croix River Valley, southeast of historic Stillwater, Paul and Ann Emerson have been raising and breeding

Arabian horses for more than 25 years. They began with Shetland and Welsh ponies purchased for their three young children in 1955. After ten years of raising quarterhorses and Palominos in addition to the ponies, the Emersons decided to make a commitment to breeding Arabians.

Horseshoe Lake Arabians has been established for about seven years on a beautiful 350-acre farm just off of I-94 between the Twin Cities and Stillwater. It is a nationally known Arabian horse breeding, training, and sales facility where visitors are welcome to drop in for a tour. The sizable establishment includes a 44-stall barn, one 12-stall barn, six pastures, five runs, an outdoor arena, a large indoor arena, and an outdoor work ring. Expansion plans include additional paddocks and possibly a racetrack. Approximately 75 horses are on hand at any given time at the farm. Visitors may view horse training sessions and a video presentation. The Emersons are happy to share the experience they have gained through breeding and showing quality horses. Riding lessons and seminars with topics ranging from basic horse care to specific riding techniques have not only served to educate

new clients, but have also brought new people into the Arabian horse business. The Horseshoe Lake Arabians have outstanding success in competitions. From spring to fall, horses are shown two and three times a month.

Through the combination of hard work, good stock, and commitment to the Arabian horse; the Emersons have made Horseshoe Lake Arabians the successful breeding and marketing venture it is today, with sales around the country as well as overseas. In spite of their busy schedule, they also find time to operate a land development business and collect antique cars.

ART GALLERY

■ KELLEY FRAME AND FINE ART GALLERY
312 S. Main Street
Stillwater, MN 55082
Tel: (612) 439-6246

Additional Location:
783 Radio Drive
Suite 117
Woodbury, MN 55125
Tel: (612) 738-7776
Hrs: Mon., Tue. 10 a.m. - 6 p.m., Wed. - Fri. 10 a.m. - 8 p.m.
　　Sat. 9 a.m. - 6 p.m., Sun. noon - 5 p.m.
Visa, MasterCard, and AmEx are accepted.

Located in historic downtown Stillwater, the Kelley Gallery features excellent service and quality artwork and prints. This family-owned business was established in 1984 and specializes in wildlife art. Recently, wildlife artist Rick Kelley's painting "Common Golden Eye" was selected as the 1989-1990 winner of the Wisconsin Duck Stamp Competition. He was also named the 1990 National Eagle Conservation Print Artist of the Year with his prize-winning entry, "Soaring the Peaks," a painting depicting two bald eagles.

The gallery houses a colorful selection of original paintings, posters, serigraphs, lithographs, as well as limited editions, creatively framed and displayed on the wood paneled walls. Artists include Bateman, Doolittle, Brenders, Redlin, Smith, Kelley, Jarvi, Isaac, Olson, Asaro, Hatfield, Roman, and Plasschaert. There is also an excellent selection of porcelain, bronze, and wood sculptures, along with limited-edition plates. Experienced staff provide consultation services, as well as unique framing ideas at competitive prices. The gallery has special showings of different artists throughout the year. Out-of-state shipping is also available.

Kelley Frame and Fine Art Gallery offers a wide range of artistic styles by highly acclaimed artists. Whether visitors are purchasing fine art or framing their own creations, Kelley Gallery will help them reflect the personality and value of their investment.

BED & BREAKFASTS

■ASA PARKER HOUSE
17500 St. Croix Trail N.
Marine on St. Croix, MN 55047
Tel: (614) 433-5248
Visa and MasterCard are accepted.
No smoking and no pets allowed.

Just on the outskirts of William O'Brien State Park nestles the Asa Parker House, a restored lumber baron's home and now a four-star bed and breakfast. Built in 1856, the house overlooks the spectacular St. Croix River Valley and offers guests a choice of five individually decorated rooms.

Each room has its own, charming ambiance and is named after an historic person who actually lived in Marine on St. Croix. The three-room Alice O'Brien suite even has a whirlpool bath and a large, private flower-filled deck. Innkeeper Marjorie Bush

brightens the rooms with her own arrangements of fresh and dried flowers and serves her guests a three-course breakfast served on antique china and Bavarian crystal. Her outstanding breakfasts earned Marjorie an entry representing Minnesota in *Better Homes and Gardens.* The *Chicago Tribune* travel section has recognized her culinary talents, rating her hospitality and cooking the best in the Midwest. After breakfast, explore the paved bike and walking paths, and cross-country ski trails at the nearby William O'Brien State Park or join other guests in a game of croquet or tennis on the Parker grounds. Guests also can stroll through the historic village of Marine on St. Croix, admire the vintage homes and shops, or take a ten-minute drive to Stillwater.

A stay at the Asa Parker House is definitely a one-of-a-kind vacation. When guests step inside this stately, romantic bed and breakfast, they feel they have entered a quieter, gentler era.

■ THE RIVERTOWN INN

306 W. Olive
Stillwater, MN 55082
Tel: (612) 430-2955
Visa and MasterCard are accepted.

The Rivertown Inn, Stillwater's oldest bed and breakfast, overlooks the picturesque St. Croix River. John O'Brien, a prominent lumberman, built this large three-story mansion in 1882 for his family. Many of the family's pictures and portraits still adorn the walls and hallways of the Inn. The Rivertown Inn transports guests and passers-by to the 1800s and the tradition of the old lumbering days and era of horse-drawn carriages.

Looking through the Rivertown Inn, one can appreciate the quality of the gracious furnishings and nostalgic atmosphere. Guest rooms are impeccably designed and decorated with special charm. The John O'Brien room is a true tribute to the Inn's past, surrounded by elegant woodwork, private whirlpool and fireplace. Faith's room, also known as the Inn's bridal suite, features an 11-foot high walnut canopy bed, marble top dresser, fireplace, and whirlpool. Each room is named after a person who might have lived in it.

Breakfast usually begins with a fresh fruit cup. The owner, Chuck Dougherty, has won the Bed and Breakfast Conference's "Best Fruit Muffin" contest with his apple muffin. The Doughertys utilize their extensive baking skills to prepare the most exquisite breakfasts for their guests. Homemade pastries, breads, and delectable entrees await guests in the morning and are served in the Inn's dining room or the screened porch, weather

permitting. A short walk from the Inn brings guests and visitors to downtown Stillwater where there are countless antique stores, specialty shops, and other historic buildings. The St. Croix River provides for an array of outdoor activities and excellent swimming, boating, and picnicking.

Step into the Victorian ambience of the Rivertown Inn and leave modern-day stress behind. The Rivertown Inn is undoubtedly an elegant historic experience that guests will cherish.

COUNTRY INN

■THE OUTING LODGE AT PINE POINT
11661 Myeron Road
Stillwater, MN 55082
Tel: (612) 439-9747
Hrs: Bed and breakfast, Fri. - Sun. Business conferences, Mon. - Fri.
   (Weekday bed and breakfast guests accommodated on short notice if no business conferences are booked.
Visa and MasterCard are accepted.

Imagine a stately European country home or chateau of the 18th century, surrounded by lawns and gardens, and 300 acres of wooded walking paths. A place where people would go to get away from the city and enjoy an "outing" in the country. The Outing Lodge at Pine Point provides that perfect atmosphere for an intimate dinner or formal meeting or banquet.

The decorating style at the Outing Lodge is a combination of Georgian, early American, and Louis XV. The emphasis is on the warm and cozy relaxed country atmosphere. All of the nine private suites are spacious and quiet, some with attached sunporches. A continental breakfast is brought to each guest room in the morning; or by special arrangements an elegant champagne breakfast with pan-fried brook trout can be served. Overnight guests and groups can dine by candlelight in front of one of the seven-foot wide fireplaces. The Outing is well-known for its special dinner offered monthly, "Babette's Feast," a memorable seven-course French meal recreated from the Academy Award-winning Danish film by the same name. The Lodge is a departure point for outings. The well-kept grounds offer a serene atmosphere for a quiet, contemplative walk. A typical Sunday afternoon might feature croquet on the lawn in the English style. The peaceful and unique surroundings are stimulating for meetings and creative work sessions. A meeting planner assists customers to design the meal, lodging, and meeting program to best suit their needs. Complete catering services are available for

weddings, receptions, and other special occasions.

The Outing Lodge has a special character that inspires fresh approaches to problems and stimulates new ideas and attitudes. It offers receptive guests the added opportunity to recreate for themselves the experience of life as it was in the great country homes of Europe.

GLASS GALLERY & GIFTS

■ GLASSPECTACLE
402 Main Street
Stillwater, MN 55082
Tel: (612) 439-0757
Hrs: Mon. - Sat. 10 a.m. - 5 p.m.
    Sun. noon - 5 p.m.
Visa and MasterCard are accepted.

While in Stillwater, be sure to visit the Glasspectacle — the only gallery in the area specializing in hand-blown glass. Beautiful glass work is displayed in a comfortable, informal atmosphere.

Visitors will be fascinated by the wide spectrum of colors, styles, techniques, and forms of contemporary glass art. From sculpture and vases to lamps and goblets, from marbles and paperweights to perfume bottles and jewelry, the Glasspectacle has it all. The store features a host of U.S. glass artists ranging from the famous to the soon-to-be-famous, and also includes a stained glass studio. The studio's artists specialize in custom-designed as well as traditional stained glass windows, lamps, door inserts, and other works of art.

Whether customers are serious collectors, just looking for a unique decorating accessory, or seeking a beautiful and unusual gift item, the Glasspectacle is the place to see.

HISTORIC HOTEL

■ LOWELL INN
102 N. Second Street
Stillwater, MN 55082
Tel: (612) 439-1100
MasterCard and Visa are accepted.

A Williamsburg-style country inn located in historic Stillwater opened its doors in 1927 and was managed by Arthur Sr. and Nelle Palmer since 1930. They purchased the Inn in 1945 and were joined by Arthur Jr. and Maureen Palmer in 1951. Their goal was to create an atmosphere that would make their guests feel that they were in a real home, with fine art pieces, antiques, linens, tableware, and glassware. This collection may be seen throughout the Lowell Inn today.

The Lowell Inn is a striking three-story, red brick, colonial mansion. The broad veranda is supported by 13 columns, each flying the historic flag of the original colonies. There are 16 guest rooms plus five suites, all with private bath. Each room features an eating/sitting area and complimentary wine and liquor, a service originated by the Lowell Inn. The George Washington Room was the original dining room. It has Williamsburg Colonial furnishings. Sheffield silver services and a Dresden china collection are displayed on sideboards about the room. The Garden Room was the first addition to the Lowell Inn in 1939. It features an indoor trout pool formed by natural springs from the adjoining hillside. The earthy atmosphere of the room is accentuated by huge, round, polished-agate tables. The Cocktail

Lounge was added in 1957. In 1959 Arthur and Maureen added the Matterhorn Room, to reflect their Swiss ancestry. They decided the beauty of Swiss woodcarving would be the basis of the decor for the new dining room. Also featured are imported table settings and stained glass windows.

Stillwater has many other historic buildings. A tour visiting the many antique shops, the Minnesota Historical Museum, or a Paddlewheel Boat ride at St. Croix Falls can make an ideal weekend at the romantic Lowell Inn. Gift certificates are available.

J EWELRY & COLLECTIBLES

■ FANCY NANCY'S
317 S. Main Street
Stillwater, MN 55082
Tel: (612) 430-2648
Hrs: Mon. - Sat. 10 a.m. - 6 p.m. Sun. noon - 6 p.m.
All major credit cards are accepted.

Fancy Nancy's is located in downtown historic Stillwater in the St. Croix River Exchange Building. Nancy takes special pride to make sure customers are happy and enjoy their visit.

Customers are able to find something special at Fancy Nancy's for anyone and any occasion. One of the popular specialty items is Fancy Nancy's Festive Faces and personalized cups. Each of these fine ceramic items is meticulously hand-crafted and painted. "Lucky Leaves" are a gold-tone jewelry made from natural objects that have been hand-selected and preserved. These leaves are nature's symbolic treasures and said to bring good fortune. Other unique items include gems and diamonds, rings, fashion jewelry, and also shirts, leather items, antiques, and many more fine collectibles. Exceptional custom work for wedding rings, cocktail rings, pendants, and earrings is also available.

L ADIES APPAREL

■ RIVER RATS
233 S. Second Street
Stillwater, MN 55082
Tel: (612) 439-3308
Hrs: Tue. - Sat. 10 a.m. - 6 p.m., Sun. noon - 5 p.m. Closed Mon.

Built in the mid-1800s, the River Rats is located in one of Stillwater's oldest buildings. The high ceilings, bare brick walls, and hardwood floor definitely makes visitors feel like stepping back a century in time.

River Rats has a fine selection of domestic and imported natural fibered clothing at very reasonable prices. The cut-loose and "real clothes" clothing line features a wide range of colors and quality styles for mixing and matching wardrobes. Accessories such as hats, belts, scarves, boots, shoes, and imported jewelry and ladies' totes from Africa, Indonesia, and Thailand complement a clothing selection. River Rats offers fresh styles from season to season to help create comfortable ensembles for any occasion. There is also a wide assortment of imported, hand-crafted baskets and pottery items displayed by local craftsmen. After shopping, discover and enjoy historic downtown Stillwater. Main street offers a variety of antique, gift and souvenir shops, art galleries, and restaurants. When hectic shopping malls and "trendy" fashions won't do, River Rats is the place to shop.

R ESTAURANTS

■ CLYDE'S ON THE ST. CROIX
101 S. Fifth Ave.
Bayport, MN 55003
Tel: (612) 439-6554
Hrs: Sun. - Thur. 11 a.m. - 9 p.m., Fri. - Sat. 11 a.m. - 10 p.m.
All major credit cards are accepted.

When in Bayport, visit Clyde's On The St. Croix. Just a short drive south of Stillwater, this fine restaurant is located on the grounds of the former Pavilion — a 1920s dance hall hotspot that attracted such star performers as Benny Goodman and the Memphis Five. With style and class, Clyde's recalls those long ago days of glamorous entertainment.

As befitting the history of the area, Clyde's is devoted to exquisite dining, offering a tantalizing array of chicken, veal, beef, and pasta entrées. How about Champagne Breast of Chicken — a tender breast of chicken lightly breaded and glazed with champagne sauce? Or the marvelous Chicken Bolo — chicken breast stuffed with prosciutto ham, spinach, and mozzarella cheese served with Bolognese sauce? For lunch, don't miss the outstanding broiled crabmeat croissant served with celery and onions, and layered with cheddar cheese.

Every day, Clyde's offers enough chef's specials to satisfy the most discriminating taste: veal of the day, pasta of the day, and seafood of the day. On Sundays, Clyde's serves a brunch with more than 40 different items, and every weekend the special feature is prime rib. Fridays, a fish fry takes center stage. For those who visit during the summer, Clyde's offers outdoor dining complete with an outstanding view of the St. Croix River, one of the cleanest and most scenic rivers in the world. When boaters on the St. Croix feel the hunger pains setting in, they simply land at Clyde's dock and let the chef handle the rest.

■ ESTEBAN'S OF STILLWATER
324 S. Main Street
Stillwater, MN 55082
Tel: (612) 430-1543
Hrs: Daily 11 a.m. - 1 a.m.
All major credit cards are accepted.

Esteban's of Stillwater is located in one of the most historic and unique buildings in Stillwater, The Grand Garage, which was originally built in 1882. Freshly prepared menu items feature traditional American to authentic Mexican cuisine.

The restaurant's ambience reflects the Spanish environment with its decor and furnishings. With good health in mind, Esteban's offers menu selections that are high in fiber and complex carbohydrates that are recommended to promote good health. Original Mexican specialties include "camarones," extra large gulf shrimp, and "chuletas," Mexican-style pork chops, both prepared with South of the Border spices. Popular appetizers and entrees include nachos, quesadillas, combination plates featuring tacos, burritos, enchiladas, and chili rellenas smothered in special homemade sauces.

Fajitas, chimichangas, tostadas, and burritos are all prepared with a variety of meats and vegetables. Thursday is enchilada night. On Friday the chef prepares a special seafood entree. There is an excellent choice of American entrees to choose from. Relax in the lounge Monday through Friday during Happy Hour or join family and friends for a Sunday champagne breakfast. For special occasions, meeting and banquet rooms are available for large or small groups with complete catering service.

The excellent food and genuine Spanish warmth make Esteban's of Stillwater outstanding. Before or after the meal, guests often take time to browse Grand Garage and Main Street or stroll along the riverfront.

■ GASTHAUS BAVARIAN HUNTER
8390 Lofton Ave.
Stillwater, MN 55082
Tel: (612) 439-7128
Hrs: Lunch Mon. - Fri. 11 a.m. - 2 p.m., Sat. noon - 4 p.m.
    Dinner Mon. - Thur. 5 - 9 p.m., Fri. - Sat. 4 - 10 p.m., Sun. noon - 8 p.m.
Visa, MasterCard, AmEx, and Diners Club are accepted.

Approaching this alpine chalet nestled in the pines one can hear a faint echo of accordion music drifting through the air. The sounds blend with Old World accents and New World enthusiasm. Banners are displayed from Munich, Regensburg, and Inzell. Waiters and waitresses wear beautiful Bavarian dirndls and lederhosen. Hear the German band, see the dancers twirling in traditional colors of Bavarian blue and white, smell the aromas of authentic Bavarian specialties welcoming guests to Oktoberfest at the Gasthaus Bavarian Hunter restaurant.

Enjoyment is something that happens year-round at the Gasthaus Bavarian Hunter restaurant. In the middle of September it is time for Oktoberfest in Germany and here in the beautiful wooded countryside of eastern Minnesota. Whether reveling in the sights and sounds of an outdoor festival or watching the snow settle softly in the surrounding pines, one can be transported to another time and place.

Authentic in every detail, the Gasthaus offers traditional Bavarian specialities such as sauerbraten, jaegerschnitzel, schnweinshaxe, and sausages. Enjoy the wide selection of Munich beers on tap, as well as the extensive array of liqueurs and alcohol-free favorites. Sing along with the strolling accordion player on Friday nights and Sunday afternoons during the lavish Bavarian buffet. Dance to the music of traditional German bands on selected Saturday evenings.

For 23 years, Karl Schoene and his son, Carli, have built upon the traditions of their native Bavaria to create a tradition in Minnesota. Raise a stein of Munich beer, Prosit! and sing along. Welcome to a centuries-old German tradition of having fun!

■ LAKE ELMO INN
3442 Lake Elmo Ave.
Lake Elmo, MN 55042
Tel: (612) 777-8495
Hrs: Lunch Mon. - Sat. 11 a.m. - 2 p.m.
    Dinner Mon. - Thur. 5 - 10 p.m.
    Dinner Fri. - Sat. 5 - 11 p.m.
    Champagne brunch Sun. 10 a.m. - 2 p.m. Dinner Sun. 4:30 - 8:30 p.m.
All major credit cards are accepted.

The Lake Elmo Inn was originally built in 1881 as an inn. John and Kathy Schiltz, owners, now provide customers with the same country, yet sophisticated atmosphere in elegant dining. The restaurant and lounge area provide a country-French ambience complemented by a friendly, professional staff creating a very memorable dining experience. On display are salt and pepper shakers in a showcase along the wall in the dining room, which also is decorated during the holiday seasons. A garden patio with a waterfall is exceptional for outdoor seating.

Bringing the classical dishes back, this award-winning restaurant's continental cuisine features game dinners of roast duckling and veal. Gracing the menu are daily fresh selections of fish and seafood, such as lobster, Salmon Wellington, scallops, seafood platter, prawns and pasta, and walleye pike. Other entrees include chicken specialties, rack of lamb, hickory-smoked ribs, and an excellent choice of steaks and chops. Dinners are served with fresh sauteed vegetables, along with a choice of wild rice, potato of the day, pasta, or baked potato. There is a pleasing selection of appetizers and an extensive wine list to complement the menu selections. A light Lemon Sorbet Intermezzo is served before the main entreé, and a chocolate-dipped strawberry is a perfect finish after the meal.

Special preparations can be made for restrictive diets and light appetites. Sunday and holiday brunches provide a culinary extravaganza with a variety of entrees and desserts. Banquet facilities and catering are also available. Enjoyment and quality of food are assured at the Lake Elmo Inn.

V ICTORIAN PUB

■ MAD CAPPER SALOON AND EATERY
224 S. Main Street
Stillwater, MN 55082
Tel: (612) 430-3710
Hrs: Mon. - Sat. 11 a.m. - 1 a.m.
    Sun. noon - midnight
Visa, MasterCard, and AmEx are accepted.

Located in the heart of downtown Stillwater and listed on the National Register of Historic Places, the Mad Capper Saloon and Eatery is the meeting place for Stillwater locals and visitors.

This century-old building has a beautiful Victorian interior with a sports accent. The Mad Capper Saloon and Eatery has been a bar for over 100 years and once had live boxing in the back. A unique assortment of hats adorn the interior walls along with many antiques throughout the restaurant. The sandwich selections are extraordinary and available on three different types of bread.

Specialty burgers are individually smothered in favorites such as sauteed mushrooms and onions, barbeque sauce, or cheddar cheese. Other menu selections feature daily luncheon specials, homemade soups and chilis, and a tasteful choice of popular appetizers. Also available is a large selection of imported and domestic beers.

In addition to the delicious food served, friendly and courteous staff reflect the Mad Capper Saloon and Eatery's healthy attitude of Stillwater.

Wayzata

The history of this busy suburban town with its many upscale specialty shops is intrinsically tied to the late railroad baron James J. Hill. In the early days, when Wayzata was still a small farming village nestled on the north shore of Lake Minnetonka 12 miles west of Minneapolis, James J. Hill laid his St. Paul and Pacific railroad line straight down the middle of Wayzata's main street, blocking the tiny village's only access to Minneapolis. Wayzata proceeded to sue the Empire Builder, requesting that he move the line to a neighboring street. Hill, however, was so miffed by this audacity that he not only moved the line — he moved it one mile out of town so the people of Wayzata would have to, as he put it, "walk a mile for the next 20 years" to catch the train. Eventually, the city and the railroad baron came to terms, and in 1906 Hill moved the line back into town and built a new depot.

ATTRACTIONS

Today, the *Wayzata Depot* is a national historic landmark and focus for numerous community activities. An ideal way to recapture the mood of the young Victorian town at the turn of the century is to take a free *Wayzata Trolley* ride from the depot, through town and back to the *city beach* on Lake Minnetonka — one of the Twin Cities area's most popular lakes, ideal for fishing, boating, windsurfing, and swimming. Local events also focus on the depot, most notably *James J. Hill Days* in September, featuring an arts and crafts fair, children's games, a parade, and athletic events for the entire family. From late June through July, the depot is the venue for weekly, free *family concerts* featuring a great variety of music and artists. In the winter, local residents flock to the February *Chilly Open* to enjoy hot chili, a pancake breakfast, dinner, cabaret entertainment — along with ice fishing and golf on the frozen Lake Minnetonka.

For more information on Wayzata, contact:
GREATER WAYZATA AREA CHAMBER OF COMMERCE
402 E. Lake Street
Wayzata, MN 55391
(612) 473-9595

ART GALLERIES

■ THE GALLERY WAYZATA
635 E. Lake Street
Wayzata, MN 55391
Tel: (612) 476-4522
Hrs: (Summer) Tue. - Sat.10 a.m. - 5 p.m.
    (Winter) Tue. - Sat. 10 a.m. - 5 p.m.
Visa, MasterCard, AmEx and Diners Club are accepted.

The Gallery Wayzata is certainly a treat to the senses: a riot of color and texture, featuring the works of local and nationally known contemporary artists. Paintings, sculptures, prints, and unique original pieces adorn the Gallery Wayzata, offering a special opportunity to purchase fine contemporary art without going to California or New York. The work of local artists such as Carisch, Evans, Foty, Hegman/Fogg, as well as nationally known artists are available for purchase in a range of prices.

Owners Don Miller and Jeff Brown chose Wayzata as the location for their gallery because they were impressed by its strong arts community. Located in a charming building overlooking Lake Minnetonka, the Gallery Wayzata is a perfect place to browse, purchase, or simply to learn about contemporary art from knowledgeable owners who are happy to take the time to educate the public.

The Gallery Wayzata will work with customers to accommodate their needs — acquiring pieces from other parts of the country, or art design consulting, a specialty of this gallery. The Gallery Wayzata also provides delivery and hanging. Interior designers, corporations, serious collectors, or simply the interested and curious public are all welcome.

■ MEADOW CREEK GALLERIES
771 E. Lake Street
Wayzata, MN 55391
Tel: (612) 476-1664
Hrs: Mon. - Wed., Fri. 10 a.m. - 5:30 p.m
   Thur. 10 a.m. - 8 p.m. Sat 10 a.m. - 5 p.m.
   Closed Sun.

Additional Location:
3560 W. 70th Street
Edina, MN 55435
Tel: (612) 920-7123
Hrs: Mon. - Fri. 10 a.m. - 9 p.m.
   Sat. 10 a.m. - 6 p.m. Sun. noon - 5 p.m.
Visa, MasterCard, AmEx, Diners Club, and Discover are accepted.

Meadow Creek Galleries specializes in original and limited-edition artwork by the top area and nationally known artists. Classical, Impressionistic, Americana, Western, and Wildlife art are well represented. Meadow Creek Galleries also offers an impressive array of customer services that go beyond those of traditional art galleries. Consultation, leasing, delivery, lay-away, gift certificates, art search (a secondary market service for collectors), and a recently added gift registry are some of the services offered. Skilled designers will assist in choosing the perfect combination of mats and frames for artwork. The galleries offer the finest in museum-quality custom framing. Artwork may be commissioned.

The galleries also offer a delightful collection of original wood carvings by local artists, and schedule frequent events such as art openings, receptions, and trunk shows. The galleries are distributers for Greenwich Workshop, Millpond Press, and others. Meadow Creek Galleries has been in business since 1984, and is located in both Wayzata and Edina.

B OOKSTORE

■ THE BOOKCASE
607 E. Lake Street
Wayzata, MN 55391
Tel: (612) 473-8341
Hrs: Mon. - Sat. 9:30 a.m. - 6 p.m.
   Thur. 9:30 a.m. - 8 p.m.
Visa and MasterCard are accepted.

The Bookcase has been a community favorite since the early 1960s, drawing a wide cross-section of patrons from near and not so nearby areas. This cornerstore faces Lake Minnetonka and offers breathtaking scenery of the lake area year-round. Planters and tables beckon patrons during the summer months to gather their reading material and savor it near the lakeshore.

An outstanding selection of children's books occupy the shelves of The Bookcase in a vibrant section. Monthly story hours are filled with stories being related to children by famous local authors. Field trips for local schoolchildren explain how a book is made. The Bookcase is the first store in the area to sponsor author breakfasts, where local authors can bestow their experiences on an admiring audience. Journalist Charles Kurault has been a revered guest in the past.

The customer base extends from the metro area all the way to Japan, France, and South America. Special orders and out-of-print searches are specialty services. Free gift wrapping and shipment of packages are also services offered year-round. In addition to books, an assortment of calendars and stationary are on the shelves. The staff at The Bookcase is knowledgeable and well read. The Bookcase holds temptations for a variety of patrons.

G IFT SHOP

■ BLANC DE BLANC
691 Lake Street
Wayzata, MN 55391
Tel: (612) 473-8275
Hrs: Mon. - Wed. and Fri. - Sat. 9 a.m. - 6 p.m.
    Thur. 9 a.m. - 8 p.m.
    Holiday hours may vary; call ahead
Visa and MasterCard are accepted.

"Blanc de blanc" means white on white in French, and that's what this unique gift shop is all about. Serenely located on the shores of Lake Minnetonka just west of downtown Minneapolis, Blanc de Blanc specializes in white items for every room.

The gift shop is a treat by itself, all white, light and airy. From the showroom, the view of the lake, fiery red at sundown or glittering in the midday sun, is a stunning complement to the delicate beauty and elegance of Blanc de Blanc's merchandise. In the shop, mother-daughter owners Heidi and Sharon Carisch have tenderly displayed plate settings, ceramic jugs and figurines, clothes, knick knacks, and a myriad of other items. Although all their products are top-quality, the price range is still very wide and most who stop find something to take home.

The Carisches are proud of the variety of services they offer customers, such as personal assistance and complimentary gift wrapping. Blanc de Blanc also offers personal, bridal, and baby registries. If customers are looking for just the perfect gift for a housewarming, a new job, a special newborn, or a bride and a groom, this innovative two-year-old shop might have just what they need. Or maybe the time is just right to be pampered with something white, clean, and beautiful.

G IFTS & HOME ACCESSORIES

■ FROST & BUDD, LTD
750 E. Lake Street
Wayzata, MN 55391
Tel: (612) 473-1442
Hrs: Mon. - Sat. 9 a.m. to 6 p.m.
Visa, MasterCard, and AmEx are accepted.

Frost and Budd, Ltd. opened in 1983 in an historic building near Lake Minnetonka and later expanded to a location in "Cross Creek" at the east end of town. Still adjacent to Lake Minnetonka, this store contains two levels of unique and exquisite home accessories. The store is arranged like a private home. Kitchen accessories are displayed in a pine-floored kitchen complete with an antique wood cookstove. Outdoor and gardening merchandise are on the brick-floored patio complete with a running fountain.

Several gallery concepts are found at Frost and Budd. The Colonial Williamsburg shop contains 18th century reproductions of small accent furniture pieces, lamps, and tabletop pieces. The

china room contains over 125 fine china and porcelain dinnerware patterns as well as sterling silver and stainless steel flatware. Also available are hand-cut and -blown crystal, domestic and imported casual dinnerware from England, France, Italy, and Portugal. Gift items such as cards, books, stationery, lifestyle gifts, gourmet foods, and picture frames offer a wide selection of choices to suit the person who has everything. The Garden Gallery features concrete sculptures, birdbaths, lawn and garden items, wind chimes, picnic baskets, mailboxes, games, and barbeque accessories. A complete selection of birdfeeders and birdhouses is in the outdoor patio and garden room.

Frost and Budd was nominated for the Best Retailer Award in the Mid/Southwest Speciality Store category by the National Tabletop Association in 1989. Also in 1989, Frost and Budd received the "Finest Presentation" award by the Williamsburg Foundation. A bridal registry and UPS shipping services are available. A second Frost and Budd, Ltd. is located in The Conservatory in downtown Minneapolis.

R ESTAURANT

■ SUNSETS ON WAYZATA BAY

700 E. Lake Street
Wayzata, MN 55391
Tel: (612) 473-LAKE (5253)
Hrs: Mon. - Sat. 6:30 a.m. - 1 a.m., Sun. - 9:30 a.m. - 1 a.m.
    Call for breakfast, lunch, dinner, and brunch hours.
Visa, MasterCard, AmEx, and Diners Club are accepted.

Residents of Wayzata have gathered at this beautiful spot on Lake Minnetonka for decades, coming in the early days by train, bus, and on foot. Today, Sunsets on Wayzata Bay is still a popular rendezvous spot for folks from Wayzata and beyond. The landmark Clock Tower ticks away the hours as business people gather for breakfast meetings, shoppers drop in for lunch, and workers relax at the Happy Hour. A meal at Sunsets on Wayzata Bay is a spectacular affair — where else can one be treated to a front row seat of the best in panoramic color that Minnesota has to offer? Voted as one of the top views in the seven-county metro area by *Minneapolis/St. Paul* Magazine, this all-season restaurant supplements the view with a fine selection of food and drink.

Breakfast features Eggs Benedict, Sour Dough French Toast, or the Marinaro Special (scrambled eggs with Italian Sausage, peppers, and onions). Lunch features a wide selection of appetizers and entrees ranging from Szechuan Spicy Green Beans to Shrimp Linguini and an array of chicken and seafood salads. For dinner, guests may choose from a variety of steak and seafood dishes or sandwiches.

Come by car, by foot, or even by boat. No matter how guests arrive, they are sure to experience what Wayzatans already know — that Sunsets on Wayzata Bay is the perfect place to enjoy a good meal and a good view, with good friends.

S PECIALTY SPORTING GOODS

■ SKI HUT
1175 E. Wayzata Blvd.
Colonial Square
Wayzata, MN 55391
Tel: (612) 473-8843
Hrs: Mon. - Thur. 9:30 a.m. - 7:30 p.m., Fri. 9:30 a.m. - 6 p.m.
Sat. 9 a.m. - 5 p.m., Sun. noon - 5 p.m.
All major credit cards are accepted.

Ski Hut prides itself on personalized service that can make recreational outfitting choices easier. Owners Jim and Laurie McWethy and their staff offer experience, expertise, and a genuine concern for the safety and pleasure of their customers.

At Ski Hut, customers find the equipment and advice they need to enjoy a variety of such demanding sports as cross-country and downhill skiing, hockey and figure skating, road and mountain biking, waterskiing, snowboarding, and rollerblading. Always wanted to take up tennis, soccer, or softball? Come to Ski Hut for the latest outfits and equipment. And, for those who are between the ages of eight and 18, a winter's worth of fun awaits at the store's Skijammers Ski School, one of the largest in the United States. In addition, Ski Hut offers the Ski-A-Way Ladies Program, a series of ski instruction outings for women. The McWethys also stock unique seasonal sports clothing and beachwear in the hottest styles and the most sought-after colors. The shop offers a variety of special services, too, such as custom-built insoles for boots or skates, custom, stone-finished tune-ups for skis, and a balancing service to give the best position and control while skiing.

Check out Ski Hut's great inventory of used boots, bindings, poles, skis, skates and rollerblades. Here find some of the best used equipment in town along with expert recommendations, so customers will get only what they need, and they'll know exactly how to use it. The people at Ski Hut know how to enjoy a sport, and they want to pass their knowledge on to their customers. Ski Hut really is the ticket to outdoor fun.

White Bear Lake

This city of 25,000 skirts the shores of White Bear Lake, the second largest lake in the Twin Cities metropolitan area. Located 15 minutes north of St. Paul, White Bear Lake is a subtle combination of country and city — of the natural beauty of lakes and the industrial determination of corporations such as Johnson Boat Works and Weyerhaeuser, a leading corrugated box manufacturer. Before the days of these large companies, White Bear Lake was a popular resort frequented by the likes of F. Scott Fitzgerald and Mark Twain, who eloquently described the serene beauty of the lake. Memories of those early days come alive during a visit to the *Rockin' R Ranch,* offering horse-drawn carriage trips into the countryside surrounding the city, and at the restored Victorian cottage *Fillebrown House,* furnished with antiques and memorabilia. Two community theaters top the list of other attractions in White Bear Lake; the *Lakeshore Players* features musicals, drama, and comedy in an intimate setting from August to June, while *Shakespeare & Company* presents classical plays in a relaxed outdoor setting during the summer. Other events of note include the weekly *farmers' market* with its profusion of local produce; fun-filled *ice fishing competitions* in the winter; and the art shows *A Fair in the Fields* and *Northern Lights,* held in the summer and the winter, respectively. An art show is also on the agenda for *Manitou Days,* a giant festival in late June that also includes a parade, beach dances, big wheel races, and other sporting events.

For more information on White Bear Lake, contact:
WHITE BEAR LAKE CHAMBER OF COMMERCE
2189 Fourth Street
White Bear Lake, MN 55110
(612) 429-7666

Skiing Minneapolis, St. Paul

by John G. Shepard

Ask any cross-country skier. He or she will tell you that the bad press often given Minnesota's winter weather is actually a ploy to keep too many people from discovering how great the skiing is here. And, truth be told, you don't even need to drive outside the Minneapolis-St. Paul city limits to find some of the best skiing the north country has to offer.

When the snow falls, any surface flat enough to hold it is almost guaranteed to have tracks by the time the streets have been plowed. The newscasts following each winter storm invariably feature stories about impromptu snow parties, citizens performing charitable feats on their skinny skis, and workaholics who defy common sense by skiing to the office only to find that no one else is there.

But as much fun as the carnival atmosphere of a Minnesota blizzard can be, it certainly isn't the only time to enjoy the uncommonly good skiing that the Twin Cities have to offer. A half-dozen urban parks offer groomed and tracked trails that wind for a total distance of more than 50 miles across the rolling Midwestern landscape through stands of elm, oak, and pine. More than a dozen additional parks and golf courses boast the same inviting terrain without prepared tracks. Even the Minnesota Zoo in Apple Valley has ski rentals and groomed trails past its outdoor exhibits. Both cities also provide lighted trails for night skiing, frequent races, instruction programs, and ski rental facilities. Among these compelling options, two parks in particular stubbornly refuse to accept their civilized status.

The deep tree-lined canyon carved by the Mississippi River at its confluence with the Minnesota River is the site of a special skier's haven. Here the steep river bluffs are topped by the ramparts of an historic military post from the early 1800s called Fort Snelling. Along the banks of the river at the foot of the old fort are approximately 20 miles of easy to intermediate ski trails, most of them within the confines of Fort Snelling State Park. Besides an occasional passing airplane or glimpse of a bridge through the stately trees, little reminds skiers that they are within the limits of a decidedly cosmopolitan pair of cities. With some imagination, it's easy to mentally reconstruct the steamboat landing, warehouses, and riverside gambling dens that stood more than a century ago in the protective shadow of the fort.

The second ski area with a deceptively woodsy feel given its location less than five minutes from downtown Minneapolis is Theodore Wirth Park. Here an oak-studded golf course and wooded wildflower sanctuary provide over five miles of novice and intermediate trails, some of which are lighted. For more advanced skiers, a two-mile racing trail meanders through some steep and densely forested hills. A couple of rope-tows, a 30-meter ski jump, and a grand lodge offering a comfortable place to warm up before heading home round out the scene.

Each winter, St. Paul puts on a spectacular Winter Carnival reflecting the area's strong Scandinavian influence. This century-old celebration depends on such traditional outdoor activities as speed skating, ice fishing, tobogganing, ice carving, and snow sculpting. Cross-country ski races are held in Phalen Park.

All season long, Phalen Park is center stage for St. Paul skiing. With over ten miles of double-set tracks and more flat-packed trails for ski-skating, the park hosts weekly races and a special race on New Year's Day. Some trails are lighted and video instruction is available.

Hennepin County, which includes downtown Minneapolis, has 13 parks in its Park Reserve system with a total of over 140 kilometers of trails and special provisions for ski-skaters. While skiing inside the city is geared to beginners and intermediates, trails for advanced skiers can be found in a park 40 miles south of downtown Minneapolis: Murphy-Hanrehan Park Reserve. Here some 20 kilometers of hilly oak forest offer the best collection of difficult trails in the area. Enjoy one of these trail networks on a fine winter's day, and you'll find yourself thanking those news reports that so effectively keep the crowds at bay.

For more information on Twin Cities skiing, contact the Minnesota Office of Tourism, 375 Jackson St., Room 250, St. Paul, MN 55101; (612) 296-5029. The state requires a ski pass on all non-federal public lands.

©MARTIENA R. RICHTER

Wheaton

Ortonville

Benson
New London
Spicer
Willmar
Litch-
field

Montevideo
Hwy. 212
Granite Falls
Olivia
Hutch-
inson

Belle Plaine
Glencoe
New Prague

Redwood Falls
Morton
Gaylord

Marshall
Le Sueur
Northfield

New
Ulm
St.
Peter
Le Center
Faribault

Tracy
Walnut
Grove

Mankato
Pipestone
Slayton
Hwy. 169
Waseca

St. James
Owa-
tonna

Luverne
Hwy.
60
Windom
Blue
Earth
I-35

I-90
Jackson
Albert Lea

Worthington
Fairmont
Frost

Twin
Cities

PRAIRIELAND

by John G. Shepard

Though bison and nomadic bands of Dakota Indians no longer occupy southwestern Minnesota's once ocean-like prairie, it is still a land rich with opportunities for the curious traveler. There are patches of remnant hardwood forests and an occasional lake oasis—but this gently rolling, largely treeless landscape reflects the fact that before the plow, most of the region was covered with a dense carpet of colorful native grasses that could grow over a man's head. Fortunately, there are places where one can still go to recapture the magnificence of how this land once looked.

One of Minnesota's largest remaining areas of virgin prairie is found at Blue Mounds State Park near Luverne. The Blue Mounds, formed by a protrusion of quartzite bedrock that burst through the area's fertile soil, received their name from settlers traveling west. Approaching families in their lumbering wagons noticed the bluish hue of a steep escarpment (as much as 100 feet high) along the mounds' eastern flank that is lined at its base with stately oaks.

In the spring, when the wild flowers are in bloom, the Blue Mounds are a riot of color, peppered by blooming prickly pear cacti and large quartzite boulders covered with lichens. A resident bison herd completes the image of the past coming to life.

History buffs will also enjoy the Pioneer Village at Worthington and the End-O-Line Railroad Park and Museum at Currie. "Fragments of a Dream," an outdoor pageant presented at Walnut Grove, depicts the life of Laura Ingalls Wilder's family in the 1870s. Hallowed Native American cultural traditions are living still at Pipestone National Monument, while cryptic evidence of prehistoric life can be pondered at the Jeffers Petroglyphs.

The valley of the Minnesota River from its elbow at Mankato upstream to Montevideo brings a sudden change to the prairie. The gentle bluffs of the valley and the floodplain are lush with tall hardwoods. Nearby, lazy river currents flow, affording a pleasant relief from the expanse of agricultural lands that now roll oceanlike to either horizon.

Though the serenity of the countryside wouldn't suggest it, for six weeks in the late summer and early fall of 1862, this river valley was the site of one of America's most tragic and brutal wars between Indians and European settlers. It is possible to piece together the events of the Dakota conflict of 1862 by visiting and studying the many landmarks and historic sites that note locations of battles, ambushes, and ugly encounters between the Santee Dakota and the soldiers and settlers. Also along the Minnesota, visitors can enjoy the proud German heritage of New Ulm, where an excellent county historical museum, a well-preserved general store, and a century-old family brewery offer interesting tours.

Round out a Prairieland tour by visiting the communities that prospered at the expense of what was once called the Big Woods— a stretch of hardwood forest that cut through the northeastern part of the region. Drop by the Geldner Sawmill near Cleveland for a hand's on education about how the elm, basswood, maple, and oaks succumbed to the needs of an expanding civilization.

Albert Lea

The city's somewhat incongruous name stems from a U.S. Army cartographer by the name of Albert Lea who passed through the unsettled area on an expedition in 1835, and stopped to survey one of the numerous lakes dotting the region. This lake was later named in his honor, and the community that eventually grew up along Albert Lea Lake assumed, naturally, the name of the lake. As the years wore on, Albert Lea grew up to become one of the largest and most prosperous cities in southern Minnesota, thanks to its strategic location at the junction of Interstates 35 and 90, the two major highways transecting the Upper Midwest. This city of 18,000 has attracted companies such as Streater's (a major store fixture manufacturer), Naeve Health Care Association, and two leading meat processing firms — Farmstead Foods and Hudson's Foods — which is not surprising since Albert Lea's home county, Freeborn, is among the top three percentile of all agriculture producing counties in the nation.

ATTRACTIONS

History is, in fact, an important part of everyday life in Albert Lea. The city has maintained scores of historical buildings, and an excellent way to view them is on a Freeborn County Historical Society self-guided *historic walking tour.* (The society also maintains a *county museum* and an outstanding *historical village* with 18 buildings — well worth a visit.) Following a brochure available at the convention bureau, the tour originates among the Victorian residences surrounding *Fountain Lake Park,* a recreational community area in the heart of the city, and includes 27 buildings. Four of these — including the *Liquor Rail Depot,* the former *City Hall,* and the *Jones Residence* — are listed on the National Register of Historic Places. Two of the most notable sights, however, are the imposing Romanesque grandeur of the *Freeborn County Courthouse* and the unique French classical *Albert Lea Art Center.* The Art Center is an important aspect of Albert Lea's cultural life, presenting monthly art exhibits and regular educational programs. Another cultural keystone in Albert Lea is the *Minnesota Festival Theatre,* a widely recognized community theater presenting a variety of summer performances, covering the span from dire drama to fun-filled farce. The city is also known for its many country *specialty shops,* including *Country Pleasures* and *The Heart of the Artichoke,* both of which cater to visitors looking for that genuine prairie gift.

EVENTS

Albert Lea's events calendar is filled from January through October with a variety of happenings, including the January *Mid-America Drag Snowmobile Races* on local lakes; the February *Winterfest* with polar bear golf, ice bowling, and dancing; and the *Black Powder Trade Fair & Gun Show,* also held in February and featuring furtraders in full costume from throughout the United States. Other outdoor-related events are the *Minnesota Wild Game, Fish and Domestic Meat Cook-Off* and the *Maple Syruping* workshop in March; the June *Eddie Cochran Music Festival* in memory of the native '50s rock 'n' roll legend; and the *Art in the Park* open-air art exhibit in July. The season's most celebrated event, however, doesn't come to town until October. It's the *Big Island Rendezvous & Festival,* one of the state's largest reenactments of an 1840s fur trader encampment including 200 Indian teepees and lodges, black powder shooting, Native American dances, and ethnic foods.

For more information on Albert Lea, contact:
ALBERT LEA CONVENTION AND VISITORS BUREAU
141 E. William
Albert Lea, MN 56007
(800) 345-8414

A CCOMMODATIONS

■ DAYS INN
2306 E. Main Street
Albert Lea, MN 56007
Tel: (507) 373-6471
Hrs: Open year-round
All major credit cards are accepted.

Conveniently located close to the intersection of Interstates 35 and 90, the Days Inn of Albert Lea provides excellent lodging at a reasonable price. There are 129 tastefully decorated rooms, each of which is spacious, clean, and comfortable. The motel also features fine family dining in the Courtyard Restaurant with daily specials, a children's menu, and a Sunday breakfast buffet. The popular Nite Out Lounge has live entertainment on weekends, dancing, and offers a tempting variety of wine, beer, and mixed drinks to suit every taste. A relaxing swim in the large, indoor, heated swimming pool is a perfect way to end a day on the road.

The town of Albert Lea, often called "The Crossroads of the Upper Midwest," offers a wide range of recreational opportunities with 39 parks, many historic sites, and a civic theatre. This city, with its one million square feet of retail space and 40 restaurants, holds a number of annual events, such as The Winter Festival in February, Art in the Park in July, and the Big Island Rendezvous in October. Snowmobiling on the hundreds of miles of groomed trails or cross-country skiing at Helmer Myre State Park are perhaps the most popular winter activities — and the trails are only minutes from the Days Inn doorstep.

There are as many reasons to visit Albert Lea as there are days in a year. But no matter why visitors come, Days Inn offers them reasonably priced, comfortable accommodations.

B ED & BREAKFASTS

■ FOUNTAIN VIEW INN
310 N. Washington Ave.
Albert Lea, MN 56007
Tel: (507) 377-9425
Hrs: Open year-round
Visa and MasterCard are accepted.

The Fountain View Inn, located in the heart of town on Fountain Lake, has a tradition of being occupied by people who loved it. This tradition is being carried on by Dick and Kathy Paul who have made it possible for many to appreciate this beautiful home. The turn-of-the-century house was once occupied by Madame Beatrice Bessesen, an opera singer who earned her fame in Europe. Madame Bessesen and her husband, Dr. William Bessesen, started their family in this stunning home. Now Dick and Kathy Paul provide an opportunity to share the warmth and charm of this lakeside refuge.

The Fountain View Inn currently has three guest rooms, all offering a lake view. Each room has a private bath and is air conditioned. The Jorgenson room contains natural brick walls and a queen-size bed. The Sullivan room also has a queen-size bed and a picturesque bay window. The Miskell room is located in a corner of the house providing a different angle view of the lake and a double-size bed. The rooms maintain a blend of antiques with cozy creature comforts.

Each morning a continental breakfast of fresh seasonal fruit, juice, homemade muffins and breads, and coffee or tea is served. During warm weather, breakfast is served on the porch overlooking Fountain Lake. Fountain View is located only two blocks from downtown Albert Lea and is a short drive from Helmer Myre State Park, Freeborn County Museum and Historical Village, or to a golf course. Pontoon boat rides are available in season by arrangement.

■ THE VICTORIAN ROSE INN

609 W. Fountain Street
Albert Lea, MN 56007
Tel: (507) 373-7602 or (800) 252-6558
Hrs: Open year-round
Visa and MasterCard are accepted.

Built in 1898 in Queen Anne Victorian Style, the Victorian Rose Inn is a majestic presence in Albert Lea. Upon entering the inn, a beautiful open staircase awash with sunlight streaming through the stained-glass windows overhead greets each visitor. The hand-crafted woodwork has been maintained throughout the

house over the years and is enhanced by period light fixtures scattered inside.

Four rooms are available, the first of which is The Kensington Suite. This sleeping chamber is reminiscent of the palace of the same name and provides the comfort of a queen-size poster bed, private bath with a shower, sitting room, and turret surrounded by lace and gingerbread. The Queen Victoria room is decorated in deep, dramatic colors around a marble fireplace and lace canopied queen-size bed. The Windsor room could aptly be called the rose room due to its decor. This room has a flowered canopy over the oak queen-size waterbed. The Duchess room is tucked away in the rear of the house and contains a writing table and double-size antique spoon-carved bed. In the morning a full breakfast is served featuring quiche, fresh baked muffins and breads, pancakes with blueberry sauce, fruit, and coffee.

The Victorian Rose Inn provides excellent lodging for members as well as non-members of the royal family.

B OOKSTORE

■ THE CONSTANT READER
238 Broadway
Albert Lea, MN 56007
Tel: (507) 373-6512
Hrs: Mon. - Fri. 9:30 a.m. - 6 p.m.
    Thur. 9 a.m. - 8 p.m.
    Sat. 9:30 a.m. - 4 p.m.
Visa and MasterCard are accepted.

Step inside the turn-of-the-century building on Albert Lea's main street to find a one-of-a-kind bookstore. New and used books, magazines, comics, bookmarks, and bookplates make this store a reader's delight. The front of the store features new books with strong sections of regional books and nature guides. Children's books, bestsellers, and books on tape are also available.

The back half of the store is a wonderful mixture of used books, slightly hurt books, and other book bargains. The atmosphere is informal with customers sitting on the floor while they look through baskets of craft patterns, sheet music, or school materials. Tall shelves contain half-price paperbacks arranged by genre and author. A children's nook lets children sit and read while allowing parents to browse. The values are excellent, even volumes are featured at bargain prices.

The Constant Reader is a delightful bookstore and is able to satisfy any taste, from top 10 bestsellers to that title customers always wanted to read but never had the time. It also provides a great opportunity for parents to browse with their children and share interests or break ground on new ones.

S TUDIO & GALLERY

■ ORIGINALS STUDIO AND SHOP
1322 Fountain Street
Albert Lea, MN 56007
Tel: (507) 373-4153
Hrs: Mon. - Sat. 9 a.m. - 5 p.m. (Or by appointment)
Visa and MasterCard are accepted.

In the heart of Albert Lea sits Originals Studio and Shop, a 100-year-old Victorian house which has served as home and business for 20 years to owners and artists Jack and Eloise Adams. This stunning Victorian structure offers the perfect setting in which to display the pottery and paintings of Jack and Eloise. The business

portion, the attached two-level studio, is fitted with beautiful stained glass decor throughout, which complements the vast selection. The residence portion can be appreciated on Fridays, which are tour days. Tours of the main house provide an opportunity to view the antiques and artwork that decorate the interior, as well as the charm of the home itself. Demonstrations of how the Adams' craft their art are also included on Fridays. Jack and Eloise make items ranging from greeting cards to original paintings and drawings. Eloise also creates beautiful animal sculptures. Custom order work is available on all of their wares. A wide selection of stoneware and functional pottery items are also featured in the studio. Originals Studio and Shop provide unique handcrafted merchandise in an affordable price range.

Belle Plaine

I n a rush of Victorian romanticism, Minnesota Territorial Judge Andrew Chatfield selected this serene prairie spot for his new home in 1853 and called it 'Belle Plaine' — French for 'beautiful prairie.' In the century-and-a-half since its eloquent founding, this town of 3,000 has attracted a small but vital share of industry — most notably the exercise equipment manufacturer Nordic Track. Still, it remains a beautiful, quiet spot, nestled near the woods of the Minnesota River in a setting that has changed little since it captured the heart of the itinerant judge. The scenic Minnesota River today provides excellent recreational opportunities for Belle Plaine residents and visitors alike, most notably within the confines of *Minnesota Valley Trail State Park* — a 21-acre area ideal for camping, fishing, picnicking, and birdwatching, and featuring 72 groomed miles of trails for hiking, skiing, horseback riding, and mountain biking. In town, there are over four blocks of *city parks* with playground equipment and shelters with kitchen facilities. The city's most notable sight, however, is the rare — possibly unique — restored *two-story outhouse* attached to the *Hooper-Bowler-Hillstrom House,* an 1870s home with period furnishings. Also on the grounds of the Hooper House is a carriage house that has been turned into the *Carriage House Museum,* complete with numerous items from Belle Plaine's past. The Hooper House is also site of one of the city's main events, an *Old-Fashioned Christmas Party* featuring sleigh rides through the snow-covered streets. Other events of note include the three-day summer festival *Bar-B-Q Days* with its parades and entertainment; the *Downtown Cookout* in June, when Belle Plaine merchants set up barbecue grills on the sidewalks and serve free food; and the *Scarecrow Festival* in October, featuring scarecrows designed by local residents.

For more information on Belle Plaine, contact:
CITY OF BELLE PLAINE
P. O. Box 6
Belle Plaine, MN 56011
(612) 873-2000

A PPLE ORCHARD & RESTAURANT

■ EMMA KRUMBEES RESTAURANT AND APPLE ORCHARD
Highway 169 S.
Belle Plaine, MN 56011
Tel: (612) 873-4334
Hrs: Daily 6 a.m. - 11 p.m.

Emma Krumbees is located just south of Shakopee and is well worth the drive. This restaurant/apple orchard/bakery/ice cream parlor/gift shop/candy shop/country store is truly a "one stop" shop. Located here since 1979, this establishment has become a real favorite in the area and has drawn visitors from all over to enjoy the excellent food and friendly atmosphere.

Everything in the restaurant is made from scratch including soup, pies, and the honey bread, which is fresh baked hourly.

After sampling some of the bakery items, visitors will be happy to know that they are available for sale. Monster cookies, cakes, muffins, and scrumptious cinnamon rolls will satisfy the sweet tooth of all generations. The restaurant is famous for its baked chicken and BBQ ribs in addition to the local favorites of chicken dumpling soup and Swedish meatballs (a natural in Minnesota). Prime rib is the specialty on Fridays and Saturdays. Breakfast is served daily along with a great cup of coffee and conversation.

The apple orchard and country store are located next to the restaurant. Apples and fresh produce are sold in the orchard building in addition to ice cream, fudge, jams, and maple syrup. Upon entering the gift shop, visitors are greeted by wind chimes, Christmas decorations, and wall decorations. The featured items allow customers to take a reminder of their visit home. Each fall the Great Scarecrow Festival and Pumpkin Contest is held at Emma Krumbees. These unique designs provide a charming way to enter autumn and witness the true talent of the contestants.

Blue Earth

This city of 3,700 owes its prosperity not to the blue riverbank clay that gave it its name, but to the extremely rich soil in the area. Never in recorded history has Blue Earth suffered a general crop failure due to lack of moisture, and rarely has this area failed to lead the country in soybean and corn production. It is an excellent location for food product industries, a fact underscored by the overwhelming presence for more than half a century of the Green Giant Company, a leading canned pea and corn supplier. In fact, the city's close ties to Green Giant can hardly be missed by any visitor to Blue Earth. A 55-foot statue of the *Jolly Green Giant* looms above the trees and picnic areas in the *Green Giant Park,* site of the Blue Earth *Tourist Information Center.* Blue Earth citizens are quick to note that the city is not only a corn-lovers delight — it is also the heralded birthplace of the ice-cream sandwich. Among sites of more historical interest are the *Blue Earth County Historical Society Museum,* located in an 1871 Victorian mansion and featuring exhibits of pioneer life and Native American culture; the *Etta C. Ross Museum,* housing historical settler artifacts; the *Faribault County Courthouse;* and the unique *Music Museum Store* featuring player pianos, custom-built pipe organs, grandfather clocks, and antique pump organs to view, rent, or purchase. Many of the city's annual events also have an historical and artistic flair, including the *Fine Arts and*

Antiques Festival in June, the *Upper Midwest Woodcarvers Exhibition* later in the summer, and occasional performances by the community troupe *Town and Country Players.*

For more information on Blue Earth, contact:
BLUE EARTH CHAMBER OF COMMERCE
111 N. Main Street
Blue Earth, MN 56013
(507) 526-2916

ACCOMMODATIONS

■ BLUE EARTH SUPER 8
Junction I-90 and Highway 169
Blue Earth, MN 56013
Tel: (507) 526-7376 or (800) 843-1991
Hrs: Open year-round

The Blue Earth Super 8 Motel is truly an exception among motels. Ernie and Mickey Wingen have custom-crafted each room in the hotel in its own unique design. Some visitors have called it Spanish style, some Swiss, Oriental, Bavarian, or Early American. The style really depends upon which room customers visit. The Wingens have made most of the furnishings that now occupy the rooms. Mickey has painted murals on the walls in each room, in lieu of paintings, adding a personalized touch.

In the winter Ernie scrapes the iced-over windows of guests' cars in the parking lot. Customers would be hard pressed to find that kind of service anywhere else. A continental breakfast is served each morning in the cozy atmosphere of the lounge. The Blue Earth Super 8 is a real original in a chain of quality motels.

Fairmont

F airmont is a prosperous industrial center — a home to corporations like Harsco, Weigh-Tronix, and Teledyne Aerospace Systems, issuing no less than 263 building permits in 1990. But times weren't always that good. During the early 1860s, the city became a hotspot during the Dakota Indian uprising and in all haste, a fort was erected to protect the tiny, struggling farming community. After the Indian wars and the tribulations of the Civil War, years of grasshopper plagues followed, driving many of the impoverished farmers from their hard-won land.

Fairmont was just barely saved from depopulation by the railroad, which arrived in 1878, bringing scores of English colonists who brightened the hills surrounding the town with their colorful fox hunts. Traces of these English transplants appear in the many historical buildings in the area, including the lavish *Fairmont Opera House* — patterned after the renowned Illinois Theater in Chicago and, today, venue for a summer series of theater events — the classical *Martin County Courthouse;* and the extravagant, Victorian *George Wohlhuter Mansion.* For history buffs, the list doesn't end there. The agriculture interpretive center *Heritage Acres* — located on the northwest shore of *Sisseton Lakes,* one of five interconnected lakes in town — features a pioneer church, schoolhouse, homestead, and barn. In a similar vein, the *Martin County Historical Museum* includes an old-fashioned schoolroom, old newspapers, and war memorabilia. Also an historical sight, but of a decidedly newer date, is the *Dale A. Gardner Aerospace Museum & Learning Center,* named after the city's native son and space shuttle astronaut, and featuring Gardner's flight suit, "Challenger" space tiles, and numerous videos. A different mode of transportation is celebrated by the members of the *Sisseton Sioux Model Railroad Club,* who have built an enormous model train layout featuring 1,500 feet of track, more than 100 turnouts, and lifelike scenery created by 1,000 pounds of plaster. Another notable model construction is an 18-foot city sculpture located in the family restaurant *The Ranch;* a competitor, the *China Restaurant,* comes without sculptures but with the best Chinese food in the area. The list of local events

begins with *Interlaken Heritage Days* in late June, a week of hearty food, parades, and top national entertainers. The city also offers races at *Fairmont Speedways* every Friday during the summer months, and in December, *Fairmont Glows,* a city-wide display of Christmas lights.

For more information on Fairmont, contact:
FAIRMONT CONVENTION & VISITORS BUREAU
P.O. Box 976
Fairmont, MN 56031
(507) 235-8585

GALLERY & FRAME SHOP

■ On the Wall

72 Downtown Plaza
Fairmont, MN 56031
Tel: (507) 238-9555
Hrs: Mon. 9 a.m. - 9 p.m.
   Tue. - Fri. 9 a.m. - 5:30 p.m.
   Sat. 9 a.m. - 5 p.m.
Visa, MasterCard, and Discover are accepted.

Since 1983, On the Wall has provided the public with a fine selection of framing services. It recently has expanded to handling a wide variety of prints for home and office decor. The expansion of services has led to a large clientele base and has drawn the works of some noted artists.

The P. Buckley Moss limited edition prints are very popular items. Moss's scene of Fairmont's Heritage Acres is on display and was also the site of a personal visit from the artist who is originally from Virginia. On the Wall is an exclusive dealer for the Moss collection, which depicts wholesome, rural scenes of the countryside. Limited edition prints from additional artists include Terry Redlin, Jerry Raedeke, and D. Morgan. Plates by Terry Redlin and P. Buckley Moss add another selection dimension.

Greeting cards and photo frames complete the variety of items available. Framing and mounting services have been a mainstay at On the Wall. Either for prints featured at the gallery or for your own creations, the frames add the finishing touch to a fine print. A visit to On the Wall will long be remembered.

Faribault

F aribault was named after the itinerant fur trader Alexander Faribault, who in 1853 erected a trading post at the confluence of the Straight and Cannon Rivers, to trade with the native Dakotas. At first, the town of Faribault was nothing more than a log cabin, but soon scores of Indian teepees dotted the riverbank, and a community of settlers sprang up. In 1872, when Faribault was finally incorporated as a city, 5,000 called the town home. By the time the enlightened founding father passed away ten years later, he had established many of the private schools the city is noted for today, as well as donated the land for the country's first, imposing *Gothic Episcopal cathedral.* Today, the city maintains a host of historical buildings — arguably the greatest number in a Minnesota community its size. On top of the list reigns the *Alexander Faribault House,* a poignant memory of the generous patriarch; the Gothic *Shattuck-St. Mary's School* buildings; the architectural masterpiece *Tate Hall* on the 1864 campus of the State Academy of the Deaf; and the restored, late-18th-century *heritage preservation commercial district.* In addition to the *Rice County Museum of History,* which relates the pioneer and Indian history of the area, history buffs may want to explore the unique state hospital museum *Dr. Engberg Museum;* and the *Faribault Woolen Mill Co.,* one of the few remaining active woolen mills in the country. The mill has an outlet store for its famous blankets. Other shops of interest to visitors are the *Ivan Whillock Studio* with its amazing wood carvings; the *Faribault Art Center,* featuring regular exhibits; and *Uhlir's Apple Orchards,* which offer tours of the orchards and mounds of mouthwatering apples. Outdoor sights not to be missed include *Nerstrand Woods State Park,* a rare remnant of the native hardwood forest that once covered this area; the *Sakatah Lake State Park* with campsites and trails; and the magnificent *River Bend Nature Center* where naturalists are available for guided tours of the 600-acre, carefully protected riverine habitat. The town is not a hotbed of special events, but it does put on *Heritage Days* in June with artists, craftspeople, and musicians from around the area; and the September *Fall Feast-ival* with musical events, special shopping, and a fun-filled hot air balloon rally.

For more information on Faribault, contact:
FARIBAULT CHAMBER OF COMMERCE
P. O. Box 434
Faribault, MN 55021
(507) 334-4381 or (800) 658-2354

B ED & BREAKFAST

■ CHERUB HILL
105 N.W. First Ave.
Faribault, MN 55021
Tel: (507) 332-2024
Hrs: Open year-round
Visa and MasterCard are accepted.

Cherub Hill was designed in 1896 by the first deaf architect in America, Olaf Hanson, for Dr. Jonathan Noyes and his wife Elizabeth. Dr. Noyes was one of the first headmasters at the Minnesota Academy for the Deaf and was instrumental in

founding the school for the blind and mentally disabled children in Faribault. The house is a late Victorian design and is on the National Register of Historic Places. Dr. Noyes's affection for children is apparent in the decor of the home, which is accented with cherub figures throughout.

Current owners Keith and Kristi LeMieux have restored this charming home, which will be accepting guests in May 1992. There are three rooms from which to choose at Cherub Hill. Jonathan's room is reminiscent of an English Manor house with its antique dresser and cozy queen-size bed. A private bath and double whirlpool tub make this room a luxurious hideaway. Alice's room is dedicated to the memory of the Victorian woman. The flower and lace decor surround the white iron queen-size bed with a subtle feminine air of grace. Elizabeth's room has a sunny southeastern view and a high oak double bed. The handmade quilt covering the bed and the pressed tin ceiling make visitors feel as if they are hiding away deep in the country.

The antiques are quite interesting and some are for sale. During the week a continental breakfast of yogurt and pastry bars, fruit, juice, and gourmet coffee is served. Weekends rate a full breakfast which may include wild rice crepes, eggs Benedict, apple tarts, waffles with peach topping, and freshly ground coffee, espresso, tea, and fruit juice. Cherub Hill is also available for special occasions such as weddings, or teas. No matter what the reason, Cherub Hill provides an exquisite getaway.

MILL & FACTORY OUTLET STORE

■FARIBAULT WOOLEN MILL COMPANY
FARIBAULT WOOLENS FACTORY STORE
1819 N.W. Second Ave.
Faribault, MN 55021
Tel: (218) 334-1644
Hrs: Mon. - Sat. 9 a.m. - 5:30 p.m. Sun. noon - 4 p.m. Closed holidays
Visa, Mastercard, and AmEx are accepted.

Beginning in 1865 with a one-horse treadmill, five generations of skilled craftsmen have developed this family-owned company into a thriving business through pride and motivation. Faribault Woolen Mill Company survived three fires from 1888 to 1892, rebuilding and expanding from selling yarn to producing fine woven cloth. In an historic brick mill on the banks of the Cannon River, Faribault Woolen Mill Company employees use high-tech equipment to practice an ancient manufacturing process.

In the 125 years that Faribault has been in business, blanket making has gone from hand operation to micro-chip control. One of only a few "fully vertical" woolen mills existing in the U.S., the mill is capable of changing raw wool into woven blankets. Scouring and blending, dyeing, carding, spinning, weaving, and burling all occur under one roof. In fact, the Faribault Woolen Mill manufactures throws and blankets exclusively. These include fine wools, wool blends, cotton, and acrylic, designed and woven by its 175 workers. The Faribault Woolens Factory Store offers these in current first-quality colors, as well as slightly irregular items and discontinued colors. Other items include men's, women's, and children's clothing, toys made from blanket patterns, and hand-woven throws and blankets produced by its mill in Houston. Monogramming and shipping are available. Faribault Woolens invites visitors to the outlet store where warmth, integrity, and excellence can be found in every product.

NURSERY

■DONAHUE'S GREENHOUSE
420 Tenth Street S.W.
Faribault, MN 55021
Tel: (507) 334-8404
Hrs: Mon. - Sat. 8:30 a.m. - 5 p.m.
    (Apr., May, Nov., and Dec.) Sun. noon - 5 p.m.
Visa, MasterCard, and Discover are accepted.

What started as a perennial nursery in 1932, has grown with the 1940s introducing garden mums, and the 1950s and 1960s bringing spring bedding plants and garden center business. In 1972, Dick and Lois Donahue, along with their family, took over and substantially increased the wholesale and retail business. Donahue's Greenhouse is now a four-acre plus greenhouse.

The greenhouse has one of the largest displays of spring plants and poinsettias under one roof in the Midwest. There are over 40 varieties of clematis, a Minnesota hardy vine, and over 100 varieties of garden chrysanthemums. There is a wide variety of colorful greenery and multi-colored geraniums, petunias, marigolds, fuchsias, hibiscus, and bougainvillea, among many others. Christmas time brings a "sea of red," with over two football fields of poinsettias on display!

Donahue's Greenhouse is a complete garden center offering beautiful flowering and foliage plants, along with a friendly, knowledgeable staff. It is truly a unique and enjoyable experience, one in which visitors can take a little bit of the atmosphere home with them.

■R ESTAURANT

■ THE LAVENDER INN
2424 Lyndale Ave.
Faribault, MN 55021
Tel: (507) 334-3500
Hrs: (Rose Room and Gold Room) Daily 11 a.m. - 10 p.m.
(Gallery Dining Room) Sat. evening and Sun. noon

The Lavender Inn, that famous "little oasis" 50 miles south of the Twin Cities, just off I-35 at Exit 59 and 50 miles further to the Iowa border, is the perfect place to stop as visitors are traveling. It began as a drive-in in 1960 and became well-known for its one-dollar broasted chicken and 25-cent hamburger.

The Lavender Inn now has three different dining rooms, each with its own personality, exquisite decor, and elegant furnishings. The classic interior, the aroma of gourmet feasts, and the warmth of family greet customers. Chef Sonny Craig brings 30 years of experience and serious commitment to the art of cooking. The careful selection and preparation of choice meats and seafoods are enhanced by fresh, locally grown vegetables. The Lavender Inn menu features favorites such as broasted chicken, fresh scallops, walleye pike, jumbo shrimp, prime rib, and many other enticing entrees. Dinner is complemented by fresh bread and distinctive beverages. Aside from the dining rooms, the Lavender Inn proudly features an art gallery displaying artwork by Terry Redlin, Jim Killen, Elaine Wadsworth, Lou Roman, and other popular wildlife, landscape, and impressionist artists. The art gallery also offers a fine selection of porcelain collector items, hand-carved jade and ivory, Strauss crystal, and costume jewelry, all reasonably priced.

For a unique experience, choose the Lavender Inn. After dining, be sure to visit other local sites such as the Faribault Woolen Mill, Tilt-A-Whirl, and the Treasure Cave Blue Cheese.

Frost

L ocated just south of I-90 in lush, rolling southern Minnesota farmland, Frost is usually not on passing motorists' itineraries. It is a hidden jewel, a unique city of less than 250 people supporting an amazing variety of cottage industries. In fact, Frost is steadily attracting new residents who work in neighboring industries, but who wish to return at night to the peace and quiet of a genuine small town. The area has a strong Norwegian heritage, which becomes transparently obvious at a visit to the extravagant *Nordic World,* the area's largest Scandinavian gift shop featuring an extensive collection of Scandinavian imports, original rosemaling (a Scandinavian art form involving elaborate drawings of flowers and leaves), as well as Minnesota crafts. The *Main Street Coffee Shop,* meanwhile, is about as Middle America as they come, a favorite meeting ground for townspeople to enjoy a little gossip over a cup of steaming coffee and a plate of hearty home cooking.

For more information on Frost, contact:
FROST ECONOMIC DEVELOPMENT AUTHORITY
P. O. Box 548
Frost, MN 56033
(507) 878-3106

S|CANDINAVIAN GIFTS

■NORDIC WORLD
100 Pioneer Trail
Frost, MN 56033
Tel: (507) 878-3110
Hrs: (May - Christmas) Tue. - Sat. 10 a.m. - 5 p.m.
    (Winter) Tue. - Fri. 1 p.m. - 5 p.m.
Visa and MasterCard are accepted.

Just five minutes south of I-90 on Highway 254 near the edge of Frost sits Nordic World. This gift shop is located on a farm that has been owned by the same family since before the Civil War. Sonja Anderson is the owner, and she spends her time filling the shop with treasures. Many of the treasures she has made herself and others are imported from Scandinavian countries. Nordic World boasts the largest collection of Scandinavian imports and Minnesota gifts in the area.

Since 1982 Nordic World has attracted shoppers from all of the United States as well as countries outside the U.S. The inventory crafted by Anderson includes breadboards, Christmas ornaments, jewelry boxes, and trunks. All of the items made by Anderson are handpainted in the form of rosemaling. Import items include Norwegian sweaters; jewelry from Norway, Sweden, and Finland; a large variety of candleholders, candles, table runners; and Scandinavian records and tapes.

Cookbooks and bakeware invite customers to try new and different recipes when setting the table with pewter and crystal atop an imported tablecloth, all of which can be purchased at Nordic World. Greeting cards can also be found to accompany purchases. This intimate and comfortable setting entices customers to browse and thoroughly enjoy the selection and quality provided by Nordic World.

Glencoe

Little Glencoe is an industrial giant in miniature. This community of 4,700 is home to the world's largest corn packing plant and a disproportionate number of leading manufacturing firms such as the feed manufacturer Glencoe Mills, the hearing aid producer Starkey Labs, and Delta Manufacturing, a firm specializing in metal electrical enclosures. The city aggressively promotes its industrial parks and its convenient location just an hour southwest of the Twin Cities, and is steadily enlarging its commercial base. But despite its industrial focus, Glencoe is one of the few cities in the state with its own wildlife park, the 40-acre *Sportsmen Club Wildlife Sanctuary.* Located at the west end of *Oak Leaf City Park* — an attractive facility with picnic shelters and outdoor pools — the sanctuary features deer, Canadian geese, wild ducks, pheasants, and peacocks. Glencoe also supports its own community theater — the *Buffalo Creek Players* — which presents traditional and children's plays in the historical *Crystal Theater Building.* The main event of the year, *Glencoe Days,* takes place in Oak Leaf Park during the second weekend in June and includes a mouthwatering, free corn-feed provided by the local Green Giant plant, along with a carnival, dance, sporting events, and other family fun.

For more information on Glencoe, contact:
GLENCOE AREA CHAMBER OF COMMERCE
630 Tenth Street E.
Glencoe, MN 55336
(612) 864-3650

Granite Falls

G ranite Falls owes its name to the abundance of granite found here along both shores of the scenic Minnesota River. Geologists have determined that the Granite Falls granite, a rock appearing in a variety of colors ranging from grey to dark red, is among the oldest in the world — older even than the Grand Canyon. The granite deposits in this area are remnants of mountains that once stood four miles high, but were slowly eroded during the past four billion years to form today's bedrock. An outcrop of this bedrock is displayed at the *Yellow Medicine County Historical Museum,* which also features excellent exhibits of pioneer and Native American artifacts. Another historical sight worth visiting is the Upper Sioux Agency, located in the scenic *Upper Sioux Agency State Park,* complete with a horse campground, and horse and hiking trails. The Upper Sioux reservation agency was established by the U.S. government in the mid-1800s, but was destroyed in the Dakota Indian wars in 1862. One building has been restored and is available for viewing, along with a natural history center with a "touch and see" room. For those hungry for more outdoor activities, the city is an excellent vantage point for surprisingly good catfish and walleye fishing in the *Minnesota River, Yellow Medicine River,* or *Hawk Creek* —

maybe combined with a camping trip to *Memorial Park* south of town. Also outdoor-related, the main annual event in Granite Falls is the huge *Western Fest and Stampede Rodeo,* a must for anyone interested in the professional rodeo excitement of bareback riding, calf roping, steer wrestling, and bull riding.

For more information on Granite Falls, contact:
GRANITE FALLS AREA CHAMBER OF COMMERCE
P.O. Box 220 A
Granite Falls, MN 56241
(612) 564-4039

GAMING CASINO

■ FIREFLY CREEK CASINO
P.O. Box 96
Granite Falls, MN 56241
Tel: (612) 564-2121
Hrs: Mon. - Thur. 10 a.m. - 2 p.m., Fri. open 24 hours
Visa, MasterCard, and Discover are accepted.

The Firefly Creek Casino offers gambling in an authentic Indian environment. This casino shies away from the Las Vegas type atmosphere and creates a more earthy feel with Indian theme decorations. Blackjack and video slot machines provide gambling excitement and highly valued jackpots. Keno is also featured on video machines throughout the casino.

The Firefly Restaurant is located inside the casino and serves breakfast and lunch menu items in a casual setting. The house speciality is Indian tacos, or try the freshly made Indian fried bread. For a gambling experience in an original setting, the Firefly Creek Casino has much to offer.

Hutchinson

In 1855, the singer Asa Hutchinson and two of his musical brothers settled in this frontier village along the banks of the Crow River in southern Minnesota. A few years later, Asa, his wife Elizabeth, and their four children traveled to the East on a concert tour to raise funds for the expansion of the modest village church. The citizens of the Massachusetts town of Martha's Vineyard were so impressed by the Hutchinsons' altruism that they donated a sizeable sum of money, some of which was spent to purchase the bell that today still tolls in the clocktower of the *Vineyard's Methodist Church.* The same year as the fateful arrival of the Hutchinsons (who, needless to say, had the young town named after them), the city set aside 15 acres of parkland, making Hutchinson's park system the second oldest in the country. Today, these 27 city parks still form a comforting heart for the community, with picnic grounds, paths, and playgrounds. For a better chance to view wildlife, however, visitors and residents make tracks to the *Wildlife Sanctuary Park* located along the banks of the Crow River. Founded by the Gopher Campfire and Gun Club, the oldest conservation club in the United States, the 25-acre sanctuary offers excellent opportunities to observe deer and waterfowl. Also overlooking the Crow River is a life-size statue of *Chief Little Crow,* erected in honor of the leader of the Dakota uprising in 1862. Another sight of historical interest is the *McLeod County Heritage & Cultural Center,* featuring a century-old log house, period room, and the *Les C. Kouba Gallery* with its permanent display of 200 paintings by the internationally renowned wildlife artist. Among the city's annual events, the most notable are the *Taste of Hutchinson* arts and crafts festival and *Water Carnival* celebration held each summer; the fall *McLeod County Fair and Heatwole Threshing Show;* and the winter *Sno Break,* featuring magnificent, illuminated ice sculptures.

For more information on Hutchinson, contact:
HUTCHINSON CONVENTION AND VISITORS BUREAU
45 Washington Ave. E.
Hutchinson, MN 55350
(612) 587-5252

ACCOMMODATIONS

■ VICTORIAN INN LODGING & CONFERENCE CENTER
1000 Highway 7 W.
Hutchinson, MN 55350
Tel: (612) 587-6030
Diners Club, AmEx, Visa, and MasterCard are accepted.

The Victorian Inn/Conference Center meets the needs for nearly any type of gathering. Banquet rooms are available with a capacity for up to 300 guests. The smaller meeting rooms are perfect for seminars or private parties. Victoria's Dining Room provides full dinners or hors d'oeuvres for any occasion. The dining room also provides delicious breakfasts, lunches, and

dinners for anyone who enjoys good food and good service. Sir Lancer's Lounge has a full-service bar and a lighter menu for a more casual outing. The rooms at the Victorian Inn are all individually decorated emphasizing the Victorian era. Suites provide king-size beds, jacuzzis, and wet bars. Inside and outside rooms are also available, offering queen-size beds. A swimming pool and game room complete the attractions for guests to visit.

B ED & BREAKFAST

■ HARRINGTON HOUSE
325 Hassan Street
Hutchinson, MN 55350
Tel: (612) 587-2400
Hrs: Open year-round
All major credit cards are accepted.

The Harrington House was built in 1892 and provides guests with the opportunity to enjoy a turn-of-the-century atmosphere in lodging and dining. Located just one block east of the main street in Hutchinson, this bed and breakfast offers a variety of ways to pass the time. A player piano and Edison crank phonograph occupy the living room, which is enhanced by stained-glass windows, hardwood floors, and a beamed ceiling. The guest suites consist of a bedroom, parlor, and bathroom.

One of the suites has a fireplace and large double whirlpool with a shower. Another of the suites has a double shower, clawfoot tub, and marble floor. Each has a private phone line, remote color television, and a refrigerator. Antiques and handmade quilts adorn each room. The gourmet restaurant provides one seating per meal in which to enjoy excellent food and relish the surroundings over a long, leisurely meal.

A full gourmet breakfast is included in the stay as well as evening hors d'ouevres. This Victorian-style bed and breakfast invites visitors to enjoy the pace and hospitality of a bygone era.

GIFTS & COLLECTIBLES

■ THE VILLAGE SHOP

134 S. Main
Hutchinson, MN 55350
Tel: (612) 587-2727
Hrs: Mon. and Thur. 9 a.m. - 9 p.m.
    Tue., Wed., Fri., and Sat. 9 a.m. - 5 p.m.
Visa, MasterCard, and Discover are are accepted.

The Village Shop contains gifts in all price ranges for all occasions. Customers return again and again because new treasures are discovered with each visit. The shop is the perfect place to browse, it has intriguing merchandise on every shelf with plenty of space in which to comfortably linger. Collectibles include The Heritage Village and Snow Village Collection, Hummels and Maude Humphrey figurines along with many collector plates.

Wedding, anniversary, and novelty gifts are in abundance along with free gift wrapping and delivery service. Bath items, T-shirts, wind chimes, stuffed animals, candles, and jewelry are just a small listing of the extensive inventory. This is truly one of Minnesota's unique gift shops.

Jackson

V iolent conflicts between the native inhabitants of these prairie lands and the early European settlers color the history of Jackson. Two times, young Jackson was completely deserted after settlers and Indians shot it out among the rickety shacks of the struggling settlement. Even after the Dakota War of the 1860s had once and for all settled the conflict, Jackson was left to suffer through droughts, grasshopper devastations, blizzards, and prairie fires. Life is easier in this farming town of 3,600 today, but the memories of these early days are vividly present in several historic sites. Most notable among these is historic *Fort Belmont,* erected in 1864 during one of the Indian conflicts. The reconstructed fort contains a sod house common on the prairie 100 years ago and the only water-wheel operated flour mill in the Midwest. In the neo-classical *Jackson County Courthouse* there's a display of rock fossils and Indian relics; while the Jackson Historical Museum with its giant wall mural features extensive pioneer collections. Also a must for history fans is *Jackson*

County Fair Village, a fascinating collection of restored log cabins, a schoolhouse, a depot, a hotel, a printshop, and more, available for viewing during the month of August. In addition to history, Jackson offers excellent boating, canoeing, camping, and fishing opportunities on the *Des Moines River* and in *Kilen Woods State Park,* as well as golfing at *Jackson Country Club* and *Loon Lake Golf Course.* Special events include nationally famous car races every Saturday at the *Jackson Speedway,* and the *Fort Belmont Renegade Days* in July, featuring demonstrations of old-fashioned spinning and embroidery, lefse baking, butter churning, early blacksmithing, and fur trapping.

For more information on Jackson, contact:
JACKSON CHAMBER OF COMMERCE
1000 Highway 71 N.
Jackson, MN 56143
(507) 847-3867

GIFT SHOP

■WELLS DESIGN STUDIO
213 Third Street
Jackson, MN 56143
Tel: (507) 847-4292
Hrs: Mon. - Wed., Fri. 9 a.m. - 5 p.m.
    Thur. 9 a.m. - 8 p.m., Sat. 9 a.m. - 1 p.m.
Visa, MasterCard, and Discover are accepted.

Wells Design Studio originated in humble beginnings, but Dave and Teresa Wells had big plans which were to be realized. In 1974 a log cabin served as the setting; this was soon outgrown and in 1977, the move to a renovated two-story house took place. Currently located in downtown Jackson, this paint and decorating store has expanded to include selling gifts and maintaining a year-round Christmas room. Just two blocks south of the downtown stoplight, Wells Design Studio provides two full floors of gift and decorating items.

One of the most popular events to take place at Wells is the annual Christmas Open House held the first weekend of November each year. This much anticipated event boasts five rooms of gift and decorating ideas for the holidays. The Scandinavian corner, stocking stuffer corner, and German wood collectibles are among the most favored browsing areas. Free gift wrapping is available as well as an inviting cup of hot apple cider and a plate full of homemade gingersnap cookies. During the rest of the year, Wells Design studio also functions as a full interior design service. Teresa Wells specializes in designing colors and interiors that complement the house or building she is working on at the time. Accent pieces such as clocks, kitchen accessories, and wall prints abound at decorators' fingertips. Other pieces include Dickens Village, Snow Babies, and also beautifully designed silk flower arrangements.

Le Sueur

O ne of the oldest settlements in southern Minnesota, Le Sueur was named in honor of the Frenchman Charles Pierre le Sueur who explored the area in the early 1700s. In the mid-19th century, Le Sueur enjoyed a brief hiatus as the county seat of Le Sueur County — a distinction it lost in 1875, fortunately without succumbing to depopulation like many other towns that lost county seat status. Instead, Le Sueur matured and eventually spawned two great native sons, William Mayo, who founded the world-famous Mayo Clinic in Rochester, and the Jolly Green Giant — the fictitious spokesman for the Le Sueur-based Green Giant vegetable processing company. Today, the *Mayo House* — where, incidentally, a former president of Green Giant once lived — has been restored and opened to the public. Next door to the Mayo House, the *Mayoview History Center & Gift Shop* features changing exhibits of state or area history; while the *Le Sueur Museum* includes eclectic exhibits of an early hotel room, post office, and school room, as well as a unique veterinary display. Another historic building that doubles as a fine bed-and-breakfast inn is the *Cosgrove Home,* built in 1893 by one of the founders of Green Giant. Some of the most challenging and picturesque golfing is also ready at hand in Le Sueur at the 165-acre *Le Sueur Country Club.* Other than golfing, residents join in five- and ten-kilometer runs, street dances, and corn feeds during the *Giant Celebration* in early August, and in the old-time fun of the *Pioneer Power Threshing Show* later in the month.

For more information on Le Sueur, contact:
LE SUEUR AREA CHAMBER OF COMMERCE
500 N. Main Street
Le Sueur, MN 56058
(612) 665-2501

Litchfield

L ocated 70 miles west of Minneapolis in prime corn country, Litchfield represents the very heart of Minnesota's farming tradition. It's the kind of town where visitors feel right at home — not a flashy spot, but a place filled with hometown hospitality and low-key friendliness. A variety of visitors' services are available, including fine dining for reasonable prices at *The Blue Heron's Daughter Restaurant & Lounge.* But Litchfield is primarily a place to soak up farm culture, and there's nowhere better to start than at the *Nelson Turn-of-the-Century Farm* where the kids can cuddle chicks, pet sheep, play in the hay, or enjoy other traditional country fun. The *Meeker County Historical Museum,* meanwhile, is an ideal choice for more insight into settler history, as well as an intriguing display of Civil War artifacts. The Civil War is also memorialized in the fortress-like *Grand Army of the Republic Hall,* one of the nation's last remaining memorials entirely built by Civil War veterans. Memories of yet another conflict come alive at the reconstructed *Forest City Stockade,* erected in 1862 six miles north of town to serve as protection during the Dakota uprising. Many of the city's events have a farming connection, including, of course, the *Meeker County Fair* in August, as well as the *Peanut Butter and Milk Festival* in February. The most boisterous event of the season is *Watercade* during the first weekend following Fourth of July, featuring parades, water shows on *Lake Ripley,* and a queen pageant.

For more information on Litchfield, contact:
LITCHFIELD AREA CHAMBER OF COMMERCE
P.O. Box 820-G
Litchfield, MN 55355
(612) 693-8184

R ESTAURANT

■ THE LIBRARY SQUARE RESTAURANT
201 S. Sibley
Litchfield, MN 55355
Tel: (612) 693-7947
Hrs: Mon. - Sat. 7 a.m. - 10 p.m., Sun. 8 a.m. - 3 p.m.

Originally built in 1904 as Litchfield's public library, the building was purchased by Bill and Laura Harper in 1983. With extensive renovation, this historic library was restored to its original condition and turned into the Library Square Restaurant.

Befitting its former function, the restaurant is quiet and peaceful. Everything served at the Library is prepared from scratch, with out-of-the-ordinary menu selections for each meal. Breakfast offers a variety of wholesome country entrees from scrambled eggs and hearty omelettes to pancakes, french toast, and Belgian waffles.

Lunch and dinner selections are numerous and include a variety of tempting appetizers, sandwiches and salads, homemade soups, tender steaks, fresh fish, turkey, and chicken items. Dinners are prepared or sauteed to perfection, with individual selections smothered in special sauces. Conclude a meal with one of Laura's famous homemade desserts featuring a variety of pies. The Library also offers complete catering services for banquets and private parties.

S PA

■ BIRDWING SPA
R.R. 2, P.O. Box 104
Litchfield, MN 55355
Tel: (612) 693-6064
Hrs: Open year-round
Visa and MasterCard are accepted.

Birdwing Spa — the Minnesota Spa with a national reputation and a European touch — is on a 300-acre private estate with 20 kilometers of beautiful wooded trails abundant with wildlife.

Birdwing Spa offers days of revitalizing exercise, healthful gourmet dining, absolute pampering, and evenings of country serenity. There are several spa packages to choose from, whether it be a one-day, weekend, one-week, or an extended visit. Packages offer exquisite accommodations, gourmet meals, fitness programs, speakers, cooking classes, beauty makeovers, and much more. Customers can indulge in massages, facials, manicures, and pedicures. Relax in the sauna, jacuzzi, or by the fireplace. Discover health tips and customized exercise routines that work. The Birdwing's highly qualified staff will consult with visitors to design the best schedule according to their individual needs.

Whether here for a day or an entire week, guests leave feeling renewed, relaxed, a little healthier, and a bit spoiled. Birdwing is one of the few authentic European spas in the Upper Midwest.

Luverne

L uverne is a most intriguing mixture of farming tradition, prairie wilderness, and industry. Primarily a farming community, Luverne is engulfed by cornfields and echoes to the sounds of combines and cattle auctions. But it was also in Luverne that the "big brown Luverne" automobiles were made in the early 1900s (in the same building where Luverne Fire Apparatus has built fire fighting equipment ever since), and it is in Luverne today that a Kosher processing plant produces beef for Jewish communities throughout the nation. Most notably, however, just five miles to the north of the city lies *Blue Mounds State Park*, one of the few remaining, untouched areas of prairie left in the country. The park, featuring an interpretive center, is home to the largest herd of buffalo in the state, as well as another rare, overlooked state resident: the delicate prairie cactus. Other interesting sights in Luverne include the *Palace Theatre & Museum* — built in 1915 as a vaudeville theater, it today serves as a community movie house and as a venue for the three yearly performances by the local community theater *Green Earth Players.* Along with the Palace Theatre, the *Hinkly House Museum* from 1892 is another fascinating historical site. The Hinkly family mined the granite seen in many of the buildings in the area, and they stored the dynamite they used in their quarries in a unique cavern system beneath the house. In the way of events, Luverne is site of the *Tri-State Band Festival* attracting marching bands from across the country each September. In June, the city hosts *Buffalo Days,* with an auto show, arts and crafts fair, and horseshoe pitching contest.

For more information on Luverne, contact:
LUVERNE CHAMBER OF COMMERCE
102 E. Main
Luverne, MN 56156
(507) 283-4061

Mankato

A lthough Mankato's name resulted from a misspelling of the Dakota Indian word for "greenish blue earth" — which abounds in the area — few other things have gone wrong for this city of 40,000. (Actually, Mankato is two cities in one; Mankato to the south of the Minnesota River and North Mankato, rather self-explanatory, located to the north.) The city was founded on the extensive river boat traffic, which flourished along the Minnesota in the 1800s, and is beautifully located on the bluffs where the river joins with the Blue Earth River. Once, ferries provided the connection between the two Mankatos, but in 1880 the first bridge was built, and the city never stopped growing. In intervening years, it has attracted some of Minnesota's largest companies, including Carlson Craft (one of the largest printing operations in the country), Hubbard Milling (the world's largest processor of private label pet food) and Johnson Fishing, a leading international producer of fishing rods and reels. Today, Mankato ranks as the major trade, medical, and educational center of southern Minnesota, complete with a university, several colleges, hospitals, numerous restaurants and hotels, and a flourishing cultural life.

ATTRACTIONS

Mankato is home to famed children's author Maud Hart Lovelace, and some of Mankato's unique culture-related attractions are the tours of the various homes and sites she described in her *Betsy and Tacy* series, well-known among children nationwide. The *Mankato Symphony Orchestra*, along with various theatres such as the *Mankato State University Theatre Arts Department, The Merely Players*, and *Cherry Creek Theatre* located in the beautifully renovated *Carnegie Library;* make their own lively contribution to the city's culture scene. In addition to the Carnegie Library, there are numerous fine historical buildings in town, most notably the *R. D. Hubbard House*, a magnificent 1871 French Second Empire style mansion; the Queen Anne style *Judge Lorin P. Cray Mansion;* and Blue Earth County Courthouse with its local Mankato stone. Also a fascinating piece of local history, the *Seppmann Mill* — located in *Minneopa State Park* — was one of Minnesota's first stone gristmills. The state park, however, with its waterfall, campgrounds, and trails, is itself worth a visit, as are some of the other parks in the area. Magnificent hiking or bicycling are available along the 39-mile *Sakatah Singing Hills Trail,* which meanders through rich farmland along an abandoned railway line, or the *Flood Wall Trail* along the scenic Minnesota River. Those looking for more physical activity often visit the ski resort *Mount Kato,* which features eight chairlifts, 18 slopes, and a chalet and rental shop. *All Seasons Arena,* meanwhile, arranges skating lessons and clinics in addition to ice shows and figure skating performances; while *Skatin' World* offers some of the best roller skating around.

EVENTS

To some, the biggest annual event is also sports-related. It's the late summer *Minnesota Vikings Training Camp,* when the professional players can be seen working out on Blakeslee Field at Mankato State University. A little later in the year, the town is filled by the sounds and colors of the fascinating *Mahkato Mdewakaton Pow-Wow,* with its dancing, traditional foods, and exquisite crafts. Yet later on, in mid-November, it's time for the *1800s Historic Festival,* featuring fur traders, historic artifacts, music, and other family fun. The final event of the year comes on the heels of the Historic Festival. It is the *Celebration of Lights* — a month-long event when residents and businesses light thousands of Christmas lights all over town and numerous smaller events are held.

For more information on Mankato, contact:
MANKATO AREA CONVENTION & VISITORS BUREAU
P.O. Box 999
Mankato, MN 56001
(507) 345-4519 or (800) 426-6025

ACCOMMODATIONS

■ BEST WESTERN - GARDEN INN
Highway 169
111 Range Street
North Mankato, MN 56003
Tel: (507) 625-9333
Hrs: Open daily year-round
Visa, MasterCard, Discover, and AmEx are accepted.

The Garden Inn, nestled in the valley of the other Twin Cities (Mankato/North Mankato), offers gracious lodging for business or pleasure. A complimentary continental breakfast and newspaper awaits guests during the week, 6 a.m. to 8 a.m. There are 147 spacious rooms from which to choose, as well as meeting, banquet, and convention space for up to 500 guests. An enclosed recreation area with pool, sauna, whirlpool, and putting green is also available for the ultimate in relaxation. Bus tour groups may choose from many entertaining packages available.

The Garden Inn dining room features a Heart Healthy menu for the diet conscious guest. The lounge is completely stocked and provides entertainment Friday and Saturday evenings. The Best Western Garden Inn is a full-service advantage motel offering fine accommodations.

ANTIQUE STORE

■ SAVE MOR ANTIQUES/MAXFIELD HOUSE
816 N. Second
Mankato, MN 56001
Tel: (507) 345-5508
Hrs: Mon. - Sat. 9 a.m. - 5:30 p.m.
Discover, Visa, and MasterCard are accepted.

Save Mor Antiques makes its home in The Maxfield House. Originally built in 1861, this house was constructed by George Maxfield, a prominent businessman who owned the stone quarry. This was the first stone house built in Mankato as well as the oldest still standing.

Save Mor deals in fine glassware, light fixtures, and furniture. Indian artifacts, rare coins, and jewelry are also available. Collectible items from estate sales are on display, creating a wide variety of items from which to choose. Artwork and fine paintings round out the selection. A wealth of items to enhance the decor of homes or offices is Save Mor's speciality.

M USEUM

■ HERITAGE CENTER MUSEUM

Blue Earth County Historical Society
415 Cherry Street
Mankato, MN 56001
Tel: (507) 345-5566
Hrs: (Exhibit Gallery) Tue. - Sun. 1 - 5 p.m.
     (Research Library) Tue. - Fri. 1 - 5p.m.
     Tours and additional visits by appointment

The Heritage Center Museum highlights Blue Earth County and Mankato in the areas of settlement, development, history, and culture. The museum includes hundreds of artifacts from the Blue Earth County Historical Society's collection. Attractions include the Native American artifact collection, the farming and industrial development exhibit, and the Maud Hart Lovelace exhibit.

The Research Library is available to the public for studying family and regional history. The library maintains an extensive manuscript collection. The fee for use of the Research Library is $2 per day. Research assistance is available. Special programs are sponsored, including the Tour of Historic Homes in June and "Ghosts from the Past" in October. The gift shop offers handmade items from the area as well as period gifts and books on local history. Admission to the Exhibit Gallery is $2.50 for adults, $1.50 for students and seniors, and free to children under six.

S HOPPING

■ HARPIES BAZAAR

605 N. Riverfront Drive
Mankato, MN 56001
Tel: (507) 387-2736
Hrs: Open daily
Visa and MasterCard are accepted.

Harpies Bazaar, tucked off by itself in the Old Town area of Mankato, occupies three connected storefronts with nine rooms of gift and home accent ideas. Harpies began in 1971 as a tiny craft shop but has evolved into almost a mini-mall. Merchandise in Harpies ranges from area suppliers to world imports.

The fragrance of potpourri and strains of relaxing music provide a backdrop for creative displays that are a visual delight. The coffee pot is always on for customers to sample a gourmet flavor while browsing through the book room, which features fine children's books. The lace room displays European curtain lace and table coverings. Additional rooms include the fireplace room and the kids' stuff and rubber stamp department. Selections vary from Crabtree & Evelyn soaps to an irresistible sweatshirt collection as well as unusual jewelry and dried flowers.

Harpies has always been a little off of the beaten path so the staff firmly believes in good customer service. Pictures, lamps, and lace samples often go home with customers for a trial run. Tapes and CDs can be heard before being purchased. The goal at Harpies is to give visitors many reasons to return. Being in business for more than 20 years indicates that Harpies Bazaar succeeds in making customers into friends.

TOURS

■R.D. HUBBARD HOUSE
606 S. Broad Street
Mankato, MN 56001
Tel: (507) 345-5566 or (507) 345-4154
Hrs: (Summer) Tue. - Sun. 1 - 5 p.m.
(Winter) Sat. - Sun. 1 - 5 p.m.

Tours and other visits by appointment

The residence of Rensselaer D. Hubbard, founder of Hubbard Milling Company, celebrates its 120th anniversary this year. The Hubbard House was built in the second French Empire style and has long been recognized for its historical and architectural significance. Both the house and the carriage house are on the Minnesota State Historic Register and the National Register of Historic Places.

The house is constructed of local red brick painted white on a Mankato Stone foundation. The maid's call register on the pantry wall still lists the room designations as they were in 1888 and the green silk brocade wall fabric, Tiffany light fixtures, and marble fireplaces transport visitors to an earlier time in Mankato's history.

The R.D. Hubbard House gift shop offers handmade items from the area as well as period gifts and books on the history of the area. Admission is $2 for adults, $1 for students and seniors, and free to children under six. Family admission is $5, providing the opportunity for an inexpensive trip through time.

Marshall

U nlike many other southwestern Minnesota towns, Marshall was founded by a colorful cross-section of ethnic groups. The French, Scots, Welch, English, German, Norwegians, Belgians, and Poles all settled along the rolling hills lining the Redwood River west of the Twin Cities, and apart from isolated ethnic squabbles in the early days, they all got along remarkably well, considering the conflicts on the European continent at that time. These early settlers left behind a spirit of cooperation and friendliness that served Marshall well in its painful transition from railroad town to regional agri-business center. But despite the changes, the Redwood River today continues to be a focus for much of the outdoor activities in Marshall, including canoeing, fishing, hiking, and cross-country skiing in one of the many parks that line the river. Two of the most notable parks in the area are the 1,175-acre *Lake Shetek State Park* 33 miles to the southeast, and *Camden State Park* with its river valley, prairie meadows, and maple forests located ten miles to the southwest. In the cultural arena, Marshall has a variety of offerings, including its own community theater — the *Four Winds Community Theater* — as well as the *Marshall Men's Chorus, Marshall Municipal Band,* and *The Southwest Minnesota Orchestra.* The city also has its share of historical sites, including the *Lyon County Historical Museum,* featuring a fascinating, original 1892 courtroom; and the *Southwest State Historical Center,* with an extensive regional research collection. One of the finest local service businesses, the Greek Revival *Blanchford Bed & Breakfast,* is also an historical site in itself, while *Strawberry Fields* and the *Chalet* simply offer fine antiques and dining, respectively. The major events in Marshall are the unique *International Rolle Bolle Tournament,* a

Belgian game reminiscent of bocce ball; and *Fifties Revival,* a nostalgic celebration of 1950s cars, music, and games.

For more information on Marshall, contact:
MARSHALL AREA CONVENTION & VISITORS BUREAU
501 W. Main Street
Suite 65
Marshall, MN 56258
(507) 537-1865

ACCOMMODATIONS

■BEST WESTERN MARSHALL INN
Junction Highways 19 and 23
Marshall, MN 56258
Tel: (507) 532-3221 or (800) 422-0897
Hrs: Open year-round
All major credit cards are accepted.

The Best Western Marshall Inn has provided the finest in lodging over the past ten years for this bustling campus community. The Marshall Inn is located adjacent to Southwest State University and often serves as lodging for visiting parents or opposing teams. One-hundred tastefully decorated rooms are available to choose from; two suites are available with private whirlpools for the ultimate in relaxation. An indoor pool, sauna, whirlpool, and game area provide an opportunity to lean back and enjoy.

The Camden Country Inn Restaurant in the hotel serves breakfast, lunch, and dinner and has become very popular within the community. Prime rib is the specialty on Friday and Saturday evenings along with a full menu featured every night. The International buffet on Fridays is a real crowd pleaser. The Camden Country Inn Lounge is the perfect retreat in which to socialize and unwind with a favorite cocktail. Meeting rooms are also available for groups from 10 to 500 as well as banquet facilities for up to 400 people. Camden State Park, Lake Shetek State Park, Garvin Park, and the Pipestone National Monument are all within driving distance.

Montevideo

Montevideo and its namesake, the capital of Uruguay, have maintained close ties for more than a century. Montevideo's founder, Cornelius Nelson, had visited Uruguay and was taken by the resemblance between the rolling hills surrounding the two towns. He proposed naming the Minnesota pioneer town in Montevideo's honor, and his persuasive gifts apparently carried the day. Only a few years later, in 1905, the mayor of the Uruguayan Montevideo presented his country's flag to the blooming prairie town, and in 1949, the people of Montevideo, Uruguay, gave their North American friendship town an impressive 11-foot bronze statue of the Uruguayan independence leader *José Artigas.* Today, the statue dominates *Artigas Plaza,* the celebrated heart of downtown Montevideo complete with comfortable outdoor furniture, decorative lights, and recorded music. Still, the most interesting sights in Montevideo are outside town. Eight miles to the northwest lies the reconstructed, 19th-century Indian *Lac Qui Parle Mission;* closer to town visitors find *Chippewa City Pioneer Village,* a fascinating collection of 23 restored historical buildings and a gift shop. The *Olaf Swensson Farm Museum,* located six miles to the east, consists of a 17-acre farmstead, barn, and well-furnished living quarters, while *Camp Release* to the southwest commemorates the spot where the battle-weary Dakotas in 1892 released 269 white prisoners of war to General Sibley. Still on the outskirts of Montevideo, the *Lac Qui Parle State Park,* site of an annual stopover of more than 100,000 migrating Canada geese, offers excellent hiking, fishing and camping opportunities, while in town, *Smith Park* and *Lagoon Park* provide a chance to spend a restful afternoon in secluded, wooden areas. On a hot day, the *Montevideo Outdoor Pool & Waterslide,* featuring a 6,544 square-foot basin and 151-foot waterslide, is a popular gathering place for locals and visitors alike. The main event of the year, the June *Fiesta Days,* is a fun-filled celebration of the friendship between the two Montevideos and includes mouthwatering food, parades, and arts and craft shows.

For more information on Montevideo, contact:
MONTEVIDEO CHAMBER OF COMMERCE
Artigas Plaza
Montevideo, MN 56265
(612) 259-5527

GIFT SHOP

■ CREATIVE CRAFTS
111 N. First Street
Montevideo, MN 56265
Tel: (612) 269-5493
Hrs: Mon. - Sat. 10 a.m. - 5 pm.
   Thur. 10 a.m. - 9 p.m.

Creative Crafts is the brainstorm of ten Montevideo women who are skilled craftspeople and found an outlet for their designs. Originally the idea was to make their items available only in November and December for the holidays but the venture turned out to be so successful that it evolved into a year-round business.

Each owner has an individual skill, which includes folk art painting; artificial flower arrangements and woods; stained glass; clay sculpting of clowns, animals, and people; creation of wreaths, baskets, and woods; restoration of antiques; sewing of quilts and animals; and crocheting. Consignment sales are also a part of the inventory to add even more diversity to the already impressive stock. Creative Crafts combines small town charm with a personal touch to each item sold.

Morton

E very major city in the United States has a little piece of Morton. This scenic Minnesota River Valley community is the source of Rainbow Granite, one of the oldest and hardest stones known, and a preferred building material for hundreds of major municipal and private buildings nationwide. In Minneapolis, Rainbow Granite has been used in the Powers department store building, the Baker Building, and the Public Health Center. Appropriately enough, the two monuments erected to the east of Morton to commemorate the Dakota uprising of 1862 are also made of local granite. One of the bloodiest events of the uprising took place just outside town, at the *Birch Coulee Battlefield* one mile north of the city, where the Dakota surrounded the U.S. cavalry for 36 hours in a pitched, violent battle. Memories of the Dakota Wars come alive in the interpretive center at *Lower Sioux Agency,* one of the two agencies erected by the U.S. government to administer the newly established Dakota (Sioux) reservation. The *Renville County Historical Museum,* as well, maintains extensive exhibits on Dakota life, along with the pioneer tradition of the area. At the *Lower Sioux Indian Community* four miles southwest of Morton, visitors are invited to the high-stakes thrill of *Jackpot Junction,* the largest casino between Las Vegas and Atlantic City. More low-key action takes place at the *Lower Sioux Pottery Shop,* where visitors can see local Dakota artists at work or buy exquisite handmade pottery items. Rounding off a series of Native American-related sights is the colorful *Lower Sioux Pow Wow* and the poignant *Harvest Gathering* at Birch Coulee.

For more information on Morton, contact:
CITY OF MORTON
P.O. Box 127
Morton, MN 56270-0127
(507) 697-6912

■CHANLY CHEESE & GIFT SHOP
Highway 19
Morton, MN 56270
Tel: (507) 697-6294
Hrs: Mon. - Sat. 9:30 a.m. - 7 p.m.
      Sun. 1 - 6 p.m.
Visa, MasterCard, Discover, and AmEx are accepted.

Chanly Cheese and Gift Shop is not just another small town store along the wayside. There are several special features customers will find connected with this shop not found anywhere else. First of all, it is owned and operated by a former bank president and his wife, a former real estate agent. Carl and Phyllis Lokker escaped from the high-pressure career track to pursue their own business, and very successfully.

The name Chanly comes from the first two letters of their children's names, Christopher, Ann, and Lynn. This shop also has its own parking meters, claiming that this gives the store that downtown feel. The small town of Morton is home to this unusual store where cheese of all kinds can be found as well as some unique gift items.

Phyllis has a knack for finding one-of-a-kind treasures to display in the store. Barbecued Iowa corn, funny T-shirts, handmade pottery, and Christmas collectibles with a Ho-Ho-Ho are just a partial listing of the inventory. Gifts that are unlikely to be duplicated are the specialty of the house along with some of the best choices of cheese in the state.

HISTORIC SITES

■ FORT RIDGELY

A Minnesota Historical Society Site
(In Fort Ridgely State Park, 7 miles south of Fairfax on Minn. Highway 4)
Mailing Address: R. R. 1, Box 32, Fairfax, MN 55332
Tel: (507) 426-7888 or (507) 697-6321
Hrs: (May 1 - Labor Day) Open daily 10 a.m. - 5 p.m.
There is no admission charge.

Constructed in 1853 on a high plateau near the Minnesota River in southwestern Minnesota, Fort Ridgely lacked a stockade and was made mostly of wood. Deep, wooded ravines surrounded it on three sides. The fort, in the opinion of many soldiers banished to this western outpost, was impossible to defend.

Only nine years later, after a period of peace and routine to the point of boredom, the soldiers' assessment was put to the test. The Dakota Indians, confined to a small reservation along the Minnesota River, had long resisted the sudden, imposed change in lifestyle from hunting to farming. In 1862, tensions reached the breaking point. When the yearly June payment for their ceded land hadn't arrived by August, the Dakota declared war. On August 20, they attacked Fort Ridgely, but withdrew after five hours of fighting. Two days later, they returned, but fire from the fort's five cannons prevented them from organizing an effective assault. One month later, after repeated skirmishes along the upper Minnesota Valley, the Dakota surrendered.

Today, very little is left of Fort Ridgely. After the war ended and the Indians were forced to relocate to the Dakotas or Nebraska, the fort was closed, and settlers tore down the buildings to use the materials for homes and barns. Only a restored stone commissary and a handful of scattered stone foundations littering the windswept plateau remain. Here, the Historical Society operates historical exhibits and a gift shop to help visitors remember the last Indian war in Minnesota.

■ LOWER SIOUX AGENCY AND INTERPRETIVE CENTER

A Minnesota Historical Society Site
(Nine miles east of Redwood Falls on Redwood County Highway 2)
Mailing Address: R.R. 1, Box 125, Morton, MN 56270
Tel: (507) 697-6321
Hrs: (May 1 - Labor Day) Open daily 10 a.m. - 5 p.m.
    (Post Labor Day - April 30) Open daily 1 - 5 p.m.
There is no admission charge.

When the first white settlers entered Minnesota in the late 18th century, the Dakota Indians began to lose their land — the very foundation of their traditional hunter-gatherer culture. Their dispossession culminated in treaties signed in 1851, when the U.S. government confined them to a reservation along the upper Minnesota River in southwestern Minnesota.

The U.S. built two agencies on the new reservation, the Upper and the Lower Sioux Agencies. Both were crucial elements in the design to change the lifestyle of the Indians and turn them into stable, self-sufficient farmers. By 1862, the plan had partly succeeded. The land under cultivation around the Lower Sioux Agency had increased to 1,357 acres, and more than 100 white and mixed-blood residents lived in the thriving prairie settlement. But the government's efforts to "civilize" the Indians were heavy-handed, taking little or no account of Indian culture and traditions. Many Indians resented the pressure to change and to give up their traditional life. Their resistance eventually led to the U.S. - Dakota conflict of 1862.

A single stone warehouse is now the only remnant of the Lower Sioux Agency; most of the other buildings were burned during the six-week war. The Minnesota Historical Society operates a visitor center featuring a film and an exhibit called "A Harvest of Sorrow." The film, exhibit, and museum shop books help visitors recall the tragic story of the Dakota and their last stand in the Minnesota Valley. In addition, unmarked trails explore the 240 acres of grassland, river bottom, and wooded bluffs surrounding the center.

G AMING CASINO

■ JACKPOT JUNCTION CASINO
P.O. Box 420
Morton, MN 56270
Tel: 1-800-LETTER-X
Hrs: Open daily, 24-hours-a-day
Discover, Visa, and MasterCard are accepted.

Jackpot Junction Casino has evolved from its origins as a bingo hall into a very successful casino. This casino is located on the Sioux Indian Reservation and is owned and operated by that tribe. Jackpot features Vegas-style gambling, a 24-hour fine dining restaurant, and live entertainment nightly.

The two-story casino is loaded with a variety of gaming entertainment. There are over 40 blackjack tables with betting limits from $2 to $500. Jackpot offers over 700 coin drop slot machines including ¢5, ¢25, $1, and $5 slots. Progressive jackpots and video poker are available. A live Keno lounge and nightly Mega Bingo invite even the novice gambler. Jackpot's new campground can accommodate 90 campers and motorhomes with full hook-ups and bathhouses. Complimentary shuttle service is also provided to area hotels in the neighboring towns of Willmar, New Ulm, Olivia, and Redwood Falls.

Impressions restaurant is open 24 hours a day and includes a wide variety of dining entrees. Fine cocktails are also available from the full service bar. Jackpot Junction's new entertainment center features live entertainers nightly. For Las Vegas-style fun in America's heartland, there is Jackpot Junction Casino.

New Prague

N ew Prague's rich Czech heritage is celebrated with much ado, maybe more so because the city was settled by mistake. The founding fathers, new from the old country, took the wrong ferry from St. Paul and ended up on the Minnesota River west of today's Shakopee, instead of their intended destination in the St. Cloud area further to the north. They liked what they saw in the picturesque Minnesota River Valley, and decided to settle here. Naturally, they named their new home Praha after the Czech capital; through the years, the name was Anglicized to New Prague. Today, this city of 3,500 is replete with Czech culture and traditions, from the many historical buildings in town to food such as the cookie *kolacky,* card games like *euchre,* and dances and songs. Passers-by can even hear old-timers rattle off a few phrases of Czech as they stroll in the street or shop in the neighborhood drugstore. Some of the quaint shops that feature traditional gifts and foods are *The Country Store of New Prague; Milo and Ruth Tuma's Country Boutique; The Elegant Era, A Taste of Gourmet,* and *Lau's Czech Bakery & Coffee Shop.* A fun way to start exploring New Prague's heritage is by studying the many historic wall murals scattered through town. After this, a self-guided walking tour will take visitors to the most renowned historic buildings. These include the restored *Schumacher's New Prague Hotel,* designed by famed architect Cass Gilbert in 1898; *St. Wenceslaus Church,* once one of the largest churches in the state; the Old World-designed *Gateway Tower;* the *Bean Mansion,* once the home of the founders of International Multifoods; and, of course, the site of New Prague's founder, *Anton Philipp's Home.* The main event of the year is inspired by the old country. *Dozinsky,* which means harvest festival, is held at the end of

September and features authentic Czech and German food, live ethnic music, dancing, and singing; and demonstrations of intriguing, almost lost Bohemian skills such as lace making and blacksmithing.

For more information on New Prague, contact:
NEW PRAGUE CHAMBER OF COMMERCE
P.O. Box 191
New Prague, MN 56071
(612) 758-4360

HISTORIC HOTEL

■ SCHUMACHER'S NEW PRAGUE HOTEL
212 W. Main Street
New Prague, MN 56071
Tel: (612) 758-2133 or (612) 445-7285 (Twin Cities Metro)
Hrs: (Restaurant) Sun. - Thur. 7 a.m. - 9 p.m., Fri. - Sat. 7 a.m. - 10 p.m.
   (Cally's Bar) Mon. - Sat. until 1 a.m., Sun. until midnight
   (Gift Shop) Daily 9 a.m. - 9 p.m.
All major credit cards are accepted.

When guests arrive at Schumacher's New Prague Hotel, they step into the warmth and charm of a central European inn. Set in a lovely Georgian revival style building, the hotel features a nationally renowned restaurant and provides personal touches that guests will fondly remember.

Superb cuisine established the reputation of Schumacher's New Prague Hotel. Owner John Schumacher's quest for excellence has resulted in a menu featuring excellent ethnic food with an emphasis on homemade freshness. Schumacher, the hotel's executive chef, makes his creativity evident in all the restaurant's offerings. The staff of 60 prepares Czech, German, and Polish sausages from Schumacher's own recipes, debones and dresses all meats and bakes over-size cinnamon and caramel rolls, kolacky, and rye rolls. Diners can feast on delicious entrees like sauerbraten in gingersnap sauce, wienerschnitzel, venison steak saute, creamed rabbit, pheasant in heavy cream, fresh trout with shrimp in dill sauce, or the house specialty — roast duck. The hotel's gift shop reflects Kathleen Schumacher's determination to acquire exclusive hand-crafted gifts and glassware from central Europe. Furniture, lamp shades, and dolls from the Menzel workshop in Bavaria create an authentic setting for this charming shop.

Guests should remember that Schumacher's New Prague Hotel is more than a restaurant. Its 11 guest rooms feature Bavarian hand-carved furniture and lamps, original paintings and imported

Eiderdown comforters, pillows, and linens. Overnight guests receive a complimentary half-bottle of German wine. Gas fireplaces, and private bath with whirlpools add to the romance of this luxurious Bavarian hotel.

New Ulm

New Ulm is southern Minnesota's hidden jewel, an architectural wonder set amidst the rolling hills of the Minnesota River Valley. The German heritage of the town is strong and immediately evident, from the name of the city itself, to the smattering of German speech heard on the street, to the colorful dances and songs of the many German festivals celebrated in earnest each year. Situated on the confluence of the Minnesota and Cottonwood rivers, the town didn't grow up haphazardly overnight like so many other frontier towns. Instead, the early German settlers carefully platted a townsite complete with parks, market squares, and public areas to create their home away from home in the image of the land they had left behind. The foresight of these early settlers contributed to making New Ulm the attractive, prosperous town it is today — as a regional educational center and home to leading corporations such as the cheese processor Kraft, Inc. and several large trucking firms.

ATTRACTIONS

Since it is a German city, New Ulm is a natural location for a beer brewery. Indeed, the *August Schell Brewing Company,* founded in 1860 and family-operated ever since, is one of the most successful specialty beer breweries in the nation; and tours of the brewery and the *Schell Mansion* are musts for beer lovers. In addition to the Schell Mansion, the home of another noted resident of New Ulm is also worth a visit. Erected in 1887 by Minnesota's 14th governor, the stately Queen Anne *John Lind Home* was once a center of New Ulm's cultural life. Today, the focal point for most visitors is the unique *Glockenspiel* with its animated figures, at 45 feet one of the few free-standing carillon clocks in the world. Located in the restful *Schonlau Park,* the Glockenspiel's 37 bells chime the time of day, and play special programs at noon, 3 p.m., and 5 p.m. Another towering testimony to the industriousness of the early residents of New Ulm is *Hermann's Monument,* a 102-foot tall monument to a warrior who united Germany in the ninth century. Other historical sites of interest include the *Harkin Store* eight miles north of town — an 1870s country store restored to its smallest, fascinating detail; the *Doll House Museum* with antique doll displays — hand-crafted dolls are also available for sale on consignment to collectors; the magnificent *Holy Trinity Cathedral Church;* and *Brown County Historical Museum* — in the old New Ulm Post Office, a building reminiscent of guild halls from medieval Europe. Also in the spirit of Germany, New Ulm has many renowned bands specializing in polka and other old-time music, including the world-renowned *Concord Singers.* Finally, thanks to the city's founders, New Ulm's many parks make it possible to spend a relaxing afternoon after traipsing through the city's historical sites. *Flandreau State Park* located just outside town, is ideal for camping and hiking for those who want a touch of wilderness.

EVENTS

The festival season kicks off in late July with *Heritagefest,* a four-day extravaganza billed as one of the top ten community festivals in Minnesota, featuring music and crafts from many European countries. *Oktoberfest,* meanwhile, is an all-German celebration with music and entertainment from the old country; and in February, New Ulm's "Mardi Gras" — *Fasching* — heats up town with its costume party and German music. After all the ethnic celebrations, the final large event of the year, the April *Minnesota Festival of Music,* features Minnesota music makers in all categories from polka via country to jazz.

For more information on New Ulm, contact:
NEW ULM CONVENTION AND VISITORS BUREAU
P.O. Box 862 C
New Ulm, MN 56073
(507) 354-4217

ACCOMMODATIONS & RESTAURANT

■ HOLIDAY INN OF NEW ULM
2101 S. Broadway
New Ulm, MN 56073
Tel: (507) 359-2941
All major credit cards are accepted.

The Holiday Inn of New Ulm, "Home of Oktoberfest," provides exceptional accommodations and meeting facilities for its guests. The Bavarian decor throughout the hotel offers a charming ambience of old Germany.

The hotel's accommodations offer singles, doubles, king, king executive, poolside, and the famous Burgermeister Suite. For banquet parties, the German Cafe offers informal dining for breakfast or lunch in a relaxed outdoor courtyard atmosphere. Complimentary cocktails are offered 5 - 7 p.m., Mon. - Thur. for hotel guests. For breakfast, lunch, and dinner, relish fine dining in Hermann's Heidelberg and Stein. To top off the evening, there is live entertainment and dancing in Hermann's Stein.

The Holidome Indoor Recreation Center includes a heated pool, whirlpool, sauna, exercise room, game room, children's play area, and indoor sunbathing.

A visit to the area's Glockenspiel, Hermann's Monument, and August Schell's Brewery is a must. Relive and celebrate New Ulm's European heritage. Partake in New Ulm's Oktoberfest festivities the second and third weekend in October and Fasching — the weekend before Lent — the German version of Mardi Gras.

For a memorable and affordable experience, come to the Holiday Inn of New Ulm. Come and experience "Gemütlichkeit" — the charm, hospitality, and enjoyment of good things in life.

B REWERY & TOURS

■ SCHELL'S BREWING COMPANY
Schell Park
New Ulm, MN 56073
Tel: (507) 354-5528
Hrs: Tours Available: (Memorial Day - End of October)
    Mon.-Fri. 3 - 4 p.m.
    Sat.-Sun. 1 p.m., 2 p.m., 3 p.m.
    (Nov.-May) By appointment only

August Schell, a young German immigrant, founded the brewery in 1860. During the Sioux uprising in 1862, New Ulm was almost completely destroyed, but the brewery was left untouched due to the family's friendship with the Indians. By 1880, the August Schell business had grown to become the dominant brewery in the region and is the third oldest family brewery in the United States. It has remained in continuous operation at this same historic site for the last 130 years and is still family owned by two brothers, George and Ted Marti.

Schell's Brewery offers a distinctive line of beers in a variety of style unmatched by any other domestic brewery. Schell produces extraordinarily good beer in eight different styles of beer: Pilsner, Bavarian wheat beer, pale lager, dark beer, bock beer, American lager, low-calorie beer, and weiss beer. Their product has won two gold medals at the Great American Beer Festival.

The museum exhibits the original operating equipment and brewer's tools used over the years, along with pictures and other historic remnants. The unique gift shop offers glassware and many items with the Schell logo. There is a minimal charge for tours of the museum and brewery. The gardens of the August Schell Brewery are open to the public and visited by thousands of people each year.

Also worth the visit is the Hermann Monument, which rises 102 feet on the bluff just west of the city. The statue commemorates the deeds of Hermann, who united Germany and defeated the Roman forces in the ninth century.

GIFT & CRAFT STORE

■ DER ULMER SPATZ, INC.
16 S. Broadway
New Ulm, MN 56073
Tel: (507) 354-1313
Hrs: Mon. - Fri. noon to 5 p.m.
Sat. 10 a.m. - 5 p.m.
Call for special hours during Christmas and Heritage Fest
Visa and MasterCard are accepted.

A trip to New Ulm won't be complete without a stop at Der Ulmer Spatz, Inc. Located just one-half block from the Brown County Historical Museum, this castle-like house intrigues tourists and locals alike.

Visitors will be able to find something special in this unique gift and craft store. Discover original paintings, pottery, wood carvings, handmade quilts and needlework, South American baskets, other locally crafted gifts, and unusual imports from around the world. There are many one-of-a-kind gift ideas here not found anywhere else, including the famed "Ulm Sparrow." Purchases may be gift-wrapped or shipped.

Tours of this historic residence are available with one week advance notice. Artist demonstrations can be arranged for tour groups. Guests are also served donuts, cookies, and coffee.

Here in New Ulm where the old legend of the Sparrow of Ulm, Germany still lives, guests explore Der Ulmer Spatz and its charm.

GIFT SHOPS

◼ DOMEIERS, NEW ULM'S GERMAN STORE
1020 S. Minnesota Street
New Ulm, MN 56073
(Located ten blocks south of downtown in a residential area of New Ulm.)
Tel: (507) 354-4231
Hrs: Open Mon. - Sun.
   Closed Wed. Closed a few weeks after Christmas

What began as a neighborhood store in 1934 has since flourished under the guidance of the Domeier family. Filled to the brim with imported German gifts and collectibles, the charming little shop has a real storybook quality and has attracted tourists from around the world.

From the window of the chalet-style building that houses Domeiers, a delightful little gnome greets customers with German folkmusik on his accordian. Inside, the shelves are brimming with enchanting imported treasures. German music filters through the cheery atmosphere; there is so much to see that visitors return again and again for new surprises. Bright wooden nutcrackers, smokers, steins, Bavarian blown glass ornaments, Swiss music boxes, records, tapes, and greeting cards abound.   There are also imported cookies, candies and food, German books and magazines, and more.

During festivals in the City of New Ulm, 13 flags representing the different areas of Germany decorate the street on which the store has stood for more than 50 years. A very special Old World treat that will be enjoyed by the entire family, a visit to Domeiers is like stepping into a corner of Germany's Black Forest region.

◼ LAMBRECHT'S GIFT SHOP AND CHRISTMAS HAUS
119 N. Minnesota Street
New Ulm, MN 56073
Tel: (507) 354-4313
Hrs: Mon. and Thur. 9 a.m. - 9 p.m.
   Tue., Wed., Fri., and Sat. 9 a.m. - 5 p.m.
   Sun. noon - 4 p.m.
Visa, MasterCard, and Discover are accepted.

Built in 1898 as a harness shop and fine leather goods store, this shop was owned by several different families and was the first gift shop in the New Ulm area. Purchased by Curt and Donna

Lambrecht in 1983, it is located on the main street of New Ulm. A Christmas shop was recently added to the upstairs.

Throughout the store are an assortment of greeting cards, nutcrackers, beer steins, baskets, leather goods, collector dolls, T-shirts, beautiful linens, and placemats. The Lambrechts are also dealers for these limited edition collectible lines: Carin Studio Gnomes, Artina Gnomes, Precious Moments, and Department 56 lighted Christmas villages. There is a large variety of glass, crystal, china, and brass. For the bride-to-be, there is a large wedding registry.

The Christmas Haus is separated into different rooms: the Scandinavian Room, Victorian Room, Christmas Village Room, German Christmas Room, Kids Christmas Room, and the Country Christmas Room. Creatively displayed are large Santa figurines, treetops, Nativity sets, nutcrackers, and much more. Many more selections of gifts for the home and every occasion imaginable are available. Free gift wrapping is offered. Lambrecht's Gift Shop and Christmas Haus offers a broad selection and quality of gifts in the area.

■ THE NUTCRACKER
Zentral Platz Building
First S. Minnesota
New Ulm, MN 56073
Tel: (507) 354-7466
Hrs: Mon. - Sat. 9 a.m. - 5 p.m.
    Sun. during special events
Visa, Mastercard, and Discover are accepted.

This enchanting shop of imported gifts has an old world charm. It is located in the Zentral Platz Building, which means "center of the downtown" in German.

The shop specializes in German clothing, so customers can find a good selection of lederhosen, dirndl dresses, and German scarves and hats.

German beer steins and many other collector items are on display. The Nutcracker also carries many antiques, Black Forest clocks, German jewelry, nutcracker toys, stationery, tablecloths, European candies, greeting cards, linens, and many other souvenirs and all occasion gifts. Selections can be gift-wrapped or shipped. For something different or unusual, the Nutcracker is the place to stop.

S AUSAGE & MEAT SHOP

■ THE SAUSAGE SHOP
Third Street N. Broadway
New Ulm, MN 56073
Tel: (507) 354-3300
Hrs: Mon. 8 a.m. - 8 p.m.
     Tue. - Fri. 8 a.m. - 6 p.m.
     Sat. 8 a.m. - 5 p.m.
     Sun. 10 a.m. - 3 p.m.
Visa and MasterCard are accepted.

Located in the center of New Ulm, tourists and locals alike can walk into this shop and smell the aroma of homemade sausage and fresh meat, bringing back memories of the old-fashioned, small town meat shop.

In 1982 Lenny and Donna Donahue renovated an old gas station building into The Sausage Shop, providing the finest and largest variety of homemade sausage for miles around. They have been in the meat business for 30 years. The Sausage Shop offers a full line of fresh meat, homemade sausages, home-cured hams, Landjaegers (German link sausage), and deli food grocery items.

An antique sausage stuffer and grinder is used for demonstrations during Heritage Fest and other festivities. Local festivals buy their meat for their stands from The Sausage Shop. Special services include hog roasts and catering. Visitors "Taste the German Heritage of The Sausage Shop."

Northfield

N orthfield soon became the center for the development of Holstein cows, the descendants of whom can be seen lolling around the many dairy farms surrounding Northfield. It is also the headquarters of major corporations like Malt-O-Meal — responsible for the bulk of the country's hot breakfast cereals. And finally, the city has spawned two renowned colleges, St. Olaf's and Carleton; as well as the celebrated economist Thorstein Veblen — who in his brooding studies coined the phrase "conspicuous consumption"; the Republican governors Edward Thye and Karl Rolvaag, and, in all fairness, the very Democratic U.S. Senator Paul Wellstone. But despite these respectable achievements, it took a gang of outlaws to put Northfield firmly on the map. On September 7, 1876, the infamous Jesse James and his gang tried to rob the First National Bank, but the cashier,

Joseph Lee Heywood, refused to open the safe. In the ensuing, blazing shootout, Heywood and a passer-by were killed along with two members of the gang. Jesse James was eventually shot in Missouri, while his brother Frank was cleared of all crimes and died a free man.

ATTRACTIONS

The site of the bank raid, today known as the *Northfield Historical Society Bank Museum,* has been restored in fastidious detail, including authentic artifacts from the James gang. The Bank Museum is located in the downtown area, much of which today is an historic preservation district with no less than 65 intricately carved, stately buildings, including the *Central Block Building* and the *Scriver Building,* where the bank museum is located. Other historical buildings of note are the sprawling, French Second Empire *Archer House,* now an elegant inn, and the modest home of *Thorstein Veblen.* While in downtown, many visitors take a break with some popcorn purchased from the antique wagon located on Bridge Square, or sample the pies and breads at the traditional *Ole Store bakery.* For those looking for a sampling of the arts instead, many galleries in town present exhibits, including the *Northfield Arts Guild Gallery,* the *Steensland Gallery* and the *King's Room Corridor* at St. Olaf College. Theater plays, musicals, and concerts are performed regularly by the *Northfield Arts Guild Theater,* as well as by students and professionals alike at the St. Olaf and Carleton College theater and concert halls. The *St. Olaf Choir* is renowned worldwide, representing the United States at the 1988 Olympic Arts Festival in Seoul, South Korea. Finally, Northfield offers a relaxing game of golf for those who are so inclined at *Northfield Golf Course.*

EVENTS

The major event of the year is *Defeat of Jesse James Days* on the weekend following Labor Day. The highlight of this major festival — which also includes tractor pulls, rodeos, and parades — is a reenactment of the Great Northfield Bank Raid. The musical events at the *St. Olaf Christmas Festival,* meanwhile, are usually telecast on national public television during the holiday season.

For more information on Northfield, contact:
NORTHFIELD CONVENTION AND VISITORS BUREAU
P.O. Box 198
Northfield, MN 55057
(507) 645-5604 or (800) 658-2548

DELI & CAFE

■ TREATS, LTD.
214 Division Street
Northfield, MN 55057
Tel: (507) 663-0050
    Hrs: Mon. - Fri. 7 a.m. - 7 p.m.
    Sat. - Sun. 8 a.m. - 5 p.m.

Located in the historic Archer House, Treats, Ltd. is a delicatessen and cafe providing a cosmopolitan continental atmosphere and menu selection.

Owner and chef Barbara Hill takes pride in the quality and variety of food served. Treats offers specialty ethnic cuisines and authentic Indian curries. Daily specials feature hot entrees such as chicken and leek pie, steak pie, lasagna, moussaka, shepherd's pie, and curry and pasta dishes. Meat-eaters and vegetarian palates are easily pleased by the variety of menu selections. Bakery items include muffins, caramel rolls, croissants, shortbread, and much more. There is a full range of intriguing beverages of juices, beers, and seltzers. Stupendous desserts of French Chocolate Mousse, Mozart Cake, Amaretto Mousse, and Dutch Apple Cheesecake are a select few to sample. Imported and domestic cheeses, meats, and patés provide a tempting selection from the deli. A wide selection of imported oils, vinegars, olives, pine nuts, and other hard-to-find ingredients can also be found at Treats. For special occasions, conferences, and banquets, complete catering arrangements can be made from the simplest cheese tray to the finest gourmet meal.

Treats offers everything from coffee to a banquet. For the adventurous diner and those hosting special guests, friends, or colleagues, Treats, Ltd. offers superb quality and service with exceptional food.

HISTORIC HOTEL

■ THE ARCHER HOUSE
212 Division Street
Northfield, MN 55057
Tel: (507) 645-5661
Visa, MasterCard, and AmEx are accepted.

The Archer House, built in 1877 by James Archer in the French Second Empire architectural style and renovated in the 1980s by owners Dallas and Sandra Haas, is located in historic downtown Northfield, a bustling town on the banks of the Cannon River.

Visitors are first greeted by the casual elegance of the lobby with its amber-stained glass portal, pressed-tin ceiling, and carved winged-back chairs. This elaborate hotel captures the old-fashioned, homespun graciousness of its 38 rooms. Quaint wallpapers, handmade quilts, and dried flowers add style to the atmosphere. Lavish suites offer the luxury of a whirlpool. Continental breakfast is available upon request. Arrangements for conferences, banquets, or other special occasions are also available. The first floor of the Archer House provides a haven for a variety of specialty shops and restaurants that guests and visitors alike frequent. The Tavern restaurant is located at the riverfront entrance of the Archer House, providing excellent menu selections for breakfast, lunch, and dinner.

While in Northfield stop at the Northfield Historical Society Museum, located in the former Northfield Bank where in 1876 the notorious Jesse James and his gang attempted a robbery. Relive the excitement during the town's celebration dedicated to the event, "Defeat of Jesse James Days." Northfield is rich in past and promise. The historic downtown or the area parks are worth a visit. Visitors enjoy biking, canoeing, fishing, and nature walks on the riverfront. Guests step into the warmth and comfort of an Old Country inn. Midwestern hospitality awaits them at The Archer House, "One of Minnesota's Oldest River Inns."

Olivia

The "Corn Capital of Minnesota," Olivia lies at the heart of an extremely fertile agricultural region. It's a sleepy example of the typical small farming towns dotting the Minnesota countryside, and an ideal representative of the calm friendliness that's cultivated with as much dedication in rural Minnesota as are potatoes and barley. Not surprisingly, the main attraction in town is a *Giant Ear of Corn* located in *Memorial Park,* one of the seven spacious city parks that feature attractive, sheltered picnic areas and tennis, softball, and basketball fields. (Memorial Park also offers free overnight camping.) Golfing, bowling, roller skating, and swimming in the indoor municipal pool are options for the physically inclined. For those looking for historical sights, check out the imposing, prairie-style *Renville County Courthouse* and *St. John's Historical Church.* Farming is, naturally, the focal point for the top event of the season — the four-day celebration *Corn Capital Days* in late July featuring street dances, arts and crafts shows, parades, and a corn feed. Also in July, the *Polka Fest* takes over town with its traditional, fun-filled music and dance.

For more information on Olivia, contact:
OLIVIA CHAMBER OF COMMERCE
P. O. Box 37
Olivia, MN 56277
(612) 523-1350

A CCOMMODATIONS & RESTAURANT

■ THE SHEEP SHEDDE
2425 W. Lincoln
(On west Highways 212 and 71)
Olivia, MN 56277
Tel: (612) 523-5000
Hrs: Open year-round
All major credit cards are accepted.

Entering the Sheep Shedde is like traveling to an olde English pub, restaurant, and inn. In the same location since 1938, the Sheep Shedde has become an institution of quality food and pleasant service in the community of Olivia.

American cuisine is featured on the three restaurant menus. Selections range from tender prime rib to bountiful sandwiches and cool salads. Sunday brunch offers a tantalizing array of traditional favorites — warm muffins, salads, homemade soup, french toast, and baked ham with mashed potatoes and country gravy. This immense selection beckons the diner to a multitude of other savory dishes. Several banquet rooms provide ample facilities for weddings, reunions, or business meetings.

The inn features comfortable, quiet, country rooms with room service and a complimentary continental breakfast. Suites are available for special occasions and business travelers.

Owatonna

L egend has it that Owatonna was named after the daughter of the Dakota Chief Wadena, who brought his sickly girl to bathe in the bubbly mineral springs here. Miraculously, she recovered, and so the tribe decided to settle in this area and name it after the fortunate Owatonna. Be that as it may, Owatonna is no longer a traditional Native American village but a prosperous industrial city, doubling as the transportation hub of southern Minnesota and northern Iowa. It prides itself on being one of the wealthiest cities in the state, measured in per-capita income, and is home to more than 40 large corporations. Two higher education institutions — Pillsbury Baptist Bible College and Owatonna Technical Training Center — smooth the edges of this regional business center and make it an attractive Minnesota destination.

ATTRACTIONS

Owatonna boasts 19 spacious parks, including Morehouse Park with its plethora of play equipment and ducks inhabiting the nearby river; and the 38-acre *Mineral Springs Park,* source of the waters that cured the legendary Owatonna. It's also a good city for golfing, featuring three of the finest courses around — the nine-hole *Havana Hills* and the *Brooktree-Municipal and the Owatonna Country Club* — both challenging and scenic 18-hole courses. A particularly fine day in the outdoors can be had in the *Kaplan's Woods Parkway,* a 225-acre natural wonderland where all vehicles are prohibited, providing a perfect setting for peaceful hiking, skiing, swimming, or canoeing excursions. In the downtown area, two historic buildings — the *Adair House* and the *National Farmers' Bank* (now the Norwest Bank) — provide intriguing insight into a little-known architectural style, the prairie school. A movement during the first two decades of this century, the prairie school style was uniquely American, noted for its linear qualities, long low roofs, and horizontal bands of windows. Other historical sites include the Romanesque *Steel County Courthouse and City Hall,* and the *Union Depot,* complete with the *Old Engine 201* driven by the legendary Casey Jones. The restored *Northrup House* today provides bed-and-breakfast lodging. The *Village of Yesteryear,* meanwhile, consists of eight historical buildings representing early settler life, including a church, fire station, schoolhouse, and general store. In the way of arts and culture, the main attraction is certainly the *Owatonna Arts Center,* featuring a sculpture garden as well as changing displays of the works of local artists. The arts center is also the venue for frequent musical and performing arts programs. For other fine performances, the *Little Theater of Owatonna* presents an eclectic series of drama, comedy, and music several times each year.

EVENTS

The main annual events in Owatonna include *Arts in the Park* in June; the *Historical Society Extravaganza* in July — held in the Village of Yesteryear and featuring blacksmiths, weavers, and spinners plying their traditional trade — the *Car Nuts Antique & Auto Show,* also in July; and the *Pumpkin Festival,* offering fun-filled square dancing and other activities in October.

For more information on Owatonna, contact:

OWATONNA CONVENTION AND VISITORS BUREAU
P.O. Box 331
Owatonna, MN 55060
(507) 451-7970

ACCOMMODATIONS

■ WESTERN INN

Junction I-35 and Highway 14
Owatonna, MN 55060
Tel: (507) 455-0606
Hrs: Open year-round
All major credit cards are accepted.

The Western Inn is a prime choice for lodging between the Twin Cities and Rochester. This handsome inn was originally built as a Holiday Inn in 1975. As a Western Inn it has evolved into a comfortable home away from home for its guests. The hotel offers an indoor pool, sauna, whirlpool, full service restaurant, lounge, and 120 rooms from which to choose. The Executive Suite includes a kitchenette and living room, the remaining two suites provide a private jacuzzi. The Mineral Springs Lounge features live entertainment six nights a week along with hot hors d'oeuvres during happy hour. The Sunset Cafe provides relaxing dining and tasteful specials such as stirfry, pasta dishes, and prime rib on the weekend.

Sunday brunch is also a special attraction running from 10 a.m. to 2 p.m. Meeting rooms are available for conferences, reunions, or special occasions. The Minnesota Executive Boardroom offers the perfect environment for those all-important business sessions. Non-smoking and handicapped rooms are available on request.

ART GALLERY

■ OWATONNA ARTS CENTER
436 Dunnell Drive
Owatonna, MN 55060
Tel: (507) 451-0533
Hrs: Tue. - Sat. 1 - 5 p.m.
Sun. 2 - 5 p.m.
Closed Mon. and during Aug.

The wide variety of artwork at the Owatonna Arts Center is both delightful and astonishing. Even the century-old Romanesque building housing the Center is an unexpected treasure. The Center's main gallery features rotating exhibits of regional artists using a variety of media, while the outdoor Sculpture Garden highlights the efforts of Minnesota sculptors.

Works of music and drama are performed regularly in the Performing Arts Hall — a sound-balanced room decorated with six 12-foot stained-glass panels. The Center also includes the Marianne Young Costume Collection of over 100 costumes from more than 25 countries. Owatonna Community Education and the Mankato State University Extended Campus often hold classes in the Center's working studios.

ART GALLERY & FRAME SHOP

■ CEDAR GALLERY
303 N. Cedar
Owatonna, MN 55060
Tel: (507) 451-3460
Hrs: Mon. - Fri. 9 a.m. - 5:30 p.m.
Thur. 9 a.m. - 8 p.m.
Sat. 9 a.m. - 4 p.m.
Visa, MasterCard, and Discover are accepted.

The Cedar Gallery is located in an historic building of Italian design, rare in southern Minnesota. The historic Zamboni building, built in 1929, is designed in a 16th century Italian style. The design of the building is not the only attraction of this gallery.

The gallery carries limited edition signed and numbered prints as well as watercolors, oils, and original art. A large assortment of custom frames and photographic frames for the featured works or for that special picture at home are also available. A variety of bronze works from local artists such as John Idstrom are special items on display. Collector plates, woodcarvings, and posters created by national and local artists round out the selection.

GIFT SHOP

■ COUNTRY TREASURES

143 W. Broadway
Owatonna, MN 55060
Tel: (507) 451-6384
Hrs: Mon. - Fri. 9 a.m. - 5:30 p.m.
  Thur. 9 a.m. - 9 p.m.
  Sat. 9 a.m. - 5 p.m.
  Hours extended during holidays
Visa and MasterCard are accepted.

Country Treasures is an exceptionally charming gift shop located in historic downtown Owatonna. It is filled with gifts of every shape and size and has expanded to include furniture, bedding, and accessories. Owner Debbie Liskow started this shop because of her affinity for crafts. After attending many gift shows she felt she had enough insight and knowledge to open her own shop. The store is designed with different display areas so clients can see how a particular item would look in their own home. Debbie also assists clients with designing room decor and ideas appealing to their own personal taste. The inventory is constantly changing with a steady influx of new merchandise arriving daily. A wide assortment of country-related items occupy the shelves, including pottery and stoneware made in Northfield, MN. Heritage curtains and table lace provide an elegant accent for the floral designs on display. Wall hangings and Amish, country, and Victorian prints are featured eye catchers.

Reproduction country furniture and bath accessories including soaps and gift packages are favorite items always in stock. Minnesota-related items — including clothing, coffee cups, greeting cards, jams, and jellies — are a well-deserved treat or a great gift for another deserving soul. Wicker baskets, porcelain dolls, kitchen accessories, and candles complete the all-encompassing inventory. Country Treasures is owned and operated by someone who truly enjoys her work, and this quality shows through in every corner of the store.

Pipestone

An intriguing combination of Native American heritage and Midwestern farm culture makes Pipestone unlike any other town. For centuries, Native Americans — most notably the Dakota — quarried the soft, red sandstone found here and fashioned it into ceremonial pipes. Tribes from all across the country coveted the stone, making the Pipestone area one of the last pieces of Minnesota land to be ceded to white settlement. Not until 1876 was the city officially founded by settlers Daniel Sweet and Charles Bennett — 40 years after noted artist George Catlin visited the area and spread the story about the quarry around the world. Bennett had been attracted to Pipestone by Henry Wadsworth Longfellow's famed poem about the area, "Song of Hiawatha", but the droughts, blizzards, prairie fires, and grasshopper plagues did much to destroy the founder's romantic illusions about life on the untamed tallgrass prairie.

ATTRACTIONS

The major attraction in Pipestone is, without doubt, the renowned *Pipestone National Monument.* Covering 283 acres, it encompasses the ancient quarry, where the Dakota still ply their trade, quarrying the red sandstone and fashioning pipes as in centuries past. The monument also includes a fascinating culture center, exploring the Native American heritage of the area as well as the art of pipemaking; and a visitors' center with interpretive displays, films, and other information. While at the monument, most visitors choose to walk the beautiful, mile-long circle tour past the quarries, the waterfalls, and the fantastic stone formations. (The presence of the Dakota Indian community also makes gambling an option at the full-service *Royal River Casino.*) At the entrance to the national monument, meanwhile, looms the pioneer fort replica Fort Pipestone, and just to the south lies *Split Rock Creek State Park* with its unusual stone bridge constructed in the 1930s and its excellent camping, boating, and swimming opportunities. Back in town, the *Pipestone County Museum* features local history exhibits, as well as an impressive Native American exhibit and an extensive collection of paintings by George Catlin. The county museum is located in the *Old City Hall* which — along with the *Calumet Hotel,* the magnificent Courthouse, and 17 other buildings — forms the *Pipestone Historic District.* Most district buildings are built with hand-hewn Pipestone quartz, and all are listed on the National Register of Historic Places. (Most visitors don't leave town until they have admired the details of the carved gargoyles on the building at 102 East Main Street, on the corner of Hiawatha and Main.) A final unique historical site is the concrete *Historic Watertower* located in *Watertower Park.* A 132-foot structure built in 1920, it is one of only two still in existence.

EVENTS

Watertower Park is also site of the season's first major event, *Watertower Park Festival* in June, featuring an art show, sidewalk sales, and a street dance. The top event of the summer is the July *"Song of Hiawatha" Pageant,* a unique, colorful performance with a cast of 200 held in the spirit of Longfellow's poem. The *Civil War Festival* in August, meanwhile, features fascinating reconstructions of soldier's camps, infantry maneuvers, and a Civil War battle performed by reenactors hailing from a wide area, many of whom were in the filming of "Dances With Wolves." The *Festival of Trees* starts after Thanksgiving and features a wide variety of decorated Christmas trees and much more.

For more information on Pipestone, contact:
PIPESTONE CHAMBER OF COMMERCE
P.O. Box 8
Pipestone, MN 56164
(507) 825-3316

GIFTS & SOUVENIRS

■ FORT PIPESTONE
104 Ninth Street N.E.
Pipestone, MN 55164
Tel: (507) 825-4474
Hrs: (May 15 - Aug. 15) Mon. - Sat. 9 a.m. - 9 p.m.
     (Aug. 16 - Sept. 30) Mon. - Sat. 9 a.m. - 7 p.m., Sun. 10 a.m. - 8 p.m.
Visa and MasterCard are accepted.

Fort Pipestone is a replica of a Minnesota fort. The original fort was built as a refuge from the 1862 Sioux uprising. This defensive fort has been replicated for visitors to enjoy. Today, the fort carries gifts and souvenirs reminiscent of the settlers' era.

Upon entering, visitors can't help notice the authentic mounted trophy-size buffalo head. Less intimidating items are made up of predominantly Indian-style gifts and souvenirs. Minnetonka moccasins, Minnesota grown wild rice, and Carlson dolls are all famed state originals. Replicas of Indian bow and arrows, hand-painted shields, and Man-del-las are particularly interesting; and hand-painted buffalo and cow skulls are available.

A beautiful selection of Navajo and Zuni turquoise and silver jewelry are special items over which to ponder. Tipi Maka Duts (House of Red Clay) pottery is produced at the fort and is individually painted by local artists. Craft demonstrations are scheduled throughout the season as are buffalo feeds, which feature grilled or barbecued buffalo as the main entree.

H ISTORIC HOTEL

■ THE CALUMET INN
104 W. Main
Pipestone, MN 56164
Tel: (507) 825-5871 or (800)535-7610
Hrs: Open year-round
All major credit cards are accepted.

The Calumet Inn is located in one of the largest historic districts in Minnesota. Originally built in 1888, this exquisitely decorated hotel is a three-star, three-diamond hotel facility and is listed on the National Register of Historic Places. There are 38 rooms that are richly designed to provide the utmost in comfort and charm for each guest. The original Victorian furnishings come from period mansions in Louisiana, Boston, and England.

In addition to the attraction of the hotel itself, The Calumet Inn hosts the Pipestone Festival of Trees each year. This festival starts after Thanksgiving and runs though New Year's. This has been rated one of the top 25 annual festivals in the state, featuring sleigh rides, music, and dinners. A wonderful dinner and concert theatre operates mid-October through March in the dining room, offering a wide variety of entertainment.

The hotel restaurant serves some of the best meals in the area. House specialties include the seafood platter, prime rib, and fresh Canadian walleye pike. The mouthwatering steaks served are hand-cut from certified Angus beef. Tasty lunches are also served, highlighting a different dish daily. The gift shop in the hotel features handmade Native American crafts, including pipes made from stone taken out of the local pipestone quarries. Pipestone is a wonderful and friendly community; visiting this historic town is like taking a step back in time.

Redwood Falls

B eautifully set along the banks of the scenic Minnesota River, Redwood Falls was the birthplace of the country's largest retail conglomerate. Richard Sears sold his first watch just two miles north of the city in the village of North Redwood. The extraordinarily successful Sears Roebuck & Co. he later created eventually grew to become an American institution. The history of Redwood Falls was also influenced by another colorful figure, the Army Colonel Sam McPhail, who platted the town in 1864 after defeating the Dakota Indians. McPhail, who was an opportunist with the skills of a politician, promoter, lawyer, writer, and orator, financed the entire county of Redwood for a period of two years while the county government was being organized. A view of the fascinating history of Redwood Falls is presented at *Redwood County Museum,* housed in the 1908 former county rest home and containing hundreds of relics, photos, tools, and Indian artifacts. For more Native American history, visitors venture the few miles east to the *Lower Sioux Agency Interpretive Center,* which is also the site of the excellent *Lower Sioux Pottery* workshop and retail outlet. The main attraction in Redwood Falls, however, is not an historical site, but the magnificent *Alexander Ramsey Park,* at 217 acres Minnesota's biggest municipal park. The area includes a spacious campground with electrical hookups and restrooms with free hot showers, picnic areas, beautiful Ramsey Falls, miles of hiking trails, the *Vita-Course* exercise course, and the *Ramsey Park Zoo* with buffalo, deer, pheasants, hawks, and owls. In the way of events, Redwood Falls is, in the spirit of Richard Sears, host to the nationally renowned *Minnesota Inventors Congress.* The oldest of its type in the country, the congress is held during the second weekend in June and features displays of every invention imaginable. During the same weekend, Redwood Falls is also site of a pow wow, bed races, pork chop feed, and an arts and crafts fair. In neighboring North Redwood, residents honor their famous native son during *Richard Sears Park Day* in mid-August.

For more information on Redwood Falls, contact:
REDWOOD FALLS CHAMBER OF COMMERCE
140 E. Bridge Street
Redwood Falls, MN 56283
(507) 637-2828

S PECIALTY SHOPS

This small group of shopkeeper craftspeople in Redwood County is establishing itself in the public eye as a reliable source for multitude interests. Antiques, ceramics, woodwork, flower arrangements, and many other gift and personal items abound. Operating fairly independently, this collection of entrepreneurs has also recognized the ties which bind them, and they work together to achieve a greater ability to meet the growing demands of local patrons and travelers who seek their wares. They provide "Simple Pleasures from Simple Treasures."

■ GERI'S PALACE

230 S. Washington
Redwood Falls, MN 56283
Tel: (507) 637-3023

Geri Dahmes's shop in downtown Redwood Falls is a pleasant haven for many in the area. She is a certified ceramicist, and hundreds of her creations line the aisles of her spacious store. Geri provides custom work when asked, teaches ceramics classes, and maintains a solid product line of Duncan paints and supplies for those who prefer supplying much of the personal touches themselves. Geri's Palace also provides tanning facilities, and passive exercise equipment is available as well. Sandy Hindermann's painted wooden gifts, dolls, miniatures, and floral arrangements provide a uniquely special touch to the surroundings. Geri also puts particular attention into satisfying custom orders for special events and occasions; her one-of-a-kind pieces reflect the personal touch often lacking in the franchised gift shops.

■ TIMBERLINE WOOD PRODUCTS

404 Galles Drive
Redwood Falls, MN 56283
Tel: (507) 637-5304

Paul and Rae Fischer co-own this family-operated business. They create quality, hand-crafted wood furnishings and decorative items for the home or office. Handsome, attractive, functional, and durable; these pieces represent the attention to service and people which are the hallmark of Timberline's success. The Fischer's wares are available wholesale or by catalog; just call or write for information. They are also on display and available at Geri's Palace.

■**HOMETOWN TREASURES**
719 Main Street
Wabasso, MN 56293
Tel: (507) 342-5212

Located in the heart of Redwood County — in fact, within the town's old barber shop — is a unique craft and collectible shop called Hometown Treasures. Customers will find books, yankee candles, craft supplies, and many hand-crafted items. One-of-a-kind floral arrangements and wall decorations are also featured for some stylish design options for the home. Locally crafted collections of country wooden items — many hand-painted — round out the selection available. Many other sorts of wares are on display as well. Several appear and are then replaced with the seasons, so there is always something new. Closed Sundays and Mondays, owner Donna Peterson's place is open the rest of the week with hospitality and friendly service.

St. Peter

If not for a backhanded state legislator, St. Peter would have been the capitol of Minnesota today. Originally named Rock Bend because of its location near the only rock bottom crossing of the Minnesota River, St. Peter's main street was even widened in anticipation of the day the town would steal the capitol away from St. Paul. But a legislator by the name of Joseph Roulette managed to hide the bill authorizing the move until the deadline passed. Roulette was opposed to St. Peter on the grounds that it would be too far for him to travel from Pembina in the northern part of the then-Minnesota Territory, but ironically enough, Pembina soon became part of the new State of North Dakota. In the years following this fateful turn of events, St. Peter nevertheless prospered, eventually producing far more than its share of governors (five, including turn-of-the-century presidential hopeful John Johnson), the respected *Gustavus Adolphus College,* and the state hospital *St. Peter Regional Treatment Center.* The first psychiatric treatment center of its kind when it opened in 1866, it is today the city's largest employer. A museum located on the facility's campus explores the fascinating history of the center. The other main museum in town is the *Nicollet County Historical Society Museum* with 3,000 Indian and pioneer artifacts. In addition, the town has a number of historic buildings, including the magnificent *Julian Cox House* — once home to St. Peter's first mayor — the *1869 Episcopal Church of the Holy Communion,* and the beautifully restored *Nicollet House.* Also in a traditional vein, *Granni's Country Crafts & Gifts* features a wide selection for souvenir-minded visitors. For those looking for a broader selection of various arts, the *St. Peter Arts and Heritage Center,* located in a Victorian school building, showcases the work of local artists, while the dinner theater *North Star Summer Theatre* features professional comedy productions at Gustavus Adolphus College. The college is also venue for *Minnesota Valley Sommarfest* classical performances in July, the October *Nobel Conference* attended by scholars from around the world, and the *"Christmas in Christ Chapel"* Scandinavian music festival. Music of a different type is featured during the *Rock Bend Folk Festival* in September, while the *Traditional Fourth of July Celebration* features — among other events — an evening drum and bugle competition followed by fireworks.

For more information on St. Peter, contact:
St. Peter Area Tourism and Visitors Bureau
101 S. Front Street
St. Peter, MN 56082
(800) 473-3404

B ED & BREAKFAST

■ Park Row Bed & Breakfast
525 W. Park Row
St. Peter, MN 56082
Tel: (507) 931-2495
Hrs: Open daily year-round

Park Row Bed and Breakfast, nestled in picturesque St. Peter, is a beautiful Victorian home that has been remodeled to accommodate guests. The featured rooms are the English room, the parlor bedroom on the first floor, and the German and Scandinavian rooms upstairs. The home was built in the 1870s and each room's decor retains the charm of the era. The large windows offer a view of the well-kept town that sits in the heart of the lush Minnesota valley.

Upon awakening in the morning, guests are greeted by a breakfast made from scratch.

Owner Ann Burckhardt, a home economist, prepares a scrumptious breakfast featuring a blended fruit juice, an egg dish, hot bread, a fruit dessert, and pots and pots of coffee. Heart-shaped coffeecakes are baked especially for newlyweds, who are always served breakfast in bed. The cookie jar in the parlor is kept stocked with treats to satisfy every sweet tooth. For a cozy retreat close to the Twin Cities, Park Row is close enough for comfort.

■B OOKSTORE

■ THE BOOK MARK
Gustavus Adolphus College
800 College Ave.
St. Peter, MN 56082
Tel: (507) 933-7587
Hrs: Mon. - Fri. 8:30 a.m. - 4:30 p.m.
    (Spring and fall semesters) Sat. 10 a.m. - 1:30 p.m.
Visa, MasterCard, and Discover are accepted.

The Book Mark is located on the campus of Gustavus Adolphus College. It has occupied several different spaces throughout the years but has remained in its Student Union location since 1960. In 1972 a contest was held to find a distinctive name, thus "The Book Mark" was dubbed. All the required and recommended textbooks and supplies for classes can be found here as well as a large selection of general books. Books with regional and Scandinavian titles also line the shelves, offering a complete history of the area and its roots. Gift and card items as well as a variety of college imprinted clothing round out the inventory. The King and Queen of Sweden have managed to make several stops at the college — chances are they couldn't resist taking home a souvenir for themselves!

■M ILL & YARN SHOP

■ ST. PETER WOOLEN MILL
& MARY LUE'S YARN AND NEEDLECRAFT
101 W. Broadway
St. Peter, MN 56082
Tel: (507) 931-3702
Hrs: Mon. - Sat. 9 a.m. - 5 p.m. Most Sundays noon - 4 p.m.
Most major credit cards are accepted.

Specializing in the manufacturing of hand-tied quilts, wool mattress pads, and bed pillows, The Brinker Family continues to carry on the family tradition of four generations in the woolen mill business. The St. Peter Woolen Mill is believed to be the first in Minnesota and the oldest business in St. Peter, providing service to the community for the last 127 years.

This mill is one in about five in the country that does custom carding. They have one of the very best selections and the largest rainbow array of color and textures of yarn and stitchery products in the Midwest. There is an extensive supply of handcrafts for crocheting, needlepoint, cross-stitch, crewel embroidery, and weaving. Customers can also choose from a large selection of comforters, wool batting, and fabrics for comforters. Spinning wheels, looms, and knitting machines are also available to purchase. Take a tour of the mill and and have the opportunity to watch the carding of wool and tying of the comforters. Group tours by appointment only.

After a tour of the mill, visitors should explore the town. Rich in historic heritage, St. Peter is often referred to as the "Williamsburg of the Midwest" for its prominent preservation of colonial homes and churches with 13 sites on the National Historic Register.

NATURAL FOOD & GROCERIES

■ ST. PETER FOOD CO-OP
100 S. Front Street
St. Peter, MN 56082
Tel: (507) 931-4880
Hrs: Mon. - Sat. 9 a.m. - 6 pm.
     Sun. 11 a.m. - 5 p.m.

The St. Peter Food Co-op is a grocery store with a mission. That mission is to promote for the health, dignity, and well-being of all. This goal is achieved through cooperation with customers, members, and the environment.

Grocery selection includes fresh produce, bulk and packaged foods that are natural, organic, international, and gourmet. The Sandwich Shop is located within the St. Peter Co-op and features a complete deli with delightful meals, beverages, and snacks.

A unique shopping experience awaits customers whether they are after a fast and healthy meal from the Sandwich Shop or they need to replace food items in the kitchen.

R ESTAURANT

■ MITTERHAUSER'S GRILL & RESTAURANT
429 S. Minnesota Ave.
St. Peter, MN 56082
Tel: (507) 931-3833 or (800) 657-4783
Hrs: (Lunch and dinner) Tue. - Sun.
    Sun. Brunch 11 a.m. - 2 p.m.

Mitterhauser's Grill and Restaurant provides a unique opportunity to dine by the books. Mitterhauser's is located in an historic library, which was one of 3,500 originally donated by Andrew Carnegie and is currently on the National Historic Register. In addition to truly original food, there are also books for browsing.

Created by its owner, chef, and gold medalist in the Culinary Olympics in 1972, Klaus Mitterhauser displays his award-winning ability in each dish on the menu. The cuisine in this cozy but informal atmosphere consists of a wide range of dishes such as grilled poultry, game or pork medallions with exotic chutney sauce (six varieties), and incredibly tasty vegetarian entrees. Light and healthy combinations include organic salads and California-style dishes plus regional wild rice specialties or sizzling steaks for traditional folks.

The lobster tail wrapped in chicken breast is a signature dish. The wienerschnitzel a la holstein and the Hungarian paprika chicken with spaetzle are mouthwatering treats. Austrian hospitality for guests near and far boasts the experience of "love at first bite." Mitterhauser has more than 800 original recipes up his sleeve, so there is always a surprise in store. Mitterhauser's is easy to find in the center of St. Peter on Highway 169.

S CANDINAVIAN GIFT SHOP

■ SWEDISH KONTUR IMPORTS
310 S. Minnesota Ave.
St. Peter, MN 56082
Tel: (507) 931-1198
Hrs: Mon. - Thur. 9 a.m. - 5:30 p.m.
    Fri. 9 a.m. - 8 p.m.
    Sat. 9 a.m. - 5 p.m.
Visa and MasterCard are accepted.

Since its opening in 1962, Swedish Kontur Imports has maintained its title as the oldest Scandinavian gift shop in Minnesota. Swedish Orrefors crystal is a treasure as a gift for someone or to oneself. Dansk dinnerware is the perfect wedding gift and can be found in abundance at Swedish Kontur. Sterling silver jewelry from Denmark and Norway are also on display for a more personal gift selection. Christmas ornaments and toys bring an Old World quality to the holiday season. Scandinavian jams and ginger cookies are tempting treats year-round and are extra tasty when accompanied by the imported Swedish coffee. All of the items in Swedish Kontur Imports are authentic and add a special touch to every gift given.

Slayton

S layton is tucked into the southwestern periphery of the state, with Iowa to the south and South Dakota to the west only a short jaunt away. But to the farmers who settled this area, Slayton was — and is — set at the very heart of the best Midwestern farmland. As in the early settler days, farming dominates this quiet small town, and a drive along the outskirts of town will reveal some of the finest farms in the area. For insight into the agricultural history that shaped Slayton, visitors beat a path to *Murray County Historical Museum,* featuring an old fire hall, a farm wagon, railroad and Indian artifacts, a country store, and old tools and machinery. Next door stands the century-old, restored *Wornson Cabin.* For those looking for recreational opportunities, *Slayton Country Club* offers a round of fine golf; *Slayton Swimming Pool* is the place to cool off on a sizzling summer day; and *Lake Shetek State Park* features abundant wildlife, 88 campsites with electrical hook-ups, picnic areas, and groomed trails for hiking, cross-country skiing, and snowmobiling. Slayton is also the venue for one of the area's most exciting events, *Power Days Farm & Home Show* featuring some of the rowdiest demolition derbies and antique tractor pulls around, as well as somewhat more restful parades and exhibits.

For more information on Slayton, contact:
SLAYTON CHAMBER OF COMMERCE
2438 26th Street
Slayton, MN 56172
(507) 836-6902

GIFT SHOP

■ THE HUT
2620 Broadway
Slayton, MN 56172
Tel: (507) 836-6800
Hrs: Mon. - Sat. 9 a.m. - 5 p.m., Thur. 9 a.m - 9 p.m.
Visa and MasterCard are accepted.

For 23 years The Hut has brought the finest in gifts and collectibles to residents and visitors passing through Slayton. The Hut carries a wide range of country and traditional items as well as those on the humorous side. It is the headquarters for Lake Shetek, Lake Sarah, and Slaytona Beach shirts.

The Hut is known in the area as one of southwestern Minnesota's finest gift shops. The expansive selection supports this statement. Oak and pine shelves on which to place favorite keepsakes or on which to place newly purchased ones are available. Precious Moments collectibles, Black Hills gold and silver jewelry, and Noritake crystal and china decorate the shelves. Heritage lace doilies and curtains create a light breezy atmosphere and the stoneware selection ensures a charming table.

Every fall, starting in mid-October, the back area is transformed into a Christmas showcase. This showcase features decorated trees, assorted ornaments, and special holiday gift items. Items that convey the true meaning of Christmas are in abundance in The Hut. This display is a sight to see and a great way to start the holiday shopping season.

Sleepy Eye

W hen it was founded in 1872, this community of 3,600 took the name of the scenic Lake Sleepy Eye. Years before, the lake had been named for the chief of a band of Sisseston Dakota Indians, and today, the town of Sleepy Eye maintains the spirit of this wise chief through its many community services and its far-sighted industrial development. In fact, the commercial future of Sleepy Eye was secured as early as 1883, when the Sleepy Eye Milling Company opened. During the next 40 years, the mill drew many people to the area and helped build the foundations of the agricultural industries that still dominate the city's economic life. Today, the main attractions on an historic sites tour of Sleepy Eye include the old *Sleepy Eye Mill Elevators*, the *Long Building*, the *Engine Building*, and the *Five Story Building* — so named because of its five floors: the packing, roller, shaker, purifier, and bleaching floors. Other notable historic buildings in town include the *Chicago & Northwestern Passenger and Freight Depots*, built in 1902 and 1887, respectively; and the 1900 *Dyckman Free Library* erected by Frank Dyckman in gratitude for the business opportunities awarded him in Sleepy Eye (he was a prosperous partner in the milling company). Like most towns its size, Sleepy Eye also offers several city parks with playgrounds and picnic facilities, and access to the wilderness of *Fort Ridgely State Park* and *Flandrau State Park.* Golfing is available at *Sleepy Eye Golf Club,* and bowling at *Sleepy Eye Lanes.* The two main events in town fall in the late summer; *Buttered Corn Day* where the local Del Monte corn packing plant offers unlimited, free buttered corn; and the *Great Grassroots Gathering* featuring a flea market with numerous displays of hand-crafted goods.

For more information on Sleepy Eye, contact:
SLEEPY EYE AREA CHAMBER OF COMMERCE
108 W. Main Street
Sleepy Eye, MN 56085
(507) 794-4731

Spicer/New London

L ocated in the midst of the lake-studded Little Crow Lakes region in western Minnesota, Spicer and New London rank among the most popular tourist destinations in the state. This rolling, wooded region shelters in excess of 50 lakes, offering excellent walleye and bass fishing, and hiking and swimming opportunities. Sinclair Lewis, the great Minnesota writer, once compared New London to a Cape Cod village. This friendly town along with its twin, Spicer, does indeed offer the type of quaint, restful respite from the demands of everyday life that visitors may expect to find along the country roads of New England. In addition to all this natural beauty, these resort communities also include the 18-hole, championship level *Little Crow Country Club;* and the 2,400-acre *Sibley State Park* with excellent swimming, canoeing, hiking, and camping opportunities, as well as environmental education tours led by a resident naturalist. *Monongolia Historical Society,* located in the old Lebanon Church, features a traditional newspaper office, country store, and an assortment of old farm machinery; while the 1893 Victorian *Historic Spicer Castle,* once a private house, has now been turned into an elegant bed-and-breakfast inn. But it is, after all, the multitude of annual events that make Spicer and New London special. Spicer starts out the list with a grand *Independence Day Celebration,* including a flea market, street dance, road race, arts and crafts fair, and music in the park. One of the largest Fourth of July celebrations in the area, it attracts 12,000 to 15,000 people annually. New London's main events include two vintage car runs, the *Mt. Tom Tour* in May and the huge *Antique Car Run* between New London and New Brighton just north of Minneapolis. Patterned after a similar run between London and Brighton in England, it attracts participants from the United Kingdom eager to drive the 120 miles through rolling Minnesota countryside. *New London Water Days* in late July, featuring amazing water ski shows and *Little Britches Rodeo* — which offers teenagers a chance to try their hand at this all-American sport, are only two of a long series of additional events in the Spicer/New London area.

For more information on Spicer/New London, contact:

SPICER COMMERCIAL CLUB   or   NEW LONDON CHAMBER OF
P.O. Box 244   COMMERCE
Spicer, MN 56288   New London, Mn 56273
(612) 796-0066   (612) 354-2011

B ED & BREAKFAST

■ROSE MANOR ON-THE-PARK
152 Lake Ave.
Spicer, MN 56288
Tel: (612) 796-6030
Visa and MasterCard are accepted.

For an intimate, romantic, unforgettable interlude, don't miss Rose Manor On-the-Park in Spicer, just 11 miles north of Willmar, on Highway 23.

Built in 1896, the building was a center of railroad tourism activity. Remodeled many times over the years, it came into its own under the ownership and direction of Frank and Lori Morrell. The Morrells remodeled the complete second floor, carefully constructing each room with as much authenticity for the earlier era as possible. The Morrells collected artifacts and furniture from all over Minnesota to complement the architectural style that they created. A wide promenade, ballastraded stairway brings visitors into an inside courtyard boasting an eight-foot skylight adorned with bluebirds centered above a continental fountain. The courtyard is surrounded by the four rooms available. Two artifacts, which are the center of attention in the Manor, are the chandelier in the dining room and a large circular French window at the entrance landing. The chandelier dates to 1710 and was purchased in France in 1962. The six-foot window was originally in a French chalet in 1740. Guests will enjoy hors d'oeuvres for two nightly, along with complimentary champagne and a full, lusty breakfast. If guests prefer, nightly dinners are served in the formal dining room in a romantic setting of candlelight. Pre-arranged reservations are required for dinner. Rose Manor On-the-Park is a marvelous bed and breakfast for couples to enjoy each other in an uninterrupted, ultra-romantic atmosphere. It must be experienced to be appreciated.

C OUNTRY GIFTS

■MINNESOTA COUNTRY
12011 Highway 71 N.E.
Spicer, MN 56288
Tel: (612) 796-2199
Hrs: Mon. - Sat. 10 a.m. - 5 p.m., Sun. noon - 5 p.m.
All major credit cards are accepted.

For the elegance and charm of traditional country gifts, look no further than Minnesota Country, conveniently surrounded by 15 lakes and 30 resorts and campgrounds. Originally established in 1980 as a fur trading center, it has expanded into gift items and is west-central Minnesota's largest gift store. It represents 75-90 artisans and craftspersons, providing hand-crafted or gift items and accessories from the five-state region.

The store is attractive and inviting, displaying merchandise on unique shelving. The Christmas Room features Christmas tree skirts in patchwork or star design; stockings and applique designs of Santa, scotty dog, reindeer, mother goose, and other heart-warming designs; ornaments; string Santa dolls; and much more. Victorian hand-crafted items and accessories are elegantly displayed in the Victorian Room. Other gift items include wreaths and floral arrangements, quilt items, a wide selection of handmade dolls, Amish string dolls, rugs and blankets, cabinets and spice racks, hand-crafted pottery, porcelain figurines, and that's not all. Customized special orders and shipping are also available. It's no secret that Minnesota Country offers only the best quality in all of its hand-crafted gift items.

R ESORT

■ CEDAR POINT RESORT
4808 132nd Ave. N.E.
Spicer, MN 56288
Tel: (612) 796-5146
Hrs: Open May to Oct. 1
Visa and MasterCard are accepted.

On the southwest shore of Nest Lake is Cedar Point Resort, originally built in 1940. Nest Lake covers approximately 1,200 acres and is fed by the Little Crow River. The rough and wooded shoreline and many peninsulas and bays make good fishing and beautiful scenery available to Cedar Point Resort guests.

Cedar Point has 18 modern housekeeping cottages, fully equipped, and two lakefront cabins with full wheelchair access. The cottages are attractive and comfortable, each offering a beautiful view of Nest Lake. There is a choice selection of one-, two-, three-, and four- bedroom cottages to meet individual needs. Each cottage has its own picnic table and table grill, and many of the cottages have deck porches. Guests enjoy free use of the paddlebikes, playaks, canoes, innertubes, horseshoes, volleyball, and Fun Bugs. Campground facilities are also available. The recreation center is open daily, and the lounge area provides a relaxed area for the adults to socialize. Also available at the resort are groceries, gas, oil, tackle and live bait, licenses, boats and motors, and pontoon boats. Area attractions include museums and historical sites pertaining to the Indian heritage, shopping, restaurants, golf courses, and other amusements activities. Cedar Point Resort's well-kept grounds offer a safe and relaxed recreation area for the whole family.

RESTAURANT

■ SAFARI SOUTH ON BEAUTIFUL GREEN LAKE
149 S. Lake Ave.
Spicer, MN 56288
Tel: (612) 796-2195
Hrs: Daily 11 a.m. - 1 a.m.
All major credit cards are accepted.

Once a country club facility in the early 1900s, the main building of Safari South and the fieldstone entry, "Porte Cochere" or buggy port, are still in evidence today.

The restoration of this grand building by owner Chuck de Cathelineau is set off by his private collection of artwork, antiques, and animals, which are on display. The animals were collected from around the world — Russia, South Africa, Iran, and North and South America. Some of the animals on display are a Montana Rocky Mountain bighorn, dall sheep from Alaska, cape buffalo, lion and its cub, stone sheep from British Columbia, and rhinoceros. Aside from this natural history museum, Safari South provides customers with quality food, drink, service, and a beautiful view of Green Lake. Menu items offer popular appetizers, fresh garden salads, seafood and beef specialties, chicken and pork entrees; and "on the wild side" each weekend, the chef prepares a wild game entree.

Safari South specializes in weddings, banquets, receptions, reunions, and business meetings. In the summer, there are docking facilities and excellent beaching for pontoon airplanes. In the winter, there is room for snowmobile parking, and weather permitting, a cleared ice runway for wheel or ski planes.

Antiques, art, and good food complement one another to make a dining experience at Safari South memorable for the whole family. There is not a dining place like this anywhere else in Minnesota.

S PECIALTY SHOP

■ MILL POND MERCANTILE ARTISTS' COOPERATIVE
18 Main Street
New London, MN 56273
Tel: (612) 354-5557
Hrs: Mon. - Sat. 9 a.m. - 5 p.m.
       Sun. noon - 5 p.m.
Visa and MasterCard are accepted.

Mill Pond Mercantile Artists' Cooperative is a unique specialty shop located in a turn-of-the-century building in New London, the "City on the Pond." The shop is represented by 15 local artists and crafters, all of whom formed the Artists' Cooperative in 1987.

The interior boasts Victorian pressed-tin walls and ceiling. The artist takes pride in preserving this tradition of finely crafted objects. The merchandise is tastefully displayed in groupings that reflect a home-like setting. Customers can explore the rich diversity of quilts, pine furniture, dried flower wreaths, Scandinavian gifts, stenciled work, needlework, and hardanger Norwegian embroidery. Other handmade items include rugs, dolls, pottery, tapestry weave baskets, stained glass, watercolors, wood burning, folk art, and much more. The art objects are enhanced by a fine collection of restored antiques provided by a local antique dealer.

Mill Pond Mercantile Artists' Cooperative takes pride in the quality and timelessness of their products. An artist is always in the store to assist customers. This is where artist and customer can meet, talk, and sometimes look on as artists work.

S PORTING GOODS & CONVENIENCE STORE

■ MEL'S SPORT SHOP
Highway 23 S. and Ruth
Spicer, MN 56288
Tel: (612) 796-2421
Hrs. Daily 7 a.m. - 10 p.m.
All major credit cards are accepted.

Mel's Sport Shop has the largest selection of sporting goods in the Crow Lakes region. Located on Highways 23 and 10, in Spicer, it serves the area resorts and travelers alike.

Trophies of big game and fish adorn the walls of this convenience and sporting goods store. With an unbelievable selection of fishing gear, guns, and clothing; Mel's Sport Shop easily can handle all its customers' needs. A complete line of guns and ammunition is available, with over 500 guns in stock from which to choose. The shop has a complete selection of fishing gear, rods and reels, tackle, live bait, trolling motors, and other marine items. Clothing for fishing and hunting includes rain gear, camouflage, and other outdoor articles. For convenience needs, gasoline, groceries, filling of propane tanks, and diesel fuel are also available. For miscellaneous and souvenir shopping, there are plenty of gift items and T-shirts to choose from. Services include taxidermists, gun and reel repair, hunting and fishing licenses, and fishing and tourist information for the area's lakes. Mel's Sport Shop is one of the best sporting goods and accessory stores in west-central Minnesota.

Walnut Grove/Tracy

These southwestern Minnesota farm towns are known for their fascinating settler heritage. From 1874 to 1876, Walnut Grove was the home of Laura Ingalls Wilder, author of a series of children's books. The family, whose life here was the basis of the television show "Little House on the Prairie," left Walnut Grove after swarms of grasshoppers destroyed their wheat crop two years in a row. The *Laura Ingalls Wilder Museum* is dedicated to the author and her work, and markers originating at the museum show the way to the site of the family's dugout along a creek bank. Tracy, meanwhile, has some historical sites of its own, most notably the *Wheels Across the Prairie Museum,* featuring a wide variety of settler-era machines and equipment; and *St. Mark's Church Museum,* also featuring historical artifacts collected from residents in the area. Another fascinating historical site and a must for railroad fans is *End-O-Line Railroad Park and Museum,* located 15 miles south of Tracy. The museum includes a caboose, locomotive, railroad memorabilia, as well as the only hand-operated turntable still in operation in the United States. This area is also the site of *Lake Shetek State Park,* a 4,000-acre haven of wildlife, trails, campgrounds, and serene lakes. The main annual events organized by the two prairie towns are the historical pageant *Fragments of a Dream* based on Wilder's children's books, and the *Pioneer Festival* with its pioneer crafts, heritage booths, and food; both are held in Walnut Grove. Tracy also hosts *Box Car Days* in late August, featuring parades, a teen dance, and a concert in the park.

For more information on Walnut Grove and Tracy, contact:

WALNUT GROVE   or   TRACY AREA
TOURISM CENTER   CHAMBER OF COMMERCE
P. O. Box 58   Masonic Building
Walnut Grove, MN 56180   Tracy, MN 56175
(507) 859-2358   (507) 629-4021

Waseca

The early settlers who decided to farmstead here made an excellent choice. The ancient Dakota name for this patch of rolling tallgrass prairie was "Waseca" — fertile — and in the century that followed the immigrant settlement, Waseca lived up to its name. Today, while still maintaining its connections to a rural past, Waseca has grown up to become a prosperous industrial town. In fact, the rural heritage of Minnesota has never been explored better than at *Farmamerica* near Waseca; a 120-acre cluster of restored farmsteads from the 1850s, 1920s, and 1970s. Complete with costumed interpreters conducting long-forgotten farm activities, Farmamerica provides excellent insight into the lives of Minnesota's settler families. *Waseca County Historical Society,* as well, is dedicated to farm history with its intriguing collections, including a rural school house, a reconstructed log home, and a profusion of agricultural implements. Other historic buildings in town include the *Ward Home* and the distinguished *Waseca County Courthouse;* the work of local artists, meanwhile, are beautifully exhibited in the *WAC Gallery.* For those physically inclined, there's scenic biking and fishing available along the many lakes surrounding Waseca; and picnicking, hiking, or camping in *Maplewood Park* or *Courthouse Park* along the *LeSueur River.* The outdoors is also the venue for the main events in Waseca, most notably *Happy Days* with goldfish-eating and bubble gum-blowing contests, as well as an antique car show; and the *Sleigh and Cutter Parade,* a 40-year-old tradition featuring old-fashioned sleighs pulled by sturdy Morgan and Belgian horses.

For more information on Waseca, contact:

WASECA AREA CHAMBER OF COMMERCE
Department 3
108 E. Elm
Waseca, MN 56093
(507) 835-3260

A GRICULTURAL INTERPRETIVE CENTER

■ FARMAMERICA
County Roads 2 and 17
P.O. Box 111
Waseca, MN 56093
Tel: (507) 835-2052
Hrs: (June - Sept.)
    Fri. - Sun. 10 a.m. - 4 p.m.
Visa and MasterCard are accepted.

Minnesota history comes alive at Farmamerica, the state agricultural interpretive center four miles west of Waseca in southern Minnesota. On a sprawling 120 acres complete with farm buildings, gardens, and farm animals; Farmamerica brings to life the history of farming in Minnesota from the pioneer days of the 1850s to the present. The land, the people, and the future they made for themselves on the vast open prairie are all covered through history reenactments and restored buildings.

Visitors to the non-profit center start their journey at a restored school that serves as an admissions center. Continuing on the circular "Time Line Trail" — either on foot or in a horse-drawn wagon — the first stop is a true replica of a pioneer homestead. Built from roughly-hewn logs, the diminutive buildings echo to the sound of Farmamerica staff demonstrating the lifeways of the pioneers. Across from the settlement farm, a nine-acre swath of original prairie waves in the wind just as it did in the settlers' days. Meanwhile, in a nearby blacksmith shop, a smithy reenacts the centuries old craft, while a complete farm from the 1920s furnished with authentic period furniture rests in solitude further along the trail. Finally, a modern farm completes the circle.

In addition to enjoying history reenactments, don't forget to examine the vegetables grown at the settlement farm; they are the same varieties as those grown by the settlers. Also, Farmamerica hosts a rambunctious corn-shucking or horse-plowing contest. They are all part of the educational fun that makes Farmamerica a must for anyone interested in the heritage of Minnesota.

CAMPGROUND

■ KIESLER'S CAMPGROUND ON CLEAR LAKE
Highway 14
(East edge of Waseca)
Waseca, MN 56093
Tel: (507) 835-3179
Hrs: Open Apr. 15 - Oct. 15
Visa, MasterCard, and Discover are accepted.

Nestled in southern Minnesota's quiet farmland near the Iowa border is one of the most exciting and entertaining RV parks found anywhere. The owners take pride in the five-star rating.

Since 1972, Kiesler's Campground has enjoyed a prestigious location on the 700-acre Clear Lake, situated in the friendly community of Waseca in the "Deep South of Minnesota." The park boasts 250 spacious sites with water and electric hookups, 132 with sewer, free cable television, and picnic tables. Recessed fire pits and graveled parking pads are surrounded by manicured grass; landscaping includes plenty of shade trees. Kal and Barb Kiesler play host and hostess to a summer full of activities for the whole family. Children enjoy the playground and activities planned by "Jolly Jon," the recreation director. There is also volleyball, basketball, shuffleboard, horseshoes, and softball. Special events include bingo, kite flying, camper's auction, teen sock hops, bike parade, mini-golf tournaments, tug-o-war, kiddie carnival, fireworks, and much more. Plenty of prizes are awarded for outdoor contests. For the avid golfer, there is Kiesler's 18-hole mini golf; next door is the Clear Lake Country Club and 18 holes of golf. Water sports enthusiasts enjoy waterskiing and swimming. A large heated pool is on the campgrounds. The camp store and recreation hall provide additional conveniences and activities. Fishing licenses, bait, tackle, and boat and motor rental are also available. Kiesler's Campground is a vacation center for the entire family.

Willmar

A s a city of predominately Scandinavian heritage, it is hardly surprising that Willmar's coffee consumption is outrageously high. Whether due to this huge daily dose of caffeine or not, Willmar is today one of Minnesota's fastest-growing cities, a prosperous community of 18,000 with well-known industries like Jennie-O Foods, Supersweet Feeds, and ASI-AGRI Products. As these firms indicate, agriculture forms the foundation of the economic life of the city, as it should in this pastoral farm setting 100 miles west of the Twin Cities. But the fields of corn, grain, and potatoes surrounding Willmar are conveniently interspersed with a multitude of small and large lakes set among the rolling hills, making the city a busy gateway for vacation fun in the Little Crow Lakes region.

ATTRACTIONS

Upon arrival in Willmar, visitors are encouraged to take a self-guided tour along the *Glacial Ridge State Trail.* This trail gives a good sense of the changing, hilly landscape formed by the retreating glaciers that once covered the area; and the many historical markers found along the route bring to life the local history. But this is not the only trail found in Willmar. Bikers, snowmobilers, and cross-country skiers will have a field day on the 18.5-mile state *Glacier Lakes Trail,* as well as on the many trails criss-crossing beautiful *Sibley State Park.* These include 18 miles of foot trails; a one-mile, self-guided interpretive nature trail; 15 miles of biking trails; ten miles of groomed cross-country ski trails and six miles of snowmobile trails. Other parks and parkgrounds abound in the area, but one deserves special mention. *Robbins Island,* located between *Foot Lake* and *Willmar Lake,* was once a hideaway for settlers retreating from conflicts with the Native Dakota, and now provides picnic shelters, a playground, and a public beach in a serene setting. The area also has numerous golf clubs, including the *Willmar Golf Course* with the adjacent restaurant *Blue Heron on the Green,* both overlooking scenic *Swan* and *Willmar lakes.* History buffs, meanwhile, can trace the heritage of the area in the *Kandiyohi County Historical Society Museum* with its artifact collection, agriculture exhibits, and the *Great Northern Steam Locomotive No. 2523* — one of the last great steam engines ever built for the mighty Great Northern. Willmar also offers music and theater performances, beginning with *Willmar Community Orchestra,* which offers five classical concerts every year; the *Willmar Community Band,* performing ten outdoors "pops" concerts in the summer and several indoor concerts in the winter; and the *Barn Theatre,* offering professional performances ranging from "Fiddler on the Roof" to "Steel Magnolias" throughout the entire year.

EVENTS

The best-known event of the year is actually four festivals in one. *Willmar Fest* in June combines the *Kaffe Fest, Frameries Fest, Aqua Fest,* and *International Fest* into one extravagant week of parades, fireworks, carnival rides, and other family fun. The *West Central Concert Series* offers a variety of highly popular professional concerts throughout the year, while the Kandiyohi County Historical Society sponsors area *folk entertainment* on Tuesday evenings during the summer. The city's main events conclude with an *arts and crafts fair* in October.

For more information on Willmar, contact:
WILLMAR CONVENTION & VISITORS BUREAU
518 W. Litchfield Ave.
Willmar, MN 56201
(612) 235-0300 or (800) 845-8747

ANTIQUES

■D.B. VICTORIA AND COMPANY
629 First Street S.
Willmar, MN 56201
Tel: (612) 235-0303
Hrs: Mon. - Sat. 9:30 a.m.- 5 p.m.

D.B. Victoria and Company has nine individual dealers and is this area's only antique mall. An outstanding collection of antiques and collectibles are beautifully displayed in a quaint,

turn-of-the-century Victorian home, creating a very relaxed and charming atmosphere. The owner, Donna, has been an antique collector and enthusiast for 20 years, and that love shows in the conception of this shop.

The selection and range of a general line of antiques and collectibles are unmatched in the area. It is typically stocked with quilts and linens, stoneware and pottery, Christmas and holiday collectibles, furniture, and other related home decorating accessories. Customers will find baseball cards, souvenir and advertising pieces, art and photographs, postcards, and other paper ephermeral. Cookie jars, cookie cutters, rolling pins, granite and enamelware, and a host of other kitchen collectibles are regular fare. Also expect to find vintage clothing, hats, and jewelry, and several hunting and fishing items. As a special service to her customers, Donna will work with her associates to search out and find a specific item just for them.

This grand old home also offers The Porch Peddler, a beautiful shop brimming with gifts and collectibles. Together these two shops provide visitors with a truly unique and pleasurable shopping experience.

A RT GALLERY & FRAME SHOP

■ SHOREWOOD GALLERY
1700 S. First Street
Willmar, MN 56201
Tel: (612) 231-2730
Hrs: Mon. - Fri. 10 a.m. - 5:30 p.m.
     Sat. 10 a.m. - 3 p.m. Closed Sun.
     Extended hours at Christmas or by appointment
Visa, MasterCard, and Discover are accepted.

Shorewood Gallery is located on Highway 71 in Willmar, across from the Kandi Mall. The gallery elegantly displays limited edition wildlife and western prints that will delight customers in decorating their home or office. There is a beautiful display of Minnesota loons, stunning sunsets, and carefree puppies. For stamp collectors, often the gallery has new selections of stamps and matching prints available.

Limited edition collector plates, custom hand-carved decoys, and many other artworks are also available. Artists represented at the gallery include Terry Redlin, Les Kouba, James Meger, Rosemary Millette, Dan Smith, Michael Sieve, David Maass, Penny Ann Cross, and Jessy Barnes, to name a few.

The gallery specializes in custom framing of artwork, prints, photographs, needlework, stamps, and collector plates. When framing artwork that a customer has created or selected, staff will discuss several options and ideas with customers to help achieve the look they want. Shorewood Gallery can also mount and frame precious documents, photographs, and much more.

G IFTS & COLLECTIBLES

■ THE PORCH PEDDLER
629 S. First Street
Willmar, MN 56201
Tel: (612) 235-5338
Hrs: Mon. - Sat. 9:30 a.m. - 5 p.m.
     Closed Sun.
Visa and MasterCard are accepted.

The Porch Peddler is an antique and gift shop located in a quaint Victorian home originally built around the turn of the century. D. B. Victoria and Company, located on the second level of the building, offers wonderful antiques and collectibles. The "two stores in one" delight customers with Willmar's only antique mall.

Inside, the wood floors — along with a country and Victorian blend of decor, kitchen and pantry, stained-glass windows, Victorian porch, and open stairways — create a warm, enchanting atmosphere. The scent of potpourri complements the display of merchandise. Everything imaginable is available from collectibles by Jan Hagara, Sarah's Attic, and Charles Wysocki, to kitchen and plate settings, recipe books, pottery, hand-carved ducks, and country furniture. Gift and other home accessories include floral wreaths, afghans, brass and copper items, and a varied assortment of pictures. The Porch Peddler offers shoppers unhurried assistance in finding just the right gift or home accessory. It has charming country and Victorian gifts, for gracious living and thoughtful giving.

Windom

A pleasant farming town of 4,500 located on the scenic Des Moines River, Windom was named after a prominent 19th-century statesman, William Windom, who served as a U.S. congressional representative, senator, and Secretary of Treasury during an impressive career spanning 33 years. Only one year after the city's founding, the railway was constructed through town and Windom was named county seat — two events that ensured the young town's future. In later years, Windom's economic life has received valuable injections from two large firms located here, The Toro Corporation (a leading manufacturer of lawn care and snow removal products) and The Caldwell Packing Company, an international supplier of beef. For an insight into the farm heritage of Windom, visitors may choose to pay a visit to *Cottonwood County Historical Society*, featuring agricultural implements, antique clocks, and a one-room school house. Two historical buildings also deserve mention. The *Windom Public Library,* erected in 1883, is an imposing edifice of Bedford stone and marble pillars; the 1904 *Cottonwood County Courthouse* with its unusual Corinthian columns has earned a spot on the National Registry of Historic Places. Another historic spot, located 15 miles north of Windom, is *Jeffers Petroglyphs,* a magnificent collection of more than 2,000 ancient Indian rock carvings viewed by more than 6,000 visitors annually. The top event of the year, *Riverfest,* is a week-long celebration featuring a live bear as grand marshal, numerous contests, ethnic foods, and much fun-filled entertainment. The *Dickens Christmas,* meanwhile, is a city-wide reenactment of the story A Christmas Carol, including special music performances to create a festive Christmas atmosphere.

For more information on Windom, contact:
WINDOM AREA CHAMBER OF COMMERCE
P.O. Box 8
Windom, MN 56101
(507) 831-2752

HISTORIC SITE

■ JEFFERS PETROGLYPHS
A Minnesota Historical Society Site
(32 miles south of Redwood Falls on U.S. Highway 71, then 3 miles east on Cottonwood Co. Highway 10 and 1 mile south on Co. Highway 2)
Mailing Address: Bingham Lake, MN 56118
Tel: (507) 877-3647 or (507) 697-6321
Hrs: Open daily May 1 - Labor Day 10 a.m. - 5 p.m.
     Weekends through Sept. 10 a.m. - 5 p.m.

On a windswept, 40-acre patch of virgin prairie near Jeffers in southwestern Minnesota, the earliest inhabitants of Minnesota have left a riddle to ponder. As early as 3,000 B.C., the Late Archaic People started carving figures known as petroglyphs in a quartzite bedrock ridge poking through the grassland. Using only the resources at hand — chisels and hammers made of hard antlers and stone — they painstakingly created animals and human figures that still have archaeologists mystified.

The petroglyphs most commonly depict animals native to the region, such as bison, rabbits, wolves, turtles, and elk, which probably symbolize the significance of wildlife for a people living off the land. Alongside the animal figures, carvings of arrows, lances, spearpoints, and atlatls — (a spear-throwing device only found in Jeffers and a handful of other sites) — represent the human struggle for subsistence. Other figures, such as thunderbirds and humans with bison-horn headdresses, probably represent shamans or other spiritual leaders, while yet other, more complex carvings depict important events and sacred ceremonies.

Although Indians still carved petroglyphs at Jeffers as late as the mid-18th century, the decorated quartzite ridge known as Red Rock Ridge is now just a last remnant of a vanished civilization. Administered by the Minnesota Historical Society, the site includes an interpretive trail with 22 marked stations that describe to visitors the meaning of the petroglyphs. There is no admission charge. As visitors walk the trail, they are surrounded by the undulating tallgrass prairie, looking as vast as it did when the first Minnesotans left their cryptic messages in Red Rock Ridge.

Worthington

O nce an obscure stop on the Sioux City and St. Paul Railroads named Okabena — "nesting place of herons" in Dakota — Worthington soon changed names in honor of a large group of settlers from Worthington, Ohio. These early settlers belonged to a strict religious group that believed in abstinence and high moral standards, and one of their descendants, famous evangelist Billy Sunday, began his revivalist career here. Eventually, Worthington grew to become a diverse regional trade center with major employers like the pork processor Monfort and Campbell Soup Company. The heritage of this prairie town is captured through a multitude of exhibits in *Nobles County Historical Museum,* as well as the impressive *Pioneer Village* with its 35 restored buildings from the early years of Nobles County. A special attraction is a museum of farm machinery, also located in the Pioneer Village. One of the more unique sights in the southern Minnesota region is the *Peace Avenue of Flags,* a summertime display of 36 flags in celebration of Worthington's designation as "World Brotherhood City" in 1959. A must for art lovers is *Nobles County Art Center,* featuring 12 annual shows of the works of area artists. Other works of art (including signed prints by star photographer Jim Brandenburg), as well as a wide collection of books, are available at *The Cows' Outside* store. For those so inclined, a game of golf can be had at the traditional Scottish link design *Prairie View Golf Course.* Main annual events in Worthington include *Art in the Courtyard,* an annual summer showcase for area artists hosted by the Nobles County Art Center; the *Worthington Labor Day Golf Classic;* and the *Grand National Tractor Pull* and *Flying Turkey Hot Air Balloon Races,* both held in the summer.

For more information on Worthington, contact:
WORTHINGTON CONVENTION & VISITORS BUREAU
P.O. Box 608
Worthington, MN 56187-0608
(507) 372-2919

INDEX

Pathways Through Minnesota Reader Survey

To make our next edition even better, please take a minute to answer the following questions. Mail the completed form to the address below for a chance to win a weekend at one of Minnesota's Historic Hotels or Bed & Breakfast Inns.

1. How did you obtain your copy of *Pathways Through Minnesota?*
a) Bookstore
b) As a gift
c) At a gift or specialty store
d) Other

2. Do you plan to use this book for your own city as well as travel throughout Minnesota?
a) Own city
b) Minnesota travel
c) Both

3. How many people, other than yourself, plan to use this copy of *Pathways Through Minnesota?*___

4. When planning a vacation or travel excursion through Minnesota, what other sources do you look to for help in your decision?
a) Other travel guides
b) State Office of Tourism
c) Word of mouth
d) Newspaper
e) Other _____

5. What are the three features you like most about *Pathways Through Minnesota?*
a)
b)
c)

6. What features, if any, do you dislike about *Pathways Through Minnesota?*
a)
b)
c)

7. Please list any features you would like to see added to our next edition of *Pathways Through Minnesota.*
a)
b)
c)

8. On average, how many books do you read per year?
a) 1-5
b) 6-10
c) 11-20
d) 21 or more

Clark & Miles Publishing
1670 S. Robert St., Suite 315
St. Paul, MN 55118

9. How many trips, in Minnesota, do you take per year?
Business ___ Pleasure ___

10. How many times per month do you dine out? _____

11. Which area(s) of Minnesota do you visit most?
a) Arrowhead
b) Bluff Country
c) Heartland
d) Metroland
e) Prairieland

12. Which area of Minnesota do you live in?
a) Arrowhead
b) Bluff Country
c) Heartland
d) Metroland
e) Prairieland

13. Which of the following recreational activities do you enjoy?
a) fishing
b) camping
c) boating
d) hiking
e) skiing
f) canoeing
g) general pleasure traveling
h) antiquing
i) snowmobiling
j) golf
k) other _____

14. Age
a) Under 20
b) 21-35
c) 36-50
d) 51-65
e) 66+

15. Household income
a) $10,000-20,000
b) $21,000-30,000
c) $31,000-45,000
d) $46,000-60,000
e) $61,000-$99,000
f) $100,000+

16. Education level
a) High school
b) Trade school
c) Some college
d) College graduate
e) Master's degree
f) Doctoral degree

Please fill in the address form below for your chance to win a weekend for two!

Name _____

Address _____

City and state _____

Zip _____

Phone (optional) _____

I would like to order _____ additional *Pathways Through Minnesota* books at $14.95 each. In the U.S. include $2.00 (U.P.S. shipping charge) for the first book, and $1.00 for each additional book. Outside the U.S., include $3.00 and $1.00 respectively. Please add 6.5% for books shipped to Minnesota addresses. Enclosed is my check or money order (U.S. funds only) made out to Clark & Miles Publishing, for $_____

Name _____

Address _____

City _____ State _____ Zip _____

Country _____